CONTEMPORARY CASES IN CONSUMER BEHAVIOR
Fourth Edition

CONTEMPORARY CASES IN CONSUMER BEHAVIOR

Fourth Edition

ROGER D. BLACKWELL
The Ohio State University

■

KRISTINA S. BLACKWELL
The Ohio State University

■

W. WAYNE TALARZYK
The Ohio State University

The Dryden Press
Harcourt Brace College Publishers

Fort Worth   Philadelphia   San Diego   New York   Orlando   Austin   San Antonio
Toronto   Montreal   London   Sydney   Tokyo

Acquisitions Editor: Lyn Keeney Hastert
Marketing Manager: Lise Johnson
Production Manager: Trisha Dianne
Manager of Production: Diane Southworth

Project Management: Elm Street Publishing Services, Inc.
Compositor: G&S Typesetters, Inc.

ISBN: 0-03-097038-5

Library of Congress Catalog Card Number: 93-6545

Printed in the United States of America
345-090-987654321

The Dryden Press Series in Marketing

Preface

■ ■ ■ ■ ■

We are excited about writing and completing this book. We hope you are excited about using it because there are some truly fascinating companies and issues described in the following pages. "The wise teacher makes learning a joy," says one of the Proverbs. We have prepared a collection of cases with the intent of adding to the enjoyment of studying consumer behavior in a marketing setting.

The purpose of this book is to develop the student's ability to interpret the environment—especially the consumer environment—using the tools of research and logic and to develop effective strategies and policies based upon that interpretation.

We have attempted to compile a balance of cases. Some cases deal with very large corporations and the problems they face, such as Ford Motor Company and AT&T. Others deal with much smaller, entrepreneurial companies such as Cheryl & Co. and the Longaberger Basket Company. The cases cover a wide spectrum of industries, businesses, and services including food, automobiles, dry cleaning, electronic banking, retailing, computer services, and medical services. One of the more interesting cases is on the development of a national poinsettia market.

Global thinking is essential today. Several cases are designed to develop global thinking. Two of these are Miele & Co. and Center Parcs, which raise issues about how successful European firms market in the United States. Singapore Airlines raises the question of how a firm in a small Asian country markets throughout the world and achieves for itself the enviable image of the best airline in the world. Cross cultural analysis of global markets is also an issue in the Avon and Wendy's cases. Perhaps the case likely to bring about the most spirited discussion is Pick 'n Pay, which raises issues of whether a South African firm should sell to other countries and whether firms in other countries should sell to a South African firm, as well as the entire issue of the involvement of business in social and political issues. Social responsibility is also an important issue in cases such as The Body Shop and McDonald's.

Several emphases form the foundation of this book. The first emphasis is on growing profits. In an age of mergers and acquisitions, firms must grow profits to achieve a respectable price/earnings ratio. Cases such as The Limited, Bank One of Columbus, and The Home Depot raise this challenging issue. Emerging from Chapter 11 bankruptcy is an issue in the Paul Harris case.

A second emphasis is on the use of research data for managerial decisions. The book is based on the premise that contemporary managers must be able to obtain and interpret research. Many of the cases either present data for students to analyze or raise the question of what research should be conducted. Worthington Foods (B), City Police, and Marketing a City—Discover Columbus are examples of cases containing research. The cases are developed in such a way that the instructor may ask students to develop a sophisticated analysis and intrepretation of the research or may require the student to emphasize strategy issues more than research sophistication.

A third emphasis is on using actual companies for cases. The cases report actual research (with all of its inadequacies) in real company settings. In most cases, we have secured permission to include the real name of the company rather than to use a "masked" case. Experience indicates that students are more interested in studying a case about an actual company. In our own teaching of these and similar cases, we encourage students to secure annual reports or 10-K reports filed with the Securities and Exchange Commission for the latest financial or operating information. The information service described in one of the cases, CompuServe, is a source for much of these data for the increasing number of students with a PC, a modem, and an account number.

This book contains cases on some truly exciting companies. Students will learn much by understanding the basis of these companies' successes. The Ford Taurus, for example, is the most successful American car development of recent years. This case will help students understand why Detroit needed a truly revolutionary approach to new product development. Two of the five most successful retailers in America are The Home Depot and The Limited. Both are in this book as is Consolidated Stores, another high-growth firm in a very competitive industry. Bank One is probably the most innovative bank holding company in the world, with new product developments such as bank cards, ATMs, drive-in banking, EFT, cash management accounts, and other innovations that have truly transformed America and the world. Yet, many will find just as exciting the problem of rejuvenating a retailer such as Paul Harris. If you have students who are concerned with difficulty in getting good grades or the problems of overcoming physical handicaps, they should find The Longaberger Company (A) of special interest.

This is a "high tech" book in the sense that we have included cases about new high tech products such as CheckFree and CompuServe as well as Checkpoint. Students will have to access the data base for such cases, however, with the "old tech" of the printed page.

This case book, designed especially for courses in consumer behavior, is organized around the contents of the seventh edition of *Consumer Behavior,* by James F. Engel, Roger D. Blackwell, and Paul W. Miniard. The case book is useful, however, with other consumer behavior texts. Judging from adoptions of the previous edition, it may also be used in marketing research, advertising, and communication courses. These disciplines are either explicitly or potentially included in almost every case in this edition. This book has a strong managerial orientation, continuing the orientation of earlier editions of this case book.

When an earlier edition of this book was reviewed in a leading journal, the reviewer reported that it was valuable reading as a guide to contemporary consumer research and strategy. This confirmed the experience of the authors in preparing the case book. Although designed for pedagogical purposes, the book provides a vehicle for describing the decision processes, marketing strategies, and research of leading organizations. We have been pleasantly surprised by the large number of business firms and managers who have purchased earlier editions of this case book as a source about contemporary, mostly successful organizations.

We enjoyed working with people from the companies who supplied materials for these cases and greatly appreciate their time and assistance. In many instances, a large number of persons became involved in obtaining materials, granting permissions, and checking final cases. We have listed some of them on the Acknowledgments page. We appreciate the work they did and that of others who helped develop this book. Many of the cases grew directly out of the "live" cases that were prepared by the MBA class in Consumer Behavior at The Ohio State University and we gratefully acknowledge the contributions of these students to many of the cases. We are particularly appreciative of the contribution of Kelley Hughes, who prepared the manuscript.

Finally, we would like to thank our families, Dr. and Mrs. Blackwell, Mr. and Mrs. Stephan, and Rosey Talarzyk for their support during the writing and editing processes. Working closely with a spouse on such a project has made it a unique and wonderful experience for two of us. It also made the late night writing sessions necessary to produce this book a little easier.

Roger D. Blackwell
Kristina Stephan Blackwell
W. Wayne Talarzyk

February 1993

Acknowledgments

■ ■ ■ ■ ■

Many individuals were very helpful in the successful completion of this collection of cases. It is with much appreciation that all of these people are acknowledged for their contributions to this book. Sincere appreciation is given to Lyn Hastert, The Dryden Press, and Betsy Webster, Elm Street Publishing Services, for their guidance and attention to detail in the preparation of this manuscript.

In addition, appreciation is specifically expressed to the following individuals for cooperating in the development of cases on firms and organizations with which they are associated:

Anita Roddick
Cheryl Kreuger
Dale Twomley
Steven Dunson
Al Dietzel
Bill Kelley
Dan Evans
Emil Brolick
Bill Krestel
Todd Barnum
Karen Brennan
Gerald Paul
Paul and Mary Gelpi
Leonard Jennings
Dave Wible
Maurice Cox

Peter J. Kight
A. E. Wolfe
Vicki Limbach
Harry Rosen
R. A. Ackerman
Sarah Patterson
Carlo Tunioli
Tami Kaido Longaberger
David Lida
Paul Ecke
Wilfried Huettemann
Peter Rhode
Henk Westerlaken
John Russell
Dick Karn
Dennis Karn

Contents

■ ■ ■ ■ ■

CONSUMER INFLUENCES ON THE ORGANIZATION

ENVIRONMENTAL INFLUENCES ON CONSUMER BEHAVIOR

INDIVIDUAL DIFFERENCES

DECISION PROCESSES

MARKETING STRATEGY

COMPREHENSIVE CASES

P A **1** R T

CONSUMER INFLUENCES ON THE ORGANIZATION

■ ■ ■ ■ ■

CASE 1
Ford Motor Company

CASE 2
The Body Shop

CASE 3
Pepsi Cola

CASE 4
Cheryl & Co.

■

Ford Motor Company

■ ■ ■ ■ ■

"It's a global war and we're under attack on every front." That's the way one automobile executive described the market for cars in 1992. What once was a cozy national market shared by the Big Three automakers has turned into a free-for-all in which U.S. manufacturers are fighting for their lives against strong competitors from Japan, Germany, Korea, Sweden, and other countries.

An indication of the intensity of global competition was the decision of the Board of Directors of General Motors in 1992 to shake up top management by replacing the Chairman of the Executive Committee with a new chairman—a Canadian, John Smale, who formerly had headed Procter & Gamble. Both General Motors and Chrysler recently turned to Europe to find a new company president. *USA Today*, with headlines announcing "Reins Go to Globally Oriented," described the new leadership at GM by saying, "Unlike GM executives of the past, whose frame of reference seemed to be southeastern Michigan, the new triumvirate has solid global credentials."[1]

The Big Three are not only competing for sales in other countries of the world, but even in the United States, where the Honda Accord has become the number one selling car in the nation in 1991. It replaced Ford's Escort, which formerly held the title of largest selling car in the United States. "Japan bashing" was a popular sport with union leaders, auto management, politicians, and others, who often placed blame for America's deteriorating position on Japan rather than on U.S. practices.

Some observers believe that Ford Motor may be the best positioned of Detroit's Big Three automakers for global marketing. With policies begun under former Chairman Peterson and extended by current Chairman "Red" Poling, Ford has quietly set about to make itself into a world-class

---

[1]Micheline Maynard and James R. Healey, "Reins Go to Globally Oriented," *USA Today*, April 7, 1992, B1.

competitor. In the darkest hours of the 1980s, Ford North America was helped greatly by Ford Europe. Not only did profits flow from Europe to Detroit, so did key executives as well as new approaches to manufacturing and marketing. Ford is highly successful in the United Kingdom and reasonably successful in competing with European firms throughout Europe.

In the U.S. market, Ford has declared all-out war on both foreign and domestic competitors. The central combat area in this war lies in the midsize market, where Ford hopes to go head-to-head with Accord and dislodge it from the number one spot.

More is at stake than simple pride or the desire to be number one. Midsize family sedans such as the Accord, Camry, Taurus, and the Chevrolet Lumina make up 34 percent of the total car market. More importantly, they generally return an average of 16 percent to 18 percent profit margin. On smaller cars such as the Escort, manufacturers generally lose money. With swelling numbers of aging baby boomers, midsize sales are expected to increase 20 percent during the next five years.[2]

The key weapon in Ford's battle for dominance is the Taurus (and its sister car in the Mercury line, the Sable). Sometimes called a "jellybean," a "flying potato," or a copy of Germany's best cars, the Taurus is a distinctively different approach to producing cars.

Cars typically were produced in Detroit first as a gleam in somebody's eye, then a burst of passion, and finally a long period of intense labor pains and a messy delivery. U.S. automakers competed aggressively with one another but their products and methods all sprang from the same family of ideas, which typically resulted in similarity and active procedures for creating supposedly new products.

When Ford first introduced the Taurus in 1986, it might have followed the ordinary pattern of development for new products. That might have resulted in an undistinguished product that would have done little, if anything, to improve the company's chance of survival.

Sequential Product Development

The conventional process of developing new cars was described by Ford executives as "sequential." It consisted of a series of unrelated, uncoordinated activities by people insulated from one another in their own narrowly defined areas of specialization. The unwritten rule previously was that certain things had to be done before others and that each area of specialization was sacrosanct. No set of experts had any business meddling in other experts' affairs.

The development of a new car typically began with product planners, who generated an overall concept of the vehicle's basic dimensions, style,

[2]Greg Bowens, "Taurus Goes for the Title," *Business Week*, May 18, 1992, 50–51.

and equipment content. These product planners had a narrowly defined area of creative freedom, working within the constraints of the vision for the car that top management felt the public ought to have. From product planners, the vehicle's development was given to design engineers, who translated the more or less abstract design into concrete form: clay scale models and mock-ups. Next, the job was passed along to specifications engineers, whose job was to draw up the nuts-and-bolts requirements that would determine and demonstrate how the artistic creation could actually be turned into a car.

After various engineers had done their work, the manufacturing specialists were responsible for figuring out how all the components would be built and brought together and how the car would be built on the assembly line. Some specialists were internal company people. Others were outside suppliers who were expected to build components according to the specifications of the automaker's engineers. As the cars rolled off the assembly line, the company's marketing department had the task of selling them. Later, when an unpredictable number of cars broke down, the dealer and sometimes the company's own service specialists had to fix them.

At various times, or in various stages of the car's progression from concept to service bay, there were still other specialized jobs and events going on that would affect the car's ultimate success. Company finance people had to compute costs and establish budgets for producing and marketing the car and price it to suit the intended market and yield the intended profit. The legal department had to make sure the car met various government regulations concerning safety, fuel efficiency, noise, and pollution controls. Labor relations people were interested in whether or not the car could be built within union work rule constraints. Procurement and inventory control specialists arranged for the purchase and timely availability of materials. Public relations experts had to prepare the public for the new car and seek favorable attention from the automotive press.

The results of this system were poor communication, territorialism, buck-passing, and squandered opportunities. People from different departments or specialties didn't speak the same dialect or share a common purpose. There were professional jealousies, interdepartmental rivalries, and a widespread tendency to blame somebody else for anything that went wrong. If too many cars were coming off the line with defects, the manufacturing specialists, designers, and engineers found it easy to blame one another. If a car didn't sell as well as expected, the marketing people might blame the finance people for pricing it too high. The situation was something described as civil war. Donald Peterson, former CEO of Ford, described the situation as a collection of vertical "chimneys." Each function was a self-contained, vertical unit, and one chimney's managers usually didn't communicate very well with their counterparts in other chimneys.

■ EXHIBIT 1.1   The Sequel That Improves on the Original

**THE SEQUEL
THAT IMPROVES ON
THE ORIGINAL.**

Buckle up — together we can save lives.

**HAVE YOU
DRIVEN
A FORD
LATELY?**

You've been waiting for it. The evolution of the revolutionary Ford Taurus. Be prepared to cast aside the limits of traditional sedan expectations.

THE REINTRODUCTION.
And here it is. The 1992 Ford Taurus. An innovative wonder that gives refinement and subtlety their due. The new Taurus has a completely redesigned exterior that gives you a distinct new edge of sophistication. The interior is quieter, more comfortable. And the instrument panel flows smoothly from door to door, with controls put in places that will pleasantly surprise you.

THE SAFETY STORY.
But this Taurus is not just a testament to

smoothing rough edges. It's taking the best of new ideas and putting them to use. Anti-lock brakes are available. And Taurus offers *dual air bags* (standard driver and optional right-front passenger air bag supplemental restraint system to be used with your safety belts) — a Ford Motor Company exclusive in this class.

THE SATISFYING CONCLUSION.
The 1992 Ford Taurus. An excellent reminder that the best sequels are the ones that know why the original was a success.

For more information call 1-800-34-FLEET.

NEW TAURUS 🔵 *Ford*
THE FORD FLEET DIFFERENCE.

Team Taurus[3]

Ford's leadership wanted "no more heroes," a dismantling of the chimneys. The result was a new atmosphere that encouraged the creation of coordinated, project-oriented teams of people with diverse talents, such as the team that developed the Taurus.

Development of the Taurus began in late 1979 under the code name "Sigma" and was originally a project of the company's advanced vehicle department. Heading the department at that time was Lewis C. Veraldi, who later became the vice president for car programs management. The team eventually grew to include several hundred people, and in the spring of 1980, the team received a new name: "Team Taurus."

The name Taurus evolved from conversations between Veraldi and planning director John W. Risk, who discovered that their wives shared the astrological sign Taurus. Taurus became the working name for the team. Later the company tested the name through consumer research and got very positive reactions. Taurus seemed appropriate for a product that bore the burden of saving its company. In Greek mythology, Taurus is a cosmic constellation containing seven stars that represent the seven daughters of Atlas, who was the titan bearing the weight of the world on his shoulders. Astrologically, the Taurus personality is supposed to be faithful, deliberate, determined, and practical—qualities that might be desirable in a family car. To consumers, Taurus suggested brute power, tenacity, and the pride of a bull.

The Sable, companion to the Taurus, is virtually identical to the Taurus mechanically but has a somewhat sleeker, more stylish exterior and interior. It is also 2.5 inches longer than the Taurus, giving it 1.5 cubic feet more interior space and a different front-end appearance. The net effect of the subtle styling differences is enough to make the Sable appear sportier and a little more dashing, targeted to a market of younger, style-conscious buyers. The Taurus, on the other hand, looks heavier, more substantial, and slightly subdued in style to appeal to young and middle-aged, family-oriented buyers.

The Target Customer

Team Taurus grew in size as well as in clarity of purpose, which Lewis Veraldi segmented into four basic parts:

1. The team was to create a *world-class car*, with quality second to none—either domestic or foreign.

2. The *customer* would be the focal point in defining quality.

---

[3]The quotations and most of the facts in this case about Taurus are abstracted from Alton F. Doody and Ron Bingaman, *Reinventing the Wheels* (Cambridge, MA: Ballinger Publishing Company, 1988).

3. *Product integrity* would never be compromised.

4. To accommodate the first three objectives, the team at the very beginning had to involve people from both *"upstream"* and *"downstream"* in the car-making process: that is, from the CEO's office to the design studios to the end of the assembly line—and even beyond, to the supplier, the ad agency, the dealership, and, ultimately, the customer.

To make the first three objectives more attainable, Veraldi's fourth objective had a corollary purpose: to replace *sequential* development with *concurrent* development. For example, soliciting manufacturing's input upstream in the design process would make manufacturing's job easier and better integrated with design objectives when the project later came downstream through engineering to the factory floor. With all the departments working concurrently rather than sequentially, all the benefits of real teamwork would be more achievable.

The team aspect was very important in the development of the Taurus. The great legends in the automobile business were about *individuals* rather than groups or teams. Bold, colorful workaholic, domineering personalities stir the emotions and fascinate the imaginations and feed the presses of the business and popular media. The Henry Fords, Lee Iacoccas, and John DeLoreans are typical of such legends. With the Taurus, the "hero" was the *product* rather than an individual. This represented a transformation of the *corporate culture* at Ford and involved both company executives and union leaders as well as engineers and stylists, accountants and manufacturing people, marketers and lawyers. Getting such diverse types of people to listen to one another, to respect one another's ideas and problems, and to collaborate to satisfy the customer was the objective of Team Taurus.

With the Taurus program, Ford made a different type of commitment than in the past. For the first time, the *customer* came first. This meant serious research from the beginning and continuing throughout the development process to ensure that Team Taurus remained on target. Furthermore, Ford needed to understand more clearly its overall position in the marketplace. Things were getting bad, but it wasn't enough simply to blame imports or even to admit that Ford quality was unacceptably low. The company needed to know what was on consumers' minds. What, specifically, did consumers dislike about Ford, its products, or its dealers? Exactly what did they find better about both domestic and foreign competition?

Marketing Research

Marketing research at Ford had long been a central corporate staff function operating out of Ford's world headquarters. This position separated the research people from many of the day-to-day operating realities of the company. Many of the manufacturing and other personnel viewed marketing research with distrust. In 1980, a large part of the marketing research staff was reassigned to Ford's North American Automotive Operations

(NAAO), headed by Red Poling. A few researchers remained part of the worldwide corporate marketing staff but most were transferred out of the world headquarters and placed in the operating unit responsible for actually producing and selling cars in the United States. Louis Ross, head of NAAO's Car Product Development Group, told his staff, "If you ask these people to do research, you'd better listen to them, and if you don't want to follow their research findings, you'd better have a very good reason."

Once marketing research became part of NAAO, its top priority was Team Taurus, and research personnel became working members of the team. Working side-by-side with designers, engineers, manufacturing specialists, finance people, marketers, and other key operating personnel, they could become sensitive to the complexities of putting an automobile together. Research would be focused tightly on practical, day-to-day knowledge requirements. Marketing researchers were *team* members.

A master plan was developed for the marketing research group within NAAO, headed by Ray Ablondi. The objective of this plan was to identify the specific, concrete ways in which research could contribute to or reinforce the overall team effort. Research for the sake of research was of no interest. The *timing* of research activities was of crucial importance, geared to specific make-or-break decision points in the continuing development of a new car.

An example of the flexibility that occurred with the new approach to research came more than a year after development had begun. As Lewis Veraldi put it, "We scrapped the whole car." Although an overstatement in the sense that the basic conceptual design and quality standards were not changed, the size was engineered to be bigger than originally intended, because of a perceived change in the targeted market. When planning had first started, the national and world economies were still experiencing rapidly rising oil prices. Gasoline prices were then expected to keep climbing to as much as $2 or $3 a gallon. Fuel efficiency had been an overriding priority, and since a car's size and weight are major determinants of fuel efficiency, the Taurus had started out as a rather small car. In early 1981, there were signs that by 1985 when the Taurus was scheduled to reach the market, gasoline prices would level out and Americans would again prefer larger cars. Team Taurus reached a consensus that the car as originally designed would be too small. The small prototype was expanded by enlarging the wheelbase, widening its trance and increasing overall volume. Veraldi was convinced that such a midcourse change in direction could not have occurred in the previous culture: "Without the simultaneous process of the team approach, so much time would have been lost that we probably wouldn't have been able to accomplish all the changes in design. With the team approach, everyone was in on the change. It came as no surprise, and thus could be planned for and adjusted to accordingly."

An important finding during the early marketing research projects concerned consumer perceptions of Ford. Some Ford officials had presumed that the public was angry with the firm. Research showed that Americans, especially those on the West Coast, were not really angry with

Ford; they simply didn't care. They were indifferent and were now getting their cars from sources that provided what they really wanted. The only thing that mattered, according to the research, was *customer satisfaction*. If Ford made the right kind of car available at the right price, convinced people that it really was good, and then serviced it properly after it was in the customer's hands, the company would be able to sell more cars.

The overall marketing research program for Team Taurus was far more extensive and exhaustive than any such program ever conducted by Ford or by any other U.S. auto manufacturer. Researchers interviewed more people than had ever been interviewed before in connection with a single new car model and covered more territory geographically. In Marin County, California, the research team interviewed 4,500 people in group sessions and conducted consumer tests using fifty Fords, thirty European cars and twenty Japanese cars.

Researchers asked questions about specific car features and drive concerns. The team showed Taurus mock-ups to a group of people, let those same people drive prototypes of the cars, and then went back to them yet a third time for additional feedback after recommended changes had been made. This was different than previous approaches in which a company would hold a "product clinic" and invite a small number of consumers to look at either an exterior or interior mock-up of a new car in its early design stage. Previously, those same people were rarely ever asked back or given a chance to drive a prototype; they hardly ever saw the car again until the finished product was on the market.

The styling of the Taurus was the most important focus of consumer research in the early stages. The soft, oval style was so different from the boxy, angular shape of mainstream American cars that many people at Ford were uneasy about how the public would react. It was true that Ford was already committing to the production of other models of similar shape, such as Thunderbird and Cougar, but these cars were targeted for markets considerably different from the ones Taurus and Sable were intended to reach. The Thunderbird and Cougar were targeted to youthful, sporty, nonconservative buyers, the type of people who are fashion-conscious and who like to think of themselves as being in the vanguard of new styles and trends. The Taurus, in contrast, was to be Ford's meat-and-potatoes car. It had to appeal to a much broader assortment and greater number of buyers, described as the "mid-market"—buyers concentrated among middle-and upper-middle-income families, a larger number of whom tend to be conservative in taste and oriented more toward utility and economy than toward cutting edge style. Ford was hoping this market would include many young professional families—the vast number of "baby boomers"—who might otherwise buy European or Japanese family size cars. The danger was that too many mid-market buyers might consider Taurus styling to be uncomfortably strange, too futuristic, or perhaps even too European.

In automotive marketing research, one of the important variables is geography. Regardless of how car buyers may be classified according to income, occupation, age, or other market segmenting characteristic, many also tend to follow a geographical bias in their choice of cars. Size and styling preferences, especially, vary by region or even by state. Certain types of cars sell better in Texas than in Ohio; New Yorkers buy more of a certain car than Kentuckians. Perhaps no car buyer stands out more distinctly than the California driver.

With its penchant for youth worship, sportiness, and offbeat life-styles, California is a bellwether for new trends, unconventional ideas, and innovative products of all types. California drivers are especially interested in the "cockpit," or the way the car feels and looks from the driver's seat. They are particularly aware of the personal, even intimate, car-driver relationship, which involves the features surrounding and affecting the driver's own space in the car. Californians spent a great deal of time sitting in the driver's seat and absorbing the aura of the car's cockpit and the Taurus's drastically new dashboard design, instrument configuration, and other driver-friendly accessories. By contrast, when the car was previewed in Rochester, New York, consumers were more interested in the *back seat*. After a rather cursory inspection of the cockpit, most upstate New Yorkers opened the rear doors, climbed in, and tried out the rear seat compartment, which would have to be suitable for hauling around tots and teenagers, as well as mothers-in-law.

The research revealed that many people might initially be uncomfortable with the car's aesthetics, but through persuasion and understanding could come to appreciate the practical benefits of its aerodynamic design. Ford was more interested in lasting relationships than in initial reactions and wanted to build a solid constituency of repeat buyers. This would require education to change attitudes and preferences through two-way marketing research. In short, the market was to be educated, briefed, and conditioned to appreciate the Taurus for what it really was rather than what it might initially seem to be.

The Product

The aerodynamic styling was essential to Ford's belief that form should follow function in the design of the car using the new total process of development. Even though there was uneasiness about how America's mid-market car buyers would accept the radical new styling, there were simply too many practical benefits to the aerospace design. The more aerodynamic the style, the less wind resistance, or drag. This principle is known as "coefficient-of-drag," or Cd for short. The lower the Cd number, the better. A compact car with a Cd of .36, for example, gets about two miles per gallon better highway mileage than a car of similar size with a .40 Cd. Most American cars in the early 1980s, with the exception of Ford's Thunderbird and LTD, had .48 Cd. The best standards up to that time had been developed in Europe, especially with the Mercedes-Benz and Audi 5000, which had .33 and .32 Cd ratings, respectively.

Ford's goal with the Taurus was to come as close to these pacesetting drag coefficients as possible. When the first models came out in December 1985, the rating was .33 for the Taurus sedan (and .32 for the Sable) and .34 for the station wagon, which beat Ford's own best standard up to that time of .35 for the 1983 Thunderbird. These principles have since been introduced to other Ford products; the Probe, for example, achieved an outstanding .30 Cd.

The aerodynamic design not only delivered better gas mileage but also enhanced handling and roadability. It also cut down wind noise, giving a quieter ride, reflecting Ford's concern for the passenger. A company press release proclaimed, "The drive is the focus for all engineering, design, performance, dynamics, and functions. The Taurus will be designed from the driver outward."

The "driver-outward" concept affected many aspects of the Taurus. Using ergonomics, the science of relationships between humans and machines, Team Taurus studied every facet of the driver's interaction with the car. This meant designing a cockpit that brought all the instruments and control systems within quick and easy reach of the driver, making the job of driving as manageable as possible, including *safety* as well as comfort. If all the details that confront a driver can be simplified, then the driver can pay more attention to watching the road, traffic signals, and other cars.

Since drivers and passengers come in as many sizes and shapes as the human race affords, it is next to impossible to build a "universal" car seat that will comfortably fit everyone. But Team Taurus, aided by an unprecedented research investment in seat design, did about as good a job as could be expected. For one thing, front seats are offered in three configurations: (1) a full length bench seat with a fold-down center armrest and a driver's seat back recliner that allows half degree incremental adjustments; (2) a split-bench seat, with individual center fold-down armrest and dual seat back recliners; and (3) individual "bucket" recliner seats. All seats have lower back supports and are made of heavy density foam to help alleviate fatigue on long trips. All front seats have headrests that adjust both horizontally and vertically.

At one point during its research, Ford learned of a common customer complaint involving the forward and backward floor level adjustment of front seats. People said it was irritating to have to grope under the edge of the seat for a small release lever, which was located in different spots on different models of cars. It was especially inconvenient to people in two car families and to people who frequently drove cars, such as rentals, that didn't belong to them. Ford's ergonomical solution was to equip the Taurus with a horizontal release bar running almost the entire width of the seat beneath its front edge. The driver only needed to reach down, at any point, and the release bar would be there. Under the old Detroit philosophy this improvement might have been considered an insignificant detail affecting only a small number of drivers. Had it cost, say, an incremental $1.00 per car for a car that was expected to sell 500,000 units a year, then it would have been viewed as $500,000 in "lost" profit—maybe $2–3 million over the life span of the model.

Taurus also has dual sun-visors. Most late model cars have adjustable sun-visors that can be swung to the front or to the side, depending on whether you're driving toward or parallel to the sun's glare. But in real life, streets and roads don't always run in straight lines for long distances. One moment, the sun is directly in front of you; the next, it may be directly to your side. It is not only an inconvenience but also a compromise of driving safety to be constantly switching the visor as you follow the bends in the road. In the Taurus, however, dual visors block the sun's rays from both the front and side simultaneously, and built-in visor extensions offer further protection when the sun is low on the horizon.

Throughout the car, Team Taurus pursued similar customer-oriented ideas and opportunities—any one of which might have been viewed as relatively unimportant but when taken together added up to the most user-friendly car Detroit ever produced. The driver, for example, was given a left footrest and an oversized accelerator pedal for more comfort on long road trips. Cockpit controls were backlighted for easy visibility at night, and the map light was designed to give clear view to the front seat passenger while remaining almost invisible to the driver. Rope netting was installed in the trunk of the sedan, so that the grocery bags could get from the supermarket to the driveway without falling over.

Best-in-Class Program

Quality was of critical importance. But quality can be a nebulous concept. If Ford was to build not a "good" car, but the "best" quality car of its kind in the world, some objective standard of measurement would be needed to help keep score. As with virtually everything else connected with the Taurus program, Ford had to invent its own standard. The result was the "Best-in-Class" program, or "BIC" for short.

The idea of BIC was not attributable to any one person, but arose from early brainstorming sessions among designers, engineers, and product specialists. Under the BIC program, the development team identified every major car in the world and then evaluated those cars in terms of 400 separate components, features, and functions. The key idea was not to rate every competitive car as a whole, but to evaluate each of the designated components or features on a car-by-car basis and to single out the best among them. The "best" then became Ford's target for the Taurus. The company tried to match or exceed the competition in as many of the 400 categories as possible.

The 400 BIC items were grouped into twelve major categories and forty-nine subcategories. The major areas covered were: ride, steering, handling, power-train performance, power-train smoothness, body chassis, performance feel, driveability, brakes, climate control, seat performance, and operational comfort. Subcategories covered an exhaustive list of functional as well as image-oriented features such as driver's rearward visibility, brake-lining life, ease of checking fluids, glove compartment size and accessibility, ignition key size and weight, and many others.

The team even measured the number of times you had to turn the handle to roll a manually operated window up and down. The Mazda 626 won Best-in-Class for this particular function with a performance beyond the reach of the Taurus. BIC couldn't be achieved in competition with Mazda. But the reason for this "failure" illustrates a serious issue in car design. The more severe curvature of Taurus's flush glass required a trade-off. The aerodynamic styling of the Taurus required that the windows be flush with the car's rounded body, and this meant that the window glass had to be curved to an unusual degree. The result was a somewhat less efficient window cranking system—a problem most people might consider minor, but one that Ford made an effort to modify in later models of the Taurus. This example reflects the complexity of designing a car as an integrated totality. Change one thing, and you'll most likely have to change a number of others. And if you do not follow up with those changes, the result is a hodgepodge in which many of the components work at cross purposes, as had been the case with many Detroit products over the years, such as Chevrolet's Caprice.

The first Taurus released in December 1985 met the target on 320 of the 400 selected BIC features. In other words, it matched or bettered a full 80 percent of the best features found on the best cars of its class in the world.

Throughout the development, Team Taurus had to make decisions about when to disregard or override certain consumer likes and dislikes, even when those likes and dislikes were explicitly revealed in marketing research. The goal was to create a rationally conceived, coherent, functioning piece of equipment rather than tacking together an assortment of features to satisfy any and all of the perceived wants and whims that might be expressed in the marketplace.

The issue of white sidewall tires presented Team Taurus with one such judgment call. For as long as people could remember, large and midsized American cars had been rolled onto the market on gleaming white sidewalls. It was almost an article of faith. Even though whitewall tires were used nowhere else in the world as original new-car equipment, Americans seemed to consider them an almost indispensable accessory. Until Team Taurus, no Detroit automaker dared to offer a major new model in the Taurus class without white sidewalls, at least as an option. Members of Team Taurus considered white tires as incompatible with either the car's styling or the overall image of a world-class car. Europe and Japan had been designing and building quality cars that looked just as good without "white spats." If Taurus was to claim its place among world-class cars, it should be able to do so on the strength of its simplicity and symmetry of design, which white tires would only serve to disrupt visually.

■ **EXHIBIT 1.2   Have You Ever Thought Life Could Use a Wake-Up Call?**

HAVE YOU EVER THOUGHT LIFE COULD USE A WAKE-UP CALL?

HAVE YOU DRIVEN A FORD LATELY?

THE 24-VALVE, 220 HORSEPOWER FORD TAURUS SHO.
It's a wake-up call in a world of sleepy sedans. The 24-valve, 220 horsepower shot of adrenalin called Ford Taurus SHO.

When its Super High Output V-6 comes alive, a special sport-tuned suspension and anti-lock brakes sync up with a *new, improved five-speed shifter* to create a responsive and invigorating performance.

The SHO's new dash flows into the doors in a seemingly seamless manner. SHO also has performance gauges and articulated sport seats with optional leather trim.

Outside, ground effects enhance a new shape to create a dramatic look. One to be noticed both coming and going.

NEWS ABOUT SAFETY.
All it takes is some rapid eye movement around the cockpit to see what's new. For safety's sake, there's a *newly available front passenger-side air bag*. A driver-side air bag comes standard. Both supplemental restraint systems should be used with your safety belt.

Take your daily routine down a new route. The 1992 Ford Taurus SHO.

FORD. THE BEST-BUILT AMERICAN CARS...ELEVEN YEARS RUNNING.
Based on an average of consumer-reported problems in a series of surveys of all Ford and competitive '81-'91 models designed and built in North America.

NEW TAURUS SHO

Competition

The new research philosophy of Ford contrasted sharply with the approach that General Motors appeared to use during this period. GM's 1985 and 1986 Cadillacs, for example, had been downsized and restyled with trimmer, cleaner, sleeker lines. But consumer research showed that some customers were beginning to view GM's lineup of Buicks, Oldsmobiles, and Cadillacs as a parade of look-alikes. Many Cadillac owners, especially, seemed dissatisfied with the smaller look of their cars. The new Cadillacs apparently were not "Caddy" enough for them. GM, perhaps fearing a full-scale revolt by Cadillac traditionalists, hastily responded in a superficial, stopgap manner. On the 1987 Cadillac, the company extended both the front and rear bumpers by a few inches to make the car look longer and heavier. The change was purely cosmetic. It added or improved nothing in terms of the car's efficiency, driving ease, or safety. In fact, the opposite was the case. The only things added were cost, weight, and bulk; the changes even made the car more difficult to park. Furthermore, the integrity of the car's original design had been compromised. Part of the gracefulness and balance of the car's styling was sacrificed in order to allow a few people to feel they were once again driving a "big" Cadillac. General Motors had invested about $3 billion in developing its new larger car series, which included the 1985–86 Cadillacs. This was identical to the sum that Ford committed to the Taurus-Sable program. Ford executives were reported to say, "GM is going through the motions, but they're still not *really* listening to the consumer." It was not until 1990 that the effects of their concern began to be observed with the winning of the Malcolm Baldrige award for quality.

When Taurus was originally introduced, promotional effort was not extensive but soon word of mouth and much favorable publicity began to build awareness of Taurus among the consuming public. In 1987 and 1988, Ford outsold Chevrolet, a feat that had not been accomplished for many decades. Chevrolet and the entire General Motors family of cars began a precipitous decline in market share, culminating in the management shake-up by the outside directors of GM in 1992.

But Ford and the Taurus were also under attack, most directly by Japanese firms. While Japanese firms had originally entered the market with low price, fuel efficient cars following the fuel shortages of the mid-1970s, the Japanese brands had evolved over time and in response to the changing age of the baby-boomer cohort. The Honda Accord became America's number one selling nameplate in 1991. But at the same time, the Lexus and the Infiniti luxury cars were tied at number one in quality, based on ratings by J.D. Powers, Inc.

Taurus had achieved great success—perhaps the most successful new car introduced by an American manufacturer in recent decades. For 1992, Toyota had introduced a dramatically restyled and higher priced Camry. But Ford was not sitting still either. For 1992, Taurus introduced new styling and began pushing its safety edge as the only midsize family car offering both a driver's air bag as standard equipment and, for an extra $400, an optional passenger side air bag. Taurus also offered a top of the line Taurus—the SHO, capable of speeds in excess of 150 miles an hour and rated by some car magazines as the fastest sedan in America.

In its television advertising, Taurus featured the dual air bags as well as the new styling of the 1992 model. In specialized print ads, Taurus featured on a more limited basis the luxury and highly acclaimed performance of the Taurus SHO. The Honda Accord was expected to introduce extensive restyling in its 1994 model, but Taurus as well as Toyota's Camry offered a more powerful V-6 engine compared to Accord's four-cylinder power plant. Ford felt that its cars, its organization, and its vision were positioned for the global marketplace better than were its domestic competitors, but Ford was well aware of the intensity of competition it would face on many fronts.

Focal Topics

1. Should Ford be considered "customer oriented" in the development of Taurus? Has Ford successfully implemented the marketing concept?

2. Is Ford justified in focusing on the midsized car market? Who are the core market segments for the Taurus?

3. How do consumers buy cars in the core market segments you have identified as the Taurus market targets? What are the variables that determine whether or not they buy a new car and which specific brand is bought?

4. What promotional strategy would you recommend for Taurus in the mid-1990s? Be specific about creative appeals and media.

5. Can Taurus be classified as a "world-class car"? What principles used to develop the Taurus should be applied to other areas at Ford or to its competitors?

■ ■ ■ ■ ■

The Body Shop

■ ■ ■ ■ ■

The Body Shop was founded in 1976 by Anita Roddick; its first shop was located on a side street in Brighton, England. Ms Roddick envisioned a store where customers could buy beauty items such as shampoo and skin cream in the quantities they desired, just as consumers shopped for fruits and vegetables. She had experienced some tough times of her own and could not afford to buy large quantities of shampoo and beauty care items at one time. When she opened her store she figured there were other people in the same situation and, therefore, offered five different sizes of products. These same bottle sizes are available in each store today.

The first shop sold a variety of twenty-five different natural skin and hair care products in hand labeled bottles. The labels were round and green in color only because they were inexpensive and the color was bright. People like to speculate today that the labels were green because of issues of environmental concern. Today there are over 800 Body Shops worldwide with a variety of over 350 products sold in each store. Still headquartered in West Sussex, United Kingdom, The Body Shop employs over 5,850 worldwide. The Body Shop through its concept, staff and founder, continues to have an impact on consumers, retailing, and people throughout the world.

Products

The company is committed to the research, development, manufacturing, and distribution of healthy beauty care products for men and women. Body Shop products are designed to cleanse, polish, and protect the skin and hair naturally. Consumers can buy avocado soap, apple shampoo, clay facial masks, fragrance derived from vanilla, spearmint, and cinnamon, and natural peach bath crystals. The Body Shop has also expanded into natural and non-allergenic makeup, including eye shadow, mascara, foundation, and blush. A photo of products and list of products are shown in

■ **EXHIBIT 2.1   The Body Shop**

■ **EXHIBIT 2.2   The Body Shop Retail Environment**

Exhibit 2.1. Exhibit 2.2 shows a typical Body Shop store. Product categories are listed in Exhibit 2.3, which also details the depth and variety of soaps available.

The product line at The Body Shop has evolved dramatically in the last decade. Colourings, a cosmetics range, was launched in the stores in

■ **EXHIBIT 2.3   Product Categories and Soap Categories**

SOAPS

HAIR SHAMPOOS

HAIR CONDITIONERS

HAIR TREATMENTS

HAIR STYLING

FACIAL CLEANSERS

CLEANSING MASKS

SKIN FRESHENERS

FACIAL MOISTURIZERS

SKIN TREATMENTS

LIP CARE

BODY LOTIONS

BODY CARE

MASSAGE

BATH/SHOWER

NATURAL OILS

FRAGRANCE RANGES

PERFUME OILS

SUNDRIES

MOSTLY MEN

ALOE RANGE

SUN CARE

MAMATOTO

COLOURINGS

The Body Shop
45 Horsehill Road,
Hanover Technical Center,
Cedar Knolls, NJ 07927
© The Body Shop. All rights reserved.

SOAPS

All The Body Shop's soaps are vegetable based. Instead of the traditionally used animal oils and fats, our soap base is made with Palm Oil and Coconut Oil.

Soapworks
Soapworks is The Body Shop's soap-manufacturing base at Easterhouse in Scotland which currently produces the majority of our soaps. Easterhouse is an area with high unemployment and few facilities. Soapworks provides work for local people and products for The Body Shop.

Coconut Milk Soap
Contains pure coconut oil, a fine-grade emollient oil expressed from the kernels of the coconut pod. Skin type: all types.

Fruit Soaps
Very mild transparent glycerin soaps colored according to fragrance: Green Apple, Fresh Lemon, Mandarin, Apricot, Strawberry, Dewberry, Grapefruit and Fuzzy Peach. Skin type: all types except very sensitive skin.

Fun Fruit Soaps
A range of small fruit-shaped soaps, looking and smelling just like the real thing. These mild glycerin soaps are available in Apple, Strawberry, Lemon and Banana and are great for all skin types, except very sensitive.

Lily Milk Soap
Extra mild glycerin soap especially recommended for sensitive skins.

Evening Primrose Oil Soap
A gentle soap containing evening primrose oil well known for maintaining healthy skin. Herbalists in Europe used this oil so much it became known as the "Kings Cure All"! Skin type: all types except very sensitive skin.

Tea Rose Soap
A gentle soap delicately fragranced with Tea Rose - grannies, aunts and moms will love it! Skin type: all types except very sensitive skin.

Camellia Oil Soap
Contains camellia oil for its light non-greasy texture. Skin type: all types except very sensitive skin.

Jojoba Oil Soap
Contains jojoba oil, a superb alternative to sperm whale oil, remarkable for its skin softening properties. Skin type: all types except very sensitive skin.

White Musk Soap
Fragranced with our most successful perfume oil, it is the most accurate copy of musk we have ever found. Skin type: all types except very sensitive skin.

Mini Vegetable Soaps
These vegetable-based soaps are great as guest soaps or for travelling! Available in White Musk, Jojoba Oil, Camellia Oil, Tea Rose and Evening Primrose Oil fragrances. Skin type: all types except very sensitive skin.

Aloe Soap
(See the Aloe Range)

Seaweed and Loofah Soap
A chunky body bar with an ocean-fresh fragrance. It contains loofah particles to exfoliate and seaweed to condition the skin. The Shinnecock Indians of Long Island traditionally used seaweed as a skin treatment. Skin type: all types except very sensitive skin.

Wheatgerm Oil Soap
This is an extra mild transparent soap containing wheatgerm oil to benefit those with blemished and problem skins. Skin type: all types especially blemished skin.

Endangered Species Soaps
A range of soaps in the shape of animals in danger of extinction: Rhino, Panda, Elephant, Whale and Turtle. Free educational leaflet available.

September 1986 and has been very successful. Mostly Men, a collection of skin and hair care products designed specifically, but not exclusively, for men debuted in November 1986. Mamatoto, The Body Shop's comprehensive mother-to-be and baby range, was launched in the United Kingdom in September 1990 and in the United States in September 1991. The Body Shop is looking forward to the introduction of a line of products which contain sustainable ingredients from the Rainforest in Brazil.

Unlike many major cosmetic brand name products, The Body Shop's products contain a relatively high percentage of natural base ingredients. For example, the Aloe Vera range contains as much as 98 percent pure gel from the aloe plant. Cocoa Butter Suntan Lotion is 13 percent cocoa butter.

It is not just the products that make this company unique. It is its innovative formulations, passion for the environment and social issues, and sensitivity in retailing that make The Body Shop a corporation of the future. The Body Shop cares about its consumers. Because the company has no advertising overhead and uses minimal packaging, the product cost is low compared with those products of similar quality and efficiency produced by other cosmetic companies.

The approach of The Body Shop is unique in the cosmetic industry in that it focuses on health and well-being. It is an approach that is nonexploitative. The company does not promote or sell beauty "fantasies" in its advertisements or point-of-purchase displays, as other cosmetic companies do. The Body Shop sees its consumers as beautiful in a healthy way, not from use of heavy cosmetics but because of a natural beauty enhanced by natural products. Because of this belief, there are no images of "perfect" or idealized women in its shops or in its literature.

The Body Shop has gone from serving a select niche of customers interested in natural beauty care products to serving a variety of consumers, some aware of the company's environmental ties and others who just like the products. When customers enter The Body Shop, their senses are delighted by the smells, sounds, sights, and atmosphere of the store. Retail stores have a natural and clean feel to them with the corporate commitment to the world and its inhabitants evident in the literature, brochures, and point-of-purchase information items. Shopping at The Body Shop is not a chore; it is an experience that, when coupled with quality products, keeps customers coming back.

There is an electricity that runs through the stores—from the products and their bright green labels to the friendly sales staff. Although trained to help consumers when they ask for assistance, the sales staff will not bother customers when they are shopping. The staff is trained to be sensitive to the needs of the customers and to not make them feel pressured into buying something but to help them make informed purchase decisions. Instead of pressure selling, the staff's role is to educate consumers and tell them stories about different products, their origin, and how they finally made it onto The Body Shop shelves. All of The Body Shop products are backed by information available from either brochures or the sales staff. Staff members are knowledgeable about the products as well as social/environmental issues such as animal testing.

Profitability and Philosophy

The Body Shop has learned effectively the lesson on how to grow profits. With an approximate market value of $1 billion and great stock performance, the company has earned the reputation in the City, London's equivalent of Wall Street, as the 'share that defied gravity.' Since the company went public in 1984, the share price has increased 10,944 percent. Some analysts predict that the company will grow its profits at an annual rate of 30 percent to 40 percent for the next 5 years.

While understanding the need to increase profits as it grows in sales and number of stores, The Body Shop is concerned about the using of these profits to better the world in which we live. The company believes that with profitability comes responsibility and that profits should be partnered with principles. Simply stated by Ms. Roddick, "The company operates within the world, the environment, the community. That is where our responsibilities lie—we want to give something back to society." And it does.

The Body Shop is a company that has grown quickly and successfully but has never lost sight of its corporate philosophies. Since its inception in 1976, The Body Shop's ties and commitments are to the environment and the world's inhabitants, animals, and human beings alike. One goal of the organization is for its products to reflect its philosophies. Its strong foundation and corporate philosophies can be summarized as follows:

- Use vegetable rather than animal ingredients in products whenever possible
- Prohibit testing of ingredients or final products on animals
- Respect the environment
- Use naturally based, close-to-source ingredients as often as possible
- Offer a range of sizes so that customers can buy quantity needed without buying extra

The Body Shop exemplifies its commitment to the environment by offering recycling in its stores. Consumers receive a discount on their next purchase if they participate in this program. The Body Shop feels customers should be able to buy its products without having to pay for elaborate and expensive packaging. To reduce waste and keep prices down, packaging is kept basic and to a minimum. In fact each store has a refill policy which will refill a customer's old product bottles with new products to save on packaging materials and create less waste. This policy has been in place since the store opened. At that time Roddick could only afford to buy 700 bottles in which to package her products. She asked people to bring them back to be refilled to cut costs for her and her customers. Today all Body Shop products are biodegradable, and the stores participate in recycling waste when needed. The company's commitment to recycling is further displayed in its use of recycled paper for brochures and shopping bags.

A variety of organizations involved in protecting the environment have benefited from The Body Shop's efforts. It became involved with Greenpeace in England to "Save the Whales" and with The Friends of the Earth to raise public awareness about the dangers of acid rain. In 1986 the company formed The Body Shop Environmental Projects Department to develop and coordinate environmental and community projects. While these projects might be initiated by the company or individual stores, employee participation is voluntary. The Body Shop has been involved in various projects, ranging from providing massage for the elderly and psychiatric patients to sensory therapy for the blind. By encouraging individual stores and employees to get involved, The Body Shop hopes that each store will support specific projects to help their own communities.

The organization strives to have its products reflect its philosophies. In developing "futuristic" products, The Body Shop relies on knowledge and wisdom from the past regarding natural ingredients used for remedies and preventive purposes. Traditional ingredients such as almond oil and vanilla, which are used in Body Shop products, have been used for centuries and have a history of safety and health on which The Body Shop relies in its "return to basics" approach to cosmetics. The Body Shop respects the world of nature and tries to use the ingredients in their most natural forms. Not only does the company look to nature for many ingredients, it looks to nature for inspiration.

Product formulation and business operations are also based on respect for its customers and different cultures. Roddick, still actively involved in the growth of the organization, travels the world to learn how different cultures care for their skin and hair. These beauty secrets are used in the formulation of new products for people of various cultures to enjoy. Understanding and respect for other cultures has also helped The Body Shop to be successful in a variety of markets because of the cultural empathy the company has developed. Regardless of location, The Body Shop expresses its respect for all of its customers by offering them a variety of choices of products, product sizes, and information.

Animal Testing and Cosmetics

The use of animals in the testing of cosmetics continues to be a controversial debate fought in many arenas throughout the world. Animals primarily serve two purposes in cosmetic testing: they provide raw ingredients for formulations and perfumes, and they are used in laboratory testing. The Body Shop questions the need for such practices and considers them to be cruel and unnecessary. Over 7,000 U.S. organizations with over 10 million supporters are dedicated to animal welfare and animal rights. The Body Shop, its employees, and many of its customers as well are dedicated to similar goals.

The Body Shop's position on animal testing is clear. While it understands the need to test for eye irritation, toxicity, and skin irritation to assure human safety, alternative methods should be used. This principle has been a part of The Body Shop foundation since 1976. Some of the alternative testing methods employed by the company are:

1. Use of "old and tested" ingredients. Such ingredients include beeswax and honey, which have been used by humans for hundreds of years. Even when new formulations with "old" ingredients are made, the histories of the ingredients allow the products to be tested safely on people. The Body Shop has established a panel of Animal Aid volunteers for testing conducted at The University Hospital of Wales.

2. Use of ingredients derived from plants or vegetables. These ingredients have been tested by human beings for years through food consumption. The Body Shop selects its raw ingredients and its suppliers carefully. It requires suppliers to confirm in writing that they have not used animal testing for cosmetics in a 5-year period prior to association with The Body Shop. Continual monitoring of suppliers helps ensure that this standard is always met.

New testing methods are also being developed as alternatives to animal testing. They include:

- bacterial tests
- in vitro tests: testing on cells rather than live animals
- mathematical models and imaging techniques
- computer analysis to predict how a substance will react when used on human skin

The Body Shop encourages its employees and customers to become involved in animal rights and other environmental concerns. It provides literature in its stores on such topics and invites consumers to make suggestions, ask questions, and raise issues to increase the company's level of consciousness. The Body Shop also initiates and supports letter writing campaigns for various causes. The stores become letter writing and collection stations for weeks until every customer has voiced his or her opinion on the topic at hand. Over 4 million letters were delivered by Roddick and her staff to the doors of the British government protesting animal testing. Once again, Roddick and The Body Shop made national and international headlines.

A Global Company

The Body Shop has grown into a global company with a network of retail stores spanning the continents and including such markets as Denmark, Australia, Sweden, Singapore, Hong Kong, and the United States. Although The Body Shop operates in many diverse countries, trades in seventeen languages, and employs staff members representing a variety of cultures, all retail shops look basically the same and carry the same products. The image and reputation of the company have remained strong and constant through the expansion process by staying true to corporate philosophies. Customers throughout the world respect The Body Shop's goals, philosophies, and products.

The global concern of The Body Shop extends beyond selling in foreign markets; it includes sourcing in Third World countries. By using ingredients from Third World countries, the company hopes to encourage local communities to grow specific ingredients and develop trade practices. This method of sourcing allows The Body Shop to get fresh, unique ingredients and helps Third World countries develop jobs for its people. Corporate philosophy dictates that such relationships be based on equality and respect.

When Roddick finds a group of people who have ingredients which she can use in beauty products, she shows the people, in many cases tribes in Third World countries, how they can make money with their products by adding value. For example if a South American tribe is efficient in gathering Brazil nuts, she will show them that by extracting the oil, they have something of great value for which The Body Shop will pay. Roddick is committed to fair business. If it costs The Body Shop $30.00 for a liter of extract from a wholesaler, that is the price she will pay to the South American tribe as well. She and her staff also spend time with various groups of people from whom they buy ingredients and help them establish schools and housing from the money they earn.

The Body Shop has developed a relationship with the Boys' Town Trust in Southern India, designed to provide education and training for underprivileged children who learn trades and skills such as farming, woodwork, basket making, and silk screen printing. The goal of the Trust is to help these children to become skilled and valued members of their communities. The Body Shop has also raised funds to build The Body Shop Boys' Town, a community project developed by the company to house, educate, and train underprivileged boys. The Athoor site houses eighty-five boys who work on a productive farm to support the community. Sponsorship money from The Body Shop, its employees, and customers helps sustain the boys through their schooling.

Although The Body Shop enjoyed a somewhat unique positioning for many years, recently the number of "green" cosmetic companies has grown dramatically. Some of the companies and their products that now compete with The Body Shop include the major cosmetic manufacturers as well as other specialty shops and specialty lines handled by other retailers.

Reflecting on the Future

Anita Roddick feels the thing that will keep The Body Shop growing throughout the 1990s will be its *passion*. Her definition of business is *the activity needed to keep a company alive and breathlessly excited*. She is dedicated to protect the company's employees and remain a force in society. After those goals, concerns over profits arise. Although profits are necessary to stay in business and keep growing, fun and love are what keep management on the cutting edge.

It is ironic that a company which does not have a formal marketing or advertising department is cited as a company which will sell successfully in the next decade. The Body Shop accomplishes this in many ways. First, it relies heavily on word-of-mouth advertising, but without excitement, word-of-mouth will cease. Second, the company believes in educating its consumers by giving the staff unusual product information. The staff is told anecdotes about the history and ingredients of its products and humorous stories on how some of its exotic products wound up on The Body Shop shelves. This type of information hopefully will stimulate interesting conversation between staff and customers.

Finally, it is the enthusiasm of its management which makes The Body Shop poised for growth this decade. Roddick and her team have an electricity that is contagious. It is evident in management philosophy and in the stores.

Anita Roddick has become a CEO of the future, one to be studied, admired, and understood. She has three distinct values which she carries into her business. The first one is to have fun. The second is to put love where your labor is. The third is to go in the opposite direction of everyone else.

Anita Roddick says this about running a business successfully, "I think you can trade ethically; be committed to social responsibility and global responsibility; empower your employees without being afraid of them. I think you can rewrite the book on business."

Focal Topics

1. What attributes of The Body Shop products are most important to consumers?

2. How large is the market for products of The Body Shop? Is it a small, specific segment or a mass market?

3. What promotional program would you recommend for The Body Shop in order to expand its sales?

4. What changes in retailing or other distribution methods should be considered by The Body Shop?

■ ■ ■ ■ ■

Pepsi Cola[1]

■ ■ ■ ■ ■

The Cold War may have ended in 1992, but the great cola war was hotter than ever. Pepsi Cola, originally an upstart cola with the audacity to attack mighty Coca Cola in the 1930s and 1940s with slogans such as "Twelve Full Ounces—that's a lot for a nickel," has done it again in 1992 with the help of Ray Charles, singing about Diet Pepsi, "You've got the right one baby, Uh-huh." The battle between Pepsi and Coke is one of the mightiest marketing wars ever, and one fought on many fronts over many decades.

The Pepsi Challenge

On a particular July 4 in the 1980s, the fireworks boomed in Austin, Texas. Steve Choate, district manager for Pepsi-Cola, signed a misdemeanor assault complaint against Skip Morgan, a Coca-Cola salesman. In this instance, the great cola war was being fought in the trenches in a yelling and shouting match in Austin's largest supermarket. Choate claimed Morgan yelled obscenities at him and shoved him after he found Choate and another Pepsi worker dismantling a Coke display. Even the customers began choosing sides as the cola salespersons fought over who was going to get the space between the potato chips and the charcoal. The war was being fought at every level of strategy and tactics.

Coke had to do something pretty dramatic in response to one of the most effective promotional programs of all times—the Pepsi Challenge. In this program, Pepsi set up a taste test program throughout the United States in which consumers were asked to compare Pepsi and Coke in blind samples.

---

[1]Pepsi and Pepsi-Cola and Coke and Coca-Cola as well as the advertising slogans mentioned in this case are registered trademarks or service marks of the respective parent companies. The facts in this case were developed from published sources as well as public documents of the companies.

With the Pepsi Challenge, Pepsi went to state fairs, malls, and supermarkets and involved millions of people in taste tests. Pepsi choices were reinforced with a smile and a coupon, in classic behavior-modification form. The results of the taste comparison showed a high preference for Pepsi, a fact which was featured in Pepsi's advertising, point-of-purchase materials, and publicity. Even the cans reinforced the theme of "Pepsi Challenge" as consumers read the words with every use. Many people participated in the taste tests but even more vicariously learned the theme because of the publicity and reinforcing nature of the advertising and sales promotion programs.

Coke has produced some of the best advertising in the world—with such memorable themes as "I'd like to teach the world to sing in perfect harmony . . ." and "Coke is It." Even with highly memorable and pleasing advertising, Coke became subject to continual erosion of market share during the Pepsi Challenge. According to some observers in Atlanta, Coke management was in disarray, failing to yield an effective, strategic counterattack to Pepsi's challenge. Pepsi was increasing market share fast, especially among younger market segments who responded to Pepsi's sweeter taste and youth-oriented advertising.

New Coke

Coke management began one of the most extensive testing programs of its own to find a better tasting Coke with which the company could respond to the Pepsi Challenge. After spending millions of dollars in carefully controlled experiments, Coke introduced new Coke in April 1985. The taste tests were so clear in preference for a new formula that Coca-Cola replaced its 99-year-old formula with the new Coke. Pepsi immediately took out ads claiming victory in the cola war.

Consumers rebelled at new Coke. Some of the most loyal customers began a class action suit to force Coke to return to the original formula. More importantly, market share began to plummet almost one point per week. Bottlers across the country became so alarmed that they called a special meeting in Atlanta with Coca-Cola management, demanding relief. On June 6, in one of the most dramatic and fastest reversals in marketing history, old Coke was renamed and brought back as "Coca-Cola Classic."

New Coke continued to be available in theory until the 1990s, but in reality it nearly dropped from the marketplace with a market share of less than 1 percent. Coca-Cola Classic had a market share of almost 20 percent. Coca-Cola, faced with evidence that people preferred the slightly sweeter taste of new Coke, decided to rename it and try a new marketing campaign. The new name was Coke II. With new packaging but the same formula as new Coke, Coke II was test-marketed in Spokane in 1990 where it gained a 2.4 percent market share (compared with 1.3 percent for new Coke in that market) before being introduced in Chicago and other test markets.

▪ EXHIBIT 3.1   Can People Tell a Difference between Pepsi and Coke?

Taste is such a subjective matter that *Consumer Reports* usually does not conduct preference tests for food. Even a gourmet's preference is simply one person's opinion. But because the two big colas are marketed so relentlessly, *CR* set up a taste test that challenged people who identified themselves as either Coca-Cola or Pepsi fans to find their brand in a blind tasting.

Volunteers were recruited who professed a strong liking for either Coca-Cola Classic or Pepsi and diet Coke or Diet Pepsi. These people thought they would have no trouble telling their brand from the other brand. They were given samples of all four colas.

Of nineteen regular cola drinkers and twenty-seven diet cola drinkers, only seven of the (19) regular cola drinkers correctly identified the brands, and only seven of the (27) diet cola drinkers correctly identified the colas. While both groups did better than chance would predict, nearly half the participants in each group made the wrong choice two or more times. Two people got all four samples wrong. These preference test results suggest that only a few Pepsi and Coke fans may reliably be able to tell their favorite based on taste alone.

Source: Summarized from "Preference or Prejudice," *Consumer Reports*, August 1991, 519.

Some industry observers believe Coke II will be rolled out by Coca-Cola because the results from Spokane, if they could be achieved on a national basis, would yield additional retail sales of $475 million for Coca-Cola. Other observers believe Coke II lacks a clear niche and will complicate production and distribution for bottlers attempting to carry two sugar-based colas under the Coca-Cola brand. Coke II might gain shelf facings but it also might eliminate some of Coke's more successful brands from retailers' shelves.

Although Coca-Cola had invested billions into marketing research for taste tests, new packaging, advertising, and promotion, the new Coke strategy was a major failure. Perhaps, as Exhibit 3.1 seems to indicate, taste is not as important as image or positioning through advertising.

Pepsi Advertising

When Pepsi first attacked Coca-Cola (a brand that has existed since 1886), it did so on the supermarket shelves. While Coke has dominated the "fountain" business for over 100 years, Pepsi focused on the supermarket shelves and on the economy segment in vending machines with its "12 ounces for a nickel" approach during the 1940s and 1950s.

For the past 30 years or more, Pepsi has developed advertising slogans appealing to youthful segments of the market. Some of these eras and slogans include the following:

- 1958–1961: "So young at heart."
- 1961–1963: "For those who think young."
- 1963–1968: "Come alive, You're in the Pepsi generation."

- 1974–1976: "Join the Pepsi people, feelin' free."
- 1980–1983: "Catch the Pepsi spirit! Drink it in."
- 1984–1988: "Pepsi, The choice of a new generation."
- 1988–1989: "Pepsi. Generations ahead."
- 1989–1992: "Pepsi. The choice of a new generation."
- 1992: "Pepsi: Gotta Have It."

In recent years, Pepsi-Cola has spent about 6.3 percent of sales on advertising. For decades, Pepsi's memorable advertising has been prepared and placed by one of Madison Avenue's most successful ad agencies, Batton, Barton, Durstine, and Osborn, now BBDO Worldwide. See Exhibit 3.2 for examples of some of these campaigns.

In a major shift away from the "Pepsi Generation" strategy, Pepsi switched in 1992 to a campaign that would position Pepsi as a soft drink more oriented to the masses. Coke has generally always positioned itself toward a broader audience.

In the 1992 campaign for Pepsi, 60-second TV commercials featured celebrities such as Bo Jackson and Yogi Berra explaining that the taste of Pepsi appeals to everyone. In one commercial, various celebrities try to phrase a slogan that explains why Pepsi is the best tasting. Talk-show host Regis Philbin offers "Pepsi, What a cola. *What* a cola" as a potential slogan and tennis star Jimmy Connors suggests the slogan, "Pepsi, I drink it. So should you." Finally, a young child introduces the slogan that becomes the tag line for all ads when she asks, "Why don't they just say: Pepsi, Gotta Have It?" Dr. Joyce Brothers provides an opinion that "Gotta Have It" strikes a chord in everyone.

In another spot, a hip teenager wearing sunglasses and a black leather jacket says: "At first, I was upset that all these old folks starting drinking it, and then I said, 'Hey, they're people, too.'" In the feature commercial, a little girl says: "Maybe . . . the taste of Pepsi is so big, it should be the choice of everyone." Other commercials feature celebrities such as Leeza Gibbons and John Tesh, who report on the "Gotta Have It Movement" sweeping America.

David Novak, Pepsi's vice president of marketing, explains that the campaign represents the evolution of the Pepsi generation to a new level to maintain the Pepsi attitude for people who think young and want to celebrate life. Bill Katz, executive vice president of BBDO Worldwide, explains that it is an expansion of the basic positioning of the Pepsi generation over the past 30 years.

Novak says that Pepsi's previous positioning does not exclude older consumers and is meant to express an attitude rather than represent a certain demographic target. The basic shift apparently is due to the substantial drop in the number of 18–34-year-olds that is occurring in the United States and other industrialized countries. Some concern exists, however, that moving to a broader target may weaken Pepsi's positioning strategy, which has set it apart from Coke for several decades. Tom Pirko,

■ **EXHIBIT 3.2   Examples of Pepsi Ads**

a marketing consultant, voiced concern that the new Pepsi campaign makes it amorphous. He says, "Before Pepsi was focused and now they seem to be giving multiple, mixed messages. When you change your basic positioning, isn't that a revolution? My concern is that there is simply too much at one time," noting Pepsi's recent logo change, new slogan, and the new positioning.

The "Pepsi Gotta Have It" campaign appeared during major network TV programs such as the Super Bowl, as well as on Fox Broadcasting Co.'s live edition of "In Living Color" during the Super Bowl halftime. Pepsi is expected to spend about $80 million in measured media on all Pepsi brands in 1992 and currently achieves 31 percent of the $46 billion soft-drink market, compared to Coca-Cola's 41 percent share.

Diet Pepsi

In an attempt to improve its market share of 6.3 percent for Diet Pepsi compared with diet Coke's 9.3 percent share, about $50 million of Pepsi's advertising budget was spent in 1992 on its "uh-huh" campaign featuring Ray Charles. In addition to a substantial schedule of TV ads, Pepsi filled supermarkets with life-size cutouts of Ray Charles and the Raylettes with which consumers can have their pictures taken. Consumers can also record their own versions of the "uh-huh" jingle at *karoaoke* booths. Pepsi has also named April as national uh-huh month and shipped one million cases of Diet Pepsi to confirmed diet Coke drinkers via UPS. Pepsi also ran updates in *USA Today* and other media about uh-huh events in specific locations.

Pepsi stumbled upon the current campaign when the "uh-huh" slogan made a big impact during its introduction during the 1991 Super Bowl. Before that, Diet Pepsi had been trying a number of slogans, none with much memorability. The slogan officially was "Diet Pepsi—the Right One." While preparing a commercial featuring Ray Charles, the creative staff of BBDO found they had two-syllables left over, even after Ray Charles threw in his obligatory "baby." "It could have been 'doo-wap,' " says Creative Director Alfred Merrin, but it was a two-syllable grunt of affirmativeness that became history with the Ray Charles touch.

In the past, diet Coke had lead Diet Pepsi in a forced choice of preferred brands by 70 percent to 30 percent according to David Novak. Since the "uh-huh" campaign, this image gap has been reversed and Diet Pepsi leads diet Coke 52 percent to 48 percent.

The campaign was introduced with an ad during the Super Bowl, showing Ray Charles and the Raylettes as witnesses in a Senate committee room. When asked to explain why Diet Pepsi tastes the way it does, Ray Charles responds with "uh-huh." In other commercials, the Raylettes coo "uh-huh" whenever someone pops open a can of Diet Pepsi.

Pepsi and BBDO have produced highly memorable ads although competitor diet Coke produced an ad named in 1992 by *Ad Age* as the best commercial of the year. The Coke ad features Elton John singing "There's just one; just for the taste of it—diet Coke." The ad is set among a historical montage of stars such as Louis Armstrong and Humphrey Bogart from movies such as *Casablanca*.

The key question about advertising concerns sales. Unfortunately for Diet Pepsi, there was little movement between the two major brands. Consumers often buy what is on sale at the supermarket and one of them almost always is. From 1991 to 1992, the sales gap between diet Coke and Diet Pepsi stayed the same according to *Beverage Digest*. As a result, the two competitors' diet cola market shares are exactly the same as before the first "uh-huh" became Pepsi's watchword. Jesse Meyers, publisher of *Beverage Digest*, explains, "This is a distribution business. The bottler decides what goes on the shelf, and all the rest is just conversation."

Some bottlers are questioning the expenditure of such large amounts on advertising. A Super Bowl commercial costs $850,000 for 30 seconds of time and Pepsi spent between $6 and $7 million on the show in 1992. Production costs are very substantial and some observers estimate that Ray Charles may be paid as much as $3 million for his part in the commercials. Pepsi has long-term contract rights to Mr. Charles's participation, but the president of Pepsi's largest bottler expresses the concern of some bottlers when he says, "I think Ray has a good year left, and then you better start looking for a new slogan and a new guy."

The Next Real Thing

While Pepsi and Coke are busy firing their heavy artillery at each other, they are both faced with a wide range of flak from smaller competitors nipping at the heels of the giants. The substitute competitors include a wide variety of bottled water marketers such as Perrier, Crystal Springs, and Evian, as well as juice distributors and companies such as Clearly Canadian, which has a highly successful line of sweet sparkling drinks. And there is always competition going on between the makers of colas and the marketers of coffees and teas, including some successful new herbal teas and new specialty coffee drinks. There are also adult juices and juice-based products, powdered drinks, and gourmet and sports beverages.

According to the 1991 Consumer Expenditures Study conducted by the U.S. government, sales of diet soft drinks in bottles grew by 3.5 percent in the most recent study compared to 1.8 percent annual growth for sugared products. Sales of diet soft drinks sold in cans increased 12.6 percent versus 11.5 percent for sugared. But bottled water sales advanced 15.6 percent. Distribution of sales for some carbonated soft drinks and all drinks is shown in Exhibit 3.3.

Pepsi is introducing a number of new products and exploring the introduction of others. One such product is Wild Bunch, its trademarked cola product mixed with flavors including strawberry and tropical fruit. It is also testing a sports drink. Gary Gerdemann, manager of public relations for Pepsi, explains, "We pioneered the juice-added category with Slice. But it makes sense for big companies to let smaller companies pioneer many niches. Companies like Coke and Pepsi are best at getting products ready for supermarkets and getting them on the shelves and selling."

Some of the smaller "niche" companies include Snapple Natural Beverages (Valley Stream, New York), Nora Beverages U.S.A. (Stamford, Connecticut), Artesia Waters, Inc. (San Antonio, Texas), Ocean Spray (Lakeville, Massachusetts), and the Gatorade division of the Quaker Oats Company (Chicago). Carl Gilman, vice president of sales and marketing at

■ **EXHIBIT 3.3   What People Drink**

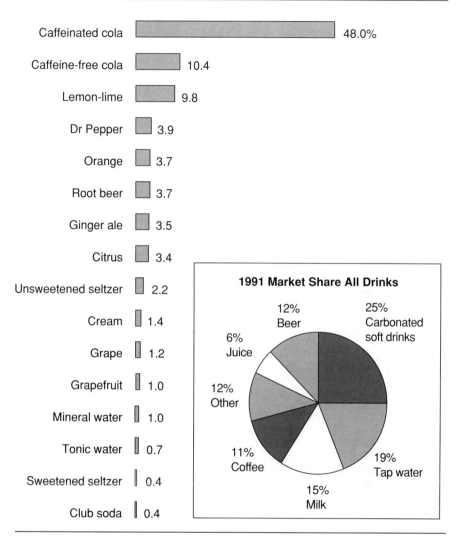

Caffeinated cola	48.0%
Caffeine-free cola	10.4
Lemon-lime	9.8
Dr Pepper	3.9
Orange	3.7
Root beer	3.7
Ginger ale	3.5
Citrus	3.4
Unsweetened seltzer	2.2
Cream	1.4
Grape	1.2
Grapefruit	1.0
Mineral water	1.0
Tonic water	0.7
Sweetened seltzer	0.4
Club soda	0.4

1991 Market Share All Drinks

25% Carbonated soft drinks
19% Tap water
15% Milk
11% Coffee
12% Other
6% Juice
12% Beer

Source: Eben Shapiro, "Looking for the Next Real Thing," *The New York Times,* May 5, 1992, 19, 21.

Note: Figures for supermarket sales only, which reflect approximately 40 percent of the total soft-drink market.

Snapple, targets concerns of older, more aware, and more demanding consumers. He explains, "Our niche, really, is people who care what they ingest. Our audience is skewed to the older and higher educated. Our slogan is: Made from the Best Stuff on Earth. Everything is natural and that's on the label. Our teas are fresh brewed and our lemonade is all natural as well, with no preservatives or additives. New age, natural products are the beverages of the 90s."

According to Stu Levitan, vice president for marketing at Nora Beverages U.S.A., which imports water from its parent in Canada, health consciousness, influenced by demographics, has created the market for these products. He explains, "There is a heavy focus on being healthier and the diet itself has become something of concern. People are concerned about the environment and the beverages they consume. They're starting to worry about what's going into their bodies. People are drinking alcoholic beverages less. Baby boomers are the swell of the population and their bones are starting to creak."

Rick Artesia, president of Artesia bottled water states, "You can't get what we offer out of the tap. A lot of people won't drink what comes out of the tap. Water supplies are becoming tainted." Adult-oriented beverage companies do occasionally run into credibility problems. Perrier got a blitz of bad publicity when its lab work revealed traces of benzine in the "Earth's First Soft Drink." Even after this event, some media questioned how the product was processed and bottled and Perrier had to remove its "Naturally Sparkling" claim from the product when it was discovered that carbon dioxide from its well was removed and reintroduced during the bottling process.

In its efforts to find higher sales growth than in the sluggish cola markets, Pepsi is testmarketing three fruit-flavored colas under the name Wild Bunch. Fruit flavors are mixed with regular Pepsi-Cola and named Tropical Child (pineapple-orange taste), Raging Razzberry, and Strawberry Burst. The cans have colorful graphics of the various fruits.

Soft drink companies traditionally took a conservative approach to any change in the basic cola formula. Consumers can drink much more cola because it has a lower level of so-called "flavor wearout" than other soft drinks, such as grape or orange. The one notable exception, cherry-flavored colas, has met with mixed success. The Wild Bunch may offer additional growth to counter the slippage of sugared sodas from 75 percent of the total market to 70 percent currently. Some market analysts believe the new flavored colas might be especially appealing to young adults and pre-teens, as well as to minority groups like blacks and Hispanics, all of whom show a preference for sweeter-tasting drinks and fruits.

Another product test-marketed by Pepsi is Pepsi A.M., a cola drink with about 28 percent more caffeine an ounce than regular Pepsi but 77 percent less than coffee or tea. Coca-Cola has been providing its bottlers with advertising for use at their discretion to promote Coke in the morning.

Crystal Pepsi is another new product introduced by Pepsi and positioned as a clear cola "that's more refreshing and has a clean, smooth taste." It is less sweet, contains 100 percent natural flavors, and has no preservatives. It is also caffeine free and low in sodium. A 12-ounce can has 130 calories, compared with 154 calories in a can of regular Pepsi and less than 1 calorie in Diet Pepsi. Consumer analysts have also commented that "clear" has a positive connotation for many buyers. Clearly Canadian has achieved enormous success with a sweetened, clear product, and the trend to clear products has a parallel in the liquor business where gin, vodka, and tequila are outselling Scotch and bourbon. One possibility would be to position Crystal Pepsi as a mixer, perhaps with lemon and rum. When 7UP was introduced in 1920, it had caramel color and achieved success only after its brown color and lemon-lime flavor was changed to a clear drink.

Pepsi has a number of other possibilities for future development. It is now selling canned ice tea, as is Coca-Cola. Pepsi also has a deal with Ocean Spray to distribute juices and is testing a new sparkling water called H2Oh!. Pepsi continues to market Slice aggressively as well as expand distribution of its All-Sport to compete with Coca-Cola's Powerade. Both are direct competitors to Gatorade, the best-selling product of the Quaker Oats Company with nearly $1 billion of sales worldwide. Seagram Beverage is marketing a low calorie flavored mineral water and General Foods is test marketing Cappio, a bottled iced cappuccino product.[2]

Focal Topics

1. Why do consumers buy Pepsi?
2. How important should advertising be in Pepsi's marketing program?
3. What theme should Pepsi use for positioning regular Pepsi?
4. What theme should Pepsi use for positioning Diet Pepsi?
5. What should Pepsi's strategy be for development of products in addition to regular Pepsi and Diet Pepsi?

■ ■ ■ ■ ■

[2]Sources used in the preparation of this case include: Joshua Levine, "Affirmative Grunts," *Forbes*, March 2, 1991, 90–91; Alison Fahey, "Pepsi Bridges 'Generation' Gap in Ads," *Advertising Age*, January 20, 1992, 1 ff; Eben Shapiro, "Looking for the Next Real Thing," *The New York Times*, May 2, 1992, 19, 21; Michael J. McCarthy, "New Pepsi Soda Will Seek To Break the Coffee Habit," *The Wall Street Journal*, September 28, 1989; The Associated Press, "A New Pepsi Adds Caffeine," *The New York Times*, September 20, 1989, 41; Michael J. McCarthy, "Pepsi-Cola Testing New Cola Drinks With Fruit Flavors," *The Wall Street Journal*, February 25, 1991, 5C; Kent Phillips, "Critical Vending," *Beverage World*, February 1991, 99–100; "Soft Drinks," *Supermarket Business*, September 1991, 175.

Cheryl & Co.

■ ■ ■ ■ ■

Constant change and innovation are perhaps the best words to describe Cheryl & Co. and its entrepreneur manager, Cheryl Krueger. Cheryl's started with one cookie store in 1981 in the French Market shopping center in Columbus, Ohio. By 1992 it had become a firm operating seventeen cookie/gourmet gift stores in three states, a catalogue business, and a wholesale division selling cookies and other desserts to grocery stores, restaurants, and airlines.

Cheryl's fundamental success is attributed to a commitment to high-quality products and the best possible service along with a creative shopping atmosphere. Over the past few years, the award-winning cookie line has expanded to gift tins, custom baskets, and imported mugs, complemented with a broad assortment of dessert related items.

An exciting white and black design characterizes the stores in each shopping mall, inviting customers to help create the perfect gift for any occasion. A gift wrap station helps in this process. The company also designs and prepares packages, free of charge, to ship anywhere in the United States.

Cheryl Krueger—Cheryl's Story

Flexibility, determination, hard work, a solid retail background, and Grandma's cookie recipes are the ingredients that make up this gourmet dessert entrepreneur's success. Cheryl Krueger has built a booming business of retail stores and a national mail-order business.

Cheryl had always baked cookies for friends and relatives. The reviews were so good that she and college roommate, Caryl Walker, decided to market the cookies that have now won awards throughout the Midwest. "Most small businesses fail because people aren't willing to make sacrifices for the business," says Cheryl. She held down a full-time job in order to keep the cookie company financed in its initial years. Friends and family managed the business during the week while Cheryl commuted from New York City to Columbus, Ohio, every weekend for three years.

Comments Cheryl, "I've made personal sacrifices, most of the time not without a sense of guilt toward my family and friends, but sometimes it just becomes necessary. Excellence cannot come without sacrifice." Her efforts have paid off and her management and marketing successes have earned her numerous awards as small businessperson of the year and other awards for entrepreneurship and women in business.

Her strong family ties are evidenced in the way she manages her company. Her associates use such words as visionary, dynamic, compassionate, outstanding, aggressive, and confident when describing this lady of never ending energy and determination. Her husband, John Green, is director of corporate sales at Cheryl & Co. Her young son also is often in Cheryl's office or in the stores—she first brought him to the office in his crib.

Cheryl received a bachelor's degree from Bowling Green State University with a major in home economics. She began her professional career in 1974 as a buyer for Burdine's department store in Miami, Florida. It was not long before this fast-growing and innovative retailer recognized her talents. In 1976, she began her career with the Limited Stores and eventually became their "youngest ever" merchandise manager. With responsibility for a multimillion-dollar business and four solid years of performance behind her, she moved on to New York City in the very competitive sportswear industry. She spent three-and-a-half years as vice president of sales for Chaus Sportswear, commuting between New York City and Columbus to begin operation of Cheryl's Cookies. It became clear that a decision had to be made for the sake of the cookie business and her involvement with the company. She came back to Columbus and The Limited in 1984. The cookie business was growing at a steady pace, but was not yet ready for a full-time, dynamic, chief executive officer of Cheryl's caliber. The Limited offered Cheryl the opportunity to continue her successful retail career and personal growth. Running an accessory business for 600 stores offered Cheryl the experience that eventually enabled her to become the full-time manager of her cookie business in 1985.

Time is valuable to Cheryl Krueger. Yet she constantly gives back to the community by participating in the Lung Association, Women's Business Board, YWCA, Private Industry Council, Arts Council, and the College Board of Advisors for Home Economics at Ohio State University. She also gives many speeches to emerging entrepreneurs, high schools and universities, and other groups. She has also helped several businesses to get started through advice, consultation, and business leads.

In her many speeches to entrepreneur groups, Krueger explains, "You have to be willing to work harder than anyone else in your company and you need a good staff. You can't do it all yourself so you better surround yourself with good people." Many of her employees have been with her since the beginning but she has also attracted outstanding people as key executives from other successful firms.

Krueger believes her key to success is giving the public what it wants. Krueger spends two and a half days a week in her stores, often waiting on customers herself. She believes the best advice she receives comes from customers.

Product Line

The original cookie recipes came from Cheryl Krueger's grandmother, who taught her how to be the best baker in all of Bellvue, Ohio. Even when Krueger grew up and went to college, her hands never really left the mound of cookie dough. While home for holidays and vacations Krueger continued to bake cookies for her family and friends. After joining Burdines, busy though she was, Krueger remembered her friends back home with birthday gifts of cookies. One grateful recipient suggested that she start her own business.

"One of the first cookie brands I noticed was David's, which is popular on the East Coast. Although their product was totally unlike what I had in mind," Krueger says, "I liked the way they were being merchandised to the public. They were in little open shops similar to ones I had seen in Europe. I thought it gave them a touch of exclusivity, something I wanted to portray." She tested her original recipe to make sure it could be made in large quantities without affecting the taste and quality. "I wanted to be absolutely positive my cookies would taste exactly like the ones I used to bake for my family," she says.

Today all the dough is prepared in the headquarter's commissary under exacting standards using only natural ingredients with no compromises on quality. The dough is delivered frozen in the firm's own trucks to each store where the cookies are baked fresh each day, throughout the day. The cookies are produced in mouth-watering varieties such as chocolate chunk, chocolate chip, white chocolate pecan, macadamia coconut, sugar, oatmeal raisin, spice, and one of the most popular recent additions, butter cookies with delicious icing—originally produced for holidays but now so popular that they are baked throughout the year. Some of the varieties can be seen in Exhibit 4.1.

Originally the stores carried only cookies, in an area of about 250 square feet. Later, brownies and other innovations were added. A problem faced by the company, however, is that large shopping malls usually want cookie stores in regional shopping malls to be placed in the food court. Unfortunately, much larger chains such as David's and Mrs. Field's are able to compete for these locations better than Cheryl's even though Cheryl's believes its products are generally much better in taste.

Cheryl's has expanded and converted some of its early stores into gourmet gift stores. The original store of 250 square feet has been renovated to a store with an area of 1,000 square feet, dramatically increasing sales to the point where the newest stores gross as much as $500,000 a year.

The new concept store is a gourmet gift store in the Ross Park Shopping Center in Pittsburgh. The gift stores offer specially flavored cheesecakes, breakfast rolls, gourmet coffees, chocolate sauces, and other gift items. Some of the older stores include a few of these items. When the Pittsburgh store was opened, the company changed its name from Cheryl's Cookies to Cheryl & Co., in order to better communicate the wider product line. Such a change raised the issue, however, of whether or not consumers might be confused or less attracted by the name Cheryl & Co. rather than Cheryl's Cookies, which emphasizes the mainstay of the company's product line. Cookies continue to account for the majority of sales, even in the concept gourmet gift stores. The store is shown in Exhibit 4.2.

Product development is an ongoing process at Cheryl's. Not only is there a broad assortment of scrumptious cookies, but delicious gourmet treats such as homemade ice cream, party size cookies, award winning fudge brownies, and Cheryl's own line of gourmet coffee. Cheryl's supplements its product line with a wide variety of specialty foods and contemporary gift items such as sauces and cookbooks from the Silver Palate, imported chocolates from Droste and Neuhaus, preserves, crackers and candy from Crabtree & Evelyn, and gourmet cheesecakes and mousse pies.

A major issue facing the company is how to position itself in the face of America's increased interest in health and fitness. Cheryl's emphasizes the quality and taste that is achieved by using all natural products such as butter. The company has also tested low-cholesterol cookies. Krueger enlisted food and nutrition experts from a university to help find a low-cholesterol shortening. Several combinations of butter and margarine or margarine and vegetable oil were tested in the stores. While low-cholesterol cookies have been offered by other companies such as Entenmann's, they have more often been distributed through health-food stores. The prototype cookies of this type developed by Cheryl's have excellent taste and are low in cholesterol. Despite these attributes, the initial tests in stores were disappointing. Most consumers bought the traditional cookies and sales of the low-cholesterol products were so low that they were withdrawn from the stores. The company is currently evaluating these products and now faces the decision of whether they might be distributed through alternative channels, such as health-food stores or supermarkets or whether the idea of low-fat and low-cholesterol cookies is incompatible with the overall product strategy of Cheryl & Co.

One of the most innovative new products introduced by Cheryl's is cookie roses (see Exhibit 4.3). A basic chocolate chip cookie is mounted on a stick that appears to be a rose stem; it is then wrapped in red cellophane and packaged in a rose box with appropriate greenery and florist paper. For Cheryl's, the margins on products such as these are good—a rose cookie sells for $1.95 in contrast to the normal 50–60 cents for a cookie, depending on weight. The product has been so dramatically successful that Cheryl's has become one of the largest buyers of florist supplies. Cheryl's feels rose cookies are an excellent alternative to traditional roses because of the novelty and price of $19.95 per dozen, much lower

■ **EXHIBIT 4.1   Cheryl's Famous Cookies**

(*continued*)

than the usual cost of a dozen roses from a florist. Cheryl's arranges low price delivery to local locations through a commercial delivery service and ships nationwide.

Corporate and Catalogue Division

Cheryl's has placed major emphasis on developing a corporate and catalogue division, which in recent years has become the fastest growing part of the company. Through the division, businesses are able to send gifts of Cheryl's cookies and baskets to customers and employees. Many large

A. Twelve Cheryl & Co. fresh-baked gourmet chocolate chip cookie flowers make this a special Christmas wreath! Each grapevine and baby's breath wreath is handmade and wrapped with bright Holiday ribbon. After the cookies have been enjoyed, the wreath will be a lasting reminder of your thoughtfulness. **G2371 $39.95**

■ **EXHIBIT 4.2**   **Cheryl & Co. Store**

■ **EXHIBIT 4.3   Cheryl's Cookie Roses**

organizations such as New York Telephone, Digital, Hewlett-Packard, Bordens, and General Motors have been customers, sometimes ordering hundreds or even thousands of gift boxes or tins during holidays. Companies with large sales potential are called directly by Cheryl's staff; telemarketing is used for other firms.

Recognizing the need for constant change and innovation to ensure the growth and future of the business in the 1990s, the corporate sales division has been expanded to include a national mail-order business and catalogue division. Unlike building new stores, the development of these divisions requires less capital investment.

As one part of corporate sales, tins of cookies are shipped to customers of firms such as automobile dealers. For approximately $10, firms have shipped for them a special tin that includes their logo on the top, a note of appreciation for the customer's sale, and a follow-up questionnaire that provides the dealer with marketing research information. Cheryl's has achieved considerable success in marketing this program to auto dealers and is analyzing what other types of businesses might be appropriate markets for the service.

The catalogue division is also growing rapidly. Exhibit 4.4 shows typical products. Full color brochures and special fliers are distributed through the

■ **EXHIBIT 4.4   Cheryl's Catalogue**

CREATE YOUR OWN ASSORTMENT

Does someone you know have a soft spot for fresh-baked cookies? Is your best friend especially deserving of a midweek treat? Or maybe you've had a craving for an extra moist brownie and a cold glass of milk after a long day at work? Now you can personalize an assortment of Cheryl & Co. award-winning cookies or brownies in the gift container of your choice.

First, select a tempting assortment of up to four varieties per gift item (up to two for the snack tin) from fourteen delicious varieties.

CHOCOLATE CHIP
CHOCOLATE CHUNK
WHITE CHOCOLATE PECAN
OATMEAL RAISIN
OATMEAL CHOCOLATE CHIP
SPICE
BUTTERSCOTCH
MACADAMIA COCONUT
SUGAR
PECAN CHOCOLATE CHIP
HEATH BAR
PEANUT BUTTER CHOCOLATE
NO-CHOLESTEROL CHOCOLATE CHIP
NO-CHOLESTEROL OATMEAL RAISIN

Next, choose your favorite gift tin or gift box from an exciting assortment of nine Cheryl & Co. designs.

A. Teal Gift Box
G2511 12 Cookies $9.95
G2521 8 Brownies $12.95

B. Hostess Tin
G141 12 Cookies $12.95
G1071 8 Brownies $16.95

C. Red Gift Box
G1081 12 Cookies $9.95
G1091 8 Brownies $12.95

D. White Gift Box
G3111 24 Cookies $19.95
G3121 16 Brownies $24.00

E. Teal Tin
G3131 16 Cookies $18.95

F. Black Tin
G131 16 Cookies $18.95

G. Snack Tin
G151 6 Cookies $6.95
G3141 4 Brownies $9.95

H. Small Bow Box
G231 36 Cookies $24.95
G3151 24 Brownies $36.95

I. Large Bow Box
G3161 48 Cookies $29.95
G3171 60 Cookies $35.95

Cheryl & Co. cookies and brownies are baked fresh the very day we ship them. Order anytime and we'll bake and ship your gift for the special dates you request. If you're planning a family reunion, club or business meeting, or even an informal gathering with friends, order now and we'll see that the dessert is delivered fresh to your door or anywhere you choose.

CALL FREE 24 HOURS A DAY
1-800-443-8124

(continued)

■ **EXHIBIT 4.4**   *continued*

(continued)

stores and to previous buyers. The company maintains a computerized data base to send to its previous customers and also buys mailing lists from other mail-order companies. The company is now considering the best way to extend this part of the business.

Cheryl & Co. also has a fund-raising part of the business with two variations. In one part of the business, schools or other organizations take orders for packages of cookies and deliver them to customers. A substantial portion of the price is retained by the organization as a fund-raising activity. Cheryl's has also developed a program for health related organizations, such as the American Cancer Society, in which persons who make major donations are given a tin of Cheryl's cookies with special logo covers. The organizations can also inform members of the availability of Cheryl's gift items, and for each order received, a significant portion of the proceeds is given to the charity.

Promotional Programs

The cookies are the most important part of the marketing program; the cookies are so good that people repeatedly come back to the stores or the catalogue—to find not only the great taste of quality ingredients and

■ **EXHIBIT 4.4**   *continued*

recipes but constantly changing varieties and products. A distinctive black-and-white design of the store also invites people from the malls into the stores. This creative store design and concept has won awards and was featured in numerous local publications, as well as in *Interior Design*. The store design directly reflects the dynamic personality of the business and the people who run it.

The company has been fortunate to receive a great deal of publicity, due to the personality and visibility of Cheryl Krueger. She has been featured in a number of local and national magazines and newspapers. The company has won rave reviews in various local magazines including "Best Cookie" in *Indianapolis Magazine*, "Best Brownie," in *Indianapolis Monthly*, "Best Retail Store Design," by the Institute of Business Design, and "Best Cookie" by the *Columbus Monthly*. Many newspapers have interviewed Krueger and carried stories about her views on product quality, entrepreneurship, the importance of people in the business, and the need to give time to the community in which a businessperson operates.

The company is also facing the issue of what other promotional activities should be implemented. The company has tried some television advertising scheduled on local stations in 10- and 20-second spots featuring Cheryl Krueger inviting people to the stores for Mother's Day purchases. The company received a lot of comments from customers mentioning the ads and felt that sales were stimulated, although it was difficult to determine the actual effect.

The company has also used print ads in local media for special occasions such as Mother's Day, Valentine's Day, Father's Day, and Secretary's Week. Some ads were also used at Christmas but the company was unsure how much to budget for such activities, which media were most effective, and the market targets and appeals that would be most effective.

Cheryl's tested a small national advertising campaign with an ad in *Working Woman* (see Exhibit 4.3). Since these ads featured the toll-free telephone number, sales could be tracked fairly accurately. The ads, which featured Cookie Roses and ran in the spring, produced sales in February, March, April, and May. The cost of the ad was $8,886 and produced sales of over $20,000 in roses. After deducting the costs of the ad and the materials used to produce the roses, the ad produced a direct profit of $5,489. These results caused the company to raise the issue of whether or not such advertising should be continued, whether additional national magazines should be used, and, if so, which ones and for what occasions. In the *Working Woman* ads, sales were concentrated during the Valentine sales period with a small increase (but far less than at Valentine's Day) for Mother's Day. The company considered the initial attempt at national advertising to be very successful. But could it be duplicated? Was *Working Woman* a unique market target and this time period a unique opportunity, or could the success and profitability of direct sales be duplicated in other media and at other times of the year?

Wholesale Division

Cheryl & Co. has also developed a wholesale division. Although several attempts have been made to sell cookie/ice cream sandwiches and other specialty products, these distribution activities had been generally unsuccessful until 1992. Although Cheryl & Co. had sold cookies to Midway Airlines (until it ceased to operate), Cheryl & Co. had not been very successful in selling to the major airlines until USAir signed a large contract in 1992 to serve Cheryl's cookies on a regular rotation on many of its flights. United Airlines also began to buy cookies from Cheryl & Co. for use on some first-class food service. Cheryl viewed these contracts very positively for reasons beyond their immediate profitability. First, these contracts created sales throughout the year in contrast to the retail business, which was highly seasonal. The catalogue business required capital to create and distribute hundreds of thousands of catalogues as well as a substantial inventory of ingredients, tins, packaging materials, and other items, with little way of predicting or realizing sales until after Thanksgiving.

An additional reason for the attractiveness of sales to airlines is the fact that the labels carry the toll-free number which customers who like the cookies can call and receive a catalogue. Cheryl is aware that Otis Spunkmeyer and other cookie companies have begun to sell cookies at Subway, McDonald's, and other restaurants. Cheryl is actively investigating the possibilities of sales through restaurants based on what she believes is the superior quality of her cookies compared to most of the competitors. She also believes that her production facilities and strategic location in terms of logistics provide a cost advantage over many of the competitors.

Cheryl & Co. has also developed other dessert items to sell through the wholesale division. These include brownies, pumpkin pies, and a special Kentucky Bourbon pie. These products are currently marketed to regional and national chains of restaurants.

Focal Topics

1. Who are the most important targets for Cheryl's retail stores? How do they typically make a decision to buy cookies? Would this differ for the other products sold by Cheryl's?

2. What are the most important reasons Cheryl's has experienced rapid growth in the face of much larger competitors such as David's and Mrs. Fields? What policies should be maintained or implemented to continue the growth in the 1990s?

3. Should Cheryl's add gift and other items as it has done or would the company be better positioned if it "sticks to its knitting" of being the best cookie company?

4. Should the major emphasis at Cheryl's be on retail stores, catalogue and corporate, or the wholesale division?

5. Recognizing the small size and resources of Cheryl's, develop a recommended promotional strategy, including market targets, media plan, and creative appeals.

■ ■ ■ ■ ■

ENVIRONMENTAL INFLUENCES ON CONSUMER BEHAVIOR

■ ■ ■ ■ ■

■

Avon Products

■ ■ ■ ■ ■

How can a Chinese pediatrician increase her earnings if she wants more money than her typical $120 per month? Sell Avon, of course. And Linag Yungjuan, age 40, has done just that.[1] As a part-time Avon representative she has increased her earnings to $1,500 per month by selling $5,000 worth of makeup products—something, which to say the least, is changing the lives of Chinese women. Avon ladies are gaining self-confidence and increasing their standards of living dramatically, while their customers are experiencing glamour for the first time.

Avon: Positioned for the 21st Century

Avon is a company focused on beauty and direct selling, the company's heritage and strength. Avon businesses are doing well, with sales in 1991 of $3.59 billion, up from $3.45 billion in 1990 and $3.29 billion in 1989, representing the sixth consecutive year that its core business has generated increased sales and pretax profits. Net income in 1991 was $135.7 million, or $1.89 per share, compared with $195.3 million in 1990, or $2.60 per share.

Five years ago Avon ventured into the health care market and experienced severe losses from the unsuccessful venture. It eventually withdrew that product line, thus ending a diversification strategy into health care services. The irony is that, in the final analysis, Avon did not need to diversify into health care. Worldwide beauty and direct selling are healthy and appear to provide ample opportunities for the company.

Avon Principles

Avon is committed to a statement of principles developed by the founder of Avon more than a century ago. These principles commit the company to certain specific human values:

---

[1]Andrew Tanzer, "Ding Dong, Capitalism Calling," *Forbes*, October 14, 1991, 184.

We will provide individuals an opportunity to develop and earn in support of their betterment and happiness.

We will serve consumers throughout the world with products of the highest quality, backed by a guarantee of satisfaction.

We will provide a service to Representatives and customers that is outstanding in its helpfulness and courtesy.

We will rely with full confidence on employees and Representatives, recognizing that our corporate success depends on their individual contributions and achievements.

We will share with investors and others the rewards of growth and success.

We will be responsible citizens of the country and the communities where we do business.

We will cherish and maintain the friendly spirit of Avon.

The Role of Beauty   The world of beauty is a timeless world. Adornment of the face and body began before recorded history and persisted through the millennia. Egyptian women used an ancient eye shadow. The Greeks loved rouge and powder. Cosmetics were popular in imperial Rome and the courts of eighteenth-century Europe. Today they are ubiquitous.

Throughout history, beauty products have satisfied a profound and enduring human need—the desire to look one's best. Fashions change but the fundamental truth does not: When people look good, they feel good about themselves.

Avon is proud of its more than a century of service to its customers. The company expresses a dedication to serving their changing needs with products of quality, value, and constant innovation.

U.S. Direct Selling

Avon is well-known for its sales force of "Avon Ladies" ringing doorbells. In fact, 425,000 (as of 1989) U.S. representatives are selling products, many of them receiving their total income as Avon salespersons. But they are no longer just ringing doorbells of suburban homes. They are also selling in the workplace, where management often encourages sales calls that keep employees on the premises rather than running out to do shopping which might delay their return to work. The turnover rate for U.S. sales representatives is now lower than at any time during the past decade.

In recent years, the company has implemented a comprehensive training program for representatives that boosted sales of those who participated by 20 percent, and it encouraged representatives to remain active longer. Productivity-improvement programs have helped President's Club members, the top-selling representatives, increasing their average order size. New representative recruiting programs have also started to pay off. The company believes both the quantity and quality of representatives is show-ing improvement.

Avon produces and markets a wide variety of beauty products. Some of the newer products include "Avon Color," an entirely new line of more than 350 shades of lip, eye, face, and nail colors to assure customers that Avon has just the right shade for them and that their total "look" can be coordinated. Avon representatives have a powerful high-technology tool called the Avon Beauty Vision Personal Color Computer. In less than five minutes, it analyzes a customer's skin tone, categorizes it in one of four color groups, and prints out recommended shades. "Avon Color" is consid-ered a major success throughout the country, contributing to an increase in sales of color cosmetics.

Other recent products are described in the category of Visible Im-provement Products. Avon's "BioAdvance" and "Collagen Booster" have received praise from outside experts in magazines and on television. "Vi-sible Advantage" is another product in this category.

Other major product categories include bath products, fragrances, jewelry, and fashion. In the bath products area, a product benefiting from wide publicity was "Skin So Soft." Sales of this product have risen sharply recently. Fragrances is a category that is highly competitive, and Avon has been holding its share and has introduced several new products through its retail fragrance company. Avon is also attempting to increase the ap-peal of its jewelry products. New manufacturing techniques at the com-pany's two jewelry plants in Puerto Rico—which produce 70 percent of U.S requirements—will allow them to economically produce more designs in small quantities. The Fashion division experimented with sleepwear, and Avon believes it has found a successful niche with this product line.

Avon has developed special marketing programs for African-American and Hispanic consumers. Almost six million black consumers receive a spe-cial, 16-page *Holiday Beauty Guide* designed to attract them to Avon. Re-lated print advertising appears in magazines targeted to African-Americans. The division is also expanding sampling programs and devoting more adver-tising in its sales brochures to products for black consumers.

Avon uses Spanish-language television commercials, reaching about 85 percent of Hispanic-American women. Some commercials use a direct-response telephone number to recruit Hispanic Avon representatives in each of twenty-one selected local markets.

International Direct Selling

Avon has major operations in twenty-six countries around the world, nearly all of which are meeting or exceeding sales and earnings expecta-tions. This division produced sales of $2.08 billion in 1991, up 9 percent from the previous year on unit sales increases of 6 percent. Pretax profits rose 5 percent to $326.7 million, and the division had over 1.5 million rep-resentatives in 1991.

Avon Japan is the division's largest international company, followed by Brazil, Mexico, and the United Kingdom. In Mexico, Avon has a 25- to 30-percent market share; in Brazil, 35 to 38 percent; in the United Kingdom, 16 to 17 percent. The company is strong in Canada and Italy as well. While Avon is the eighth largest firm in the beauty business in Japan, that country is the largest profit market for Avon. Avon does poorly in France.

Japan   Avon recently implemented a three part strategy to increase business in Japan and to have it remain one of its most successful and profitable foreign cosmetics companies. It expanded its product line to include jewelry, which contributed significant incremental sales and earnings. Lingerie was added to the product line. Sales in small towns and rural communities were also targeted for strong sales efforts. Avon Japan is a publicly held company in Japan with about 40 percent of the shares held by Japanese investors.

Contributing to Avon Japan's success was the growing direct response operation, in which products are sold by mail order to inactive and former representatives. Direct response now generates 25 percent of Avon Japan's sales and 35 percent of profits. The program brings in 30,000 to 40,000 additional orders per three sales campaign. General managers in other Avon companies are working on similar programs.

China   Before Avon came to town, Chinese women found themselves with the money to buy things they wanted but nothing much to buy. Avon changed that when it began its march on China.

After years of failing negotiations with government officials for a northern China venture, Guangzhou (Canton) was targeted by Avon as the city where it would begin its entrance into China. Avon's direct selling concept was too complicated and too new for them to support. However, David Li, chief executive of Hong Kong's Band of East Asia and advisory board member of Avon, steered the company to Guangzhou because of the acceptance of capitalism among its people. An agreement with government authorities was reached in late 1989.

In its first full year of operation, Avon's joint venture in China (60 percent of which is owned by Avon, 35 percent by Guangzhou Cosmetics Factory, and 5 percent by Mr. Li and a partner) greatly exceeded expectations. The Chinese company outgrew its initial distribution center and added three more. Another two are planned for 1992. More than 6,000 representatives were selling Avon products in China at the beginning of 1992.

The Chinese joint venture operates differently from its U.S. counterparts in that it does not distribute its products to its representatives; they pick them up from branch depots to avoid communication and transportation problems. Chinese Avon ladies do not ring doorbells for cold-call sales as is done in the United States. Because the majority of them have other jobs, most sales occur in the workplace, among friends and family, and in schools. The most frequently sold items are skin care products, yet as

Chinese women learn how to apply makeup more proficiently, sales in this category are expected to increase.

European Region   Avon U.K. experienced problems in prior years but has recently been turned around and is experiencing significant sales increases annually. The improvement reflects refocusing the product line to appeal to core customers and a new spirit of enthusiasm in the organization. In addition to its core beauty products business, Avon U.K. improved market penetration through new product categories—lingerie, fashion accessories, and preschool educational toys. These new lines were chosen after Avon researchers studied market demand for 140 types of products. It also improved representatives productivity and increased gross margins by tightening controls over manufacturing overhead costs.

Avon continues its dramatic expansion into the postcommunist East, but the greater part of the European surge was due to the solid performance of established Western markets. Avon Germany, the cornerstone of Avon's continental operations, put together a new sales and marketing management team, improved consumer access, and launched a new advertising campaign with much success in the early 1990s. Excellent field coverage in the first full year of operations in the former East Germany helped Avon gain a 20 percent market share there. Czechoslovakia became a new market for Avon in November 1991, while Hungary has had steady growth in its first full year of operation. Further expansion opportunities being considered for 1992 include Poland and parts of the former Soviet Union.

Other Foreign Markets   Also showing rapid growth in sales and earning are other Avon companies around the world—in the Philippines, Thailand, Taiwan, and Malaysia in the Pacific Rim; Portugal and Austria in Europe; and Mexico, Venezuela, and Chile in Latin America.

Avon Mexico is currently achieving sales and profit increases despite an uncertain economy. One reason for the gains was the national rollout of "Modavon" (Fashions by Avon), which includes lingerie, sleepwear, hosiery, and some sixty other items. Research showed—and experience proved—that Mexican women prefer to shop at home for intimate apparel because they like the privacy and convenience. Among the stars of Avon's international markets is "Au Naturel" skin care line from Mexico and the "Colourama" line from the United Kingdom.

Avon Spain is receiving excellent response from a new type of sales brochure. The core pages of the brochure display all products and remain constant for three months. But "wraparound," which changes every three weeks, highlights new products and those on sale. Like Avon Japan's direct response program, the Spanish brochure concept is likely to be adopted by other Avon countries.

Among all Avon markets, Brazil continued to have the most volatile and challenging economic and political environment. Avon Brazil responded by adjusting prices, changing the product line to include more inexpensive items, and launching an aggressive program to recruit and retain representatives. Sales have increased and the company manages to produce a modest profit. A new international company is Avon Indonesia, a joint venture formed in 1988.

One of the factors in Avon International's overall success was a strategic change in organization. Individual countries have been given more decision-making responsibility, and area management has been moved closer to markets. The objective was increased sensitivity to consumers and market dynamics. The continuing change will put Avon International in an even better position to serve potential high growth areas such as the Pacific Rim.

Another factor that is believed to be key for Avon International is the spreading of new ideas across national borders. When a new product or program proves successful in one country, it's then tested in other countries where market conditions are similar. Under this system, Avon companies often increase their chances of a successful innovation while decreasing product development costs. A good example of this process is lingerie, which began in Brazil in the mid-eighties and was then expanded to Mexico, Argentina, Venezuela, Japan, the United Kingdom, and continental Europe.

In each case, the local Avon company studied the market to learn what kind of lingerie its consumers wanted—lively and glamorous in Brazil but conservative in Japan. Local Avon companies are also established for manufacturing and distributing the products to representatives. Avon studied the risk that lingerie sales might reduce sales of traditional Avon products. Tests showed that, in most cases, lingerie sales produce incremental sales, increasing average customer orders and winning Avon a larger share of total household budget. Avon lingerie is available in about two-thirds of Avon International markets.

Retail

Avon also manufactures a number of brand name products that are marketed through major retailers. The retail division produced sales in 1991 of $152.3 million. While this reflected an increase of 13 percent in unit sales, expenses are high and pretax profits for the division were only $13.8 million for the division.

The two major units in the retail division are Giorgio Beverly Hills and Parfums, both acquired in 1987. While both are in the same division of Avon, each company maintains a separate identity and unique personality, which makes them the "jewels" of the $1 billion retail fragrance industry.

Both companies have begun a stepped-up program of new products. In 1988, Giorgio introduced sixteen new products and line extensions. Among them was the company's first nonfragrance line, the successful "Giorgio Beverly Hills Tan Collection."

The major attention at Parfums Stern was focused recently on the new brand "Uninhibited by Cher." An aggressive cooperative program was developed by Parfums Stern, Avon support groups, and suppliers to introduce "Uninhibited by Cher" to 250 stores in 10 major cities in one month. These stores included Macy's in New York and Atlanta, Marshall Field's in Chicago, and Foley's in Houston. The introductions featured a carnival atmosphere and enormous sales of the new fragrance. With store appearances by Cher amid tumultuous special promotions, the fragrance was literally bought out by the public.

"Red," a Giorgio fragrance, was introduced after months of research and testing aimed at developing a scent for women who were attracted to the "Giorgio Beverly Hills" image but were reluctant to use the strong floral scent of the original. "Red" was introduced via direct mailings to more than a million target consumers with results that far exceeded plans. Although sales in this category are down sharply in 1991, "Red" remained the country's top-selling prestige fragrance for the third consecutive year. Giorgio's newest scent, "Red for Men," had a highly successful launch and ended the year among the top five men's prestige fragrances. Giorgio also began its first licensing ventures with Giorgio handbags, eyewear, and sunglasses.

Giorgio approached its ten-year anniversary and still ranked in the top five fragrances in the United States, with a double-digit volume increase worldwide. Overseas, the fragrance volume increased in the fifteen European countries where it was distributed. It also expanded to Australia and to many duty-free markets. Parfums Stern has expanded its products overseas, strengthening management to be able to do so.

Focal Topics

1. Can Avon expect to use the same products and marketing programs in its international division as its U.S. division?

2. If choices must be made, would you recommend that more resources be devoted to the U.S., the international, or the retail division?

3. Within the international division, which countries do you recommend to target for maximum growth in the future?

4. Which products or marketing methods of Avon are likely to be the most successful with African-American and Hispanic markets in the United States? How do you recommend Avon expand sales to these market segments?

■ ■ ■ ■ ■

Worthington Foods, Inc. (A): Meat Analogues

■ ■ ■ ■ ■

Worthington Foods was founded in 1939 to produce nutritional, vegetarian foods for members of the Seventh-day Adventist Church. Miles Laboratories purchased Worthington in 1970. Worthington Foods, Inc., in a management-led buyout, acquired the business and assets of the previous company in 1982.

Today, Worthington Foods, Inc., develops, produces, and markets high quality, zero-cholesterol, vegetarian and egg substitute food products for consumers seeking healthful food choices. Offering more than 150 product items, the company is one of the leading independent producers of healthier alternatives to meat, egg, and dairy products. For more than 50 years Worthington Foods has been dedicated to producing meat alternative products that simulate the taste and texture of meat and which are made primarily from soy and wheat proteins. Since the 1970s it has produced egg substitute products made primarily from liquid egg whites.

Worthington Foods, Inc., is made up of four separate product brands—Morningstar Farms, Worthington, LaLoma, and Natural Touch. All brands offer products of healthy food alternatives. Exhibit 6.1 shows how Worthington Foods' sales have increased steadily over the last 5 years; Exhibit 6.2 shows net sales by brand name for 1989 through 1991.

Worthington and LaLoma

For the last 50 years, Worthington Foods has offered the most complete line of vegetarian products under its Worthington label. In 1990, Worthington Foods acquired the LaLoma brand product line to provide vegetarian consumers with even greater product variety and availability. LaLoma, founded in 1906 by the General Conference of Seventh-day Adventists, made whole wheat breads and health cookies for the patients and staff of what has become Loma Linda University Medical Center. After its purchase, Worthington Foods consolidated the production, sales, and distribution of the product line at its central Ohio plant.

■ **EXHIBIT 6.1   Selected Consolidated Financial Data for Worthington Foods**

	Years Ended December 31,				
	1987	1988	1989	1990	1991
	(In thousands, except per share data)				
Statement of Operations Data:					
Net sales..	$36,891	$47,538	$61,157	$66,385	$70,182
Cost of goods sold	22,710	28,587	41,098	42,229	42,516
Gross profit	14,181	18,951	20,059	24,156	27,666
Selling and distribution expenses......	9,200	12,593	16,521	15,359	17,134
General and administrative expenses	1,326	1,576	1,795	2,234	2,459
Research and development expenses	729	940	1,131	1,218	1,123
Total expenses	11,255	15,109	19,447	18,811	20,716
Income from operations.............	2,926	3,842	612	5,345	6,950
Write-down of non-operating assets	—	—	—	—	440
Interest expense.................................	558	611	1,169	2,565	2,340
Income (loss) before income taxes.........................	2,368	3,231	(557)	2,780	4,170
Provision (benefit) for income taxes	931	1,205	(264)	1,033	1,613
Net income (loss).......................	$ 1,437	$ 2,026	$ (293)	$ 1,747	$ 2,557
Net income (loss) per share...............	$ 0.46	$ 0.63	$ (0.09)	$ 0.49	$ 0.69
Dividends per share	$ 0.07	$ 0.10	$ 0.11	$ 0.11	$ 0.11
Weighted average common and common equivalent shares outstanding	3,150	3,231	3,420	3,566	3,689
Balance Sheet Data (at period end):					
Working capital..................................	$ 5,584	$ 5,589	$11,169	$ 7,553	$ 9,472
Total assets	16,904	22,367	36,431	42,208	44,163
Total long-term debt	4,248	3,801	17,980	19,253	18,783
Total shareholders' equity	7,788	10,580	9,931	12,268	14,360

■ **EXHIBIT 6.2   Worthington Net Annual Sales by Brand Name**

	Years Ended December 31,					
	1989		1990		1991	
	(Dollars in thousands)					
Morningstar Farms..........................	$41,344	67%	$38,270	58%	$39,228	56%
Worthington	17,530	29	18,939	28	21,140	30
LaLoma	—	—	7,002	11	7,370	11
Natural Touch	2,283	4	2,174	3	2,444	3
Total......................................	$61,157	100%	$66,385	100%	$70,182	100%

■ **EXHIBIT 6.3   Worthington and LaLoma Products**

Worthington Foods manufactures and markets more than 150 canned, dry, and frozen items under its four nationally distributed brand lines.

Annual Report, 1991

Developed initially to meet the dietary preferences of Seventh-day Adventists, these popular brands now serve a growing market of vegetarians and semivegetarians with nearly 100 canned, dry, and frozen items shown in Exhibit 6.3. Worthington and LaLoma products have been available for many years in specialty and health food stores, but now they are found increasingly on supermarket shelves.

Nearly four generations of vegetarian consumers have enjoyed the healthy benefits and taste advantages of these products. Worthington and LaLoma products are cholesterol free and low in saturated fat. They are also rich in protein, and many offer a good source of dietary fiber. Moreover, they are lower in calories than their meat counterparts and provide essential vitamins and minerals. CrispyChik patties, shown in Exhibit 6.4, are breaded vegetable protein patties that are completely meatless but taste like chicken. Worthington Foods has helped educate people on ways to enjoy and cook with its products. It offers cookbooks to consumers that contain recipes for dishes such as those shown in Exhibit 6.5, a promotional piece created by the company.

Recent consumer research confirmed that Worthington products are perceived as the "premium tasting" brand in the Seventh-day Adventist marketplace. It was rated as the brand of choice for family dining and entertaining because of its taste, meatlike texture, and variety of recipe applications. LaLoma products, according to the same tests, were said to contribute to nutritionally balanced meals by providing Seventh-day Adventist consumers with an even greater assortment of vegetarian products.

Worthington and LaLoma brands' broad acceptance among vegetarians and other health conscious consumers is one reason that annual dollar

■ **EXHIBIT 6.4   CrispyChik Patties**
  CrispyChik Patties taste and look like chicken.

NEW! **Crispy Chik Patties!**
You're only minutes away
from great "chicken" taste.

Like our popular Worthington® Crispy Chik nuggets,
these new patties let you enjoy great "chicken" taste in
minutes. Plus, they're meat-free and cholesterol-free.
Just heat in your regular oven or microwave. Savor
the light breading and delicious
tenderness in a sandwich. Or serve
as an entree with other healthful
trimmings. Look for them in
your favorite store's
frozen-food section.

Worthington®

Taste Plus

CrispyChik Patties
A Breaded Vegetable Protein Product
Completely Meatless
NET WT. 10 OZ. (284 GM)

sales in recent years have increased steadily within both Seventh-day Adventist markets and grocery stores. While some sales increases can be attributed to expanded distribution, much of the lines' successes are the result of Worthington Foods' ability to reward the brand loyalty of its core
vegetarian consumers.

- **EXHIBIT 6.5**   'Worthington. For All the Right Reasons'
A sampling of delicious dishes made with Worthington and LaLoma Products

Morningstar Farms

Morningstar Farms offers the most readily available line of zero-cholesterol food items sold nationally through supermarkets. These frozen, easy-to-prepare products offer healthier, vegetarian options to many familiar processed meats, as well as eggs. Because of their hearty, meatlike flavor and texture, Morningstar Farms products provide consumers with one of the easiest ways to reduce their meat consumption and eat more healthy. The Morningstar Farms product line includes Breakfast Links, Patties, and Strips, which provide the taste satisfaction of sausage and bacon but are completely free of meat and animal fat. Grillers® offer a tasty zero-cholesterol alternative to hamburger patties. Because they are made primarily from soy and wheat protein, Morningstar Farms products contain two-thirds less saturated fat and about half the fat and calories of their meat counterparts. Exploratory research by the National Cancer Institute also suggests that the soy protein found in such meat substitutes may help to prevent certain types of cancer. These products are precooked so they can be reheated in just minutes using a microwave or conventional oven.

Complementing this assortment of meatless alternatives is an expanding line of egg substitute products. First introduced in the mid-1970s, cholesterol-free substitutes for whole, shell eggs are one of the fastest growing categories in the frozen breakfast section. Morningstar Farms Scramblers® have half the fat and one-third fewer calories than whole eggs. Made from egg whites, they have no cholesterol. Scramblers frozen egg product has maintained a strong presence in this category as the number two selling egg substitute nationally. Egg Beaters, produced by Fleishmann's, and Scramblers have battled for the number one and two market share positions for years. Scramblers has become Worthington Foods' largest selling product. This versatile product can be used in virtually any recipe calling for whole eggs.

Natural Touch

All items within the Natural Touch brand line adhere to a purity pledge that they are "100 percent free of anything artificial." These nutritionally balanced products are intended to help health-active consumers not only perform better today but to invest in a healthier tomorrow.

Starting with an initial offering of four frozen products launched in 1984, Natural Touch is now rapidly becoming the leader in wholesome, vegetarian products for natural food shoppers. The brand encompasses nearly all departments of a health-food store, including frozen, canned, and dry products in the forms of entrees, beverages, and confections. High fiber Okara Patties and Lentil Rice Loaf lead the natural foods category of frozen entrees and have registered double digit annual increases in dollar sales. Kaffree Roma, a roasted grain beverage, also leads the category of coffee substitutes among health food stores. This popular product offers natural food consumers a robust, coffeelike flavor, but without caffeine or tannic acid. Natural Touch spicy chili is popular among many consumers. While it contains no meat, it has a hearty flavor packed with zest and zing.

The latest Natural Touch entry is its Garden Pattie, a frozen vegetarian pattie distributed through health-food stores and made with a wholesome blend of garden vegetables and grains. Each pattie is made with real garden vegetables—bell peppers, carrots, water chestnuts, onions, mushrooms, black olives, rolled oats, and brown rice. It is precooked for heat-and-serve preparation in microwave or conventional ovens. It can be used as an entree or in a sandwich, as a substitute for luncheon meat or hamburger.

The Vegetarian Market

The trend toward more healthful food choices is expected to accelerate during the 1990s as consumers seek a greater variety of products offering the desired balance of taste, convenience and nutrition. Consumers of all types and of all demographic profiles are changing their diets to lower fat, sodium, cholesterol, and calorie levels. Most of these consumers can be grouped into the health-active consumer category, which participates in some type of activity to promote good health in their diets. Such activities might include buying reduced fat or cholesterol products, participating in physical activities, and reading food labels and nutritional information. A 1990 survey by HealthFocus, a Pennsylvania-based market research firm, concluded that 90 percent of U.S. adult food shoppers "purposefully selected foods for healthful reasons."

People eat healthy foods for a variety of reasons according to the HealthFocus study. More than half of "health-active" consumers were making food choices to reduce their consumption of fat, especially saturated fat, and cholesterol. By contrast, fewer than 30 percent were making dietary changes to control weight. Exhibit 6.6 examines people's attitudes toward healthy foods and why they eat them. Surprisingly, over three quarters of health-active consumers say they enjoy eating healthy foods,

■ **EXHIBIT 6.6   Attitudes toward Healthy Foods**

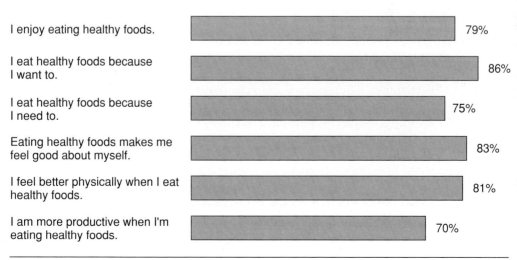

I enjoy eating healthy foods.	79%
I eat healthy foods because I want to.	86%
I eat healthy foods because I need to.	75%
Eating healthy foods makes me feel good about myself.	83%
I feel better physically when I eat healthy foods.	81%
I am more productive when I'm eating healthy foods.	70%

HealthFocus, Inc., 1990. Courtesy of Worthington Foods.

and 86 percent say they eat healthy foods because they want to, not just because they have to. But only one in five said they would be willing to give up good taste for health benefits, and less than one third said they would compromise convenience.

While many consumers choose to eat healthy, for others it is a struggle they endure for health reasons or to reduce weight. Exhibit 6.7 shows that for most health-active consumers it is most difficult to restrict diets and eat healthy during holidays. Approximately 50 percent of these consumers find it difficult to find healthy snack alternatives.

Over the past decade, nutritional and biomedical studies have shown that not only is it possible to be a well-nourished vegetarian, but also that vegetarians experience lower disease rates and generally live longer. Vegetarianism might have been considered "trendy" in the 1980s, but reduced meat and egg consumption have become mainstream approaches to healthier eating in the 1990s. Red meat consumption dropped by more than 12 percent during the 1980s, and according to one study, nearly one out of two adults has reduced his or her use of whole shell eggs over the past two years, while sales of cholesterol-free egg substitutes have grown in excess of 10 percent annually. The number of vegetarians and semi-vegetarians in the United States has increased nearly eightfold over the past decade. Today over 12 million Americans consider themselves vegetarians and another 15 million sometimes eat soy-based alternatives to meat, according to reports from the American Soybean Association. Twenty-six percent of health-active consumers eat vegetarian foods at least occasionally as shown in Exhibit 6.8. Some eat soyfoods and meat analogues as well. The National Restaurant Association discovered in a Gallup Poll of its patrons that one in five sought more vegetarian dishes among restaurant offerings. The most popular vegetarian menu items were pasta, vegetable pizzas, and meatless casseroles.

Growing interest in low-fat, cholesterol-free vegetarian food choices is sure to increase competition among food companies seeking health-motivated consumers. More than 10 percent of the 15,000 products new to grocers' shelves touted reduced fat or cholesterol claims in 1991. But Worthington Foods is one of the few companies who can claim its products contain no meat or animal fat and have zero cholesterol.

To maintain its industry leadership, Worthington Foods continues to focus on the unique vegetarian positioning of its products and dedicates even greater resources to introduce healthful products that meet the taste and convenience expectations of today's consumers. Worthington Foods has doubled the number of food scientists and product engineers in its Research and Technology Department over the past three years. Among their priorities are the development of value-added foods that place meatless products in more familiar eating contexts like single serving meals and sandwiches. Many resources are devoted to developing delicious vegetarian foods that make no attempt to resemble meat. Already, Okara Patties and Lentil Rice Loaf are top-selling frozen entrees in natural food stores, and Garden Patties are among the first vegetarian patties to contain real garden

■ **EXHIBIT 6.7**   Meals and Occasions When It's Most Difficult to Eat Healthy (by different age groups)

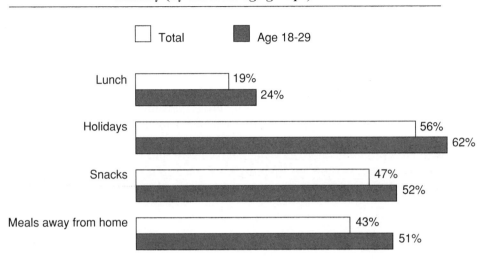

HealthFocus, Inc., 1990. Courtesy of Worthington Foods.

■ **EXHIBIT 6.8**   Frequency of Using Vegetarian Foods, Soyfoods, and Meat Substitutes/Analogues

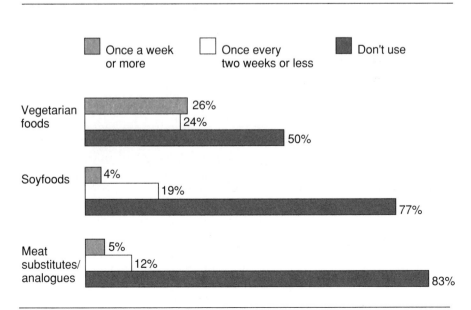

HealthFocus, Inc., 1990. Courtesy of Worthington Foods.

vegetables. Worthington Foods' scientists have also spent more than four years developing the patented process to manufacture new Better'n Eggs™, a premium quality egg substitute with zero fat and cholesterol.

The HealthFocus study concluded that the health-active market is no longer a small niche market. This group has grown so large "that for a food company to be successful, it must develop and target products to segments within the market and not attempt to position one product as the Holy Grail of healthy foods." Through its four nationally distributed brand lines, Worthington Foods offers these health-active consumers more than 150 different food choices. Each product provides a healthier alternative to any of the high-fat, high-cholesterol foods in the typical American diet. Worthington products offer the same hearty flavor and taste satisfaction as the processed meats they are intended to replace. And nearly all are precooked for heat-and-serve convenience in microwave or conventional ovens.

Distribution

Worthington Foods understands the increasing demand for healthy food products in specialty markets and also among mainstream consumers, but it has not always been easy knowing how best to get products to consumers. Worthington, LaLoma, and Natural Touch products can be found in health and natural food stores. Morningstar Farms products are available in most grocery stores. While Scramblers and Better'n Eggs have the widest appeal among mainstream consumers, the meat analogues are increasing rapidly in acceptance among this group. The 1991 HealthFocus study shows that over 50 percent of health-active consumers always shop at grocery stores, which makes it easy for consumers to buy their favorite Morningstar Farms products. In addition to supermarkets, 70 percent of health-active consumers shop at produce/farmers' markets, 44 percent shop at convenience stores, 30 percent shop at health food stores, 20 percent shop at gourmet stores, and 15 percent shop at ethnic food stores.

Worthington Food products are distributed efficiently to its consumers in different markets. In 1989, 67 percent of all Worthington Foods' products were sold in supermarkets and grocery stores, 19 percent in Seventh-day Adventist retail facilities, and 7 percent in health food stores. By 1991, 55 percent of all products were sold in supermarkets, 26 percent in Seventh-day Adventist retail stores, and 9 percent in health food stores.

Worthington Foods has addressed the issue of distribution in another way. In 1990 it established the food service division to move its vegetarian products beyond the retail market. It was put in place to tap opportunities for healthier fare among restaurants and institutions. It has been successful in securing the placement of the Scramblers egg product with American Airlines for its passengers requesting low-cholesterol breakfasts. Several Worthington Foods' meatfree products have been added to the menus of colleges and universities such as Boston College, University of Pennsylvania, and Yale. Efforts have also led to authorization of several vegetarian selections by the Marriott Corporation within its contract feeding division.

Products represented by the company's food service division are marketed under the Morningstar Farms identity to capitalize on the brand's retail awareness and popularity. In addition to institutional sizes of Morningstar Farms products such as Breakfast Links, Patties, Strips, Grillers, and Scramblers, the food service division has developed new product applications such as "Burger" and "Sausage" Crumbles, which can be used as ingredients for pizzas, tacos, casseroles, and gravies. Also, more natural forms of vegetarian products such as the vegetable-rich Garden Pattie are being added to food service sales. The food service division's revenues doubled in 1991 and aggressive advertising through magazines and direct mail are expected to continue this rapid growth trend.

Worthington Foods is also reaching beyond the bounds of the United States. It is pursuing opportunities for expanding the distribution and availability of these egg and meat substitutes in foreign countries. The company already has sales in the Caribbean and has developed modified versions of some chicken and hamlike products for distribution in Taiwan and the Far East.

Long-Term Objectives

Worthington Foods has spent significant time developing long-term strategies to lead the company through the nineties and into the twenty-first century. It has set several objectives to satisfy its shareholders, consumers, trade partners, employees, and community. Its primary objective is to provide its shareholders with increasing value from their investments. As a 50-year-old growth company, it recognizes the necessary balance between consistent dividends and additional shareholder value created through the internal use of generated profits. Worthington Foods evaluates its strategies in terms of enhancing shareholder value as measured by the market appreciation of its stock and dividends, not just in terms of increased sales and net income.

Worthington Foods is also committed to its consumers and strives to provide them with good tasting, nutritionally sound vegetarian choices for healthful living. It is dedicated to offering its consumers a variety of high quality, convenient products appealing to the full spectrum of health concerned consumers—from those wanting to reduce their fat and cholesterol intake to those seeking only vegetarian foods.

Another objective of Worthington Foods is to meet the needs of its trade customers by offering them a wide assortment of healthful, high quality products to satisfy the needs of their shoppers, whether motivated by health or philosophical reasons. Worthington Foods believes its products will provide consumers with good value while permitting the trade to realize a competitive profit. Trade promotions, consumer advertising, and merchandising support are designed to generate demand through the channels, from both nationally and targeted international markets.

Worthington Foods is also committed to its employees. Employees are provided with challenging and satisfying employment in a pleasant working environment. Stable employment with appropriate financial rewards for outstanding work accomplishments can be expected, while personal growth and development are encouraged. All employees are given opportunities to be well-informed and meaningfully involved in their company.

Finally, Worthington Foods is determined to provide its local community and those it serves with a good corporate neighbor that practices the highest values of honesty, integrity, and mutual trust. Worthington Foods strives to help the environment by promoting vegetarian foods to vegetarians and mainstream consumers. Worthington Foods will assume a responsible leadership role in economic, social, and industry matters in which it believes it can have a positive influence on the public welfare.

Focal Topics

1. What factors in the environment account for the increasing acceptance of vegetarian foods?

2. How should Worthington Foods segment its market target? What should be the most important segments in planning its marketing strategy?

3. Given the limited resources of the firm, which product lines and brands should receive the largest allocation of resources and effort?

4. How should Worthington Foods sell effectively to the international market?

■ ■ ■ ■ ■

AT&T Global

■ ■ ■ ■ ■

AT&T is determined to grow. Short-term profitability is important but long-term growth in revenues, earnings, and shareowner value is essential. AT&T is determined to grow in the United States and in markets around the globe, with a planning objective of an average annual earnings growth rate of at least 10 percent.

By early in the twenty-first century, AT&T hopes to be getting half of its revenues from international markets. To do so AT&T intends to offer a wide range of communications services and equipment that enable any AT&T customer, anywhere in the world, to complete transactions easily and efficiently, and by designing, engineering, and managing end-to-end networks for customers on a global basis.

Growth will come also from successfully assisting customers as they integrate computing and communications to serve their business and personal needs. That is what the merger with NCR Corporation, now a wholly owned AT&T subsidiary, was all about. The AT&T competency in networking is now linked to NCR's capabilities in computers and transaction processing. NCR, with its substantial presence in more than 130 countries, is an essential component of the acceleration of the globalization of AT&T.

To achieve its objectives in international trade, AT&T believes it is important that it be allowed the same freedom in other countries to sell its products and equipment as other companies enjoy in the United States, where telecommunications services and equipment markets are wide open. That freedom exists in some countries but not in others.

With its goals for growth, AT&T is pursuing strategies to firmly establish AT&T as a global company; to strengthen and build on leadership in its core business; and to become the world leader in the area of networked computing, where the technologies of computers and telecommunications converge. The business units of AT&T are grouped in major divisions known as communications products, communications services, AT&T Network Systems, AT&T Capital Corp., NCR, and other divisions. These organizations and their products are described in Exhibit 7.1. Highlights of fi-

- **EXHIBIT 7.1   AT&T 1991 Annual Report**

COMMUNICATIONS PRODUCTS

AT&T Computer Systems Transition Operations is responsible for closing down AT&T Computer Systems. Major goals are to place 100 percent of CS people who want to stay with the corporation; shift customer commitments to NCR; maximize financial benefits to AT&T; transfer operations quickly and effectively out of Computer Systems; and help make the acquisition of NCR the most successful in computer industry history. Headquarters: Parsippany, N.J.

AT&T Ventures Corp., a new business unit, is an internal venture capital firm that will create and foster growth of new businesses in AT&T by commercializing AT&T technology into information industry markets not addressed by other business units. Initially it will manage the following businesses: Advanced Decision Support Systems, Migration Technologies, Pixel Machines and UNIX System Laboratories, a subsidiary of AT&T.

AT&T Paradyne develops and manufactures data communications equipment for large and small customers and provides domestic and international sales and service. Products include modems, multiplexers, data service units, channel extension equipment and network management systems. It also sells *Accumaster* Integrator network management systems to international customers. Headquarters: Largo, Fla.

Business Communications Systems develops, manages, markets and supports large communications systems. It offers AT&T's largest business and government customers a complete range of premises-based systems with advanced capabilities like voice mail and sophisticated telemarketing/call center features, and service-support offerings. Products include the *Definity* communications system, System 75 and System 85 PBXs and terminals, *AUDIX* voice messaging systems and *Conversant* voice information systems. Headquarters: Bridgewater, N.J.

Communications Products Sourcing and Manufacturing Division manufactures communications products for 10 business units serving consumers, business and government customers worldwide. Headquarters: Bridgewater, N.J.

Consumer Products designs, develops, manufactures, markets, sells, leases and services communications products and services for personal use within and outside the home and in very small businesses in domestic and international markets. The product line includes basic and high-feature corded telephones, cordless phones, cellular phones, telephone answering systems and telephone accessory and wiring products. The unit also offers home security systems, public telephones and communications products for people with hearing, speech, motion and vision impairments. Headquarters: Parsippany, N.J.

Federal Systems Advanced Technologies markets AT&T business communications equipment, computers and networking services to meet the needs of the federal government. While most sales involve products and services available to AT&T's commercial customers, some custom equipment is developed, manufactured and marketed in Federal Systems' own facilities. Headquarters: Greensboro, N.C.

General Business Systems develops, markets, sells and services telecommunications equipment, including the *Partner* and *Merlin* communications systems, System 25 PBX, Partner and Merlin cordless multi-line telephones, voice messaging systems and facsimile machines for small- and medium-size businesses. Headquarters: Parsippany, N.J.

COMMUNICATIONS SERVICES

AT&T American Transtech, a marketing services company and a leader in the telemarketing industry, provides inbound and outbound services, calling market research services and list and data-base management. It also offers various financial and recordkeeping services. Headquarters: Jacksonville, Fla.

AT&T EasyLink Services is a global electronic messaging business created in 1991 by combining assets acquired from Western Union with various related AT&T products, services and people. This business unit develops, markets, sells and supports electronic mail, telex, enhanced facsimile, electronic data interchange and information services. The unit has representatives in 28 countries and provides service to 160 countries. Headquarters: Parsippany, N.J.

Business Communications Services includes: Inbound 800 Services, which manages such domestic business long-distance services as basic 800 Service, 800 *ReadyLine* and *Megacom* 800; Inbound Applications Services, responsible for such business offerings as teleconferencing and *MultiQuest* services; Outbound Networking Services, which manages Software Defined Network, Software Defined Data Network, Megacom WATS and *Accunet* Switched Digital services; Outbound Business Services, which manages basic, one-line and *PRO* WATS; Network Management Services, which manages the *Accumaster* family of network management products and services; Business Special Services, which manages the Accunet family of private-line services, Digital Data services and Accunet packet services; and Satellite Communications, which manages the *Skynet* family of satellite services and AT&T Tridom's Skynet *Clearlink* VSAT services and equipment. Headquarters: Basking Ridge, N.J.

Consumer Communications Services manages AT&T domestic long-distance services, the away-from-home calling market, domestic and international operator services, directory information services, calling cards and AT&T Gift Certificates. AT&T Español provides translators to assist Spanish-speaking customers, and Dual Party Relay services enable hearing- and speech-impaired customers to communicate with the hearing and speaking world. Its AT&T Message Service enables customers to record and send messages anywhere in the world, and *AT&T Language Line* provides on-line translation of phone calls in 140 languages and dialects. AT&T College and University Systems (ACUS) offers colleges and other institutions specialized long-distance billing and management systems. Headquarters: Basking Ridge, N.J.

Integrated Communications Systems Division, a part of Business Communications Services, addresses customer needs for integrated services and equipment. The division also manages AT&T's FTS 2000 contract with the federal government and promotes sales of products and services through relationships with other firms, through new business opportunities and through industry consultants. The organization also includes two BCS strategic business units: Business Special Services and Satellite Communications. Headquarters: Basking Ridge, N.J.

International Communications Services provides basic and custom long-distance services to consumers and businesses. The international fiber-optic portion of the AT&T network now connects the United States to Europe, Asia, South America, Central America and the Caribbean. ICS offers: private lines; AT&T Mail connections to electronic mail systems; Enhanced FAX Service; International 800 Service; International PRO WATS service to more than 170 countries; a switched digital service for voice, videoconference and data transmission; a Global Software Defined Network; *USADirect* Service from more than 90 countries; and the *Reach Out* World plan, offering discounts on calls to more than 40 countries. Headquarters: Morristown, N.J.

Network Services Division manages AT&T's Worldwide Intelligent Network in support of long-distance services. The network handles 125 million to 130 million calls on a typical business day. With more than 2 billion circuit miles of virtually 100-percent digital lines, it reaches 273 countries and territories, with direct-dial capability to 177 countries. AT&T has been investing approximately $3 billion a year in digitization of the network and new network reliability features since 1984. Headquarters: Bedminster, N.J.

Universal Card Services Corp. markets and provides customer services for the AT&T Universal Card, a combined long-distance calling card and general credit card accepted by Visa or MasterCard merchants worldwide, with more than 6.6 million accounts and more than 11 million cardholders. The business unit also conducts credit checks and handles collections. Headquarters: Jacksonville, Fla.

AT&T CAPITAL CORP.

AT&T Capital Corp. provides a diversified range of equipment leasing and financing services through its six strategic business units: AT&T Credit Corp., AT&T Commercial Finance, AT&T Capital Holdings International, AT&T Capital Services, AT&T Systems Leasing and Eaton Financial Corp. While the business unit's primary focus is

---

nancial performance for the last two years are shown in Exhibit 7.2. In 1991, some of the company's actions to reposition for growth resulted in $4.5 billion in charges that reduced net income by $2.9 billion. There were also one-time gains from selling some equity investments. Without these charges and gains, per share earnings were $2.51 and annual revenues were over $63 billion.

■ **EXHIBIT 7.1** *continued*

financing AT&T products, it also supports a growing array of non-AT&T products, including complex computer systems, medical diagnostic equipment, automobiles and major transportation equipment. Headquarters: Morristown, N.J.

AT&T NETWORK SYSTEMS

AT&T Network Systems is the world's leading manufacturer and marketer of network telecommunications equipment. It offers communications service providers virtually everything they need to build and operate their networks. Its major customers include local telephone companies around the world, AT&T's Network Services Division, the federal government, large companies that own their communications networks, cable television companies and cellular service providers. Unless otherwise noted, all Network Systems business units and divisions are headquartered in Morristown, N.J.

Switching Systems develops, manufactures and markets digital switching systems and software for business and residence service applications. Major products include the *5ESS, 4ESS* and 1AESS switches.

Transmission Systems develops, manufactures and markets systems for transporting data, voice and image. Major products include the 2000 Product Family of cross-connect systems, digital multiplexers and lightwave systems.

Network Cable Systems develops, manufactures and markets copper and fiber-optic cable and apparatus for telecommunications, cable television and computer applications. Major products include *Systimax* premises distribution systems.

Operations Systems develops, makes and markets software and hardware for network management and operations, as well as data networking. Major products include *Datakit* virtual circuit switch and Total Network Surveillance operations systems.

Cellular Systems develops, manufactures and markets software and hardware for wireless communications systems. Major products include *Autoplex* cellular radio system and quality management tools.

A number of divisions support these five business units:

U.S. Marketing and Sales— Two divisions represent Network Systems products and services to the regional Bell operating companies and to service providers in Canada and Mexico. Headquarters: Morris-

town, N.J., and San Ramon, Calif.

A third division represents Network Systems products and services to U.S. national accounts, such as non-Bell telephone operating companies, the federal government, end users who own their networks, cable television companies and non-wireline cellular service providers; it also manages a network of national distributors.

International Marketing and Sales—Two divisions represent Network Systems products and services outside the United States. One division covers Europe, the Middle East and Africa. It also represents the company's interests in AT&T Network Systems International, a joint venture of AT&T, STET and Telefónica, and its subsidiaries in the United Kingdom, Switzerland, Belgium, Spain, Italy and the Netherlands. Headquarters: Hilversum, Netherlands. The other division covers Asia, the Pacific, the Caribbean and Latin America. It also represents the company's interests in such Asian joint ventures as AT&T Taiwan Telecommunications and Gold Star Information and Communications. Headquarters: Hong Kong.

Customer Support and Operations provides engineering services, installation services and technical support to Network Systems customers.

Strategy and Market Development does market research, strategic planning, business development, architectural and standards development and sales support for the Network Systems strategic business units and sales division.

Engineering Division provides AT&T business units and divisions, as well as external organizations, with engineering services and technology in the following areas: environment and safety, material management and resource planning, manufacturing, logistics, quality assurance and order fulfillment.

AT&T Microelectronics develops, markets and manufactures electronic components and subsystems for telecommunications, computer and industrial applications. Major customers are other AT&T business units, original equipment manufacturers and telephone companies. Headquarters: Berkeley Heights, N.J.

OTHER DIVISIONS

AT&T Bell Laboratories, the world's foremost research and development organization, designs and develops new products, systems and services for AT&T's business units,

and is funded primarily by those units. Bell Labs also pursues a broad program of basic research to sustain AT&T's technological leadership. Most R&D focuses on three technologies common to AT&T's markets: microelectronics, software and photonics (lightwave). Headquarters: Murray Hill, N.J.

AT&T International Division coordinates and oversees AT&T's global interests and provides common support functions to business units operating outside the United States. Provides market and environmental intelligence, develops and maintains relationships with key decision-makers around the world and identifies and helps develop international business opportunities. Headquarters: Morristown, N.J.

Chief Financial Officer organization is responsible for accounting, financial reporting, financial planning and budgets, financial operations and systems, tax planning and compliance, auditing and security, overseeing investing of the AT&T pension funds and employee savings plans, actuarial services, financing activities, investor relations, cash management and risk management. Headquarters: Basking Ridge, N.J, and Berkeley Heights, N.J.

Contract Services Organization provides such services as purchasing and transportation, support services, corporate education and training, and real estate management to all AT&T business units and divisions. Headquarters: Berkeley Heights, N.J.

Corporate Strategy and Development is responsible for strategic planning at the corporate level, including long-range planning and new business development. It also provides information on the current and future conditions of the business to support corporate decision-making, oversees protection of intellectual property and supports merger-and-acquisition efforts. Headquarters: Basking Ridge, N.J.

Human Resources works to create a competitive advantage by attracting, developing and retaining talent needed to fulfill AT&T's vision. Two important groups include Labor Relations, which develops, negotiates and implements policies and collective bargaining agreements for occupational employees, and Health Affairs, which helps employees maintain optimal health and promotes a safe and healthy work environment. Headquarters: Morristown, N.J.

Information Management Services provides information movement and management products, services and technology to AT&T businesses and divisions. Partnering with other groups, it also functions as a corporate information office for AT&T. Headquarters: Warren, N.J.

Law and Government Affairs represents AT&T and its business units and divisions to all branches of government. It encompasses three divisions:

Law provides advice, counsel and legal representation required to support the policies, business activities and strategic objectives of AT&T and all of its businesses. Headquarters: Basking Ridge, N.J.

State and Federal Government Affairs interact with all branches of federal, state and local governments on matters affecting operations and interests of AT&T and its business units, including managing relations with state and federal regulatory agencies and legislatures. Headquarters: Washington, D.C., and Basking Ridge, N.J.

Public Relations provides services that articulate the direction and policies of the AT&T corporation and its business units to the company's employees, customers, investors and national and local opinion leaders. These services include media relations, employee communications, executive speechwriting, marketing public relations, corporate advertising and public relations counseling. Headquarters: Basking Ridge, N.J.

NCR

NCR is responsible for development, manufacturing, marketing and servicing of enterprise-wide information systems throughout the world. A product line based on an open cooperative computing architecture and the NCR System 3000 line of computers provides systems to meet the information processing needs of customers in a wide variety of markets, including commercial, industrial, government, financial, retail, medical and education. Customer needs are addressed in nine categories: processing platforms, telecommunications platforms, networking hardware, network and systems management, network services and protocols, transaction processing, workgroup computing, cooperative computing solutions, and document management systems. Headquarters: Dayton, Ohio.

October 1991

Global Leadership

AT&T recently appointed Randy Tobias to a new position, vice chairman to oversee AT&T's globalization efforts. Tobias says, "For six years, AT&T has fundamentally not been in a growth mode. Now, we're saying growth is our focus, our priority, and the global market is our target. It's

▪ EXHIBIT 7.2   AT&T Financial Highlights

Dollars in millions (except per share amounts)	1991	1990	Percent Change
Revenues:			
Telecommunications Services	$38,805	$38,263	1.4%
Sales of Products and Systems	15,941	16,124	(1.1)
Rentals and Other Services	6,959	6,993	(0.5)
Financial Services and Leasing	1,384	811	70.7
Total Revenues	$63,089	$62,191	1.4%
Income:			
Operating Income	$ 1,358	$ 5,496	(75.3)%
Net Income	522	3,104	(83.2)
Earnings Per Share	.40	2.42	(83.3)
Other Information (at year-end):			
Total Assets	$53,355	$48,322	10.4%
Total Employees	317,100	328,900	(3.6)
Stock Price	$ 39¹/₈	$ 30¹/₈	29.9

- We continued taking actions in 1991 that will make us more competitive and help us accelerate our growth worldwide.

- Some of our actions resulted in $4.5 billion in charges that reduced net income by $2.9 billion. We also had one-time gains from selling some equity investments. Without these charges and gains, per-share earnings were $2.51.

- Because of the AT&T and NCR merger, all financial and other data for the companies are now combined for 1991 and earlier years.

- And we changed our reporting of the amounts we pay telephone companies to connect our customers to our network. The change didn't affect earnings, but it increased reported revenues and costs in 1991 and earlier years.

AT&T vs. Dow Jones Industrial Average
Relative Stock Performance
Index: December 31, 1990 = 100

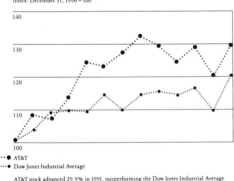

··● AT&T
···● Dow Jones Industrial Average

AT&T stock advanced 29.9% in 1991, outperforming the Dow Jones Industrial Average.

a target analysts like because they see tremendous opportunities for us there, too."

"The trick for us now," Tobias says, "is to develop the wisdom to decide what, where, when, by whom, and with what technology we are going to act in a particular country or region of the world. Part of our strategic direction also requires that we tell ourselves what we aren't going to do. We have finite resources. That's a challenge. Our decisions must be made against a set of priorities. If we don't set them, then resources tend to be allocated based on someone's internal selling skills or the emotion of the moment. We want vision, not a collection of projects."

Tobias believes the key to unlocking AT&T's global strategy lies in the eyes of the beholder—the customer. "Not how they see us now, but how we would like them to describe us in 1996 or 2001. What would they say about what we do for them and the way we do it? What makes our service, our technology better than anyone else's?"

AT&T wants global growth, but the task is not simply convincing the world to buy whatever it is AT&T has to sell. "Countries and companies are going to spend billions of dollars with somebody in all manner of activities related to the things we do," Tobias says. "We have brought focus to the U.S. market with our business-unit approach. The global market demands a similar focus. Global markets are driven by different cultures, different product needs, and a fairly dramatic change in business style from country to country, and sometimes from market to market within a country."

Emerging markets also demand an understanding of local dynamics. "We need to bring together local market knowledge and our global product and service offerings in such a way that they give us a competitive advantage. How we market telephones in Kuwait is going to be very different than how we market them in South Carolina. From a technological point of view, we have tremendous products, services, and global opportunities. But the differentiating factor is going to be how we market locally, whether we're in Poland or Kansas. A successful company is both global and local simultaneously."

Globalization of Products and Services

Demand for information—when, where, and in the form people want it—is spurring a global information revolution. To reach a worldwide marketplace, multinational companies demand communications services that transcend boundaries. AT&T has the unique combination of resources and resolve to enable customers the world over to access a gold mine of information. Delivering on this promise means enormous growth potential for AT&T. Calls throughout the world are handled with AT&T direct-dial service, made possible by use of the AT&T 5ESS® international gateway switch and digital transmission facilities. International business currently accounts for approximately one fourth of total revenues, but the target for early in the next decade is for half of all revenues to be generated internationally.

To become a leading global enterprise, AT&T is forming partnerships, making strategic acquisitions, increasing its international presence, making and selling its products in more and more countries, and offering services that span the globe. AT&T's first investment in ownership of another country's telephone company occurred by joining a consortium led by GTE in a successful bid to buy part of Venezuela's CANTV. In 1992, AT&T formed a joint venture to bill, own, operate and modernize much of the communications network in Ukraine. Partners in this project include the PTT Telecom of the Netherlands and the State Committee of Communications in Ukraine.

Communications between the United States and other countries is expanding by 15 to 20 percent annually. To serve this burgeoning market, four AT&T cable ships crisscross the seas with cables of hair-thin glass fiber of amazing capacity. The TAT-9 cable under the Atlantic, which went into service in 1992, handles 80,000 transmissions at one time. It has the capacity to carry in one day what the first cable, installed in 1956, carried in 20 years. AT&T has also signed agreements to place two more transatlantic cables with the same capacity. A transpacific cable owned by AT&T, KDD of Japan, and other carriers will deploy new optical technology that will increase capacity to some 600,000 simultaneous calls when it begins service in 1995.

The global messaging market is red hot, worth over $3.25 billion in 1991 and growing by 40 percent a year. AT&T EasyLink Services provides electronic messaging and telex services to and from some 160 countries. A computer center in Ontario handles electronic messaging services for customers throughout Canada. A Brazilian firm now distributes AT&T EasyLink services in that country. AT&T services are the primary offering of the Hutchison AT&T Network Services joint venture in Hong Kong.

For global and globe-trotting consumers, AT&T offers convenient dial-up digital service for video conferencing now available to fifteen countries, and AT&T data transmission extends to about 100 countries. Virtual private network service, providing the advantages of private-line service and cost savings over direct-dial service, links the United States with nine countries. The expansion of this service is hampered, however, by lack of common international signaling standards.

AT&T markets the popular USADirect® service to more than 100 countries, allowing callers to reach easily an AT&T operator in the United States for completing calls. AT&T Calling Cards are available to U.S. visitors from certain countries who have Visa or MasterCard accounts.

Many countries are now upgrading their telecommunications systems. AT&T Network Systems International, which serves Europe, the Middle East, Africa, and other selected markets, has sales of nearly $1 billion. The Polish telephone company contracted for digital switching and transmission equipment and a nationwide network management system. An NSI subsidiary also won a three-year $80 million contract for a network management center in Belgium. Similar centers were installed in France and the Netherlands. In partnership with Italtel, NSI sold an intelligent network to Italy's telephone company, SIP. In Spain, AT&T Network Systems Espana, a joint venture with Amper, delivered 350,000 lines of digital switching for the Spanish telephone company.

Sales are also strong in the Pacific Rim and Latin America. These include a contract valued at $300 million for NSI to provide Indonesia with an additional 400,000 phone lines; about a million lines of 5ESS switching for Taiwan, sold through a joint venture in that country; a gateway switch for Brazil; switching and operating service equipment for Mexico; and switching, cellular, and cell-site equipment in the Dominican Republic.

AT&T intends to become a world leader in supplying wireless infrastructure equipment for mobile systems and personal communications networks, which increasingly will be served by its 5ESS digital switch. Eventually, 5ESS switch owners, worldwide, will be able to provide their customers with access to multiple networks using pocket-sized portable phones. AT&T has reached a significant agreement to provide microwave radio equipment for a cellular service operator in Germany, its first major wireless business in Europe.

Establishing factories around the world is viewed as another strategy that can open new markets to AT&T and increase its global presence. AT&T Consumer Products began producing telephone answering systems at a new factory in Guadalajara, Mexico and announced plans to make cordless phones in Monterey, Mexico and at a new facility in Indonesia. AT&T Microelectronics is making electronic power systems in the United Kingdom for European customers. AT&T and its venture partners now manufacture in more than thirty countries, primarily for sales abroad.

Strategic alliances with multinational companies also open international markets and spread the cost of research and development. For example, with the Japanese firm NEC, AT&T Microelectronics is developing a chip manufacturing process that will advance hand-held digital phones, computer disk drives with all the electronics of a single chip, and economical signal-processing solutions for advanced television technology. Global expansion of AT&T's microelectronics business is on the fast track with sales growing at 60 percent a year. AT&T also provides value-added network services through AT&T ISTEL in the United Kingdom and AT&T JENS in Japan.

AT&T has marketed its "smart card" domestically for applications in personal banking, transportation, health care, security, and auto and equipment maintenance. The size of a credit card, the smart card conveniently stores and processes information. Development and marketing agreements for the "smart card" have been established with Vapor Canada, Inc., for a smart card based electronic toll collection system. AT&T has an agreement with Toyota Group's Nippondenso Co., Ltd to develop applications and market card systems in Japan.

With its NCR division, AT&T hopes to become the global leader in networked computers. For example, a businesswoman in Hong Kong can insert her credit card into an automatic teller machine and request a video link to see her banker in New York to arrange for a loan. She signs an electronic tablet and a computer verifies her signature. Then she dials a multilingual operator, using her credit card to charge a call home to her office.

AT&T and NCR believe that the computer industry is moving from an era of closed, proprietary computing with incompatible machines and systems, to an era of open computing in which multiple machines, applications, and networks form an integrated, enterprise-wide environment. By combining AT&T's networking capability with NCR's products and international strength, the firm believes it has the ingredients needed to link departments, buildings, campuses, and worldwide institutions.

In 1991, international revenues from operations located in other countries accounted for 9 percent of total revenues of AT&T. International revenues from U.S. operations (international telecommunications services and export sales) were 15 percent of total revenues. Combined, these products were 24 percent of the total. The goal for early in the next decade is over 50 percent.

Focal Topics

1. Is the target of 50 percent of sales from global operations soon after the turn of the century a reasonable goal for AT&T?

2. What geographic areas of the world do you recommend as AT&T's primary targets? Why?

3. What products or services do you recommend as the top priorities for AT&T's marketing strategy? Why?

4. Is AT&T a "global" company? What other steps do you recommend to achieve its goals?

■ ■ ■ ■ ■

The Limited

■ ■ ■ ■ ■

"Our goal is to make The Limited a $10 billion company by the mid-1990s. We'll accomplish this by having the right merchandise and an ability to execute all the details. In fashion retailing, we're only as good as what we can deliver to the customer tomorrow; it doesn't matter what we did yesterday or even today. If we ever think we've got things really figured out, we will be steering our business away from our customers and right off a cliff. But when we're asking questions, finding answers, and acting on them, that's when we know we're thinking. And there's a good chance we're finding another way to be faster and smarter."

These were the words of Mr. Leslie Wexner, founder, chairman, and CEO of The Limited, a firm described as one of the five best retailers in the nation by *Business Week* in a 1992 special issue on "power retailers." With net income of 6.6 percent as a percentage of sales and return on average shareholders' equity of over 23 percent, the description seems appropriate.

As of December 31, 1991, The Limited consisted of 4,194 stores from twelve divisions. Exhibit 8.1 shows the number of stores in each division for 1990 and 1991 along with projected stores for 1992.

Throughout its history, The Limited has focused on the customer, advocating a philosophy that nothing happens in a business until the customer says, "I'll take it." At The Limited, the philosophy is advanced that no one can predict exactly what the customer is looking for; no one can create fashion trends. Yet, the key is to be successful at anticipating the customer. As an explanation of its success, management of The Limited stresses the importance of the people within the organization and their ability to anticipate what the customer wants.

Wexner explained in 1989 how his organization responds to change:[1] "The key is our ability to change. Of course we're proud of what The

---

[1] All of the quotes from this case are from the various years' annual reports of The Limited, Inc.

■ **EXHIBIT 8.1**   Summary of Stores for The Limited, Inc.

		Goal–1992	1991	1990
Limited Stores	# of Stores	781	773	778
	Total Selling Sq. Ft.	4,351,000	3,927,000	3,526,000
Lerner New York	# of Stores	955	910	858
	Total Selling Sq. Ft.	7,185,000	6,515,000	5,721,000
Express	# of Stores	671	611	549
	Total Selling Sq. Ft.	3,629,000	2,926,000	2,151,000
Lane Bryant	# of Stores	829	786	752
	Total Selling Sq. Ft.	3,873,000	3,522,000	3,295,000
Victoria's Secret Stores	# of Stores	557	507	447
	Total Selling Sq. Ft.	2,073,000	1,666,000	1,286,000
Structure	# of Stores	360	240	152
	Total Selling Sq. Ft.	1,191,000	676,000	355,000
Limited Too	# of Stores	187	172	108
	Total Selling Sq. Ft.	571,000	514,000	268,000
Abercrombie & Fitch	# of Stores	42	36	27
	Total Selling Sq. Ft.	350,000	287,000	192,000
Henri Bendel	# of Stores	4	4	4
	Total Selling Sq. Ft.	93,000	93,000	72,000
Cacique	# of Stores	74	54	51
	Total Selling Sq. Ft.	195,000	127,000	115,000
Bath & Body Works	# of Stores	105	95	27
	Total Selling Sq. Ft.	111,000	99,000	24,000
Penhaligon's	# of Stores	6	6	7
	Total Selling Sq. Ft.	3,000	3,000	3,000
Total Retail Divisions	# of Stores	4,571	4,194	3,760
	Total Selling Sq. Ft.	23,625,000	20,355,000	17,008,000
	Increase in Selling Sq. Ft.	3,270,000	3,347,000	2,634,000

Limited has become, but that's yesterday's news. Our customer doesn't give a damn that we've been in the business for 25 years or that we have 3,400 stores . . . and why should she? When she goes into a store she wants to see something new and she wants to see it now.

"There is no formula for creating excitement. No computer can tell you today how a customer will react tomorrow. To anticipate, we have to lead and follow at the same time. We keep up with the customer's changing needs by acting on our most creative impulses.

"Nothing is taken for granted: Ideas are constantly being sought out and tried. We don't schedule creativity. We don't just fuss with details—we're continually questioning basic premises. You can see that restlessness expressed in every business. We are constantly in the stores looking for ideas and listening to our customer. If we listen carefully enough she'll tell us all we need to know.

"Creativity and innovation are essential to our success . . . and risky. The best informed hunch is just a hunch and the smartest merchant's instinct is still an instinct. We will have failures. We work hard to make risk acceptable. We reward the risk taker who succeeds; we don't penalize the one who fails.

"It's natural for small companies to think big . . . but it takes a deliberate effort for a big company to think and act small. When I opened the first Limited store in 1963 I made an incredible effort to see that every detail was as perfect as I could make it. Today we open approximately 300 stores every year—and each one gets the kind of attention given to our first store. When we recently opened our large format Limited store at the Northland Shopping Center in Columbus, Ohio, the team had been at work until three a.m. the night before . . . and that was the associates' thirteenth 18-hour day in a row.

"Our presidents get involved in these kinds of efforts because they have the basic hands-on skills to sell to a customer, select a style, or change something in a store to make it better. Our performance during this past year suggests that we not only survived the women's apparel recession, but emerged stronger than ever.

"I am proud of what our retail associates have accomplished and of the vital role played by our support businesses. Marty Trust and the associates of Mast Industries achieved record profits on near-record sales. Charlie Hinson and the Store Planning associates created new designs for several divisions and new formats for Limited Stores, Express, Lerner, and Victoria's Secret. The associates of Limited Real Estate added a total of 1.5 million selling square feet during the year. Ralph Spurgin and the associates of Limited Credit Services continued to provide our customers with the best service of any retail credit company in the country, having reduced their average response time to a telephone call to 5 seconds. A record number of shipments were handled by Lee Johnson and the associates of Limited Distribution Services, who reduced transit times by 10 percent in 1988.

"In the future no one will succeed—or even survive—without a solid financial base. We continue to pay close attention to the basics: asset management, cash flow, expense control, and efficiency. We have enormous resources and financial flexibility. While we are aggressive about growth, we are equally conservative in our financial view.

"The future will belong to those retailers who can respond to the changing needs of their customers . . . and do it fast! If the recent past has been tough on the women's fashion industry, the future will be even tougher. Retail companies without merchant leaders, financial stability, and real skills will not be able to successfully manage change in the coming years.

"We've been serving our customer for 25 years, and we know that tomorrow it will be a different business—because it's a new business every day! We think this is the most exciting aspect of our work. I believe, in fact, that the future is going to be different in ways that we can't possibly imagine. Our company has demonstrated the ability to anticipate and manage change: We are uniquely positioned today . . . and determined to be even better prepared for the future."

The major divisions of The Limited have evolved over the past 25 years, some by external acquisition; all by internal growth as well. As it prepared for the future, The Limited described its major divisions and the people who manage them as the following.

Express

The Express offers fashion-forward "Compagnie Internationale Express" brand sportswear and accessories in dramatically designed stores. Express for men was introduced in 1987 and eventually evolved into the highly successful division called Structures.

Express is a new business today, totally different from the company of a year ago. It has developed a new look and a new merchandising concept. The Express customer has responded dramatically to the more sophisticated "Compagnie Internationale" assortment and store design, propelling the business to record levels of sales and profitability. It was the Express customer, and the men she often shops with and for, who led management to the idea of a collection for men that has become Structures. Management believes Express has the potential to be more than a $1 billion business in its first decade!

Limited Stores

The international fashion source has offered brands including Cassidy, Forenza, Outback Red, Axcess, Lingerie Cacique, and Limited Too, although merchandise is increasingly featured under The Limited brand itself.

There are times when the best way to get at the answer is to ask a different question. Years ago Limited associates needed an answer to the question of how to build Limited Stores into a $1 billion business. With nearly 600 stores and a very limited number of potential new sites, conventional wisdom said that the company had crested. The question that was asked instead was: How do we grow Limited Stores into a $3 billion business? In the midst of a retail recession, Limited Stores, the industry leader, implemented totally new merchandising and marketing strategies. In addition to unveiling Limited Too, fashion for kids, and Lingerie Cacique, Limited Stores opened twenty-five dramatically different stores. The larger (12,000–20,000 square foot) International Fashion Store is opening up significant opportunities for Limited Stores. In their first year the International Fashion Stores were as productive, on a sales-per-square-foot basis, as the Limited Stores average. This extraordinary customer response suggests to management the Limited team was on its way to its sales goal of $3 billion.

Victoria's Secret

Purveyors of fashionable intimate apparel and personal luxury items are now featured in the larger "Bond Street" format. To achieve new sales and earnings records, the associates of Victoria's Secret stores successfully introduced major new product lines, including toiletries, fragrances, bath products and accessories, and an expanded men's line. Larger format stores maximize the visibility of the new lines. The distinctive new "Bond Street" store environment reflects the English influence that will transform the business in the 90s. Today Victoria's Secret is the dominant intimate apparel store in the world.

Henri Bendel

This is a line of international designer clothes and accessories. Mark Shulman and the team he has assembled are preparing to take an important step in the growth of Henri Bendel, transforming a single store business into a national and international presence. International design talent is at work on the new Henri Bendel. The 57th Street location in New York was used as a laboratory for constant experimentation, and in 1990 Henri Bendel moved to an 80,000-square-foot landmark location on Fifth Avenue. Some have described the store as the most elegant women's store in the world. Henri Bendel stores have also opened in City Center in Columbus, Ohio, and Michigan Avenue in Chicago, and more openings in similar high-fashion centers of other cities are planned.

Lerner

The largest women's specialty apparel business under one name in the country is spearheading dramatic change in the moderate-price business. Lerner provides consumers fashion clothing and accessories at reasonable prices.

Lerner was the sleeping giant of The Limited: Its market is not only the largest, but the one management believes is the least served by other national retailers. Since the acquisition in 1985, Bob Grayson and his associates have taken a tired, unprofitable, 80-year-old business and given it a whole new future. It will take persistence, vision, and a continued focus on the customer, but management believes Lerner has the potential to be a $2 billion business within the next few years.

Lerner Woman

Formed by the merger of Sizes Unlimited and Lerner Woman, this company offers sportswear, dresses, and accessories, sizes 14 and up. Lerner Woman is not simply an altered company but a brand new business. The merging of Sizes Unlimited and Lerner Woman in 1987 has created the second largest specialty business in the large-size market. In 1988 Raphael Benaroya and his associates emphasized offering the greatest possible value to the customer—the highest quality at the best price. This not only means anticipating the customer's needs, but working constantly to simplify the business. Management expects that Raphael and his associates will move toward fully realizing the profit potential of their business.

Lane Bryant

Lane Bryant, the nation's first retailer exclusively for large sizes, offers sportswear, ready-to-wear, intimate apparel, career apparel, and accessories to the fashion conscious woman wearing sizes 14 and up. It has become the dominant retailer in the special size business.

Lane Bryant's performance has steadily improved. Why? Because Ira Quint led his associates through some major changes—implementing a shorter merchandise cycle, launching a new store design, and placing greater emphasis on fashion—all to make the business more appealing to the woman who shops Lane Bryant. Lane Bryant is giving the customer what she wants.

Brylane

Brylane is a fashion catalogue business with the industry's most sophisticated shipping and receiving operation. Great merchandise and convenience have contributed to its success.

Through its Lane Bryant and Roaman's catalogues, Brylane dominates the direct sales market for large-size fashions. Brylane also serves the junior and misses customers through the new Lerner catalogue. Brylane's better inventory control, quicker deliveries, and improved quality all arise from the determination of Pete Canzone and his associates to be as service-oriented as the best of the retail operations.

Victoria's Secret Catalogue

One of the fastest growing mail-order operations in the United States, this offers intimate apparel and ready-to-wear merchandise. Since its acquisition in 1982, Victoria's Secret Catalogue has made steady progress. In 1988 record sales and earnings were achieved. In 1989 the customer responded to the more sophisticated offering as Cynthia Fedus and her associates invigorated the business with improved customer service and a new, classic format. Today this is the dominant lingerie catalogue in the world.

Structure

Structure has been a member of The Limited family since it was developed in 1987 when management noticed young men were buying unisex sportswear from the Express for their own use. Structure provides men with a store full of fashionable sportswear alternatives. In fact some young women shop the stores and buy some items for their own use.

Structure is the fastest growing major chain in the country, and projections indicate it may reach the $1 billion mark in fewer years than it took Express to reach the same sales benchmark. It plans on growing to 360 stores by the end of 1992.

Bath & Body Works

Bath & Body Works was founded in 1990 as a skin and body care company to complement the other Limited, Inc. stores. The apparel stores provide women and men with clothing to make them look and feel beautiful. Now Bath & Body Works allows consumers to take that beauty one step deeper . . . to their skin and hair. The new concept offers a wide line of personal care products including fragrances, lotions, and shampoos to name a few. Ultimately, the customers decide which products and fragrances are carried in the stores. It keeps the most popular fragrances in stock while it introduces new scents into the line based on customer acceptance.

Most of the growth of Bath & Body Works is expected to come from increasing the depth and breadth of its categories. Some of the products to be added to current offerings include bath oil, sun care, and a relaunched men's line. The goal is to increase customer awareness of the products and stores by featuring the items on tables in more than 300 Express stores. It is also distributing brochures and has established a toll-free number for telephone orders to add to its customer base.

From Ideas to Customers

In addition to the retailing divisions of The Limited, the company has one of the most advanced distribution systems in the world. Logistics management is highly computerized, linking sources in such places as Taiwan and Hong Kong directly with The Limited's headquarters. The Limited is distinctive in that much of its merchandise is shipped by air from these locations to its massive distribution center in Columbus where, after extraordinarily quick turnaround, the merchandise is shipped to local stores throughout the United States. The goal of this division is simply stated, "To take apparel from the idea to someone wearing it in 1,000 hours." Design and manufacturing, sourced on a worldwide basis, is accomplished through the wholly owned subsidiary of Mast Industries.

Focal Topics

1. Is The Limited a marketing oriented organization? Describe your reasons for the position you take.
2. What demographic or psychographic trends will have the most impact on The Limited during the next decade?
3. Which divisions of The Limited are best positioned to grow in the future? Why?
4. What changes or additions should The Limited make to continue its growth in the next 25 years?

■ ■ ■ ■ ■

Consolidated Stores Corporation

■ ■ ■ ■ ■

Consolidated Stores Corporation entered the arena of close-out retailing in 1983 with the Odd Lots concept. In less than a decade the company grew from 2 to 390 stores, making it the largest retailer of its kind in the United States. Consolidated Stores unveiled its All For One concept in 1991. By August 1992 there already totaled 125 All For One stores in the company's operating region. Consolidated Stores also operates a wholesale division that complements the Odd Lots and All For One concepts. Exhibit 9.1 shows the locations of the Odd Lots, Big Lots, and All For One stores and how many openings are planned for 1992. Additional locations have been added since this graph was produced in 1991, including Wisconsin, Florida, Colorado, and Maryland.

Close-Out Retailing: Consolidated's Niche

The philosophy of providing good products at low prices is relatively simple, but the execution of the process is much more complex. Product supply is critical to the success of any close-out retailer. Regardless of economic condition, manufacturers need to liquidate billions of dollars worth of quality products annually due to overruns, packaging changes, bankruptcies, and discontinued product lines.

Manufacturers have several options in getting rid of their excess inventory. One option is warehousing or destroying the inventory, but this can decrease bottom-line results dramatically. Dumping the goods on the market is also possible, but this often results in brand image problems and unstable relationships with established traditional vendors. Close-out stores provide a third alternative.

Manufacturers rely on close-out retailers to liquidate their excess inventory without disrupting their reputations or regular channels of distribution. Consolidated understands the delicate position of the manufacturer in such situations and is willing to negotiate mutually satisfactory agreements. This

- **EXHIBIT 9.1   Locations of Consolidated Stores**
Consolidated Stores plans to open an additional 15 Odd Lots and 35 All For
One stores in 1992.

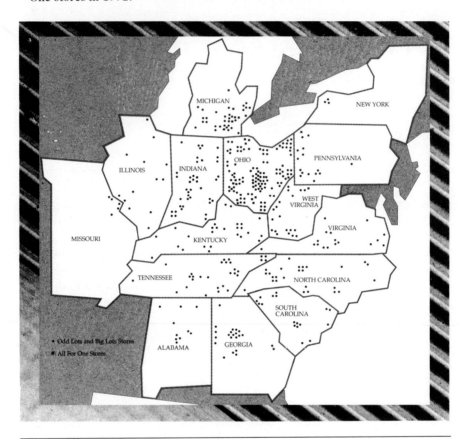

1991 Annual Report, Consolidated Stores Corp.

requires a trust between supplier and retailer. With a new supplier, it requires the retailer to have a reputation of trust, which Consolidated has
worked diligently to establish in the marketplace. Consolidated Stores' reputation is based on long-term personal relationships between its people and
the manufacturers, resulting in contracts with over 165 suppliers of over
$1,000,000 each in products annually. Consolidated also relies on more
than 3,000 additional sources of supply, many of which are small vendors
who provide the interesting and unique merchandise that keeps the Odd
Lots and All For One shopping experiences exciting and new each time.

The Buying Process

Buying is one of the most sophisticated aspects of close-out merchandising. While there is never any shortage of close-out deals, it takes special
people to find them, evaluate them, and strike a profitable deal, some-

times in a matter of hours. Consolidated strives to employ the best buyers in the industry, with years of experience and personal contacts critical in delicate negotiations. To ensure they have the freedom they need in this type of opportunistic business, they have substantial latitude in striking a deal. They are treated as entrepreneurs, and their success is judged by results.

Consolidated Stores' experienced buying team plays a critical role in its success in both retail and wholesale operations. At Consolidated, a single buying team supplies both the wholesale and retail operations, which increases synergy and gives it greater flexibility in putting together package deals, making it more competitive in every way. Each Consolidated buyer specializes in a product category, developing in-depth expertise on the product and cultivating long-term relationships with suppliers. These buyers search the world looking for the best deals to bring to Odd Lots, Big Lots, and All For One customers.

Logistics Systems

Consolidated Stores' ability to meet the demands of its stores in different regions and consumer groups successfully depends largely on its logistics system. Any organization as fast-paced and diverse as Consolidated needs support systems that can keep pace. It relies on its 2.5 million square-foot computerized distribution center located on 270 acres for the speed and flexibility needed to keep the shelves stocked and products moving. A state-of-the-art, point-of-sale system tracks over 4,000 Macro-SKUs, providing Consolidated with current sales information that helps determine the changing product mix on a daily basis.

Consolidated employs an advanced training program by which it identifies and promotes its best operations associates to create a loyal and motivated team from which to draw store managers and other front-line personnel. This helps ensure that the people managing the stores understand the importance of good logistics systems and how they can remain a part of the distribution chain. Logistics does not stop at the warehouse. These philosophies are carried through to the individual stores when items must be shipped to a different location for quicker sale or for purposes of inventory control.

The Consolidated Philosophy

One of the goals of Consolidated was to be the largest close-out retailer in the country, a position it has already reached. The simplicity of providing customers with the best goods at the best prices possible is the reason cited by management for its success in the marketplace and its steady growth.

The late 1980s were tough years for Consolidated Stores. It performed poorly financially and the Big Lots and Odd Lots stores' images dropped substantially in the minds of consumers. Although consumers were willing to accept lower levels of service and in-store atmosphere in return for savings, it became apparent that in some ways Consolidated was not meeting consumers' expectations. Because of poor performance and the need for change at Consolidated Stores, William Kelley was brought in as chairman, president, and CEO in January 1990.

Changes began immediately when Kelley took charge at Consolidated Stores. His growth orientation became apparent by examining the number of stores planned to open in 1992—40 Odd Lots and 120 All For One stores. He attributes recent growth and strong performance to improvements in gross margins by reducing low-margin items from store shelves, namely food items. Some of the items dropped included brand name snack foods and colas. There was a time when such items helped build traffic through the stores, but Kelley believes that by replacing these low-margin items with higher margin merchandise, profits will ultimately increase.

Consolidated showed impressive performance in 1991. Its primary goal during that year was to demonstrate through sales and profits the validity of its exciting turnaround. It wanted to re-establish Consolidated Stores as the premier close-out retailer in the United States. Exhibit 9.2 shows its financial performance in 1991.

Sales in fiscal 1991 grew by 13.7 percent to $752.6 million, and it achieved increased margins of 19.9 percent. Net earnings grew 342 percent to $20.1 million.

Kelley believes that the single most important factor in Consolidated Stores' turnaround and recent success is its new "corporate culture." More than anything else, it is this culture which he feels will guide the company successfully through the 1990s. Consolidated has made the commitment to embrace open-minded, stimulating reviews of operations and careful analysis of exactly what employees can do to help get the most out of

■ EXHIBIT 9.2   Consolidated Stores Corporation and Subsidiaries Financial Highlights (Dollars in thousands, except per share data)

	Fiscal Year	
	1991	1990
Net Sales:		
Retail	$752,581	$662,050
Other	18,916	17,253
	$771,497	$679,303
Net Income	$ 20,098	$ 4,545
Earnings Per Share of Common Stock	$ 0.44	$ 0.10
Working Capital	$120,275	$100,033
Total Assets	$329,321	$288,119
Number of Stores Open	398	337

themselves. It encourages employees to achieve extraordinary contributions in every area of the organization. The Consolidated team is not afraid of what it does not know. It only wants to learn from it.

Consolidated Stores: A Great Shopping Experience

Some of Consolidated Stores' objectives in recent years have been developed to help reach the goal of enhancing the shopping experiences in Odd Lots, Big Lots, and All For One stores. Consolidated has worked on training the sales staff better to meet the needs of the diverse group of consumers. Managers are given the opportunity to change the product mix, alter merchandising, and tailor promotional activities to meet the needs of their local communities. Trust among members of the supply chain coupled with an advanced distribution system allow Consolidated to custom-tailor the merchandise in each store, cut costs, and keep items in stock. In turn, customers are able to buy the items they need, when they need them, and at low prices. By encouraging the different regional stores to adapt to the buying preferences in their area, Consolidated Stores' retail outlets are better able to meet the demands of the different groups of customers and make the shopping experience satisfying for each of them.

Consolidated has revived the entrepreneurial spirit among its individual stores and among its sales associates. Individual stores are encouraged to respond to local customers and communities through a results-oriented evaluation process based on sales and profits. Such performance evaluation has created a group of highly motivated and loyal associates who equate company success with their own interests. Because associates of all levels work together, Consolidated has created a base of employees with common vision and interest in the long-term success of the company and each division. Management believes that, ultimately, their caring reaches down to the customers as well, making the shopping experience better and keeping customers coming back to Consolidated.

Odd/Big Lots

The Odd Lots and Big Lots outlets were the original stores resulting from Consolidated Stores' close-out retail concepts. The primary appeal to consumers is brand name products at low prices. It is savings that entice customers to experience Odd Lots shopping for the first time, but it is the "treasure hunt" experience that keeps them coming back. Each time consumers enter the store, they find new items—some they look for and others they discover while there. Consolidated nurtures this "treasure hunt" atmosphere by carrying as many product categories as possible, constantly developing new sources, and adding new items to the product mix. The company also gives its customers extraordinary bargains stemming from "one of a kind" deals with suppliers. Consumers are motivated to buy the bargain product now whether it is a planned purchase or not because they realize that these special bargains may disappear in a matter of hours and never return to the store.

Odd Lots and Big Lots have gained their reputations primarily through word-of-mouth advertising. By capitalizing on this reputation, they drive traffic with their product circulars, generally published forty times per year. These colorful pieces, shown in Exhibit 9.3, focus on approximately thirty-five items featured in the stores during that week. Each item reflects a bargain designed to make a trip to the store the first item on a customer's shopping list.

Odd Lots and Big Lots have also become involved in community activities and social programs. They have created the campaign "Lots More Literacy," designed to motivate people to teach someone to read and help fight illiteracy in their community. Odd Lots asks people to volunteer one and a half hours, twice a week, through their local agencies listed in the literature to help people to learn how to read. In turn, the Odd Lots stores pledge to recruit and help train more than 10,000 new teachers in thirteen states during the 1990s. The company feels that making a difference in the quality of life in the communities where its stores operate will make a difference in the quality of life for its employees and its customers.

All For One

Consolidated Stores likes to think that its All For One stores are changing the way people look at a one dollar bill. When shoppers see what each dollar buys at an All For One, a contagious kind of excitement begins to build. While each item might not cost much individually, customers leave the store having bought on an average of four to six items. Although unusual, some customers have bought nearly $200 worth of items at one time! Good value attracts a wide range of customers, but the changing variety of name brand merchandise presented in an exciting, upscale environment, as seen in Exhibit 9.4, keeps them coming back. The inventory is ever-changing so each time shoppers visit the store, they find different products to keep that enthusiasm alive. Consolidated is able to offer such variety because of its extraordinary buying power.

Today's value shoppers find themselves filling up their baskets with name brand products that they use every day: health and beauty aids, gift wrap, automotive goods, household cleansers, kitchen utensils, and much more. People are able to stock up on seasonal items such as candles, gift wrap, and decorations while they are still in season. The toy section offers a rare opportunity for parents—the luxury of allowing children to choose anything they would like without the fear of the price tag of the chosen toy. Consumers recognize that All For One products are things for which they normally pay considerably more than a dollar, especially when they carry brand names such as Hawaiian Tropic®, PlaySkool®, Gerber®, Panasonic®,

■ **EXHIBIT 9.3** A Weekly Flyer Highlighting
Specials at Odd Lots/Big Lots

■ **EXHIBIT 9.4   All For One Stores**

Esprit®, and Gitano®. A selection of audio tapes and CDs are usually available, also for one dollar.

All For One creates a synergy with Odd Lots and Big Lots. The size and upscale, contemporary look and feel of the new All For One stores have opened the door to hundreds of mall locations unsuitable for the much larger Odd Lots and Big Lots stores. This gives Consolidated Stores another retail format almost at the other end of the spectrum from its established outlets. A synergy is created by minimizing competition between its stores while increasing its flexibility in selecting a large variety of goods from around the world. The majority of All For One store managers are chosen from a pool of talented Odd Lots and Big Lots assistant managers, creating a consistency in corporate culture among the divisions of Consolidated Stores.

The addition of the All For One concept has given the company a wide range of retail stores to serve its customers—large stores dominating their shopping centers with a broad assortment of merchandise and a small, upscale specialty store that one can fit in anywhere. All For One, in fully enclosed malls or high-traffic strip centers, draws from heavy pedestrian traffic by appealing to the value shopper who buys on impulse. And, since All For One is unlike any other store in the mall, it generates foot traffic as well by becoming a destination store with its own loyal shoppers.

Future Perspectives

Consolidated Stores sees the 1990s as the decade of the "value shopper." While it recognizes there will always be a segment of consumers who will have money to spend, it feels that many consumers believe it is no longer fashionable to do so frivolously. Consolidated appeals to consumers who may have more or less disposable income, but want to save for a rainy day. The company believes that in tough economic times people feel productive and smart when they are able to save money and spend wisely. "Getting a deal" on a product for some is a source of pride in an era when smart shopping has become a reflection of a smart person.

Consolidated wants to achieve high growth in the 1990s. It plans to do this by increasing the number of stores of its existing concepts and by expanding into other discount retail concepts. Management believes that its culture and other resources could support the development of other value-oriented retail concepts that would be consistent with Odd Lots/Big Lots and All For One.

Focal Topics

1. What economic, social, and other factors influence the previous success and potential growth for Consolidated?

2. What market segments are the core market target for Odd Lots/Big Lots? For All For One?

3. How can Consolidated continue to increase the number of Odd Lots/Big Lots and All For One Stores? Outline the location strategy and promotional programs you recommend the firm use.

4. What additional concepts in "value retailing" would you recommend Consolidated develop or acquire? What factors in the Consolidated organization are likely to make this development successful?

■ ■ ■ ■ ■

Benetton

■ ■ ■ ■ ■

Benetton is a global apparel manufacturer with approximately 6,500 licensed retail stores in almost 100 countries on six continents. Founded in 1965 by the Benetton family in Treviso, Italy, where it is headquartered today, the company quickly created and filled a niche in the market for the colorful fashion-forward knitwear and sportswear that has become Benetton's signature around the world.

The Benetton family, Luciano, Guiliana, Gilberto, and Carlo, began their entrepreneurial venture in 1965 with the establishment of their first factory at Ponzano Veneto, near Treviso. Today the Group has more than 3,000 employees, 14 factories in Italy, France, Spain, the United States, and Brazil. Benetton owns 50 percent of the shares of Linz Co., Ltd. of the Seibu/Saison Group in Japan. It also has a joint venture company, Ajas-Benetton, with its headquarters and a plant in Armenia to produce and distribute cotton clothing in the former USSR.

The success of the company's collections is based on color, design, and the quality of raw materials. Careful attention is paid to trends in fashion and the desires of the marketplace. Twice a year Benetton presents its rich range of styles, totaling about 5,000 annually. The system of production is flexible and highly decentralized, utilizing a network of outside suppliers. The system relies heavily on advanced technology, such as electronic knitting machines (programmed to produce complex designs) and automated cloth-cutting machinery.

Distribution is handled by a network of eighty representatives, each one of whom is responsible for a precise geographic area and the 6,500 independent stores that agree to sell Benetton products exclusively. Orders are fed through a computerized network that enables the representatives to link up to the central system in Ponzano.

Part of the Group's marketing strategy is to allow the customer to experience a direct relationship with the merchandise. So in all Benetton stores, products are visible and can be handled. Store furniture and layout have been designed with this objective in mind. All stores are light and airy, conveying youth and energy as well as accentuating the color of the clothes.

Benetton opened its first store in North America in 1979 and by 1992 had almost 500 stores in the United States and Canada. Benetton attributes much of its success to its unique and highly automated design, production, warehouse, and distribution facilities. Benetton stores are independently owned and operated by licensees, which sell the Benetton sportswear collection for men and women, the 012 (pronounced Zero-Twelve) collection for children, the Zerotondo collection for infants, the Sisley collection of contemporary sportswear, as well as fragrances, cosmetics, and accessories. Each Benetton product is marketed under the United Colors of Benetton logo. Illustrations of a Benetton store (in Tokyo) and signage are shown in Exhibit 10.1.

Benetton Group S.p.A. is a public company traded on the Milan, Frankfurt, Toronto, London, and New York stock exchanges. Consolidated sales exceed Lire 2,303 billion in 1991, up 11.9 percent from the previous year. Over 83 million items were sold with operating income totaling Lire 312 billion or 13.5 percent of total revenues. Capital investment amounted to Lire 50 billion. Sisley growth has been over 30 percent for the past two years and is expected to double within the next three years. Consolidated net income rose 23.6 percent to Lire 164.8 billion, partly as a result of the contribution made by products sold under license for such things as watches, perfume, and other accessories. In 1992, the company paid a dividend of 300 Lire per share.

The company has demonstrated its ability to tackle world markets, exporting not only its products but also its creativity, technology, and production know-how. The most recent examples of this have been in China, Turkey, Egypt, and India, where joint ventures with local companies have been set up to produce and distribute clothing and other products under the Benetton name. Benetton Japan now owns four new Japanese manufacturers and distributors of footwear, stationery, and accessories.

The range of products sold under Benetton labels is expanding. In particular, Benetton Legs was formed to produce pantyhose for distribution under the Benetton name throughout Europe, while both styling and marketing efforts were stepped up in the footwear sector. In addition, corporate investment was increased to 50 percent in Benetton Undercolors, which produces accessories such as key chains, hats, gloves, tights, bags, and shoes.

The company has numerous license agreements, covering more than thirty countries throughout the world, involving the production of clothing and other items carrying the Benetton name. These are intended to spread brand awareness. The products concerned vary from spectacle frames (regular eyewear and sunglasses) to stationery, from cosmetics to linen, from watches to toys, and from steering wheels for automobiles to clothing for Barbie dolls.

The company invests about 4.7 percent of total revenues in communications for advertising and sponsorship. Advertising campaigns are

■ **EXHIBIT 10.1   Benetton Store in Tokyo**

dedicated to social topics of universal importance designed to raise the Group's profile throughout the world.

Benetton Advertising

The company's advertising is a unifying element for all Benetton marketing and communications. Since 1984, advertising has been conceived and directed by the photographer Oliviero Toscani. The universality of Benetton's appeal is reinforced by its theme: United Colors of Benetton.

Benetton has pursued a campaign of public communication based on a few key concepts that contain the essence of the company's philosophy. The goal is to create a long-term, homogeneous, international image that focuses on the ethos of the company. The campaign intends to capture the infinite variety and use of colors and the fact that the Benetton label is accessible and affordable to everyone. The advertising has evolved over the years in the following manner. Exhibit 10.2 shows some of the most recent ads of Benetton.

1983

Until this year Benetton had an advertising presence only in Italy and France. The image was limited to showing the product only.

1984

In the spring of 1984, Benetton started along the road toward a new communication strategy, beginning with the campaign "All the colors of the world." Jumping groups of young people were pictured together laughing. This campaign appeared in fourteen countries and the slogan was translated into various languages.

1985

The campaign developed as colors and nationalities were mixed. Flags and symbols of various countries were added. Above all, this year the slogan "United Colors of Benetton" was born. This slogan was not only repeated in successive years but also eventually became the new trademark of the company. The 1985 campaign had a strong impact, alluding to historical conflicts, past and present. Depicted side-by-side were the United States and the USSR, Germany and Israel, Greece and Turkey, Argentina and England. The people photographed were all happy and smiling, the images seemed to be a call for peace in the world. With this campaign, Benetton made a real leap into the area of worldwide communications.

1986

The symbol of the new Benetton campaign was the globe. The campaign strived for and achieved an image that was even more multiracial and international by choosing models with accentuated ethnic features and

■ **EXHIBIT 10.2   Benetton Advertising**

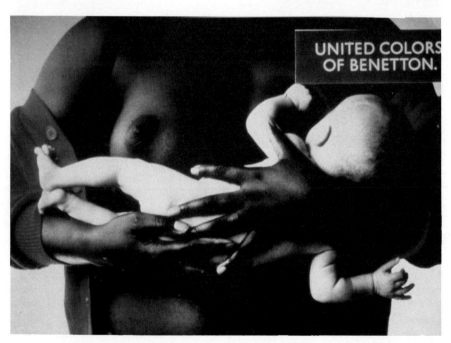

(continued)

■ **EXHIBIT 10.2**   *continued*

Courtesy of Benetton.

names written in their own languages—Chinese, Russian, and so forth. Although they were dressed in Benetton apparel, it appeared that they were wearing national costume.

1987

The autumn/winter campaign carried the slogan "United Fashions of Benetton." The pictures portrayed young people dressed in Benetton apparel but with accessories that reflect the style of the great names in fashion.

1988

United Superstar was the slogan for the spring/summer campaign. Joan of Arc and Marilyn Monroe, Leonardo da Vinci and Julius Caesar, Adam and Eve, are portrayed alongside each other, again in a mixture of history and culture.

1989

The campaign initiated the subject of equality between black and white. The images included: two men, one white the other black, handcuffed together; a black woman breastfeeding a white baby. The product had only a symbolic value.

The campaign created controversy in the United States. Benetton U.S.A. decided to withdraw the image of the black woman and white baby prior to publication because the campaign was intended to promote equality and not friction. This particular image became the most highly awarded in Benetton's advertising history, receiving acclaim in France, Holland, Denmark, Italy, and Austria. In 1989 the company decided to adopt as its trademark, "United Colors of Benetton."

1990

The campaign again promoted equality between races. This time the images became more symbolic, but still with strong contrast and without the presence of any product. Two hands (one black, one white) passing a baton. Two children on potties. A white wolf and a black lamb.

1991

The 1991 spring/summer ad campaign continued to address the major social issues of the time, including AIDS, overpopulation, and racial harmony. The following five subjects comprised the print and outdoor advertising campaign for spring/summer 1991: A white boy gives a big kiss to a happily surprised black girl; three children (white, black, and Asian) stick out their tongues in an expression common to children all over the world; an image of several Pinnochio puppets each made of a differently colored wood; a photo of brightly colored condoms takes the "united colors" theme one step further to promote social responsibility relating to over-population and sexually transmitted diseases such as AIDS; in a military cemetery, human beings of different races and religions die for common ideas and adverse causes—there are no winners in a war.

In the campaign for fall/winter 1991, as in the past, the themes were socially oriented and universal because Benetton was speaking to audiences in 100 different countries around the world. The theme of this campaign was as timely and timeless as the universal value—love: the underlying reason for life. The images featured a newborn baby seeing the world for the first time; a priest and a nun sweetly kissing; two children: one black, one white, hugging; colored leaves floating in a sea of oil; a zebra and a brightly-colored parrot; and a roll of pure white toilet paper.

The photo of the newborn baby became an exhibit at the Baymans-van Beuningen Museum of Rotterdam in Holland as part of an exhibit dedicated to images of motherhood through the centuries. It is typical of the Benetton advertising, which has sparked high commendation and honors while at the same time provoking sometimes violent criticism.

It was in Holland that the first of a long series of awards was bestowed on a Benetton advertising campaign. This occurred in 1984 with an award from the magazine *Avenue* (which has continued to honor Benetton advertising practically every year since) for the campaign titled "All the Colors of the World." The ads spotlighted groups of young people of different races and colors as they jump and laugh together.

In 1985, the campaign accentuated its unique international flavor with the presence of flags of deliberately chosen countries in the same photo. The photo featuring the flags of the United States and the former USSR was criticized in the United States for the prohibition—then in effect—of representing the national flag in advertising. The same picture was lauded in Europe. In France, it won the Gran Prix de la Publicite Press Magazine and the Grand Prix de la Communication Publicitaire. Also in France, the overall campaign won an unusual prize from the Banque de l'Union Publicitaire: one million francs, which were reinvested in advertising space.

Also part of this campaign was a photo with two black children kissing, one was wrapped in the stars and stripes, the other in the red Soviet flag. Benetton, on the occasion of the meeting in Paris between Mitterand and Gorbachev, used this photo to carpet the entire route of the presidential motorcade along the Champs Élysées. The effort paid off, and Gorbachev demanded of his colleagues, "Who is this Benetton anyway?"

In 1986, the symbol of the advertising became the globe. Models with pronounced ethnic characteristics wore Benetton clothing that suggested their national costumes. In one of these photos, a young Jew embraced a young Arab; money emerged from the globe, which both held in their hands. Protests from the Jewish community in Paris, concerned about the possible repercussions evoked by the combination of Jews and money, resulted in the covering up of the bank notes. This photo was, however, a prize-winner in Holland.

The 1988 campaign featuring personalities such as Joan of Arc and Marilyn Monroe and Adam and Eve combined different cultures and stores. The naked breast of Eve peeping out from a jeans jacket was enough to scandalize some Americans, but the same photo was again a prize-winner in Holland. Also in 1988, the children's campaign, "United Friends of Benetton," won the prize for best print campaign in Italy, in a competition organized by Confindustria, the Italian Association of Industries.

The controversy continued with the campaign supporting equality between black and white. Two photos aroused fervent opposition: the black woman breastfeeding a white baby, and two men, black and white, handcuffed together. The black community in the United States reacted most strongly against the former photo because, in their opinion, it portrayed the stereotypical image of the black wet nurse relegated to a subordinate role. The spirit of the picture intended by Benetton, however, that equality goes beyond knee-jerk reactions and conventional perceptions, was well perceived internationally. The photo received awards in Austria, Denmark, France, and Holland. In Italy, it won the Confindustria prize for the best print campaign in the textile category and the overall Grand Prize for best photo in any print advertising. This photo became the most-awarded image in Benetton's advertising history.

The campaign of 1990 was presented with the slogan "United Colors of Benetton," which by then had been adopted as a trademark for the company. It consisted of highly symbolic photos where the product was no longer in evidence: Two hands, one black and one white; a black child sleeping on a blanket of white stuffed bears; a series of test tubes filled with—according to their labels—the blood of important heads of state; two boys, one black and one white, sitting together on a potty.

This last photo initiated a typical Italian story. It could be called "the censure of the Plaza Duomo." As if in a script of "commedia del l'arte," the left-wing administration of the city of Milan and the Cardinal of the city (and its most powerful religious leader) agreed to prohibit the image from being displayed in Plaza Duomo, on the largest billboard in the world (770 square meters). The pretext was to defend the sensitivities of the faithful exiting from Sunday Mass in the Duomo Cathedral.

In sharp contrast to this reaction, the 1990 Benetton campaign was extremely successful abroad, gathering awards in Australia, France, Great Britain, Holland, and the United States. The ad won many awards including the prestigious Internationally Addy Awards of Excellence in the United States and the Media and Marketing Europe in Great Britain, for the best print campaign in Europe.

The two campaigns of the spring/summer and the autumn/winter of 1991 reached the height of controversy. The themes selected were of social and universal importance, designed to capture people's interest by breaking through their indifference. The first photo was that of a war cemetery, with long rows of crosses symmetrically aligned as if to say, "Attention! In wartime nobody wins. Beyond uniforms and races and religions, death is the only victor."

The photo was published in Italy a few days after the start of the Gulf War in two major daily newspapers, *Corriere della Sera* and *Il Sole 24 Ore*. Subsequently the ad was blocked by the Grand Jury, the Committee of Self-regulation of Italian Advertisers. The photo, after furious debate in newspapers worldwide, was also refused in France, Great Britain, and Germany.

A second subject, "Prophylactics" (colored condoms on a white background photographed in stark graphic style), caused a great deal of confusion, above all in Italy and the United States. At the same time this campaign was released, condoms were distributed in Benetton shops all over the world. The move was met with general disapproval from older adults and enthusiastic approval from younger customers. Meanwhile, in New York City, Benetton contributed to a program sponsored by the city's mayor to distribute condoms and information about AIDS prevention in the public schools.

The photo of three children—black, white, and yellow—sticking out their tongues (the point of which is that all tongues are the same color) serves to illustrate the fact that the universality of Benetton advertising sometimes encounters unforeseen cultural barriers. This image was deemed "pornographic" and subsequently withdrawn from display in Arab countries, where the depiction of an internal organ is prohibited. Yet the same photo won two awards in Europe, in Great Britain (another International Advertising Award), and in Germany.

The 1991 autumn/winter campaign was severely criticized for two photos in particular. The first, a priest and a nun kissing, created a scandal in a number of countries, but was blocked in effect only by the Grand Jury in Italy. Its message of love beyond conventional barriers was better understood where the impact of the church is less strong. In England, for example, it won the Eurobest Award. But a more important tribute came in the words of Sister Barbara of Alzey, Germany, who wrote to Benetton, ". . . I think that his photo expresses a great deal of tenderness, serenity, and peace."

It was, however, the photo of newborn Giusy trailing her still attached umbilical cord that set off controversy just about everywhere. In Italy the protests began in Palermo, where the local government asked Benetton to remove the billboards. In Milan, the censure was preventive, and the aforementioned billboard on the Plaza Duomo remained "off-limits." The official explanation of city authorities was "excessive impact and vulgarity of the subject." Afterward came condemnation by the Grand Jury, which claimed the photo "does not take into account the sensitivities of the public." Similar criticism forced Benetton to remove the ad from billboards in Great Britain, Ireland, and France.

The negative reactions and the criticism seemed to be triggered more by the billboards than by the print campaign, almost as if the dimensions of the photo were what bothered the critics most. Giusy's advertising journey is peculiar in that, once the period of rejection was over, the photo began to be understood and appreciated. It won the Swiss prize from the

Societe Generale d'Affichage, and the Poiclinic Sant'Orsola of Bologna requested a copy to hang in its labor room.

The tumultuous campaign of 1991 produced one more controversy about the photo that perhaps would have been least suspect in the series, the colored parrot atop a black-and-white zebra. In Riyadh, the billboards had to be removed because a rule of the Koran (subject to ambiguous interpretation) prohibits the visual depiction of living creatures.

Not all of Benetton's advertising is of the controversial nature. Benetton also provides its store owners with ads featuring clothes rather than causes plus assistance for cooperative local advertising. To a degree, such programs answer the complaints that some store licensees have expressed against Benetton's social awareness advertising. One licensee in Biloxi, Mississippi, objected to the condom ads so strenuously that she closed her store and filed a lawsuit against Benetton, alleging that the ads helped drive her out of business. Another store owner in Chattanooga, Tennessee, has closed two of his five Benetton shops, believing that the Benetton advertising is at odds with the new customer it hopes to attract. He explains, "Our market is now the 25- to 49-year-old woman, and she isn't impressed to see the teeny-bopper ads." Another store owner in Tampa, Florida, who has closed 12 of the 27 Benetton shops once owned, complains, "It is not our function as retailers to raise the consciousness of people. I've had long, hard fights with Italy over the advertising."[1]

Focal Topics

1. What should the objectives be for Benetton's advertising? Does the campaign achieve these objectives?

2. Which, if any, of the ads produced by Benetton should be withdrawn and should not have been originally placed?

3. What marketing research or consumer analysis techniques would be helpful to the development of Benetton's communications program?

4. Should government agencies or other organizations be able to prohibit Benetton from releasing controversial ads? What are the legal rights of Benetton in the United States or other countries?

■ ■ ■ ■ ■

---

[1]Teri Agins, "Shrinkage of Stores and Customers in U.S. Causes Italy's Benetton to Alter Its Tactics," *The Wall Street Journal*, June 24, 1992, B1ff.

Cantina del Rio

■ ■ ■ ■ ■

Mexico. The hot sun shines down on the porch of the local cantina. The old ceiling fans keep the hot air moving, and the cool, sweet margaritas and the warm, freshly made tortilla chips make for a lazy afternoon. A couple sits with friends and discusses plans for the rest of the day. They could see the sights in the city or just stay in the cantina until dinner time. No pressure, no deadlines. Is this a pleasant little town in Mexico? Or is it Columbus, Ohio?

Bob Evans Farms, under the leadership of Daniel Evans, chairman of the board and CEO of Bob Evans Farms, announced on April 26, 1991, that it was ready to expand into the casual dining market. While the original Bob Evans Farms restaurants were doing extremely well during breakfast hours, sales in the dinner category were lagging. It chose to enter the market with a unique Mexican restaurant, unique in that it would be truly Mexican. So authentic that one could hardly tell whether it was in Mexico or in Ohio.

The concept and the restaurant were developed to appeal primarily to young adults and dual-income families, the emphasis falling on "families," consistent with the image of its parent company. The restaurants would not operate under the Bob Evans Farms name. Rather they would stand alone on the Cantina del Rio (cantina by the river) name, although the restaurant would be frequently related to the parent company in publicity campaigns. The average check was estimated to be $8 for lunch and $13 for dinner. "Food value and fast service—that's everything today," states Evans[1].

Project Authenticity

The development of Cantina del Rio began with a project team formed in 1990. This team traveled south to Texas and Mexico in search of a Mexican

[1]Carolyn Walkup, "Bob Evans' Cantina Del Rio Pledges: No Gringo Food Allowed," *Nations Restaurant News*, February 17, 1992, 50.

restaurant that the company could buy. It was during its stop in Houston, Texas, that the team discovered Guadalajara Mexican Grille and Bar, a Mexican restaurant owned and operated by Phillip Torres. In talking with Torres, the team found what they were looking for in a restaurant concept. Torres, while not interested in selling Guadalajara Grille and Bar, joined the team as a consultant.

Phillip Torres traveled with the project team through Texas and Mexico in search of restaurant styles and artifacts. Cities they researched included Guadalajara, Acapulco, Mexico City, and Juarez, Mexico; and El Paso, San Antonio, Dallas, and Houston, Texas. The research and travels done by the project team resulted in what consumers experience in a trip to Cantina del Rio—a restaurant that captures the 1940s architecture of Mexico with Spanish and southwestern influence. This experience is brought to each table with the taste of fresh, authentic ingredients following the Torres family tradition of quality food.

Columbus, Ohio was chosen for the first Cantina del Rio location. It did not have many Mexican restaurants, but consumer demand was there. It was also the corporate headquarters of Bob Evans Farms and top management also wanted to be close to its new restaurant to learn and be involved in every process. Although operations are a Bob Evans Farms specialty, Mexican culture was not. The Bob Evans team, however, wanted to make Cantina del Rio and its food as authentic as possible. It wanted to be different from the popular but Americanized chains. It realized that consumers, unfamiliar with true Mexican cuisine, would have to be educated by the staff on southwestern taste.

Before construction began, the Bob Evans team was committed to authenticity in the development of the Cantina del Rio building. The company wanted it to be as authentic as possible without being stereotypical or offensive to any segment of the community (see Exhibit 11.1). The Hispanic Alliance of Ohio became an ally and supporter of the restaurant prior to its opening. Its members endorsed the building and the interior and exterior of the restaurant. For instance, in the United States people say air is air-conditioned if it is cooled by an air cooling system. In Mexico it is called refrigerated air. Therefore, Bob Evans placed the words "Refrigerated Air" on the outside of the building, to add to the experience of dining in Mexico. Other phrases were added to the outside of the building in either graffiti form or neon lights. All of the effort made the building look old and somewhat run down, yet very authentic. The Hispanic Alliance of Ohio understood the company was not poking fun at the Hispanic culture, but representing the buildings accurately.

The Cantina del Rio team and the Hispanic Alliance of Ohio worked on identifying artifacts to include in the restaurant. The management team traveled through Mexico to locate just the right ones. They returned with two semi trucks full of things that have made the restaurant what it is today: authentic Mexican. The company spent about $2 million on the property, equipment, and artifacts.

■ **EXHIBIT 11.1** Cantina del Rio

Courtesy of Cantina del Rio.

The welcome station is hand-carved Mexican pine wood and was crafted in Guadalajara, Mexico. The hand-carved wood columns, hand painted porcelain sink bowls, doors, wrought iron fences, stone bar countertop, pictures, and all of the pottery were made and purchased in Mexico. In fact, even the tile on the walls of the "baños" to the inset tile in the dining room floor and on the table tops are a result of the team's Mexican treasure hunt.

The Cantina team also brought back some ideas. A cantina in Guadalajara could not afford to repair a broken window, so it mortared old bottles into the wall to keep out the weather yet welcome in sunlight. This was replicated in Cantina del Rio with old water jugs. The salt and pepper shakers at each table are genuine Coronita (small Corona) beer bottles. And the restaurant proudly displays Corona and Coca Cola coolers that come from Mexico. They are used now to store silverware.

A focal point of the restaurant is a mural depicting an outdoor Mexican marketplace. It was hand painted by Trinidad Cordero, of Houston, on antique wood planks that can be disassembled and displayed in future Cantina del Rio locations. This mural, shown in Exhibit 11.2, is featured on the menus and brochures.

The Hispanic Alliance group was proud of a job well done; however, some people were skeptical. The owner of an area business contacted Bob Evans Farms' corporate headquarters and complained about the building.

■ **EXHIBIT 11.2   Mural by Trinidad Cordero**

Courtesy of Cantina del Rio.

Among his complaints were that he felt it looked rundown and was offensive to the Hispanic community. Evans immediately contacted his friends at the Hispanic Alliance of Ohio with concern. Representatives of the Hispanic community who had worked on the project issued a statement to the business owner and the media to assure all skeptics that no offense was taken. They explained their role in the development of Cantina del Rio and pride in "their" restaurant. The business owner was satisfied and never heard from again. Once the restaurant was opened a large opening party was thrown for the Hispanic Alliance of Ohio in return for all of its help.

Cantina del Rio's relationship with the Hispanic Alliance of Ohio continues to be strong. The restaurant presented the organization's scholarship fund with a check for $10,934. The president of the Hispanic Alliance accepted the donation for his group and thanked Cantina del Rio for supporting its young people, respecting the Hispanic culture, and contributing to the Hispanic community. The money was raised when more than 4,000 guests were treated to practice meals during a 2-week, pre-opening period.

Eat, Drink, and Be Mexican

There were few good Mexican restaurants in Columbus, Ohio; therefore, Cantina del Rio has enjoyed phenomenal success in the few months it has been open. Due to its popularity and no reservations policy, most evenings one can expect a wait of at least 45 minutes for one of the 300 available seats. Some critics say the lines and policy are driving away those customers likely to become regulars. But most customers do not mind waiting. They sit in the reception area or wander into the bar area, which is filled with long tables and bar stools. A server immediately brings warm tortilla chips and fresh salsa to the tables. The weekend crowds, which often face a 2-hour wait, enjoy their time in the casual bar, but Evans is quick to stress that he and the company do not want Cantina del Rio to get the reputation of being a bar. In fact in the original construction, the bar area was much smaller in order to be consistent with the company's values not to emphasize excessive alcohol consumption. Because of the long waits, a few more tables were added and the waiting area, now the bar, was expanded.

Evans makes it clear that alcohol is offered in the restaurant so that people can enjoy a margarita or Mexican beer with their food, not so that people will think of Cantina del Rio as a place to drink. If for some reason the restaurant acquires this type of image, Evans says he will consider reformulating the Cantina del Rio concept regardless of its success. Those are his values; those are the values of the company.

Mexican Cuisine

"Not for Gringos" warns the Cantina del Rio menu. Customers are instructed to leave their gringo tastes at the door and not to expect the usual "Americanized" form of Mexican fare because the Cantina cuisine is unlike what most people have ever tasted. While fajitas, tacos, and enchiladas appear on the menu, they are different from those served in most "Mexican" restaurants. The chefs use over three cords of hickory logs a week to grill meat used in entrees to enhance flavor.

Cantina del Rio prides itself on the authenticity of its food. Many of the recipes come directly from Mexico through Phillip Torres and his family, and many of the chefs have been recruited from the Hispanic Alliance. It is proud to serve dishes like quail legs and shrimp wrapped in bacon in addition to the entrees and menu items listed in Exhibit 11.3. Items made fresh daily at the restaurant include garden fresh salsa made with vine ripe tomatoes.

Only the finest spices such as cilantro, cumin, and fresh chiles are used in the recipes to add authentic flavor to the dishes. Cantina del Rio has also gone the extra mile to use ingredients straight from Mexico, such as Mexican asadero cheese, a mild white cheese. Authenticity and great taste are further enhanced by the handmade flour tortillas, made by skilled tortilla makers on the premises. Exhibit 11.4 shows Evans behind the tortilla station during a busy lunch hour when over 300 tortillas are made fresh every hour.

When dining at the Cantina del Rio, customers must remember to save room for dessert. Just like the entrees, desserts are made fresh daily on site. The margarita pie and the cool, caramel flans are very popular.

- **EXHIBIT 11.3   Some of the Authentic Offerings Featured on the Cantina del Rio Menu**

ANTOJITOS
[appetizers]

Nachos Regulares - Our crisp corn tortilla chips with layers of refried beans, picadillo meat and melted cheddar. Garnished with jalapeños, pico de gallo and sour cream.. lg $5.95   reg $3.95

Nachos del Rio - Your choice of marinated chicken or beef fajita meat over crisp corn tortilla chips with layers of refried beans and melted cheddar. Garnished with jalapeños, pico de gallo, sour cream and guacamole................. lg $7.95   reg $4.95

Quesadillas de Pollo o Carne - A fresh flour tortilla lightly grilled to a golden brown and filled with a mild Mexican asadero cheese, fresh vegetables and your choice of marinated chicken or beef fajita meat cooked over hickory. Served with sour cream, pico de gallo and guacamole.. lg $8.45   reg $5.45

Chili con Queso - Fresh green bell peppers and onions added to a blend of melted cheeses, served with or without chorizo (our spicy Mexican sausage) and crisp corn tortilla chips .... lg $5.95   reg $3.50

Tamales - An authentic Mexican tradition! Four savory tamales, made of Masa (dough), stuffed with shredded pork, wrapped and steamed in corn husks. Served with sour cream, pico de gallo and guacamole $5.95

Fajita Fondue - Choose our marinated chicken or beef fajita meat cooked on our hickory grill, in a creamy cheese and mushroom sauce. Served with plenty of our warm, crisp flour tortilla chips $6.50

Queso Mexicanos - A mild Mexican asadero cheese melted, served with our fresh flour tortillas and blended with your choice of:

  Parilla (from the grill) - Marinated chicken fajita meat cooked over hickory and sauteed onions $6.95

  del Jardin (from the garden) - Sauteed garden fresh vegetables $5.95

  del Mar (from the sea) - Succulent sauteed shrimp and crab meat $7.50

  Flamedo (served flaming) - Chorizo (spicy Mexican sausage) $5.95

SOPAS Y ENSALADAS
[soups and salads]

Sopa de Poblano - A creamy soup made with mild poblano chilies, rich cream, Mexican seasonings and garnished with strips of our crisp corn tortillas... bowl $2.95   cup $1.95

Sopa de Tortilla - Our special chicken broth slowly simmered with large chunks of garden fresh vegetables. Garnished with strips of crisp corn tortillas, mild Mexican asadero cheese and fresh avocado............................. bowl $2.95   cup $1.95

Sopa de Frijoles - A rich broth made from pinto beans, bacon, fresh tomatoes, onions and our special Mexican seasonings all simmered to perfection .... bowl $1.95   cup $ .95

Guacamole Salad - ¡Ingredientes Frescos! Fresh, tender avocados, lime juice and garlic, blended together and served with warm tortilla chips .... lg $5.25   reg $3.50

Chalupas Compuestas - We start with two crisp corn tortillas, layers of refried beans, picadillo meat, shredded cheese, lettuce and tomatoes. Topped with sour cream and fresh guacamole $6.50

del Rio Salad - Choose marinated chicken or beef fajita meat cooked on our hickory grill, piled high on a bed of crisp salad greens, smothered with chili con queso and topped with a slice of fresh avocado $6.95

Grilled Camarones Ensalada - Jumbo shrimp delicately grilled over hickory, in a bed of crisp salad greens, grilled chunks of pineapple and our honey-lime vinagrette $8.95

ENCHILADAS
[served with refried beans and Spanish rice]

Cheese Enchiladas - A rich blend of cheeses and onions wrapped in soft corn tortillas and smothered by our special enchilada sauce.. (3)$6.35   (2)$5.35

Beef Enchiladas - Picadillo meat, cheese, onions and our own special seasonings wrapped inside soft corn tortillas. Topped with our own enchilada sauce and melted cheese .... (3)$6.95   (2)$5.95

Chicken Enchiladas - Shredded chicken, cheese, onions and special seasonings wrapped inside soft corn tortillas. Topped with Spanish sauce and melted cheese .... (3)$7.95   (2)$6.95

Fajita Enchiladas - Choose our tender marinated chicken or beef fajita meat grilled over hickory, cheese and onions wrapped inside soft corn tortillas. Topped with enchilada sauce and melted cheese .... (3)$7.95   (2)$6.95

Chicken Enchiladas Verdes - Shredded chicken, cheese, onions, special seasonings, wrapped inside soft corn tortillas and smothered in our special verde (green) sauce. Topped with a mild Mexican asadero cheese, pico de gallo and sour cream... (3)$7.95   (2)$6.95

TACOS, FLAUTAS & BURRITOS
[served with refried beans and Spanish rice]

Beef Tacos - Your choice of two crisp corn or soft flour tortillas overflowing with picadillo meat, lettuce, tomatoes and shredded cheese $5.75

Chicken Tacos - Your choice of two crisp corn or soft flour tortillas generously filled with shredded chicken, lettuce, tomatoes and shredded cheese $6.25

Tacos al Carbon - Your choice of marinated chicken or beef fajita meat hickory grilled, wrapped inside two soft flour tortillas and served with fresh guacamole and pico de gallo $7.95

Chicken Flautas - Three crispy flour tortillas loaded with shredded chicken and special seasonings. Served with sour cream, fresh guacamole and pico de gallo... $6.95

Burritos de Carne o Pollo - Choose strips of marinated chicken or beef fajita meat hickory grilled, wrapped inside two soft flour tortillas and topped with chili con queso. Served with sour cream, fresh guacamole and pico de gallo...................... $7.95

(continued)

During the practice week, Evans and his Cantina team listened closely to what customers said about their dining experiences. One of the only complaints they heard about the food came from Mrs. Evans. After reading the dessert menu, she told her husband Dan that the Cantina must be the only restaurant in the midwest that did not have

■ **EXHIBIT 11.3**   *continued*

PLATO COMBINADOS
[served with rice and frijoles charros]

1. **del Rio Especial** - Chicken Enchilada, Tamale, Beef Taco al Carbon, pico de gallo and guacamole $8.45

2. **Jalisco Plate** - Beef Taco al Carbon, Cheese Enchilada, Tamale and Soft Chicken Taco $8.45

3. **Palenque Deluxe** - Beef Enchilada, Cheese Enchilada, Soft Chicken Taco and a tender marinated Fajita Steak grilled over hickory $8.95

4. **Mariachis Plate** - Hickory grilled beef Fajita Enchilada, Cheese Enchilada and Chicken Burrito topped with chili con queso. Served with guacamole $8.45

5. **Enchilada Dinner** - Two Cheese and onion Enchiladas and a crispy Beef Taco served with guacamole $6.95

6. **Acapulco Especial** - Beef Enchilada, Cheese Enchilada, guacamole, and pico de gallo $11.95
   Served with your choice of:

   Three Camarones Pacificos - Succulent bacon wrapped shrimp, grilled over hickory.

   One Seafood Skewer - Hickory grilled shrimp, scallops, whitefish and vegetables served sizzling on a skewer.

   Three Piernitas - Stuffed quail legs wrapped in bacon and grilled over hickory.

7. **Cadillac Combo*** - Beef or Chicken Fajitas, guacamole, pico de gallo $11.95
   Served with your choice of:

   Three Camarones Pacificos - Succulent bacon wrapped shrimp, grilled over hickory.

   One Seafood Skewer - Hickory grilled shrimp, scallops, whitefish and vegetables served sizzling on a skewer.

   Three Piernitas - Stuffed quail legs wrapped in bacon and grilled over hickory.

GRILLED OVER HICKORY

Our grill is fired-up naturally with hickory logs, giving our chicken, beef, shrimp, ribs and quail legs a savory flavor.

del RIO COMBINATION GRILLE*

Your choice of any three of the following marinated and hickory grilled specialties served sizzling. Served with guacamole salad, pico de gallo, rice and frijoles charros $15.95

   Three Camarones Pacificos - Succulent bacon wrapped shrimp, grilled over hickory.

   Costillas - Tender, hickory grilled ribs.

   Three Piernitas - Stuffed quail legs wrapped in bacon and grilled over hickory.

   One Seafood Skewer - Hickory grilled shrimp, scallops, whitefish and vegetables served sizzling on a skewer.

   Beef or Chicken Fajitas - One quarter pound of our famous hickory grilled fajitas.

FAVORITOS del RIO
[served with rice, frijoles charros and warm flour tortillas]

8. **Fajitas del Rio*** - One half pound hickory grilled, marinated chicken or beef $8.95
   One pound marinated chicken, beef or combination $15.95
   Served with pico de gallo, guacamole and sour cream.

9. **Costillas** - Tender barbeque pork ribs grilled over hickory, served with pico de gallo and guacamole.
   Half Rack $8.95
   Whole Rack .... add $3.95

10. **Enchiladas Mariscos** - (A house specialty) Succulent shrimp, crabmeat and garden fresh vegetables wrapped inside two flour tortillas, topped with a creamy avocado sauce and mild Mexican asadero cheese. Served with cilantro rice, guacamole and pico de gallo $11.95

11. **Alambres*** - Two delicately seasoned hickory grilled skewers of jumbo shrimp, scallops wrapped in bacon, whitefish and a medley of garden fresh vegetables. Served with cilantro rice $11.95

12. **del Mar Especial** - One hickory grilled Seafood Skewer, one Enchilada Mariscos and cilantro rice. Served with fresh guacamole and pico de gallo $11.95

13. **Camarones Pacificos*** - Six jumbo shrimp delicately seasoned, wrapped in bacon, stuffed with fresh jalapeños, asadero cheese, and charbroiled over hickory to perfection. Served with garden fresh vegetables, cilantro rice, pico de gallo and guacamole $11.95

14. **Piernitas*** - Six marinated quail legs wrapped in bacon, stuffed with fresh jalapeños, asadero cheese, and charbroiled over hickory. Served with cilantro rice, garden fresh vegetables, guacamole and pico de gallo $10.95

15. **Pechuga Y Amigos*** - Our marinated chicken breast, charbroiled over hickory, smothered with Mexican asadero cheese, and sauteed garden fresh vegetables. Served with cilantro rice, guacamole and pico de gallo $8.95

* Served on a Sizzling Platter

Fresh Homemade Flour Tortillas Served with all Dinners.
Please No Substitutions on Our Menu Items. ¡Muchas Gracias!

something chocolate on its menu. Being a big chocolate fan, she was disappointed. However, the next time she ate at the restaurant she was served a Mexican ice cream dessert with, much to her liking, chocolate sauce. Now the Cantina del Rio satisfies chocolate lovers as well.

■ **EXHIBIT 11.4   Cantina del Rio Tortilla Stand**
Dan Evans visits Cantina del Rio about five times a week. He is pictured here helping make fresh tortillas in the tortilla station.

Future

If sales performance of the first 6 months of operation is any indication of Cantina del Rio's future, it is sure to be a bright one. Bob Evans Farms is working out the quirks in its operations by concentrating its efforts on perfecting its first location before it expands. The company will be faced with site location decisions as it plans for expansion. It plans to open its second Cantina del Rio in Centerville, Ohio, just outside of Dayton, and the third is set for Reynoldsburg, Ohio. Six locations should be open by the end of 1993, with additional locations in Cleveland and Cincinnati.

Management believes that Cantina del Rio's long-term success is dependent upon the quality of the restaurant and the reputation of the parent company. But the restaurant business is very fickle. It is uncertain what sales levels will be achieved once the newness of the concept dies down and competitors enter the market. But growth is on the horizon. Bob Evans Farms plans to open six Cantina del Rio restaurants in Ohio by early 1993. Each restaurant is expected to cost approximately $2.5 million and estimated to generate roughly $4 million in revenues annually. Evans feels the cantinas fit well with the goals of 12 to 15 percent annual growth of restaurants and food retail products. While each cantina will be unique because of different artifacts, consistency in food and service quality will be a key in its long-term success.

"This is one of the most exciting projects the company's ever done," says Evans, "and we've only just begun!"

Focal Topics

1. How important is the company's philosophy about authenticity? Is it necessary to go to the lengths the company has to achieve authenticity or would it be more profitable to use more Americanized approaches?

2. Should future locations be in the Midwest where there is little experience with Mexican restaurants or should the company locate future expansion in areas nearer Mexico?

3. Considering market conditions and the company's philosophy, prepare a policy statement that can be used by management and other personnel at Cantina del Rio concerning the serving of alcohol.

4. What recommendations do you have for the marketing program of Cantina del Rio? Be specific concerning menu, pricing, restaurant appearance, promotion, etc.

■ ■ ■ ■ ■

Wendy's International

■ ■ ■ ■ ■

Wendy's management believes the best way to succeed in creating shareholder value is to build customer value. Customer value is created when customers come to Wendy's and receive the superior quality and competitive prices they expect. There is a direct relationship between customer value and shareholder value, and Wendy's has developed four main points of its strategic plan to ensure both customer and shareholder value:

1. Exceed customer expectations
2. Build a performance-driven culture
3. Build brand equity plus value
4. Grow a healthy restaurant system

Exceed Customer Expectations

Wendy's main objective is to fulfill and surpass customer expectations by delivering total quality every day. Customers give Wendy's high marks for quality, variety, and atmosphere. They do not rank Wendy's as high on price/value, operational consistency, and convenience. Thus, in addition to building on its current strengths, Wendy's has aimed its strategies at improving customers' perceptions of the latter three, as well. All six characteristics together—quality, variety, atmosphere, price/value, operational consistency, and convenience—are referred to as the "total quality equation."

One key to operating a successful restaurant is balance—balance between satisfying the customer and satisfying sales and profitability goals. It means establishing priorities and doing many things well. Increased profitability in a restaurant comes from either higher sales or improved efficiency and productivity. Wendy's managers are trained to strike the balance to achieve both.

The Sparkle program, developed in 1989, is an incentive program designed to measure quality, service, and cleanliness in every restaurant. It is a concentrated effort to ensure consistent customer satisfaction. The result, when all is working well, is a sales increase that directly measures the delivery of customer satisfaction. More customers plus greater satisfaction equal higher sales and profits for Wendy's.

Wendy's achieves enhanced profitability by implementing the Total Quality Equation. Total Quality equals the retention of quality, variety, and atmosphere plus the building of the price/value relationship, consistency, and convenience.

Building a Performance-Driven Culture

Wendy's believes that building a performance-driven culture is essential to accomplishing the goals it sets for itself. This commitment to its employees means that Wendy's strives to articulate thoroughly the expectations of employees, give people the tools they need to perform well, reward them for excellence, and provide leadership with a focus on strategy. Wendy's wants to become the employer of choice by giving people the proper training and offering competitive wages, incentives, and benefits. Wendy's also feels it is important to give employees a sense of involvement and continuing recognition. On the management level, Wendy's compensation and incentive programs are also highly performance-oriented.

Building Brand Equity Plus Value

The year 1991 ended with America accompanying Wendy's founder, Dave Thomas, on his "world tour" in search of new product ideas—at least in the "anything is possible" world of advertising. The campaign topped off what was a banner year in terms of advertising awareness for Wendy's.

Wendy's marketing approach was developed with two objectives: first, reinforce Wendy's heritage of superior quality food (brand equity) while providing for specific price and product promotion (value); and second, increase Wendy's advertising awareness, thereby closing the gap on the competition. Given recent successes on both fronts, this strategy remains in place.

Wendy's, as a total system, spends in excess of $125 million in paid advertising. The Wendy's National Advertising Program (WNAP), the administrator of both company and franchise advertising dollars, will oversee a budget in excess of $60 million in 1992, representing the required 2 percent of domestic systemwide sales. Another 2 percent, at minimum, is spent at the local level on television, radio, newspaper, and direct mail.

Wendy's menu is known for the wide variety of fresh, nutritious choices. As the menu evolves throughout the 1990s, the key requirements set for new products respond to consumer desires: quality, value, and convenience, supported by nutritional merit and variety. Wendy's tries to balance new products that increase the average check and those geared toward increasing volume or transactions. Both build total sales. Chicken Cordon Bleu, for example, a premium chicken sandwich with a relatively higher price point, falls most directly into the check-building category, while a new product idea for the Super Value Menu is more clearly transaction building.

Grow a Healthy System

When Jim Near became Wendy's president in 1986, he quickly took steps to eliminate plans to build new company restaurants. He felt that it was not wise to open new restaurants until the existing ones were operating better. Today existing stores are operating extremely well. Following five years of earnings improvements and greatly improved quality, service, and cleanliness ratings, Wendy's is implementing a plan that anticipates aggressive company and franchise growth. Enormous opportunities exist to increase market penetration and enhance location convenience for customers. Yet the company recognizes it is just as important to grow responsibly as it is to grow aggressively. Targeting its strongest markets for growth and ensuring the buildings are cost effective and efficient are two ways it plans to grow responsibly. According to Jim Near, Wendy's goal of 5,000 restaurants by the mid-1990s is within reach.

Wendy's Goes Global

While the advertising of Wendy's in the United States featured founder Dave Thomas in his global visits, something more serious was occurring in the firm's strategy. Wendy's International was in an expansion phase of international development. It has just begun to tap into the vast opportunities offered by global expansion with a very profit-oriented strategy. Its global expansion plan calls for 75 new international restaurants to be opened in 1992. Wendy's currently has 3,820 stores worldwide, 188 of those outside the United States and Canada. Wendy's operates in 28 countries outside the United States, with contracts signed or negotiated to develop in 15 more in 1992. Exhibit 12.1 lists the countries in which Wendy's is currently operating and those for which it has expansion plans.

Although Wendy's plans to enter new markets in 1992, its primary goal is to increase market penetration in existing foreign markets through 1993. A primary expansion period is planned for 1993 as Wendy's plans to open approximately sixty-seven new stores worldwide in countries including Japan, Mexico, Poland, Honduras, and Egypt. By the end of 1993, Wendy's plans to have well over 300 international operations, nearly twice its 1990 operations.

Wendy's sees much growth potential in the international market. Its goal, however, is not to see how rapidly it can build stores and how many different exotic locations it can find. It is looking for opportunities that

■ **EXHIBIT 12.1** International Stores Open and International
Department Projected 1993 Openings

International Stores Open		*International Dept. Projected 1993 Openings*		
Country	Total	Country	Projected Openings	
Aruba	2	Egypt, Morocco, Tunisia	2	
Bahamas (Freeport 1; Nassau 1)	2	Greece	5	
Dominican Republic	1	Gulf States	9	
El Salvador	1	Hungary	1	
Grand Cayman	1	Poland	1	
Greece	3	Switzerland (Weneco)	1	
Guam	2	Turkey	2	
Guatemala	2	U.K.	2	23
Honduras	1	Antigua, Barbuda, Barbardos, St. Lucia	1	
Hong Kong	3	Argentina	1	
Iceland	1	Aruba, Bonaire, Curacao	1	
Indonesia	4	Bahamas - Nassau	1	
Israel	6	Chile	2	
Italy	9	Colombia	2	
Japan	30	El Salvador	1	
Korea	39	Guatemala	1	
Kuwait	1	Honduras	1	
Mexico	5	Mexico (Hamburg.)	4	
New Zealand	4	Mexico (Wend Jal)	2	
Philippines	20	Mexico (Other)	2	
Puerto Rico	19	Panama	1	
Saudi Arabia	6	Puerto Rico	3	23
Spain	0	Australia	1	
Switzerland	3	Hawaii	2	
Taiwan	15	Hong Kong	2	
Turkey	2	Indonesia	4	
United Kingdom	2	Japan	3	
Virgin Islands	4	New Zealand	2	
(St. Croix 2; St. John 1; St. Thomas 1)		Philippines	4	
TOTAL	188	Thailand	3	21
		TOTAL PROJECTED '93 OPENINGS		67

■ EXHIBIT 12.2   Ad of Wendy's Worldwide

Note: numbers denote number of restaurants per region.

make sense from a financial and economic standpoint both in the short and long term. Exhibit 12.2 shows the number of restaurants per region in its worldwide operations.

Wendy's largest market outside the United States and Canada is Korea. One of the challenges Wendy's faced when it entered Korea was name recognition. Dr. Y. I. Kim, owner of thirty-three Korean Wendy's, decided to locate his restaurants in high-traffic, prime visibility locations that kept Wendy's in the public eye constantly. Every morning when thousands of commuters pour from the subway into the main intersection of Seoul, South Korea, the first thing they see is a striking, seven-story Wendy's sign above an attractive restaurant. Another restaurant borders the largest women's university in Korea, while a third is in the Itaewon shopping district. There is even a Wendy's in the Korea World Trade Center. With a population of 40 million and an increasing per capita income, there is great continued potential to capitalize on Korea's growing appetite for American-style, quick food service.

Another challenge for companies entering foreign markets is adapting to cultural norms and tastes. Before Japanese cars were introduced into the U.S. market, the cars had to be redesigned so that the steering wheels were on the left side of the car. One of Wendy's products in the Pacific stores is spaghetti. It added this special item because of a recognized demand for spaghetti among Filipinos and other Asian consumers. Similarly, Wendy's has included items such as teriyaki hamburgers and shrimp cake sandwiches in Japan, bone-in-chicken in the Pacific and Caribbean markets, and corn soup in Taiwan.

Wendy's has experienced its fair share of growing pains during its international expansion efforts. The company is honest about some of the mistakes that were made in the past and intends to make its international expansion as successful as the turnaround in domestic operations that has occurred in the past few years. Wendy's management recognizes that the international openings were not always done right the first time out but believes the present approach is much sounder.

The global expansion vision of Wendy's is built upon the premise that people may differ in specifics but that they are universally similar in the important attributes of quality and service. While Wendy's may not have as much recognition as some competitors, it has something more important. Wendy's can describe itself as having the best hamburgers in America. This premise is based upon the fact that in a highly competitive environment Wendy's has been named as having the "best hamburgers in America" for the past 13 years. Wendy's may not be the largest restaurant, but it intends to be number one in quality and service in whatever country it may be operating.

As part of its vision for excellence in global operations, Wendy's has closed stores in some countries in which it formerly operated. While Wendy's currently maintains an interest in operating or franchising restaurants in countries such as Germany and Belgium, it has closed stores formerly operated in these and some other countries. The reasons for closing operations varies between countries. In some cases, the stores were not operated in conformance with the quality expectations of Wendy's management. In other cases, political and social changes caused management to believe closings were necessary. In other countries, the company believed that cash available from selling the restaurants could be used more effectively in the restructuring process that occurred in Wendy's domestically during the late 1980s. Although the company closes stores in countries cautiously and sometimes regretfully, management believes that such moves are sometimes necessary to accomplish the mission of quality in products and service on a global basis.

■ **EXHIBIT 12.3**   Company- versus Franchise-Owned Restaurants

	1986	1987	1988	1989	1990	1991
Company	129	115	97	87	88	82
Franchise	102	119	144	178	203	234

Source: Wendy's International Annual Report 1991

Franchising

Wendy's has expanded globally by concentrating on franchise operations. Of its 316 stores outside the United States, 82 are company owned and 234 are owned by franchisees. Exhibit 12.3 shows how the number of company owned Wendy's stores has decreased since 1986 and how the franchised stores have increased.

Wendy's is reviewing its policy on joint ventures with a view to assessing the advantages of joint ventures over franchising. Currently, Wendy's international operations award an exclusive franchise to an operator in each country. The franchisee has the right to operate within the country in which the franchise has been awarded. Wendy's is looking for strong local business people who understand the culture and the infrastructure. Franchisees often have other businesses and always have contacts and personnel in the foreign market. Finding these partners and conducting the required research for opening a new store in a new market often takes several years. Wendy's has been doing basic background research in Russia and the Eastern European countries for some time. Although the process has been time-consuming, this initial work helps ensure good business decisions.

The franchise operations have led to many countries having only one or two stores, which has hampered Wendy's ability to advertise effectively and to impact the market. In a few instances Wendy's has entered into joint ventures. The idea is to build several restaurants with a partner to test the market with limited financial exposure. It is an approach that will be used cautiously. Joint ventures are expected in the United Kingdom and Australia in 1992.

Wendy's has also utilized a third distribution system to expand internationally. It has joined the U.S. Navy. Wendy's restaurants can be found on the naval base in Naples, Italy, and the naval air station in Sigonella, Sicily. A third restaurant just opened at the Keflavik Naval Base in Iceland. Although only three restaurants have opened by means of this new expansion strategy, the potential for further expansion is great.

European Fast Food Market

The European fast food market has developed substantially over the last decade. Because it is not as saturated as the American fast food market, there exist many opportunities for new entrants into the market. The European market is dominated by McDonald's, which has been there longer than any other American fast food company. After 20 years, McDonald's has assumed a lead in Europe. Its early entry into the market has helped McDonald's secure its premiere locations in most markets.

Even when all indicators seem positive, no organization is invincible, including Wendy's. It entered Germany in the late 1970s and early 1980s with thirty-seven restaurants and by 1989 had closed them all. Similarly, the four Belgian restaurants opened in the early 1980s were all closed within 2 years of operation. Yet, other European locations, such as those in Switzerland, Greece, and the United Kingdom, have remained open and have performed well. This leads Wendy's to believe that many opportunities exist to increase its profits, enhance its image, and compete with its competitors effectively.

Wendy's is looking to Europe and the United Kingdom for one area of expanded profits in the 1990s. McDonald's opened more than half of its new restaurants in 1991 in Europe, and Burger King has followed suit. Other American format restaurants are also opening under both American and European ownership. One reason for growth in the European market is the fact that it has been underdeveloped in the fast food market in the past. The European Economic Community has a population of approximately 320 million people, many of whom are waiting for more fast food restaurants to open.

Another reason for expected growth is the increase in the number of working women in Europe. Many of the trends taking place in Europe are similar to what has happened in the last decade in the United States. The demographics are changing more toward food away from home. Home life is changing, and a meal at Taco Bell or Pizza Hut is becoming part of the daily expectations of families. This trend means profitability for European Wendy's. The three Wendy's restaurants in Greece had sales averages in 1991 of over $2 million per unit, and the Greek operations are regarded as highly successful and a good base for future expansion.

Market Analyses

Before entering any market, Wendy's conducts primary and secondary research to better understand the environmental conditions of its new potential market. Wendy's, once present in Germany, does not want to repeat unnecessary mistakes should it reenter Germany. To avoid such problems, Wendy's has conducted some limited research into the German fast food market. Some of the results are summarized below to serve as a guideline for the types of information needed to evaluate global opportunities. This information may also help evaluate why closings were necessary in some countries during the past few years and serve as a base for reopening these countries. Additional information about other European markets is outlined to provide insights into some of the differences and similarities among European fast food consumers.

Germany

Country Data   The latest census taken in 1990 showed total German population to be the largest population base in Europe since reunification. The Eastern portion of Germany represents a large population that had been denied American fast food for many years.

Much of Germany has experienced a decline in expenditures on food and drink at home when compared to other types of expenditures on items such as clothing, education, and leisure activities. However, expenditures on eating out of the home have continued to grow, particularly in single person households.

Wendy's is evaluating potential new restaurant openings in Germany, with four tentatively planned for 1993. All stores in the country were closed in late 1980s for various reasons, including operational and service problems and a lack of adaptation to the German cultural climate. Wendy's international approach has been the same as McDonald's in the past. Thus, German consumers often do not differentiate the two restaurants. In order to achieve success in the new Germany, Wendy's believes it must develop a more thorough understanding of the decision processes of German restaurant patrons.

Motivation and Need Recognition   German consumers tend to eat fast food because it is convenient, quick, and inexpensive. Most of these fast food customers do not plan their purchases, which often occur while shopping, after an evening at the local discotheque, or when returning home from work. Very few German families eat at fast food restaurants as a family unit. They prefer to eat at home. The typical Wendy's customer is a teenager, who goes to meet friends after playing soccer or seeing a movie. More and more business people are going to Wendy's for lunch rather than going home for the traditional large midday meal.

Some observations and conclusions drawn by German consumers about Wendy's and its appeal to the market include the following:

- The prices are low compared to the typical German restaurants and to European restaurants in general
- Wendy's is on the way (to work, etc.)
- Families never meet at fast food restaurants
- Wendy's gets the most business on weekends, when people come home from discotheques

Search for Information   German consumers can find Wendy's conveniently located on busy city blocks. To this consumer group convenient location is very important in its fast food choice. They consider Wendy's to be the best American fast food restaurant, based on the quality of the food, citing the salad bar as the most preferred product sold. The purchases are generally done on impulse; thus, the most convenient source of food is chosen without a great deal of consideration of the alternatives available.

Yet many Germans state they would not go to Wendy's, or any fast food restaurant, if they were concerned about nutrition.

Exterior signage is important when the consumer is interested in making a fast food purchase. Convenience, however, is the main focus of the search for Wendy's fast food, with taste and price of the menu items being the main product determinant characteristics.

Alternative Evaluations   The main criterion for selection is convenience. When asked which German fast food restaurants were most similar to Wendy's many Germans named two other American restaurants, McDonald's and Burger King. They consider these restaurants to be symbols of America and different from their European counterparts, but very similar to each other. German consumers do have various alternatives from which to choose, including convenience food from street vendors, cafes, beer gardens, pizza delivery services, and small, privately owned, inexpensive restaurants.

Several product attributes are used to evaluate these alternatives. The issue of packaging and waste is an important consideration for the majority of Germans. They tend to avoid American fast food restaurants because of the restaurants' lack of environmental concern and actions. Wendy's is preferable to the other American fast food restaurants, however, because of its more traditional restaurant atmosphere, which is very important since Germans enjoy meeting friends and acquaintances in restaurants. The quality of food in local restaurants is perceived as better, especially the meat dishes and the small details they associate with small, privately owned establishments.

Germans also value taste and nutritional quality of food. They feel that American fast food buns and bread are too soft and spongy. Consumers are accustomed to whole grain, chewy breads. Germans also insist on cleanliness, and they view McDonald's as cleaner. Several of these attributes are used when choosing fast food, with convenience and lack of excessive packaging being the most salient. While service is considered to be important, it is viewed differently according to the food source. In a fast food restaurant service is expected to be quick, but in local restaurants, it is expected to be personal.

Purchase Behavior   German consumers spend little energy choosing one fast food establishment over another, except for the packaging/recycling issue. Germans prefer to eat at home when simply hungry and wish to spend time with their families at home over meals. Eating out is viewed as a social occasion and rarely a hurried activity. Drive-through restaurants, however, are seen as potentially useful, especially for commuters returning home after work.

Different Strokes for Different Folks

Belgium   Wendy's opened stores in Brussels and Antwerp in the early 1980s and closed them two years later. Belgian consumers apparently did not see Wendy's as representative of the typical American fast food restaurant because of the emphasis on the salad bar rather than on hamburgers. For Belgian consumers American fast food means hamburgers. In general most fast food is consumed on the premises rather than taken home and is consumed primarily by teenagers who buy from restaurants they perceive as American. As they grow older, the importance of American image diminishes, and they tend to frequent Pizza Huts or similar restaurants which have good seating and service and relatively inexpensive prices.

Spain   Spanish consumers perceived Wendy's as representative of a typical American fast food restaurant, although they tended to be somewhat suspicious of the ingredients of the various food items. Many consumers mentioned they would enjoy drinking beer with their meals at Wendy's and would be appreciative of the stores staying open longer because many Spanish people do not eat dinner until 10:00 P.M. and stay out until 5:00 A.M.

Turkey   While the Turkish people are not yet as environmentally sensitive as the Germans, there is a sense that they will be soon. This is a country which embraces the American image, but Wendy's is not differentiated significantly in the minds of the Turkish consumer. It is viewed as just another American restaurant. Turkish consumers often make their fast food eating experiences a part of a larger occasion, such as getting a hamburger and fries before going to a movie or to a disco with friends rather than family. They usually spend at least 30 minutes at the restaurant and do not appear to be interested in drive-through service.

The United Kingdom   Consumers in this country often turn to fast food restaurants for snacks rather than for meals and use the take-out services often. Speed of filling orders is not as important to this group; they would prefer to see more personal service at a slower pace. They also did not like having their orders announced over loud speakers for cooks to fill. This system seemed too impersonal.

How Different Consumers Evaluate Different Attributes

An American Image

An American image continues to attract many European consumers to Wendy's and the other American fast food chains. The European consumer views the fast food restaurant, particularly the hamburger restaurant, as very American. They go for the American "experience" first rather than primarily for the food. Therefore, they do not expect many local dishes to appear on the menus. Although some adaptations are wise, European consumers want the menus to remain American and not to focus too much on their countries' local flavors. They can go to local restaurants if they want that type of cuisine.

European consumers also want the American image to carry through to the actual restaurants. They expect the buildings to appear modern, clean, and nicely decorated, and they expect them to be consistent in appearance from one location to the next. Minor variations in details and appearance in business districts or central city areas are acceptable and often encouraged, with the American image remaining predominant.

Most Europeans, representing a variety of countries, like the American image of Wendy's and the other American fast food restaurants. However, the degree to which this image should be emphasized changes from country to country. For example, in Greece and Turkey, the American image was highly desired and played an important part in the purchase decision, but in Germany, while the American image was acceptable, it was not considered to be a highlight or strength of the restaurant. Wendy's is evaluating how to emphasize or de-emphasize the American image in different European countries.

Focal Topics

1. Why do consumers choose Wendy's rather than its competitors? Is Wendy's emphasizing the proper attributes in its domestic operations?

2. Can Wendy's achieve its growth objectives best by domestic expansion or global expansion? Would it be better to place most of its resources into domestic locations instead of global locations?

3. If Wendy's does expand globally, to which countries of the world do you recommend most resources be committed? What can be learned from decisions to enter and later close stores in some countries?

4. If Wendy's reenters the German market, how should it be done? Outline the most important elements of a plan for reentering the German market.

■ ■ ■ ■ ■

INDIVIDUAL DIFFERENCES

■ ■ ■ ■ ■

■

Max & Erma's

■ ■ ■ ■ ■

In 1993, Chicago loomed large in the horizon for Max & Erma's. It was in this city and in this year, that Max & Erma's faced a major turning point in its 21-year history. While the restaurant chain had experienced its ups and downs over 2 decades, it had established an enviable record of success in pleasing customers and expanding restaurants. With a base of twenty stores in seven cities appealing to midwestern lifestyles, Max & Erma's was now developing a taste for the Chicago market.

Max & Erma's Restaurants, Inc., is a regional dinner-house chain operating nineteen stores and franchising one in seven markets in five midwestern states:

Market	Units	In Market Since
Columbus, Ohio	7	12/72
Detroit, Michigan	4	11/83
Indianapolis, Indiana	3	4/77
Pittsburgh, Pennsylvania	3	3/80
Dayton, Ohio	1	12/75
Lexington, Kentucky	1	9/78
Canton, Ohio (franchised)	1	7/88

Max & Erma's features a fairly diversified, approximately 65-item menu of "American favorites," including hamburgers (30 percent of entree sales), sandwiches (20 percent), pasta (10 percent), and salads (10 percent), as well as charbroiled steaks, chicken, and fish. Food accounts for 71.5 percent of restaurant sales, beverages including soda for 28.5 percent.

Management believes that the Max & Erma's concept has four main competitive advantages:

- *higher cuisine quality*: almost all food is cooked to order, and the company strives to offer only the "best" possible item in its category. Thus, Max & Erma's juices are fresh-squeezed and many items hand-made; local media have consistently named the burgers the best in each of the chain's markets.

- *superior value*: the combination of quality food, ample portions, and moderate prices (average checks of $7.50 for lunch, $10.00 for dinner) creates this perception of value.

- *more personal service*: unlike other concepts, Max & Erma's does not employ "runners" to deliver orders; instead the waiter or waitress handles service throughout the meal. Having a single server rather than several promotes accountability and personalizes the dining experience.

- *homier atmosphere*: from the logo and menu cartoons to the barstools with handcarved "human" legs (with varying footwear), Max & Erma's decor is designed to impart the fun, relaxed feeling of a "gathering place," which is how the chain positions itself.

Though stores range from 5,000 to 15,000 square feet, average and current standard unit size runs from 5,500–6,500 square feet. Most restaurants are open seven days a week, from 11:00 A.M.–1:00 A.M., except Fridays and Saturdays, when they are open until 2:30 A.M.

Headquartered in Columbus, Ohio, Max & Erma's has approximately 1,100 employees, none unionized. The company has few minimum-wage employees and thus little vulnerability to an increase in the minimum wage.

History and Operating Strategies

In the early 1970s, there was a sleepy and slightly funky bar in Columbus, Ohio run by a guy named Max Visconik and his wife Erma. It was bought by entrepreneur Barry Zacks, who along with Todd Barnum, operated another restaurant a few blocks away. After going through a list of two hundred new names, they finally decided the old name was the best. They redecorated the place with antiques and quirky artifacts.

At the end of fiscal 1986, Zacks stepped down to pursue other interests. Cofounder and current Chairman and CEO Todd B. Barnum, COO Mark F. Emerson, and CFO William C. Niegsch, Jr., purchased a major interest in the company and together with its vice president of marketing, Karen A. Brennan, assumed leadership.

Over the past 2 decades, the original location has become something of a landmark and a "neighborhood gathering place" in Columbus' German Village. The overall effect is a chummy, fun sort of place where service is friendly, relaxed, and personal and where the food is the biggest and best around. The emphasis at Max & Erma's is on quality—the fresh burgers are still cooked to order and remain the mainstay of the menu.

Each Max & Erma's restaurant is different and has a unique personality of its own. The strategy in each location throughout the Midwest remains to create a "neighborhood gathering place" where people can relax and enjoy themselves amid friends. There is always something novel to see and discover.

The new management team has built customer traffic and loyalty and honed operating efficiency through three specific strategies.

Strategy 1: Increasing promotion and targeting it better   It reduced radio advertising and replaced year-round with soft-season-only couponing, redeploying funds saved into directional billboards and a television campaign. The company's marketing efforts have also emphasized publicity-generating special events, such as the annual "Max & Erma's Jingle Bell Run for Arthritis," a 5-kilometer, costumed winter run held in several markets. Such events are cosponsored by local radio and television stations. Examples of promotional materials are shown in Exhibit 13.1.

Strategy 2: Streamlining and making the menu more "user-friendly"
Guided by customer preferences indicated in historical data, surveys, and focus groups, management eliminated 30 percent of the old menu items and added 10 percent new items. Deletions included trendy but hard-to-prepare dishes such as fish fajitas and "frozen hot chocolate," which were unfamiliar, and thus slow-moving, in the company's midwestern markets; additions included prosaic but popular items such as club and reuben sandwiches and a fried cheese appetizer. The slimmed-down menu has not only improved food quality and consistency, but it has helped pare the cost of sales and operating expenses by 1.6 and 3.1 percentage points, respectively, over a 2-year period. In response to greater health consciousness and lighter dining habits, management began to promote its 6-ounce burger in addition to its traditional 10-ounce hamburgers and half portions of salads and entrees. Permitting patrons to order individual servings instead of sharing dishes has increased customer satisfaction and spurred appetizer sales so that average checks have fallen only nominally.

Strategy 3: Upgrading existing facilities   A $1.4 million renovation and remodeling program enhanced ambiance and facilitated service. All stores have been upgraded within the past four years, and the system should require only some $500,000 per year to maintain high standards. Most importantly, Max & Erma's new leadership has instilled an ongoing, organization-wide commitment to planning, financial performance, and maximum customer satisfaction. This has been accomplished through:

- wider management input: general and regional managers have been enlisted to develop the annual budget and strategic plan. This has strengthened "pride of ownership" and thus dedication to meeting goals.

■ **EXHIBIT 13.1   Max & Erma's Promotional Materials**

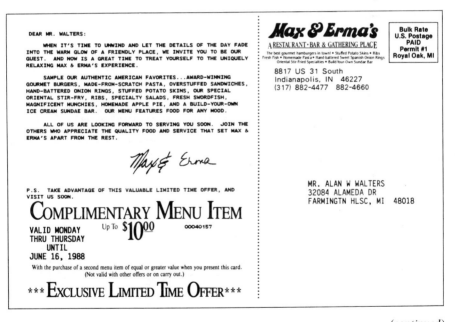

(continued)

■ new incentive compensation system: this system reinforces corporate priorities by enabling store managers to earn up to 20 percent of their base salary for attaining sales and controllable (i.e., prerent and depreciation) profit targets, and up to an additional 20 percent for achieving dining experience quality goals as measured by shoppers' reports.

YOUR NEAREST MAX AND ERMA'S:
630 Stanwix Street
(In Horne's)
Pittsburg, PA 15222
471-1140

Mr. Jose Valverde
P.O. Box 22023
Pittsburgh, PA 15222

Dear Mr. Valverde:

DON'T OPEN THAT ENVELOPE!
READ THIS FIRST!

How strong is your ability to resist temptation? If you can refrain from opening the prize envelope, you will receive one of the prizes in the MAX & ERMA'S "WE-BET-YOU-CAN'T-RESIST-THE-TEMPTATION" SWEEPSTAKES!

Here's how it works. Go to MAX & ERMA'S as soon as possible and order some of your MAX & ERMA'S favorites. When your check is presented, give your server the enclosed envelope. When your server opens the envelope, you will receive one of the prizes! That's all there is to it.

Dining at MAX & ERMA'S will really put your will-power to the test. Do you think that you can resist the temptation of one our award-winning gourmet hamburgers? Can you mount a defense against our made-from-scratch pasta? Can you say no to our overstuffed sandwiches, hand-battered onion rings or our delicious stuffed potato skins? Will you be able to turn your back on our sensational oriental stir-fries, our succulent ribs, our specialty salads? Can you refrain from our magnificent munchies, homemade apple pie, or our build-your-own sundae bar?

We're betting you can't. But, don't feel bad. Everyday, many people who think they have good self control, give in to the temptation to really enjoy themselves at MAX & ERMA'S.

So, when you feel like relaxing, and you want to unwind in the warm glow of a friendly place, bring your prize envelope to MAX & ERMA'S and let us try to tempt you in our very special way.

Max & Erma

P.S Hurry! Your envelope expires on June 15, 1989. Remember, every envelope contains a prize, so even if you were born under a bad sign and have had evil voodoo curses cast upon you, at the very least, you will receive $5.00 off your check. But, you could very well have won a PICKETT SUITE RETREAT WEEKEND. You won't know until your envelope has been opened at MAX & ERMAS'S located at 630 Stanwix Street.

Max & Erma's
RESTAURANT · BAR & GATHERING PLACE

Store managers increasingly elect to receive part or all of these quarterly bonuses in stock, at a one-third discount from market price.

- competition and recognition: "break-outs" for each restaurant have been added to store managers' four-weekly "Key Results Reports," which present sales and profit variances, food and labor percentages, shoppers' reports, and kitchen productivity scores. Peer awareness of a manager's performance spurs him or her to achieve first-place and avoid last-place ranking. Additionally, management has established three contests to stimulate and acknowledge employee excellence. First, in the monthly "Only the Best—Take The Extra Step" competition, each store manager gives a pair of Reebok athletic shoes to the employee who contributes the most toward enhancing customer satisfaction. Second, the quarterly "Top Shop" contest awards special sweatshirts to the staff of the unit with the best shoppers' report average scores. Third, the quarterly "Top Team" competition provides $1,500 in discretionary funds to the staff of the store with the best actual versus budgeted sales.

- leadership by example: An "Executive Work Experience" program has been instituted in which each corporate manager spends one week per year in a line position; assignments have included hosting, waiting tables, and food preparation. Besides bringing executives "closer to the customer" and operations, this enables them to "practice what they preach" in terms of focusing on customer satisfaction. The program also conveys top management's appreciation of the importance of line work, as does the company practice of referring to employees as "associates."

The new management team's strategies and organizational focus on performance resulted in dramatic same-store sales growth through 1989, a particularly noteworthy performance in light of annual menu price inflation of under 3 percent and of the unforgiving environment prevailing throughout the industry. Because same-store growth involves minimal incremental fixed costs, it tends to contribute significantly to overall profits.

Exhibit 13.2 shows that Max & Erma's has not fared well financially in recent years. After a dramatic turnaround, the firm ran into trouble when faced with a recession and the Gulf War. A product liability suit beyond insurance limits also dramatically reduced profits in fiscal 1991. Two new stores were initially unprofitable although the one location had become profitable by 1992.

The record of opening new stores slowed, perhaps due to fear of further failures, with only one opening in 1991. The new store was a highly successful location in downtown Columbus. Only one new store was opened in 1992, in Ann Arbor, Michigan. As could be expected, the decline in earnings in 1990 and 1991 resulted in a drop in the stock price from a high of $8.50 to about half that amount trading in the $4.50 to $5.00 range.

■ **EXHIBIT 13.2**   Max & Erma's Restaurants, Inc.:
                       Five-year Financial Highlights

Financial Highlights

(in thousands, except per share data)	52 Weeks Ended October 27, 1991	52 Weeks Ended October 28, 1990	52 Weeks Ended October 29, 1989	53 Weeks Ended October 30, 1988	52 Weeks Ended October 25, 1987
Total Revenues	$36,402	$30,344	$24,330	$19,672	$15,533
Net Income	$ 429	$ 836	$ 1,188	$ 774	$ 303
Net Income Per Share	$ .15	$ .25	$ .41	$ .30	$ .14
Total Assets	$14,820	$15,263	$12,737	$ 6,991	$ 6,767
Long–Term Obligations– less current maturities	$ 2,925	$ 2,958	$ 1,107	$ 919	$ 1,588

Annual Report 1991

Market Targets and Situations

Max & Erma's target market may appear to be broad-based, but the core of
frequent users is quite a bit narrower and easier to define. The demographics show them to be young (age 21–45), highly educated (at least

some college), and affluent (household incomes over $35,000). But the values and lifestyles of Max & Erma's customers show them to be generally of two distinct groups: "Individualists" (38 percent) and "Achiever-Oriented" (38 percent). (The remaining 24 percent fall into the "Other lifestyles" category.) *Individualists* tend to be sophisticated and nonconformist. They eat out a lot and enjoy unusual foods. They, like the *achiever-oriented* customers, tend to be from professional, dual-income households. *Achievers* tend to care more about status.

To really focus marketing efforts, it is important to evaluate which groups come to Max & Erma's on which occasions. All groups tend to see Max & Erma's as a good place to go for a *fun* occasion. More upscale segments such as "Achievers" may very well view Max & Erma's as an appropriate "family occasion" restaurant, but they might not even consider it for a special evening such as a "date occasion." The following lists begin to explain why and how people choose Max & Erma's. They also indicate how to best appeal to the specific customers of Max & Erma's market targets.

Individualists	Achiever-oriented
▪ Business Occasion	▪ Convenience
▪ Convenience	▪ Family Occasion
▪ Date	▪ Fast Occasion
▪ Family Occasion	▪ Fun Occasion
▪ Fast Occasion	▪ Regulars
▪ Fun Occasion	
▪ Regulars	

Competition

Among restaurants in the casual/theme segment of the market, competition is intense, and growth within this segment has outrun the population growth. This segment of the market is showing signs of increased concentration through acquisitions, mergers, and a shake-out of smaller chains. Lower earnings and lower growth rates are further evidence of the shakeout, which many believe will slow down the entry of new competitors in this segment of the restaurant industry. As some firms leave, new entrants replace them.

Declines in alcohol sales appear to be leveling off, but most major chains continue to seek marketing advantages to offset loss of liquor sales. Menu changes and value-added promotions are at the center of marketing efforts. The competitive environment in which Max & Erma's operates includes several strong *national chains*, such as Friday's and Bennigan's; *gourmet burger concepts*, such as Chili's, Applebee's, and Fuddrucker's, which have broadened the concept to become more mainstream; *ethnic concepts*, such as Chi Chi's and the Olive Garden, which compete in the same price range; and strong *regional chains*, such as Cooker and Rafferty's, which remain close to the customers. Much of the growth in the industry is among regional chains such as Houston's, Ruby Tuesday's, Tony Roma's, Ryan's Steak House, O'Charley's, and Charlie Brown's. There are many other competitors that appeal to specific market segments including T.G.I. Friday's, Houlihan's, Red Lobster, Stuart Andersons, and others.

Take-out Market

Max & Erma's is currently developing strategies to address the rising number of consumers wanting to take out their food rather than eat it on the premises. Exhibit 13.3 shows how the "sit-down" share of sales has decreased in the last 5 years. It also shows the percentage of off-premise purchases by category. A few reasons exist for the take-out phenomenon.

More and more of the lunch hour crowd is asking for take-out orders. The reason for this is that in a time when job security seems to be an oxymoron, people want the image of being dedicated to their jobs; therefore, they spend more time in the office. One way to do this is to eat lunch at the office, or even better, at one's desk. While some people bring their lunches from home, many time constrained consumers rely on take-out or office delivery services. To expedite the take-out process, some restaurants have installed fax machines to receive orders quickly and help fill them accurately.

More and more families are dual-income families; both partners are tired when they return home after a long day on the job. Often they are too tired to cook. In the 1980s people solved this problem by eating out. But with some return to "family life," couples, especially those with children, are finding themselves too tired to eat out. They want to be able to come home, put on comfortable clothes, take off their makeup, and relax for the evening. They want to eat at home.

Most Americans cannot afford the luxury of having a full-time cook prepare their meals for them, so they either resort to frozen/microwaveable meals or to take-out food. But many casual format restaurants, such as Max & Erma's and many of its competitors, are apprehensive about offering the take-out option. From the restaurant's point of view, take-out is more of a problem than an opportunity. The restaurant has to worry about customers getting the wrong orders, a decrease in food quality level during the drive home, and an overloaded, untipped staff. It is far easier to prevent problems from happening with in-store sales or to correct customers' problems if they are on the premises, rather than if they have taken the food home. The danger is that unsatisfied customers might too often become lost customers. The bigger danger, however, is not offering a service customers want while your competitors do offer it.

Max & Erma's has been experimenting with take-out for a few years. Operations problems associated with take-out orders are substantial. Understanding and writing up orders requires considerable training and daily adaptation. When a take-out order is received currently at Max & Erma's,

■ **EXHIBIT 13.3**   Make Mine To Go

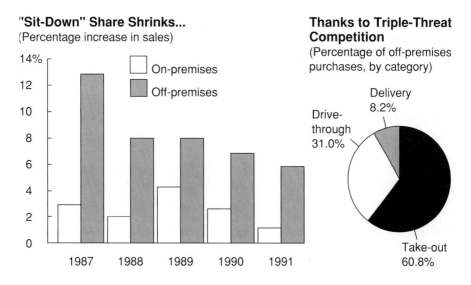

"Sit-Down" Share Shrinks...
(Percentage increase in sales)

On-premises
Off-premises

1987 1988 1989 1990 1991

Thanks to Triple-Threat Competition
(Percentage of off-premises purchases, by category)

Delivery 8.2%

Drive-through 31.0%

Take-out 60.8%

Reprinted from Kevin Helliker, "Forget Candlelight, Flowers—and Tips: More Restaurants Tout Takeout Service," *The Wall Street Journal*, June 18, 1992, B1.

it is necessary to pull a wait-person away from his or her normal station to fill the take-out order. The waits do not like that because it reduces tip income substantially and compromises their ability to service the customers on the premises. Additionally, Styrofoam packaging keeps food in the best condition, but the firm has concern about the environmental impact of such packaging. Nevertheless, Max & Erma's does provide take-out service when requested. While the demand has not been great, Max & Erma's does offer the option to its customers and is evaluating the possibilities of expanding this service since many of the existing stores are at capacity during peak times. Thus additional same-store sales growth is difficult to achieve even if the firm were able to attract more customers through advertising or some other method.

Future Growth

Plans for the future include three resources necessary for successful new store growth. First, Max & Erma's has a low-risk expansion strategy. The company plans to improve penetration of familiar territories where the concept is well established and to gradually move outward from its heartland, into markets where the concept already enjoys a fair degree of consumer awareness (an expansion strategy similar to that of Chili's, Cracker Barrel, Shoney's, and other successful regional chains). Four leases are being negotiated in Chicago and others are in negotiation in suburban Detroit, Cleveland, Akron, Indianapolis, Dayton, and Cincinnati.

Over the next 24 months, the firm wants to expand at a prudent pace of four restaurants, or one per region, each year. The year of 1993 will be challenging for Max & Erma's as it plans to open two to three restaurants in Chicago, and the new management team will need to continue demonstrating its store opening proficiency when it enters this market. While Chicago is attractive to Max & Erma's in terms of demographic and psychographic profiles of its markets, it is very competitive. It is developing specific site location strategies to address issues of where to locate the new restaurants—in shopping centers, residential areas, or downtown areas. The challenge is to find locations that match Max & Erma's customer base or core market target.

Max & Erma's is also faced with some higher operations costs associated with Chicago and Cleveland, cities that are more expensive markets compared to smaller midwestern cities. Leases are more expensive and often tougher to negotiate in markets such as Chicago. It will also be more difficult for Max & Erma's to enter a region where its name is not recognized and its employee base (primarily college students) does not previously know the restaurant and its image.

The Chicago expansion will demand most of Max & Erma's time and efforts in 1993, but the company will continue to seek out new, potential sites. It might further stimulate new store growth by turning to franchising, which it is testing with a seasoned operator. This firm which runs five hotels, all with food service, and franchises a chain of rib-houses, opened a Max & Erma's in 1988. Although the franchise has been profitable, the amount of profit that can be generated from a franchise location is approximately 10–15 percent of the amount that can be generated from a successful company owned store.

Second, the company has construction financing in place: strong cash flow—estimated to be approximately $3 million per year—plus an untapped bank line of credit of several million dollars. Moreover, low annual debt service (currently under $100,000) leaves ample room for additional borrowing, if necessary.

Third, and most important for the company's future, Max & Erma's is believed to have outstanding management depth for a firm its size. The new management team has an average of nearly 12 years of experience at Max & Erma's, and the average team member's age is 43; the team holds an 18 percent stake in the company plus options for another 10 percent. Thus Max & Erma's corporate leadership is experienced, youthful, and "incentivized." Backing them up are four regional managers, averaging over 10 years at Max & Erma's, two of whom have worked their way up from busboys; twenty store managers, averaging over 4 years with the firm; and nearly forty assistant managers, all of whom have undergone 14 weeks of intensive field training.

As Max & Erma's faces the future, it also faces many issues about how to increase earnings. Can same store sales increases be achieved as they have been in the past? How can the firm open new locations with a minimum risk? What should it do to ensure the planned openings in Chicago and how should it seek other sites in Chicago or other cities? Its experienced management team will challenge itself and its store managers to answer these questions and implement successful strategies for the 1990s.

Focal Topics

1. Who should be the primary market targets for Max & Erma's? What products or operational attributes should Max & Erma's emphasize to attract these segments?

2. What promotional program should be used by Max & Erma's? Prepare a budget showing the percentage allocation you recommend for each media. What creative appeals should be used?

3. Should Max & Erma's develop a major emphasis on take-out products? What should it do to implement your recommended policy?

4. What should be Max & Erma's strategy for future expansion of new stores? Prepare specific recommendations that will achieve successful entry, if possible, in Chicago.

■ ■ ■ ■ ■

Paul Harris

■ ■ ■ ■ ■

Gerald Paul and Earl Harris, two entrepreneurs from Indiana, joined forces in 1952 to start Paul Harris, a specialty retail clothing store. It catered to Indiana housewives who wanted known brands but who did not want to drive to urban department stores to find them. The original Paul Harris stores carried clothing and accessories for women, men, children, and infants. But when Mr. Paul and Mr. Harris decided to expand into the Indianapolis area, they had to limit their offerings to remain competitive. They concentrated on men's and women's apparel, but by the 1960s, had become primarily a women's fashion store.

The 1960s were a time of transition for the company. The emergence of mass merchandisers located in big malls and the continued growth of department stores caused Paul Harris to reexamine its image. It focused on young women—16- to 24-year-olds—by stocking smaller sizes and changing its product mix. Although this concept appealed to the new target market, it drove away the former Paul Harris family-oriented consumer.

As shopping activity moved from shopping centers (today's strip centers) to shopping malls, Paul Harris moved along with it. Rather than pull out of the strip centers, which became down-scale compared to their modern counterparts, the company decided to open Clothes Out Junction, which sold popular brand name merchandise and leftover Paul Harris clothes at reduced prices. All merchandise was grouped according to price points. In 1988, these stores were converted into new stores with a new name, The $5, $10, $15, $20 Place. These stores sell merchandise at either $5, $10, $15, or $20, with the lowest price at two items for $5 and the highest price at $20.

In the 1980s Paul Harris was positioned for the working woman and offered primarily conservative clothes, suits, and dresses to its customers. As lifestyles changed, Paul Harris tried to stay positioned strictly to the conservative working woman, but women took on a new dimension of excitement. This excitement became apparent in their attitudes, lifestyle choices, and fashion needs. While many apparel retailers changed to meet these needs, Paul Harris did not. In 1985 Paul Harris formulated a strategy to liven up the stores. Enter Pasta.

The Pasta brand was designed with a youthful, playful image in mind to provide a variety of clothes so that the working woman could buy both business and leisure clothes in the same store. Pasta departments, which displayed the fun, exciting, and colorful fashions, were established in Paul Harris stores. The concept was so well accepted and sales were so strong that the company opened over seventy freestanding Pasta stores by 1989, some of which were connected to Paul Harris stores with a walk-through. Recently, these stores have been closed, but the Pasta label was integrated back into the existing Paul Harris stores. The expansion efforts had strained the company's financial and human resources too much to retain a separate chain of Pasta stores.

The company now operates two divisions, Paul Harris with 143 stores and The $5, $10, $15, $20 Place with 52 locations. While the Paul Harris stores are located primarily in malls and in some downtown shopping areas, the $5–$20 stores are found primarily in strip centers.

Perspectives from Gerald Paul

From inception, Paul Harris stores have always strived to provide quality to fashion-conscious consumers. Paul Harris has prescribed the Value Formula shown in Exhibit 14.1.

Simply stated, the formula defines "value" as the sum of quality, fashion, and price, and it recognizes that with every fashion purchase, a trade-off between these variables is made. Research indicates that the customer's perception of value is based on an uneven relationship among these variables. The consumer is willing to sacrifice a little quality to get current fashion. Her perception of price is dependent upon the direct relationship between the cost of a piece of clothing and the emotional satisfaction of the article. Her sense of value is heightened when fashion is perceived as higher than the price she is asked to pay. These are perceptual and emotional motivations that help Paul Harris understand its customers and learn how to satisfy them with its merchandise and in-store atmosphere.

In a recent Paul Harris annual report, Mr. Paul discussed some of the changes in the fashion industry and how its customers are changing.

> *Our industry is going through a period of instability. Many major retailers are in serious financial difficulty, and their problems create serious price competition. In addition, women are telling us to give them styles that reflect the image they have of themselves, instead of what we (the retailer) think they should wear. Niche marketers that develop styles to fit a specific image a woman has of herself will be successful during the 1990s. This is how Paul Harris will position itself.*

■ **EXHIBIT 14.1   Paul Harris Value Formula**

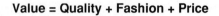

Value = Quality + Fashion + Price

In addition to fine-tuning our fashion focus, we put major emphasis on techniques for getting the garments from the drawing board into our stores quickly and then from our stores to the consumer. We are addressing a wide range of disciplines needed for successful retailing in the 1990s. These include advanced sales training, updated internal controls, and advanced technology. We've made greater use of computers for design, planning, scheduling, shipments, and financial controls. We are also improving our approach to sourcing, particularly toward getting faster shipments and better quality merchandise.

We realize and are committed to improving leadership training and maximizing associate involvement. Customer satisfaction depends on the attitude and know-how of (the Paul Harris) staff. In order to be a great company, much effort is directed toward making our people great.

Paul Harris

Today, Paul Harris finds itself competing for women's fashion dollars with stores such as The Limited, Express, Lerner, Casual Corner, and many others. Its positioning strategy among some of its competitors is shown in Exhibit 14.2.

$$$
|
|
|
Bergdorf Goodman
|
Saks
|
Ann Taylor
|
Liz Claiborne
|
The Limited
|
Express
|
The Gap
|
Merry-Go-Round
|
PAUL HARRIS / PASTA
|
|
Lerner
|
Brooks
|
Rave
|
T.J. Maxx
|
|
$

As economic times tighten the belts of many Americans, competition becomes even more fierce. Paul Harris has learned quickly that in order to survive and be successful in an increasingly competitive marketplace, it must provide its consumers with exactly what they want, which has led the company to the question: What does the American woman want and expect from her clothes and fashion retailers in the 1990s?

Paul Harris attempts to answer such questions frequently by getting close to the consumer. The Paul Harris "look" changes with the passage of time because of ongoing market studies that reveal subtle shifts in attitudes year by year as women adapt to an ever-changing world. In 1989 consumers indicated they wanted a higher level of quality and workmanship. Paul Harris created a department whose sole responsibility is quality. Another department has since been established to find better sources for fabric and garment assembly. Consequently, Paul Harris is selling the best-made garments in its history, and customer response has been very positive. This has also decreased the amount of unsold clothing at season's end.

It is difficult to define consumers based strictly on demographics, especially since 50-year-olds in 1992 are not the same as 50-year-olds in 1970. Consumers have become far more complex. Women are juggling careers, children, families, and social responsibilities, and they have many different and distinct facets in their hectic lives. The company has identified the Paul Harris woman as a value-conscious working woman who wants to be fashionably dressed and contemporary without being avant-garde. She is stylish, very feminine, up-to-date, and a bit of a romantic. She supports traditional American values. She values hard work and often manages the twin careers of working woman and mother. Paul Harris develops its clothing to match her lifestyle, her values, and the image she wishes to project.

How does an apparel company satisfy consumers with such diverse needs? Paul Harris feels that versatility is one answer. Paul Harris understands that each customer has a mature, reflective, and basic side to which it must be positioned. It also understands that each of its customers has a younger, more impulsive side. Pasta is designed to appeal to this side of the consumer.

Paul Harris offers a variety of smart, casual apparel at modest prices. Each store is divided into two different conceptual sections, one located on the left side of the store and the other on the right. While the left side displays casual apparel such as shorts, tee shirts, and leggings, the right side displays dressier items such as silk tanks, blazers, pants, and skirts. Between these two sections is a center isle that integrates the two concepts. Not only does it contain some "in-between" fashions, it combines some of the casual items from the left and some of the dressier items from the right to show women how they can combine different pieces in their wardrobes to achieve different looks and how to get the most versatility of each Paul Harris item.

■ EXHIBIT 14.3   A Paul Harris Store

The concept of versatility is becoming more and more important to Paul Harris as it positions itself for the 1990s. Paul Harris feels that women do not want to have segregated closets containing clothes only worn for work, those only worn for parties, and those only worn for play. It feels that the woman of the 1990s wants to be able to reach into her closet and pull out mix-and-match separates that are compatible based on color and material. The integration of casual and dressier items for a unique and different look each time makes women feel good about themselves and the money they spend on clothes. Paul Harris encourages integration of shorts and blazers, appropriate for work and for a casual evening out, and tee shirts and blazers, a great look for day and evening functions, so its customers get the best and a variety of looks from their items. Versatility is a thread that has become deeply woven into Paul Harris's strategy. Providing clothes that can be worn for a variety of occasions is valuable to the Paul Harris consumer.

Pasta

The Pasta line was developed to give Paul Harris consumers a leisure-wear alternative. Like the Paul Harris clothes, Pasta does not dictate fashion; it responds to consumers' wants. Pasta evokes "leisure wear" or "weekend fun." It is an understanding of women's attitudes as much as a line of women's clothing. Pasta fits the niche of being stylishly casual. In some areas of the work force, it is an accepted "uniform."

A key element to the success of the Pasta line is that it is easily changed. Pasta merchants tell management what the women that they talk to want, and the clothing is then designed, manufactured, and delivered to the stores. Until recently, while there had been much change and evolution in workplace apparel, there had been little change in what was available for weekend fun clothes. With Pasta came a multitude of stylish tops, pants, skirts, and shorts, and the latest in complementing accessories. The Pasta line integrates well into the other Paul Harris offerings; in fact, it dominates the casual section of the store.

The $5, $10, $15, $20 Place

This discount clothing store provides a unique treasure hunt experience for its customers. Upon entering the store, they are presented with many racks of attractive clothing, including shorts, tee shirts, tops, pants, jeans, dresses, and complementary accessories, all of which cost either $5, $10, $15, or $20. Consumers like to look for bargains on name brands. Some of the labels carried in the $5–$20 stores include Forenza, Outback Red, LA Gear, Lee, Levi, Calvin Klein, and The Gap.

The $5–$20 Place is able to keep its prices low because it keeps its costs down. Although its goal is to provide a pleasant atmosphere to complement the attractive merchandise mix, it concentrates on keeping overhead down. One way it does this is by locating in strip center malls, as seen in Exhibit 14.4, which have substantially lower lease costs than either freestanding stores with expensive addresses or highly visible stores in trendy mall locations.

■ EXHIBIT 14.4   A $5, $10, $15, $20 Store in Columbus, Ohio

Another way it keeps costs down is to purchase its merchandise from manufacturer overruns and manufacturer cancellations due to circumstances such as retail credit problems. Because of its lower costs, the $5–$20 Place is able to compete effectively with mainstream stores that sell at full retail prices and incur higher operating costs.

The $5–$20 Place currently finds itself competing with large merchandisers such as the Dress Barn, K Mart, Target, and Marshall's. But perhaps the greatest challenge for the $5–$20 Place will come from stores like Ten Below, which offers all merchandise for under $10. These types of stores are frequented often by teenagers, who like to spend their tight budgets on fashion-oriented clothing, but do not want to buy in a mass merchandise atmosphere. The $5–$20 Place and Ten Below provide a more sensitive clothes shopping experience and atmosphere than stores such as K Mart. Whether the customers are teenagers or value-conscious consumers, they tend to be loyal.

Financial Situation

Paul Harris achieved moderate to high growth through much of its evolution. Its stock increased in value to $20 in 1988. Soon after 1988, however, problems became apparent and the stock began to drop, reaching a value of only $1–2 by 1991.

The U.S. economy was entering a recession. Consumers were reluctant to spend money freely; competition was intense. The company had expanded the Pasta stores. To finance the expansion, Paul Harris borrowed substantial amounts of money from banks and Prudential Capital. By the end of the 1990 Christmas season, it was clear that inventories were much larger than could be moved through the stores. Paul Harris was experiencing great difficulty in meeting its debt service. As the stock plummeted, some personnel left and creditors became reluctant to extend additional credit, fearing the company might be headed toward insolvency.

The fears were justified. Paul Harris entered bankruptcy in 1991, operating under protection of Chapter 11 of the bankruptcy law.

Management believed that Paul Harris could still be a successful specialty retailer and a number of changes were implemented. Overhead was reduced, the number of stores was decreased, stores and product lines were updated, and the firm began to plan for the future. A reorganization plan was developed with the cooperation of the creditors committee and included delay of debt payment to give Paul Harris an opportunity to find a niche in the marketplace, develop a strategic plan, and move toward operations as a profitable firm. The creditor committee and management sought a new board of directors to assist in the creation of a retailing firm that would be successful in the competitive American marketplace of the 1990s.

In August 1992 Paul Harris came out of bankruptcy. The management, with Gerald Paul still at the helm, is excited about the future of the retailer. While the next few years will be challenging, they are happy to face them.

Focal Topics

1. What marketing research or analysis would you recommend to develop a positioning and marketing plan for Paul Harris?

2. What segments of the market do you recommend Paul Harris pursue as its core market targets?

3. Given the very limited financial resources that will be available under terms of the bankruptcy reorganization, on what type of stores should Paul Harris place highest priority?

4. Assuming you were a member of the new board of directors, what should be your most important activities during the first year following reorganization?

■ ■ ■ ■ ■

C A S E

Swan Cleaners[1]

■ ■ ■ ■ ■

One recent spring morning, the Swan Cleaners at 6690 Sawmill Road in Dublin, Ohio, was a concert of activity. The dry-cleaning machine hummed in the background, while the steam iron hissed in accompaniment. A conveyor belt chugged around its track at one side of the store as associates waited on customers.

It might seem like an unusual place to find the president of a company. But Paul Gelpi, dressed in a button-down oxford shirt and burgundy sweater, didn't look out of place.

The president of Swan Cleaners, a local institution for more than 50 years, is more at home in one of his company's forty-nine locations than in an office. Sitting behind a desk and conducting business on the telephone do not hold up in the wash. "I've got a nice office, but I don't spend much time there at all because the action is right here," he said during an interview that took place at a small table in a corner of the Sawmill Road store.

It's not unusual to find other Gelpi family members in the store as well. One recent Sunday, Mary Gelpi, Paul's wife and Swan's senior vice president who oversees human resources and marketing, and daughter, Lisa Kollat Gelpi, a district supervisor, were working the counter at one of the stores. The hands-on, all-in-the-family approach to running the business is not new at Swan, according to Paul Gelpi, whose parents, Andre and Eleanor, founded the company in 1937. Neither is the emphasis on employees.

His parents' philosophy: "Be in your store. Treat your customers, employees, and associates well. Then good things will happen." According to Paul Gelpi, "Tom Peters (coauthor of *In Search of Excellence* and *A Passion*

[1]This case is adapted from Sarah Mills Bacha, "Swan Cleaners Presses On," *The Columbus Dispatch*, May 14, 1989, p. G-1; Marshall Hood, "Pressing Business," *Columbus Dispatch*, January 14, 1992, B-1 and other materials. The Motivation Research summary is from *Today's Drycleaning Customer*, © August 1982 by the International Fabricare Institute, Silver Spring, Maryland, and is reprinted by permission of the Institute.

for Excellence) is out making millions of dollars every month telling people that. My dad used to tell me that and didn't charge me anything." Paul Gelpi credits this corporate strategy for Swan's accomplishments, which include more than a 40 percent market share, about 99 percent name recognition, and around 600 associates.

Andre and Eleanor Gelpi, both deceased, opened the first Swan near the center of the city. Laundering and tailoring were part of the Gelpi family before that. Paul's grandfather, a tailor in the area, and his grandmother had a dry-cleaning store, City Cleaners, in the mid-1920s.

"My mom and dad had the vision. They put the dedication and effort in it and made it a great company," Paul Gelpi said.

Swan's track record has been recognized in the industry. Earl Fischer, editor of *American Drycleaner*, a trade publication based in Chicago that has written about the company, called Swan "well-run and respected" in the industry. "We've never done any rankings, but I can say that they are one of the largest chains in the country," he said.

While many features of the corporate climate at Swan have not changed, some have. In response to industry trends during the past half century, the company has adapted. There are more service jobs and more women in the work force today, which means the need for cleaning services—especially for dress shirts—has increased, according to industry officials.

Shirt Laundry

The demand for shirt laundering is so great that in the northeastern United States, which has a high number of professionals, some companies are moving into the shirts-only business, according to Ed Easley, editor of *Drycleaners News*, a Connecticut-based regional trade publication.

To meet the demand for shirt laundering locally, Swan opened a 10,000-square-foot dress-shirt plant in 1985. Approximately 1.5 million shirts are laundered there each year. Dry cleaning is done at outlets throughout the city, but all shirts go to the central facility and into the hands of forty markers, shakers, pressers, and inspectors.

When truckloads of shirts arrive at the laundry, the tail of each garment is affixed with a cloth label marking its origin and assigning it a lot number. The shirts then are separated by amount of starch (light, medium, heavy, or none) and type of service (same-day, next-day, or regular 3-day). Shirts are washed in net bags to protect them from the pounding of the agitation of a 125-pound washer-dryer. A computer controls the water temperature and amounts of detergent and starch and regulates the moisture content while the shirts dry. "Moisture content is critical," Gelpi says. "It can't be too damp or too dry, or the shirt just won't press right."

The shirts are handled with precision throughout the process until they are placed on hangers for their conveyor-driven, cool-down cruise around the plant. "Shirts are like eggs," Gelpi explains. "You can crush the finish if you handle them when they're too hot."

The pressing machines are built to accommodate men's standard size shirts. Extra-extra-large shirts, kids' sizes, and women's blouses are done primarily by hand, for the same price as a man's shirt. "It costs more, but we've decided not to differentiate between the price of men's and women's shirts." Many competitive laundries have a two-tier pricing system, charging more for women's and children's blouses because of the higher costs incurred in processing them.

Before an order is twist-tied together and shrouded in plastic, an inspector checks for creases, stains, rips, and missing buttons. Problem shirts are redone or touched up by hand. Broken or missing buttons are replaced—at the rate of 500 to 1,000 buttons per day.

Despite the careful attention given, handling over a million shirts a year yields to problems, which leads to unhappy customers. "If we legitimately screw things up, we'll make it right," Gelpi says. To keep customers, mistakes that were caused by the manufacturer are sometimes handled by Swan's customer service department. "If somebody buys a garment, washes it at home and it's ruined, they wouldn't hesitate returning it to the store," Gelpi says. "But if it's laundered, they blame it on the laundry."

The price charged for laundering a shirt is about $1.40; the cost is approximately $1.25. A substantial number of shirts are priced at $.99 for promotional purposes with the result of the shirt laundry being a persistent break-even operation at best. "It's a tiny profit, if at all," Gelpi says. "But you do the shirts to get the dry cleaning. And you've got to do the shirts right. If not, everybody is mad at you." Gelpi's financial advisors constantly challenge whether or not investing capital in the multimillion dollar laundry with all the problems of a large work force can be justified but Gelpi believes it is a necessary part of the total success of Swan.

Changing Clothing Patterns

Today, customers are busier and demand quicker service. "People want to get things back in a hurry," Paul Gelpi said. "You know the pace we all go at: 'Right now, I've got to have it.'" As a result, Swan has increased store hours and is beginning to computerize operations to reduce waiting time.

The dry-cleaning business is experiencing sparkling growth nationwide, as more cleaners open to meet the demand, according to industry experts. Helping create the demand is a population wearing more cotton, wool, silk, and linen garments that require professional cleaning.

Today, most dry-cleaning companies still have one store, but the number adding stores is growing, officials said. According to a recent survey conducted by *Drycleaners News*, 70 percent of the businesses in the Northeast have one plant, but 16 percent have a second location, up from 9 percent 4 years ago.

Traditionally, dry-cleaning businesses have been family-owned and located in one metropolitan area. But that also is changing, as more entrepreneurs enter the industry. "In recent years, there have been people—although relatively few—who have designs on national expansion," Fischer said.

Included in that trend is the Johnson Group, a British-based company with U.S. headquarters in Cincinnati that is buying chains nationwide. The company has reportedly over 400 U.S. locations.

"The economy has been good the last several years and has lent itself to a lot of business openings," Paul Gelpi said. "The dry-cleaning industry has not been immune to that."

According to the International Fabricare Institute, a trade association in Silver Spring, Maryland, the estimated 24,000 U.S. dry-cleaning establishments generated more than $4 billion in sales last year. However, the increased competition is not a major concern for Swan. "It's fashionable right now to open a business and call it something other than a dry cleaner, such as wardrobe care specialist," Paul Gelpi said. "A lot of equipment people in the industry have touted that it's a quick way to make money. It is not an easy industry to be in and do a job well. It is very equipment intensive and labor intensive. You've really got to love this business to be in it. There are a great many other businesses that will give you a much higher return on your investment or risk capital than the dry-cleaning industry will."

Locally, Swan is the market leader. Other chains with more than five locations include Callander Cleaning Co., Bright & Clean Laundry and Cleaners, and Sunshine Cleaning Co., which operates the Sunlight Cleaning Centers. Most companies in the area have one or two operations.

In addition to dry-cleaning operations and the shirt laundry, Swan also has ten laundromats, a sewing and alterations department, a suede and leather cleaning and repair center, a drapery center, and a fur vault. Dry cleaning is the largest revenue-generating segment of the business, followed by shirt laundering, Paul Gelpi said.

The fur vault, "the only one of its kind between New York and Chicago," is where "several thousand" furs are stored annually, he said. The company also sells and custom-designs new furs and offers repair and relining services.

Swan's dry-cleaning plants are about 2,000 square feet in size. Dry-cleaning machines, which can clean 50 pounds of clothing at a time, resemble oversized washing machines.

Dry cleaning is not totally dry. The process, which takes about 30 minutes, involves adding perchloroethylene, a dry-cleaning solvent, detergent, and a small amount of water to each load. Moisture is necessary to work the solvent and detergent through the garments.

At the Swan plants, seven to ten associates dry-clean and press thousands of garments annually. According to *Drycleaners News*, plants in the Northeast dry-clean on average between 1,000 and 1,500 pounds per week.

The work is intensive, but there are light moments as well. Before garments are cleaned, they are inspected. And that means checking the pockets. "There are a lot of interesting things in pockets," Mary Gelpi said, including the $11,000 in cash someone left behind. The money was returned.

Swan does a lot of the dry cleaning for state legislators and celebrities who come to town. "We do almost all the big acts that come through the city," Mary Gelpi said. Swan even altered a pair of pants for Ronald Reagan when he was passing through as President. "We've even taken the blame for wives who have ruined husband's shirts or trousers," Paul Gelpi said.

Swan recently expanded outside of the county in which they have always operated by opening stores in Lancaster and Delaware, but it has no plans to grow beyond central Ohio, Paul Gelpi said.

"People in those areas have been asking us when we're going to do this," he said. "They've been bringing their dry-cleaning to stores in Columbus."

Concerning future store openings, Gelpi said Swan does not have a specific program. Typically, from two to five stores are opened per year. The rate of new shopping centers appears to be slowing, however, and the company is beginning to question how to achieve additional growth in the future.

"I don't want to make it sound too casual. We really do look at the future, and we plan. But as far as 5-year plans, I just don't do that," Paul Gelpi said.

"We don't have any aspirations to own 2,000 stores. We like central Ohio and the areas contiguous to it. If we see that we can provide opportunity for other people, and if we can keep it well-managed, interesting and *fun*, then we may see some additional growth beyond Franklin County."

Paul, age 45 and the youngest of three sons, said he acquired an interest in the business at an early age. The business is a job he would like to keep, and he has shunned bids from companies to purchase Swan or offers to go public.

"I've never really been tempted to do it. Swan has always been a family-owned business. Actually, I think I want to keep it that way." He also doesn't have any immediate interest in franchising. "We might consider something like that at some point, but we're not pushing it."

Paul Gelpi feels that one of the keys to Swan's success is its employees or "associates." Swan pays competitive wages and is a leader in employee benefits. More importantly, Swan associates become part of the "family," and Swan strives to promote teamwork and individual performance. A variety of incentives and company outings support this philosophy. In recent years, however, Swan has experienced difficulty recruiting employees for either counter work or the skilled categories of cleaner or presser. "Probably our most pressing problem," Gelpi states, "is how to find and keep good people."

Marketing efforts at Swan are supported by the store associates who are trained to sell additional services to customers. A separate training center is located in one of the stores, where the director of training conducts orientation, preliminary training, and ongoing training sessions for all associates. In addition, refresher courses and special seminars on everything from pressing to interviewing techniques are offered. All new associates receive one day of general orientation covering Swan's benefits, policies, and procedures.

There are six district managers responsible for the operation of the forty-nine stores. Each district manager oversees six to nine stores to ensure that everything is running smoothly and consistently.

Each store is staffed by a store manager, assistant manager, presser, cleaner, and counter clerks. The store manager is responsible for timely delivery and the work of the associates in the store. They do most of the hiring and supplemental on-the-job training of their own full-time and part-time associates. The exact number of associates per store varies with the volume. The store managers conduct performance evaluations and handle the administrative tasks, such as store reports. The store managers and assistant managers attend management training courses and special seminars. The pressers and cleaners receive apprentice-type training in the stores with experienced associates. The counter clerks have the most customer contact. They receive one week of intensive training on point-of-sale equipment and how to market Swan's services. The training includes role play and study of the procedures manual.

Corporate Culture

Because Swan has grown from a one-store, family-run business, and is still controlled by the same family, management has paternalistic views of its obligations to its employees. Swan has never laid off a non-front-end employee. In tough economic times, Swan has reluctantly cut back work hours of its counter employees, and usually this reduction was met by volunteers.

The corporate culture emanates from the president. Paul Gelpi has both process knowledge and managerial skills. His goal is to provide the customer with quality service and convenience at a competitive price. His people orientation applies to both sides of the counter. He regards Swan's associates like family and strives to treat them with understanding, goodwill, and fairness. He is hard-working and dedicated and expects the same from each associate. The ongoing training programs and opportunities for promotion demonstrate his respect and concern for the associates as individuals. Periodic visits to the stores give associates accessibility to top management.

Competitors to Swan generally are "mom-and-pop" businesses, which seldom have branches. In Swan's market, more than fifty new dry cleaners have opened within the last few years, some operated by families who use family members to perform much of the work at low or no pay. Many of these have gone out of business a few years after opening.

Market Strategy

Swan strives to give friendly and personal attention to its customers. Swan maintains high-quality standards (i.e., spot removing, special care, etc.) and offers convenience through extended store hours. Swan has a policy of opening the majority (85 percent) of its stores from 7 A.M. to 8 P.M. With this schedule, the stores are open for morning drop-offs and evening pick-ups and some stores are open on Sunday afternoon as well. Many of the stores are located in shopping centers and some locations offer drive-through windows.

Fast service is an important feature. For most dry-cleaning items, Swan has 1-day service (morning drop-off, evening pickup). For shirt cleaning and pressing, Swan has a 4-day service or a premium 2-day ser-vice. These services meet or exceed competitors' service. Swan feels that the shirt laundry, although not highly profitable, is a key strategic factor to attract new and keep the current dry-cleaning customers.

Swan's services are priced at the medium to high level. In order to compete on price, Swan aggressively promotes coupons. Swan has also pi-oneered unique sales promotions in the dry-cleaning industry, which in-clude an annual spring household cleaning sale, the Frequent Customer Club, an Express Bag, and free flag cleaning.

Maximum efficiency and self-reliance are important aspects of Swan's competitive strategy. Swan has constantly maintained state-of-the-art equipment. The recent completion of Swan's computerized shirt laundry is an example of continued commitment to efficiency. Self-reliance is ex-hibited by the fact that Swan handles all of the dry-cleaning and related services in its own facilities. In the majority of dry-cleaning companies, services such as suede and leather cleaning or fur storage are subcon-tracted out to specialized companies. However, Swan feels it is important to control the quality of all services provided to its customers.

Swan's market strategy of friendly, personal attention, convenience, quality standards, fast service, full service, competitive price, maximum efficiency, and self-reliance has resulted in its market leadership position in the dry-cleaning industry. Nevertheless, Gelpi is looking to the future. He has been approached with the idea of franchising his method of dry cleaning in other cities beyond his initial market or perhaps merging into a national chain. He is also concerned about the many new entrants to the market. If Swan does not build new locations, can Swan retain loyalty of customers who might be nearer one of the new locations?

In recent years, Swan began to suspect the possibility of some erosion in its market share and wanted to determine the best way to attract and keep customers in the face of the many new entrants to the marketplace. Through his trade association, Gelpi found a study conducted for members of the International Fabricare Institute designed to understand the motiva-tions of consumers in purchasing dry cleaning (Exhibit 15.1). Gelpi thought that this study was interesting but that a local study should be conducted to focus more on Swan's position in the marketplace and to

■ EXHIBIT 15.1   Summary of Motivation Research for the Dry-Cleaning Industry

Introduction

In the spring of 1982 Dr. Ernest Dichter, of Ernest Dichter Motivations, Inc., was commissioned by the International Fabricare Institute to conduct an indepth motivational study of consumer attitudes about drycleaning. The purpose of the study was to give drycleaners a tool to understand the modern customer and his or her motivations in order to help increase sales volume, improve customer retention, and prepare for the future by understanding the needs of the customers of the 1980s.

The basic purpose of this study was to assist the drycleaner in understanding opportunities to retain and increase business and to understand the factors of the 1980s that will help him to do this. The following factors are those that the study emphasized.

Part 1: Knowing Your Customer: A New Type of Woman

A new type of woman customer, the "balanced woman" seems to have emerged in the 1980s. It is important for the drycleaner to recognize this type of customer as well as the more traditional "housewife" and "career woman." The housewife was characterized by some guilt and insecurity. Since she felt that her place was in the home and the care of her family and their clothes entirely her responsibility, she felt some reluctance about giving this responsibility to the drycleaner and was more likely to be upset when something went wrong. The career woman, on the other hand, wanted to hand over entire responsibility to the drycleaner to get rid of as much household work as possible. Her main criterion was convenience and she was less emotional about clothing care, although as a professional she would appreciate quality and perfection.

The balanced type of woman is more and more the customer of the present and the future. She combines a job with home duties and tends to be more creative in her cooking, her home decorating, and her attitude toward clothes. Because she goes out to work, she needs and buys more expensive clothes and is willing to pay for their care. She is interested in keeping up the quality of her life in this as in other spheres. The balanced type of woman has more income than the other two types.

The balanced type of woman has the most positive attitude toward the drycleaner. Over three-quarters of these women rated the drycleaner as "great" or "good." Only seven percent rated him negatively, as opposed to 12 percent of the housewives and 31 percent of the career women.

As discussed further on, the career woman expects too much of the drycleaner while the housewife feels that she should do all "housework" herself. The balanced type of woman is most likely to cooperate with the drycleaner and accept some responsibility when things go wrong.

It is important that the drycleaner be aware of which kinds of customers he is dealing with in order to understand their expectations and characteristics.

Recognizing the Three Types of Women

As mentioned before, women customers can be roughly divided into three types: the housewife, who is characterized by being overly concerned and guilty about the care of her family's clothes; the career woman, who may be too demanding, too much of a perfectionist; and the "balanced" woman, who tends to be a reasonable and appreciative customer. These types were identified with the following questions.

		Percent
1.	"I hate housework. I just hate having to do it."	30
2.	"I'd rather pay more to enjoy more. It's easier to pay someone to clean my home and clothes so I am free to do what I want to do."	32
3.	"I enjoy being at home. I was brought up believing a woman's place is in the home and that is where I'm happy."	14
4.	"I like cleaning my home. It gives me a good feeling. But I like my job too."	24
5.	"Since I have small children I'm at home so I clean. But if I were working it would be easier to have someone else come in."	3
6.	"I don't feel right having someone else cleaning up after me. I find myself cleaning before they come and after they leave. They don't clean the same way I do."	25

Answer 1 is characteristic of the career woman. Answers 3 and 6 indicate the housewife. Answers 2, 4, and 5 indicate the "balanced" woman.

Naturally you are not going to question your customers about their attitudes toward housework, but you can determine which type they are by observing their behavior. The following is a sort of test to help you identify what type she is and how she should be treated.

(continued)

■ **EXHIBIT 15.1**   *continued*

For each customer check off description a, b, or c, figure out the score, and refer to the treatment suggestion.

Identifying the Customer

1. Watch how the customer brings clothes in
   __ a. In a heap
   __ b. Sorted out
   __ c. With a list

2. What does the customer say about clothes?
   __ a. Please take really good care of them.
   __ b. They are hardly worth cleaning.
   __ c. Discusses individual stains and problems.

3. How is time of delivery treated?
   __ a. Be sure you have them ready.
   __ b. Whenever you get around to it.
   __ c. Within a few days is fine.

4. Price consciousness
   __ a. Takes clothes back because it is "too expensive."
   __ b. Complains about price.
   __ c. Asks about price or not; accepts it.

5. Picking up clothes
   __ a. Looks each garment over.
   __ b. Just takes them without comment.
   __ c. Makes positive comments.

6. Special requests
   __ a. Fix whatever is wrong.
   __ b. Be sure pleats are sharp, wool fluffy, etc.
   __ c. I never have time to sew on buttons. Please do it.

Scoring and Customer Treatment   All "a" answers score 1, "b" answers score 2, and "c" answers score 3.

Someone with mostly "a" answers, with a score of 6 to 8, is probably a housewife type who feels guilty and overly concerned about having her clothes taken care of.

Treatment   Reassure her; compliment her on the care she takes of her clothes and her family.

Someone with mostly "b" answers and a score of 9 to 12 is probably a career person for whom cleaning of clothes is a sober necessity.

Treatment   Be businesslike; reassure the customer about your efficiency.

Someone with mostly "c" answers and a score of 12 to 18 is probably a balanced type and more clothes conscious than the other two.

Treatment   Compliment her on her taste and interest in clothes. Sell her on the advantages of coming more often.

Men can be scored and treated similarly. If they are bringing in the family's clothes, add 3 points to their score.

The Liberated Relationship

The liberated relationship or partnership marriage is becoming more prevalent. This means that it is no longer the woman who necessarily takes full responsibility for the clothing and seeing to it that it gets cleaned. Men are more often taking responsibility for their own clothes, both to decide when they need cleaning and to actually take them to the fabricare plant. In addition they may be bringing in the clothing of other family members.

This may offer new opportunities in itself. Men may not know how to sew on buttons or repair seams. And they may be more likely to want to have their clothing repaired or their clothing altered. Making these services conspicuously available may have a particular appeal to male clientele.

In addition, men may not be as knowledgeable about clothing care. It may be worthwhile to help to educate them through brochures, posters, and the advice of the counter personnel.

Part 2: Clothing Has Renewed Importance

A recent article in *Time* magazine featured clothing and fashion. The headline was "clothes are the fabric of history, the texture of time." In the 1980s, more than ever and for more people, clothing is an extension of personal lifestyle. Clothing is recognized to influence mood, professional and personal success, outlook on life. As a corollary to this, well-kept clothes are an expression of quality of life. While one would expect that people are trying to get more mileage out of their clothes as clothing becomes more expensive, the real motivation seems to be more related to an increased clothes consciousness. Designer jeans provide a good example. Jeans used to be casual wear. Now they are "dress" wear and it is important that they look pressed and neat. Having clean and well finished clothes is more an expression of psychological attitudes than of economic status. Modern families reject sloppiness and negligence about clothing. They want clothing that is alive and expressive rather than dull and dead.

(*continued*)

■ **EXHIBIT 15.1**   *continued*

Greater Clothes Consciousness

While people did not express very much interest in preserving clothes, despite their higher cost and the costs of drycleaning, there is a greater appreciation of wearing and owning clothes that are well taken care of. Being clean and having well finished clothes is definitely part of this new consciousness.

There seems to be a bipolar attitude about clothes. People either wear their "grubbies"—old, sloppy clothes—or they dress up. Even when clothes are not expensive, they must be "chic," "in." People are very style conscious.

The more a drycleaner can relate to this fashion consciousness, the better.

There seems to be a realization that the best way to preserve a garment is to have it cleaned regularly.

Respondents were asked the following:

The basis for deciding that a garment needs cleaning is: (Check as many as apply)

Reason	Percent
"I like to have clothes drycleaned before putting them away for the summer or winter."	61
"I get my things cleaned when they are spotted or soiled or look bad."	58
"After wearing a garment X times, I just have the feeling it should be cleaned."	52
"When I am going to a party or the theatre I check to see if the clothes I'm going to wear need cleaning."	22
"I believe in getting my clothes cleaned often and send them out regularly."	15
"I'm a seasonal cleaner. I have clothes cleaned at the beginning of the season."	12
"When I'm on a business trip I have all my clothes cleaned as a business expense."	4

In response to the question "What is the best way to preserve a garment?" 40 percent responded, "Clean it after three to five wearings." Twenty percent said, "Clean it whenever it gets wrinkled or dirty," and 20 percent said, "Clean it when it has a spot or looks dirty."

New Fabrics

For a certain period of time "miracle" fabrics were considered just that, but now there is dissatisfaction. People have discovered that synthetics often look artificial and cheap and do not hold up well to wear.

Washable men's suits, for example, have lost their appeal and consumers are no longer willing to buy them.

So the new fabrics are really the old fabrics—silks and pure cotton and wool, or blends of natural and artificial fibers. And with this return to natural fibers there is also a return to the professional drycleaner. People very easily grant the superiority of drycleaning.

"You're better off drycleaning. The clothes come out nicer,"

is a typical remark.

People are well aware of Woolite, and of the advertising campaign that amounts to an attack on drycleaning, but they still have doubts about washing at home.

"I just don't feel that it's as clean as drycleaning."

"It's an expensive shirt and I thought it would get ruined if I didn't get it drycleaned."

"I bring shirts that are either silk or polyester and I don't want to ruin them in the washing machine."

"I bring my corduroy pants, because when you take them out of the washing machine they always look icky."

"If it's a garment that can't be washed in the washing machine I take it to the drycleaner."

Wool, silk, and many of the new synthetics all require expert care. Consumers have become disenchanted with many of the "wash and wear" fabrics, and have returned to the perceived high quality of natural fabrics. In addition, many consumers reported trying to wash some of these articles at home, with disastrous results. They realize that their expensive and good-looking articles require, and are worth, the professional care the drycleaner can provide.

Part 3: The Concept of Quality

Quality means a number of things to the consumer. It is an expression of his own refinement, in that he has an appreciation for quality, and it means that he feels appreciated in turn, that "someone cares for me."

Quality means reliability. It means "I can relax, not have to worry about every detail." Another aspect is not having to spend emotional energy on being anxious about or suspicious about the job that will be done.

Quality also means "something extra." For a hotel patron it may mean a chocolate on the pillow. For the drycleaning patron it may mean coat sleeves stuffed with tissue. It implies something that goes beyond the call of duty.

(continued)

■ **EXHIBIT 15.1** *continued*

Specific expectations have to do with stain removal, with odor, with the feel of the garment after cleaning, and with creases and pleats. To ascertain what criteria customers used in judging the drycleaner, the following question was asked.

How do you judge whether your articles have been well cared for? (Check as many as you like.)

Pressed	Percent
Fresh in appearance	77
Comes back really clean	67
Article did not shrink or stretch	66
Feels crisp	43
Seems almost like new	34
Seems just like new	21

Many of the responses center around the idea of freshness and rejuvenation of clothing.

Cleanness Clean clothes mean, in a way, getting a fresh start. We take a renewed interest in clothes that are freshly cleaned. It is not quite the same as a new garment, but there is something of the same feeling.

Appearance of the Fabricare Plant

Consumers today are more spoiled and more demanding. They are accustomed to glittery malls and modern movie houses and greatly glamorized restaurants. Even banks have changed their design to become more friendly and inviting. By comparison, fabricare plants, with some exceptions, seem to be rather old fashioned and sometimes dingy looking.

"Drycleaning places are generally not very attractive and generally smell pretty bad."

was one comment. On the other hand,

"You could have the most beautiful drycleaning place in the world and if they don't treat you with courtesy and the clothes don't come out looking very nice, what's the point?"

But consumers do care how the plant looks to some extent. Cleanliness is often mentioned. This does not mean, however, that the fabricare plant should look sterile and ultramodern. There is a more recent trend to give an impression of warmth, in tune with the feeling of humanness and of quality. Natural materials like wood and stone are more appropriate than the "plastic" look that yesterday's supermodern architecture often had.

In general the consumer wants an atmosphere that is pleasant, quiet, well ventilated, and fresh. They do not seem interested in being able to see the drycleaning process.

"I'd like a bright white wall with beautiful pictures on it."

"It should be very friendly, very nice."

Warmth, space, and cleanliness were the features that were mentioned most often as desirable.

Personal Care

Related to the perception of quality as expressed in the appearance, smell, and feel of the garment is the idea of quality of service, and this has to do with the consumer's perception of personal care. The more tender loving care the drycleaner can bestow, the better. Getting clothes clean is expected as a self-evident service. The customer wants more than that.

Some respondents told little human interest stories that expressed this desire, and determined their feelings about their drycleaners. One woman told of an instance in which her drycleaner had cleaned her daughter's doll, and sewed on a severed arm. She felt it was an expression of love on his part. The more helpful a drycleaning plant can be, the more it can convey this feeling of personal service and contribution to customer well-being, the more it will convey the feeling of quality.

There is also a feeling that a person who is directly involved is less likely to do a sloppy job. He is more like a friend, and there is no expectation that he will take advantage of the customer. (In a study conducted for doctors a few years ago it was found that regardless of patient outcome, doctors who were perceived to take a personal interest in their patients were far less likely to experience malpractice suits.)

It cannot be emphasized strongly enough that personal care is all important to the customer. When customers were asked what they appreciated most about their drycleaner these were the answers received.

Attitudes/Qualities of Personnel	Percent
Personable	62
Helpful	59
Speedy	59
Knowledgeable	58
Efficient	57
Careful in handling my articles	51
Careful attention to special instructions	51
Mature	45
Knows me by face	39
Pays individual attention to me	31
Doesn't get involved with me personally	29
Knows my name	24
Young	22
Attractive	21
Leisurely	18

(continued)

■ **EXHIBIT 15.1**   *continued*

The highest ratings are given to helpful and personable personnel.

Part 4: Psychological and Sociological Changes

A number of specifically psychological and sociological factors emerged as relevant to the consumer and drycleaning. Several of these points have been touched on before but they are discussed here in terms of psychological and sociological meaning.

Desire for Individuality

Related to the sense of quality and to the importance of personal care is the desire that consumers have today to be treated as individuals. This is a trend which is going to increase in the next few years. It is a form of reaction against the mass society and the depersonalization of an industrialized and highly mobile society.

As drycleaning chains increase, people want the assurance that their clothes will be handled personally. Often they will continue to patronize the same cleaner even when they move to a new neighborhood. This is especially true if they feel that they are known and receive individual attention.

It is just as true of the fabricare industry as it is of others that the more work is taken over by machines, with greater efficiency, the more important is, and the greater opportunity there is, for creative and individual attention.

In training counter personnel, more attention should be paid to their dealings with people than to technical knowledge about drycleaning. Employees should be encouraged to give the impression that they are running the place and that they are as concerned about the customer's clothes as if they were their own.

Customers don't like the feeling of being lumped all together.

"I'd feel better if I know my clothes were being cleaned separately, but at least if I don't see the operations, I don't have to recognize that they're being thrown together with everyone else's dirty laundry."

The modern consumer looks back with nostalgia on the personal care and service that was more common in the past and hopes for a recurrence of that attitude. She or he wants to be recognized by name and to have personal requirements acknowledged.

The Psychology of Cleanliness

Cleanliness has moral overtones. "Cleanliness is next to godliness"; dirt is felt to be sinful. Angels are white and devils are black. The "good guys" wear white hats and ride white horses. The desire for cleanliness is a deepseated human desire. Dirt is also heavy in a psychological sense. Clean garments seem lighter.

When we watch television commercials for detergents, there is a lot of emphasis on "before and after," and a lot of dramatization of the "deep down" cleaning effect of these cleaners. It might be worthwhile to place a similar emphasis on the "magic" of drycleaning chemicals.

Stains   The whole idea of a stain has an even deeper meaning than that of "plain dirt." Dirt is just the result of normal wear. A stain is like a blemish, "a stain on one's honor," a thing to be ashamed of, a violation of purity.

For this reason people feel emotionally involved and hope that stains will be removed without a trace. They appreciate it when they feel the drycleaner is paying special attention to stains. It might be helpful to remind them that stains are harder to remove the longer they remain, and that they can be set by heat. Customers react better if they are warned in advance that a stain may not be removable, especially when they have the assurance that every attempt will be made.

Odor   How clothes smell when they come back from the drycleaner is extremely important. People strongly dislike a chemical smell.

"I can't ever remember smelling an odor in the drycleaning and if I did, I would never go back."

People would like for their clothes to smell like new. Wool, leather, freshly laundered cotton all have a characteristic smell.

Failing that, they would like their clothes to have a "fresh" smell. People distinguish between a "dead" smell and an "alive" smell. At all costs, a chemical smell or any unpleasant odor should be avoided.

Crispness and tactile quality   People touch garments before and after cleaning, and use "crispness" as a description of quality results. New, clean wool is fluffy and springy. Old, dirty wool feels matted and dead. People want their clothes to feel, as well as look, clean and new.

Pleats and creases   There is an emotional reason that pleats and creases in skirts and trousers are important. They indicate sharpness in a psychological sense. Baggy pants and ill-defined pleats look sloppy, as if people had slept in their clothes. Sharp creases are an expression of preparedness and courage and readiness to face the challenges of the day. One thinks of the importance of sharp creases in military uniforms. Even on a civilian level, one feels prepared

(continued)

■ **EXHIBIT 15.1** *continued*

for "the battle of life." On a deeper level, there is probably a relationship with the idea of potency.

All of the above attributes enter into the customers perceptions of "quality."

Authority Versus Choice

An additional psychological consideration with the modern consumer is the general resentment of an authoritarian approach. People dislike being told outright what to do, and may even resent care labels that say "dryclean only." Losing claim checks can also be seen as a small defiance of authority.

A study of farmers using an insecticide revealed that they often deliberately used too little or too much and then blamed the manufacturer for poor results. This was a symptom of revolt against authority, a desire for free choice. When the instructions were changed to be more suggestive than directive—"Most farmers use about X amount per acre"—conformance with the instructions improved.

In the same way, the drycleaner can suggest that drycleaning will give better results, that stain removal should be left to the professional, without seeming authoritarian and arousing the resistance of the customer.

Claim tickets are accepted and desired but they also seem to represent a form of authority and are often lost. It might be interesting to study the shape and size of tickets, to make them more conspicuous and more attractive, or perhaps to present them in the form of a boarding pass or a passport—"your passport to a well cared for wardrobe," or in the form of a coupon for a small discount on a subsequent order.

Another suggestion is that items could be logged in on a computer, so that no one would have to have a paper record. The customer's name could be entered on the computer and tag numbers could be recalled in a similar way to airline flight information.

Again, the key is to give the impression of cooperation with the customer.

Delegation of Clothes Care

In delegating the task of keeping clothes clean, the consumer may feel some guilt, especially the housewife, who feels that she is primarily responsible for her family's clothes, or the career woman who may feel she is shirking this duty. This feeling may be unconscious and irrational, but it is still there. This feeling of guilt may be behind the disproportional anger a customer feels when clothing is damaged, whether or not it is the drycleaner's fault.

To counter this attitude the best approach is to create a feeling of cooperation right from the start. This means careful inspection of a garment on receipt, questioning the customer about special problems, and informing the customer when a stain may not be removable or when a garment may be too fragile to withstand drycleaning.

Aggression and Defense

In trying to get at some of the underlying feelings consumers have about drycleaning, one of the sessions included a "role play" in which one respondent was asked to play the role of the drycleaner and another the role of the garment. In this situation the drycleaner was perceived as the aggressor, and the person representing the garment felt that she had to defend herself. She feared that the drycleaner would shrink her, or make her look thinner.

This finding can be used by the drycleaner. Making a point of treating clothes gently, with consideration and concern, can dissipate this subconscious feeling of defensiveness. For this reason clothing should never be wadded up or thrown on the floor in the customer's presence, and the use of staples in clothing for identification tags should be avoided.

Naturalness—the New Psychological Buzzword

In the past several years there has been an emphasis on what is "natural." This seems to be a reaction to the overly manufactured and artificial world we seem to live in. The idea of "naturalness" perhaps provides a feeling of reassurance and perhaps of greater permanence. Cosmetic manufacturers are one group that has actively and conspicuously both taken advantage of and promoted this concept.

A desire to return to more "natural" things is beneficial to the drycleaner since silks and wools, which are natural fabrics, usually require drycleaning.

Reassurance should be offered to customers that chemicals used in drycleaning are not "unnatural" and are not harmful to fabrics, and also that they do not leave a residue that would be harmful to sensitive skin.

In addition, the drycleaner can take advantage of this taste for the natural in considering the appearance of the plant. Even if remodeling is not possible or needed, extra touches like fresh flowers or live plants could be considered to enhance the feeling of naturalness and attractiveness.

The Modern Consumer Is Spoiled

Modern consumers expect convenience. Banks, supermarkets, and other businesses are increasingly open during evenings and

(continued)

■ **EXHIBIT 15.1**   *continued*

weekends. Banks are offering 24-hour service through automated equipment. The consumer expects similar innovations from the fabricare industry. In addition, he or she expects a higher quality of service. Deluxe finishing and presentation of clothes, availability of tailoring and repairs and of clothing care related products from the drycleaner are examples of the "creative considerateness" that has become almost an expectation of the modern consumer.

Convenience—Today's Most Important Motivation

Respondents reported staying with the same plant for many years. This was a response both to convenience and to satisfaction. When asked what factors were most important to them, convenient location ranked highest.

Factor	Percent
Convenient location	77
Reliability in having clothes ready	61
Adequate cleaning process	59
Ample parking	57
Reasonable prices	57
Convenient hours	49
Packaging or wrapping	46
Ability to handle problem items	28
Appearance of interior of shop	28
Adjustment policy for loss or damage	23

Clearly convenience factors are of primary importance, apparently even more than quality of work.

Integration with the Customer's Timetable

People are busy, more so than ever. When they drop off their clothes, they want them ready again when they need them.

"I expect them to have it ready when they tell me it's going to be ready."

Offering an express service as well as regular service might be a worthwhile customer convenience, but the important thing seems to be to have the order ready when it is promised.

Part 5: Relationship between the Fabricare Plant and Today's Customer

Certain aspects of the relationship between today's family and the drycleaning establishment offer opportunities for the drycleaner to respond to the customer's more hidden or unconscious desires. Aspects of this relationship and suggestions about ways to improve it are discussed in this section.

A Relationship of Trust

Consumers feel that they are entrusting their valuable clothes to a drycleaner in a similar way that they entrust their money to a bank. Most people do not realize that the drycleaner does not have special insurance to protect them against damage to clothing. They do expect that he will make good in the case of damage.

"If they damage your article you should get compensation—money back or free drycleaning."

Drycleaners are well aware of this attitude. One drycleaner mentioned the protection that garment analysis service offers in this respect. The customer tends to accept a written report from the garment analysis laboratory whether it indicates manufacturer responsibility, customer responsibility, or drycleaner responsibility.

People want to talk with someone who is knowledgeable about the drycleaning process, who can explain what stains won't come out or what chemicals may ruin a piece of fabric. They also assume professional competence.

"I don't check the suit when it is returned. I trust the drycleaner."

Along with the feeling of trust there seems to be a feeling of loyalty. Over seventy-five percent of those questioned had been using the same drycleaner for many years.

Sympathy for the Drycleaner

An interesting finding that emerged from the in-depth interviews was a feeling of sympathy for the drycleaner. Drycleaning is seen as an energy intensive business, both physically and emotionally. There was also an appreciation that the drycleaning establishment is often a small, family owned business. And there was concern about the possible discomfort of heat in the plant and the possible danger of the chemicals used.

Drycleaning Seems Mysterious

Consumers did not seem to have a very clear understanding of the drycleaning process, and in some ways seemed not to want to know more about it, just as people may find the details of flying an airplane threatening to think about. On the other hand, lack of knowledge seemed to lead to a feeling of apprehension. A fear was expressed, for example, that drycleaning would "dry out the wool and break down the fibers."

For this reason customer information in the form of posters and brochures that

(continued)

■ **EXHIBIT 15.1**   *continued*

explain more about the process and enable consumers to have realistic expectations, yet without going into great technical detail, can give customers a feeling of reassurance.

Few People Blame the Fabricare Operator

At first glance respondents seemed to remember incidents where they thought the drycleaner had been negligent, but in discussing specific problems customers admitted that they might also have been negligent, for example in failing to point out or remove a button they know is loose. Consumers do blame the drycleaner for shrinkage, inefficient stain removal, and sometimes for broken buttons. But they are also realistic. "If I had a stain and it didn't come out, I would assume that it wasn't possible to get the stain out."

A Good Feeling about Drycleaners

"I am basically pleased with most things when they come back from the drycleaner."
"I think good thoughts about the drycleaner."
These quotes were fairly typical when people were asked about their relationship with their drycleaner.
"They are a little higher priced than average, but they do a nice job and they are convenient."
This last response indicates that price plays a role but is often compensated by positive feelings about quality and convenience.

"My Drycleaner"

The term "my drycleaner" is used often. It implies pride and possessiveness, a sense of relationship that it is important for the fabricare plant to recognize and take advantage of. The customer sees the drycleaner as a professional with whom he or she has entered into a kind of partnership to take care of his or her clothing. In some ways it is not unlike the relationship between doctor and patient. The customer expects professional expertise, and also a sense that the drycleaner *cares* for him and his clothes.

Customers See the Fabricare Plant as Anonymous

Although most customers seemed to have a positive relationship with the drycleaner they patronize, what seems to be lacking is any sense of human interest or humor about the idea of drycleaning. This implies that more could be done to "personalize" the plant.

The plant operator should be alert to every opportunity to make his plant more personal and more personable.

Household Changes

As national demographic statistics show, there are more single adult and single parent households than ever before. There are households shared by two or more unrelated adults. And there are more "partnership" households in which household responsibilities are shared.

The implication for the drycleaner is that he is no longer catering to the traditional family in which the woman is solely responsible for clothes care. He may also be catering to the man of the house and to the single, divorced, or widowed man or woman.

This implies a new opportunity for the drycleaner to enter into a partnership with the customer in the care of his or her clothes. When questioned about their present drycleaner's attitudes and how they would like him to be or remain, cooperative attitudes received the highest ranking.

More Double Income Families and Working Women

There are many more women working today than 18 years ago. This means both that households have more income and that family members have less time.

This in turn has implications for the fabricare industry. Many items that could be cared for at home are brought to the drycleaner for the sake of convenience.

"I have a limited amount of time to get my clothes ready so I can wear them. Twenty-four-hour service is really important to me."
"Sweaters take too long to dry and I don't feel they are easy for me to do. Besides, I don't have the time to do it."
A fabricare operator says,

"The tendency today is a lot of your younger couples have two working people and the woman is not coming home at night and handwashing her clothes. She'd have to go to work, come home and cook, and then spend another hour or two handwashing her sweaters and blouses."

The more the modern fabricare plant can stress that they understand and cater to the customer's need for convenience, the better.

Another renewed opportunity is the cleaning of shirts. About forty percent of the people have shirts cleaned professionally. This tendency is especially strong among younger people. Not only is the time

(continued)

■ **EXHIBIT 15.1**   *continued*

saved important to them, but they feel the appearance of the shirts is more professional than when they are washed at home.

***Price Is More Important,
But Not a Deterrent***

Consumers surveyed complained about the high price of drycleaning, but recognized that all costs have gone up. Indications of price acceptance included several rationalizations:

> *"For the time I'd have to spend ironing them and everything, I'd rather pay for the drycleaning."*
> *"My drycleaner is very reasonable, . . . They have to make a living too."*
> *"I take care of my clothes because clothes are very expensive today and you can't afford to ruin them."*

Economics

As mentioned before, customers complain readily about the price of drycleaning even while they realize that prices for everything are going up. In some cases the response is to cut back. There is also a feeling that they are not getting anything new although they are paying more money. In this sense, extra little things, little additional considerations, mean a lot.

Although there are complaints about increased prices, this is offset for the customer against savings of their own time and energy and against the prolonged life of clothing through proper care.

Consumers do want cut rate prices, in the form of specials, discount coupons, volume discounts (e.g., five garments cleaned for the price of four), and refunds on returned hangers.

When asked about willingness to pay "a reasonable amount" for special services, responses were as follows:

Service	Willing to Pay (percent)	Unwilling to Pay (percent)
Individual attention to missing buttons, loose threads, etc.	60	26
Hand blocking for spreads, comforters, lace, etc.	47	31
Home delivery	45	35
Hand pressing	39	52
Separate washing for own clothes	23	44
Hand laundry service	16	46

As is apparent from the table above, although wishing for cut rate prices, consumers are also willing to pay more for special attention.

Contrary to expectations, the most important reason for using the drycleaner seemed to be to save time, even more than to preserve clothes. and quality of service seems to mean more than saving money. Thus quality and convenience seem to be the keys to success in the 1980s.

Cooperation and Partnership

Many families are now two-income families, and taking care of the home and of clothing has become more and more a shared duty. This idea of cooperation also extends to the drycleaner. While he is still blamed if something goes radically wrong, there is also a recognition that keeping clothes and household articles clean is a joint responsibility.

Men Have Taken a New Role

With the emergence of the balanced woman, men have also learned to become more interested and involved in taking care of their clothes. Clothes care is no longer strictly the woman's domain. Either a man or a woman, married or single, is likely to visit the drycleaner.

Part 6: Advertising and Communications

As in many businesses, word of mouth advertising seemed to be considered most effective, with over seventy percent of respondents reporting that they would be influenced by this method. There was also a strong response to the idea of special discounts, which could presumably be advertised in the window, by means of flyers, in a local newspaper or "shopper" publication, or over radio or television.

But it is well known that consumers are not always aware of what influences them in advertising. In a recent study reported in *Advertising Age*, it was revealed that consumer behavior is actually more easily influenced than consumer attitudes.

Whatever kind of advertising the drycleaner elects to do, whether it is handing out flyers or promotional items or advertising in the newspaper, on the radio, or on television, he should keep in mind that customers are looking for convenience, quality, and a sense of personalized service as much as for discounts or bargain buys.

Related to advertising is a more public relations oriented kind of communication. In this category could be handouts or brochures treating various aspects of garment care and care of household articles. Another idea is a "garment care hotline" that people could call for advice about stain removal and other cleaning problems. Service columns in newspapers could be spon-

(*continued*)

■ **EXHIBIT 15.1** *continued*

sored by a group of cleaners as a way to offer consumers information about cleaning and caring for garments and household articles. All of these things could contribute to the image of the drycleaner as a professional in partnership with the family in helping to keep clothes and other articles clean and attractive.

Some form of advertising is necessary to make people aware of a newly offered or innovative service, such as alterations, rental of formal wear, express service, or some form of "creative financing." It is also a means to reach a particular group of customers. Newlyweds, individuals or families who are new to the neighborhood, people who have received a promotion, are all logical targets for special advertising. Even the recently bereaved might appreciate an offer to clean the clothes of the deceased so that they can be given away. Senior citizens might be offered special discounts. Young people might be attracted by an offer to take care of their designer jeans.

Various kinds of situations can be used as triggers for new sales. For example, a change of season can bring the suggestion that customers prepare their clothes for storage or for the new season's wear. Inviting travelers to start out with clean clothes could provide a theme.

Reminder cards could be sent in the mail, as they often are by dentists and doctors. When a new fashion or style appears, drycleaners could emphasize that they are prepared to take care of the new kind of garment.

These are only a few of many advertising possibilities.

Part 7: Consumer Desires for the Future

Increase Desire for Progress

When asked what they hope for in the fabricare plant of the future, many people have the wish that new types of miracle fabrics will be invented that don't have to be cleaned at all. This is not a realistic hope, but meanwhile the plant operator should probably emphasize the progress that drycleaning has made and consider offering extra services to extend the image of clothing renewal and clothing care.

There does seem to be a strong desire among consumers for additional conveniences, specifically pressing while you wait, after hours pickup and drop off service, a drive-through window, and computerized receipts.

Another suggestion was that the drycleaner should care about all fabrics, not just drycleanable items, and should help educate the customer about home care between cleanings, care of washable items, and so on.

Every interviewee expressed the desire to have personal contact with another person involving their drycleaning. Although there was interest in the automated machine for drop offs and pickups, this was seen as something only to use in an emergency, as it was felt to be cold and impersonal.

New Expectations

In keeping with the modern concern about "quality of life," the consumer has high expectations of the fabricare plant. Thus the appearance of the plant is very important to the image of quality and cleanliness that the consumer expects. Also, although the consumer has no very specific ideas about what new developments might take place in the drycleaning industry or the drycleaning process, there seems to be a desire for progress and innovation.

Wishes for Future Service

To discover what consumers would like to see in the drycleaning plant of the near future, they were offered a set of possible services and asked both whether the drycleaner they now use offers them and whether they would like to use a drycleaner who offers them.

These services were as follows:

Service	Now Offered (percent)	Would Like to Have (percent)
All work is done on premises	65	23
Wash and wear cleaning services	31	22
Pressing while you wait	16	42
Drive-through pickup & delivery	13	29
Computerized receipts and organization	6	24
Shirt laundry service	46	20
Off-premises outlet for pickup and delivery	6	30
After hours machines for pickup and delivery	4	37
Special offer when moving on cleaning and delivery of rugs and draperies	7	20

The most significant services are those that people want and are not getting now. Some of the services that are available now, such as work done on premises and shirt laundry service, do not seem to be highly valued. On the other hand there seems to be significant desire for pressing while you wait, machines for off-hours

(*continued*)

■ **EXHIBIT 15.1**   *continued*

pickup and delivery, drive-through windows, computerized receipts, and special service on rugs and draperies. These five categories represent all new opportunities for increasing business by taking advantage of the strong desire for customer convenience.

Dormant Desire for Drycleaning

One of the questions asked in the survey was "Suppose that you could get free drycleaning for a year, how many more garments or other articles would you take to the fabricare plant?" Sixty-eight percent responded that they would have more things cleaned more often. When asked what specific items they would have cleaned more often, drapes, shirts, quilts, and bedspreads led the list by a large margin.

Of course the plant operator cannot offer free drycleaning to take advantage of this dormant desire, but such innovations as charge accounts, subscriptions, monthly fees, or other forms of "creative financing" might be used to take advantage of this potential chance to develop new business.

Source: *"Today's Drycleaning Customer,"* copyright August 1982 by the International Fabricare Institute, Silver Spring, Maryland is reprinted by permission of the Institute.

specifically answer the question of how consumers choose Swan in preference to competitors. Gelpi also felt that a study could be useful in deciding how to structure the firm's promotional program. The firm currently uses extensive newspaper and considerable radio advertising. Television is occasionally used. Major media are backed with billboards and other special promotions. Gelpi wants to know, "Which is best? What should we be saying in our advertising and how should we say it?"

Focal Topics

1. How do consumers choose a dry cleaner?

2. What marketing research would you recommend be conducted by Swan?

3. What are the most important issues facing Swan in the future? What recommendations do you have for the firm for future growth?

4. Should the shirt laundry be continued as a major investment of capital for Swan?

■ ■ ■ ■ ■

■ **EXHIBIT 15.2**   Newspaper Advertisement for Swan Cleaners

Sew Easy!

Depend on Swan for all your repair and alteration needs

Our expert repair & alteration staff specializes in mending seams, linings and buttonholes. We make size alterations, shorten or lengthen hems and replace zippers, buckles, snaps and worn-out elastic.

Plus we offer custom monogramming and reweaving. Most work is completed in three days.

It's sew easy to depend on Swan!

Swan cleaners keeps you looking great!

41 Convenient Swan Cleaners Locations

Columbus • Dublin • Worthington • Arlington • Westerville • Bexley
Grandview • Powell • Hilliard • Gahanna • Clintonville • Grove City
Whitehall • Reynoldsburg • Pickerington • German Village • Downtown
Check Yellow Pages under CLEANERS for store nearest you!

Advertisement courtesy of Swan Cleaners, Columbus, Ohio.

PART 4

DECISION PROCESSES

■ ■ ■ ■ ■

■

City Police Department

■ ■ ■ ■ ■

The City Police Department is facing a tremendous challenge in recruiting new police officers, as are many police departments nationwide. Disturbances during 1992 in Los Angeles and other cities, a general increase in violence against police officers, and perhaps even music by recording artist Ice-T referring to "kill a cop" contribute to the difficulty of attracting men and women to major urban police departments. It is particularly challenging to attract qualified minority candidates. City Police Department has initiated a project to determine if the process of recruiting and training minority candidates can be improved by undertaking a marketing analysis and promotional program.

The current recruitment program of the City Police Division is governed by the city charter and regulations adopted under the charter. These limitations limit the flexibility of the recruitment process. In many cases the charter regulations work against the best interests of the minority recruiting program. Yet, changing the city charter is very difficult and largely out of the control of the police department.

The process of becoming a police officer begins with taking the Civil Service Examination. A major problem to be addressed is how to keep candidates interested in a career as a police officer during the extended selection process for the police academy. It is believed that marketing techniques may be helpful in the process.

To have a reasonable opportunity to be selected for a class at the police academy, potential candidates must do more than merely pass the Civil Service Examination. The name of each examinee passing the examination is placed on a rank-ordered list with the candidate scoring the highest at the top of the list. Then, pursuant to civil service regulations, the city safety director selects the candidates for the police academy class by working downward from the top of that rank-ordered list of candidates. The safety director reviews test scores and performance of each candidate before the oral interview board. In order for candidates to be selected, they must score high enough on the examination to be among the thirty-five people chosen for a police academy class. The number of classes and the dates they are conducted vary depending upon staffing needs and the availability of funds from the city council. Currently the city is conducting two classes a year. Staffing requirements indicate a need for several more but funds are not available.

During the application process, candidates must apply in person at the recruitment office at police headquarters during normal business hours. The city provides a Civil Service Study Guide, which gives a cursory overview of the exam. The police department maintains a recruiting office staffed by two officers. Among other duties, they attend career days, community festivals, and other events likely to attract a substantial number of people of recruiting age. All recruiting funds are held in the city general fund, making flexibility in such activities or accessibility of funds difficult without support from city council and the mayor's office.

A manual file system is maintained of all persons who become involved in the recruiting process. From an operational perspective, it is difficult or impossible to maintain any contact with persons who have indicated an interest in becoming a police officer or who have taken the Civil Service Test. Since the exams are given every 12 to 16 months, a period of up to two years may lapse between successfully completing the test and entering the academy. The motivation of the candidate as well as practical considerations concerning the individual's current career, education, and residence determine how much, if any, contact is maintained between the police department and the potential recruit. For the candidate who wants to join the police department and successfully completes the Civil Service Examination, a high degree of motivation is required to survive the long, drawn-out process.

Becoming a Police Officer: The Decision Process

A preliminary analysis of how persons become police officers indicates that it involves a five-step decision process, similar to many other consumer decisions. The research and strategic analysis conducted for City Police Department (CPD) focused on the five-step process: need recognition, search for information, alternative evaluation, "purchase," and outcomes.

Step 1: Need Recognition

In the first step of consumer decisions, people perceive a difference between the desired state of affairs and the actual situation sufficient to arouse and activate the decision process. Within the context of an employment decision, need recognition might occur if the person were either unemployed or were employed in an occupation that did not fulfill his or her needs.

To measure this process, CPD developed a survey to be completed by students in local educational institutions and by members of other community organizations. The first half of the survey was designed to assess what needs these people saw as being satisfied in a job, and what needs they thought a career as a police officer might satisfy. In the other half of the survey, which involved similar questions asked of existing members of CPD, police officers answered questions that sought, among other things, to identify needs that these officers felt were satisfied by their careers. People were identified by race in both surveys, allowing CPD to assess whether minorities have different needs fulfilled by their employment than nonminorities and whether minority police officers find that their careers fulfill different needs than the nonminority police officers.

As part of the marketing project, the promotional materials of CPD were analyzed and compared with those of other police departments in twenty similar cities. The purpose was to determine how promotional materials of CPD might trigger need recognition in potential police candidates.

Step 2: Search for Information

In this step of the process, the consumer searches for information in memory (internal search), or acquires information relevant to the decision from the environment (external search). In the context of considering a police career, a consumer's memory would include such things as personal encounters with police officers and encounters he or she is aware of through word of mouth or the news media; fictional accounts of police work on television, in movies, or in books; the influence of family, friends, or acquaintances who are police officers; and exposure to police recruiting materials or presentations.

One of the open-ended questions asked students and community members whether they ever considered a police career and their reasons for their answer. This question was intended to identify what experiences or information either attracted people to, or dissuaded them from, a possible career as a police officer.

In the context of the police career, the potential candidates obtain information from advertising, police recruiters, other police officers, the media, or friends and family. While it is somewhat difficult to control the information disseminated by the media, or by friends and family of potential police candidates, it is possible to develop advertising for recruiting purposes. It is also possible to use police recruiters and other police officers to assist in encouraging minority candidates to consider a career as a police officer.

Step 3: Alternative Evaluation

In the third step of the consumer decision process, the consumer evaluates options in terms of expected benefits and narrows the choice to the preferred alternative. Among other things, the survey of students and community members is intended to elicit their opinions on what benefits and detriments they believe a police career might offer, and the importance (or salience) given to each of these factors. Respondents were also asked what factors would attract them to a career as a police officer.

Comparing the responses of students and community members with the responses of police officers on the actual benefits and detriments of a police career provides information on those benefits of which the public is and is not already aware and what misconceptions of the public need to be corrected. This information can be used in developing promotional materials for the recruiting process.

Step 4: The "Purchase"

In this step of the decision process, the consumer acquires the preferred alternative or an acceptable substitute, if necessary. For potential police candidates, this involves actually signing up to take the Civil Service Examination and starting the process for consideration as an active candidate for the police academy. This process can occur in many different settings.

A candidate could come to the police recruiting office (analogous to consummating the purchase in the store). The person could also respond to a targeted mail or "door hanger" solicitation, which could come to the home. A police recruiting team might take recruiting presentations to schools and colleges where the process could also be commenced. The team might also appear at job fairs and in career day settings in the city, in other cities in the state, and in nearby states.

In some instances the Civil Service Examination is given to prospective candidates in connection with these events. In an effort to understand people who were involved in part of the process but who did not "purchase" a CPD career, the marketing project included a survey of security guards, some of whom had been involved in part of the CPD recruiting process.

Step 5: Outcomes

The final step of the consumer decision process involves the consumer evaluating whether or not the chosen alternative satisfies needs and meets expectations. In the context of attracting qualified police candidates, there are actually two relevant considerations in assessing the outcome of the "purchase" decision. The ultimate result of the process is to become a police officer, and the question arises as to whether or not this career will satisfy the needs and meet the expectations of those who signed up to take the Civil Service Examination.

The marketing project was expected to focus on attracting qualified minority candidates to take the Civil Service Examination and for them to pass it at a high enough level to be selected for a position in the police academy. The people who are attracted may have their satisfaction with the "purchase" adversely affected by the laborious, complicated, and frustrating process faced because of the city charter and civil service regulations, even before starting at the police academy. Thus, there is a strong degree of relationship between marketing and operations. Reducing the frustration with the process and encouraging minority candidates who score well on the Civil Service Examination to endure the process and actually enter the police academy involves both marketing and operations programs.

Exploratory Research

Before conducting primary research in the community and among police officers, the marketing project began with interviews in twenty other cities. These interviews were qualitative in nature and solicited the opinions and experiences of the departments to determine what was already known about minority police recruiting.

Two of the cities were under federal court orders to integrate minorities into the force. In one of these cities, the mandated hiring of minorities was achieved by lowering standards and helping marginal people with additional training. The training consisted of mathematics and reading skill enhancement training. The other city succeeded in achieving mandated quotas by developing a point system that favored local residents who were veterans. Neither of these cities used a marketing approach to attract minorities.

Interviews with the police departments of other cities indicated extensive usage of time-honored methods such as recruiting at high schools, job fairs, and unemployment offices. A few departments described novel ideas that had attracted minority recruits, which included police cadet or high school programs.

The interviews with other police departments revealed that the most common reasons people became police officers are (1) to help others, (2) pay and benefits, (3) respect, and (4) power. The major negative factors about police work appear to be (1) danger, (2) irregular hours, (3) pay and benefits, and (4) lack of respect. These results from the exploratory study were used to develop questionnaires for local research of a primary nature.

Secondary research included many articles on police recruiting, although no articles were found about minority recruiting in police departments. The literature indicates that to qualify to be a police officer, a person needs to have reasonable intelligence, good moral character, U.S. citizenship, good health, and no felony record. These five attributes are the minimum standards to qualify for police work.

Intelligence is usually evaluated on the basis of receipt of a high school diploma or its equivalent. Good moral character generally is interpreted as having no personal problems such as bad credit or a drug dependency. Small offenses are usually forgiven, but felony convictions prevent one from becoming a police officer. Good health is generally defined the same for police departments as in the military.

There are many articles in newspapers and journals about minority pressures in police departments but little directly related to recruiting. Many published accounts report racially biased practices in police departments. Incidents indicating racial discrimination are reported in Miami, San Francisco, Dallas, New York, and other cities. A perception of widespread racial discrimination is believed to be one of the factors inhibiting minority recruiting in many cities.

Primary Research

The primary research used in the marketing analysis consisted of a survey of students and community members, a survey of police officers, and a series of interviews with security guards. Because there were no funds available for research, the surveys were completed without any interview costs by administering printed questionnaires to classes at two of the local universities as well as to members of a large urban baptist church. The church was a predominantly black church with members generally aged between 20 and 40. This survey is referenced as the "student" questionnaire despite the fact that the church members include students as well as other respondents who have completed their education. From the church, 158 questionnaires were obtained from respondents who were black. Nearly 1,000 student questionnaires were collected in several undergraduate classes. From the total, 259 were randomly selected for tabulation, providing a total of 407 in the "student" survey.

A second questionnaire was administered to 218 police officers to identify those aspects of the career that officers viewed as positive or negative and to determine how important those aspects were to them. In addition to data on the officer's education, sex, race or national origin, and years on the force, the questionnaire also asked each responding officer to offer suggestions on how minority recruiting efforts might be enhanced and how the public image of the city police force might be improved.

The purposes of the surveys were (1) to identify the factors respondents to the student questionnaire believe are important when they consider a career, (2) to determine if significant differences exist between minority and nonminority respondents, and (3) to assess which of those factors the police officers feel are present in their careers as police officers. In addition to these questions, demographic information was requested from the student questionnaire respondents, who were also asked whether or not they ever considered becoming a police officer and the reasons for their answer. These respondents were also asked what factors would attract them to a career as a police officer.

The data from all questionnaires were prepared for data processing, and statistical analysis was performed on a pro bono basis by a second-year MBA class at one of the local universities. Exhibit 16.1 shows this questionnaire.

■ **EXHIBIT 16.1   The Ohio State University Graduate School of Business Columbus Police Department—Student Survey**

The following is a short survey of your opinions on career related topics.
Thank you for your help.

1. Identify highest education grade completed. (Please circle)
    a. High School Grade — 10   11   12
    b. College — Year: 1   2   3   4   5   6
    c. Graduate School — Year: 1   2   3   4

2. How important are the following factors to you when you consider conducting a job/career search?

    (Please rate on a scale of 1 to 5 with 1 being not important and 5 being very important.):

		Not Important			Very Important		Don't Know
a.	High Pay/Salary	1	2	3	4	5	DK
b.	Power & Authority	1	2	3	4	5	DK
c.	Job Security	1	2	3	4	5	DK
d.	Ability to help others	1	2	3	4	5	DK
e.	Excitement and challenge	1	2	3	4	5	DK
f.	Respect you will receive from others	1	2	3	4	5	DK
g.	Working with people in the community	1	2	3	4	5	DK
h.	Employee Benefits (i.e. sick leave, vacation, health insurance, pension, etc.)	1	2	3	4	5	DK
i.	Variety in work assignments	1	2	3	4	5	DK
j.	Opportunity for advancement	1	2	3	4	5	DK
k.	Other (please list and rate—use back of sheet if necessary):						
	_____	1	2	3	4	5	
	_____	1	2	3	4	5	

Student Responses

Exhibit 16.2 displays results from the student survey. The numbers in each cell represent the rank order of the average score for each factor rated by the identified group. If two factors have the same average score, their rank order is identified by ".5." The numbers in parentheses represent the average score for that factor on the 5-point rating scale (with 5 being "very important" and 1 being "not important").

Exhibit 16.3 shows general consistency in relative importance of most of the factors among the various groups. With the exception of the white males, who ranked it ninth, every group on average ranked "power and authority" last in relative importance. On average, every group except the black females ranked "opportunity for advancement" as the most important score. For black females, it was a close second.

▪ EXHIBIT 16.2   Student Responses to Importance of Career Positive Attributes

Factor	All	All Black	All White	All Males	All Females	Black Males	Black Females	White Males	White Females
Opportunity for Advancement	1 (4.68)	1 (4.68)	1 (4.69)	1 (4.72)	1 (4.66)	1 (4.76)	2.5 (4.66)	1 (4.71)	1 (4.67)
Employee Benefits	2 (4.54)	3 (4.65)	2 (4.43)	3 (4.51)	4 (4.54)	3 (4.63)	2.5 (4.66)	2.5 (4.47)	4 (4.38)
Job Security	3 (4.51)	2 (4.67)	3.5 (4.40)	2 (4.52)	2 (4.56)	2 (4.67)	1 (4.67)	2.5 (4.47)	3 (4.40)
Excitement/ Challenge	4 (4.50)	4 (4.61)	3.5 (4.40)	4 (4.49)	3 (4.55)	4 (4.53)	4 (4.63)	4 (4.38)	2 (4.43)
Respect	5 (4.20)	6 (4.23)	5 (4.20)	7 (4.12)	6 (4.28)	9 (3.92)	6 (4.32)	5 (4.18)	5 (4.22)
Help Others	6 (4.17)	5 (4.58)	8 (3.90)	8 (4.01)	5 (4.33)	5 (4.47)	5 (4.61)	8 (3.87)	8 (3.94)
Variety in Assignments	7.5 (4.15)	9 (4.14)	6 (4.15)	6 (4.13)	7 (4.17)	7 (4.16)	8 (4.14)	7 (4.12)	6 (4.20)
High Pay	7.5 (4.15)	8 (4.16)	7 (4.09)	5 (4.17)	8 (4.08)	6 (4.27)	9 (4.13)	6 (4.14)	7 (4.02)
Work in Community	9 (3.76)	7 (4.17)	9.5 (3.50)	9 (3.62)	9 (3.92)	8 (4.08)	7 (4.20)	10 (3.49)	9 (3.52)
Power/ Authority	10 (3.34)	10 (3.01)	9.5 (3.50)	10 (3.44)	10 (3.17)	10 (3.11)	10 (2.98)	9 (3.54)	10 (3.44)

Note: Cell numbers represent rank of each attribute. Numbers in parentheses represent rating on a 5-point scale.

Exhibit 16.3 contains the results of ratings by the students on the ten positive factors of a police career. The fact that all of the ratings are on average over "3" indicates that all ten factors listed are somewhat important to all groups responding. The perceptions of respondents to the student questionnaire relative to potential negative aspects of a police career are summarized in Exhibit 16.4.

Question five of the student questionnaire was an open-ended question asking whether or not the respondent ever thought about being a police officer and the reasons for the answer. Black females answering "yes" listed "ability to help others" and "excitement and challenge" more often than any other reasons to explain their answers, but expressed concern about the danger of a police career. Black females answering "no" gave "danger," "lack of appeal of the career to them," "stress and psychological pressures," and "violent nature of the job" most often as the reasons they had no interest in a police career.

The black males answering "yes" also listed "ability to help others" most often as the primary attraction of a police career to them. The most prevalent reason listed by those answering "no" was "other career plans."

- **EXHIBIT 16.3**   Student Ratings of Positive Factors of Police Career

Factor	All	Black Males	Black Females	White Males	White Females
Helping Others	1 (4.67)	2 (4.76)	1 (4.85)	1 (4.53)	1 (4.62)
Employee Benefits	2 (4.56)	1 (4.86)	3 (4.73)	3 (4.49)	3 (4.38)
Job Security	3 (4.52)	5 (4.51)	4 (4.66)	2 (4.50)	2 (4.43)
Work in Community	4 (4.48)	4 (4.54)	2 (4.74)	5 (4.34)	4 (4.33)
Opportunity for Advancement	5 (4.44)	3 (4.68)	5 (4.59)	4 (4.38)	7 (4.18)
Respect	6 (4.36)	7 (4.38)	6 (4.48)	6 (4.31)	6 (4.28)
Excitement/ Challenge	7 (4.32)	8.5 (4.22)	7.5 (4.35)	7 (4.25)	5 (4.32)
High Pay	8 (4.16)	6 (4.49)	7.5 (4.35)	8 (4.00)	9 (4.02)
Variety in Assignments	9 (4.08)	8.5 (4.22)	9 (4.26)	9 (3.96)	10 (3.96)
Power/ Authority	10 (3.80)	10 (3.86)	10 (3.50)	10 (3.83)	8 (4.10)

Note: Cell numbers represent rank of each attribute. Numbers in parentheses represent rating on a 5-point scale.

- **EXHIBIT 16.4**   Student Ratings of Negative Factors of Police Career

Factor	All	Black Males	Black Females	White Males	White Females
Low Pay	1 (4.08)	4 (3.95)	4 (4.03)	1 (4.19)	1 (4.11)
Race Discrimination	2 (4.04)	1 (4.57)	1 (4.65)	6 (3.27)	4 (3.96)
Danger	3.5 (3.98)	2 (4.05)	3 (4.21)	4 (3.67)	2 (4.10)
Lack of Respect	3.5 (3.98)	3 (3.97)	2 (4.23)	2 (3.81)	3 (4.05)
Poor Image	5 (3.75)	5 (3.92)	5 (3.89)	3 (3.68)	5 (3.76)
Irregular Hours	6 (3.46)	6 (3.28)	6 (3.56)	5 (3.36)	6 (3.58)
Good Officer	7 (2.79)	7 (2.80)	7 (3.29)	7 (2.49)	7 (2.67)
Difficult Training	8 (2.58)	8 (2.51)	8 (3.16)	8 (2.18)	8 (2.51)

Note: Cell numbers represent rank of each attribute. Numbers in parentheses represent rating on a 5-point scale.

No single reason was prevalent among those listed by white females who said they have considered a police career. The overwhelming reasons listed by the white females to explain why they never considered a police career were the danger and the fact that the career does not appeal to them. Low pay, irregular hours, stress, and lack of physical ability or strength needed to be a police officer were also listed by many of these women.

The white males who have considered careers as police officers listed "ability to help others," "excitement and challenge," and "always wanted to be a police officer" as the prevalent reasons for their answers. Those who answered "no" overwhelmingly listed "danger," "low pay," or "doesn't interest or appeal to me" to explain their answers.

In the open-ended questions in the student questionnaires asking what would attract the respondent to a police career, the overwhelming response among all groups was, "nothing could attract me to such a career," or words to that effect. Low pay and danger were the most prevalent explanations given for this response. For those listing the factors that would attract them to a police career, the prevalent response among all groups was "high pay," followed by "ability to help others." Both the white males and the white females listed "excitement and challenge" as an attraction to them of a police career, to a greater extent than blacks of either gender. Some white males and black females stated that they would be attracted to a police career if they could have their choice of assignments. A few of the white males and females answered this question with responses like, "being able to beat up people," "using confiscated drugs or drug money," or "ability to frisk prostitutes." Such responses were coded as "ability to take advantage of improper opportunities offered to a police officer."

Police Officer Responses

A total of 218 usable questionnaires were collected in the survey of 223 police officers. Of these respondents, 25 were black male officers; 5, black female officers; 5, male officers of "other" minority status; 147, white male officers; 20, white female officers; and 21 refused to identify either race or gender. These responses approximate the current composition of the CPD.

The results of the police survey relating to officers' feelings about the importance of various positive aspects of their careers as police officers are summarized in Exhibit 16.5. The data relating to the police officers' perceptions about the negative aspects of their careers are summarized in Exhibit 16.6.

In the question relating to negative aspects of a police career, the respondents were asked to list "other" negative aspects. The most prevalent single answer among white male police officers was "reverse discrimination," followed by "lack of backup or support from police administration,"

- **EXHIBIT 16.5**   Police Officer Ratings of Positive
  Factors of Police Career

Factor	All	All Blacks	Black Males	Black Females	All Whites	White Males	White Females	Other Males
Job Security	1 (4.59)	1 (4.84)	1 (4.88)	1.5 (4.60)	1 (4.59)	1 (4.60)	2 (4.55)	4 (3.40)
Employee Benefits	2 (4.50)	2 (4.66)	2 (4.68)	1.5 (4.60)	2 (4.49)	2 (4.48)	1 (4.60)	1.5 (4.00)
High Pay	3 (4.02)	4 (4.19)	4 (4.20)	4 (3.80)	3 (4.01)	3 (3.99)	3.5 (4.20)	3 (3.80)
Helping Others	4 (4.00)	3 (4.37)	3 (4.36)	3 (4.40)	4 (3.95)	4 (3.92)	3.5 (4.20)	1.5 (4.00)
Excitement/ Challenge	5 (3.73)	9 (3.38)	9 (3.40)	8 (3.00)	5 (3.81)	5 (3.82)	6.5 (3.70)	7.5 (2.60)
Variety in Assignments	6 (3.66)	5.5 (3.88)	5 (4.04)	9 (2.80)	6 (3.68)	6 (3.70)	9 (3.55)	6 (2.75)
Work in Community	7 (3.63)	5.5 (3.88)	6 (3.92)	7 (3.40)	7 (3.65)	7 (3.59)	5 (4.15)	5 (2.80)
Opportunity for Advancement	8 (3.49)	8 (3.72)	8 (3.75)	5.5 (3.60)	8 (3.51)	8 (3.50)	8 (3.60)	10 (2.20)
Respect	9 (3.38)	7 (3.75)	7 (3.84)	5.5 (3.60)	9 (3.36)	9 (3.31)	6.5 (3.70)	7.5 (2.60)
Power/ Authority	10 (2.56)	10 (2.73)	10 (2.92)	10 (1.80)	10 (2.54)	10 (2.50)	10 (2.80)	9 (2.40)

Note: Cell numbers represent rank of each attribute. Numbers in parentheses represent rating on a 5-point scale.

- **EXHIBIT 16.6**   Police Officer Ratings of Negative
  Factors of Police Career

Factor	All	All Black	All White	Black Males	Black Females	White Males	White Females	Minority Other
Lack of Respect	1 (3.63)	1 (3.97)	1 (3.60)	1 (4.00)	2 (3.40)	1 (3.52)	1 (4.15)	3.5 (3.00)
Low Pay	2 (3.29)	4 (3.23)	2 (3.21)	4 (3.28)	4 (3.00)	2 (3.22)	4 (3.10)	1.5 (4.00)
No Job Guaranty	3 (3.08)	5 (3.07)	3 (3.13)	5 (3.08)	5 (2.80)	3 (3.06)	2 (3.65)	1.5 (4.00)
Danger	4 (3.00)	2 (3.58)	5 (2.95)	2 (3.67)	3 (3.20)	5 (2.94)	5 (2.95)	5 (2.60)
Irregular Hours	5 (2.98)	6 (2.69)	4 (3.03)	6 (2.71)	6 (2.60)	4 (2.99)	3 (3.33)	3.5 (3.00)
Race Discrimination	6 (2.09)	3 (3.48)	6 (1.81)	3 (3.29)	1 (4.60)	6 (1.81)	6 (1.78)	6 (2.00)

Note: Cell numbers represent rank of each attribute. Numbers in parentheses represent rating on a 5-point scale.

and "need to improve police administration." No particular answers were prevalent among the responses of any of the other groups.

Another question answered by the police officers was whether they agreed or disagreed with the following statements: (A) Minority officers receive less desirable assignments than nonminority officers; (B) Minority officers receive fewer promotional opportunities than nonminority officers; and (C) Racial discrimination exists within the city police force and is visible to the general public, especially new minority police officers.

Statistical analysis of the results indicate that white police officers on average strongly disagree with each of the statements. Black female officers on average decidedly agree with each of the statements, and black male officers slightly disagree with the statement about worse jobs and slightly agree with the statements about inferior promotional opportunities and the existence of visible discrimination on the police force.

The police officers were asked two additional open-ended questions, the first of which requested suggestions for enhancing minority recruitment. The most prevalent responses of the white and black male officers were either "none" (i.e., they wrote that they have no suggestions for enhancing minority recruitment), or "recruit the most qualified, regardless of race." A number of white males also said "do not lower standards," "the department has already done all it can do," or "do not do any more, there is no need to enhance minority recruitment." The most prevalent suggestion among all groups was to recruit on college campuses and in high schools.

The second open-ended question in the police officer survey asked police officers for suggestions that would enhance the public image of the City Police Division. The most prevalent response among all groups was that more positive media relations and coverage were necessary, and that negative publicity should be "controlled" or "stopped." Other prevalent responses were to increase support for the police officers from the police administration, or otherwise to improve the administration. Some white officers said the police should stop all emphasis on race matters.

Demographic Analysis

The 1990 Census places population of the city at approximately 800,000 people. Of these 81.5 percent are white, 15.9 percent are black, .21 percent are Native American, 2.02 percent are Asian, and .35 percent are Other. About 1 percent are of Hispanic descent, and can be of any race.

The population varies considerably in educational attainment. Since a high school diploma is a minimum requirement for becoming an officer, the following statistics are relevant, indicating the percentage of people over age 25 in each racial group who are high school graduates.

Ethnicity	Percent High School Graduates
White	73.3
Black	59.4
Native American	61.5
Asian	82.4
Hispanic	68.8

During the period of 1990 to 2000, the city's population in the 15–24 ages is projected to change in the following manner.

Age Group	1990 to 2000: Percent Increase (Decrease)
Age 15–19	
White	3%
Other Races	20%
Total	5.4%
Age 20–24	
White	(6.8)%
Other Races	4.1%
Total	(5.50)%

The city's black population is largely centralized into a geographic area across the central and southern portion of the city, concentrated in twelve zip codes. Of the city's twenty high schools, about five have black student concentrations in excess of 50 percent.

Current Promotional Materials

The CPD has developed various recruiting materials in recent years. Two printed materials are available. One is a color brochure describing the advantages of living in the city, not related specifically to being a police officer. It has a great deal of copy and statistical information, and is used largely by various city government units at job fairs outside the immediate area of the city.

The second printed material is a low-cost, high-volume brochure titled "A Career in Law Enforcement." It clearly explains the process of applying for an officer position and the reasons that might disqualify a prospective applicant. It describes technical issues that recruiters believe are important details in the recruiting process.

The CPD also has a 13-minute recruiting video. It provides a good overview of advancement opportunities and future career needs. It details the enrollment process and the specific requirements needed to enter the police academy. It addresses the character requirements of potential candidates.

None of these materials address the social, cultural, and educational needs of potential applicants. They do illustrate the time-consuming nature of the qualification process, the stressful waiting period, and the worrisome nature of the enrollment process but do not emphasize job satisfaction attributes of law enforcement opportunities or the various law enforcement technology fields.

The CPD also has available a 30-second public service announcement, which illustrates many positive aspects of law enforcement careers. These include personnel, activity, diversity of opportunity, diversity of responsibility, and the opportunity to help others. Although it is of high quality, it has not been used extensively by local television stations.

Currently, the city budget provides approximately $50,000 a year for purchase of promotional materials, media advertising, public relations, and other direct elements of recruiting. Two full-time police officers are assigned the task of coordinating the overall recruiting program as well as the specific task of increasing minority representation on the CPD.

Focal Topics

1. What attributes should be the primary emphasis in recruiting minority and nonminority police officers?

2. What promotional materials should be used or developed for the CPD?

3. Assuming the limitation of $50,000 for recruiting purpose is continued in the future, prepare a marketing program that will use this budget most effectively.

4. If additional funding were available, what additional marketing research should be undertaken?

■ ■ ■ ■ ■

Sigrid Vogt, M.D.

■ ■ ■ ■ ■

"Lose 10 pounds in 10 days; it's easy with our new seaweed diet." "Now you can look as young as your eighteen-year-old daughter." "Thunder thighs? Squeeze your way to slim thighs in just thirty days." "Work out. Lose weight. Firm up. Smooth out those wrinkles." Everywhere you turn, companies and their celebrity spokespersons are touting products to help Americans become slim, trim, healthy, and "young again." The decade of the body has arrived . . . and with a vengeance.

It is a long way from Pittsburgh to Orange County, California. At least that was the thought of Dr. Sigrid Vogt, M.D., who grew up with her parents in Pittsburgh after they emigrated from Germany to the United States. After diligent study through secondary school, Sigrid (Sigi as she is known among her friends and associates) attended the University of Pittsburgh for her undergraduate education. She had worked very hard scholastically to maintain the 3.7 grade point average needed for admission to medical school. She also worked a part-time job at a restaurant on weekends and during summers to earn most of the money required for her undergraduate degree. With her diploma in one hand and loan application in the other, she left for medical school—one of the finest in the East—with high hopes to become a surgeon.

During her internship, she listened carefully to a lecture one day by a plastic surgeon. Although not a part of the rotation, plastic surgery was a topic that intrigued young Vogt. She listened intently to the chief of plastic surgery explain the advances that had been made in restorative plastic surgery—replacing fingers that had been severed by lawnmowers, correcting cleft palates, correcting congenital disfigurations, helping scar tissue heal in such a way that it would be almost unnoticeable, and providing relief to the social discomfort felt by what the public called "elephant man" disease. She saw that these and other corrective procedures demanded the highest level of both science and art.

When Sigi was accepted for a residency in plastic surgery at Northwestern University, she entered a new era—one in which she knew what she really wanted to do. After finishing her residency with distinction, she was ready, she thought, to perform a service to humanity and enjoy the lifestyle for which she had prepared over the past 14 years since high school.

During the residency, Dr. Vogt had thought little about the practice she might later have, except to look forward to it. Training under Dr. Christine Demos, one of the finest surgeons in America, Dr. Vogt assumed she would be in high demand after finishing her residency, perhaps even be asked by Dr. Demos to join her in her own practice. However, when the topic came up at a social occasion, Dr. Demos indicated no interest in such an expansion and advised Dr. Vogt to look for a practice location in Phoenix or Southern California rather than in midwestern states such as Illinois.

Other than a few brief discussions of this nature, Dr. Vogt had not seriously studied the topic of how to select a practice location. At a medical meeting, Sigi talked with some recent graduates and began thinking about how she might begin her career. Quite a few of the recent graduates had moved to western states. Others had accepted offers from established doctors in small towns. While there was a need for doctors in small towns, she thought, the level of medicine that could be practiced in such places was very much inferior to that practiced near the major medical centers to which she—and most of her fellow doctors—were attracted. She also thought about some of her colleagues who had joined various types of groups or institutional practices. Some were working for HMOs—Health Maintenance Organizations—which might not be so bad, she thought, but they did not employ many plastic surgeons. Other friends were working as staff doctors, including one of her friends from the plastic surgery residence of another school who was working for an urgent care center on specified days as a general physician and surgeon.

Vogt talked about the location decision with her fiancé, who would also soon face the same issue after he received his MBA, with a major in finance. He already had a good job offer from a bank in the Chicago area and had been recruited by an aerospace firm in Southern California. His best offer, however, was from a medium-sized firm in Rockford, Illinois. This firm would place him immediately in a position of major responsibility and would pay as much or slightly more than the starting salaries of either the Chicago or California position. After inquiry at the local hospital in Rockford, there appeared to be little opportunity for gaining staff privileges for an additional plastic surgeon. However, the hospital was actively seeking additional surgeons for the emergency room, and the organization that provided staff surgeons was eager to hire Dr. Vogt as a staff surgeon for ER work.

While her fiancé was in Southern California, he made a call for Sigi to a good friend, who had completed his residency in plastic surgery a few years earlier. Dr. Stacy was now practicing as an individual, fee-for-service physician in Newport Beach, California. When Dr. Stacy heard of Sigi's questions about where to locate, he immediately called her with a proposal. Dr. Stacy explained that his own practice was small and not growing rapidly. His problem was, he thought, that he could not afford as a single practitioner to advertise to get new patients. Although his patients were very satisfied and did refer other patients to his office, Dr. Stacy was convinced that he needed a partner to build the practice. Dr. Stacy explained, however, that he could offer no salary or other benefits. Dr. Vogt would be "on her own" except that they would share overhead, including advertising costs, on a proportionate basis, related to the revenues each generated.

Data Collection

To assist in making her decision, Dr. Vogt collected as many reference materials as possible. Among the things she found were materials indicating that in the 1960s and 1970s, there was much concern over the physician shortage in the United States. From 1970 to 1986, the number of active U.S. physicians increased from 311,203 to 519,411, a 67 percent increase. The number is expected to grow to 633,200 by the year 2000. In 1970 there were 150 active physicians per 100,000 persons as compared with approximately 243 active physicians per 100,000 persons in 1990.

The specialty composition of the physician population also changed during the period from 1970 to 1986. Specialties that grew very rapidly include:

- Diagnostic Radiology (605 percent)
- Gastroenterology (222 percent)
- Therapeutic Radiology (184 percent)
- Neurology (169 percent)
- Plastic Surgery (162 percent)

The proportion of physicians located in the northeast and midwest regions of the country have decreased in the 2 decades, while the proportion in the south and west increased. Another significant trend is the relative scarcity of physicians in small towns. Physicians in nonmetropolitan areas decreased from 14.6 percent to 12.3 percent between 1970 and 1986.

Dr. Vogt found that projected growth in specialties varied considerably. Emergency medicine, internal medicine subspecialties, and pediatrics are expected to have the greatest growth. Dr. Vogt found some projections (the GMENAC study) that the supply of plastic surgeons in the future would exceed the projected need by as much as 45 percent. Surpluses of physicians in other specialties were projected to be even greater, especially for areas such as pulmonary, endocrinology, rheumatology, and general surgery.

Plastic Surgery

Plastic surgery is one of the mostly highly trained specialties in medicine. Following graduation from medical school and an internship, a doctor first completes a residency in general surgery and then later a residency in plastic surgery, a process typically requiring 6 or 7 years. During the residency and in early years of practice, plastic surgeons spend most of their time with restorative plastic surgery or procedures related to trauma, burns, various accidents, and congenital defects.

Many plastic surgeons also develop an extensive practice in aesthetic surgery or what is sometimes called cosmetic surgery. Such procedures include the rhytidectory (face-lift), chemosurgery (chemical face peel), surgical dermabrasion (sanding), blepharoplasty (eyelid surgery), rhinoplasty (nasal surgery), mentoplasty (chin surgery), otoplasty (ear correction), augmentation mammoplasty (breast surgery), reduction mammoplasty (breast surgery), mastopexy (breast surgery), abdominoplasty (body contour surgery), liposuction, and other procedures.

In recent years, medical specialists other than plastic surgeons have begun to do some procedures previously limited in most hospitals to plastic surgeons. Otolaryngologists, for example, sometimes take a few weeks of additional training and begin offering rhinoplasties. General surgeons might be involved in the care of tissue that in other situations would yield different results if cared for by a plastic surgeon. Trauma cases and other facial surgery might be performed by oral surgeons rather than plastic surgeons in some instances. Either by patient choice—probably with little understanding of the relative competencies among specialties—or the call of the emergency room nurse, a plastic surgery procedure might be performed by a plastic surgeon, an otolaryngologist, an oral surgeon, a general surgeon, a dermatologist, or some other medical practitioner. This "competition" in credential battles has erupted within hospitals and among advertisements in which one group of specialists warn patients not to select a "general plastic surgeon" but instead select a member of their own group.

Because of her outstanding training, Dr. Vogt expected soon to apply for admission to the American Society of Plastic and Reconstructive Surgeons (ASPRS). This organization represents surgeons who are board certified in plastic and reconstructive surgery. ASPRS sponsors a broad range of technical and educational programs. One of its activities includes socioeconomic research and the development of communications programs that assist the public in understanding better the nature of plastic surgery and the surgeons qualified to perform it. Members of ASPRS are permitted to use a registered symbol, known as the Tiffany circle, to identify them as members of ASPRS. Educated consumers know to look for this symbol in advertisements and on literature to identify doctors who belong to this organization.

Rumors of malpractice sometimes occur within the industry. Because much of this type of surgery is "elective surgery," it is often not covered by insurance; thus, many normal rules do not apply. For example, some procedures are performed outside proper hospitals, possible side effects are not discussed in advertisements or pamphlets, and consumers do not know the records of their doctors. The American Medical Association seldom intervenes in such situations, and until recently, neither did the FDA.[1]

Much attention was focused on the industry in 1991. It was then that the silicone implant controversy erupted. While stars such as Michael Jackson, Liz Taylor, and Cher portrayed the beautiful side of cosmetic surgery, thousands of nameless, faceless women were near death from their procedures. Theirs were not stories of glamour and beauty, but of horror due to silicone implant leaks into their bodies' immune systems. Over 2 million women have had breast implant procedures, 80 percent for cosmetic reasons, 20 percent for "reconstructive" procedures after cancer.[2] Because of negative publicity, the waiting lists for such procedures have decreased dramatically, but waiting lists for other procedures have not. Dr. Vogt thought of zeroing in on those procedures with increasing demand and eliminating some of the problem procedures, but this might eliminate numerous potential clients whom her competition would not turn away. "Ethics or profits?" was a question she pondered.

If she were to locate in Southern California, Dr. Vogt would be practicing in a highly competitive market. Nearly half the world's cosmetic surgeons live and practice in America, where 15,000 doctors rely on cosmetic surgery for at least part of their income. California is home to 33 percent of these doctors practicing in America.[3] Dr. Vogt also knew that if she chose to locate in California she would have to face the issue of whether or not to advertise, and if so, how to do it effectively.

In Search of the Perfect Body

The American cosmetic surgery industry has grown in the last decade due to increased demand from people of all ages. While some people might equate upper-income groups with those most likely to buy such surgery, one survey found that nearly one in three patients had an annual income below $25,000. Procedures that cost an average of over $3,000 are a surprisingly high proportion of this group's discretionary income.

The most popular procedures in 1990 according to the American Academy of Cosmetic Surgery (AACS), beginning with the most popular, are sclerotherapy (removal of spider veins), collagen injections, nose reconstruction, lip reconstruction, liposuction, and breast enlargements (the tenth most popular procedure). The rival organization, ASPRS, lists breast enlargements, eyelid surgery, and collagen injections as the most requested procedures.[4]

People choose to have plastic surgery for many reasons. Some take body characteristics which they feel uncomfortable about, such as large

---

[1]"The Price of Beauty," *The Economist*, January 11, 1992, 25.
[2]Ibid.
[3]Ibid.
[4]Ibid.

noses, and change them to be more acceptable to themselves. While such surgery is often done to build self-confidence and make people feel better about themselves, sometimes it is done to please or satisfy others. It is also performed with the hopes of reaching perfection. These conditions often lead to dissatisfaction with procedure results. Patients often expect too much from procedures. While liposuction will help trim fat from problem areas, such as the thighs or buttocks, for safety reasons, many surgeons will not remove more than 1000cc of fat. Removing this amount will smooth problem areas, but it will not make someone automatically thin. Doctors who help their patients set realistic expectations have the most satisfied customers. Many patients are so pleased with the results they see, they almost become addicted to cosmetic surgery, having multiple procedures. They strive to have the perfect body, by means of cosmetic surgical procedures.

In the past most people would have thought that women represent the primary market for cosmetic surgery, but cosmetic surgery is not just for women anymore. As men become more concerned with looks and aging, some surgical procedures have experienced more growth among men than women. Both men and women have been working out for years to lose weight and improve their health. The result is that they do feel healthier. However, now when men look in the mirror they think they look older than they feel. The answer for many of them is plastic surgery. According to a 1990 study done by AACS and the American Society of Liposuction Surgery (ASLS), 30 percent of all plastic surgery clients in 1988 were male, an increase of 10 percent over the previous year.[5] Predictions indicate this trend will continue over the next several years. Percentages vary regionally. Major metropolitan areas with many male executives constitute a greater percentage of male patients.

Men do not necessarily want to look young. More important to them is looking rested and alert. The face of the nineties is more natural and distinctive than in the past, and surgical procedures have been adapted accordingly. Men and women may both have eyelid surgery, but if done too tightly, it can be feminizing. Surgeons will therefore arch the male brow more subtly and leave some of the fullness in the eye area. Thus men may not appear as dramatically altered following surgery as women might. In their quest to have an appearance that more accurately reflects their inner vigor, men are turning to liposuction (to diminish love handles), nose surgery, hair transplants, eyelid surgery, and face-lifts.[6]

Marketing and Competition

To mention the words *marketing* and *competition* might have been grounds for being brought up on ethics charges at some medical schools. To many members of the medical profession, these words connoted advertising,

---

[5]Linda Troiano, "Skin, Scent, & Hair," *American Health*, September 1990, 14.
[6]Ibid.

disparagement of fellow practitioners, and the possibility of overprescrib-
ing surgical procedures. They were what some doctors did when they
"went bad." In fact, a physician who allowed himself or herself to be interviewed by the press might face charges by the local medical society of "advertising" or participating in unethical behavior. In recent years, however,
the Supreme Court struck down most of the prohibitions on advertising
and competition.

As Dr. Vogt pondered these issues, her mind drifted back to undergraduate days. An economics class that she particularly liked came to
mind, especially a discussion about primary demand and secondary demand. As she thought about it, she began to think of how the total demand
for medical care might be expanded in ways beneficial to patients as well
as to health care providers.

Putting such basic issues as who should be treated and who should not
be treated aside, however, Dr. Vogt began to consider how the basic
amount of plastic surgery performed could be increased. In a $3 billion in-
dustry, how could value for such services be increased to the level that
consumers would choose to buy more? She found a national study on consumers of health care services indicating that about 6 percent of consumers now purchase cosmetic surgery, but an additional 11 percent expressed interest in purchasing cosmetic surgery. Both of these percentages
were double those to the same questions asked five years earlier in another study. If orthodontists can persuade people to spend a few thousand
dollars to improve the appearance of their teeth, Dr. Vogt reasoned, can
people be persuaded to spend a few thousand dollars to improve the appearance of their faces, noses, balding heads, breasts, or abdomens? Why
shouldn't society—individuals or their third-party payers—pay for the
correction of congenital defects, cleft palates, or fingers and toes that
could function again with plastic surgery? A rhytidectomy might improve
the appearance of a 36-year-old even more, she thought, than braces from
the dentists, a product she noticed that more and more 36-year-old persons seemed to be buying.

The concept of selective demand also raced through Dr. Vogt's mind.
How could the demand for plastic surgery be channeled to plastic surgeons
rather than other specialists, and, more specifically, how could the demand for plastic surgery—either restorative or aesthetic—be directed toward the practice of Dr. Vogt and her potential partner rather than other
plastic surgeons in the area?

To gather some input for her thinking, Dr. Vogt looked for research
that might be helpful. She found that the ASPRS had conducted a recent study on a national basis. The study was conducted for ASPRS by
Market Group One in Columbus, Ohio and involved a mail survey
completed among 865 persons, mostly female but representative of
the major demographics in the United States. A number of the general
and specific psychographic statements from this study are shown in
Exhibit 17.1.

■ EXHIBIT 17.1   Responses to General Statements about Health and Plastic Surgery

Statement	Agree		Disagree		Neither		No Response	
	#	%	#	%	#	%	#	%
I am usually aware of my appearance.	(743)	85.9	(27)	3.1	(76)	8.8	(19)	2.2
Looking good is important for my self-esteem.	(737)	85.2	(37)	4.3	(82)	9.5	(9)	1.0
I have a great deal of confidence in my doctor.	(705)	81.5	(59)	6.8	(96)	11.1	(5)	.6
I like to have brochures that explain things to me when a doctor treats me.	(697)	80.6	(43)	4.9	(122)	14.1	(3)	.3
Most physicians are ethical and responsible persons.	(677)	78.3	(63)	7.3	(123)	14.2	(2)	.2
I like to see television programs which present information about health care.	(654)	75.7	(52)	6.0	(156)	18.0	(3)	.3
I am concerned about what other people think of me.	(616)	71.2	(71)	8.2	(175)	20.2	(3)	.3
I try to dress fashionably.	(611)	70.6	(76)	8.8	(174)	20.1	(4)	.5
I regularly read articles on health care.	(601)	69.5	(115)	13.1	(146)	16.9	(3)	.3
I am trying to lose weight.	(596)	68.9	(149)	17.2	(115)	13.3	(5)	.6
I feel anxious when I speak in front of a group.	(551)	63.7	(192)	22.2	(117)	13.5	(5)	.6
I use facial creams and moisturizers regularly.	(528)	61.0	(246)	28.4	(89)	10.3	(2)	.2
People should have plastic surgery to improve their appearance if they want and can afford it.	(519)	60.0	(96)	11.1	(249)	28.8	(1)	.1
I look pretty much the way I want to look.	(517)	59.8	(210)	24.3	(132)	15.3	(6)	.7
I would prefer to save money by having an operation in a doctor's office rather than a hospital.	(438)	50.6	(256)	29.6	(166)	19.2	(5)	.6
My income is in some way dependent upon my appearance.	(376)	43.5	(291)	33.6	(189)	21.8	(9)	1.0

(continued)

■ **EXHIBIT 17.1**   *continued*

Statement	Agree		Disagree		Neither		No Response	
	#	%	#	%	#	%	#	%
I generally exercise (like push-ups or jogging) at least twice a week.	(354)	40.1	(368)	42.5	(140)	16.2	(3)	.3
I believe medical insurance should pay for cosmetic surgery.	(347)	40.1	(285)	33.0	(231)	26.7	(2)	.2
I prefer older doctors to younger ones.	(238)	27.5	(158)	18.3	(463)	53.5	(6)	.7
In most malpractice suits, the physician is not really to blame.	(208)	24.0	(192)	22.2	(458)	52.9	(7)	.8
Plastic surgeons are among the most highly trained of all physicians.	(175)	20.2	(179)	20.7	(508)	58.7	(3)	.3
I do not believe people should use surgery to alter their appearance.	(128)	14.8	(429)	49.6	(303)	35.0	(5)	.6

The study conducted for the ASPRS by Market Group One also investigated attitudes toward physician advertising. About 60 percent of consumers nationally were aware of advertising for cosmetic surgery. About one-third of those who remembered seeing ads indicated that the ad made them feel that plastic surgery is becoming more acceptable. Another one-third had no reaction to such ads. Over 11 percent indicated that physicians should not advertise. Nearly 6 percent were offended by cosmetic surgery ads they could recall, with the most often given reasons being "sexist attitude about body image," "it's not like shopping for a used car," "it exploits women, using them as objects," "it makes one think life will be wonderful if you look wonderful," and "materialistic." Responses indicated great disagreement as to the ethics of doctors' promoting their services. Advertising in the Yellow Pages was considered the most ethical means of promotion, more ethical even than TV talk shows, radio talk shows, newspaper articles, and public speeches of the type normally considered publicity rather than advertising.

Dr. Vogt began searching for additional information that might help her assess the environment in Orange County, California, or other regions. She examined a recent issue of *Orange Coast* and found numerous advertisements for plastic surgery (see Exhibit 17.2).

Sigi took all of her information and began to plan her future practice. The opportunities were exciting, but she had to answer many questions before she moved ahead.

(continued)

■ **EXHIBIT 17.2** *continued*

Shape up your SMILE

PATIENTS: MARC MILAN , NBC'S SANTA BARBARA / STACEY HALEY, T.V. GAME SHOW HOSTESS

COSMETIC DENTISTRY
*will make you smile
with advances in:*

- bleaching
- porcelain veneers
- bonding
- complete dental care

For your personal consultation please call:
William M. Dorfman D.D.S. (310) 277-5678
2080 Century Park East, Suite 1101
Century City, California 90067

(continued)

Focal Topics

1. Where should Dr. Vogt locate? How should she make this decision?
2. How do patients choose a physician such as Dr. Vogt? What research can you find or would you suggest to understand consumer decisions concerning a physician?
3. Can the demand for plastic surgery be stimulated? How?

■ **EXHIBIT 17.2** *continued*

4. If Dr. Vogt locates in Orange County, California, should she advertise? If she does, what media and creative strategy should she and her partner use?

■ ■ ■ ■ ■

McDonald's

■ ■ ■ ■ ■

The history of McDonald's is the story of a company that has succeeded on the idea that consumers want a restaurant stressing quality food, quick service, cleanliness, and good value, known within the company as Q,S,C,V. It is an ideal from which the company has not deviated since opening its first restaurant in 1955.

McDonald's has positioned itself for a decade of growth by focusing on new restaurant growth and on maximizing sales and profits. It also plans for profits in the 1990s by increasing its customer base and decreasing its operating costs. While cutting costs is key in maintaining profitability, it will not be the focus of this case analysis. Instead, consumer behavior and marketing strategy will be the areas of discussion.

McDonald's has become a global force in the world of fast food. Since opening its first international restaurant in Richmond, British Columbia, Canada, in 1967, McDonald's has made its presence known in fifty-nine countries. There are over 3,000 restaurants outside of the United States, which serve over 4 million customers per day in countries such as Japan and Italy. McDonald's foreign operations accounted for 45 percent of total revenue in 1991, up from 42 percent in 1990. In fact, of the top ten McDonald's restaurants with the highest sales, nine are located outside the United States.

The potential to serve more and more customers around the world is virtually unlimited. In the United States, McDonald's has 8,800 restaurants serving a total population of 250 million, approximately one restaurant for every 28,000 people. In the 58 countries outside the United States that host McDonald's, it operates 3,600 restaurants for a population that totals nearly 3 billion, roughly one restaurant for every 800,000 people.

McDonald's plans to grow throughout the next decade and throughout the world. Some of the strategies McDonald's follows that will keep it on

Note: Some parts of this case were excerpted from Gordon, "McDonald's Milestones," *International Parallels*, February 1992, volume 2, number 1, p. 10.

this growth track are being responsive to customers' changing needs and fulfilling its social responsibilities to the communities in which it operates.

Meeting Customer Needs for Nutrition

McDonald's continues its success in the quick-service restaurant industry by staying in tune to its customers' changing tastes. Meeting consumer demands, McDonald's finds itself serving more than 20 million customers a day worldwide. Roughly 52 percent of U.S. sales come from drive-thrus, 16 percent from carry out, and 32 percent from food eaten in the restaurants. McDonald's prepares 2 million pounds of French fries daily and buys over 3,400 tons of sesame seeds a year for its buns.

McDonald's has always monitored its customers' wants and has worked diligently to satisfy their demand for good-tasting, wholesome food. Recent improvements in the U.S. McDonald's menu include switching to 100 percent cholesterol-free vegetable oil for preparing French fries, replacing whole milk with 1 percent lowfat milk, and enriching sandwich buns with calcium. It has reduced the amount of sodium in hotcakes by 30 percent, pickles by 21 percent, breakfast sausages by 32 percent, and cheese by 10 percent. Menus also include a variety of fresh salads, reduced-calorie condiments and salad dressings, 99 percent fat-free milk shakes and frozen yogurt, and the 91 percent fat-free McLean Deluxe.

Consumer tastes and lifestyles have changed since 1955 and so has McDonald's. In 1965 Filet-O-Fish was added to the menu, followed by the Big Mac sandwich in 1968. McDonald's introduced quick-service breakfasts for people on the go in 1975 with the Egg McMuffin sandwich, and Chicken McNuggets debuted in 1983. The 1990s will bring about change as well. Now more than ever people want foods that are nutritious and healthy as well as tasty and convenient. McDonald's 1992 menu includes salads, bran muffins, and whole-grain cereals to meet these changes.

McLean . . . 91 Percent Fat Free, 100 Percent Delicious

In April 1991 the McLean Deluxe, a new lowfat ground beef sandwich, joined the Big Mac and the Quarter Pounder on McDonald's menus nationwide. The company introduced this sandwich as part of its long-term growth strategy to maximize sales and profits at existing restaurants.

McDonald's hamburgers are already classified "lean" by the USDA, but the new sandwich is even leaner. The McLean Deluxe is made with a 91 percent fat-free beef patty. It is served on a sesame seed bun with ketchup, mustard, pickles, onions, lettuce, and tomato. The sandwich contains just 320 calories and 10 grams of fat and is a great alternative for customers who love beef but want to reduce their fat intake. The company views McLean's introduction as a direct reflection of its accelerated product development program and its responsiveness to customers' expectations for variety, taste, and nutrition.

McLean Deluxe represents a true technological and nutritional breakthrough. It delivers the great taste McDonald's customers expect, with

70 percent less fat and 45 percent fewer calories than the McD.L.T., which it replaced on the menu. McDonald's and its suppliers worked closely with researchers at Auburn University to develop the lowfat ground beef. The company encouraged the research, refined the product, and became the first restaurant to offer the product to the public. Many advertising and promotional campaigns, as seen in Exhibit 18.1, focused on the new McLean to increase awareness and trial purchases.

■ **EXHIBIT 18.1**   McLean Deluxe Ad

Contains 9% fat before cooking. Lean beef patty contains beef, water, encapsulated salt, carrageenan, natural beef flavor. Ask your store manager for complete nutritional information.

Courtesy of McDonald's

McDonald's is continually testing new and promotional products and refining existing products. One of McDonald's primary objectives is to appeal to the broadest spectrum of customers and to serve them more frequently. Its goal is to give more people more reasons to visit McDonald's more often, while remaining with the limited-menu, quick-service concept that has been a key to McDonald's success and growth for many years.

McDonald's feels that consumer education is a key to good nutrition. The booklet *McDonald's Food: The Facts* is available in most U.S. restaurants and provides the complete listing of the nutritional value and ingredients of all McDonald's foods. For consumers with special needs, or who simply watch what they eat, additional information is available in the "Diabetic Food Exchange List" and the "Calorie, Sodium, Cholesterol and Fat Content Card" to help consumers follow a diabetic or weight-control diet. A special consumer hotline to the McDonald's Nutrition Information Center (708-575-FOOD) provides quick answers to consumer questions. McDonald's also placed print ads, seen in Exhibit 18.2, about nutrition in trade journals to inform health care professionals about the changes at McDonald's.

Social Responsibility

McDonald's believes that being a good corporate citizen means treating people with fairness and integrity, sharing its success with the communities in which it operates, and being a leader on issues that affect customers. This philosophy is implemented by many different people in a variety of ways throughout McDonald's.

Education

McDonald's has always been the restaurant of choice for American children for decades. They have fallen in love with Ronald McDonald, the McDonald Land characters, and the tasty Happy Meals. McDonald's is a family place. It's clean, comfortable, and friendly for people of all ages. McDonald's saved the day for many families looking for good food for adults and children and an atmosphere the children would like.

McDonald's has never forgotten the importance of children. It has always been committed to children and continues to look for ways to educate them. The company has worked with educators in developing teachers' guides and other learning tools for school use. In 1986, McDonald's introduced *Eating Right/Feeling Fit*, a video and activities guide featuring Olympic athletes Bruce Jenner and Mary Lou Retton. In 1988, a new nutrition education kit was launched called *Nutrient Pursuit*, and in 1990, the company, partnered with *Sports Illustrated for Kids*, developed a nutrition and fitness magazine insert, classroom video, and teacher's guide.

Through local mentoring, incentive, and tutorial programs, McDonald's franchisees and managers work with schools to address critical issues

■ **EXHIBIT 18.2**   Nutrition at McDonald's Is Changing

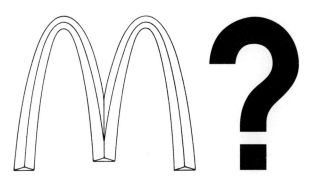

Nutrition At McDonald's...

Times are changing and so is McDonald's.® Our Menu of the '90s continues to demonstrate our commitment to making responsible menu changes as lifestyles have changed and new technologies have developed. At the same time, our menu enhancements build on our tradition of offering top-quality food that tastes good. We've revolutionized the food industry with our 91% fat-free McLean Deluxe™ beef patty. We've cut saturated fat by 45% and eliminated cholesterol in our french fries by switching to 100% vegetable oil—the only oil we use. Our milk shakes are now 99.5% fat-free, and we've switched to lowfat frozen yogurt. We offer freshly-tossed salads with reduced-calorie dressings, and whole-grain cereals with 1% lowfat milk. So you can enjoy a variety of menu selections at McDonald's that fit within current dietary guidelines.

This print ad is part of McDonald's campaign to inform healthcare professionals about
the enhancements to our menu.

Courtesy of McDonald's

such as literacy, dropout prevention, and substance abuse. Nationally, these education programs are reaching millions of school children. Recent programs include: "Exploration and Discovery," an elementary school math and science curriculum created in conjunction with the Young Astronaut Council and Ronald McDonald Children's Charities; "The Rain Forest Imperative," a video and teacher's discussion guide that explores the economic causes of deforestation, developed to support the efforts of Conservation International; and "Healthy Growing Up," a nutrition and fitness program directed to primary school students.

Charities

The Ronald McDonald Children's Charities (RMCC) was founded in memory of Ray A. Kroc, founder of McDonald's Corporation, in 1984. This organization is dedicated to helping children achieve their fullest potential. Since inception, RMCC has issued more than 1,300 grants totaling $50 million through year-end 1991. These grants develop and support programs in the areas of health care and medical research, specially designed rehabilitation facilities, and special youth education programs.

The Ronald McDonald House program is the cornerstone of RMCC, providing a "home-away-from-home" for families of seriously ill children being treated at nearby hospitals. At year-end 1991, there were 150 houses in the United States, Canada, Australia, Austria, England, France, the Netherlands, Germany, and New Zealand. Exhibit 18.3 shows an ad for the Ronald McDonald House.

Equal Opportunity

One goal at McDonald's is to attract capable minorities, women, disabled, and older people to become contributing members to the McDonald's team. It strives to develop people's potential without regard to race, sex, religion, ethnic, educational, or cultural background.

McJobs is an employment program designed to assist mentally and physically challenged individuals to develop their skills and confidence to succeed. They train shoulder-to-shoulder with a manager for about eight weeks and then graduate to a crew position. Through this program, McDonald's gains loyal, dependable, highly motivated employees who develop a professional attitude and skills. Through the McMasters program, McDonald's recruits, trains, and retains people aged 55 and over. These employees are introduced to the McDonald's work environment through a four-week training program under the guidance of a job coach and are then recognized at graduation and welcomed to the team.

In addition to its commitment to equal opportunity and affirmative action for its employees, McDonald's intends to increase both the number of minority suppliers and the amount of goods and services purchased from them. Recently, minority entrepreneurs acquired two long-term suppliers that generate $200 million of business annually. McDonald's was featured

■ **EXHIBIT 18.3   Ad for Ronald McDonald House**

Last year, we treated over 100,000 critically-ill children with advanced technology like this.

When you spend as many hours being a "patient" as some children do, it's easy to forget how to be a "kid." Fortunately, Ronald McDonald House® has a lot of ways to help them remember.

Our facilities serve as homes-away-from-home for critically-ill children and their families while they receive special care in nearby hospitals. When treatment can be done on an outpatient basis, Ronald McDonald House provides a welcome escape from the hospital. A place to unwind. To recharge. To just be a kid.

If you'd like to contribute some time or money to our House, please give us a call. With these kids, your support could be just what the doctor ordered.

Ronald McDonald House

Courtesy of McDonald's

in *Hispanic* magazine as one of the top 100 U.S. companies providing opportunities for Hispanics. The article notes McDonald's commitment to the Hispanic community in areas of recruitment and hiring, scholarships and grants, support for Hispanic organizations, and minority vendor programs. McDonald's was also recognized by *Black Enterprise* magazine as one of the twenty-five best places for African-Americans to work.

Environment

In August 1990, McDonald's announced its partnership in a unique task force with the Environmental Defense Fund (EDF), a national nonprofit organization that seeks economically viable solutions to environmental problems. Together, the task force worked to identify ways for McDonald's to reduce the amount of solid waste generated by its restaurants. Both EDF and McDonald's recognized that in order to make a real difference in the amount of solid waste generated, it would be necessary to look at the total operation, not just the restaurants' take-out business. The task force recommended activities such as source reduction, reuse, recycling, and composting programs.

McDonald's has implemented recycling and waste reduction programs throughout its company. It switched from polystyrene foam "clamshells" to paper-based wraps for packaging its sandwich items, a change that represents a 70–79 percent reduction in packaging volume, resulting in significantly less space consumed in landfills. For in-store customer service, McDonald's will test pup-style condiment dispensers in place of individual packets, a system for filling customers' reusable coffee cups and reusable lids for salads and breakfast entrees. Through the McRecycle U.S.A. program, McDonald's has committed to purchasing over $100 million worth of recycled materials for restaurant construction and renovation annually, a goal that was met and exceeded in 1991.

McDonald's is currently the largest user of recycled paper in its field. Building on this experience, McDonald's has directed its nearly 600 suppliers to use corrugated boxes that contain at least 35 percent recycled materials, a target considerably higher than the industry average. By the end of 1991, the company had programs in place designed to recycle or test the recycling or composting of more than 80 percent of all on-premise waste.

EDF is very pleased with the results. It hopes to develop a model that would work with other companies and industries as well. Other organizations are considering similar programs after seeing the results at McDonald's.

Consumers are also pleased. The reaction from the public to McDonald's recycling efforts has been very positive.

As a leader in the food-service business in the United States, McDonald's is in a position to set the pace for proactive environmental actions within the industry as well. And, given the scope of its operations abroad, McDonald's may well be the pacesetter for more environmentally sound operations in international markets.

Focal Topics

1. How significant is the market trend toward healthier foods for McDonald's? Is the company justified in changing its products to adapt to this trend?

2. How should McLean be promoted and priced?

3. Do the social responsibility programs of McDonald's increase or decrease profits? Why or why not?

4. If McDonald's were to delete some of its social responsibility programs due to cost pressures, which would you recommend for deletion and why?

■ ■ ■ ■ ■

Christina Lane Cosmetics, Inc.

■ ■ ■ ■ ■

In early 1985, Dan Brice, a southern California natural food retailer and nutritional counselor, approached Christina Lane Cosmetics about developing a personalized line of natural body care products. His plan was that he would bring the product development expertise and image to the product line and Christina Lane Cosmetics would provide the manufacturing, distribution, and marketing efforts necessary to ensure product success. The line would include a variety of products under the brand name Dan Brice Naturals and be distributed exclusively through health food stores.

Bill Wayne, vice president of marketing for Christina Lane Cosmetics, was initially very interested in the concept and strongly supported it to top management. However, as industry and consumer research began to be completed and marketing strategies were being discussed and formulated, he started to have second thoughts. He wondered about the product name, the advisability of going through health-food stores exclusively, the breadth of product mix, and, in a broader sense, whether or not a market really existed for an additional product entrant.

After some detailed evaluation, management of Christina Lane decided not to enter into a joint project with Dan Brice. They did keep the door open, however, and indicated that they wanted to see how the body care area developed and would reconsider the opportunity in the early 1990s. It is now late 1992 and Dan Brice has returned, seeking a joint partnership to develop and market a natural line of body care products. He is more convinced than ever of the potential for such a product line. Top management is again interested and asked Bill Wayne to review his previous analyses and provide his recommendations.

This case originally appeared in *Cases and Exercises in Marketing* by W. Wayne Talarzyk, The Dryden Press, 1987.

Background—Christina Lane Cosmetics

For almost a decade, Christina Lane had been one of North America's most sought-after fashion models. She appeared on the covers of many leading magazines and did a number of television commercials for major consumer companies. Around Christmas one year, two investors and a marketing executive for a large cosmetics firm approached Christina about forming a corporation to develop and distribute a full line of women's cosmetics bearing her name. While it seemed logical that her name recognition and position as a model would provide instant market exposure for such a cosmetics line, the decision was not an easy one for Christina to make. The prospects of being part of a company carrying her name seemed exciting and potentially rewarding, but it did mean that her modeling career would be severely limited as she went into competition with some of her former clients. After much personal evaluation and counsel from trusted friends and business associates, Christina decided to go ahead with the idea. Christina Lane Cosmetics, Inc. became a reality.

In many ways, the company was an overnight success. National sales distribution was achieved by developing a field sales force that personally called on all of the major department and women's specialty stores that carried full lines of high-quality cosmetics. The company decided early in the development of its marketing strategy that the product line would not be distributed through drug stores, discount stores, or smaller department stores. A multimedia advertising and promotional campaign involving national television, most women's fashion and general interest magazines, and an extensive retailer cooperative program supported the Christina Lane line of cosmetics. Christina herself was highly visible in most of the company's advertising and frequently made guest appearances at trade shows and major fashion programs at leading retail stores. During the company's first five years, sales grew at an average annual rate of 125 percent and profits increased an average of 80 percent each year.

Background—Dan Brice

Dan Brice, a southern California natural food retailer and nutritional counselor, believes that sunscreening should be an all-year affair. He has seen too many of his customers complain of skin cancer and of prematurely aging skin. One out of every four to seven people is a victim of skin cancer. The most frightening aspect of skin cancer is not knowing whether you've already been overexposed to the sun. Skin cancer is cumulative. Sunshine actually alters the molecular structure of the skin, damaging the collagen, the skin's main supporting substance.

After researching skin cancer and how to prevent it, Dan saw a need for everyday skin and hair-care products with an SPF of at least 8 to be used by everyone, regardless of skin type. Recent studies show that the UVA ray (tanning), as well as the UVB ray (burning), have been shown to cause premature aging and may also be implicated in skin cancer.

Dan met with cosmetic chemists and dermatologists to determine the best approach for developing natural products with broad spectrum sun protection and natural nutrients to condition and nourish the skin. He explained he wanted products with no fragrance, no artificial dyes, natural nutrients, a non-Paba sunscreen, and moisturizers suited to different humidity conditions. After developing some preliminary product plans, he went to people at Christina Lane Cosmetics with his ideas.

Research on Health Food Stores

Bill Wayne asked his director of marketing research, Mark Powell, to try and get a handle on the health food market. He was specifically interested in how the health food stores were doing. Mark prepared the review shown in Exhibit 19.1 from information in *Health Food Stores* magazine. The data was obtained from replies to questionnaires sent to 2,500 independent retailers throughout the nation. Major chains were not included, but were taken into account when projecting industrywide totals. Supermarkets and other mass merchants were not included at all.

Of the retailers that responded, 88 percent operated just one store. The remainder operated an average of 3.4 stores. The average length of time in business was eight years per store. The main purpose for this annual survey was to give an indication of trends at what might be termed a typical retail operation. Because the sample was taken at random and because it varied in size and character from year to year, readers were cautioned not to take the results too literally. Some of the data are based on respondents' estimates or personal interpretations of questions. Some of the main conclusions from the survey include:

1. There were 580 fewer health food stores at the end of 1984 than at the end of 1982. This alone is a major cause of the decrease in overall industry sales.

2. This is a time of adjustments for independent health food retailers, as they must learn to cope with their new competition.

3. More and more companies that once claimed they sold exclusively to health food stores are entering the mass merchandise stores. This is definitely taking away business from the health food retailer.

Marketing Research

To help ascertain the market for Dan Brice Naturals, Mark Powell contracted with a marketing research organization. The firm was asked to conduct interviews with selected manufacturers, distributors, members

■ **EXHIBIT 19.1**   *Health Food Stores* **1985 Survey Results**

■ *Total Industry Sales*
In 1984, for the second straight year sales slipped in the health food industry. Estimated industry sales were not quite $1.7 billion, down from just over $2.0 billion in 1983. That's a drop of 16.3 percent. (Last year the decrease was approximately 17 percent.)

■ *Average Sales per Store*
Going along with the drop in overall sales was a 17 percent slip in average store volume, from $211,854 in 1983 to $175,748 in 1984. In 1985, however, the majority by far of the respondents expect to see a reverse of the downtrend. Some 84 percent of the survey respondents said that they expect sales this year to be up an average of 19 percent. However, even more of the respondents to the survey last year—almost 90 percent—predicted an upturn in 1984, and it failed to materialize.

■ *Average Annual Net Profits per Store*
For profits in 1984, the drop was not quite as bad as it was in sales, but it was, nonetheless, significant. Average net after taxes among the respondents was $15,152, 14.4 percent lower than the $17,697 reported for 1983. Also, 22 percent of the respondents in the 1984 survey reported a loss, compared to just 10 percent a year ago. Another important point is that the current survey appears to report on somewhat smaller stores than it did in recent years. In this year's survey, just 22 percent of the respondents said their sales were over $300,000; that compares with 34 percent at a similar level a year ago.

■ *Average Sale per Customer*
In 1984, the amount of an average sale for the retailers dropped to its lowest level since 1980—$10.61, compared with $11.78 in 1983, $15.48 in 1982, and $10.80 in 1981. This could be another indication that the stores represented in this survey were smaller than those surveyed in recent years.

■ *Average Square Footage of Stores*
The average square footage of health stores dropped from almost 1,800 in 1983 to roughly 1,250 in 1984. Again, this may be attributed to the number of small stores in the sample.

■ *Store Locations*
Statistics on store location show some changes from the previous year, although not dramatic changes. An identical 10 percent operated out of shopping malls, while 37 percent operated from strip shopping centers (up from 33 percent in 1983) and 47 percent were located on business streets compared to 45 percent last year. The remainder of the stores were located on residential streets (8 percent).

■ *Average Dollars Spent on Advertising per Store*
The retailers in this year's survey averaged $4,530 on advertising compared to roughly $3,000 in 1983. The media they spent the most on were weekly newspaper, Yellow Pages, direct mail, daily newspaper, fliers and posters, and radio.

■ *Buying Patterns*
Direct buying by the retailer rose in 1984, with over 85 percent of the survey participants mentioning that they do at least some buying without the aid of distributors. Among that 85 percent, the percentage of goods bought directly was 28 percent. In other words, approximately one-quarter of all merchandise bought in the industry is bought direct from manufacturers (28 percent of 85 percent).

(continued)

■ **EXHIBIT 19.1**   *continued*

■ *Average Density of Competition*
In 1984, the number of other health-food stores competing with survey respondents dropped significantly—from 2.9 in 1983 to 2.0. Perhaps this was an indication of the decrease in the overall number of stores in the industry.

■ *Total Industry Sales of Body Care Products*
Sales of body care products in the health-food industry totaled $129.5 million compared to $185.6 million in 1982 and $150.6 million in 1983. This decline could be attributed to the number of manufacturers selling to the supermarkets and mass merchants. In turn, the mass merchants undersell the health food retailers, thus taking a large portion of their business.

■ *Average Body Care Sales per Store*
The average body care sales per store has followed the same path as the overall industry sales of body care products. In 1982, the average sales of body care products was just over $20,000. In 1983, it dropped to $16,000 and in 1984, to $13,500.

■ *Body Care as a Percent of Store Sales*
Since 1981, this trend has been relatively flat, and 1984 is no different. In 1984, body care as a percent of store sales was 7.7 percent, an increase of 1 percent over 1983, 1982, and 1981.

■ *Average Markup of Body Care Products*
Average 1984 markup on body care products was 53 percent. This figure is just 2 percent below the figure for 1983.

---

of the trade press, and health foods marketing consultants at various industry conferences. They were also asked to interview health food store owners, managers, and sales personnel in selected markets in Florida, California, and Arizona. In addition, several focused group interviews were held with customers of health-food stores. The criteria for participants in the focused group interviews included:

■ Women 18 to 49 years old

■ Men 18+, with about 50 percent over age 35

■ Household income $30,000+ annually

■ Must have purchased products in health food stores at least four times in the past 12 months and at least once in the past 30 days

■ Regular users of cosmetics, skin care products, sun care products

■ About one-half of participants purchase some body care products in health food stores

■ About one-half shop in health food stores, but tend to purchase most body care products in other stores

Exhibit 19.2 provides some of the general conclusions from the consumer interviews. Critical issues identified from all of the research conducted by the firm are presented in the following sections.

■ **EXHIBIT 19.2   General Detail from Customer Interviews**

Why People Shop Health Food Stores over Other Stores (Insights into what is sought in products):

- The healthy adventure—feeling that one can search out and discover wonderful, healthy things not available in other kinds of stores.

- Perception that many products in supermarkets and drug stores include harmful substances, including body care products with harmful substances that are "absorbed into my body." Included are mineral oil, bees' wax, perfumes, dyes, etc.

- Attitude that products in health food stores feature wonderful but little understood ingredients, such as vitamins, especially vitamin E; Aloe Vera, believed to be a natural miracle healing substance; and other even more exotic natural ingredients.

- For solutions to specific problems—allergies, overly oily skin, high triglycerides, low energy, etc. Older women with real or perceived health problems tend to be heavy users of health food stores.

- For "natural" products, ingredients, foods, pet foods, body care products. Natural equals *good*; natural equals *quality*; natural equals *healthy*; natural equals *gentle*. (But nobody really knows what is natural and what is not.)

- For knowledgeable, helpful advice and personal service. Store operators are consultants.

- To demonstrate individuality; to be a part of something that, clearly, is not perceived to be for everybody.

Product Mix

Limited Depth of Line Recommended   The overwhelming majority of health food stores lack the floor space, shelf space, and open-to-buy necessary for a line of some thirty skin care, sun care, and hair care products. The line should be narrowed to about twelve high-opportunity products.

Natural Ingredients Demanded   Operators and shoppers, first and foremost, want *natural* ingredients. However, neither operators nor shoppers really understand which ingredients are natural and which are not.

Sun Protection Ingredients Important   Shoppers and operators believe the sun is a major threat to healthy skin and a leading cause of skin cancer. Natural sun protection ingredients will be perceived as an effective differential advantage in skin care products.

Moisturizing Ingredients Wanted   Female and male shoppers and store operators recognize the importance of natural skin moisturizing ingredients. Many are believed to nourish and heal the skin.

Products Sought for Specific Skin Problems   Operators and shoppers seek products promising solutions to specific skin problems such as oily skin, dry skin, skin that is oily in spots, and acne.

Paba-Free Products May Provide a Differential Advantage   Paba is perceived as a positive, natural ingredient, and is recognized as a common
ingredient in body care products, but some awareness of negative publicity
is beginning.

Skin Care Sales Should Exceed Hair Care Sales   Shoppers feel that it is
less important to buy shampoo than skin care products in health food
stores. The ingredients in shampoos are thought to rinse out, anyway.

Distribution Mix

**Effective, Cost Efficient Distribution Is the Greatest Marketing Challenge
Facing the New Line**   The overwhelming majority of stores, about 6,000
or 85 percent of all health-food stores, are of the small, cramped variety.
They offer limited shelf space and limited volume and turn opportunities,
yet request frequent service. Channels of distribution to these stores are
highly fragmented.

Additional Distribution Important   In phase one of distribution efforts,
additional distribution should be sought in health-related outlets such as
large fitness centers, spas, tennis clubs, golf clubs, etc., to help offset up-
front distribution investments.

Communications Mix

- Priority 1 must be to win awareness and loyalty of distributors and
  store owners and managers.
- Brand name awareness is low for health food store body care products.
- Public relations will be important to the marketing launch.
- Local advertising will be a helpful sell-in factor with larger, more pro-
  fessional retailers.
- Sampling should be a major component of the marketing program. A
  simple, direct, no-nonsense approach to skin care and hair care will be
  effective with distributors, stores, women, and men.
- The European mystique provides an effective marketing appeal.
- The word *natural* must be featured in all communications. *Naturals*
  can be a highly productive part of the product name.

Preliminary Marketing Plan

Even though he was somewhat hesitant to move into the market, Bill
Wayne worked with members of his marketing staff and Dan Brice to develop a preliminary marketing plan. The plan was prepared in the form of
a series of questions to provide a basis for internal discussions as to how
the company should proceed with this new product line.

1. What Do We Sell?

Dan Brice Naturals Products We sell a range of natural skin care and hair care products that have been formulated to help prevent premature aging and skin cancer (see Exhibit 19.3). Protective cosmetics products can reduce the risk of long-term, in-depth skin damage caused by overexposure

■ **EXHIBIT 19.3** **Dan Brice Naturals Proposed Product Line**

	Skin and Hair Types			
Line	Oily	Combination	Dry	Special (For All Skin and Hair Types)
Skin Care	1. Cleansing bar 2. Oil-free creme	1. Thorough cleansing wash 2. Prevention age creme	1. Gentle creme cleanser 2. Skin renewal creme	1. Bath and shower soap bar 2. Hand and body lotion 3. Special protection toner 4. Anti-wrinkle creme 5. Exfoliating creme mask 6. Bath oil 7. Outdoor bronzing creme 8. Skin repair
Hair Care	1. Oil control shampoo 2. Extra light conditioner	1. Daily shampoo 2. Instant conditioner	1. Extra body shampoo 2. Extra control conditioner	1. Hair strengthener 2. Extra body styling gel 3. Conditioning spray
Sun Care				1. Dark tanning oil 2. Moderate sunscreen lotion 3. Maximum sunscreen lotion 4. Solastick 5. After-sun moisturizer

to daylight and can help preserve a young and healthy skin. The products will protect and nourish the skin and hair and prevent damage from within and without. They represent a simple, direct, no-nonsense approach to skin care and hair care. Special features include fragrance free, no artificial dyes, no mineral oil, Paba-free sunscreens, and UVA/UVB block giving broad spectrum protection.

2. To Whom Will We Sell?

- Health-concerned market segment
- Natural food store customer profile
  - Upper middle income ($25,000+)
  - Female
  - 25–44
  - Single, divorced, widowed, separated
  - College educated
  - Lives in large metro area
  - Geographic strength: (1) West, (2) Northeast, (3) South, (4) Central
  - Health is the foremost consideration, but time and convenience are significant. The customer moisturizes regularly and eats a controlled diet. This person is more brand loyal, but remains an experimenter. They see themselves as intelligent, creative, amicable, self-assured. They are prone to allergies, fever, headaches, and stress. They are exercise enthusiasts.
- Natural food retailer
  - Number of stores: Approximately 7,700
  - Average store sales: $175,748
  - Total industry sales: $1.7 billion
  - Average size: 1,700 sq. ft.
  - Sales per sq. ft.: $146
  - Average daily traffic: 71
  - Average customer sale: $10.66
  - Average annual net profits: $15,000
  - Body care sales: $129.5 million industrywide; average store sales: $13,500

3. What Are We Trying to Accomplish?

- Gain distribution in 17 percent of the health-food outlets that support 75 percent of the market.
- Sales volume first year of $500,000–$1 million depending on final product mix.
- Once final product mix is selected, a unit/volume forecast will be done.
- Market share: To replace Rachael Perry Skin Care, gain number 2 position in hair care, and gain a 10 percent market share.

4. What Techniques Will We Use?

- Competitive pricing
- Sales push strategy
- Top chains are *A* accounts (1,500 stores) and targets of Phase 1 penetration; *B* accounts are targets of Phase 2
    - Work on regional managers, who are responsible for brokers and detailers
    - Establish a strong broker network among small markets and detailers/merchandisers
    - Establish an in-store consultant network, i.e., by mail training/diplomas/lab coats/birthday cards. Sampling and P. M. (push money) program.
- Marketing theme—unique technical graphs and data to support claims. Establish M. Stowe as a credible spokesperson with script, publicity, book, video.
    - Educational approach to skin and hair.
    - Unique payment terms: Ninety-day dating to *A* credit-rating stores for launch. Not final yet.
    - Telemarketing for B—C accounts

5. How Will We Introduce the Product?

- Free goods—foil packets samples
- Floor displays/shelf displays
- Major account thrust
- Dan Brice—visit market by market—Seek free publicity through press thrust (TV, radio, newspaper)
- Regional managers—three initially for West, East, and Midwest
- Product announcement
- Mass mailing with samples to all 7,700 stores
- Trade advertising
- Trade shows

6. How Are We Going to Advertise?

- Trade journals during launch period
- Three trade journals (six times each)
- Want to make noise—lots of noise
- National sampling mailing
- Consumer—call to action in small ads in March, April, May or through direct mailing to target audience. No ads in *Vogue*, *Mademoiselle*, *Self*, etc., but target advertising.

7. How Do We Educate the Consumer about Product Features and Benefits?

Objective:	To effectively train key store personnel
Techniques	
Consumer:	In-store video, PR on damaging effects of sun. Consumer brochure, direct mail, consumer advertising, product manual
Retail	Product manuals
Stores:	Trade ad offering course
	Technical seminars
	Sales support

Focal Topics

1. Considering case facts only, what do you see as the major problems for Dan Brice Naturals?

2. Understanding that Dan Brice's research needs to be updated to reflect changes in the 1990s, what consumer research would be useful to Dan Brice Naturals at this time?

3. Suggest a final product line for Dan Brice Naturals to offer. Be sure to explain the importance of each product to the overall mix.

4. From a consumer behavior perspective, evaluate the proposed distribution channel for Dan Brice Naturals. What changes would you make, if any, and why?

5. Based on your knowledge of the industry and the changes which have occurred in the 1990s, would you advise Christina Lane Cosmetics and Dan Brice to go ahead with the project? Why or why not? How might this answer have differed 10 years ago?

■ ■ ■ ■ ■

Liz Claiborne, Inc.

■ ■ ■ ■ ■

From its first days in 1976, the Liz Claiborne team has shared one overriding goal: consumer satisfaction. The company believed that if it concentrated on giving consumers what they wanted when they wanted it, it would be successful. And it did. In the 1980s Liz Claiborne became one of the fastest-growing and most admired companies in the United States. It plans to continue growing in the 1990s by following its proven formula for success. By giving consumers around the world great designs, high quality, and good value, Liz has become the best friend of many women, and now some men.

Retail Industry Outlook

Going-out-of-business signs, bankruptcy filings, and constant sales attest to tough times in the retail industry. Such mercantile faithfuls as B. Altman and Garfinckel's have disappeared. The parent company of Bloomingdale's, Burdine's and Rich's, is in Chapter 11. R.H. Macy & Co. shocked many outsiders when it filed recently for Chapter 11. Rumors abound about other potential casualties and morale for many retail executives is rock bottom. "Retailing is not an area of hope," say Eugene Kosack, chief executive of NBO Stores, Inc., a $100 million apparel chain.

And the casualties are almost certain to keep mounting. By the end of the 1990s, half of the nation's current retailers will be out of business. "The total amount of space will contract and all marginal stuff will just be bulldozed."

Even some of the powerhouses are experiencing slowing growth and are working on more innovations to keep pulling the customers in. The companies that succeed will be the ones that avoid crippling levels of debt, focus tightly on specific customers or products, and hook into technology to hold down costs and enhance service.

It is not surprising that retailers are hurting these days. The economy is in a recession, and employers are announcing layoffs daily. Retail sales have been limping through the last year, and the latest results for chains are not encouraging. A few, such as The Gap, Inc., are reporting double-digit same-store sales. Another powerhouse, The Limited, Inc., slipped 1 percent.

Then there is the debt overload. The top thirty retailers owe more than $60 billion, on which interest rates are as high as 16.5 percent. Two giants, Federated Allied and R.H. Macy, alone account for more than $13 billion of the debt. The two went on a binge of price cutting last Christmas—before Federated-Allied filed for bankruptcy protection—that triggered a promotional meltdown throughout the industry. Retailers and vendors are still recovering from the Yuletide misery. Chain stores are bracing for a repeat this holiday.

A Harris poll conducted recently highlighted a big headache for retailers. Overall 47 percent of those surveyed said they are spending less time shopping. One reason for this is the population's demographic makeup. The prime shopping segment is aging and has less time and less money than most of their parents had. Baby-boomer families are often debt-stressed, time-stressed, and in search of quiet down-time. Consumers are growing more cautious with a lot less interest in flashy consumption. As shop-till-you-drop sprees lose their appeal, wooing such reluctant customers into stores will get tougher.

But one huge problem looms over all the others: overcapacity. There is just too much retail space—more than 18 square feet for every man, woman, and child in the United States, more than double the figure in 1972. This buildup of excess capacity was a long time in the making.

The malling of America started in the 1950s as families flocked to the suburbs. Through the 70s, malls expanded. Specialty retailers opened up stores to sell their moderately priced apparel. Their smaller, more accessible space chipped away at the department stores' customer franchise. But nobody suffered too much, since demand in the 70s grew a healthy 8.6 percent annually. In the 80s, the good times kept on rolling as the service economy flourished, baby-boomers indulged themselves, and consumer spending soared. Success came relatively easy to many up-start franchises. Many department stores prospered as millions of women took their first office jobs and acquired new wardrobes.

The frenzy seemed to peak in 1987. That year, shoppers bought more apparel than ever, and store construction seemed to be the road to riches. The prospect of scoring a 25 percent return by investing in malls attracted billions from pension funds, banks, and free-wheeling savings and loans. Between 1986 and 1989, the number of malls increased 22 percent, to 34,683. But the number of shoppers going to malls every month rose only about 3 percent, according to the International Council of Shopping Centers, the industry trade group. The development appears to have been way out of line with the realities of the retail business. Chain department stores began to compete against one another in a half-mile area. Meanwhile catalogue companies were creating their own glut by mailing up to 14 billion pieces of mail a year, up from 7 billion 10 years ago.

Closing unproductive stores is actually one strategy retailers are trying. Macy's has announced it will shut one I. Magnin location in Chicago and Bullock's in Palm Springs. Two other I. Magnin stores may go. Bloomingdale's has closed locations in Stamford, Connecticut, and Dallas. Its parent, Federated-Allied, says it plans more store closings. Federated, Macy's, and many other chains are also reducing store inventories to make sure they do not have too much merchandise on hand to mark down should Christmas business be poor.

Developers are being squeezed in other ways. Capital for projects has dried up now that many S&Ls are in the hands of government administration, and even healthy banks and thrifts are operating under tighter lending scrutiny. The number of shopping center startups dropped 41 percent in the third quarter from the year before. In Indianapolis, Melvin and Herbert Simon have had to promise personally to reimburse many of the city's costs if their $970 million Circle Centre Mall does not get built.

While keeping an eye on the immediate concerns about the economy and Christmas sales, retail executives are anxiously looking for long-term strategies. The consensus is that retailers who build their original franchise around the broad middle range of the market are most at risk. One reason, say some economists, is that income has been shifting away from the middle class, reducing the purchasing power of these crucial shoppers by billions of dollars.

A lot of middle-of-the-road merchandisers have been struggling for years to defend their market against a host of competitors that offer enormous selection in one category and a broad range of goods at low prices. To avoid second-tier status, some department stores will keep trying to emphasize their own specialties such as image, coatrooms, complimentary coffee, free local phone calls from the dressing rooms, and even diaper changing facilities in both the men's and women's restrooms.

Retailers are huddling with developers on new ways to bring back customers. The most popular ways to bring back and entice bargain hungry shoppers are with small "town square" format clothing stores and outlet malls where makers of brand name apparel and some upscale retailers sell their surplus goods. Another approach is warehouse clubs, a deep discount category that has become a key format of the 90s. Shoppers pay an annual membership fee for access to a warehouse full of name brand household items at very low prices.

Market researchers are predicting that even when the economy strengthens and consumers become more confident, they are not going to be racing to the stores with their wallets open. There are several reasons for this reluctance. One is that Americans already have spent so much on expensive apparel and gadgets. "You haven't touched your bread machine and gelato machine in 6 months," says Susan Hayward, senior vice president at the research firm of Yankelovich Clancy Shulman.

Older shoppers, who are increasing in number, complain that stores still cater too much to younger tastes. In the baby-boom generation, many shoppers are finding that they just do not equate shopping with pleasure anymore. Says Janet Coat, a 34-year-old free-lance writer and mother of two: "Ten years ago, I could shop alone, and it was a leisurely thing. Now I have two toddlers with me, and it's a nerve shattering experience." In a recent survey of women shoppers, 80 percent viewed shopping as annoying but necessary.

How to attract and keep these stressed consumers is a crucial question that is facing the retail industry. The people most likely to benefit from the struggles of the industry will be the shoppers, wooed by even more promotions, better bargains, and more attentive service. Bloomingdale's is emphasizing "kinder and gentler sale." As for retailers, the 1990s are shaping up to be the biggest clearance sale ever.

History

The daughter of a banker at Morgan Guaranty Trust Co., Liz Claiborne spent her early childhood in Brussels before her family moved to New Orleans in 1934. Claiborne returned to Europe to study fine arts in Brussels and later in Nice, although she never received a high-school diploma.

This hardly slowed her down. Liz got her first break in 1949 when she won a design contest sponsored by *Harper's Bazaar* magazine for her sketch of a high-collared coat with a "military feeling." Soon after that, she found work as a sketcher and model in New York's garment district and worked her way through the ranks at several design firms. At one of those, she met Arthur Ortenberg, who hired her as a designer. They were married in 1957.

Claiborne had already earned a reputation as a talented designer. Her creations were not avant-garde, but simple, updated interpretations of classics. She later ran the design room for dress designer Youth Guild for 16 years before she and Ortenberg and manufacturing whiz Leonard Boxer founded Liz Claiborne. One year later, the partners brought in Jerome Chazen, an industry veteran, to oversee marketing. Together they invested $50,000 in personal savings and raised another $200,000 from family and friends.

Founded in 1976, the company has concentrated primarily on identifying and furnishing the wardrobe requirements of the working woman, providing apparel appropriate in a business or professional environment as well as apparel suitable for leisure and casual dressing. Over the years the company believes that it has become the largest "better" women's sportswear and dress company in the United States. The company offers a broad selection of women's sportswear, marketed as related separates, as well as dresses and accessories. The company's better women's sportswear is offered under the company's various trademarks, including Liz Claiborne, Collection, Lizsport, Lizwear, Elisabeth, Liz & Co., and its triangular logo mark.

Sportswear and dresses are offered in "misses" and petite sizes, as well as large sizes. The company offers a higher priced "bridge" line of women's sportswear under the company's Dana Buchman label. The company shipped its first men's collection, under the Claiborne trademark, in 1985, and over the past few years has achieved a strong presence in the men's sportswear business. These collections, which also reflect a component dressing concept, were supplemented in late 1987 with a line of men's furnishings. In 1986, the company shipped its first women's fragrance collection and has since achieved a strong presence in the prestige fragrance market. The company introduced its first men's fragrance collection during 1989. In 1988, the company entered the retail market directly by opening the first of forty retail specialty stores offering collections of casual sportswear under the First Issue trademark. In 1989, the company opened seven prototype retail specialty shops, which carry exclusively Liz Claiborne and Claiborne products. The company also operates twenty-nine outlet stores.

Products

Liz Claiborne products are conceived and marketed as "designer" items, employing a consistent approach to design and quality that is intended to develop and maintain customer recognition and loyalty across product line and from season to season. The company defines its clothing as "updated," combining traditional or classic design with contemporary fashion influences While the company maintains a "designer" image, its products generally have been priced in the "better" apparel range, which is generally less expensive than most designer lines.

Substantially all items in each sportswear collection—sweaters, jackets, pants, skirts, knit tops, and shirts—are sold as "separates" rather than as ensembles such as suits. However, each collection is structured, through the use of related styles, color schemes, and fabrics, to enable the consumer to assemble outfits consisting of separate items designed to be worn together. The company intends to provide the consumer with a wardrobe that can be coordinated with other Claiborne items from season to season.

Sales and Marketing

Substantially all of the company's sales are made to over 12,480 customer accounts operating approximately 20,949 department and specialty stores located in the United States, Canada, the United Kingdom, and Spain.

Approximately 30 percent of the company's sales are made to its ten largest customers, and approximately 83 percent to its 100 largest customers; no single customer accounts for more than 5 percent of sales. However, many of Claiborne's customers are under common ownership. When considered together as a group under common ownership, sales to the eleven department stores owned by the May Department Store account for approximately 17 percent of sales; sales to the three department store customers that are owned by R.H. Macy & Co., Inc., account for approximately 10 percent of sales. While Liz Claiborne believes that, in general, buying decisions are currently made independently by each department store customer, in some situations the trend may be toward more centralized buying decisions among customers under common control.

Manufacturing

Liz Claiborne does not own any manufacturing facilities; all of its products are manufactured through arrangements with independent suppliers. It allocates production among suppliers based on a number of criteria, including availability of production requirements on relatively short notice and, with respect to foreign suppliers, their possession of the necessary quota allocation to enable the finished product to be imported into the United States.

A very substantial portion of the company's sales is represented by products produced abroad, primarily in the Far East. Its apparel, accessory products, and shoes are manufactured by approximately 350 suppliers, of which approximately fifty-one are domestic suppliers and the balance of which are located abroad, mainly in Hong Kong, South Korea, Taiwan, Indonesia, Thailand, the Philippines, and China. Approximately 38 percent of Claiborne's purchases of finished products are manufactured by its ten largest suppliers. The company purchases from its suppliers through individual purchase orders specifying the price and quantity of the items to be produced. It does not have any long-term, formal arrangements with any of the suppliers that manufacture its products. Claiborne believes that it is the largest customer of many of its manufacturing suppliers and considers its relations with suppliers to be satisfactory.

The company has been considering plant ownership particularly of knitwear factories with a healthy mix of domestic and overseas facilities. Factory ownership would enable Claiborne to respond more quickly to what the consumer wants and to impose tighter controls on deliveries for even better coordination.

The company obtains fabrics, trimmings, and other materials used in the apparel products in bulk from various suppliers. Virtually all of the fabric used in Claiborne apparel products are purchased from approximately 300 suppliers, approximately 170 of which are located primarily in Hong Kong, Japan, Taiwan, and Italy. The company does not have any long-term, formal arrangements with any of its suppliers of raw materials.

Claiborne operates under a substantial time constraint. In order to deliver, in a timely manner, merchandise that reflects current tastes, the company attempts to schedule a substantial portion of its materials and manufacturing commitments relatively late in the production cycle, thereby favoring suppliers able to make quick adjustments in response to changing production needs. However, in order to secure necessary materials and manufacturing facilities, the company must make substantial advance commitments, often as much as seven months prior to the receipt of firm orders from customers for the items to be produced. In order to support the company's continued sales growth, the company has generally been required to increase its inventory levels and commitments in order to support continued expansion, both of existing and new product lines. If the company should misjudge the market for particular product groups, it could be faced with substantial outstanding fabric and/or manufacturing commitments as well as excess merchandise inventories.

Domestic suppliers' operations are monitored by staff members based at Claiborne's New Jersey facilities; with respect to foreign suppliers' operations, these tasks are performed by company personnel based at company offices in Hong Kong, India, Taipei, Taiwan, Manila, The Philippines, Indonesia, Shanghai, Singapore, Sri Lanka, Portugal, Dominican Republic, Jamaica, Guatemala, Colombia, Brazil, Costa Rica, and Thailand, as well as by independent agents performing services in Korea, Spain, Italy, and Japan.

All finished goods are shipped to company distribution facilities for reinspection and distribution. Apparel items are generally reshipped to customers in groups consisting of coordinated items intended to be sold together.

Distribution

Liz Claiborne receives shipments from over 350 suppliers to its distribution centers located in New Jersey, Pennsylvania, and New York. The distribution process is made simple due to the fact that Claiborne customers must take order of a whole line of coordinates—blouses, skirts, pants, and accessories.

With the retail merchandise industry concentrated in New Jersey and New York, many large department stores coordinate their shipments using third-party truck companies located in that region. Other customers such as Marshall Field's have direct shipments to their distribution centers located in Chicago and in some cases directly to the stores.

Claiborne employs no regional warehouse, and therefore must make continual deliveries to maintain its 2- to 3-week infusion of new clothing. The cost of these deliveries is absorbed by the customer. The company has managed to reduce its average inventory on hand to 59.8 days, down from 67.2 days. But that is still well above the industry levels of about 47 days.

It now takes an average of about 66 weeks from the time chemicals are converted into apparel fibers to the time a consumer buys a garment at retail. Using a computerized system called Systematically Updated Retail Feedback (SURF), Claiborne is able to know what merchandise has been sold in a cross section of stores each week. SURF provides weekly reports on what is hot and what is not, allowing the company to sort and deliver fast moving merchandise to particular department stores. This system has not been rolled out to all Claiborne customer accounts, yet the company is looking to integrate new technology into its manufacturing and transportation operations.

Sales in Core Business

Now, Claiborne and her management team are being tested as never before. Sales in retail are stalling, inventories bulging, and operating margins narrowing. In 1988, for the first time ever, Liz Claiborne's net earnings dipped by an estimated 11 percent to $102 million.

What is ailing Liz Claiborne may be more serious than the dismal retailing environment. The company's women's sportswear business, which accounts for 60 percent of total revenues, is maturing. After years of 20 percent increases, sportswear sales increased by 16 percent in 1991 and by 17 percent in 1990. Now a giant by industry standards, Liz Claiborne controls an estimated one-third of the $2 billion market for better women's sportswear including missy and petite sizes. The company sells its garments though some 12,480 retailers, most in existing prime locations.

Because it is already so dominant in its market, sales gains will be increasingly hard to come by. Admits Claiborne, "We are physically limited in our ability to grow." But at maturity, women's sportswear alone had sales of $1.15 billion. There are more new products on the drawing board. In 1989 the company introduced a line of large-size women's clothing under the name Elisabeth. There are an estimated 35 to 40 million women in the United States who wear a size 14 or larger, and Liz Claiborne, with its strong presence in traditional department stores, should grab a sizable chunk of that $10 billion market. But the large-size niche is already crowded with competition. In 1991 the Elisabeth division had sales of $130.5 million.

Children's Market

Gone are the days when the younger kids dressed in a cousin's hand-me-down and prayed for a two wheeler at Christmas. Spending on kids is now one of the fastest growing sectors of the American economy. At a time when economic growth is crawling along at roughly 2 percent, spending on kids jumped an estimated 25 percent in 1991, to $60 billion. The kiddie market is expected to hit $75 billion by 1992, approaching 2 percent of the entire economy.

Adding to the spending trend, many affluent families are having only one or two children, meaning more money to lavish on each child. A well-equipped child has become a status symbol in some circles. Spending in this market on recreation and entertainment has well surpassed clothing, about 80 percent to 20 percent, respectively. Children's clothes manufacturing is dominated by companies such as Oshkosh B'Gosh. Though Claiborne sales reached a 1986 high of $16.4 million, presently the company is not in pursuit of this market.

Men's Market

Consistent with Claiborne's approach to component dressing for women, the menswear division offers it customers a broad selection of related separates—sweaters, pants, shirts, and jackets—and expanded its product offerings in 1987 to include men's furnishings, including men's dress shirts and neckwear. This division has steadily increased in sales to reach $124.6 million in 1991, an increase of 1.9 percent from 1990.

Many department stores have realized the potential of this market and plan to broaden the selection of men's clothing and install menswear boutiques. Specialty apparel companies such as The Limited and Brooks Brothers have taken special interest in this market. Brooks Brothers, along with its increased men's line, is offering smaller sizes to target the growing number of women who shop for polo and boxer shorts in the men's department. Some of the Claiborne for Men fashion items are shown in Exhibit 20.1.

Fragrances

In September 1986, ten years after entering the fashion scene with a line of stylish, comfortable, and affordable clothes for America's working women, Liz Claiborne introduced its first women's fragrance. Designed to be part of a woman's way of living, the energy and spontaneity of the fragrance make it appropriate for all occasions. Packaged in colorful, lacquer triangles, Liz Claiborne's signature scent is green, fruity and free spirited.

The success of the Claiborne fragrance inspired a complementary men's fragrance, Claiborne for Men, in Autumn 1989. The formula combines herbal, floral, and woodsy scents to produce a fresh and energetic scent.

The company's next entry in the fragrance category proved again Liz Claiborne's ability to read, interpret, and respond to the consumer. Noting a shift in the attitudes of American women toward family and relationships, satisfaction in their accomplishments, and the value of privacy, Liz Claiborne Cosmetics introduced "Realities." "Realities," a vibrant mix of floral and warm oriental scents, further demonstrates Liz Claiborne's commitment to the fragrance market. All Claiborne fragrances are available in fine department and specialty stores nationwide.

International Market

Liz Claiborne is poised to become one of the best-known fashion labels in the world. In 1988 Claiborne pursued international expansion. Within the 4 years that they launched into the Canadian market, Claiborne has become the number 1 label. It increased its Canadian volume by widening the range of products, gaining floor space, and selling to more retailers and attracting more customers.

International sales expanded steadily. In 1991, they grew by 48.2 percent to $83.6 million. This figure includes Great Britain and Spain, which Liz Claiborne pursued in 1991. Knowing that European women tend to be either very conservative or fashion forward, Claiborne was able to fill a European niche of aspirational clothing that is accessible to the international market.

■ **EXHIBIT 20.1   Tradition Updated**

Glen plaid single-breasted sportcoat in sable, in cotton/rayon/silk, $145.
English blue cotton windbreaker, $125. Blue long-sleeve cotton polo shirt, $52.
Crepe herringbone pant in sable, $80.

Photographer: Peter Zander. Courtesy of Liz Claiborne, Inc.

Publicity

Liz Claiborne has kept the fashion industry informed of changes occurring in the company and in its fashion offering. Some of the press releases used by Liz Claiborne are featured in the following pages.

Claiborne Retail Division

First Issue

Liz Claiborne's most ambitious move is into retailing. The company opened its first retail store, called First Issue, in February 1988. The specialty stores carry casual, moderately priced women's sportswear. In contrast to Liz Claiborne apparel, First Issue delivers a new line of coordinates to its stores every 2 months. Shipping more often keeps First Issue merchandise exciting and fresh.

The cost to maintain the independent operations of First Issue are of great concern to Claiborne management. There are currently thirty-nine First Issue stores with expansion plans for additional stores.

Claiborne Exclusively

During 1988, Liz Claiborne developed its concepts and strategies for company-operated specialty stores. A total of eighteen such stores, which carry company products exclusively, were opened. These stores are of three different types: (1) an approximately 10,000–12,000-square-foot store, under the name Liz Claiborne, which carries the full line of Liz Claiborne women's apparel, accessories, jewelry, shoes, sunglasses, hosiery, and fragrances; (2) an approximately 6,000-square-foot store under the name Liz Claiborne, which carries company sportswear, career dresses, shoes, and accessories; and (3) an approximately 4,000-square-foot-store, operating under the name Claiborne, which carries men's sportswear and furnishings as well as Elisabeth, which carries large-size apparel. Each store cost about $2.5 million to construct and carries approximately $1–2 million in inventory.

Though fully owned by Liz Claiborne, Inc., the specialty stores place orders and receive delivery of goods the same as would any other customer. No special distribution network or system has been established to accommodate these stores. Transportation costs are passed to each store, which increases its cost. To provide a controlled retail channel of distribution for the excess inventory generated by the company's manufacturing and wholesale operations, twenty-nine Liz Claiborne outlet stores are open at present, in areas where they will not compete with department and specialty store customers.

First Issue and retail specialty stores added $80 million in sales, but have not contributed to profits. The outlet store, requiring less investment, generated $82 million in sales.

■ **EXHIBIT 20.2   Liz Claiborne Press Release**

Liz claiborne

FOR IMMEDIATE RELEASE   JULY 1992
CONTACT: SARAH PATTERSON
212-626-5644

FALL '92 AT LIZ CLAIBORNE
A MERGING OF OPPOSITES
REDEFINES MODERN STYLE

Understated/luxurious. Tailored/feminine. Relaxed/polished. Fashion
transforms opposing inspirations into elegant statements of modern
style. These are clothes rich in cut, shape and fabric but minimal
in decoration. Deftly-shaped jackets top beautifully draped skirts
of all lengths. Colors complement clean-lined silhouettes: neutrals
and organic tones, deep, saturated brights, and classics like
heather grey, navy and khaki.

The new luxury. You see it in soft mixes of tone-on-tone neutrals,
like the layers of oatmeal and cream from **Collection**. A plush
cabled pullover, matching short-sleeve shell and soft wool flannel
trousers are all part of the new language of understatement. Animal
patterns come into play, too: a vicuna-colored short-sleeve
lambswool shell tops a tonal animal patterned jacquard knit skirt.
Black balances camel in a houndstooth jacket over a cotton winter
T-shirt and crepe pleated skirt, both in black. Dressing up is
simple, comfortable, never overdone.

His for her. Borrowing from the boys no longer means androgyny. Now
it's feminine, sexy, as seen in the casually dressed up, tough
meets tender look from **Lizwear**: the belted black leather jacket
with asymmetrical closure over a black stretch lace T-shirt and a
black georgette gently flared skirt. **Lizsport** takes a more spirited
approach to menswear-inspired style with a navy double-breasted pea
coat over a red crested cotton tunic sweater and plaid shorts.

Casual panache. From **Lizwear**, a more rugged point of view: a brown
parkskin sueded fringed jacket over the indigo denim shirt-style
bodysuit and navy corduroy slim pants, or a tooled parkskin vest
worn with the denim shirt-style bodysuit and Navaho-patterned
sarong skirt. For the ultimate in comfort, **Lizsport Elements**
continues to provide high performance fashion. Ski-inspired
activewear includes warm-up suits, T-shirts and a sleek unitard,
all in navy, yellow and orange with high-tech silver accents.

\# \# \#

212 354 4900
TELEX 621067 LIZCLAY

LIZ CLAIBORNE INC

1441 BROADWAY
NEW YORK 10018

Courtesy of Liz Claiborne, Inc.

Manufacturers versus Retailers

Though few people expect manufacturers to open hundreds of stores,
their move into retailing worries department store and specialty retailers. Department stores depend on designer clothes for much of their sales,
and privately there is a lot of grumbling about the new competition.

■ **EXHIBIT 20.3   Liz & Co. Press Release**

FOR IMMEDIATE RELEASE   JULY 1992
CONTACT: SARAH PATTERSON
PUBLIC RELATIONS
212-626-5644

FALL '92 AT LIZ & CO:
SOPHISTICATED KNIT DRESSING
WHERE COMFORT COUNTS

This season, relaxed dressing is no longer just leggings and a
T-shirt. At Liz & Co., dressing casually now means familiar,
comfortable shapes detailed with a more sophisticated flair:
richly patterned sweaters with whipstitching and embroidery, Henley
T-shirts with tooled buttons, sweatshirts updated with jean jacket
styling. The result is more fashion impact--and more fashion
mileage--from clothes that not only look good. They simply feel
great.

Sweaters are anything but basic this season. Festive patterns and
details are inspired from the American Southwest: a Western stripe
pullover with whipstitching and wooden beading, an Indian striped
cardigan, a Santa Fe star intarsia pullover. Colors, too, have a
Western sensibility--chili, navy, harvest green and Indian corn.
They're warm and wonderful in a plush blanket pattern jacket in
polar fleece. Tooled silver-toned buttons give a rugged slant to a
Henley shirt. Double knit cotton stirrup pants or Liz & Co.'s
signature sandwashed and bleached indigo denim jeans complete the
look.

At Liz & Co., style and comfort are one and the same. Sporty pieces
in cotton French terry are soft, modern--like the soft white
turtleneck over matching sweatpants. Colors--red, black, denim blue
and soft white--may be traditional but details are definitely
unique. Jean jacket styling updates the zip-front hooded denim-
colored jacket. Zippers and zipper pulls are pewter-toned for a
bold statement. Even the dependable hooded sweatshirt in red has a
zip neck for a fresh point of view. What to wear with them:
sweatpants with ribbed trim or stirrup pants in French terry and
spandex. The look is relaxed and easy. That's Liz & Co.'s style.

# # #

Liz & Co.
Liz Claiborne Inc.
1441 Broadway
New York, NY 10018
212 · 354 · 4900
Fax 212 · 626 · 1815

Courtesy of Liz Claiborne, Inc.

"Manufacturers and retailers are in a state of undeclared war," says a retail consultant.

Some department store officials concede that they are not thrilled
about having to compete more with their key vendors. "Stores like to develop exclusivity, and that works better when there are fewer outlets selling

Luggage-colored tooled vest in sueded parkskin, $160. Indigo denim shirt-style cotton bodysuit, $54, over ivory scoopneck cotton bodysuit with lace trim, $36, and multicolor Navajo ikat stripe cotton sarong skirt, $66. All items except vest available in Petite.

Luggage-colored fringed jacket in sueded parkskin, $295. Indigo denim shirt-style cotton bodysuit, $54. Ivory scoopneck cotton bodysuit with lace trim, $36. Navy cotton corduroy slim pant, $58. Outfit available in Petite.

Photographer: Pierre Scherman. Courtesy of Liz Claiborne, Inc.

■ **EXHIBIT 20.5   Western Edge**

Top left: Multicolor stripe cotton sweater with whip stitching and wooden beading, $94. Navy double knit cotton stirrup pants, $58. Top right: Multicolor stripe cotton V-neck cardigan, $84, with 5-pocket jeans in sandwashed and bleached cotton denim, $48. Navy cotton jersey turtleneck, $38. Bottom right: Navy cotton star intarsia sweater, $76. Navy double knit cotton stirrup pants, $58. Bottom left: Navy cotton Henley with pewter-colored tooled buttons, $40. 5-pocket jeans in sandwashed and bleached cotton denim, $48. Bleached white cotton T-shirt, $30, and plush blanket patterned polar fleece jacket, in polyester, $120.

Photographer: Neil Kirk. Courtesy of Liz Claiborne, Inc.

■ **EXHIBIT 20.6   Cocktail Shakers**

Black shawl collar dress with sheer sleeves, gold tone rimmed faux pearl buttons, back princess seaming and flared skirt. In satin-back crepe, $198. Accessories from Liz Claiborne.

Photographer: Tom Fogliani. Courtesy of Liz Claiborne, Inc.

the same thing," says David CarChuff of Marshall Field's. Many manufacturers introduce hundreds of styles of clothes each season, but department stores carry only a relatively small sample that they think will be sure sellers.

Through their own stores, apparel companies also gain bigger profit margins. Though their prices generally are comparable to those at department stores, manufacturers get more of each sales dollar because there are no intermediaries. Moreover, in their own stores, manufacturers can control markdown activity. They say they can outdo department stores by providing a better ambiance with a broader selection of merchandise, better displays, and more attentive service.

Many department store executives maintain that shoppers prefer to see a lot of brands in one place. The time-pressed shopper wants an edited selection of designer lines.

Specialty stores continue to eat into department store sales. Between 1980 and 1985, large specialty store chains increased their retail market share by a third, to 19.2 percent, while department stores slipped. "The wave of mergers is likely to continue as the growth of specialty stores outpaces the growth of the shopping dollar," says Kurt Barnard of Retail Marketing Report. But the pace may slow. Carl Steidtmann, Management Horizon's chief economist, noted that specialty stores are more vulnerable to slowdowns in the economy.

Focal Topics

1. What factors account for the long-term success of Liz Claiborne when other retailers are experiencing tough times?

2. Which brands have the most potential for increasing profits for Liz Claiborne in the long run? Why?

3. Should Liz Claiborne devote substantial resources to its retail division? Why or why not?

4. In view of the success Liz Claiborne has had in women's product lines, can this success be transmitted to men's product lines? What types of activities will facilitate this transition?

■ ■ ■ ■ ■

Marketing a City— Discover Columbus

■ ■ ■ ■ ■

Nonprofit marketing is one of the fastest growing forms of marketing activity. Marketing is practiced by hospitals, charitable organizations, social movements, religious organizations, and many others. It is logical, therefore, that marketing concepts also be adopted by cities and other geographic entities.

Background of Central Ohio Marketing Council

The Central Ohio Marketing Council (COMC) was formed in 1984 for the express purpose of focusing and maximizing marketing efforts for the Greater Columbus area. By combining the strengths of several organizations, which in the past individually marketed central Ohio, duplication of effort was reduced and higher quality messages were communicated to various target markets. Additionally, the COMC assured a cohesive and consistent information flow, enabling each organization to utilize standardized statistical figures for various visitor and economic development needs.

The organization's mission is as follows:

> *To achieve worldwide recognition that the Greater Columbus area is one of the best in which to work, visit and live.*

This mission was accomplished with a thorough and continuously changing marketing plan that communicated central Ohio's strengths through proactive, aggressive programming of two types. As an initiator, COMC took the lead role in funding and accomplishing defined COMC marketing programs, and as a coordinating agency, COMC oversaw the development of cooperative marketing programs. The staff consisted of an executive director and an administrative assistant, housed in the Columbus Visitors Center. The organization was administered by a board of directors appointed by the four funding agencies.

COMC operated on $250,000 annually in seed money pledged through its four sponsoring organizations:

- City of Columbus $100,000
- Greater Columbus Convention and Visitors Bureau   50,000
- Chamber of Commerce   50,000
- Franklin County   50,000

These monies were used to initiate COMC projects and to cover operating costs of the staff and office. To supplement the $250,000, COMC generated additional resources from donated or in-kind services or materials and corporate participation. The total value of the COMC's 1989 coordinated programs exceeded $2 million. Hundreds of programs were undertaken by other organizations that would otherwise have been only ideas without the coordinating and facilitating efforts of the COMC.

Marketing Objectives

The COMC identified objectives for the organization, as follows:

1. To identify and develop conditions in the Greater Columbus area that work toward attracting firms and organizations considering location of new facilities.

2. To identify and develop conditions in the Greater Columbus area likely to contribute to growth in size and profitability of firms located in Columbus.

3. To develop beliefs among businesses and other organizations that Columbus is an excellent host city for conventions, seminars, and other meetings.

4. To develop beliefs among American workers and Columbus area citizens that Columbus offers thriving economic conditions.

5. To identify the educational resources of the Columbus area and encourage their use as a business development tool.

6. To develop a growing impact on the Columbus area through increased arts activities and attendance; increased use of Columbus area cultural attractions in the tourism and convention industry; and an enhanced image nationally for the Columbus area cultural activities in order to aid in attracting and retaining businesses and their employees.

7. To enhance the quality of life in the Columbus area by housing neighborhood and community-oriented activities and special events.

Benchmarks for Measurement

The following benchmarks represent goals originally drafted in 1985 to be achieved in the 1990s. The benchmarks were used in establishing and guiding every COMC program.

1. Measured belief by 50 percent or more of top executives in identified companies that "Columbus is an excellent city in which to locate a facility."

2. Measured belief by 50 percent or more of top executives in identified companies ranking Columbus in the top twenty cities to be considered by firms for location of new facilities.

3. Measured belief by 50 percent or more of top executives in identified companies indicating awareness of specified Columbus attributes important to location decisions.

4. Measured belief by 75 percent or more of identified top executives in Columbus business firms that the environment for growth in size and profitability in Columbus is good or excellent.

5. Measured belief by 75 percent or more of identified executives in Columbus nonbusiness organizations that the environment for growth in size and attaining organizational objectives in Columbus is good or excellent.

6. Measured belief by 50 percent or more of executives in important nonbusiness organizations outside of the CMH (Columbus Metro Habitat) ranking Columbus in the top twenty cities to be considered by firms for location of new facilities.

7. Measured belief by 67 percent of executives responsible for planning meetings that Columbus is an excellent city for meetings and by 40 percent that Columbus is one of the ten best cities to consider for a meeting location.

8. Measured belief by 40 percent of a representative sample of the general public that Columbus is an interesting and exciting place they would personally like to visit and by 25 percent that Columbus is one of the ten cities they would most like to visit.

9. Measured belief by 50 percent of a representative sample of workers that Columbus is an excellent place to work now and in the future.

10. Measured belief by 75 percent of Columbus area residents that employment opportunities will be excellent in the future.

11. Measured belief by 67 percent of Columbus area residents that Columbus is a better city in which to live than other cities.

12. Measured belief by 67 percent of Columbus area residents that Columbus is a good place to start and grow a business.

13. Measured belief by 75 percent of Columbus area residents that educational facilities and opportunities in Columbus are good to excellent.

14. Measured belief by 67 percent of Columbus area residents that cultural arts facilities and activities in Columbus are good to excellent.

15. Measured awareness by 80 percent of Columbus area residents of specific visitor attractions.

Research

In 1985, one of the COMC's first projects was to do extensive marketing research. Market Group One, a marketing research and consulting firm, was engaged to interview 500 key executives and 1,400 consumers in a representative national survey to determine their perceptions of Columbus. COMC discovered that the majority of people had a neutral attitude toward Columbus resulting from little knowledge about the area. Further research identified ten central Ohio attributes, including a high quality of life and an attractive business environment, and eight target markets including local, national, and international business decision makers. Therefore, the COMC realized that its task was to build a favorable Columbus image based upon the identified attributes and to focus on the revealed target markets.

The 1985 study of business decision makers was repeated in 1988. This study was conducted by telephone with executives from small, medium, and large-sized companies nationwide. The objective of the call was to survey either the chief executive officer/president/owner or the person responsible for business location decisions. By using the same survey instrument and methodology, information obtained in 1988 could be compared with 1985 data. Demographic analysis of the responses revealed a representative sample based on geographic area, size of firm, and types of business. The results of the 1985 and 1988 surveys are presented in Exhibits 21.1 through 21.10.

■ **EXHIBIT 21.1** **Attributes Influencing the Business Location Decision Process**

	Mean Rating*	
Attribute	**1985**	**1988**
Labor force	4.04	4.23†
Operating costs	3.84	4.17†
Accessibility to markets	3.85	3.97†
Economic growth	3.74	3.84†
Quality of life	3.84	3.81
Community's attitude toward business	3.81	3.80
Taxes	3.64	3.75†
Proximity to suppliers	3.01	3.25†
Availability of technology	3.17	3.14

*Mean based on a scale of 1 to 5 where 1 = not important and 5 = very important.

†The changes in means are statistically significant at a 95% confidence level using a t-test of significance.

▪ EXHIBIT 21.2 National Perceptions of Columbus's Attributes

	Mean Rating*	
Attribute	1985	1988
Community's attitude toward business	2.24	3.58
Accessibility to markets	2.60	3.50
Availability of technology	2.34	3.49
Labor force	2.02	3.41
Quality of life	2.12	3.40
Economic growth	2.07	3.37
Proximity to suppliers	2.34	3.33
Operating costs	1.77	3.33
Taxes	1.41	3.13

*Mean based on a scale of 1 to 5 where 1 = low and 5 = high.

NOTE: The change in every mean is statistically significant at a 95% confidence level using a t-test of significance.

▪ EXHIBIT 21.3 The Most Attractive Cities for Locating a Business in 1985 and 1988

	Percentage Selecting City as One of the Three Most Desirable Places to Locate a Business	
City	1985	1988
Atlanta	21%	27%
Los Angeles	10	14
Chicago	9	13
Dallas	21	11
San Francisco	12	10
San Diego	7	9
Boston	8	8
New York City	11	8
Houston	8	5
Charlotte	7	5
Denver	6	5
Philadelphia	2	4
Tampa	7	4
Orlando	4	3
Columbus	3	3
Indianapolis	3	3
Raleigh	4	3
Kansas City	2	2
San Antonio	3	2
Austin	7	1

■ **EXHIBIT 21.4**   **Comparison of Columbus to Other Cities as a Place to Locate a Business in 1985 and 1988**

Columbus is better, about the same as, or worse than . . .

City	Percent Better		Percent Same		Percent Worse	
	1985	1988	1985	1988	1985	1988
Atlanta	9%	12%	16%	17%	60%	60%
Baltimore	40	37	24	27	16	22
Boston	25	36	15	14	43	38
Chicago	26	31	17	13	43	45
Cincinnati	22	22	45	46	12	18
Cleveland	49	46	27	33	6	9
Detroit	65	63	12	13	7	13
Houston	20	31	17	17	48	40
Indianapolis	19	23	48	46	13	17
Los Angeles	22	35	7	6	56	46
New Orleans	28	36	18	14	36	38
Phoenix	13	18	17	18	51	50
Pittsburgh	37	40	31	30	15	17
San Antonio	18	31	18	19	43	35
Seattle	21	22	20	22	39	41

■ **EXHIBIT 21.5**   **Attributes Influencing the Convention Location Decision Process**

Attribute	Mean Rating*	
	1985	1988
Hotel/meeting facilities	3.98	4.58†
Airline availability	4.22	4.43†
Safety	3.66	3.84†
Climate	3.44	3.65†
Friendliness of people	3.49	3.59†
Cultural life	3.10	3.28†
Quality of life	3.34	3.23†
Entertainment	2.87	3.16†
Shopping	2.65	2.58

*Mean based on a scale of 1 to 5 where 1 = not important and 5 = very important.

†The changes in means are statistically significant at a 95% confidence level using a t-test of significance.

■ EXHIBIT 21.6   National Perceptions of Columbus's Attributes

	Mean Rating*	
Attribute	1985	1988
Friendliness of people	2.53	3.72
Safety	2.19	3.53
Quality of life	2.12	3.40
Hotel/meeting facilities	1.79	3.15
Airline availability	2.26	3.00
Shopping	1.75	3.04
Cultural life	1.93	2.99
Entertainment	1.51	2.64
Climate	2.03	2.59

*Mean based on a scale of 1 to 5 where 1 = low and 5 = high.

NOTE: The change in every mean is statistically significant at a 95% confidence level using a t-test of significance.

■ EXHIBIT 21.7   National Attitudes toward Columbus as a Place to Locate a New Business and Hold a Convention

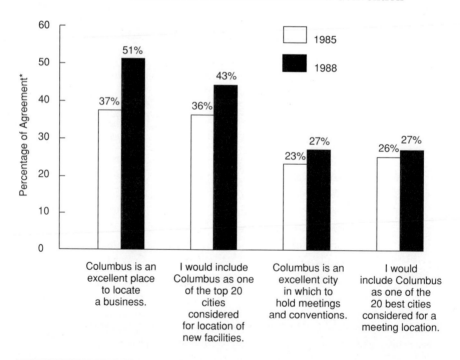

*Percentage of Agreement equals the collapsed categories of "Strongly Agree" and "Agree."

■ **EXHIBIT 21.8**   **The Most Desirable Cities for Holding a Business Meeting/Convention in 1985 and 1988**

City	Percentage Selecting City as One of the Three Most Desirable Places to Hold a Business Meeting/Convention	
	1985	1988
San Francisco	39%	36%
Atlanta	18	30
Chicago	24	27
San Diego	14	16
New York City	21	15
Dallas	18	13
New Orleans	12	13
Las Vegas	8	13
Orlando	7	11
Boston	11	11
Los Angeles	12	8
Phoenix	10	8
Honolulu	3	5
Seattle	1	5
Denver	6	4
Houston	4	3
Nashville	1	3
St. Louis	3	3
Palm Springs	1	2
Miami	6	2
San Antonio	1	2
Tampa	3	2
Ft. Lauderdale	2	1
Detroit	1	1
Indianapolis	1	1
Minneapolis	1	1
Philadelphia	1	1
Tucson	1	0
Other Hawaii	2	0
Washington, DC	5	0

■ **EXHIBIT 21.9** Comparison of Columbus to Other Cities as a
Place to Locate a Business Meeting/Convention

Columbus is better, about the same as, or worse than . . .

City	Percent Better		Percent Same		Percent Worse	
	1985	1988	1985	1988	1985	1988
Atlanta	6%	6%	11%	13%	67%	67%
Baltimore	28	27	26	26	25	31
Boston	13	17	14	15	55	53
Chicago	15	16	12	10	57	59
Cincinnati	21	19	47	45	12	20
Cleveland	43	41	31	33	8	11
Detroit	54	53	17	17	12	15
Houston	15	21	17	20	51	44
Indianapolis	18	23	47	44	14	17
Los Angeles	13	17	5	8	66	60
New Orleans	11	15	10	12	61	59
Phoenix	7	13	15	15	58	57
Pittsburgh	33	38	32	30	16	15
San Antonio	16	21	18	20	44	41
Seattle	16	18	21	21	43	43

■ **EXHIBIT 21.10** What Comes to Mind When You
Hear "Columbus, Ohio"?

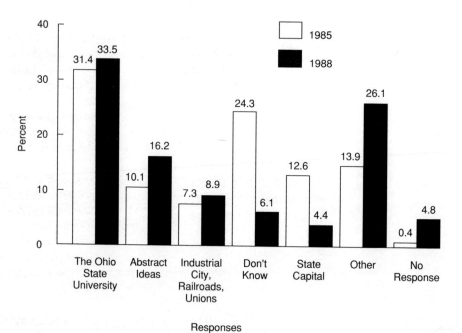

Strategy

The COMC structured its marketing strategy into a plan based on the theme: Discover Columbus. The purpose was to establish favorable, general awareness of Columbus. This purpose was based upon the 1985 research, which indicated that most people had little awareness of Columbus beyond The Ohio State University presence.

The COMC adopted Roy Lichtenstein's "Brushstrokes in Flight" sculpture as its logo for the city and as a marketing tool for the Discover Columbus phase because the contemporary artwork symbolizes the dynamic, progressive nature of Columbus. Lichtenstein, one of the top pop artists in the world, received his B.A. and M.A. degrees from The Ohio State University. The logo proved more controversial than the Eiffel Tower, however, with some people expressing satisfaction that a major piece of art was chosen to serve as a symbol for the city and other people unhappy because they did not understand or like the meaning of contemporary art. The COMC developed Columbus theme merchandise combining the logo with "Discover Columbus." The COMC produced brochures and movies promoting the quality of life in Columbus, featuring prominently the Lichtenstein "Brushstrokes" logo.

The COMC strategy was designed to produce a single, coordinated marketing effort to accommodate the interests of the four parent bodies. One of the primary tasks was to reduce duplication of marketing efforts of each of the organizations.

Programs and Major Accomplishments

During its first 4 years, the Marketing Council developed and implemented a number of marketing programs and initiatives, including the following:

- Convincing local companies to spend more than $500,000 on national advertising, incorporating the "Discover Columbus" theme and graphic, in such publications as *Forbes* and *Fortune* magazines, a marketing campaign that has resulted, over 2 years, in more than 9,000 inquiries from all over the world;

- Maintaining a public relations program to keep Columbus and central Ohio "in the news," a program that has reached more than 22 million readers. While there have been literally hundreds of electronic and print media "placements," among the most highly visible have been a *USA Today* insert and a 1989 *Newsweek* cover story, including Columbus as one of "America's 10 Hot Cities." *Newsweek* alone reached more than 3 million readers;

- Developing "Discover Columbus" as a common marketing theme and "Brushstrokes in Flight" as a common marketing graphic;

- Publishing and distributing two editions of a "Quality of Life" brochure;

- Producing and distributing "Discover Columbus—The Movie" film and videocassette;
- Licensing the production and causing the distribution of such theme merchandise as T-shirts, matches, mugs, key chains, golf balls, pens, and a trivia game to advance the "Discover Columbus" marketing theme and graphic;
- Conducting seminars for professional and community groups to encourage unified marketing efforts;
- Initiating a "Walking Ambassadors" program to provide Columbus and central Ohio business leaders, community leaders, and other individuals with a variety of marketing materials, including fact cards, "Quality of Life" brochures, and theme merchandise;
- Facilitating the translation of marketing materials into various foreign languages for use by local businesses involved in international markets;
- Participating in educational awareness programs with such groups as the Columbus public schools system, The Ohio State University, and the Columbus Board of Realtors;
- Facilitating the publication of a health care brochure to inform target markets about the high quality and reasonable cost of health care in Columbus and central Ohio;
- Participating in numerous special events including "The Brushstrokes Challenge," the Columbus Day Greeting Card Program, visits by national and international dignitaries, editors and writers, and business decision makers;
- Participating with local companies in developing uses for the "Discover Columbus" theme and graphic including their use on annual reports, corporate letterhead, airplanes, truck trailers, postage meters, advertisements, and hot air balloons.

In 1989, the COMC was at a point of evaluation. Was the marketing program on target? Was it cost effective? What should be done next? In the midst of planning by COMC, officials of the City of Columbus announced that they might have difficulty funding their part of the budget in the future because of the need to use city funds for other services provided to citizens of the city. Thus, there was need for justifying the use of taxpayer funds for activities such as marketing the city.

After many efforts to raise the required funds, COMC was dissolved in 1990. While everyone involved, including city officials and the mayor of Columbus, understood the need for such an organization and saw firsthand the results it produced, no one was able to pledge additional funds to sponsor it. Columbus had begun to shed its cow-town image, but could it continue to mature as gracefully as it had in the last decade?

The early 1990s brought with it much praise for the city as it was deemed, again, to be one of the nation's leading information centers housing organizations such as Battelle, OCLC, CompuServe, and Goal Systems. Columbus was also tagged as "the one city in America that managers consistently resist moving away from."[1] Its business environment and city leadership guided Columbus to develop jobs at triple the national average and boast unemployment averages of only 4 percent for more than a decade. Businesses continue to locate in Columbus for reasons such as its high quality of life.

The "Brushstrokes" logo for Columbus was eventually dropped from all marketing literature because of controversy surrounding the original piece of art. The logo has not been replaced. The organizations involved in COMC in the past are now all using their own versions of a Columbus logo. This means the chamber of commerce, the city of Columbus, and the convention bureau are all using different symbols to market the same product, the city of Columbus. Exhibit 21.11 shows an ad for Columbus. It incorporates a proposed new logo at the bottom reading: "Columbus America . . . discover the best."

1992: Celebrations and Reorganizations

The 1992 celebration marking the 500th anniversary of Columbus's discovery of America was designed by community officials to showcase Columbus to the rest of the nation. Columbus planned a celebration of national proportions and needed to determine the nature of that celebration and how to attract the nation to the city. While Columbus had discovered America 500 years ago, it was time for America to discover Columbus.

One of the most important elements of 1992 was AmeriFlora, an international floral event traditionally held in Europe. For the first time in history an American city would host the event. A major portion of central Columbus was turned into a giant exposition, designed to attract the general public as well as persons with floral and horticultural interests. The exhibit consisted of 88 acres of over a million flowers and featured almost 60,000 entertainers and entertainment acts in its 6-month duration. The focal point of the exhibition was "NavStar," a 30-foot-tall sculpture complete with fountains, designed by internationally recognized artist Steve Canneto. As seen in Exhibit 21.12, the sculpture symbolizes Christopher Columbus's fleet. It stands in the courtyard of the conservatory and entices people of all ages to touch it and have their pictures taken next to it. The event expected to draw 40,000 people per day, but initial counts revealed attendance at levels lower than expected.

The Columbus 1992 celebration extended beyond AmeriFlora. Community members contracted with craftsmen to build a full-scale replica of the Santa Maria, the largest of Christopher Columbus's ships. It sits on the

[1]Mark Bernstein, "Discovering Columbus," *America West Airlines Magazine*, June 1992, 51.

■ **EXHIBIT 21.11**   Where America's Top Businesses Arrive

Where America's Top Businesses Arrive

No matter where you travel on business,
there's just one place you can really arrive. Columbus, Ohio.

Established corporate leaders such as Honda of America, Lane Bryant, Wendy's, AEP,
The Limited, Borden, Bank One and Safelite call Columbus home.
So do some of the nation's fastest-growing entrepreneurial enterprises.

Here in the heartland of America, workers are dedicated. Costs are manageable.
And the living is easy.

So come to Columbus. And Arrive.

For more information, contact
The Columbus Area Chamber of Commerce Economic Development Department
37 N. High Street, Columbus, Ohio 43215 (614) 225-6940

Creative services provided by Hameroff/Milenthal/Spence, Inc.

Courtesy of The Columbus Area Chamber of Commerce

■ **EXHIBIT 21.12   NavStar Sculpture**

Courtesy of Stephen Canneto, Artist

Scioto River in downtown Columbus for everyone to examine. Visitors from near and far have flocked to see firsthand the living conditions the Italian explorer and his crew had to endure on their journey to America. People are amazed when they see how small it really was!

Although much energy has been spent on the 1992 celebration, Columbus and its leaders are now looking beyond 1992 and into the future. Community leaders will have to decide what to do with the Ameri-Flora grounds and facilities once the festivities have died down. Ameri-Flora will leave Franklin Park with flowers and landscaping, but the buildings and other structures built for the event will be torn down. Potentially, some could be moved to other sites. The Santa Maria will remain on the Scioto River. Perhaps more significant than the tangible objects, Ameri-Flora and the 1992 celebration will leave behind an image for Columbus, a portrait of how the city began its public transformation into a cultural center of the United States, described by *The Wall Street Journal* as the "Bohemia of the Midwest."

Columbus will also have to develop a new logo for marketing purposes. It will be challenging to get all of the marketing organizations to agree on one logo; they have all developed their own and are using them on letterhead and promotional materials. This creates a diversity in the city's image. The first figure is being used by the Columbus Area Chamber of Commerce. It incorporates a symbol that builds on the "Brushstrokes" symbol used until 1990. The second figure is a graphic replica of "NavStar." Its modern shape, the significance of the ships, and its visibility at AmeriFlora make it an attractive alternative as well. The third figure is a graphic replica of the Santa Maria, which is located on the Scioto River.

As 1993 nears, community leaders are debating whether or not the COMC should be resurrected. Discussions are occurring to determine if the COMC in its original form or a similar organization could be positioned among the chamber of commerce, the city of Columbus, and the convention bureau to coordinate marketing activities and to guide Columbus into the twenty-first century.

Focal Topics

1. Is it appropriate for a city to have a marketing plan? How would you justify the use of city funds for such activities?

2. Evaluate the mission and objectives of the COMC. Are they appropriate and worthwhile for marketing the city into the 2000s? What changes should be made if the COMC were to be resurrected in 1993?

3. Using the research in this case or other criteria, how would you evaluate the activities of COMC? Were they effective?

4. Given the activities of 1992, what would you do with the remaining portions of AmeriFlora or the image of Columbus if you were appointed the new director of marketing for COMC or the city?

5. If you were to develop a marketing plan for the city in which you live, how should it be done? What principles can be derived from the COMC program that would be helpful in developing the plan for your city?

■ ■ ■ ■ ■

Worthington Foods, Inc.
(B): Better'n Eggs

■ ■ ■ ■ ■

Worthington Foods was founded in 1939 as "Old Worthington" to produce nutritional, vegetarian foods for members of the Seventh-day Adventist Church. Miles Laboratories purchased Old Worthington in 1970. Worthington Foods, Inc., in a management-led buyout, acquired the business and assets of Old Worthington in 1982.

Today, Worthington Foods, Inc., develops, produces and markets high quality, zero-cholesterol, vegetarian and egg substitute food products for consumers seeking healthful food choices. Offering more than 150 product items, the company is one of the leading independent producers of healthier alternatives to meat, egg, and dairy products. For more than 50 years Worthington Foods has been dedicated to producing meat alternative products that simulate the taste and texture of meat and are made primarily from soy and wheat proteins. Since the 1970s it has produced egg substitute products made primarily from liquid egg whites. For a more complete discussion of Worthington Foods, its performance, and its product lines, please see Case 6: Worthington Foods (A): Meat Analogues.

Morningstar Farms

Morningstar Farms offers the most readily available line of zero-cholesterol food items sold nationally through supermarkets. These frozen, easy-to-prepare products offer healthy, vegetarian options to many familiar processed meats as well as eggs. Because of their hearty, meat-like flavor and texture, Morningstar Farms products provide consumers with one of the easiest ways to reduce their meat consumption and eat more healthy. The Morningstar Farms product line includes Breakfast Links, Patties, and Strips, which provide the taste satisfaction of sausage and bacon but are completely free of meat and animal fat.

Complementing this assortment of meat free alternatives is an expanding line of egg products. First introduced in the mid-1970s, cholesterol-free substitutes for whole, shell eggs are one of the fastest growing categories in the frozen breakfast section. Exhibit 22.1 shows how the egg substitute category and Morningstar Farms Scrambler brand grew in sales volume in 1989 compared to other frozen-food areas. The total frozen-food category grew by .7 percent and the frozen breakfast foods category grew 14 percent, while the egg substitute category grew by 46 percent. Within the frozen egg substitute category, Egg Beaters grew 29 percent and Scramblers grew 68 percent.

Worthington Foods entered the egg substitute market with Scramblers. Morningstar Farms Scramblers contain half the fat and one-third fewer calories than whole eggs. Made from egg whites, they have no cholesterol. Scramblers frozen egg product has maintained a strong presence in this category as the number two selling egg substitute nationally. Egg Beaters, produced by Fleishmann's, and Scramblers have battled for the number one and two market share positions for years. Scramblers has become Worthington Foods' number one product. This versatile product can be used in virtually any recipe calling for whole eggs.

While this frozen egg substitute was formulated to contain zero cholesterol, Worthington Foods placed emphasis on great taste. In numerous taste tests, Scramblers scored equal to or higher than its competitors, including Egg Beaters, Eggstrordinare, and Second Nature. Scramblers enjoyed high growth rates for several years as the egg substitute category grew rapidly, outperforming Egg Beaters, its strongest competitor, in terms of growth rates. Exhibit 22.2 examines the growth rates of the egg substitute category and Scramblers from 1986 to 1989. Total category growth increased from 14 percent in 1986 to 46 percent in 1989. Scramblers growth increased from 23 percent in 1986 to 68 percent in 1989.

Scramblers was developed to give consumers more than just nutritional benefits. Because they are frozen, Scramblers last longer than shell eggs. They are taken out of the freezer, defrosted in the refrigerator or the microwave, and then prepared as desired. Scramblers is different from Egg Beaters in that Scramblers come in smaller servings. One carton contains the equivalent of two eggs rather than four, a convenience for small families or singles.

During the formulation period, the main emphasis was on developing an egg substitute with zero cholesterol. Physicians and concerned health-active consumers were often motivated to reduce cholesterol and sodium. Thus, Scramblers and its competitors focused primarily on these factors, with taste being important as well. What was not as important in the early 1980s was fat.

As the 1980s came to an end, the issue of fat content became more important to health-active consumers as well as many mainstream consumers. According to a 1990 survey by HealthFocus, a Pennsylvania-based market research firm, people eat healthy foods for a variety of reasons. More than half of health-active consumers make food choices to reduce their consumption of fat, especially saturated fat, and cholesterol. By contrast, fewer than 30 percent make dietary changes to control weight.

■ EXHIBIT 22.1   Growth in the Frozen Foods Category (1989)

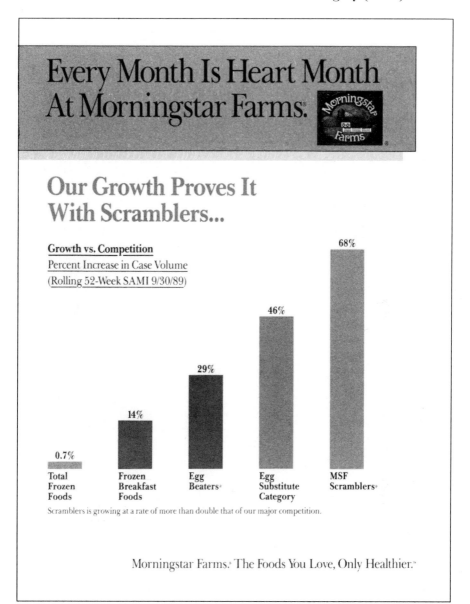

Nearly 50 percent of adults report they have reduced the use of whole shell eggs over the past 2 years.

People are still concerned about cholesterol, but awareness and concern for the issue appears to have peaked. Saturated fat appears to be the topic of most concern, and some reports cite fat as being more responsible

■ **EXHIBIT 22.2   Scramblers Growth Rates versus Total Egg
                    Substitute Category, 1986 to 1989**

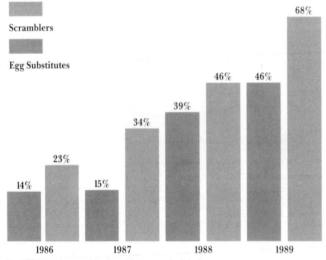

Every Month Is Heart Month At Morningstar Farms.

Your Sales Will Reflect It.

Scramblers Growth vs. Total Category
1988–1989 Percent Increases in Case Volume
(Rolling 52-Week SAMI 9/30/89)

Scramblers

Egg Substitutes

Scramblers continues to drive the explosive growth of the frozen egg category.

Morningstar Farms.® The Foods You Love, Only Healthier.™

for heart and arterial diseases than cholesterol components in the diet. Scramblers fell short of meeting the wants of some of these changing consumers because its fat content was higher than that of competitors. The trade-off was better taste.

While some consumers would rather have a reasonable amount of fat and great taste, others would rather have no fat and reasonable taste. Worthington Foods envisioned doing both by giving consumers an egg substitute with zero fat and superior taste. This objective was accomplished with Better'n Eggs, which was formulated to contain zero fat, zero cholesterol, no artificial colors, flavors, or preservatives, and the farm-fresh flavor of whole eggs.

Worthington Foods' scientists spent more than four years developing the patented process to manufacture new Better'n Eggs™. The next step was market research to assist management in naming the product and preparing the product for distribution. The research was also needed to measure respondents' intent to purchase the new egg product, assess levels of concern about perceived health problems associated with eggs, and inquire about their current diet behaviors.

Research Methodology

Three hundred and four (n=304) one-on-one mall intercept interviews were completed at mall facilities in Baltimore, Maryland (n=103), St. Louis, Missouri (n=100), and Phoenix, Arizona (n=101). Seventy-five percent of the respondents were female, while 25 percent were male.

Qualifying respondents were 45 years of age or older. Other characteristics among respondents include having some concerns about health and one or more members of their households currently using egg substitutes. No respondents had participated in any marketing research survey at any mall within three months of participating in the egg substitute interviews.

Respondents were screened and recruited, and qualifying respondents were invited into the interviewing facilities where they were shown a general description of the new egg product and asked to complete the interview. Respondents were not shown the actual product. (The questionnaire used in the data collection process is shown in Exhibit 22.7, presented at the end of the case.)

Research Conclusions

Worthington Foods tested the names Better'n Eggs, EggLite, The Good Egg, Sunnyside, and Eggz, which are ranked in the order of favorite to least favorite. Respondents gave many reasons for selecting Better'n Eggs as their first choice, shown in Exhibit 22.3. Worthington Foods considered Better'n Eggs to be the best name as well because the product was being

■ **EXHIBIT 22.3   Reasons for Preferring Name Better'n Eggs**

Reason	Percent of Respondents
Readily identifies product	24.6%
Eye-catching name	20.3
Sounds healthy	16.9
Sounds lighter/lower in cholesterol	15.3
Appealing	10.2
Sounds better than just eggs	5.9

Courtesy of Worthington Foods

formulated to be better than eggs in terms of fat and cholesterol content and taste.

When Better'n Eggs was in its developmental stages, Worthington Foods conducted research to determine what other product attributes, other than fat content, were increasing in importance among consumers. It discovered that consumers found the serving sizes of Scramblers very desirable, so the smaller serving sizes were carried over to the new product, although a larger alternative size was also added. Another area Worthington Foods addressed was the convenience factor of frozen versus refrigerated products. With many Americans living in "time poverty," the time savings associated with refrigerated egg substitutes might be worth the trade-off of lower shelf life for many consumers. They might also equate refrigerated products with freshness and being closer to real eggs. Thus, the refrigerated version was developed in addition to the frozen Better'n Eggs. Exhibit 22.4 shows how consumers in each market ranked product attributes in terms of importance.

After Better'n Eggs was described extensively to the focus groups, their intent to try the product was measured. Exhibit 22.5 shows these results.

Advertising in a Competitive Marketplace

The competitive environment for egg substitutes has changed in recent years. With more and more companies entering the market, the degree of competitiveness has increased dramatically. Healthy Choice has recently entered the market, not only with a frozen egg substitute, but also with an entire breakfast line. Rich's also entered test markets in 1992. The other refrigerated egg substitute is Second Nature, which is increasing market share rapidly.

The increase in demand for egg whites, the primary ingredient in egg substitutes, has caused the price of egg whites to increase dramatically. At one time egg whites were merely the by-product or throwaway product of shell eggs, used in the production of various food products. They

■ EXHIBIT 22.4   How Consumers Rank Product Attributes of Egg Substitutes

	Total		Baltimore		St. Louis		Phoenix	
Product Features	Very Important	Somewhat Important	Very Important	Somewhat Important	Very Important	Somewhat Important	Very Important	Somewhat Important
Zero cholesterol	94.4%	4.9%	94.2%	5.8%	93.0%	5.0%	96.0%	4.0%
Better for your health than eggs	83.2	13.2	84.5	9.7	77.0	18.0	88.1	11.9
Less fat	82.2	12.5	81.6	8.7	81.0	16.0	84.2	12.9
Tastes like fresh eggs	80.3	15.5	81.6	14.6	79.0	15.0	80.2	16.8
All natural ingredients	74.3	18.4	82.5	12.6	68.0	22.0	72.3	20.8
Fewer calories	68.4	21.1	72.8	12.6	69.0	20.0	63.4	30.7
Cooks like whole eggs	64.5	24.7	72.8	20.4	61.0	23.0	59.4	30.7
Recommended by your doctor	57.9	26.0	61.2	26.2	59.0	21.0	53.5	30.7
Used in any recipe	55.9	28.9	59.2	25.2	51.0	30.0	57.4	31.7
Ready-to-use	53.3	32.6	58.3	30.1	53.0	29.0	48.5	38.6
Real egg product	42.4	35.2	50.5	32.0	36.0	36.0	40.6	37.6
Long shelf life	38.8	35.5	38.8	35.0	39.0	34.0	38.6	37.6
Refrigerated	37.8	38.5	36.9	42.7	31.0	42.0	45.5	30.7
Pasteurized	37.5	31.9	41.7	32.0	34.0	33.0	36.6	30.7
Frozen	13.8	40.5	20.4	39.8	13.0	39.0	7.9	42.6

Importance Ratings

■ **EXHIBIT 22.5   Product Trial Intent**

	Percent of Respondents
Definitely try it	62.2%
Probably try it	27.0
Might or might not try it	7.6
Probably not try it	2.3
Definitely not try it	1.0

were very inexpensive, which allowed a high profit margin for egg substitutes. Today, the egg whites are just as pricey as the egg yolks, thus decreasing the profit margin egg substitute producers can make on a dollar of sales. Coupled with increased competition, it is more and more difficult for any individual company to increase its profits as dramatically as previously.

Worthington Foods believes that with its new Better'n Eggs, it can compete effectively in the competitive marketplace. Initial consumer research on Better'n Eggs has shown the product to be preferred to other egg substitutes. Better'n Eggs compares favorably to shell eggs in terms of appearance, taste, and texture and is better in convenience. This led one observer to comment that Better'n Eggs are better than shell eggs for every thing except coloring at Easter!

With expected national distribution in 1992 or early 1993, Worthington Foods needs to develop an integrated marketing communications campaign to introduce its new product into the marketplace. Some test markets are reviewing preliminary ads, seen in Exhibit 22.6, which are being run with corresponding television ads. Some of the ads contain coupons as well to stimulate product trial.

With the farm-fresh flavor of eggs, but without the fat, cholesterol, or guilt, Morningstar Farms' latest addition to the egg substitute category is indeed "better than eggs." The refrigerator product requires substantially different technology than the frozen product and has a shorter shelf life. To achieve national distribution, Worthington Foods must invest large amounts of capital into building a new plant. To justify the investment in a new plant, Worthington will need to achieve high levels of sales. This objective in turn probably requires high levels of investment in advertising to introduce the product and maintain market share. The company could wait and see how well the product does in a few test markets but this strategy carries the risk of allowing competitors to enter national distribution with a refrigerated product and possibly take market share that would be difficult for Better'n Eggs to regain. The balance sheet of Worthington Foods (see Case 6) does not reveal enough liquidity to make such a move without additional equity or debt.

■ EXHIBIT 22.6   Better'n Eggs Advertising

18,513,000 coupons for
Better'n Eggs from
Morningstar Farms
will appear in *VALASSIS INSERTS*
on Sunday, **May 17, 1992.**

■ EXHIBIT 22.7   Worthington Foods' Market Research Survey

			1		
1	2	3	4	**Location**	
				Baltimore	−1 (10)
				Phoenix	−2
8	2	7	2	St. Louis	−3
5	6	7	8	**Sex**	
				Male	−1 (11)
				Female	−2

(continued)

■ **EXHIBIT 22.7**   *continued*

The Answer Group Egg Product Screener

RECRUIT THE FOLLOWING:
>   75 Females: Age 45+
>
>   25 Males: Age 45+

■   Total sample: Health concerned egg users or egg substitute users.

■   Minimum of 50 respondents cholesterol-concerned (YES TO Q.D).

■   Remaining respondents must have health concerns regarding egg use (YES TO Q.C or Q.D).

SCREENING QUESTIONS

Hello, we're doing a survey today about eggs and egg usage.

A.   Does your household currently use eggs or egg substitutions?

>   –1   YES   (SKIP TO Q.C)   (15)
>   –2   NO   (ASK Q.B)

B.   Why not? (RECORD ANSWER. THANK, TERMINATE AND RECORD ON TALLY SHEET.)

>   _____   (16)
>   _____   (17)
>   _____   (18)

C.   Do you have health concerns regarding the use of eggs?

>   –1   YES   (CONTINUE)
>   –2   NO   (THANK AND TERMINATE. RECORD ON TALLY SHEET.)

D.   Would you say you are concerned about levels of cholesterol in eggs?

>   –1   YES   (CONTINUE)   (CHECK QUOTAS)   (20)
>   –2   NO   (CONTINUE)

E.   Do you, or does anyone in your immediate family, work for a marketing research firm or in a marketing department of any kind?

>   –1   YES TO EITHER   (THANK, TERMINATE AND RECORD ON
>   TALLY SHEET.)
>   –2   NO TO BOTH   (CONTINUE)

F.   Have you participated in a marketing research survey at any mall within the past three (3) months?

>   –1   YES   (THANK, TERMINATE AND RECORD ON TALLY SHEET.)
>   –2   NO   (CONTINUE)

We are introducing a new cholesterol-free, low-fat, low-calorie, food product idea to people who would like to participate in naming the product and coming up with the best way to describe it to consumers. We would like you to participate if you have a few minutes now to come to our interviewing facility here at the mall. Would you like to participate?

LEAD WILLING RESPONDENT TO THE INTERVIEWING FACILITY

IF RESPONDENT REFUSES, MARK ON TALLY SHEET.

>   TRACK INCIDENCE FOR ALL SCREENING QUESTIONS.
>
>   STAPLE SCREENER TO THE FRONT OF EACH COMPLETED QUESTIONNAIRE.

(continued)

■ **EXHIBIT 22.7** *continued*

THE ANSWER GROUP EGG PRODUCT QUESTIONNAIRE

Thank you for participating in our survey today. We are interested in talking to people who are concerned about levels of cholesterol in eggs or have other health concerns about eggs, because we would like to get your opinion about a new food product idea. First, we will read you a general description of the new product idea an then ask you to rank, according to your preferences, some features and names for the product. Finally, we will ask you some general questions about your reaction to the product idea. There are no right or wrong answers in this survey; it's your opinion that counts.

SHOW RESPONDENT THE GENERAL DESCRIPTION AND READ IT ALOUD TO HIM OR HER.

GENERAL DESCRIPTION

This is a product that can be used just like whole eggs, scrambled as well as in any recipe. It is made with real eggs, but has zero cholesterol, less fat, and fewer calories.

HAND RESPONDENT THE FIFTEEN (15) ATTRIBUTE CARDS. ROTATE THE ORDER THE CARDS ARE PRESENTED IN.

1a. Thinking about the product we have just described to you, how important would you consider these features? Please sort the cards into the following three groups, VERY IMPORTANT, SOMEWHAT IMPORTANT, or NOT AT ALL IM-PORTANT. Remember, there are no right or wrong answers. (CIRCLE –1 NEXT TO THOSE FEATURES IN "VERY IMPORTANT" GROUP, –2 NEXT TO THOSE IN "SOMEWHAT IMPORTANT" GROUP, –3 NEXT TO THOSE IN "NOT AT ALL IMPORTANT" GROUP. SHUFFLE CARDS BETWEEN RESPONDENTS.)

	Very Important	Somewhat Important	Not at All Important	DK	
All-natural ingredients	–1	–2	–3	–Y	(23)
Ready-to-use	–1	–2	–3	–Y	(24)
Real egg product	–1	–2	–3	–Y	(25)
Refrigerated	–1	–2	–3	–Y	(26)
Zero cholesterol	–1	–2	–3	–Y	(27)
Less fat	–1	–2	–3	–Y	(28)
Fewer calories	–1	–2	–3	–Y	(29)
Recommended by your doctor	–1	–2	–3	–Y	(30)
Better for your health than eggs	–1	–2	–3	–Y	(31)
Cooks like whole eggs	–1	–2	–3	–Y	(32)
Used in any recipe	–1	–2	–3	–Y	(33)
Tastes like fresh eggs	–1	–2	–3	–Y	(34)
Pasteurized	–1	–2	–3	–Y	(35)
Frozen	–1	–2	–3	–Y	(36)
Long shelf life	–1	–2	–3	–y	(37)

TAKE THE RESPONDENT'S GROUP OF "VERY IMPORTANT" ATTRIBUTES FROM PREVIOUS PAGE (Q.1a) AND CIRCLE THESE ATTRIBUTES ONLY IN THE FOLLOWING QUESTION. THEN GIVE THIS GROUP BACK TO THE RESPONDENT FOR RANKING. IF NO ATTRIBUTES WERE RATED "VERY IMPORTANT", CIRCLE 40-X AT Q.1b.)

(continued)

■ **EXHIBIT 22.7**   *continued*

1b. Looking at these attributes that you rated as "Very Important", please now rank them in order of importance to you from most important to least important. (RECORD RANKING ON THE LINES TO THE RIGHT OF THE CIRCLED ATTRIBUTES BELOW. ZERO FILL.)

CIRCLE VERY IMPORTANT ATTRIBUTES

–1 All-natural ingredients	___ (41)	___ (42)
–2 Ready-to-use	___ (43)	___ (44)
–3 Real egg product	___ (45)	___ (46)
–4 Refrigerated	___ (47)	___ (48)
–5 Zero cholesterol	___ (49)	___ (50)
–6 Less fat	___ (51)	___ (52)
–7 Fewer calories	___ (53)	___ (54)
–8 Recommended by your doctor	___ (55)	___ (56)
–9 Better for your health than eggs	___ (57)	___ (58)
–0 Cooks like whole eggs	___ (59)	___ (60)
–X Used in any recipe	___ (61)	___ (62)
–Y Tastes like fresh eggs	___ (63)	___ (64)

----
(39)

–1 Pasteurized	___ (65)	___ (66)
–2 Frozen	___ (67)	___ (68)
–3 Long shelf life	___ (69)	___ (70)

40-X NO ATTRIBUTES ARE VERY IMPORTANT

REMOVE ATTRIBUTE CARDS. HAND RESPONDENT PRE-SHUFFLED NAME CARDS.

2. Here are five (5) name ideas for this product. Please read each one of them to yourself and then rank them from 1 to 5, where 1 is most appealing and 5 is least appealing, according to how appealing you think they are as a name for this new product. (CIRCLE 1 NEXT TO FIRST CHOICE, 2 NEXT TO SECOND CHOICE, AND CONTINUE UNTIL ALL FIVE ARE RANKED. NO NAME SHOULD BE RANKED MORE THAN ONCE. ROTATE CARD PRESENTATION.)

(continued)

■ **EXHIBIT 22.7**   *continued*

	1st Choice	2nd Choice	3rd Choice	4th Choice	5th Choice	
Better'n Eggs	−1	−2	−3	−4	−5	(71)
Eggz	−1	−2	−3	−4	−5	(72)
The Good Egg	−1	−2	−3	−4	−5	(73)
Sunnyside	−1	−2	−3	−4	−5	(74)
EggLite	−1	−2	−3	−4	−5	(75)

REMOVE CARDS RANKED 3, 4 AND 5

3. Thinking again about the product names we gave you to choose from, you picked _____ (READ AND WRITE OUT FIRST NAME CHOICE FROM Q.2) as the most appealing name and _____ (READ AND WRITE OUT SECOND NAME CHOICE FROM Q.2) as the second most appealing name. In your opinion, how much better is (READ FIRST NAME CHOICE) than (READ SECOND NAME CHOICE)? Would you say it is . . . (READ LIST)?

   −5   much better   (76)

   −4   somewhat better

   −3   a little bit better

   −2   not much better

   −1   not at all better   RECORD 2

                                                                                                          dup 1–3

   −Y   DON'T KNOW (DO NOT READ)   −2 (4)

4. Could you please describe what you like most about (REFER TO Q.2. READ AND CIRCLE CODE NEXT TO RESPONDENT'S FIRST NAME CHOICE. PROBE FOR REASONS LIKED.)

Names **(10)**	**Reasons Liked**	
1. Better'n Eggs	_____	(11)
	_____	(12)
2. Eggz	_____	(17)
	_____	(18)
3. The Good Egg	_____	(23)
	_____	(24)
4. Sunnyside	_____	(29)
	_____	(30)
5. EggLite	_____	(35)
	_____	(36)

5. Could you please describe anything you dislike about (REFER TO Q.2. READ AND CIRCLE CODE NEXT TO RESPONDENT'S FIFTH NAME CHOICE. PROBE FOR REASONS DISLIKED.)

Names **(41)**	**Reasons Disliked**	
1. Better'n Eggs	_____	(42)
	_____	(43)

(*continued*)

■ **EXHIBIT 22.7**   *continued*

2. Eggz   _____   (48)
            _____   (49)

3. The Good Egg   _____   (54)
                    _____   (55)

4. Sunnyside   _____   (60)
                 _____   (61)

5. EggLite   _____   (66)
               _____   (67)

REMOVE FIVE NAME CARDS.

6. Based on what you've read and heard about this new food product (POINT TO
   GENERAL DESCRIPTION), how likely would you be to try it if you felt it was
   reasonably priced. Would you . . . (READ LIST)?

   −5 definitely try it   (72)

   −4 probably try it

   −3 might or might not try it

   −2 probably not try it

   −1 definitely not try it

   −Y NOT SURE (DO NOT READ)

(HAND RESPONDENT THE SIX (6) PRE-SHUFFLED CONCERN CARDS. SHUFFLE
THE ORDER THE CARDS ARE PRESENTED IN.)

7a. Thinking about perceived problems associated with eggs, please sort these
    cards into groups depending on how concerned you about each one. Please
    use the following three groups, VERY CONCERNED, SOMEWHAT CON-
    CERNED, or NOT AT ALL CONCERNED. Remember, there are no right or
    wrong answers.

	Very Concerned	Somewhat Concerned	Not at All Concerned	DK	
Cholesterol	−1	−2	−3	−Y	(73)
Calories	−1	−2	−3	−Y	(74)
Fat	−1	−2	−3	−Y	(75)
Saturated Fat	−1	−2	−3	−Y	(76)
Salmonella	−1	−2	−3	−Y	(77)
Illness or disease	−1	−2	−3	−Y	(78)

(TAKE THE RESPONDENT'S GROUP OF PROBLEMS RATED "VERY CON-
CERNED" IN Q.7a AND CIRCLE THESE PROBLEMS ONLY IN Q.7B. THEN GIVE
THIS GROUP BACK TO THE RESPONDENT FOR RANKING. IF NO PROBLEMS
RATED "VERY CONCERNED" CIRCLE −X AT Q.7b.)

RECORD 3
dup 1–3
−3 (4)

7b. Of these attributes that you rated as "Very Concerned", please rank them in
    order of most concerned to least concerned to you. (RECORD RANKING ON
    THE LINES TO THE RIGHT OF THE CIRCLED ATTRIBUTES BELOW. ZERO
    FILL.)

(continued)

■ **EXHIBIT 22.7** *continued*

CIRCLE PROBLEMS VERY CONCERNED ABOUT
(10)

−1 Cholesterol

‾‾‾‾ (11)   ‾‾‾‾ (12)

−2 Calories

‾‾‾‾ (13)   ‾‾‾‾ (14)

−3 Fat

‾‾‾‾ (15)   ‾‾‾‾ (16)

−4 Saturated Fat

‾‾‾‾ (17)   ‾‾‾‾ (18)

−5 Salmonella

‾‾‾‾ (19)   ‾‾‾‾ (20)

−6 Illness or disease

‾‾‾‾ (21)   ‾‾‾‾ (22)

−X RESPONDENT NOT "VERY CONCERNED" ABOUT ANY PROBLEMS
REMOVE CARDS FROM RESPONDENT.

7.c Are you currently taking any steps to control cholesterol?

    −1 YES (ASK Q.7d)   (23)

    −2 NO

    −Y DON'T KNOW/CARE   (SKIP TO Q.7e)

7.d. What steps are you taking? (DO NOT READ LIST) Any others?

    −1 Using margarine   (24)

    −2 Using egg substitute(s)

    −3 Using low cholesterol foods

    −4 Cutting back on dairy products in general

    −5 Cutting back on fried foods

    −6 Cutting back on red meats

    Other (SPECIFY) _____   (25)

    _____   (26)

    −Y DON'T KNOW/CARE

7e. Would you say you agree or disagree with the following statement with regard
    to your own diet? "I've cut down on eggs because of the cholesterol."

    −1 Agree   (29)

    −2 Disagree

    −Y DON'T KNOW

7f. In your opinion, do you agre or disagree with the following statement? "I
    really like eggs and would eat more of them if they contained less fat and cho-
    lesterol."

    −1 Agree   (30)

    −2 Disagree

    −Y DON'T KNOW

8. Have you purchased or used any egg substitute products in the last three (3)
    months?

(continued)

▪ EXHIBIT 22.7 *continued*

-1   YES   (31)

-2   NO

-Y   DON'T KNOW   (SKIP TO Q.10)

9a. What was the brand name of the last egg substitute product you bought/used?
    (DO NOT READ LIST)

-1   Scramblers   (32)

-2   Egg Beaters

-3   Second Natures

Other (SPECIFY) _____

-Y   DON'T KNOW

9b. What other brands have you bought/used? (DO NOT READ LIST) Any others?

-1   Scramblers   (35)

-2   Egg Beaters

-3   Second Natures

Other (SPECIFY) _____

-Y   DON'T KNOW

9c. Have you ever bought or used . . . ? (READ EACH BRAND NOT MENTIONED
    AT Q.9a and Q.9b.)

	YES	NO	DON'T KNOW	
Scramblers	-1	-2	-Y	(38)
Egg Beaters	-1	-2	-Y	(39)
Second Natures	-1	-2	-Y	(40)

These last few questions are for classifications purposes only.

10. What is your annual household income before taxes? (DO NOT READ LIST)

-1   Under $20,000   (41)

-2 $20,000 to less than $30,000

-3 $30,000 to less than $40,000

-4 $40,000 to less than $50,000

-5 $50,000 to less than $60,000

-6 $60,000 to less than $70,000

-7 $70,000 or more

-X   REFUSED

-Y   DON'T KNOW

11. What is the highest level of education you have completed? (DO NOT
    READ LIST)

-1   Grade school or less   (42)

-2   Some high school

-3   High school graduate

-4   Some college/Junior college/Trade school

-5   College Graduate

-6   Some Post Graduate work

(continued)

- **EXHIBIT 22.7**   *continued*

  −7   Graduate degree/Medical School/etc.

  −Y   REFUSED

12. Including yourself, how many people live in your household? (DO NOT READ LIST)

  −1   1   (43)

  −2   2–3

  −3   4–5

  −4   6–7

  −5   8 or more

  −X   REFUSED

13. How many people in your household are employed? (DO NOT READ LIST)

  −1   1   (44)

  −2   2–3

  −3   4–5

  −4   6–7

  −5   8 or more

  −X   REFUSED

14. How old are you? (RECORD EXACT. ZERO FILL.)

  _____   _____
  (45)   (46)

  REFUSED = YY

15. What is your marital status? (DO NOT READ LIST)

  −1   Married   (47)

  −2   Single

  −3   Divorced/Separated

  −4   Widowed

  −Y   REFUSED

16. Does your household have a microwave oven?

  −1   YES   (48)

  −2   NO

  −Y   DON'T KNOW

That's all the questions I have for you. Thank you for your help! There is a remote chance we will have to contact you to clarify an answer, may I please have your . . . ?

NAME _____   PHONE _____

INTERVIEWER _____   DATE _____

LENGTH OF INTERVIEW _____   minutes

Focal Topics

1. Who is the primary market target for egg substitutes? Be specific in terms of demographics, lifestyles, or variables that can be used for segmentation strategies.

2. What attributes are most important in consumer decisions to purchase egg substitutes?

3. Prepare a methodology for analyzing the data collected in the questionnaire presented in Exhibit 22.7.

4. If Better'n Eggs is introduced nationally, what promotional program should be developed for Better'n Eggs? Be specific concerning advertising, reseller support, publicity, or other elements of the program. What percentage of the advertising budget should be allocated to Better'n Eggs versus the rest of the Morningstar Farms product line?

■ ■ ■ ■ ■

WMKT

■ ■ ■ ■ ■

Dan Morris sat pensively in his WMKT office window looking toward the Sears Tower and other skyscrapers of Chicago's lakefront Loop. From the speakers that continuously monitored WMKT's music, he could hear the Red Hot Chili Peppers singing "Under the Bridge." But in his own mind, he was thinking more about "The River" flowing under the bridge and the young former marketing student who sings the song, Garth Brooks.

Dan Morris had been general manager of WMKT and eight other radio stations during his 28-year career in radio. The problems facing him now, however, were the greatest he had ever faced. WMKT was losing money, as were most of the other radio stations in the United States. An industry once viewed as a gold mine had become a salt mine with "24 hour/7 day work weeks" and almost no "rack time" for anyone at the station. In spite of cuts in budgets in every department, including reduction of staff, station revenue was still falling short of costs by over $10,000 a week. The owners of the station informed Dan that this must stop within 3 months, or they would be forced to replace the current management.

Although Dan was highly respected in the radio industry and had a track record of many successes, he knew that finding another job would be difficult. For one thing, he was now over 50-years-old in an industry characterized by youth. Many stations were downsizing, producing a surplus of experienced managers ready to accept a position at nearly any salary. Furthermore, some stations were so unprofitable that they were "going dark" and terminating the entire staff.

Ratings at WMKT had declined over the past 2 years but not dramatically. Advertising revenue had dropped more than ratings, however. The nation was in a recession that did not seem to be easing. This was one of the factors, Dan believed, that had caused advertising revenue at the station to be nearly 20 percent less than 2 years earlier.

Dan thought about some of the decisions he faced concerning the station. Should the format be changed? If the format was correct, could specific selections of music be improved? What promotions might help attract listeners? Could something be done to increase the effectiveness of the sales force? Should rates or other aspects of the station's advertising be changed? These were just a few of the questions facing Dan Morris, and he knew the answers must be found quickly.

Music Format

WMKT currently has a contemporary hit radio (CHR) format which it has had for several years. At one time, the station was the number two station of this format in the Chicago market. Recent years brought two problems, however. WMKT had dropped in its share (measured by Arbitron) compared to other CHR stations, and the CHR format had dropped overall in most cities of the United States. So many stations played CHR or AC (adult contemporary) formats that the market had also become fragmented. The result was that no single station had a very high share of the audience and consequently some advertisers turned to other media to deliver their ads to specific targeted audience segments.

Dan Morris was familiar with many formats used by radio stations. He regarded a trade publication, *R & R*, to be the most valuable source of information about the various music formats, and he regularly studied this and other publications to keep up with the changing music industry. The back page of a recent issue of *R & R*, showing the current airplay of each format, is shown in Exhibit 23.1. There are many other formats possible and currently one of the most successful seems to be "oldies."

One of the format possibilities is nonmusic. Many stations around the nation have switched to an all-talk, all-news or all-sports format, thus allowing a station to find a niche that may lead to larger total share for the station. The stations with standard music formats compete with so many stations that they fragment the market and most stations receive only a small share of the total market or of the various gender or age categories, such as "12-plus," "25–34," or "50 plus." Because WMKT is an FM station with an excellent signal throughout Chicago and the North Shore suburbs, Dan did not think switching to a nonmusic format was a good possibility, however. He felt that talk or news formats were a better possibility for AM stations.

Another possibility for WMKT is a possible switch to a country format. Dan had read numerous articles in *Time*, *Forbes*, and other publications indicating that country was increasingly the favorite of the nation's 76 million baby boomers. At one time, AOR (album-oriented rock) stations dominated the market, and Chicago's number one station was WXRT, which might be described as an eclectic AOR-based station, without the heavy metal. Another station doing well in the ratings, however, was "Route 99," a country station.

Dan Morris knew that country had always been a mainstay of American radio but usually in the country, not the city. Not since Elvis Presley had a country star gained the success currently enjoyed by Garth Brooks.

■ EXHIBIT 23.1 Airplay of Music by Formats

R&R **THE BACK PAGE**® JUNE 12, 1992

NATIONAL AIRPLAY OVERVIEW

CHR

3 WKS	2 WKS	LW	TW	
16	8	3	1	**MARIAH CAREY**/I'll Be There (Columbia)
2	1	1	2	**RED HOT CHILI PEPPERS**/Under The Bridge (WB)
7	5	5	3	**CELINE DION**/If You Asked Me To (Epic)
6	4	4	4	**SOPHIE B. HAWKINS**/Damn I Wish I Was... (Columbia)
8	7	6	5	**GENESIS**/Hold On My Heart (Atlantic)
4	3	2	6	**MICHAEL JACKSON**/In The Closet (Epic)
31	21	11	7	**VANDROSS & JACKSON**/The Best... (Perspective/A&M)
27	20	18	8	**COLOR ME BADD**/Slow Motion (Giant/Reprise)
17	14	12	9	**JON SECADA**/Just Another Day (SBK/ERG)
9	9	8	10	**MR. BIG**/Just Take My Heart (Atlantic)
12	10	9	11	**AMY GRANT**/I Will Remember You (A&M)
1	2	7	12	**EN VOGUE**/My Lovin' (You're Never...) (Atco/EastWest)
18	15	14	13	**LIONEL RICHIE**/Do It To Me (Motown)
24	17	16	14	**LINEAR**/T.L.C. (Atlantic)
21	16	15	15	**WILSON PHILLIPS**/You Won't See Me Cry (SBK/ERG)
23	18	17	16	**MICHAEL BOLTON**/Steel Bars (Columbia)
32	24	19	17	**TOM COCHRANE**/Life Is A Highway (Capitol)
—	33	21	18	**COVER GIRLS**/Wishing On A Star (Fever/Epic)
3	6	10	19	**KRIS KROSS**/Jump (Ruffhouse/Columbia)
—	40	25	20	**VANESSA WILLIAMS**/Just For Tonight (Wing/Mercury)
35	31	24	21	**SIR MIX-A-LOT**/Baby Got Back (Def American/Reprise)
34	30	23	22	**OUTFIELD**/Closer To Me (MCA)
15	13	13	23	**HOWARD JONES**/Lift Me Up (Elektra)
40	36	28	24	**ARRESTED DEVELOPMENT**/Tennessee (Chrysalis/ERG)
39	34	30	25	**ANNIE LENNOX**/Why (Arista)
5	11	20	26	**JOE PUBLIC**/Live And Learn (Columbia)
—	—	35	27	**RICHARD MARX**/Take This Heart (Capitol)
BREAKER			28	**CURE**/Friday I'm In Love (Elektra)
—	39	32	29	**EDDIE MONEY**/Fall In Love Again (Columbia)
19	19	22	30	**BONNIE RAITT**/Not The Only One (Capitol)
—	—	38	31	**TEVIN CAMPBELL**/Strawberry Letter 23 (Qwest/WB)
BREAKER			32	**GEORGE MICHAEL**/Too Funky (Columbia)
—	—	37	33	**RTZ**/All You've Got (Giant/Reprise)
—	—	39	34	**JODECI**/Come And Talk To Me (MCA)
DEBUT			35	**TLC**/Baby, Baby, Baby (LaFace/Arista)
28	26	27	36	**COLOURHAUS**/Innocent Child (Interscope)
DEBUT			37	**BLACK CROWES**/Remedy (Def American/Reprise)
—	—	40	38	**GOOD 2 GO**/Never Satisfied (Giant/Reprise)
DEBUT			39	**CECE PENISTON**/Keep On Walkin' (A&M)
BREAKER			40	**DEF LEPPARD**/Make Love Like A Man (Mercury)

N&A Pg. 134; Playlists Pg. 120; Parallels Pg. 125; Parallel Chart Analysis Pg. 132

ADULT CONTEMPORARY

3 WKS	2 WKS	LW	TW	
2	2	1	1	**CELINE DION**/If You Asked Me To (Epic)
5	4	4	2	**WILSON PHILLIPS**/You Won't See Me Cry (SBK/ERG)
3	3	3	3	**LIONEL RICHIE**/Do It To Me (Motown)
6	5	5	4	**AMY GRANT**/I Will Remember You (A&M)
1	1	2	5	**GENESIS**/Hold On My Heart (Atlantic)
17	12	7	6	**MARIAH CAREY**/I'll Be There (Columbia)
10	7	6	7	**MICHAEL BOLTON**/Steel Bars (Columbia)*
11	9	8	8	**ROBERT PALMER**/Every Kinda People (Island/PLG)
20	14	11	9	**VANESSA WILLIAMS**/Just For Tonight (Wing/Mercury)
22	19	12	10	**JON SECADA**/Just Another Day (SBK/ERG)
16	15	14	11	**SONIA**/Be Young, Be Foolish, Be Happy (RCA)
4	6	10	12	**BONNIE RAITT**/Not The Only One (Capitol)
24	22	16	13	**CHER**/When Lovers Become Strangers (Geffen)
9	8	9	14	**HOWARD JONES**/Lift Me Up (Elektra)
23	21	17	15	**EDDIE MONEY**/Fall In Love Again (Columbia)
14	13	13	16	**CARLY SIMON**/Love Of My Life (Qwest/Reprise)
—	27	20	17	**ANNIE LENNOX**/Why (Arista)
BREAKER			18	**CHRIS WALKER**/Take Time (Pendulum/Elektra)
27	23	22	19	**WYNONNA**/She Is His Only Need (Curb/MCA)
8	10	15	20	**RICHARD MARX**/Hazard (The River) (Capitol)
BREAKER			21	**KENNY LOGGINS**/If You Believe (Columbia)
BREAKER			22	**SIMPLY RED**/For Your Babies (Atco/EastWest)
BREAKER			23	**RICHARD MARX**/Take This Heart (Capitol)
13	16	19	24	**ERIC CLAPTON**/Tears In Heaven (Reprise)
7	11	18	25	**LUTHER VANDROSS**/Sometimes It's Only Love (Epic)
—	30	28	26	**BETH NIELSEN CHAPMAN**/Life Holds On (Reprise)
12	17	23	27	**KATHY TROCCOLI**/Everything Changes (Reunion/Geffen)
—	—	30	28	**K.D. LANG**/Constant Craving (Sire/WB)
DEBUT			29	**JAMES TAYLOR**/Everybody Loves To... (Columbia)
DEBUT			30	**DAN HILL/RIQUE FRANKS**/Hold Me Now (Quality)

*Keeps bullet due to continued growth.

New & Active Pg. 107
Adds & Hots Pg. 108
Associate Reporters Pg. 109

URBAN CONTEMPORARY

3 WKS	2 WKS	LW	TW	
6	4	2	1	**MICHAEL JACKSON**/In The Closet (Epic)
4	2	1	2	**R. KELLY & PUBLIC ANNOUNCEMENT**/Honey... (Jive)*
5	3	4	3	**GERALD LEVERT**/School Me (Atco/EastWest)
13	7	5	4	**LIONEL RICHIE**/Do It To Me (Motown)
23	17	9	5	**VANDROSS & JACKSON**/The Best... (Perspective/A&M)
18	11	7	6	**ARRESTED DEVELOPMENT**/Tennessee (Chrysalis/ERG)
15	10	8	7	**MINT CONDITION**/Forever In Your... (Perspective/A&M)
19	16	11	8	**PATTI LABELLE**/When You've Been Blessed (MCA)
25	22	16	9	**MARY J. BLIGE**/You Remind Me (Uptown/MCA)
22	20	15	10	**GOOD 2 GO**/Never Satisfied (Giant/Reprise)
17	15	12	11	**BOYS**/The Saga Continues (Motown)
29	23	17	12	**SHABBA RANKS**/Mr. Loverman (Epic)
26	24	18	13	**GLENN JONES**/I've Been Searchin' (Atlantic)
3	1	3	14	**CHAKA KHAN**/Love You All My Lifetime (WB)
16	12	10	15	**SOUL II SOUL**/Joy (Virgin)
—	37	22	16	**MARIAH CAREY**/I'll Be There (Columbia)
31	27	20	17	**DAS EFX**/They Want EFX (Atco/EastWest)
21	21	19	18	**HAMMER**/This Is The Way We Roll (Capitol)
38	31	26	19	**CECE PENISTON**/Keep On Walkin' (A&M)
35	28	21	20	**MEN AT LARGE**/Use Me (Atco/EastWest)
32	26	23	21	**EUGENE WILDE**/How About Tonight (MCA)
—	36	25	22	**SHANICE**/Silent Prayer (Motown)
40	34	27	23	**TROOP**/Whatever It Takes (To Make You...) (Atlantic)
—	—	37	24	**EN VOGUE**/Giving Him Something... (Atco/EastWest)
—	39	29	25	**VANESSA WILLIAMS**/Just For Tonight (Mercury)
—	38	31	26	**W. HOUSTON & S. WONDER**/We Didn't Know (Arista)
39	35	32	27	**CHRIS WALKER**/No Place Like Love (Pendulum/Elektra)
—	—	40	28	**TLC**/Baby, Baby, Baby (LaFace/Arista)
—	40	36	29	**SHOMARI**/If You Feel The Need (Mercury)
30	29	28	30	**RHONDA CLARK**/(If Loving You Is Wrong)... (Tabu/A&M)
1	5	6	31	**JODECI**/Come & Talk To Me (Uptown/MCA)
34	32	30	32	**NICE & SMOOTH**/Sometimes I Rhyme... (RAL/Columbia)
—	—	38	33	**G. WASHINGTON JR. f/L. HATHAWAY**/Love... (Columbia)
—	—	39	34	**EL DEBARGE**/You Know What I Like (WB)
DEBUT			35	**ATLANTIC STARR**/Unconditional Love (Reprise)
BREAKER			36	**BEBE & CECE WINANS**/Depend On You (Capitol)
36	33	33	37	**QUEEN LATIFAH**/How Do I Love Thee (Tommy Boy)
BREAKER			38	**ALYSON WILLIAMS**/Just My Luck (OBR/Columbia)
12	8	13	39	**PRINCE & N.P.G.**/Money Don't Matter... (Paisley Park/WB)
DEBUT			40	**DAVID BLACK**/Nobody But You (Bust It/Capitol)

*Keeps bullet due to continued growth.

New & Active, TOP 10 Recurrents Pg. 98

NEW ROCK

LW	TW	
1	1	**CURE**/Wish (Fiction/Elektra)
2	2	**XTC**/Nonsuch (Geffen)
3	3	**CHARLATANS U.K.**/Between 10th And... (Beggars Banquet/RCA)
4	4	**SOUP DRAGONS**/Hotwired (Big Life/Mercury)
5	5	**JESUS & MARY CHAIN**/Honey's Dead (Def American/WB)
7	6	**CRACKER**/Cracker (Virgin)
8	7	**MORRISSEY**/We Hate It When Our... (Track) (Sire/Reprise)
DEBUT	8	**B-52'S**/Good Stuff (Track) (Reprise)
9	9	**MATERIAL ISSUE**/Destination Universe (Mercury)
6	10	**PETER MURPHY**/Holy Smoke (Beggars Banquet/RCA)

Complete TOP 30 New Rock Chart Pg. 114

NAC

LW	TW	
7	1	**GRANT GEISSMAN**/Time Will Tell (Bluemoon)
2	2	**RANDY CRAWFORD**/Through The Eyes Of Love (WB)
1	3	**OTTMAR LIEBERT + LUNA NEGRA**/Solo Para Ti (Epic)
6	4	**GROVER WASHINGTON JR.**/Next Exit (Columbia)
3	5	**SPECIAL EFX**/Global Village (GRP)
5	6	**RICARDO SILVEIRA**/Small World (Verve Forecast/PolyGram)
9	7	**DAVID SANBORN**/Upfront (Elektra)
12	8	**NICKY HOLLAND**/Nicky Holland (Epic)
11	9	**GEORGE HOWARD**/Do I Ever Cross Your Mind (GRP)
4	10	**YANNI**/Dare To Dream (Private Music)

Complete TOP 30 NAC Chart Pg. 110

CONTEMPORARY JAZZ

LW	TW	
7	1	**DAVID SANBORN**/Upfront (Elektra)
2	2	**TONY WILLIAMS**/The Story Is Neptune (Blue Note)
5	3	**BOBBY WATSON**/Present Tense (Columbia)
8	4	**EDDIE DANIELS & GARY BURTON**/Benny Rides... (GRP)
11	5	**BENNY GREEN TRIO**/Testifyin' - Live At Village... (Blue Note)
3	6	**ROY HARGROVE**/The Vibe (Novus/RCA)
6	7	**ARTURO SANDOVAL**/I Remember Clifford (GRP)
10	8	**HAROLD MABERN TRIO**/Straight Street (DIW/Columbia)
12	9	**DELFEAYO MARSALIS**/Pontius Pilate's... (Novus/RCA)
1	10	**JOEY DeFRANCESCO**/Reboppin' (Columbia)

Complete TOP 30 Contemporary Jazz Chart Pg. 110

AOR TRACKS

3 WKS	2 WKS	LW	TW	
8	3	3	1	**DEF LEPPARD**/Make Love Like... (Mercury)
2	2	1	2	**RED HOT CHILI PEPPERS**/Under The Bridge (WB)
18	13	9	3	**BLACK CROWES**/Sting Me (Def American/Reprise)
7	6	4	4	**ARC ANGELS**/Living In A Dream (DGC)
1	1	2	5	**BLACK CROWES**/Remedy (Def American/Reprise)
10	8	5	6	**OZZY OSBOURNE**/Road To Nowhere (Epic Associated)
12	11	7	7	**PEARL JAM**/Even Flow (Epic Associated)
11	10	8	8	**LYNCH MOB**/Tangled In The Web (Elektra)
22	17	11	9	**GENESIS**/Driving The Last Spike (Atlantic)
16	15	10	10	**MEN**/Church Of Logic, Sin & Love (Polydor/PLG)
21	19	16	11	**DELBERT McCLINTON**/Every Time I Roll... (Curb)
BREAKER			12	BRUCE SPRINGSTEEN/57 Channels... (Columbia)
15	14	13	13	**MATTHEW SWEET**/Girlfriend (Zoo)
17	16	14	14	**VINCE NEIL**/You're Invited But Your Friend... (Hollywood)
5	4	6	15	**SASS JORDAN**/Make You A Believer (Impact)
24	20	18	16	**VAN HALEN**/Man On A Mission (WB)
26	22	19	17	**ELECTRIC BOYS**/Mary In The Mystery World (Atco)
BREAKER			18	TESLA/Song & Emotion (Geffen)
—	34	23	19	**STING w/ERIC CLAPTON**/It's Probably Me (Reprise)
DEBUT			20	**JOE COCKER**/Love Is Alive (Capitol)
BREAKER			21	HARDLINE/Takin' Me Down (MCA)
36	30	26	22	**TOAD THE WET SPROCKET**/All I Want (Columbia)
37	31	27	23	**CRACKER**/Teen Angst (What The World...) (Virgin)
27	23	21	24	**QUEEN**/Hammer To Fall (Hollywood)*
31	27	25	25	**JEFFREY GAINES**/Hero In Me (Chrysalis/ERG)
—	57	33	26	**KISS**/I Just Wanna (Mercury)
53	47	42	27	**NIRVANA**/Lithium (DGC)
38	32	30	28	**XTC**/The Ballad Of Peter Pumpkinhead (Geffen)
40	36	32	29	**GARY MOORE**/Story Of The Blues (Charisma)
45	40	34	30	**TORA TORA**/Amnesia (A&M)
9	9	12	31	**BRYAN ADAMS**/Touch The Hand (A&M)
54	44	40	32	**CURE**/Friday I'm In Love (Fiction/Elektra)
3	5	15	33	**JOHN MELLENCAMP**/Now More Than Ever (Mercury)
—	56	41	34	**METALLICA**/Wherever I May Roam (Elektra)
55	42	36	35	**MELISSA ETHERIDGE**/2001 (Island/PLG)
56	49	39	36	**ZOO**/Shakin' The Cage (Capricorn/WB)
34	29	28	37	**LITTLE VILLAGE**/Solar Sex Panel (Reprise)
—	54	38	38	**EMERSON, LAKE & PALMER**/Black... (Victory Music/PLG)
42	39	37	39	**ALTERED STATE**/Ghost Beside My... (WB)*
44	43	43	40	**SPIN DOCTORS**/Little Miss Can't Be Wrong (Epic)

*Keeps bullet due to continued growth.

Complete TOP 60 Tracks Chart Pg. 112; LP Chart Pg. 116

COUNTRY

3 WKS	2 WKS	LW	TW	
6	4	3	1	**TRISHA YEARWOOD**/The Woman... (MCA)
8	5	4	2	**DIAMOND RIO**/Norma Jean Riley (Arista)
12	8	6	3	**SHENANDOAH**/Rock My Baby (RCA)
13	9	9	4	**JOE DIFFIE**/Ships That Don't Come In (Epic)
14	11	10	5	**ALAN JACKSON**/Midnight In Montgomery (Arista)
11	7	8	6	**GEORGE STRAIT**/Gone As A Girl Can Get (MCA)
19	14	12	7	**WYNONNA**/I Saw The Light (Curb/MCA)
4	1	2	8	**BILLY RAY CYRUS**/Achy Breaky Heart (Mercury)
16	12	11	9	**SUZY BOGGUSS**/Aces (Liberty)
17	16	13	10	**JOHN ANDERSON**/When It Comes... (BNA Entertainment)
5	3	1	11	**McBRIDE & THE RIDE**/Sacred Ground (MCA)
18	17	14	12	**MICHELLE WRIGHT**/Take It Like A Man (Arista)
20	18	15	13	**REBA McENTIRE**/The Night The Lights Went Out... (MCA)
—	—	23	14	**GARTH BROOKS**/The River (Liberty)
21	19	16	15	**PAM TILLIS**/Blue Rose Is (Arista)
25	20	17	16	**LORRIE MORGAN**/Something In Red (RCA)
24	21	18	17	**DWIGHT YOAKAM**/The Heart That You Own (Reprise)
31	26	20	18	**BILLY DEAN**/Billy The Kid (SBK/Liberty)
23	22	19	19	**MARTINA McBRIDE**/The Time Has Come (RCA)
38	31	24	20	**MARY-CHAPIN CARPENTER**/I Feel Lucky (Columbia)

BREAKERS

BREAKER	36	**CLINT BLACK**/We Tell Ourselves (RCA)
BREAKER	37	**MARK CHESNUTT**/I'll Think Of Something (MCA)
BREAKER	39	**TRACY LAWRENCE**/Runnin' Behind (Atlantic)

DEBUTS

DEBUT	47	**MICHAEL WHITE**/Familiar Ground (Reprise)
DEBUT	48	**LITTLE TEXAS**/You And Forever And Me (WB)

Complete TOP 50 Country Chart Pg. 102; Country Song Information Index Pg. 105

Courtesy of *R & R*

This balding, former marketing and advertising major from Oklahoma State University had country roots that could be traced to people such as Dan Fogelberg and Red Foley. But Garth Brooks also displayed musical influences from Elton John, Bob Seager, and Billy Joel, as well as the stage theatrics of Mick Jagger. An NBC TV special by Garth Brooks became the number one rated TV show in the 1992 season.

Other stars such as Randy Travis, Tricia Yearwood, Clint Black, Vince Gill, Reba McEntire, and Travis Tritt characterized a new type of country star with high appeal to the baby boomers, who according to industry sales reports, now buy more records than teenagers. As one country star explained, rock music talks much about the first romances of teenagers and other feral experiences whereas country music talks about work, stress, and the third divorce of the baby boomers. One commentator explained that rock may appeal to middle-class suburban kids who have no experience of anything except what they hear on the radio, but country speaks emotional truth. Paul Shaffer of the "David Letterman Show" explains that "Country is soul music for white people, and people always return to soul music, because that's where the feeling is."

For whatever reasons, country music has been the format that has taken some stations to the number one ratings position in several cities, and Dan felt such a format should be considered for WMKT.

Dan recognizes that a major demographic shift is occurring in America. He believes that projected population changes might influence the format decision. He found statistics to indicate substantial declines in the traditional strength of hit radio (ages 12–24). At the same time, he discovered a rising number of listeners over 40. He also found that much of the future population growth was expected to be among African-American and Hispanic market segments. In some cities, urban-contemporary and Spanish language stations were achieving higher ratings than stations contending for the fragmented mass market formats.

Music Research

Even if WMKT stayed with its existing format, Dan questioned the quality of the selections in the play list of the station. He had seen many approaches to music selection over the decades he had been in the radio business. Prior to the 1960s, most on-air talent, or "disc jockeys" as they were known then, selected their own music. In the sixties and early seventies, most stations became much more disciplined in selecting music, with a play list from which on-air talent could make few if any deviations. The music director (MD) or program director (PD) made decisions, but the decisions usually reflected the instincts of the programmer. The PD or MD had to have "good ears," which they typically developed from monitoring sales in music stores, requests, and jukebox play to get a "feeling for the street."

In the late seventies and early eighties, the best programmers discovered a highly effective way to determine the music to be played—call-out research. Often the PDs or MDs of small stations either did not know how to conduct such research or did not have the budgets to do so. Smaller stations might rely on reports in trade publications to determine "what's hot and what's not."

Large share stations became sophisticated with call-out research or similar techniques conducted in auditoriums. Their research allowed them to play what the target audience rally wanted to hear. Since many stations are linked to firms that own stations in multiple markets, the research techniques and results can be shared between multiple stations, possibly achieving an advantage over other stations. Ultimately, however, many of the large share stations became very conservative, waiting 6 or 8 weeks until a record began to be played by some small stations and then testing the record.

If all major stations have good research and if they all target the largest demographic markets, the results are inevitable. All stations play the same music and sound pretty much the same. The only difference between major stations is what goes on between the records. Sometimes the research indicates that what consumers prefer most is for nothing to occur between records. As a result, some stations boast in their promotions about how many records are played "without commercial interruption." The policy of carefully researching every record worked for many years, but in the mid-nineties, the approach is not giving WMKT the ratings it needs.

Promotions

An essential component of building ratings in the radio industry is promotions and contests. Dan is concerned, however, that the contests are getting out of control, at least from a budgeting perspective. Most stations design their contests around "ratings periods," the times when Arbitron asks a sample of people in each city to complete a diary for each 15-minute period of time during the day when they listen to radio. From these diaries, Arbitron sells to advertisers information concerning each station's share by time period, as well as the age and gender of listeners.

Despite prohibitions by Arbitron against contests that distort the ratings, most stations are well aware of the ratings periods. Often stations operate contests during these periods in which listeners can call in to win prizes. In recent years, the costs of such promotions have escalated to levels of $100,000 or more. In addition to the prize money, stations have large costs associated with advertising the promotions, often using direct mail to distribute magic keys, numbers, and so forth that permit people to enter contests. The major purpose is to get people who might not normally listen to do so during ratings periods. Usually, the concentration of such promotions is on morning drive time.

Even if such promotions do not achieve many additional listeners, the effect on ratings may be significant because consumers remember the station's call letters or identifying phrase and are more likely to record them in the diary. Some people believe that the effect of the promotions, therefore, is to increase ratings regardless of actual listening. Advertising on billboards, TV, and so forth might also have the same effect as well as other promotions designed to generate publicity, word-of-mouth and media mentions. This process has caused some cynics in the industry to say that it does not matter how many listeners a radio station has; the only thing that matters is how many people write down the station's call letters in the Arbitron diaries, since that is what advertising agencies use when buying time.

WMKT had always spent large amounts of money on contests, promotion, and media advertising. During the budget problems of the past two years, however, Dan Morris was forced to make large cuts in these budgets. Large prize money was no longer available. Most of the television advertising budget had disappeared, and the overall promotion budget was less than one-half of the amount spent two years earlier.

The position of promotions director was currently unfilled following the recent resignation of Gavin Cadwallader, former PD at WMKT. Leaving it unfilled was helpful from a budget position, but Dan knew he needed to find a new person for the position soon. He was reluctant to make the appointment, however, until he made other decisions concerning format and developed a clearer policy about promotional strategy for the station.

Sales Management

WMKT has a sales force of eight persons, directed by Kelley Hughes a veteran of over 20 years in radio sales. Most of the efforts of the sales people are concentrated on Chicago area advertising agencies and advertisers. A national sales manager works closely with the "rep firm," an organization based in New York which represents the station to national advertisers and their advertising agencies.

Kelley had personally recruited all of the present sales staff. Because the station lacked a formal training program, she hired experienced sales persons from other stations or from other industries as much as possible. During the first six months of employment at the station, new salespersons are paid a draw against commissions, but after the first 6 months they are compensated on the basis of 10 percent of sales. None of the four highest paid sales persons has a college degree. Two of the saleswomen hired more recently did have degrees, one in liberal arts and one in fine arts. The youngest sales person, age 26, is pursuing a marketing degree at Loyola University on a part-time basis while employed at the station.

Challenges

Dan recently attended the Radio & Records convention in which he was confronted with a number of ideas about the challenges facing the radio industry. One of the speakers indicated that target audiences should be defined differently than in the past. Almost all stations defined market segments on the basis of two demographics: age and gender. The speaker indicated that a better approach would be on the basis of lifestyles or psychographics.

Another speaker at the national convention raised the question of "what is the business of radio?" The speaker suggested that most radio stations define their objectives mostly in terms of ratings. "Is ratings the business of radio, or is it the result?" the speaker asked. The speaker indicated that the "business of radio" should be defined as "benefits delivered to market targets," a concept that intrigued Dan.

The trade meeting also indicated that new technologies might change radio considerably. One of these is digital radio, a service in which listeners can purchase a music service of high quality, programmed to play exactly the type of format selected by the listener. The service is commercial free, mostly talk free, and available to consumers for about $10 a month. Some radio leaders see this as a threat to current radio, which is supported almost entirely by advertising revenues.

A further technology that impacts radio is the emergence of low price, high quality equipment that allows a station to be operated almost entirely by automation. Music is programmed, and the talk portion is recorded by a local announcer or a national announcing service in a short time. Four hours of on-air time can be recorded in 20 to 30 minutes with equipment that costs less than $15,000 for an entire station. While licenses, utilities, and other costs are still extensive, the net effect of new technology has been a proliferation of radio stations. It is now possible to bring a station on the air at relatively low cost with the result that stations can be targeted to very specific geodemographic market segments.

Because of the large number of stations, many are unprofitable and "going dark." As a result the FCC is considering changes in its rules that would permit national ownership groups to expand greatly the total number of stations they are permitted to own. The FCC is also considering dropping its limitation on ownership to one station of a type (AM, FM) in any market. This would open up the possibility of one company such as Westinghouse, Jacor, Nationwide, and so forth of owning several stations with a portfolio of formats in a single market.

Dan remembered that some observers predicted the demise of radio during the 1960s when television began to grow rapidly. In earlier years, people predicted that AM was the only type of radio that had significant economic value. FM stations were so limited in their signal and their audience that some FM licenses were simply abandoned; therefore, he did not want to jump to quick conclusions of doom and gloom about the present situation.

Dan Morris also knew that in an environment in which over half of all stations were losing money and stations such as his were experiencing revenue declines of 20 percent or more, other stations were gaining audience share, profitability, and community influence. His challenge was to turn WMKT around and be one of the country's winning stations.

Focal Topics

1. What is the "business" of radio? How might an understanding of this mission affect planning at WMKT?

2. What attributes determine which radio station listeners choose for most of their listening?

3. Based on trends occurring in the marketplace, what format do you recommend? How should this be implemented at WMKT?

4. Given your recommendations in the previous questions, prepare a promotional program for WMKT.

■ ■ ■ ■ ■

Singapore Airlines

■ ■ ■ ■ ■

Early in 1947 a twin-engine Airspeed Consul bearing the insignia "Malayan Airways" completed its first commercial flight linking Singapore, Kuala Lumpur, Ipoh, and Penang. Malayan Airways grew steadily during its first eight years of operation, and by 1955 a fleet of Douglas DC3s was operating flights throughout the region.

With the formation of the Federation of Malaysia in 1963, the airline was renamed Malaysian Airways. In 1966 the governments of Malaysia and Singapore acquired joint control of the airline, which was then renamed Malaysia-Singapore Airlines (MSA). Having developed a route system encompassing most of southeast Asia, MSA began to expand its intercontinental network. The airline's Boeing era began in 1968, when the company acquired three B707s and extended its northern route to Tokyo.

On October 1, 1972, MSA ceased operations and Singapore Airlines (SIA) took to the skies as its successor. The new airline continued to serve the entire international network of the previous company and retained all its B707 and B737 planes. Another B707 was added to the SIA fleet, and in 1973, SIA started to fly the wide-bodied B747s.

On May 10, 1978, SIA embarked on its fleet modernization program by signing a record $900 million order for thirteen B747s and six B727s. This was followed by a $1.8 billion order for eight 747-300s (dubbed BIG TOP) and six A300s in 1981; a $1.4 billion order for six more B747-300s, four B757s, and six A310s; a $3.3 billion order for twenty 747-400s (dubbed MEGATOP) in 1986; and a $5.5 billion order for thirty B747-400s in 1990.

By 1993, SIA's young and modern fleet will comprise twelve MEGATOP 747s, fourteen BIG TOP 747s, four B747-200s, two B747 freighters, and sixteen A310s. By the end of 1992, the SIA network stretched across sixty-seven cities in forty countries. The most recent additions to the network are Hanoi and New York.

Singapore—The Country

It is perhaps ironic that one of the world's larger airlines is located in one of the world's smaller countries. "No Crime. No Poverty. No Dirt." These are words used to describe the country by many visitors to Singapore. Even visitors from Switzerland and Germany, countries also renowned for their cleanliness, often marvel at the spotless perfection of Singapore. The tree and flower lined expressways are not only free of traffic jams; they are free of litter. Hardly ever will a scrap of paper, a cigarette butt, or a gum wrapper be found on Singapore's streets and expressways. This is accomplished not only by the well articulated values of the nation but by heavy fines for littering, smoking in nondesignated places, or failure to flush a public toilet. Visitors are clearly warned upon entry to the country that use of illegal drugs is punishable by death.

More than 24 million passengers pass through the Changi airport each year on over 1,900 flights a week. The airport is always spotless; even the restrooms are clean with flowers displayed on the tables in men's and women's facilities.

Singapore caters to everyone from businesspersons to "boat bums"—and prospers from them all. Over 250 ships enter the Singapore harbor each day to leave or pick up cargo from nearly every corner of the world. Around the clock, ships await their specific 4-hour unloading period and take their turn in one of the largest and most efficient cargo handling facilities in the world.

To say Singapore is no fun would be unfair. To say that it is "clean" fun is entirely justifiable. Dropping a gum wrapper on the street brings an automatic fine of about $250. But don't worry too much as a foreigner. The Singaporeans are so friendly and concerned about other people that should a tourist drop paper on the street a local person will often pick it up and dispose of it properly so the foreigner would not be fined.

Not only the streets are clean in Singapore but so are most options for having fun. Prostitution, drugs, and excessive forms of activity are not part of the scene in Singapore. One of the best known forms of "clean" fun in Singapore is the Jurong Bird Park, featuring the Penguin Parade. Among other things it contains 100 penguins of various species waddling among a landscape of rocks, cliffs, nesting alcoves, and burrows. Jurong Bird Haven displays over 5,000 birds of more than 430 species. In Singapore, even the bird cages are clean!

Much credit for the "economic miracle" called Singapore can be attributed to Lee Kuan Yew, the nation's leader for many years. Lee is an urban planner by discipline, and his training shines through every part of the city, no place more so than the airport. Changi airport has all the normal restaurants, duty-free shops, car rental services, and so forth that you would expect but is run more efficiently than perhaps any other airport in the world. Beyond that, the airport boasts a supermarket, children's play area, cinema, hair dressing salons, nursery, pharmacy, hotel, and a business center complete with first-rate secretarial services. Perhaps the thing that impresses visitors most are the trees lining the road to the airport. With characteristic forethought, Singapore planners planted the trees years before the airport was opened so they would be just right when the airport was completed. Trees and flowers surround Changi airport.

Planning is a key to understanding Singapore. The freeways are not crowded. This is partly due to excellence in design, but also, the government does not allow more cars to use the freeway than it can safely and swiftly accommodate. Private cars must be sold, usually to people in other countries, before they are 10 years old in order to prevent breakdowns and other problems associated with driving old cars. An even shorter period is mandated for commercial vehicles.

A striking aspect of Singapore is the low frequency of crime. This situation is created partly by the condition of having few poor people. Few people are wealthy but most people have enough to live comfortably. Low crime rates are also partly due to strict observance of law and order. Absence of crime was not always the situation in Singapore, however. A Chinese underground controlled drugs, prostitution, gambling, and other assorted vices for centuries. Neither the British nor Japanese could control these practitioners of organized crime. But Lee did, by rounding up the criminals, getting rid of them, and then maintaining a strict system of swift and certain punishment for crime.

Former U.S. President Richard Nixon wrote in his book *1999* that in his 40 years of public service and travels throughout the world, no leader had impressed him more than Lee Kuan Yew. He has helped create not only a country of enormous economic success with some of the highest levels of educational excellence and computer literacy in the world, but also a society that incorporates cultural diversity. The country's official languages are Mandarin and English, but Cantonese and other languages are common. Singapore encompasses population groups of Chinese, Malaysian, English, and other racial and national backgrounds. Significant segments of the population are Buddhist, Christian, Hindu, Jewish, or Muslim in their religious beliefs. Lee explains that the achievements of Singapore are a function of its values. In one of his most famous statements, he is quoted as saying, "We are an immigrant nation. Our values are those required for survival, stability, and success."

SIA Markets and Routes

Singapore Airlines flies around the world. Although SIA serves North America, Europe, and Africa, it is a primary server of Asia and the Pacific Rim.

Pacific Rim Economies

The economies of the Asia-Pacific area have, for 3 decades, been growing two to three times the world average growth rate, and this growth advantage is continuing. Northeast Asia produces one third of the world's vehicle output, one-quarter of world steel output, two-thirds of world consumer electronics production, and one-third of world computer output. The population and GDP (total and per capita) of key Asian countries are shown in Exhibit 24.1. Monthly wages of East Asian countries are shown in Exhibit 24.2.

Rapid growth is making for some unusual developments. The South Korean economy is now about the size of the economy of Australia. Taiwan, with a population of 20 million, has an economy half the size of China's billion population. East Asia's share of world trade has been in-

■ **EXHIBIT 24.1   Population and Economic Size of Key Asian Economies, 1990**

	Population (millions)	GDP (US$ million)	GNP per Capita (US$)
Japan	123.5	$2,942,890	$25,430
Hong Kong	5.8	59,670	11,490
Singapore	3.0	34,600	11,160
Taiwan	20.2	161,600	7,992
S. Korea	42.8	236,400	5,400
Malaysia	17.9	42,400	2,320
Thailand	55.8	80,170	1,420
Philippines	61.5	43,860	730
Indonesia	178.2	107,290	570
China	1,113.7	364,900	370

Source: THE WORLD BANK. *World Development Report 1992*, p. 222–3, and NIHON BOEKI

■ **EXHIBIT 24.2   Monthly Wages in East Asia (US$, percent change from 1990 in parentheses)**

	General Workers
Singapore	$615–846 (8–10)
Hong Kong	769–1000 (10–15)
Taiwan	639–1231 (7–21)
S. Korea (starting salaries)	515 (17)
Malaysia	208 (8–12)
Thailand	162 (5–6)
Philippines	123 (2.7)
Indonesia	54–77 (19)
China-Beijing	39 (12)
China-Shanghai	54–77 (10–15)

Source: *Nikkei Weekly*, November 30, 1991,3

creasing very rapidly and much of the increase in Asian trade is within Asia. Savings and investment throughout the area are at very high levels, with the exception of the Philippines. The levels are high enough to provide self-sustaining growth without the critical need for foreign investment.

The powerhouse economy, of course, is Japan. Alone, it totals about three-quarters of the total economies of East Asia and is nearly the size of Britain, France, and Germany combined. If growth rates continue as they have for the past 10 years, Japan's economy will overtake the United States, making Japan's the largest in the world by the year 2000 and more than twice as large as the U.S. economy on a per capita basis. Japan's current investments are increasingly focusing on Asia because of the higher growth and profitability for Japan. Asia is now a larger export market for Japan than North America.

SIA Routes

SIA dominates many routes in the Asia-Pacific area. SIA routes are shown in Exhibit 24.3.

In 1992, SIA added Madrid, Johannesburg, and Ho Chi Minh City to its fast growing international network. Madrid is served twice weekly, on Saturday and Wednesday, by B747-400 aircraft. The Saturday flight is via Amsterdam and beyond to Madrid and Paris. The Wednesday flight is via Paris and beyond Madrid to Frankfurt. As the capital of Spain, Madrid is one of Europe's most interesting destinations with famous museums, art galleries, palaces, churches, shops, and restaurants.

The flight to Johannesburg is a bi-weekly turnaround service on a circular routing. One flight uses the B747-300 and the other, the B747 combi. Flights leave Singapore for Johannesburg via Mauritius on Thursday and return nonstop to Singapore. On Sunday SIA flies nonstop to Johannesburg and returns via Mauritius. Johannesburg is South Africa's largest industrial, financial, and cultural center as well as a gateway to Cape Town in the south, Pretoria and Krueger National Park in the north, and other cities and cultural attractions.

After a break of almost 17 years, SIA has resumed its service to Vietnam. Ho Chi Minh City is served four times weekly. There is also a Hanoi service with two flights each week.

In 1992, SIA also began direct service to New York, offered six times a week. The flights are routed through Frankfurt or Brussels and fly across the Atlantic rather than the Pacific, cutting down the flight time required for the trip between Singapore and New York.

An advertisement used to announce service to New York is shown in Exhibit 24.4. This ad indicates some of the specific details of the flight as well as attempts to capture an image of the city.

■ **EXHIBIT 24.3   SIA Routes**

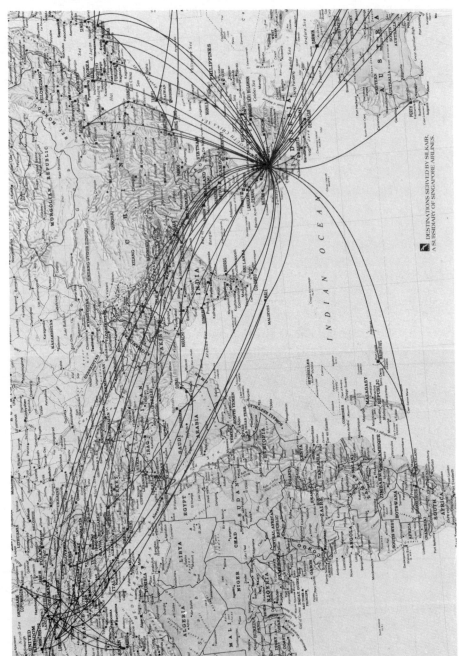

DESTINATIONS SERVED BY SILKAIR, A SUBSIDIARY OF SINGAPORE AIRLINES.

(continued)

■ **EXHIBIT 24.3** *continued*

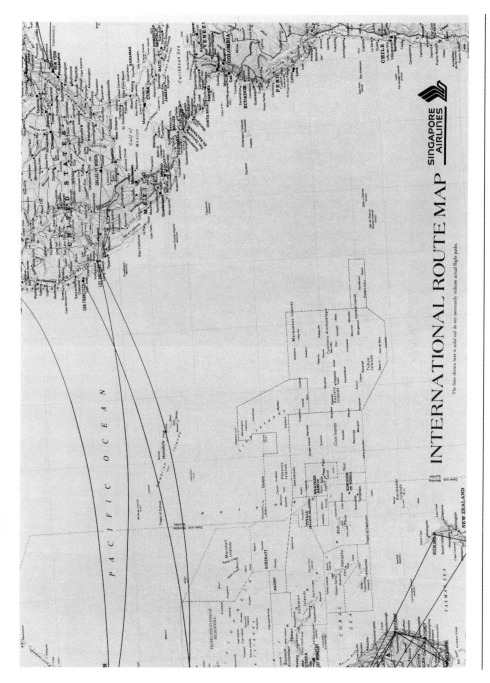

INTERNATIONAL ROUTE MAP

The lines shown here is solid red do not necessarily indicate actual flight paths.

SINGAPORE AIRLINES

281

■ **EXHIBIT 24.4   SIA New York Service**

Singapore Airlines now offers the first and only direct service from Singapore to New York. Our exclusive MEGATOP 747 departs daily except Wednesday and flies across the Atlantic (via either Frankfurt or Brussels)

(continued)

■ **EXHIBIT 24.4**   *continued*

arriving in New York (JFK) in time for lunch. So now you can fly the fastest same-plane service to the Big Apple, whilst enjoying inflight service even other airlines talk about. **SINGAPORE AIRLINES**

SIA Quality Service

Singapore Airlines provides a quality of service that is the envy of nearly every other airline in the world. Year after year, Singapore Airline is rated as the number one or two airline in the world for quality of service in a variety of polls of airline passengers and travel agents.

SIA provides three classes of service: economy, business (named Raffles Class), and First Class. Unique among airlines, SIA passengers often describe economy service on a par with the business class of other airlines and rate the Raffles Class as equal to or better than the First Class service of other airlines.

Passengers comment most on the excellence of service provided by flight attendants. They are recruited from Singapore, Taiwan, Japan, and other Asian countries and achieve a level of attention to detail that is unparalleled. In First Class and Raffles Class, passengers find it difficult to finish a glass or dish without someone immediately inquiring about additional needs or removing the used item. Hot foods are very hot and cold foods are appropriately cold, in contrast to the serving practices of some airlines. Small details are obvious everywhere. Hot towels are larger and more frequent than in competitive airlines. Earphones are top quality. The variety of foods and beverages is large, providing greater choices than among most airlines. Toilets are kept clean during the flight and stocked with a large variety of amenities such as perfume, toothbrushes, and other items. Although most of these items are found on other airlines, the quantity and quality of such items is usually better on SIA.

Perhaps First Class best typifies SIA. First Class is normally quite good in most airlines but SIA's First Class reaches new heights of luxury, with the finest champagnes, vintage wines, international beers, gourmet teas, and a choice of meals and meal times.

Renowned Krug Grande Curvee champagne is served as an additional choice on flights of two and a half hours, or more. An "Easy Meal" has been introduced to give passengers on long-haul flights the flexibility to dine at the time they prefer. Before the meal, a wide variety of hot savouries is offered. These include hot canapes and satay. The main meal is comprised of hors d'oeuvres, a main course, and fresh fruit for dessert. On SIA's Orient and Trans-Pacific flights, Sheraton Cuisine is offered as a meal choice for lunch, dinner, and supper. This cuisine is a blend of Asian spices and traditional ingredients, with emphasis on fresh, natural ingredients to create lighter, healthier meals. As an elegant finishing touch, SIA offers the best and widest choice of teas—Earl Grey, Darjeeling, Lipton Yellow label, Camomile, and decaffeinated tea. To round off the meal, there's white or dark chocolate.

Entertainment has recently been upgraded with progressive installation of in-seat videos, enabling passengers to watch movies and short features from six channels. Even the cabin has been given a new look. SIA's

B747-400 Megatops have been refitted with thicker carpets and seats that offer the highest level of comfort. The airline's most experienced stewards and stewardesses work First Class. Because of their extra years of service, they understand the needs of all types of passengers and attempt to meet every need.

Raffles Class, carrying the name of a famous hotel, street, and historical hero, provides a level of service that rivals First Class on most airlines. The seats provide less leg room than First Class and the foods and wines may not provide quite the level of luxury, but quality is just as high.

Female flight attendants wear a uniform that is as unique as the service level of SIA. The uniform is a traditional floor-length dress, including traditional sandals.

Promotional Programs

SIA engages in a wide variety of promotional programs. These include television ads in key markets such as Hong Kong, as well as print media and direct marketing in most other important markets.

A major theme or slogan in SIA advertising is "That Singapore Girl." The theme is extended to all media, including print and television, as well as to promotional and specialty items such as laminated cards to attach to luggage with the traveler's business card on one side and a picture and slogan "That Singapore Girl" on the other.

Singapore Airlines participates in the frequent flyer programs of American, Delta, and other U.S. airlines. In addition, it has special programs such as the SIA travel bonus, offered for a limited time to passengers flying the Raffles Class to the United States. Any passenger traveling the SIA Raffles Class from Hong Kong to San Francisco with SIA adult-fare tickets purchased in Hong Kong within the promotional period is entitled to an "Award MCO" (miscellaneous charges order) worth HK$700 for one way, and HK$1,400 for a round trip. The program also provides benefits to passengers heading for destinations beyond San Francisco as long as they travel Trans-Pacific on specified flights.

The Award MCOs are valid for one year from the date of issue and are good for payment of SIA tickets (including special fare tickets through agents) issued in Hong Kong, excess baggage charges, and the fare difference for upgrading. Passengers using Award MCOs for upgrading get an additional bonus. Only HK$4,200 worth of Award MCO is needed for one-way upgrading from the Raffles Class to First Class (and HK$8,400 for round trip), much less than the original fare difference between the two classes.

SIA also initiates other special promotions. Often these feature special events for travel agents, corporate travel planners, and other influential people. An example of such a promotion for the Hong Kong travel business community is shown in Exhibit 24.5.

■ **EXHIBIT 24.5**   SIA Promotional Meeting for
Hong Kong Travel Planners

SQ TOPICS

1992 MAY ISSUE   SINGAPORE AIRLINES HONG KONG

SIA'S ANNUAL DINNER "THE ASEAN ROUNDABOUT" WAS AN ALL-ROUND SUCCESS.

The Asean Roundabout Hub display was the centre of attention.

First Prize Winner, Mr. Simon Yim, Air Coal International Ltd.

The Playboy Bunnies had the place hopping.

The reception area had many welcoming Asean touches.

Once again, SIA played host to its many friends in Hong Kong's travel industry with its annual dinner. The theme of "Asean Roundabout" was to highlight Singapore as a hub for travel to the Asean countries — Indonesia, Malaysia, Brunei, Philippines and Thailand. The spectacular dinner featured spicy sensations from around the region. This year the entertainment had even more bounce, with a team of Playboy Girls high-tailing it into town. The four beautiful bunnies sang and danced their way through a long line up of songs — "Money, Money, Money", "Hanky Panky", "Get Ready", and many other pop hits. There were two Lucky Draws. Table Prizes included name card holders and calculators. Grand Prizes were round trip tickets to Singapore on Singapore Airlines and tickets to any one Asean destination served by Silk Air.

Indeed, it was a night roundly applauded by everyone.

Researching Decision Processes

A continual problem facing airline management is the question, "How do customers decide which airline to fly?" Is their decision based on schedules? Price? Service? Food and beverage? Equipment? Or some combination of these and other attributes?

Singapore Airlines maintains a marketing research group to provide information about decision processes on a continuing basis, as do other airlines. A variety of methods are employed but one of the most important is a passenger opinion survey. A copy of a recent form of this survey is shown in Exhibit 24.6. The complete form is presented in English, although the first page of the questionnaire is shown in the other languages most likely to be read by passengers.

One of the issues facing management is the question of whether or not this questionnaire contains the relevant attributes that should be measured concerning airline service. Another question facing management is how best to segment the market for airline service. The latter part of the questionnaire in Exhibit 24.6 offers many possibilities for analysis of demographic and other data.

Focal Topics

1. How do consumers decide to purchase the services from one airline or its competitors? Does the questionnaire used by SIA measure the appropriate attributes?

2. How should data from this questionnaire be analyzed to be useful to the management of SIA?

3. What markets or routes should be SIA's primary market targets? What new routes or cities should be added or increased in service based on your analysis of changing global economic realities?

4. Evaluate the promotional program of SIA. Should the theme "That Singapore Girl" and events such as that in Exhibit 24.5 which have been well received in Asian markets, be continued and used in North American, African, and European markets?

■ ■ ■ ■ ■

■ EXHIBIT 24.6   SIA Marketing Research Questionnaire

Dear Passenger

We are pleased to welcome you on board and hope that you have an enjoyable flight. We would like to ensure that we continue to provide you with the best possible service.

We therefore regularly monitor the quality of our services in order to determine areas where we can further improve our performance.

Please help us by taking a few minutes to complete this questionnaire. We are surveying only a scientifically selected sample of passengers on each flight. Your opinions are therefore of great importance to us.

One of our cabin crew will collect it prior to landing.

Thank you for your assistance.

Michael J. N. Tan
Deputy Managing Director
(Commercial)

Date: _____   Flight No. SQ _____

1.   PLEASE RATE EACH OF THE FOLLOWING SERVICES, BASED ON THIS PRESENT TRIP.

Please check ☑ one of these 5 ratings, for each service listed:

	EXCELLENT	GOOD	AVERAGE	POOR	VERY POOR
INFLIGHT SERVICE:					
Friendly, helpful attitude	☐	☐	☐	☐	☐
Prompt, efficient service	☐	☐	☐	☐	☐
Clarity of PA (Public Address) system	☐	☐	☐	☐	☐
Announcements by cabin crew	☐	☐	☐	☐	☐
Announcements by captain or cockpit crew	☐	☐	☐	☐	☐
FOOD AND BEVERAGE:					
Eye appeal of food	☐	☐	☐	☐	☐
Taste of food	☐	☐	☐	☐	☐
Quality of food	☐	☐	☐	☐	☐
Did you get your choice of main meal? 1 ☐ Yes 2 ☐ No					
Taste/flavour of coffee/tea	☐	☐	☐	☐	☐
Quality of wines	☐	☐	☐	☐	☐
Variety of choice of wines	☐	☐	☐	☐	☐
INFLIGHT ENTERTAINMENT:					
Inflight music/audio programmes:					
• Music/audio programme selection	☐	☐	☐	☐	☐
• Sound quality	☐	☐	☐	☐	☐
Inflight movies:					
• Types of movies shown	☐	☐	☐	☐	☐
• Picture quality	☐	☐	☐	☐	☐
• Sound quality	☐	☐	☐	☐	☐
AIRCRAFT INTERIOR:					
Aircraft seating comfort	☐	☐	☐	☐	☐
Clean cabin and seats	☐	☐	☐	☐	☐
Clean washrooms/toilets	☐	☐	☐	☐	☐

2.   DID YOU TELEPHONE AN SIA OFFICE TO MAKE RESERVATIONS?   1 ☐ Yes   2 ☐ No

IF SO, IN WHICH CITY IS THE SIA OFFICE? Please check ☑ one:

☐ 1 Adelaide	☐ 8 Brussels	☐ 15 Jakarta	☐ 22 Melbourne	☐ 29 Rome	☐ 36 Vancouver
☐ 2 Amsterdam	☐ 9 Colombo	☐ 16 Kuala Lumpur	☐ 23 Nagoya	☐ 30 San Francisco	☐ 37 Zurich
☐ 3 Auckland	☐ 10 Copenhagen	☐ 17 London	☐ 24 New York	☐ 31 Seoul	☐ 38 Others
☐ 4 Bandar Seri Begawan	☐ 11 Denpasar	☐ 18 Los Angeles	☐ 25 Osaka	☐ 32 Singapore	(Please write)
☐ 5 Bangkok	☐ 12 Frankfurt	☐ 19 Madras	☐ 26 Paris	☐ 33 Sydney	
☐ 6 Bombay	☐ 13 Fukuoka	☐ 20 Male	☐ 27 Penang	☐ 34 Taipei	
☐ 7 Brisbane	☐ 14 Hong Kong	☐ 21 Manila	☐ 28 Perth	☐ 35 Tokyo	

Please check ☑ one of these 5 ratings, for each service listed:

	EXCELLENT	GOOD	AVERAGE	POOR	VERY POOR
Easy to reach office by phone	☐	☐	☐	☐	☐
Fast, efficient reservations	☐	☐	☐	☐	☐
Friendly, helpful attitude	☐	☐	☐	☐	☐

3.   AT WHICH AIRPORT DID YOU BOARD THIS FLIGHT? Please check ☑ one:

☐ 1 Adelaide	☐ 8 Brussels	☐ 15 Jakarta	☐ 22 Melbourne	☐ 29 Rome	☐ 36 Vancouver
☐ 2 Amsterdam	☐ 9 Colombo	☐ 16 Kuala Lumpur	☐ 23 Nagoya	☐ 30 San Francisco	☐ 37 Zurich
☐ 3 Auckland	☐ 10 Copenhagen	☐ 17 London	☐ 24 New York	☐ 31 Seoul	☐ 38 Others
☐ 4 Bandar Seri Begawan	☐ 11 Denpasar	☐ 18 Los Angeles	☐ 25 Osaka	☐ 32 Singapore	(Please write)
☐ 5 Bangkok	☐ 12 Frankfurt	☐ 19 Madras	☐ 26 Paris	☐ 33 Sydney	
☐ 6 Bombay	☐ 13 Fukuoka	☐ 20 Male	☐ 27 Penang	☐ 34 Taipei	
☐ 7 Brisbane	☐ 14 Hong Kong	☐ 21 Manila	☐ 28 Perth	☐ 35 Tokyo	

Please check ☑ one of these 5 ratings, for each service listed:

	EXCELLENT	GOOD	AVERAGE	POOR	VERY POOR
Fast, efficient check-in	☐	☐	☐	☐	☐
Friendly, courteous check-in	☐	☐	☐	☐	☐
Efficient seat assignment	☐	☐	☐	☐	☐
IF YOU TRANSFERRED FLIGHTS AT SINGAPORE:					
Efficient transfer handling at Changi Airport	☐	☐	☐	☐	☐

(continued)

■ **EXHIBIT 24.6** *continued*

---

4. DID YOU VISIT AN SIA TICKET OFFICE?   1 ☐ Yes   2 ☐ No

IF SO, IN WHICH CITY? Please check ☑ one:

☐ 1 Adelaide
☐ 2 Amsterdam
☐ 3 Auckland
☐ 4 Bandar Seri Begawan
☐ 5 Bangkok
☐ 6 Bombay
☐ 7 Brisbane
☐ 8 Brussels
☐ 9 Colombo
☐ 10 Copenhagen
☐ 11 Denpasar
☐ 12 Frankfurt
☐ 13 Fukuoka
☐ 14 Hong Kong
☐ 15 Jakarta
☐ 16 Kuala Lumpur
☐ 17 London
☐ 18 Los Angeles
☐ 19 Madras
☐ 20 Male
☐ 21 Manila
☐ 22 Melbourne
☐ 23 Nagoya
☐ 24 New York
☐ 25 Osaka
☐ 26 Paris
☐ 27 Penang
☐ 28 Perth
☐ 29 Rome
☐ 30 San Francisco
☐ 31 Seoul
☐ 32 Singapore
☐ 33 Sydney
☐ 34 Taipei
☐ 35 Tokyo
☐ 36 Vancouver
☐ 37 Zurich
☐ 38 Others (Please write)

Please check ☑ one of these 5 ratings, for each service listed:

	EXCELLENT 1	GOOD 2	AVERAGE 3	POOR 4	VERY POOR 5
Fast, efficient service	☐	☐	☐	☐	☐
Friendly, helpful attitude	☐	☐	☐	☐	☐

5. OVERALL RATING:

All things considered, how would you rate your experience with Singapore Airlines on this trip?

☐ ☐ ☐ ☐ ☐

6 (i) Have you taken a flight of similar length as this, on another airline, in the past 12 months?

Yes ☐ Continue to 6(ii)   No ☐ Go to Question 6(iv)

(ii) Which other airline did you most recently use on a flight of similar length? Please name the airline and the route travelled on that flight:

Airline : _____ *(Name one airline only – latest travelled)*

Route travelled : _____

(iii) How would you compare that airline with SIA in the following areas?

Please check ☑ one of these 5 ratings, for each service listed:

	WELL ABOVE SIA 1	SLIGHTLY ABOVE SIA 2	SAME AS SIA 3	SLIGHTLY BELOW SIA 4	WELL BELOW SIA 5
Inflight Service					
Food and Beverage					
Inflight Entertainment					
Aircraft Interior / Comfort					
Overall Rating					

(iv) Have you flown from the same city as this occasion, on another airline, in the past 12 months?

Yes ☐ Continue to 6(v)   No ☐ Go to Question 7

(v) Which other airline did you most recently use from the same city?

Airline : _____ *(Name one airline only – latest travelled)*

(vi) How would you compare that airline with SIA in the following areas?

Please check ☑ one for each service listed :

	WELL ABOVE SIA 1	SLIGHTLY ABOVE SIA 2	SAME AS SIA 3	SLIGHTLY BELOW SIA 4	WELL BELOW SIA 5
Telephone Service					
Ticket Office Service					
Airport Service					

7. STATISTICAL INFORMATION:

I am travelling by: 1 ☐ Economy Class   2 ☐ Business Class   3 ☐ First Class

My age is: 1 ☐ Under 20   2 ☐ 20 to 35   3 ☐ 36 to 49   4 ☐ 50 and over

I am   1 ☐ Male   2 ☐ Female

I am a national of

☐ 1 Brunei
☐ 2 China (PRC)
☐ 3 Indonesia
☐ 4 Malaysia
☐ 5 Philippines
☐ 6 Singapore
☐ 7 Thailand
☐ 8 Hong Kong
☐ 9 Japan
☐ 10 South Korea
☐ 11 Taiwan
☐ 12 Other Asia
☐ 13 Austria
☐ 14 Belgium
☐ 15 France
☐ 16 Greece
☐ 17 Italy
☐ 18 Netherlands
☐ 19 Scandinavia
☐ 20 Spain
☐ 21 Switzerland
☐ 22 Turkey
☐ 23 Germany
☐ 24 United Kingdom
☐ 25 USSR
☐ 26 Other Europe
☐ 27 United States
☐ 28 Canada
☐ 29 Latin America
☐ 30 Australia
☐ 31 New Zealand
☐ 32 India
☐ 33 Bangladesh
☐ 34 Nepal
☐ 35 Pakistan
☐ 36 Sri Lanka
☐ 37 Maldives
☐ 38 Mauritius
☐ 39 Egypt
☐ 40 United Arab Emirates
☐ 41 Saudi Arabia
☐ 42 Africa
☐ 43 Others

The main purpose of my travel, on this trip, is
1 ☐ Business   2 ☐ Pleasure / vacation   3 ☐ Business and pleasure   4 ☐ Other purpose

NUMBER OF TRIPS ABROAD IN PAST 3 YEARS:
Not counting this trip, the number of trips abroad which I have made by air in the past 3 years is (count each round trip as one trip):

1 ☐ None   2 ☐ 1 – 5   3 ☐ 6 – 20   4 ☐ 21 and above

Your name and address please (optional)

Name _____

Address _____

_____

OUR CREW WILL COLLECT THIS QUESTIONNAIRE BEFORE LANDING. THANK YOU.

SINGAPORE AIRLINES

(continued)

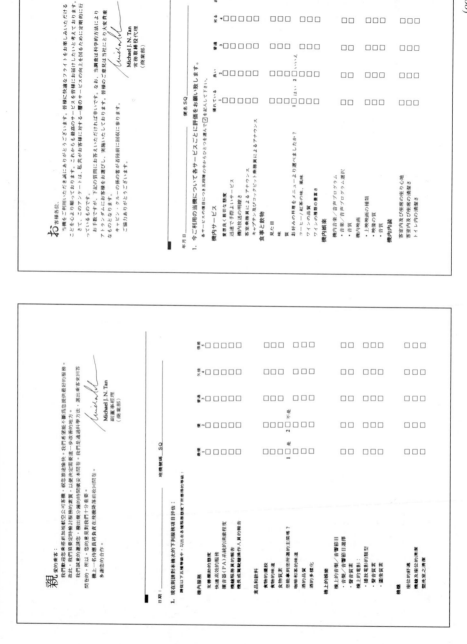

(continued)

French Questionnaire

Cher Passager,

Nous vous souhaitons la bienvenue à bord et espérons que vous faites un vol agréable. Nous aimerions continuer à vous offrir le meilleur des services.

C'est pour cela que nous continuons régulièrement à contrôlons la qualité de notre service afin de déterminer le secteur où nous pouvons l'améliorer.

Nous vous serions très reconnaissant si vous vouliez nous aider en remplissant ce questionnaire. Notre enquête est réalisée uniquement selon un échantillon de passagers choisis scientifiquement sur chaque vol. Votre avis est très important pour le succès de cette étude.

Notre personnel de cabine ramassera les questionnaires avant l'atterrissage.

Merci de votre coopération.

Michael J. N. Tan
Directeur Général Adjoint
(Service Commercial)

Date: _____ Vol No. SQ _____

1. VEUILLEZ EVALUER CHACUN DES SERVICES SUIVANTS EN VOUS BASANT SUR LE PRESENT VOYAGE

Marquer l'une des cinq appréciations pour chaque service mentionné ☑

	EXCELLENT 1	BON 2	MOYEN 3	MAUVAIS 4	TRÈS MAUVAIS 5
SERVICE A BORD:					
Attitude amicale et prévenante	☐	☐	☐	☐	☐
Service rapide et efficace	☐	☐	☐	☐	☐
Clarté du système P.A. (sonorisation extérieure)	☐	☐	☐	☐	☐
Annonces par le personnel de cabine	☐	☐	☐		
Annonces du pilote ou du personnel de cockpit	☐	☐	☐		
BOISSONS ET REPAS:					
Aspect des plats	☐	☐	☐	☐	☐
Goût de la nourriture	☐	☐	☐	☐	☐
Qualité de la nourriture	☐	☐	☐	☐	☐
Avez-vous obtenu votre choix du repas principal?	1 ☐ Oui	2 ☐ Non			
Arôme/saveur du café/thé	☐	☐	☐		
Qualité des vins	☐	☐	☐		
Variété du choix des vins	☐	☐	☐		
DIVERTISSEMENT A BORD:					
Musique/programmes d'écoute en cours de vol					
• Sélection musique/programme d'écoute	☐	☐	☐		
• Qualité du son	☐	☐	☐		
Films en cours de vol					
• Types de films projetés	☐	☐	☐		
• Qualité de l'image	☐	☐	☐		
• Qualité du son	☐	☐	☐		
INTERIEUR DE L'AVION:					
Confort des sièges	☐	☐	☐		
Propreté de la cabine et des sièges	☐	☐	☐		
Propreté des toilettes	☐	☐	☐		

German Questionnaire

Lieber Passagier!

Wir freuen uns, Sie an Bord begrüßen zu können, und hoffen, daß Sie einen angenehmen Flug haben werden. Wir möchten sicher gehen, daß wir Ihnen weiterhin den bestmöglichen Service bieten werden.

Aus diesem Grund müssen wir regelmäßig die Qualität unseres Services überprüfen, um Bereiche aufzudecken, in denen wir unsere Leistung verbessern können.

Bitte unterstützen Sie uns, indem Sie sich ein paar Minuten Zeit nehmen und diesen Fragebogen ausfüllen. Wir befragen lediglich eine statistisch ausgewählte Stichprobe von Passagieren auf jedem Flug. Ihre Meinung ist daher äußerst wichtig für uns.

Ein Mitglied unserer Crew wird den Fragebogen vor der Landung einsammeln.

Vielen Dank für Ihre Unterstützung.

Michael J. N. Tan
Stellvertretender Geschäftsführer
(Kommerz-Abteilung)

Datum: _____ Flugnummer SQ _____

1. BEWERTEN SIE BITTE DIE FLUGGESELLSCHAFT AUF DIESER GEGENWÄRTIGEN REISE.

Kreuzen Sie bitte für jede der aufgezeichneten Dienstleistungen eine von 5 Spalten an ☑

	AUSGEZEICHNET 1	GUT 2	MITTELMÄSSIG 3	SCHLECHT 4	SEHR SCHLECHT 5
SERVICE AN BORD:					
Freundliches hilfreiches Verhalten	☐	☐	☐	☐	☐
Sofortige tüchtige Bedienung	☐	☐	☐	☐	☐
Deutlichkeit der Lautsprecheranlage	☐	☐	☐	☐	☐
Durchsagen des Kabinenpersonals	☐	☐	☐		
Durchsagen des Flugkapitäns oder der Cockpitbesatzung	☐	☐	☐		
SPEISEN UND GETRÄNKE:					
Appetitlichkeit / Aussehen der Speisen	☐	☐	☐		
Geschmack der Speisen	☐	☐	☐		
Qualität des Essens	☐	☐	☐		
Haben Sie das Hauptgericht erhalten, das Sie gewählt haben?	1 ☐ Ja	2 ☐ Nein			
Geschmack/Aroma von Kaffee/Tee	☐	☐	☐		
Qualität der Weine	☐	☐	☐		
Auswahlmöglichkeiten an Weinen	☐	☐	☐		
UNTERHALTUNG AN BORD:					
Inflight-Musik-/Audio-Aufzeichnungen:					
• Auswahl der Musik-/Audio-Aufzeichnungen	☐	☐	☐		
• Tonqualität	☐	☐	☐		
Inflight-Filme:					
• Art der gezeigten Filme	☐	☐	☐		
• Bildqualität	☐	☐	☐		
• Tonqualität	☐	☐	☐		
FLUGZEUG-INNENRAUM:					
Sitzkomfort im Flugzeug	☐	☐	☐		
Saubere Kabine und Sitze	☐	☐	☐		
Saubere Waschräume/Toiletten	☐	☐	☐		

Red Roof Inns

■ ■ ■ ■ ■

Red Roof Inns is a successful motel firm in the budget motel category, a growing category in an otherwise sluggish motel/hotel business. Red Roof Inns span the entire eastern half of the United States, from Minneapolis to Dallas, Kansas City to Boston. The 200th motel opened in Orlando, Florida, in 1989, but growth began to slow in the early 1990s. All the motels are company-owned and operated, with no franchises.

On February 20, 1973, founder Jim Trueman opened the first Red Roof Inn in Grove City, Ohio. Trueman's strategy was to provide low-cost "rooms only" motels to travelers. Trueman died in 1986, leaving control of the company to his wife, Barbara. Red Roof Inns has grown from one motel in 1973 to 209 as of January 1993. On average fifteen inns were constructed each year until Red Roof Inns hit a no growth mode in the 1990s. The company had financed its growth entirely through internal operations.

Customer Orientation

Red Roof Inns is one of the most innovative economy motel chains in the United States. Red Roof Inns' success is based on the "no frills" concept of offering only the amenities most requested by travelers.

Single rooms are 192 square feet in size. Double, king, and handicapped rooms are 260 square feet. All rooms contain the following: wall-to-wall carpeting, extra long double bed or king-size bed, color television, a small table with two chairs, full tub and shower, air conditioning, individually controlled heating, and open shelving units. Guests may borrow an iron, or request a taxicab or a wake-up call from the front desk. Nonsmoking and handicapped rooms are also available on request.

Room rental includes all of the following amenities free of charge:

- Free local phone calls
- ESPN, CNN, and ShowTime

- Morning coffee in the lobby
- National weekday newspaper
- Baby crib or rollaway (on request)

Red Roof Inns instituted two more amenities to meet business travelers' needs. The Business King Room features a king-size bed, larger work area, desk with overhead lighting, padded chairs, remote control color television, modem jack for computer hookup, and touch tone telephone for calling card calls. Facsimile and copy machines are now located at the front desk of every motel. Red Roof became the lodging choice for an increasing number of business travelers in 1991 because of a tough economic business environment. In 1992, the occupancy rate declined to under 50 percent for some hotel chains, but Red Roof maintained a high occupancy rate. Companies that were trying to cut travel expenses sent their employees to budget, limited service motels. Red Roof's strong reputation in this segment allowed it to capitalize on this trend.[1]

The vending area of each motel has soda machines and a machine that dispenses ice, candy, cigarettes, razors, toothbrushes, toothpaste, aftershave, and aspirin. Some Red Roof Inns also have meeting rooms which can accommodate up to twelve people. These services were offered in response to consumer research conducted on Red Roof Inn's weekday customers.

The price varies per room type and by geographic location. For instance, in Louisiana, the price is lower than in Massachusetts.

Room Type, Number of Lodgers	Price Range
One-person, double-bed room	$24.95–41.95
Two-person, double-bed room	$30.95–47.95
One-person, two double-bed room	$26.95–43.95
Two-person, two double-bed room	$32.95–49.95
Four-person, two double-bed room	$34.95–51.95
One-person, Business King	$26.95–46.95
Two-person, Business King	$32.95–52.95

Competition

In the economy budget segment of the hotel/motel industry, competition is intense. The major competitors include:

- Days Inn
- Motel 6

[1] Sarah Bacha, "Industry Discovers Too Much Room at the Inn," *Columbus Dispatch*, March 2, 1992, E1.

- Econo Lodge
- La Quinta
- Regal 8
- Super 8
- Comfort Inn
- Hospitality International
- Knight's Inn
- Hampton Inn

Red Roof Inns' position in the market varies according to geographical area in the United States. It is the leader in most midwestern states, including Illinois, Indiana, Ohio, Michigan, and Wisconsin. Holiday Inn and Marriott are also viable alternatives for some customers, although different prices and amenities of these hotels do not make them true substitutes.

Red Roof Inns has the strongest occupancy rates in the economy sector, well above the industry average. Fiscal year 1991 translated into decreased occupancy rates for many budget chains due to the recession and excess supply of rooms. According to a study conducted by Smith Travel Research, the occupancy rates dropped from 61.8 percent in 1990 to 60.9 percent in 1991, the industry's worst year in history. However, Red Roof Inns recorded an increase in occupancy during this period.

Although it has fared well, Red Roof Inns is facing substantial competition from many new entrants. Some of the more expensive motels are also offering inexpensive weekend package deals. The high profitability of the budget category is attracting many strong entrants with considerable expertise in the industry. For instance, Marriott has launched the Fairfield Inn, with pricing in the same range as Red Roof Inns. Holiday Inn's entrant to the economy segment is the Hampton Inn, while Quality Inn entered the economy segment with Roadway Inn.

The economy segment of the hotel/motel industry has increased from 20,000 rooms and ten major chains in 1970 to over seventy chains today. Although growth has slowed recently, it is still a growing segment in the industry. One of the underlying reasons for growth in this segment is a change in consumer attitudes. Today's consumer is sophisticated enough to venture into a local restaurant rather than dine at the hotel, a reason why many budget motels choose to locate near restaurants.

Economy motels are generally more profitable than full-service luxury hotels. The budget motels have been able to keep their nightly rates in the $30 to $40 range by forsaking restaurants, swimming pools, and meeting rooms. One reason Holiday Inns has raised its prices is because of the restaurants in its hotels. For similar chains, the cost of land for a luxury hotel is usually more expensive than for an economy motel because of the amount of land required for a luxury facility.

As the competition has intensified in this segment, most chains, like Red Roof Inns, have added such free amenities as weekday newspapers and morning coffee to their offerings. In the face of such competition, Red

Roof Inns wants to maintain its leadership but is dedicated to adding only those amenities that the customers will appreciate, such as Red Room Inns' Business King Room.

Increased competition will have to be a way of life for at least the next 6 years, according to industry experts.[2] Occupancy rates are expected to remain flat for 1993 and experience slow recovery until 2000 because of over building in the industry, yet the budget, limited-service chains are expected to fare better than their higher priced, full-service counterparts. To meet this competitive challenge, some full-service competitors began aggressive pricing cuts, especially for weekend packages. In the summer of 1992, Hyatt announced a policy of "extending the weekend all summer long" by advertising the same low prices on weekdays and weekends.

Market Segments

One of the major concerns facing Red Roof Inns includes the issue of which target segments are most responsive and loyal. Currently, the typical customer is a 25–54-year-old salesperson traveling on a per diem expense account. Income ranges from $15,000 to $65,000. Nearly half have college educations and at least two-thirds are salespersons or middle management.

Demographic changes in the United States were of concern to the management of Red Roof Inns. The company hoped to continue growth by targeting travelers with the greatest growth in numbers who are most likely to be responsive to the firm's product offering and marketing mix. In 1991 and early 1992, the fastest growing segment of travelers attracted to budget motels were business travelers. While a portion of this segment has always been part of the Red Roof Inn market, the segment is growing because more and more businesses are cutting travel expenses. Economy class airline tickets and economy motels are two ways of doing just that. As mentioned earlier, some of the budget cuts were implemented by businesses to weather some tough economic times, but could this emphasis on cost control be permanent? If so Red Roof Inns will have to compete heavily with other industry members for this segment. If not, it will have to find ways to keep business travelers coming to Red Roof when they are given the option of staying in full-service hotels at dramatically reduced, though still higher, rates.

Like its competitors, Red Roof Inns was faced with the issue of what attributes should be included in the offering and the effect that any changes might have on the firm's historic price competitiveness. Studies by the company indicated that a high proportion, well over 90 percent, of the company's present customers were satisfied with Red Roof Inns and that a high frequency of repeat stays occur among Red Roof Inn customers.

[2]Ibid.

Promotion Strategy

Since its beginning, Red Roof has invested millions of dollars, with a promotional program of very high impact. The name Red Roof and its advertising slogans have achieved high awareness among consumers. In 1974, Red Roof Inns introduced "Sleep Cheap" as the company slogan. This theme was repeated many times on large billboards located near company locations. Red Roof also used other media, especially print media directed toward travelling business persons. Most of the advertising featured the logo of the company with the distinctive shape of the company's inns. The slogan "Sleep Cheap" was tremendously successful but was replaced with a newer slogan, "Hit the Roof."

In its "Hit the Roof" campaign, one ad featured comedian Martin Mull stretched out in a chaise lounge by the swimming pool of a posh, deluxe hotel. As the sun beats down on him, he sips an exotic-looking drink. He is equipped with a mirror to reflect more rays onto his body. But it's January, the pool is empty, the wind is blowing, and he is surrounded by snow drifts.

The advertisement described above is part of Red Roof Inn's first television and radio advertisement campaign. The campaign encouraged motel customers to "Hit the Roof" because Red Roof Inns has everything a customer will need at a lower price. The ad described above shows how customers of more expensive hotels have to pay for the extras even if they cannot use all of the amenities. This theme is a change from "Sleep Cheap" used by Red Roof for the past several years.

Red Roof Inns is also involved in sports marketing and sponsors a car in the Indianapolis 500 every year. Trueman was a former national champion of the Sports Car Club of America. The present management continues to support the Indianapolis 500 in the same tradition.

Red Roof Inns also has a program targeted at the growing older market. It offers a 10 percent senior citizen discount program for guests 60 years or older who become members of this Red Roof group. The discount is taken off the pretax room rate and must be mentioned by the guest at the time of check-in.

Red Roof Inns has also received an official AAA designation. As a result each motel is listed in the AAA tour books. Red Roof Inns also maintains a toll-free reservation number, which is entirely computerized.

Currently, Red Roof Inns has a very high occupancy rate on weekdays. Weekend occupancy rates are somewhat lower than during the week; the company believes that this may represent a substantial opportunity for Red Roof if an effective product offering and promotional program can be developed to reach this market segment.

The company also recognizes there may be opportunities in other areas of the hospitality business. The company recently purchased a full-service hotel previously owned by another hotel company. This property is now operated as a "Trueman Club" hotel and includes restaurants, conference facilities, a swimming pool, and other facilities.

Focal Topics

1. Who should be the most important target consumers for Red Roof?

2. What is the decision process through which target consumers choose to stay at Red Roof?

3. What research should be undertaken by Red Roof at this time? How do you recommend this research be conducted?

4. What should be the promotional program of Red Roof?

5. How do weekend customers differ from weekday customers? What marketing program should be developed by Red Roof to increase weekend occupancy?

■ ■ ■ ■

Libb Pharmaceuticals

■ ■ ■ ■ ■

In terms of understanding consumer behavior and the subsequent formation of marketing strategy, the measurement of consumer attitudes is very important. Many firms have found that it is valuable and necessary to know how consumers perceive their brands along key product attributes.

During the late 1960s, management of Libb Pharmaceuticals became quite concerned when the market share of Alive toothpaste declined from about 15 percent to 10 percent. At a meeting of the product management team it was concluded that the firm should undertake some attitude research on the toothpaste market. Specifically, the firm was interested in determining:

1. Can consumers' attitudes toward brands predict individual consumer brand preference?
2. What perceptions do people have of Alive toothpaste?
3. What are the preferences for and perceptions of the other major brands of toothpaste?
4. How can Alive toothpaste best be positioned in the marketplace?

Market share improved somewhat during the 1970s as management began a heavier emphasis on promotion. Alive's market position seemed to peak in 1980, however, with a 12 percent share. By 1983, the market share had declined to less than 9 percent. Management decided that it was time to replicate some of the attitude research it had conducted earlier on consumer attitudes toward Alive.

The toothpaste market continued to change in a variety of ways as the 1980s continued. Several brands introduced gels in addition to their regular pastes. The "pump" came along as an alternative to the traditional tube. At the same time new flavors of toothpastes were introduced and many brands began to add ingredients to emphasize tartar control.

By the early 1990s more changes had occurred in the toothpaste market. Some brands had added baking soda and others were available in "squeeze" containers. Through all of this, Alive continued to slip in market share. In late 1992, even with a gel, a pump package, and a tartar-control ingredient, Alive's total market share was at 7 percent. Most other leading brands had also lost market share as the toothpaste market became more segmented and even fragmented. Jay McCay, director of marketing research for Libb, was asked by the product team to carefully review past research and make a proposal as to what types of research should be undertaken at this time.

Background

The Company

Libb Pharmaceuticals traces its origin back to 1855 when the founder, Phillip I. Libb, developed an all-purpose skin ointment. The product achieved relatively large success within a regional trading area. From the outset Libb devoted a significant proportion of the firm's profits to the development of new product lines and the improvement of existing ones.

By the early 1900s the firm was manufacturing and distributing a wide line of pharmaceutical and personal care products. In addition, Libb was gradually expanding its marketing area and by 1920 had achieved national distribution for most of its products.

One of Libb's early product additions was in the area of toothpastes. At one point the firm was marketing four separate brands of toothpaste. By the end of World War II all of the brands had been gradually phased out with the exception of Alive. The decision was made at that time that Alive would be the firm's only brand of toothpaste and that it would be modified and reformulated as appropriate to keep the brand competitive with changing market conditions and potentials.

The Product and Promotion

In the early 1970s, Alive toothpaste was positioned almost as an all-in-one mouth care product. Promotional claims for the product included statements such as, "Alive toothpaste polishes your teeth as bright as any other brand," "Alive contains special ingredients that freshen your breath like the leading mouthwashes," "Alive now contains a special fluoride to help reduce the threat of tooth decay," and "Alive brightens and protects your teeth while it freshens your mouth."

Most of the brand's advertising budget was allocated to spot television commercials in both daytime and prime time. The basic themes of most commercials focused on boy meets girl and vice versa and "slice-of-life" type of situations. The second largest share of the brand's advertising budget went to national magazines, with some use being made of Sunday newspaper supplements.

As another form of promotion, couponing was utilized to some extent. Libb also tried several promotional efforts in which Alive toothpaste was associated with some of the firm's other products. In essence, the firm only made limited attempts to concentrate on any specific market segment with its promotional efforts. Instead, the focus was on reaching as many consumers as possible with the amount of promotional dollars available.

Based on the initial attitude research results, the firm started placing more emphasis on the issue of decay prevention. While Alive was positioned more directly against Crest, the basic promotional themes still focused on all of the characteristics of the brand. The major change in marketing centered around an increase in the promotional support for the brand, with specific concentrations on couponing and prime-time, spot television advertising.

Attitude Research

At a professional association conference in the late 1960s, Michael Leason, the director of marketing research for Libb, attended a special session on the use of attitude models to predict consumer brand preference. He learned that the elements that make up such predictive models could be utilized to assess the images and perceptions of individual brands.

A basic attitude model used in the prediction of individual brand preference was described as follows:[1]

$$A_b = \sum_{i=1}^{n} W_i B_{i_b}$$

where A_b = the attitude toward a particular brand b
W_i = the weight or importance of attribute i
B_{i_b} = the evaluative aspect or belief toward attribute i for brand b
n = the number of attributes important in the selection of a given brand in the given product category.

A consumer attitude toward a particular brand was hypothesized to be a function of the relative importance of each product attribute and the beliefs about the brand on each attribute. The logical interpretation was that the more favorable the attitude score, the more preferred the brand.

After reviewing his notes from the conference and discussing the ideas with members of the product management research team, Leason decided to conduct an attitude research project on the toothpaste market. The basic research methodology and the questionnaire used to gather the data are presented in Appendix 26A.

---

[1]Frank M. Bass and W. Wayne Talarzyk, "An Attitude Model for the Study of Individual Brand Preference," *Journal of Marketing Research* (February 1972), pp. 93–96.

■ **EXHIBIT 26.1 Frequency of Brand Preference Rankings (in percent)**

Brands	Ranking				
	1st	2nd	3rd	4th	5th
Gleem	9.0	28.1	25.0	29.9	8.0
Crest	46.4	19.6	19.8	9.8	4.4
Alive	10.5	22.7	22.3	30.1	14.5
Colgate	24.9	21.5	24.7	21.0	7.9
Macleans	9.2	8.2	8.2	9.2	65.2

■ **EXHIBIT 26.2 Brand Preference Given Educational Level (in percent)**

Educational Level	Brands Preferred						
	Gleem	Crest	Alive	Colgate	Macleans	Others	
Some grammar school	5.5	18.4	16.6	44.8	2.7	12.0	100.0
Completed grammar school	7.6	24.7	11.8	37.7	3.9	14.2	100.0
Some high school	5.1	29.7	14.1	33.9	5.5	11.6	100.0
Completed high school	5.1	33.4	10.9	31.5	5.9	13.2	100.0
Some college	6.7	42.4	10.7	23.3	4.6	12.2	100.0
Completed college	4.7	49.1	9.3	22.7	3.6	10.5	100.0
Masters or doctorate degree	4.5	53.4	7.9	17.4	3.2	13.7	100.0

Initial Consumer Research

Brand Preferences

As shown in Exhibit 26.1, Crest was ranked as the most preferred brand by 46.4 percent of the respondents. Alive was ranked as the preferred brand by 10.5 percent of the respondents, by 22.7 percent as their second choice, and by 22.3 percent as their third choice.

To gain a better understanding of brand preference across various levels of education, a cross tabulation was developed (see Exhibit 26.2). It is significant to note that, in general, as education increases the preference for Alive decreases. The same phenomenon holds true for Colgate while the opposite is true for Crest.

Attribute Importances

As part of the input to the attitude model, respondents were asked to rank the importance of five attributes of toothpaste. Exhibit 26.3 reports the ranking results for the total sample. Some 75 percent of the

■ **EXHIBIT 26.3**   **Frequency of Attribute Importance Rankings (in percent)**

Attribute	Ranking				
	1st	2nd	3rd	4th	5th
Decay prevention	75.5	11.7	5.6	3.8	3.4
Taste/flavor	11.4	26.1	24.8	25.9	11.8
Freshens mouth	4.3	21.8	32.8	32.0	9.1
Whitens teeth	5.9	31.1	23.6	22.9	16.5
Price	2.9	9.3	13.2	15.4	59.3

■ **EXHIBIT 26.4**   **Frequency of Actual Preference Rankings Given Predicted Ranking (in percent)**

Predicted Rank	Actual Rank					
	1st	2nd	3rd	4th	5th	TOTAL
1st	74.9	15.5	5.4	3.0	1.2	100.0
2nd	13.9	45.5	22.0	12.5	6.1	100.0
3rd	6.5	22.7	39.4	21.3	10.0	100.0
4th	3.2	11.7	24.5	41.1	19.4	100.0
5th	1.4	4.5	8.6	22.2	63.3	100.0

respondents ranked "decay prevention" as the most important attribute to them in selecting a brand of toothpaste. Price was ranked as least important.

Along with the model presented earlier, attitude scores were calculated for each respondent for each brand. Attribute importance (W_i) came from question 2 on the survey while the beliefs (B_{i_b}) toward each brand on each attribute came from question 1. The attitude scores for each respondent were used to predict a rank order preference for that respondent for the five brands used in the research. These predicted rank order preferences were then compared with the actual preferences given by each respondent in question 3 on the survey. Exhibit 26.4 shows the results of these comparisons.

The attitude model correctly predicted the actual most-preferred brand for 74.9 percent of the respondents. The model also correctly predicted the second most-preferred brand for 45.5 percent of the sample. The least preferred brand was successfully predicted 63.3 percent of the time. For 15.5 percent of the respondents, the model's predicted most-preferred brand was actually their second preference.

■ **EXHIBIT 26.5** Average Consumer Ratings of Toothpaste
Brands on Relevant Attributes

| | Average Score on | | | | |
Brands	Decay Prevention	Taste/ Flavor	Freshens Mouth	Whitens Teeth	Price
Gleem					
A[a]	1.83	1.33	1.33	1.78	1.95
B[b]	2.64	2.26	2.06	2.34	2.27
Crest					
A	1.21	1.32	1.44	1.99	1.96
B	1.97	2.31	2.21	2.44	2.27
Alive					
A	1.56	1.27	1.28	1.80	2.11
B	2.40	2.23	2.13	2.45	2.24
Colgate					
A	1.40	1.26	1.25	1.80	1.96
B	2.39	2.04	1.98	2.50	2.24
Macleans					
A	1.89	1.64	1.28	1.35	2.14
B	3.03	3.39	2.66	2.38	2.50

[a]Row A = average ratings given the brand by respondents preferring *that* brand

[b]Row B = average ratings given the brand by respondents preferring *any of the other* brands

Consumer Perceptions

Since the attitude model's predictions were relatively successful, the research team felt that the individual attribute ratings (question 1) would probably fairly represent the images and perceptions that consumers held toward the alternative brands studied. It was decided that the average consumer ratings for each attribute should be calculated for each brand. It was also concluded that these average ratings on each brand should be first computed for those who ranked the brand as their most preferred and then for those who stated first preference for any of the other brands. The results of these calculations are shown in Exhibit 26.5.

Alive was rated as a 1.27 (the lower the rating, the more satisfactory the brand is perceived on that attribute) on "taste/flavor" by those who prefer it and as a 2.23 by those who stated preference for some other brand. Respondents preferring Alive rated it as a 1.56 on "decay prevention" while those preferring Crest rated it as a 1.21 on that attribute.

1981 Consumer Research

After Alive's market share fell below 9 percent, Michael Leason decided it was time to replicate part of the earlier attitude research project. He went back to the consumer behavior literature to review some of the

■ **EXHIBIT 26.6**   **Frequency of Attribute Importance Rankings (in percent, 1983 Study)**

	Ranking				
Attribute	1st	2nd	3rd	4th	5th
Decay prevention	70.2	13.1	7.3	4.8	4.6
Taste/flavor	14.8	25.5	26.5	21.1	12.1
Freshens mouth	4.9	20.2	32.0	34.0	8.9
Whitens teeth	6.9	34.2	25.2	19.4	14.3
Price	3.2	7.0	9.0	20.7	60.1

■ **EXHIBIT 26.7**   **Average Consumer Ratings of Alive on Relevant Variables (1983 Study)**

	Average Score on				
	Decay Prevention	Taste/ Flavor	Freshens Mouth	Whitens Teeth	Price
Alive					
A[a]	1.40	1.39	1.47	1.95	2.40
B[b]	2.63	2.45	2.51	2.67	2.55

[a]A—average ratings given Alive by respondents preferring Alive.

[b]B—average ratings given Alive by respondents preferring brands other than Alive.

developments involving attitude formation and brand preference. He specifically studied some of the summary articles on attitude models in marketing.[2] Specialized models such as Fishbein's behavioral intentions model were also examined and critiqued.[3]

Due to budget constraints and a desire to have some comparability with the earlier study, the decision was made to stay with the same basic methodology. Selected results from the updated research project are presented in Exhibits 26.6 and 26.7.

Specific information is not provided on other brands, since the brand preferences had shifted over the years between the two studies. In most cases, for those brands other than Alive that were still among the top five,

[2]W. L. Wilkie and E. A. Pessemier, "Issues in Marketing's Use of Multiattribute Attitude Models," *Journal of Marketing Research*, vol. 10 (November 1973), pp. 428–441; and M. B. Holbrook and J. M. Hulbert, "Multiattribute Attitude Models: A Comparative Analysis," in Mary Jane Schlinger (ed.), *Advances in Consumer Research*, vol. 2 (Chicago: Association for Consumer Research, 1975), pp. 375–388.

[3]Martin Fishbein and Icek Ajzen, *Belief, Attitude, Intention and Behavior: An Introduction to Theory and Research* (Reading, Mass.: Addison-Wesley, 1975); and P. W. Miniard, "Examining the Diagnostic Utility of the Fishbein Behavioral Intentions Model," WPS 80-71 (Columbus: College of Administrative Science, Ohio State University, 1980).

there were few changes in the ways consumers perceived them. The major changes were observed for Alive as presented in Exhibits 26.6 and 26.7.

1988 Situation

As described at the outset of this case, Alive toothpaste has continued to lose market share. This loss in Alive's market share has occurred even though the company has introduced a gel, offered an optional "pump" package, and added tartar-control ingredients to its basic formula.

Jay McCay, as the new director of marketing research for Libb, is trying to decide if he should replicate the earlier two studies on Alive. Obviously the product attributes would have to be changed and other brands would have to be included. Another alternative would be to use a different research methodology to try to better understand the toothpaste market and Alive's relative position.

Focal Topics

1. How are consumers' attitudes formulated? How can marketers attempt to change or modify consumer attitudes?

2. Evaluate the research methodology used by Libb in studying the toothpaste market to date. In which ways could the research have been strengthened? What other types of analyses could have been done?

3. What research recommendations do you have for Jay McCay at this time?

■ ■ ■ ■ ■

Research Methodology
and Questionnaire

■ ■ ■ ■ ■

Four distinct steps were used in the development and execution of this
toothpaste research. First, the relevant product attributes for toothpaste
had to be determined. The second step involved designing the questions to
be asked and testing consumers' ability and willingness to answer them. It
was then necessary to test the overall questionnaire on a small sample under conditions similar to those that would prevail for the final survey. The
last step was the nationwide administration of the final survey.

Product Attributes

The first product attributes used for toothpaste were ascertained from the
results of twenty small, focus group interviews. These interviews took the
form of getting consumers involved in a general discussion about those
things that consumers think about when selecting a brand of toothpaste.
The five attributes used in this study were the ones mentioned most frequently in these interviews: (1) decay prevention; (2) taste/flavor; (3)
freshens mouth; (4) whitens teeth; and (5) price.

Initial Questionnaire

Once the relevant product attributes were decided upon, a sample questionnaire was constructed and tested on a group of consumers to determine their ability and willingness to answer the questions. The results of
this informal test indicated that the respondents in general were able and
willing to answer these types of questions.

The Pretest

In order to ensure that individuals would respond to this type of questionnaire under actual field conditions, it was decided to run a pretest of 100
panel households. A cover letter accompanied the questionnaire providing

information about how to fill it out along with an incentive to participate in the form of a promised gift upon return of the completed questionnaire. Approximately 68 percent of this sample returned the questionnaire within two weeks. In general the results were satisfactory, with no more than the anticipated number of omissions. With minor rewording of some of the questions, it was decided to go ahead with the complete sample.

Final Questionnaire

The final questionnaire was mailed to 2,000 households who were members of a national mail panel. The households were selected to provide a balanced sample which paralleled census data for the United States with respect to geographic divisions, and within each division by total household income, population density, degree of urbanization, and age of panel member. In each case, the questionnaire was to be completed by the female head-of-household. Each respondent was offered a small gift (retail value of about $2.00) for cooperating with the research. Within the predetermined six-week cut-off period, 78.5 percent of the 2,000 households had responded to the questionnaire. However, out of these 1,571 returned questionnaires, only 1,272, or 63.6 percent of the total sample, were deemed usable for the entire analysis.

Basic Questions

In addition to the standard demographic characteristics, the following questions were asked of each respondent:

1. Now we would like for you to think about these attributes for the leading brands of toothpaste. Circle a "1" if you think the brand is very satisfactory in the attribute, "6" if you think it is very *unsatisfactory* in the attribute, or somewhere in between depending how well you are satisfied with the brand. *Please indicate your "feelings" about the brand even though you have not tried it or do not currently use it.*

Gleem	Satisfactory					Unsatisfactory
Decay prevention	1	2	3	4	5	6
Taste/Flavor	1	2	3	4	5	6
Freshens mouth	1	2	3	4	5	6
Whitens teeth	1	2	3	4	5	6
Price	1	2	3	4	5	6

Crest	Satisfactory					Unsatisfactory
Decay prevention	1	2	3	4	5	6
Taste/Flavor	1	2	3	4	5	6
Freshens mouth	1	2	3	4	5	6
Whitens teeth	1	2	3	4	5	6
Price	1	2	3	4	5	6

Alive	Satisfactory					Unsatisfactory
Decay prevention	1	2	3	4	5	6
Taste/Flavor	1	2	3	4	5	6
Freshens mouth	1	2	3	4	5	6
Whitens teeth	1	2	3	4	5	6
Price	1	2	3	4	5	6

Colgate	Satisfactory					Unsatisfactory
Decay prevention	1	2	3	4	5	6
Taste/Flavor	1	2	3	4	5	6
Freshens mouth	1	2	3	4	5	6
Whitens teeth	1	2	3	4	5	6
Price	1	2	3	4	5	6

Macleans	Satisfactory					Unsatisfactory
Decay prevention	1	2	3	4	5	6
Taste/Flavor	1	2	3	4	5	6
Freshens mouth	1	2	3	4	5	6
Whitens teeth	1	2	3	4	5	6
Price	1	2	3	4	5	6

2. Please rank the following attributes for toothpaste in their order of importance to you in selecting a brand. Write a "1" by the attribute which is most important to you, a "2" by the attribute which is next most important to you, and so on until you have ranked all five attributes.

____ Decay prevention

____ Taste/Flavor

____ Freshens mouth

____ Whitens teeth

____ Price

3. Now, we would like for you to rank these five brands of toothpaste by writing a "1" next to your favorite brand, a "2" next to your second favorite brand, and so on. If your favorite brand is not listed, please write it in the space provided. However, still rank the given brands in order of preference from 1 to 5 even if you are not currently using them.

____ Gleem

____ Crest

____ Alive

____ Colgate

____ Macleans

_____ Preferred Brand

4. How many times a day is toothpaste used by all members of your family counted together?

Don't use ____

1 to 2 ____	7 to 8 ____
3 to 4 ____	9 to 10 ____
5 to 6 ____	More than 10 ____

MARKETING STRATEGY

■ ■ ■ ■ ■

■

The Longaberger Company (A)

■ ■ ■ ■ ■

The scents of crisp fabrics, spicy potpourri, new paint, and hot coffee mix in the air as the doors to shops and restaurants open and close. There is a hustle as workers sweep sidewalks, shoppers laugh, carpenters hammer, and town residents chat on street corners. The old and the new mingle on this once desolate Main Street, now lined with quaint Victorian shops, restaurants, and homes.

In the 1970s, Dresden, Ohio was one of many economically depressed small towns in southeastern Ohio. Unemployment was astronomical, the streets were barren, and the village had many empty, rundown buildings.

But native Dave Longaberger, with his multimillion dollar handwoven basket corporation, has played a strong hand in revitalizing the village, which is now an exciting place to live, work, and visit. More than 150,000 people are expected to visit the village in 1992; many come to see the Longaberger Company's production plant, where hundreds of weavers handcraft hardwood maple baskets. The facility, located just outside Dresden, is a quarter-mile long with a full mezzanine view of hundreds of craftspeople who weave baskets using a centuries-old method.

Longaberger is the world's premier maker of handcrafted, hardwood maple baskets and fine pottery. Its skilled artisans carry out age-old traditions of craftsmanship, which make Longaberger Baskets® and Longaberger Pottery® found in homes across the nation.

You will not find the smell of oil or a maze of motors, gears, and conveyor belts at the Longaberger Company's manufacturing plant. These characteristics so commonly associated with manufacturing facilities are replaced by the gentle tapping of hammers, the spirit of music and laughter, and the smell of freshly stained woods. In the scurry, hundreds of people are carrying weaving material, packing orders, and, of course, weaving baskets with the same techniques used for more than 100 years.

The few machines found in the Longaberger plant are saws, a line of carousels spinning baskets through a shower of stain, and some stampers to burn the Longaberger logo into the bottom of each basket. Largely through human effort, this quarter-mile-long facility ships 50,000–100,000 baskets, pottery items, and accessories a day.

The Longaberger family began crafting baskets, using the same methods as today, back at the turn of the century. Using hardwood maple strips, each basket is woven around a wooden form. The baskets are hand-tacked and the handmade handles and lids are manually attached with leather hinges, copper rivets, and wooden washers. Staples and glue are never used. Then, the baskets are stained, dried, and packed for shipping.

Each Longaberger basket is unique, reflecting the weaver's own style of weaving and the natural characteristics of the wood itself. This uniqueness is carried through when weavers initial and date each basket in their own handwriting.

Longaberger baskets meet extremely high standards of quality. Baskets have become quite popular and are used by many consumers to decorate their homes. While some baskets of lower quality sell for $3–50, Longaberger baskets sell for $20 to over $300 depending on the size and design. They are premium quality products sold at premium prices.

Checked numerous times during the manufacturing process, each basket is inspected for shape, wood defects, color, and tightness of weave. This process is described in Exhibit 27.1.

That is a picture of Longaberger baskets today. But the thriving business of today did not get to its present position easily.

Company Background

The Longaberger story begins over 100 years ago, in the small town of Dresden, Ohio, when J.W. left high school at age 17 to begin his career as a full-time basket maker. He applied his learned craft with patience and attention to detail, never seeming to notice the tedium of weaving endless overs and unders. J.W. fell in love with Bonnie Jean Gist; they were married in 1927 and began housekeeping in a rented home, located on the same property as the Dresden Basket Company.

The depression put the factory out of business. So, in 1926, J.W. and Bonnie purchased the home and basket shop for $1,900 and set up the Ohio Ware Basket Company, where J.W. worked for years. Bonnie Longaberger still lives in their original home today.

To support his family of twelve children, J.W. worked at the Dresden Paper Mill during the day, but continued making baskets far into every night. To assure top quality in his baskets, J.W. handpicked, then chopped down, his own straight, maple trees. These trees were then transported to Marietta, Ohio, to be made into thin strips suitable for weaving.

J.W. and Bonnie's six boys and six girls learned the family craft and helped by selling the baskets door to door. The grandfather, David Gist, would pile the children and their baskets into his Ford truck and travel to nearby villages so they could sell their wares. The pottery baskets sold

TODAY, LONGABERGER BASKETS™ ARE STILL MADE THE "J.W. WAY."

Longaberger Baskets™ are made from the finest maple trees.

Selecting

We use only the finest maple trees from forests throughout the Midwestern and Northeastern United States to make our baskets. The quality trees that are harvested to become Longaberger Baskets™ are straight and healthy. They are cut into logs which are 8- to 12-feet in length. Choosing the perfect maple is an important step in the basket process today just like it was years ago when J.W. first started making Longaberger Baskets™. We strive to find only the best so we can give you the best in quality handmade baskets.

Cooking

Once the trees are cut, the logs are delivered to the Longaberger mill where the bark is removed and they are sawed into blocks. They are now dropped into huge vats of hot steam and cooked at temperatures in excess of 200° F. The boiling time depends on the thickness of the blocks, but averages around eight hours.

Veneering

The next day, each log is hoisted out of the vat and then hooked onto the veneering lathe which rounds up the logs. Now, the hot and steamy bare wood is pliable enough to be shaved off in circles around the log to form the veneer sheets. These sheets are pulled off in 15-foot lengths and carefully laid onto a table where they are evened out for cutting. A single log can make approximately 1,000 splints.

The wood is then cut into splints, which are carefully inspected and sent to the weaving plant.

Through the veneering process, the logs are sliced into sheets of wood.

Weavers begin each basket by forming the base with splints of evenly-placed over and under weavings.

Each Longaberger Basket™ is woven by hand with care and quality craftsmanship.

Weaving

Today, each Longaberger Basket™ is still woven by hand just like J.W.'s first basket years ago. The weaver begins by attaching an interwoven bottom onto a wooden form and carefully weaving each splint over and under, making sure it is even and taut. Eventually, the basket will take shape around this wooden form. After each round of overs and unders, the weaver gently taps down the splints to make gaps disappear. The excess up-splints are cut away when the weaving is completed. Just enough of the up-splints are left to be turned under and tacked into place with a finishing band. Once the basket is finished, a hammer and paddle are used to slowly ease the basket off the wooden form. Now, it is time for the weaver to proudly sign and date this work of art.

Sorting

The splints are hand-sorted for uniform length and inspected to make sure they are free of defects and breaks. At this time, special splints which will be dyed are slowly dried on racks inside a drying kiln. Finally, the splints are bundled together into workable portions and shipped to the weaving plant.

Handmade wooden handles are attached in the finishing department.

Every Longaberger Basket™ is personally signed by the individual weaver.

Finishing

After the baskets are woven, they are sent to the finishing line department for final touches. Handles made from strong, durable hardwood are attached to the baskets. The select wood is cut, boiled for 20 minutes, then shaped around a wooden form and air dried. The next day, handles are inspected and sanded to a smooth finish. Stationary handles are attached with tacks and swinging handles are attached with copper rivets. Lids are also made at this stage. Each lid is individually cut for a perfect fit, then attached to the basket with leather "hinges"... the same way J.W. used to do it! Each basket is dipped into a brown stain developed exclusively for Longaberger, and then thoroughly dried. For the fourth time, a quality control worker inspects each basket by hand. If everything meets our strict standards, the basket is tagged and ready to go. Your Longaberger Baskets™ are hand-packed and shipped from Dresden, Ohio to you.

very well, thanks to the thriving local pottery businesses. Farmers liked the corn baskets and their wives enjoyed the large market baskets. Money was scarce, so often the farmers traded eggs for the Longaberger baskets.

Over the years, paper bags began to take the place of baskets and the Longaberger children learned new professions, but J.W. continued to make baskets. His friends and neighbors knew they could depend on J.W. to design special baskets for special occasions. Easter was always a busy time, as groups of children hovered around the Longaberger porch, waiting for their custom-made Easter basket.

In 1973, J.W.'s fifth child, David, noticed that many department stores were selling large quantities of baskets. He realized that Americans were taking a more active interest in their past. Antiques and handcrafted collectibles had become very popular. Therefore, David asked his father to weave a few baskets to sell at area specialty shops. Just as he thought, the baskets were extremely popular, so he and J.W. decided to reactivate the family's business. They taught five local Dresden residents the art of basket weaving and began filling orders.

J.W. died a year later, but his dedication to crafting fine baskets remains alive through the Longaberger Company. Today, each basket is woven with the same high quality materials and meticulous attention to detail that J.W. used, with each Longaberger employee still signing and dating his or her handiwork with pride. Since 1974, David has built the Longaberger heritage of basket weaving into a thriving business. His daughter, Tami, studied marketing during college and a decade later is now president of sales and marketing for the company, making a total of four generations of Longabergers, who have devoted themselves to sharing their family's handicrafts with others.

Dave Longaberger probably would not be the student whom teachers would have predicted to be highly successful. Suffering from a severe stuttering problem and epilepsy, Dave spent two years in the first grade and three in the fifth. When he finally completed high school, college did not seem like a promising idea. Instead, he began selling Fuller brushes door to door, raising eyebrows among people who knew Dave had a problem with stuttering and self-confidence. Dave's response was, "My only chance is to hire myself. I'll be in control and can determine my advancement. I'll have no one to blame if I don't do well. I need more self-confidence. This will help."

At Fuller Brush, Dave observed, "The more I sold, the less I stuttered. I thought of these people as *my* customers, not Fuller Brush's. I worked very hard to guarantee customer satisfaction, and I found that they liked that. I got so excited. I learned that customer satisfaction had nothing to do with intelligence."

The only problem with the job was that the customers did not have to pay until they received the brushes. Often the customers were not around when Dave returned with the merchandise, and he ended up reselling part of the merchandise. That is why years later he would collect basket sales money up front. Today, this allows Longaberger to pay weavers and consultants and grow more rapidly than if he had followed the practice of many companies of financing materials and inventory during the production process and hoping customers will pay sometime in the future.

Dave Longaberger later took a job working for Kaiser Aluminum in nearby Newark, Ohio, for $150 a week, but he did not like the working conditions of the factory. Nearly 20 years later, when he started his own factory, he used this experience to structure it the way he would have enjoyed working in a factory. Dave resigned the $150/week job to take a $75/week job as a route man for Cannon's Bakery, selling bread, rolls, and buns to stores and restaurants. And he enjoyed it, observing that money does not make a person happy.

Dave learned that work could be fun. He observes "I saw the more fun the customers had, the more they bought and continued to buy. I learned the more I enjoyed the work, the more the customers did. I found my true world. It was selling. And I believe no matter who you are, you have to continue to sell."

Later he switched to a larger company, Nickles' Bakery, where he experienced a company that takes pride in its trucks, its products, and its people. From this experience, Dave learned the importance and power of pride in what you do.

During his experience with Nickles', Dave faced serious business competitors and was aggressively victimized by one of the competitors. They would take pens and shoot ink in the packages or poke holes in the wrapper, causing the bread to get stale. They would mash the products and cover them up with their own products. Dave's solution to these problems was simple. He befriended them.

"Within 6 months, half of the competition weren't damaging my bread. The other half, well there's not too much reasoning you can do with them. We began to look out for each other, which was strange since we were competitors, but it worked. If I saw Wonder Bread was covered up, I would uncover it. If he saw Nickles' covered up, he would uncover our products. I found out there are all sorts of ways to win. And just as important to the process, I was learning to see what people wanted. Not what I wanted or the company wanted, but what the *customer* wanted. Through my bread route, I saw that the stores and restaurants who built their businesses around their customers, not themselves, won. And it was the business with the *better* product, not always the cheaper one that excelled. Those were the places that were full."

After a stint in the U.S. army, Dave wanted to start his own business— a dairy bar. The only problem was that he had no money. The bank would not loan it to him, but the current owner took a chance on Dave by taking a second mortgage on the business. Another businessman who knew what a good worker Dave was cosigned for the balance, and Dave and Laura, his wife, were in the food business—called Popeye's Restaurant, after Dave's nickname, Popeye. The restaurant grew, confirming to Dave the principle that if you provide quality and service, customers will return. Dave also joined the restaurant association and believes, "No matter what your business, join the industry association. Listen to them because at least collectively, they know more than you do. You can't do it alone."

Popeye's Dairy Bar competed with nine other eating places. Although its prices were 25 percent higher than the others, it still commanded the largest share of customers. Besides customer service, Dave emphasized quality. Dave had a fetish for cleanliness, often washing the dishes himself. The same emphasis was true on having the freshest food and even the best cup of coffee. Although many thought of it as wasteful, Dave threw coffee out after 20 minutes. Even if customers had to wait for a new pot to be brewed, Dave reasoned, the image of the restaurant would be enhanced by having great coffee.

With pain and hard work, the restaurant succeeded. But the economy of Dresden was in trouble. And so was A&P, which was trying to sell its Dresden store. Dave thought he could use part of the vacated space as well as some of its equipment. A&P was willing to sell the equipment as well as the grocery stock for $2,800. This caused Dave to consider that even though A&P was leaving, Dresden still needed a grocery store. But Dave did not have the $2,800. He finally made a deal with a supply firm to finance the grocery store in return for exclusively purchasing dairy products from the firm. Dave qualified to become an independent IGA Foodliner and was soon in the grocery business. Eventually, his became one of the most profitable businesses in town. In the process, Dave developed his skills in accounting, making product line decisions, and working with people that eventually would be a major part in the development of the Longaberger Company. In both the restaurant and the grocery store, Dave is known as a person with a sense of humor, who constantly jokes and entertains people.

Dave also observed that Dresden needed a drugstore. Although he had no knowledge of that business, he started one, and it became profitable. In the early 1970s, the restaurant, grocery store, and drugstore were providing Dave Longaberger with a combined profit of over $50,000 a year, a very comfortable living in rural America.

As he traveled around the area, he noticed that baskets were beginning to sell in department stores. He also believed that the baskets his father made were 10 times better in quality. But he also recognized that it would be hard to compete with baskets made with cheap foreign labor. Nevertheless, he asked his father to make a few baskets. He placed them on consignment in a retail store in a nearby tourist area called Roscoe Village. The baskets sold out immediately. He increased the quantity, and again, they sold out immediately. Dave thought he was onto something.

Unfortunately his father died within the next year. Although Dave had helped his father make baskets, this was not his first love. Dave enjoyed selling and merchandising more. Soon he found two people, Kenny Birkhimer and Bonnie Hague (Kenny's sister), to become the first weavers in a new business. (They are still with the company today.)

The Longaberger Company was on its way. Without the benefit of a college education himself, with the kind of company MBAs would probably question, and with the lack of ability to borrow money from either family or banks to finance the new venture, Dave asked himself three questions:

1. Will people buy the baskets?

2. Could people make the baskets on a large scale? In the face of cheap foreign labor and the scarcity of people who know how to do the skilled weaving and other basket skills, could they be produced in Dresden?

3. Was material available?

In the late 1970s and early 1980s, the company began to grow but was soon hit by a series of tragedies. The costs of producing the baskets and growing the business increased faster than revenues, and Dave eventually sold the profitable grocery and restaurant businesses in order to raise cash for the unprofitable basket business. The accounting system was inadequate, and the company found that it was behind in its payments to the IRS. To pay the debts, the firm took out a very large loan at 8 percent interest. Because of the rampant inflation during the Carter administration, the interest rate on this loan soon soared to 23 percent.

And the problems were just beginning. In February 1983, a fire completely destroyed the Hartville veneering plant. It cost over $1 million to replace the plant, yet the insurance was only $20,000. Shortages in wood caused delays in shipments, and when alternative suppliers were finally located, costs were double. The company could not meet payrolls and plunged further into debt to pay fire losses, higher material costs, and back taxes. Dave was busy with the fire and financial problems, and there was no leadership in manufacturing. Consequently, he faced a union organization effort. Worst of all, Dave learned that a lawsuit had been filed alleging that stain from a Longaberger basket had killed a baby. When Dave learned of the death, he cried for 3 days. The litigation lasted over 3 years before a jury finally decided that Longaberger and the staining company were not at fault.

The Longaberger Company took a number of actions. It decided to raise prices by 18 percent, cut out all specials (which accounted for 40 percent of their sales), and cut the product line from 170 to 70 items. (Some of the remaining products are described in Exhibit 27.2.) The company also shut down one of the plants. Then Dave had to apologize to the sales consultants and tell them he needed to raise the prices, collect the money for purchases in advance, and inform customers the delivery time would be tripled. He told the company employees and sales consultants that he thought they could save the company if they all pulled together. Sacrifice in the short term would hopefully translate into success in the long run. And it has.

Longaberger is thriving in the 1990s. Its sales have soared, much to the glee of Dave Longaberger. It is common for the company's customers to become loyal collectors. Some buy the baskets because they are "works

■ **EXHIBIT 27.2   Product Line of the Longaberger Company**

There's nothing more romantic and relaxing than a good old-fashioned picnic on a beautiful, sunny day. Like the kind near a cool Dresden stream where you can kick off your shoes, lie back and watch the clouds roll by.

Featured on next page:
Small Berry Basket
Large Picnic Basket with Liner
Cake Basket
Small Picnic Basket with Liner
Background:
Large Market Basket

Measuring baskets used to be a way of life for local farmers. J.W. realized this. That's why he made these sturdy baskets with square bottoms and round tops, so they'd be perfect for measuring feed and grain for livestock.

Featured above,
clockwise from top:
9" Measuring Basket
5" Measuring Basket
13" Measuring Basket
7" Measuring Basket
11" Measuring Basket

LONGABERGER

(continued)

■ **EXHIBIT 27.2**   *continued*

(continued)

■ **EXHIBIT 27.2** *continued*

J.W. first made these sturdy baskets for gathering fruits and vegetables on the farm. He designed them flat and wide to hold more pickings, and to fit between the garden rows. Their popularity made J.W. a regular stop for farmers ordering in time for harvest.

Featured from left to right, top to bottom:
Large Gathering Basket
Corn Basket
Small Gathering Basket
Medium Gathering Basket
Large Gathering Basket

There's no better way to begin a leisurely Saturday morning than to wake up to the smell of fresh-brewed coffee, with warm bread still baking in the oven waiting to be smothered with delicious homemade preserves.

Featured to the right:
Pantry Basket
Bread Basket
Cracker Basket with Liner

Remember picking berries with Mom on an early summer day. Red ripe berries, bursting with flavor, overflowed from the baskets. As you walked home, you could almost taste the shortcake Mom was going to make.

Featured from left to right, top to bottom:
Medium Berry Basket
Medium Berry Basket
Small Berry Basket
Large Berry Basket
Tea Basket

LONGABERGER

(continued)

■ **EXHIBIT 27.2**   *continued*

of art"; some buy because they are functional. But everyone that buys them says it is fun. Dave would want it that way.

Focal Topics

1. What are the basic motivations for buying Longaberger baskets?
2. Who are the primary market targets for Longaberger baskets?
3. Based on the description of Dave Longaberger's career development, what principles can be learned that might guide the turnaround and growth of the firm?
4. How should Longaberger Basket distribute and sell its baskets?

■ ■ ■ ■ ■

The Home Depot

■ ■ ■ ■ ■

The Home Depot is the largest retailer of do-it-yourself (DIY) home improvement products. Only 12 years old, the company reached more than $5 billion in revenues in the fiscal year 1991 with 174 stores in operation in fifteen states. Strong growth is expected over the next 5 years as new markets are tapped and existing markets are expanded. Home Depot plans to expand aggressively, taking advantage of DIY consumers' strong demand for quality products and services.

The Home Depot is one of a handful of premier retailers in the country today and has the potential to dominate the home building industry much as Wal-Mart dominates the discount retailers. Home Depot has outperformed its closest competitors by offering quality merchandise at everyday low prices with a competent and friendly sales force. Although the largest in its industry of over $100 billion, the company represents less than 5 percent of the market.

Home Depot announced 1991 fourth-quarter earnings per share of $0.31 versus $0.23 in 1990. Sales for this same period increased 29 percent to a record $1,298.7 million, spurred primarily by a 20 percent increase in new unit openings and a 12 percent increase in same-store sales. Customer transactions increased 22.6 percent to 37,241, and the average ticket price rose 5.1 percent to $34.87. Average weekly store sales rose 12.5 percent to $594,000. For the year 1991, revenues increased 35 percent to $5.1 billion and same-store sales increased 11 percent. Customer transactions increased 30.0 percent to 146 million, and the average ticket price rose 3.6 percent to $35.13. Home Depot's average weekly store sales rose 11.8 percent to $633,000.

The Home Depot now operates in numerous market areas in fifteen states. As one measure of how rapidly the DIY market has changed and grown during The Home Depot's first dynamic decade, the first warehouse home center opened by The Home Depot in Atlanta in 1979 had 60,000 square feet of store space. When the 96th store was opened in East Hanover, New Jersey, in January 1989, customers could choose quality merchandise in a warehouse covering more than 100,000 square feet.

Comparable store sales grew an impressive 11 percent in fiscal 1991, indicating the strength of The Home Depot's approach to serving the vibrant DIY market. The excellent performance in stores opened longer than one year reflects both new consumers getting started in DIY projects, as well as repeat customers "graduating" to bigger projects once they discover the many financial and personal rewards of DIY home improvements.

The increasing consumer response to The Home Depot's concept was reflected in improvements in key statistics in fiscal 1991 and is expected to continue improving through the next decade. Moreover, industry and national statistics show the DIY market continues to grow considerably faster than the total retailing sector, and at a rate far above the economy in general. Exhibit 28.1 shows The Home Depot's performance in key areas for fiscal year 1991, including some figures estimated through the year 1993.

The year 1991 also brought an increase in gross margin to 28.1 percent and a decrease of selling expense to 18.1 percent of sales. As more stores are opened in the northeast, however, selling expenses as a percentage of sales are not expected to show significant improvement and could actually increase.

The Home Depot has become a strong company because of its principles and its strategies. They are crucial to its continued superior growth during the 1990s and beyond.

Because people are the key component to the success of The Home Depot—just as they have been since the first Home Depot opened in 1979—this report features three long-term employees who typify the entrepreneurial spirit and total dedication to customer service that is so important to success in the unique market that The Home Depot has the privilege to serve.

■ **EXHIBIT 28.1**   **The Home Depot's Performance**

	1991	1992E	1993E
EPS	$1.20	$1.50	$2.00
P/E Ratio	54.1x	43.3x	32.4x
Return on Average Equity	24.4%	16.7%	18.0%
Cash Flow/Share	$1.34	$1.60	$2.11
Five-Year Earnings Growth		30%+	
Common Equity % Total Capital		56.3%	
Market Capitalization		$14.1 billion	
Fiscal Revenues (1992E)		$4.9 billion	
1992E P/E Relative to S&P 4000		230%	

J. C. Bradford & Co. Spectrum, April 1992

Finally, innovation and commitment to customer service will remain a vital part of the company's strategy as it ventures on into its second decade of operation. However, the needs of such a dynamic marketplace are bound to change in the 1990s. Innovations will be required throughout the organization, both to manage rapid growth and, more importantly, to respond to shifting conditions in a segment of the retailing industry that is really still in its infancy.

Operations Review

A great deal has changed since The Home Depot opened its first retail home center warehouse store in June 1979. As the company grew during its first dynamic decade to become a dominant force in the DIY market, however, one thing did not change—The Home Depot's dedication to total customer satisfaction. As the DIY market expands toward a projected $100 billion in annual sales, customer service will continue to be the philosophy that drives The Home Depot's success in its second decade.

The Home Depot understands that a DIY home improvement project is not just a good investment in what is the single most important asset for most people—their home. It is also a gratifying, creative venture with rewards that go far beyond any that are measured in dollars saved and property values enhanced. It is a great source of accomplishment—a feeling of pride that inspires people to "do-it-yourself" again and again.

Because The Home Depot is a company which is itself infused with an entrepreneurial spirit, its people naturally empathize with homeowners who are willing to try something different to beautify their property, enhance its value, and perfect their own abilities.

The foundation of The Home Depot's exceptional growth record comes down to the one-on-one relationship between a knowledgeable sales person and a customer in one of the stores. Rising from that foundation are several factors that make the DIY market especially dynamic and make The Home Depot a market leader. For example, significant changes in demographics, social attitudes, and the U.S. economy have contributed to dramatic growth in DIY sales. As the baby-boom generation reached adulthood, an age group oriented toward DIY moved into the housing market for the first time. In addition, the increased mobility of Americans has had a favorable impact on home improvement expenditures. Fixing up a house in preparation for sale, as well as spending to get a new house "just the way we want it" after moving in, are important spin-off effects of housing turnover.

The factors fueling the growth of the DIY market are not as vulnerable to a downturn in the economic cycle as other specialty retailing segments. While not completely immune to recessional influences or slumps in residential construction or resales, DIY revenues have grown steadily during the decade since The Home Depot pioneered the low-price warehouse concept.

In fact, many analysts assert the DIY market is actually countercyclical. During periods of weak or negative real economic growth, cost conscious consumers will save money by doing repairs themselves, and they will spend more readily to protect the value of the investment in their home, their foremost financial asset, than they will on other discretionary, consumable items.

It was into this changing consumer environment that The Home Depot introduced its cutting-edge concepts of DIY retailing a decade ago. Although they have been refined and modernized over the years—most notably through the application of state-of-the-art technology at both the in-store and corporate management levels—the basic Home Depot formula for successfully serving customers has remained unchanged for 10 years.

People

The Home Depot selects people for its stores who relish the challenge of finding the right solution to the customer's needs. The Home Depot searches for men and women who want the opportunity to grow with the company by building a career at The Home Depot. More than 90 percent of its 13,000-plus employees are full time, roughly twice the norm in the retailing industry.

Service

The Home Depot goes beyond recommending the appropriate products, tools, and materials to its customers. It teaches and demonstrates the methods and techniques of doing a job efficiently and safely. Customers are even encouraged to call Home Depot stores with questions while their projects are in progress, and many do. This unique aspect of The Home Depot's service also serves as a very personal form of market research. This on-the-job feedback keeps its employees alert to helping the next customer learn from the problems and successes of the last one.

Price

The Home Depot's policy of low day-in, day-out warehouse pricing assures the customer that he or she is getting the full advantage of its lowest prices; it curtails the "let's wait for a sale" syndrome and avoids the aggravation of stock-outs on sale items. Because The Home Depot buys in very large quantities, the vast majority of merchandise is shipped directly from the manufacturer to the individual store. This eliminates the expense of central warehousing for most items, achieving savings that are passed on to the customer through the low day-in, day-out warehouse pricing policy. Professional shoppers in The Home Depot's consumer price watch program also keep its everyday prices competitive within their markets by monitoring prices at other retail operations.

Quality

The Home Depot carries nationally advertised brands and stands behind the vast majority of items it sells. It also offers a limited assortment of its own controlled labels, manufactured to tough specifications. The Home Depot unconditionally guarantees customer satisfaction. Full refunds are cheerfully given . . . no questions asked, no hassles.

Selection

Anything the do-it-yourselfer or independent contractor needs to build, beautify, repair, remodel, upgrade, improve, add on to, or landscape a home is available—now, today, in quantity—at The Home Depot. Each warehouse store displays, literally floor-to-ceiling, some 30,000 different items, with particular attention paid to the local needs of customers in each area of the country. Up to 20 percent of the products in one of its California stores, for example, may differ from the broad selection of products offered in the new Home Depot warehouses in Connecticut and New Jersey.

In addition, The Home Depot is a major impetus behind new product development in the DIY industry. Its staff listens intently to the needs of its customers, and they work with manufacturers to improve existing lines, introduce new ones, and make products and instructions more user friendly.

Responsive Merchandising

In addition to helpful, knowledgeable personnel, low everyday pricing, enormous selection, and quality products, The Home Depot strives to make a visit to one of its stores just as pleasant for the browser as it is convenient and efficient for the professional pressed for time. For example, store hours were expanded to include earlier opening times to better serve customers who need to purchase supplies before going to the job site. Expert sales staffs are specially trained to serve independent professionals. It employs experienced tradespeople at each location to assist customers with complex projects. Free classes are offered in a variety of subjects, such as wallpapering, wiring, plumbing, and carpentry, to educate consumers and motivate them to become dedicated do-it-yourselfers by discovering the many financial and personal rewards of a job well done.

The Home Depot also caters to consumers who are putting a new twist on do-it-yourself–buy-it-yourself (BIY). Economy-minded homeowners are purchasing materials and supplies needed for a home improvement project, then contracting for the labor. Not only does relying on The Home Depot's recommendations reduce the total cost of the job, it also eliminates trade markups for materials.

Inventory Control

Merchandise inventory is by far the single biggest asset on The Home Depot's balance sheet. The efficient management of this huge investment— measured by a financial ratio called inventory turnover—is critical to both profitability and the capacity to maintain the competitive edge it gains through its low, everyday prices. Inventory turnover for 1991 increased to 6.1 from 6.0 in 1990. Increasing inventory turnover is especially vital as The Home Depot continues to expand the number and size of its stores and their formidable array of products into regions of the country with more pronounced seasonal market conditions.

The Home Depot's inventory management systems track merchandise from the time an order is placed, to delivery to the stores, through customer checkout. Daily computer reports highlight which products are selling and at what margins. Slow-moving items are indicated, and reorder quantities adjusted to match the inventory strategy. The Home Depot can quickly evaluate products on the basis of actual sales and profitability data, then take immediate action to make sure the right merchandise is in the right stores and in the right quantities.

Hands-On Management

The Home Depot management continually reviews store operations in person, listening to customers and employees. Its senior people also visit competitors' operations. The Home Depot executives, including the chairman and president, personally train all store management personnel and conduct frequent refresher courses. Management believes this personalized commitment to superior customer service and management development can be found in no other retailing operation of The Home Depot's size. It is a commitment to keeping alive the entrepreneurial spark that gave birth to The Home Depot 10 years ago. It is a commitment that management wants the customer to feel when he or she shops at The Home Depot.

The Future

As The Home Depot grows through the 1990s, the DIY market it helped to create and continues to serve will provide further exceptional opportunities for growth. By fiscal 1993, The Home Depot should have nearly 270 stores in operation, with more than $9 billion in revenues. In order to increase its leadership position in the vibrant DIY retailing market over the next 10 years, The Home Depot will be pursuing several integrated operational and financial strategies:

- The Home Depot will target growth of approximately 25 percent annually in the number of new Home Depot stores. Because its new stores will generally be larger than existing units—up to 140,000 square feet compared to an average of 86,000 square feet—selling space is expected to grow at a slightly higher rate than the number of stores. In addition, to meet new merchandising challenges, The Home Depot will be renovating and redoing its older stores, increasing overall selling space whenever possible.

- The opportunities available and The Home Depot's financial strength would enable it to add stores at an even more aggressive rate than 25 percent per year. However, management believes an orderly growth strategy will leave the company in the best position to recruit, train, and motivate the people who make The Home Depot philosophy work where it counts—on the sales floor.

- The Home Depot will continue to take advantage of innovations in data processing technology throughout its system, from the store checkout counter to decision making at the corporate level. When the first Home Depot low price home center warehouse opened in May 1979, all record keeping was done manually. Since 1989, it has adopted an on-line system with a satellite data and video transmission network and will introduce universal product code (UPC) scanning in all of its stores, improving productivity and customer service.

- The Home Depot will continue to innovate in ways that expand its markets. For example, it introduced The Home Depot consumer credit card and a credit program for certain commercial accounts, such as manufacturing companies, hospitals, and hotels, which desire the convenience of monthly billings, both under an arrangement with a major financial institution that eliminates the credit risk for its stores.

- The company will expand aggressively both into new geographic areas and into markets where The Home Depot has already established a high profile and strong consumer acceptance. Its growth strategy takes into account that new stores inevitably take away some business from existing units. However, its experience also has demonstrated that The Home Depot's overall share of the market expands in multistore markets as each store is able to maintain the critical balance between volume and service.

The future is bright for The Home Depot. The 1990s bring with them demographic trends, changing lifestyles, and a decline in service. If the next 10 years indeed turn out to be the DIY decade, The Home Depot will continue to be synonymous with quality, price, and service in a market that is growing rapidly—not only because it makes sense for the times, but also because it strikes a rewarding responsive chord in people.

Focal Topics

1. What demographic trends will impact The Home Depot most in the future?
2. How do people choose The Home Depot compared to its competitors?
3. Should The Home Depot target consumers or commercial accounts for primary emphasis?
4. How can The Home Depot stimulate the DIY market and potential customers?

■ ■ ■ ■ ■

L.L. Bean, Inc.

■ ■ ■ ■ ■

If there were ever a firm dedicated to customer service in the mail-order industry, it would probably be L.L. Bean, Inc. The firm is known throughout North America as a quality source of rugged clothing and other products for use in the outdoors and elsewhere.

In 1992, the company's reputation was extended even further in a joint venture with a Japanese firm. Many customers had ordered products from Japan in earlier years, but the company has a partner in Japan to handle marketing and distribution more extensively than before.

Background

L.L. Bean, Inc. a specialty-merchandise direct marketer based in Freeport, Maine, was founded in 1912 by Leon L. Bean. An avid outdoorsman, Bean started the company bearing his name when he acquired a mailing list of Maine hunting license holders and began advertising a superior, lightweight dry boot. In the initial 3-page brochure promoting the boot, Bean guaranteed "perfect satisfaction in every way." The beginnings of a company founded on product quality and superior service were established.

In the years since 1912, L.L. Bean has grown into a business which today mails over 70 million catalogs annually to actual and potential customers, has yearly sales of $300 million, and employs approximately 2,700 people during peak periods. Over the last decade and a half, L.L. Bean's sales growth has far exceeded average growth rates in the mail-order business generally. Between 1965 and 1979, the company grew at an average rate of 309–335 percent annually. Currently, growth is in the 20–25 percent range. In order to meet demand, the company maintains approximately 80,000 stock-keeping units (including different sizes, colors, etc.), almost 10 times the number stocked a decade ago.

During the peak customer buying season, which occurs in the first two weeks of December (and accounts for about 15 percent of annual sales),

Bean dispatches approximately 100,000 packages each day—a volume level which requires the company to stock a little over $100 million in supporting inventory, or about 9 1/2 million units. The number of vendors with whom the company works to assemble this mix of products totals about 2,000.

Product/Service Philosophy

Bean competes with companies ranging from general merchandise direct marketing giants (such as Sears, Spiegel, and J.C. Penney) to a host of specialty direct marketers (such as Land's End and Banana Republic). The heart of L.L. Bean's success has been the company's dual philosophy of premium quality in both product and service. Informally, this philosophy is embodied by what Bean's management fondly refers to as "L.L.'s Golden Rule":

> *"Sell good merchandise at a reasonable profit, treat your customers like human beings, and they'll always come back for more."*

Formally, the quality product/service philosophy finds expression in L.L. Bean's corporate purpose:

> *"To market high quality recreational products of the best functional value directly to the outdoor-oriented American consumer with the kind of superior personal service we would like to receive."*

Product

On the product side ("sell good merchandise/Market high quality recreational products") of its product/service philosophy, L.L. Bean offers a wide variety of high quality merchandise, perhaps best described as practical or functional in orientation, as opposed to stylish or trendy. Merchandise sold through the company's fourteen different catalogues includes outdoor-oriented apparel; sporting equipment for backpacking, hunting, fishing; furnishings for home and camp; and assorted specialty items. L.L. Bean merchandise, designed to meet the recreational needs (active and casual) of its outdoor-oriented customers, is durable, reliable, and moderately priced. Examples of L.L. Bean products are reproduced from the 1992 Holiday catalogue in Exhibit 29.1.

Service

As important as product quality is to Bean's success, it is probably customer service ("treat your customers like human beings/provide superior personal service") which has been most influential in the company's ability to attract and retain customers in contemporary times. At the heart of

■ **EXHIBIT 29.1   L.L. Bean Holiday Catalogue**

For 80 Years We've Made
Holiday Giving a Little Easier

We know how to make your holiday shopping easier 7 ways.

Reliable Delivery We ship your purchases to arrive reliably anywhere in the U.S.—for only $3.50 per shipping address. The lowest shipping fee of any major catalog in America*. **Free Gift Boxes** When you select an apparel item, ask and we'll send along a gift box for you to pack it in. (To add a holiday touch, see our wrapping paper sold below.) **Free Gift Cards** Let us know, and we'll be glad to send a personalized gift card along with your gift.

Holiday Greetings Direct Send your gift anywhere. We can even mark it with a "Do Not Open Until Christmas" label. **Personal Gift Advice** Stumped for a gift? Our Telephone Representatives are ready to help you choose a gift that's just

right. Our **Gift Certificates** may be the   perfect solution for those hard-to-buy-for friends and relatives.   Each certificate arrives with our latest catalog. **Shop with us anytime.** Our telephone representatives are here 24 hours a day, 7 days a week. To order call **1-800-221-4221.** For customer service *1-800-341-4341.*

We guarantee prices and terms in this catalog through January 1, 1993.

L.L. Bean Gift Wrapping Set

Festive wrapping paper featuring the scarlet, dark green and navy blue pattern of our authentic Bean of Freeport® tartan plaid. Each set includes one 43 sq. ft. roll of wrapping paper and one 32 sq. ft. roll of tissue paper, 12 gift cards and six re-sealable bows. Gift wrap is printed on recycled paper. Printed in USA.
U291GG $14.75

*Delivery dates will vary depending on where your purchases are shipped. Please call us for details and restrictions.

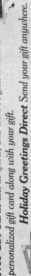

2

SHOPPING GUIDE

Christmas 1992

Shirts
Our widest variety of fabrics and styles—crisp cotton oxford cloth, warm flannels, plush chamois cloth and more.
pages 5-27

Sweaters
From the warmth of wool to the year-round comfort of cotton, our L.L. Bean sweaters are designed "from the yarn up."
pages 28-37

Outerwear
Send your warmest wishes. We have a jacket or parka for everyone from weekday commuter to weekend athlete.
pages 38-53

Gift Ideas
Need a last-minute gift to round out your shopping list or top off a Christmas stocking? Our Accessories section features belts, hats, gloves, scarves and other classic gifts. Many can be personalized with monogramming.
pages 58-71

Slippers & Sleepwear
L.L. Bean slippers and sleepwear are the perfect way to say, "to all a good night."
pages 76-89

Gifts for the Home
Our suggestions for gifts that say, "from our house to yours" will fill the home with holiday spirit.
pages 90-101

Children's
This year, we have more ways to make a child's Christmas special. Such as L.L. Bean—a Christmas morning favorite.
pages 102-107

Women's
Uniquely patterned sweaters in cotton, lambswool and mohair/silk blends. Color-coordinated separates from "versatile basics to special occasion" styles. And our luxurious blazers that go with everything.
pages 110-147

3

Bean's service emphasis is its "100% guarantee." All products sold by the company come with an unconditional guarantee of satisfaction. If for any reason a customer is dissatisfied with a product, L.L. Bean pledges to replace it or refund the purchase price.

The "100% guarantee" is Bean's most visible effort at ensuring customer satisfaction. It is not, however, the only customer service element emphasized by management. All together, Bean identifies seven customer service, Key Result Areas (KRAs). In addition to establishing customer service KRAs, Bean also has KRAs corresponding to other strategically important activities or functions, such as product-based and human resource KRAs. The customer service KRAs include: product guarantee, in-stock availability, fulfillment time (turnaround), convenience, retail service (for the store), innovation, and market standing (image).

For each KRA, Bean specifies an objective. Consider, for instance, the product guarantee, arguably the company's most important service KRA. The service objective for the guarantee is to keep at substantially less than 1 percent the number of all customers who request that their names be removed from Bean's mailing list or who state that they no longer do business with the company due to guarantee problems.

Bean's commitment to high product availability and rapid order cycle time finds expression in the company's in-stock and fulfillment KRAs. As with the product guarantee, Bean identifies specific objectives for these two KRAs. For example, objectives for the in-stock KRA include maintaining target merchandise levels, as measured by order service level, item service level, and forecast accuracy. For the order fulfillment KRA, objectives are stated in terms of turnaround times for customer orders, exchanges, and returns. Target error rates in shipping are also specified.

Convenience is another important Bean KRA. One of the advantages typically associated with direct marketing is its ability to offer customers a shopping experience free from cash register lines, parking problems, and other potential inconveniences. This advantage can easily be offset, however, if operations are conducted in a manner making it difficult for the customer to contact the company (via mail or phone), pose inquiries, register complaints, and so on. Consequently, it is vital that the direct marketer work to make customer efforts to achieve contact and/or obtain information as simple and helpful as possible. Convenience at Bean means customer dealings "must be easy and provide the service necessary for complete satisfaction." Among the objectives the company has set for convenience as a service KRA are specific telephone ordering and inquiry service levels.

Bean uses several measures to assess customer convenience in dealing with the company via telephone, including: the percentage of customer calls connected with an agent (or recorded message) within 20 seconds and the percentage of abandoned calls. The established objective for the former measure is to respond to between 85 and 90 percent of all calls within 20 seconds. From the customer's point of view, this corresponds to a response after no more than three rings. The target "abandoned call rate" is less than 2 percent. Other objectives for the convenience KRA include monitoring the quality of customer contacts and ensuring that catalogue request turnaround is at an acceptable level.

The remaining customer service KRAs defined by Bean deal with the nature of retail services to be provided at the company's single store, the attitude the company takes toward innovation in customer service, and, finally, the company's relative standing or image with respect to all areas of customer service.

Bean's customer service department is responsible for many of the customer service KRAs and is generally responsible for ensuring that customers receive the satisfaction they expect. Approximately one-third of all Bean's customer sales contacts are followed by some kind of return call or letter. About one-third of these contacts, in turn, register some kind of complaint. The balance of followup contacts include product inquiries, shipment confirmation contacts, returns and exchanges, and suggestions.

It is the responsibility of the 200 permanent employees in the customer service department to successfully resolve all post sale contacts. To ensure convenience in this area, Bean provides a toll-free (800) customer service number. This number is prominently displayed in its catalogues, and is distinguished from its regular toll-free ordering number. For telephone correspondence, Bean's service goal is to resolve 90 percent of customer contacts by the time the initial conversation ends. Unresolved problems are documented by the service phone representative, and contact is later made either by phone or mail correspondence. For those who wish, Bean also provides an address for customer service mail correspondence.

In addition to handling inquiries, suggestions, and complaints on a daily basis, Bean's customer service department also regularly tests the level of competitive services. Eight to ten competitor companies are tracked on an ongoing basis. Activities and services tracked by Bean include ease of placing an order, response to complaints, order representative courtesy and competence, return policies/guarantees, in-stock levels, order shipping costs, and fulfillment rates.

Focal Topics

1. Why has catalogue shopping increased so much in recent decades? What are the underlying trends or reasons?

2. What market segments do you recommend as the primary targets for L.L. Bean?

3. What role does Bean's service philosophy play in achieving the company's success?

4. What elements of its logistics program account for L.L. Bean's success?

■ ■ ■ ■ ■

This case is excerpted in part from Martha Cooper, Daniel Innis, and Peter Dickson, "L.L. Bean, Inc.," *Strategic Planning for Logistics,* 1992.

CompuServe

■ ■ ■ ■ ■

CompuServe Incorporated is an on-line information, communications, and software subsidiary of H & R Block, Inc. While many competitors have entered the market and failed, CompuServe has achieved a tradition of steady growth and profitability. Revenues for the fiscal year 1992 were $280.9 million, an 11.6 percent increase over the $251.6 million in 1991. Pretax earnings reached $55.4 million, up 13.9 percent from $48.6 million reported the previous year.

Despite an ongoing economic recession, CompuServe achieved strong overall growth and profitability by maintaining a strategic focus on its core business segments in a manner considered remarkable by industry observers and enviable by competitors. Careful evaluation of market needs has enabled management to maintain the company's dominant position in the consumer market, while positioning CompuServe to take advantage of new opportunities in business markets such as network services.

Background

CompuServe began in 1969 as an operator of large mainframe computers providing services to government and industry. The company earned an enviable reputation for reliability and performance in providing remote computing and information services. In addition, the company was a leader in electronic mail to large corporations and other organizations.

In the early years, the computers were spinning full time during business hours but sat idle during the evening. In the late 1970s, having attained a leadership position in business computing services, CompuServe turned its attention and expertise to personal computing services. By combining its history of reliability and innovation with its desire to utilize off-peak hours of computer power, the company created CompuServe Information Service, an information utility designed for use by the hobbyist, the professional, and the home computer user.

CompuServe Information Service is available to persons who own or have access to a personal computer or terminal. CompuServe is sold in computer stores throughout North America and much of the rest of the world. It is also available direct from CompuServe and through various manufacturers of computer software and equipment. A new CompuServe customer can purchase a starter kit for $39.95, which includes a special access number, a secret password, a user's guide, and a $15 or $25 user credit toward some services. Also included with the starter kit is a free subscription to *CompuServe* magazine, a monthly publication that keeps the user up to date on industry trends.

The CompuServe computer and common carrier networks provide access to the service through a local telephone call in most cities in the United States and Canada. Users in cities not reached by CompuServe may be able to access the service through the TYMNET system, a common carrier network, for an additional communication surcharge.

The firm has successfully integrated the use of microcomputers with large data processing mainframe computers to establish a leadership position in the steadily evolving computer information services industry. It currently provides services to nearly one million microcomputer users and continues to grow.

By 1992, CompuServe Information Service had solidified its position as the premier worldwide on-line information service for owners of modem-equipped personal computers. Though faced with aggressive competition in the on-line services industry, the information service gained more new members in 1992 than in any previous year, generated substantial profits, and developed an even more prominent position in global communications.

CompuServe Information Services

CompuServe combines menu-choice and world-search technology to provide its users with a versatile means of obtaining information. The menu-choice approach, which requires no special programming or computer language knowledge, allows the novice user to "go" anywhere on the service by simply pushing a button and entering a number into the terminal. The word-search approach, especially popular with more experienced users, allows the user to enter a word or topic into designated areas of CompuServe; the computer then looks for related information.

CompuServe has a broad data base that offers a variety of information services to its customers. For example, CompuServe gives users access to a world of financial information with news reports, reference sources, and electronic mail capabilities. These include figures on almost all securities updated throughout each trading day; current and historical information on stocks, bonds, and options; and specialized reports on commodities, today's economy, and implications for the future. CompuServe provides its users with personal financial services as well, which include basic financial tools for figuring mortgage loans, depreciation, and other financial categories. During the stock crash in October 1967, it was nearly impossible for individual investors to obtain immediate information at any place except CompuServe. The other providers of data could not meet the crushing demand, but CompuServe's massive computing capacity could be temporarily diverted from other applications to meet the surge of demands for immediate financial information.

Research on a multitude of subjects is as easy as the touch of a button. The contents of a reference library, including an encyclopedia combined with many specific data bases from throughout the world, provide a vast wealth of information available instantly.

National and international news wires give users a rundown of events as they occur, and electronic editions of many of the nation's major newspapers allow CompuServe users to know what is happening all over the country through detailed news reports, critical commentary, and sports reports. CompuServe offers electronic editions of popular consumer magazines featuring articles on a wide variety of topics as well as copies of popular TV programs such as "Wall Street Week" and "Nightline" as well as many of the Sunday morning news programs.

Playing games is popular with many CompuServe subscribers who can compete against other players across the country or with just the computer. CompuServe has electronic versions of familiar games—blackjack, backgammon, football, etc.—as well as computerized creations, such as "MegaWars," that provide users with hours of enjoyment and entertainment.

Communications possibilities are expanded dramatically with CompuServe. Users can send messages, electronically, to other CompuServe customers throughout much of the world using any of several methods. CompuServe Mail, a person-to-person message delivery system, allows users to communicate privately with one another. Less costly than a telephone call and faster than the postal service, CompuServe Mail is especially applicable to business use. CB is CompuServe's unique simulation of citizen's band radio; it puts users "on channel" so they can talk directly with one or more persons who are also tuned in. Classified ads on CompuServe allow users to post messages for all customers to read. Notices of club meetings, items for sale, and requests for information from other customers are some examples of how users can communicate via the computerized bulletin board.

Aviation   CompuServe supports the private pilot with over a dozen aviation-related on-line offerings. Three sophisticated interactive programs provide flight support. Two programs return computer-generated routes for RNAV or VOR direct flights; a third supports pilots who choose to specify a prepared flight route along selected Navaids. Pilot briefings pertinent to the specific flight plan automatically accompany route information, including weather briefings from the NWS along with reports from FAA data networks. A CompuServe aviation weather service complements flight planning, providing hourly weather reports, terminal forecasts, winds aloft, pilot reports, notices to airmen, area forecasts, radar summaries, and other resources.

Shopping The Electronic Mall is the most ambitious electronic shopping service ever launched on computers. A service of CompuServe, the mall is home for dozens of businesses, providing one-stop shopping at a single keyboard. New merchants set up shop here every week.

Selected merchants include Waldenbooks, American Express, various car manufacturers, Kodak, Godiva chocolates, Brooks Brothers, and many others. The service offers special sales, discount prices, and convenient selection and ordering procedures. Although faced with a major competitor in Prodigy (funded by Sears and IBM), CompuServe has continued to be the leader in computer shopping services.

Financial Services Several banks offer on-line financial and information systems where customers can review transactions, transfer funds, pay bills, compare current interest rates, and even exchange electronic mail with bank officers. It is possible to access a discount brokerage firm with services that include on-line purchases and sales of securities 24 hours a day, obtain current stock and option prices, portfolio management, and automatic tax–record keeping.

Clipping Service CompuServe's Executive News Service is an electronic clipping service that puts the power and scope of the Associated Press and other major news wires at subscribers' fingertips. Words or phrases of interest are entered and the Executive News Service scans the wires around the clock, filing appropriate stories in electronic folders to be read at the subscriber's convenience.

Travel With Travelshopper, Easy Sabre, and OAG Electronic Edition, a subscriber can check flight schedules and fares for virtually any airline in the world; book flights electronically; and arrange for tickets to be either mailed directly, issued by a travel agent, or held at an airline counter. The A–Z Worldwide Hotel Index provides complete reservation information and lodging descriptions for over 25,000 hotels worldwide. Travelers can shop for accommodations by a variety of criteria; price range, specific hotel name, hotel chain name, hotel location, and other factors. Once a particular hotel is selected, the index provides an address and telephone number, location description (city, suburb, airport, etc.), current rates, credit cards accepted, and an overview of meeting, health, and restaurant facilities.

Although this description of services provides a few highlights, it provides only a miniscule sample of the range and depth of services available on CompuServe. Since each area of the computer services can go deeper and deeper in a subject matter, including gateways to other data bases, perhaps no one person is capable of actually understanding all the products available on CompuServe. Studying the ads in the following pages and the price list indicates a few more than have been described in the case but still reflects only the tip of the iceberg.

Promotional Campaigns

Advertising and promotional campaigns have evolved over the years at CompuServe. Exhibit 30.1 presents ads from early years of Compu-Serve. Exhibit 30.2 displays examples of the most recent advertising campaign.

During the 1980s, CompuServe launched an advertising theme that pointed out the fact that the computer information age, long dreamed of by scientists and science fiction writers, has arrived with CompuServe Information Service. The "Welcome to Someday" campaign emphasized that the imagined "technology of the future" is a reality today and can make everyday events such as banking, reading the newspaper, and shopping take on exciting new dimensions. To carry out the "Someday" theme, four color advertisements were developed along with an education brochure which was displayed in many computer stores across the country. Exhibit 30.1 shows the cover of this brochure. The brochure was designed to introduce potential customers to CompuServe offerings and highlight the various services. The brochure also served to heighten consumer awareness regarding the many ways in which CompuServe can enhance and dramatically increase the capabilities of personal computers. The color advertisements were placed in computer-related publications and were designed to appeal to the technically oriented hobbyist, CompuServe's initial target market. The "lightbulb" ad in Exhibit 30.1 had similar objectives.

As the number of CompuServe users grew, so did the diversity of the subscriber base. No longer a hobbyist-dominated service, CompuServe began attracting users from both the business and home consumer markets. CompuServe management found that the needs of each of these market segments could be satisfied through the variety of services available on CompuServe's data base. CompuServe's promotional objectives began to change to develop advertisements that would appeal to all three market segments (business, home consumer, and hobbyist). Due to the newness of the technology, consumer awareness of on-line services, and CompuServe, initial usage was low. In order to attract attention to its product, CompuServe conducted a promotional campaign for "Mega-Wars," one of its computerized games. As shown in Exhibit 30.1, one free hour of play was offered to all entrants, and an invitation was extended to potential users to learn more about the CompuServe on-line service.

CompuServe also developed advertisements directed toward the computer retailer who sells the CompuServe subscription and software to consumers. CompuServe positioned its product as a sale closer and profit

■ **EXHIBIT 30.1   Early CompuServe Advertising**

Someday, in the comfort of your home, you'll be able to shop and bank electronically, read instantly updated newswires, analyze the performance of a stock that interests you, send electronic mail across the country, then play Bridge with three strangers in LA, Chicago and Dallas.

Welcome to someday.

Someday is today with the CompuServe Information Service. CompuServe is available through a local phone call in most major U.S. cities. It connects almost any brand or type of personal computer or terminal with our big mainframe computers and data bases. All you need to get started is an inexpensive telephone coupler and easy-to-use software.

CompuServe's basic service costs only $5.00 per hour, billed in minute increments to your charge card.

The CompuServe Information Service is available at many computer stores across the country. Check with your favorite computer center or contact CompuServe.

Welcome to someday.

CompuServe

Information Service Division, 5000 Arlington Centre Blvd. Columbus, Ohio 43220 (614) 457-8650

An H&R Block Company

(continued)

maker for computer salespersons. A modem (a device that enables computer signals to be transmitted over telephone lines) is required for users to access the CompuServe data base; therefore, a purchase of CompuServe software by a consumer means a modem sale by the dealer if the computer is not already equipped with one. CompuServe hopes to appeal to the dealer's need to sell equipment by providing a reason for consumers to buy computers and peripheral devices.

- **EXHIBIT 30.1**   *continued*

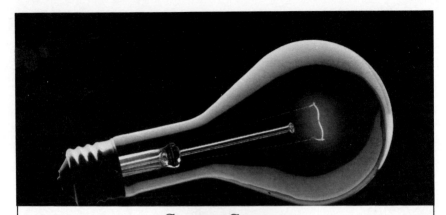

CompuServe.
You Don't Have To Know How It Works
To Appreciate All It Can Do.

CompuServe is a computer information service. You subscribe to it. In return, you have access to an incredible amount of information, entertainment, communications and services. Here are a few of the hundreds of amazing things you can do.

COMMUNICATE

CB Simulator features 72 channels for "talking" with other subscribers. National **Bulletin Boards** let you post messages where thousands will see them. Friends, relatives and business associates can stay in touch through **EasyPlex™ Electronic Mail.** More than 100 **CompuServe Forums** welcome participation in discussions on all sorts of topics. **Software Forums** help with online solutions to software problems. **Hardware Support Forums** cater to specific computers. There's even free software, and online editions of computer periodicals.

HAVE FUN

Play all sorts of sports and entertainment trivia games, brain-teasing educational games and the only online TV-style game show with real prizes. Or, for the ultimate in excitement, get into an interactive space adventure.

SHOP

THE ELECTRONIC MALL™ takes you on a coast-to-coast shopping spree of nationally known merchants, without ever leaving home.

SAVE ON TRIPS

With CompuServe's travel services you can scan flight availabilities, find airfare bargains and even book your own flights online. Plus, there are complete listings of over 28,000 hotels worldwide.

BE INFORMED

CompuServe puts all of the latest news at your fingertips, including the AP news wire, the *Washington Post*, the *St. Louis Post-Dispatch*, specialized business and trade publications and more. Our executive news service will electronically find, "clip" and file news for you...to read whenever you'd like.

INVEST WISELY

Get complete statistics on over 10,000 NYSE, AMEX and OTC securities. Historic trading statistics on over 90,000 stocks, bonds, funds, issues and options. Five years of daily commodity quotes. Updates on hundreds of companies worldwide. Standard & Poor's. Value Line. Over a dozen investment tools.

So much for so little.

All you pay is a low, one-time cost for a Subscription Kit (suggested retail price $39.95). Usage rates for standard online time (when CompuServe is most active) are just 10¢ a minute. In most major metropolitan areas you can go online with a local phone call. Plus, you'll receive a **$25.00 Introductory Usage Credit** with the purchase of your CompuServe Subscription Kit.

So easy the whole family can go online.

CompuServe is "menu-driven," so beginners can simply read the menus (lists of options) that appear on their screens, then type in their selections. If you ever get lost or confused, type H for help. Remember, you can always ask questions online through our feedback service or phone our Customer Service Department.

Before you can access CompuServe, you need a computer, a modem (to connect your computer to your phone) and, in some cases, some simple communications software. Now you're ready to order. For your low, one-time subscription fee, you'll receive:

- a complete, easy-to-understand, 170-page spiral-bound Users Guide
- your exclusive preliminary password
- a subscription to CompuServe's monthly magazine, *Online Today*
- a $25.00 usage credit!

To buy a CompuServe Subscription Kit, see your nearest computer dealer. To receive our informative brochure or to order direct, write or call **800-848-8199** (in Ohio, 614-457-0802). CompuServe. You don't have to know how it works to appreciate all it can do—for you.

CompuServe®

Information Services, P.O. Box 20212
5000 Arlington Centre Blvd., Columbus, Ohio 43220

An H&R Block Company
EasyPlex and ELECTRONIC MALL are trademarks of CompuServe Incorporated.

(continued)

■ **EXHIBIT 30.1**   *continued*

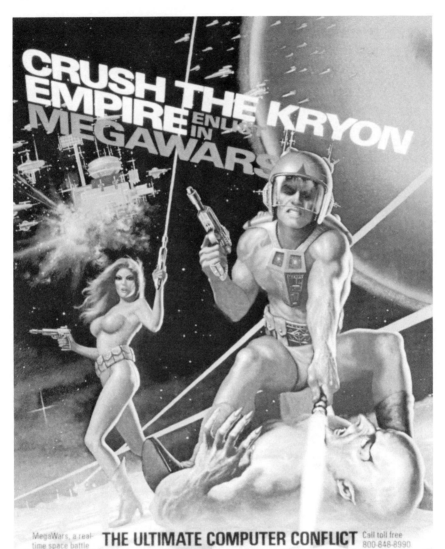

(continued)

■ **EXHIBIT 30.1**   *continued*

Exhibit 30.1 also contains one of the ads used during the late 1980s and early 1990s to appeal to consumers interested in investment information. Each CompuServe ad invites interested persons to contact the company by mail or toll-free number if they wish to receive further information about the on-line service and the procedure for becoming a

■ **EXHIBIT 30.2** Recent CompuServe Advertising

You can get your feet wet, or plumb unimaginable depths.

In a way, it's a lot like CompuServe.

CompuServe members who join for the basics quickly discover an ocean of opportunity. Like at-home shopping, financial data, travel information and reservations, entertainment, and free time to sharpen their online skills.

Computer professionals who join to access a wealth of high-tech expertise find much more. Like sophisticated research tools, hardware and software support forums, and lots of free software and shareware. In fact, no other information service offers the number and quality of choices that CompuServe does.

Now, for just $7.95 a month, and a one-time membership fee, you get all the basics as often as you like: news, sports, weather, shopping, a complete encyclopedia, and much more, plus up to 60 E-mail messages a month. And, there are lots of other valuable services available on a nominal pay-as-you-use basis.

To make the right choice in selecting an interactive service, pick the one that will always help you get the most out of your computer. For more information or to order CompuServe, see your computer dealer or call 1 800 848-8199. Outside the United States, call 614 457-0802.

CompuServe®
The information service you won't outgrow.

(continued)

CompuServe subscriber. CompuServe also ran some television commercials designed to enlist new subscribers. These were used on CNN, FNN, and ESPN as well as local spot TV.

Recently, CompuServe has begun a new series of advertisements, shown in Exhibit 30.2. Earlier ads, which contained a large amount of copy explaining services available, sometimes appealed aesthetically to the game players and hobbyists that flocked to CompuServe initially. The new

■ **EXHIBIT 30.2**   *continued*

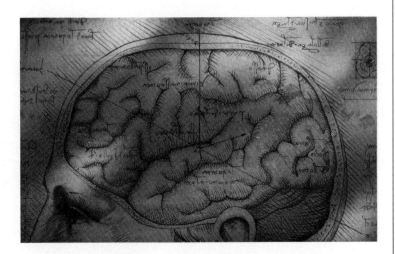

It works for beginners as well as experts.

And no matter how hard you try, you can't exhaust its potential.

In many ways, it's a lot like CompuServe.

For the beginner at interactive computer services, we've got news, travel information, stock quotes, entertainment and games, a complete encyclopedia, free time to sharpen your online skills, and more.

For the experienced user, we feature hardware and software support, special-interest forums, free software, a wealth of online computer expertise, and sophisticated research tools. In fact, no computer service offers the choices that CompuServe does.

Now, for just $7.95 a month, and a one-time membership fee, you get all the basics as often as you like: news, sports, weather, shopping, a complete encyclopedia, and much more, plus up to 60 E-mail messages a month. And, there are lots of other valuable services available on a nominal pay-as-you-use basis.

Whether you're a beginner or an expert, to choose the right interactive service, just use your brain. Pick CompuServe.

For more information or to order, see your computer dealer or call 1 800 848-8199. Outside the United States, call 614 457-0802.

CompuServe®
The information service you won't outgrow.

(continued)

series of ads reflects a more upscale image and assumes more information about computers and modems. The aesthetics are designed to communicate at the affective level rather than at the more cognitive level of ads of the past. Some of the ads also explain the new pricing options of Compu-Serve, described below.

CompuServe has competitors. One of the objectives of the firm's communications program is to convince potential subscribers to com-

■ **EXHIBIT 30.2** *continued*

When a bug showed up in a new program, the first to know was a guy in Montana. And everyone on CompuServe.

Why settle for always being the last to know when you can be among the first with a CompuServe membership? We put an entire world of up-to-the-minute information right at your fingertips.

Our online, interactive hardware and software support forums can put you in touch with thousands of experts. Even the authors of new and popular software programs.

Whether you're a novice or an expert, there's someone out there who can help you with your specific problems and concerns. Or keep you on top of the latest developments.

There are libraries of software available for each hardware and software forum that you can download for free as a CompuServe member.

And there are forums that can offer you help on just about everything: cameras, pets, model building, scuba gear—you name it.

So get CompuServe today. See your computer dealer, or call 1 800 848-8199, for more information or to order. Outside the United States, call 614 457-0802.

CompuServe®
The information service you won't outgrow.

pare wisely the availability of services at CompuServe as well as the quality and depth. The ads shown in Exhibit 30.3 are designed to achieve this objective.

Exhibit 30.4 shows selected results from a research study of CompuServe domestic subscribers. A total of 502 respondents completed the survey providing demographic information about how they found out about CompuServe.

■ **EXHIBIT 30.3**   "Choose Wisely" Ads of CompuServe

■ **EXHIBIT 30.4   Selected Information from CompuServe User Profile**

Length of Time User Has Subscribed to CompuServe

Response Categories

Less than 3 months	6%
3–6 months	14
6–12 months	16
1–2 years	28
More than 2 years	37

How User First Found Out about CompuServe

Response Categories

Advertisement in business magazine	2%
Advertisement in computer magazine	35
Retail store	7
Referral	23
Came free with hardware	24
Other	7
No response	3

Ages of Subscribers

Age

12–17	5%
18–24	7
25–34	31
35–44	36
45–54	12
55+	9

Subscribers' Levels of Education

Education

High school or less	5%
High school graduate	9
Some college	22
College graduate	36
Some graduate	6
Graduate degree	21
No response	1

Subscribers' Genders

Sex

Female	6%
Male	94

(*continued*)

■ **EXHIBIT 30.4**   *continued*

Subscribers' Occupations	
Occupation	
Professional/technical	43%
Managers/administrators/proprietors	29
Sales workers	3
Clerical workers	4
Foremen/craftsmen	7
Operatives/transportation	2
Laborers/farmers	1
Service workers	2
Military	2
Student	7
No response	2
Subscribers' Income Levels	
Income	
Under $25,000	12%
$25,000–$34,999	16
$35,000–$44,999	18
$45,000–$54,999	13
$55,000–$74,999	17
$75,000+	15
No response	9

Pricing Strategy

A major issue that has faced CompuServe management for several years is pricing. In the early years of CompuServe, pricing was designed to take advantage of excess capacity during business hours. Games and other hobbyist products could be sold during off-peak times at low rates compared to the amounts charged during business hours. In those years, users could access CompuServe for $6.00/hour in the evening hours and $20.00 during daytime business hours, for 300 baud service. At the faster speed of 1200 baud, higher rates were charged. Additional charges have always applied to certain premium-priced products.

Some competitors have introduced services that are provided for one monthly fee, such as $9.00 per month. CompuServe has been reluctant to make such a pricing move, however, because of wide variation in usage rates by its members. Because CompuServe offers a greater depth of services than competitors, serious users, who may spend considerable time to get the needed depth, also spend more money relative to the more superficial users.

Nevertheless, in 1991, CompuServe began some tests involving standard monthly fees for part of its services. In 1991, CompuServe announced a group of basic services for a standard monthly fee of $7.95. Services outside this group of basic services, offered on a pay-as-you-go basis, are referred to as Extended Services. CompuServe's Standard Pricing Plan as well as the services included in the plan are described in Exhibit 30.5.

■ **EXHIBIT 30.5**   New CompuServe Information Service Pricing

CompuServe

Corporate Headquarters
5000 Arlington Centre Boulevard
P.O. Box 20212
Columbus, Ohio 43220

Telephone 614/457-8600

New CompuServe Information Service Pricing
===

What: The CompuServe Information Service offers a group of basic services for a standard monthly fee of $7.95. Services outside this group of basic services are offered on a pay-as-you-go basis, and referred to as Extended Services. This is called CompuServe's Standard Pricing Plan.

Reading electronic mail from all incoming sources (except Internet) is free. Also, up to 60 three-page electronic mail messages can be sent free each month.

Who: Most new CompuServe members sign up with CompuServe through this new Standard Pricing Plan, with their first month's use of basic services being free.

Members can switch to pay-as-you-go for all services at any time (with a $2.00 per month membership support fee). This is called CompuServe's Alternative Pricing Plan.

Current CompuServe members can convert to the Standard Pricing Plan at any time, but are not required to convert.

How: All new CompuServe marketing materials promote the Standard Pricing Plan. Persons signing up for CompuServe through old materials will receive an "intercept message" during the online signup process so they understand they are signing up for the Standard Pricing Plan.

Why: Because extensive research has shown that current and potential members reacted enthusiastically to monthly pricing of certain popular services. Through unencumbered use of some basic services, new members are more quickly acclimated to CompuServe and are more willing to explore. Some veteran members like the flexibility of monthly pricing coupled with pay-as-you-go pricing.

Cost for using Basic Services:

$7.95 per month inclusive of the CompuServe (US/Canada) network for the basic services listed below. Surcharges for networks other than CompuServe (US/Canada) still apply.

First month of basic services usage is free for new members. Members who convert will not get a free month.

Usage credits ($15 or $25) from Membership Kits or Introductory Memberships (IntroPaks) can be applied toward pay-as-you-go services (but not toward the $7.95 monthly fee).

The $7.95 applies toward the Executive Option $10 monthly minimum.

(continued)

■ **EXHIBIT 30.5**   *continued*

Cost for using Extended Services:

Connect rates for all members include the $0.30 CompuServe network surcharge (i.e. $6.30/12.80/22.80 for 300/2400/9600 baud). Charges for supplementary networks have been decreased by $0.30 so that there will be no net increase in connect time charges to members.

Basic services:

o   CompuServe Mail*
o   Top level menus
o   Associated Press Online Hourly News Summaries, Sports, Entertainment, News, Business News, This Day in History
o   UK News and Sports from Reuters
o   Accu-Weather Maps
o   National Weather Service
o   Grolier Academic American Encyclopedia
o   Peterson's College Database
o   HealthNet
o   The Electronic Mall
o   Consumer Reports
o   Classified Ads
o   Shopper's Advantage Discount Shopping Club
o   Eaasy Sabre airline reservations, hotel and rental car information and reservations
o   Travelshopper airline, hotel and rental car information and reservations
o   Department of State
o   Visa Advisors
o   Basic Current Stock Quotes
o   Issue/Symbol Reference
o   Mortgage Calculator
o   Roger Ebert's Movie Reviews
o   ShowBizQuiz
o   Science Trivia Quiz
o   The Grolier Whiz Quiz
o   CastleQuest
o   Black Dragon
o   Classic Adventure
o   Enhanced Adventure
o   Hangman
o   Support Forums for CompuServe Information Manager software
o   Practice Forum
o   Directory of Members
o   Ask Customer Service

* CompuServe Mail costs under basic services:
Reading all in-coming mail is free (except from Internet). Outgoing messages above the equivalent of 60 three-page messages cost 15 cents for the first 7,500 characters and 5 cents for each additional 2,500 characters. Outgoing mail to TELEX/TWX, FAX, MCI and postal delivery carry nominal fees.

Global Information Services

Although CompuServe pioneered information services in the early "videotex" era of the United States and continues to employ innovative marketing strategies in this country, CompuServe has also invested in emerging opportunities in the global marketplace. Building on its earlier efforts to establish local support for European members, CompuServe instituted new product marketing activities in 1992 and dramatically reduced the communication surcharges in several western European countries. In London, a new access node on the CompuServe network decreased local members' hourly communication surcharge from $50 to as little as 30 cents.

In an effort to accommodate non–English speaking members, CompuServe introduced a number of German language offerings, including several computer support forums. To simplify use of the service of its German speaking members, CompuServe also released a German language version of the CompuServe Information Manager (CIM), the interactive user interface for the information service. Like its English language counterpart, German CIM uses pull down menus and dialog boxes to help members identify and quickly access the information they need.

As part of its ongoing effort to improve access and minimize communications surcharges for European members, CompuServe added network access points in Munich, Frankfurt, and Zurich. Other key developments in the multinational arena include the addition of several news, weather, and financial services targeted to the United Kingdom, and the debut of CompuServe Pacific, an information service developed for Australia and New Zealand.

The Pacific Rim is believed to be a key area of opportunity in the multinational market. CompuServe licensing agreements in Australia, New Zealand, and South Korea provide for local marketing and support of the U.S. service and for the development of new services based on the CompuServe model and localized to each country.

CompuServe has experienced steady growth in many areas of international market development including CompuServe mail's link with another mail system viz x.400, an evolving standard for international electronic mail interconnection. During the Persian Gulf War, CompuServe played an active part by establishing an area on the information service where members could locate breaking news, engage in on-line discussions, and send mail to military service personnel overseas via Operation Friendship. At times, the military, CNN, and other networks scanned CompuServe to receive reports more current and localized than any other source.

The Future

CompuServe is a major component of H & R Block, Inc., the world's largest preparer of tax returns. Since the company started in 1955, it has increased earnings in each of the last 20 years but one. With revenues well in excess of $1 billion, H & R Block has manned outstanding profitability and growth, with return on stockholders' equity usually over 27 percent. At a time when many companies in the computer services industry are experiencing disappointing results, CompuServe has a record of outstanding growth and profitability with pretax earnings in the 20 percent range.

CompuServe's growth and profitability has been achieved through careful planning in targeted markets and the ability to excel in computer communications, information, and software services to corporations and individual personal computer owners. It has added such innovations as the CompuServe Information Manager user interface for Apple computers; it has also grown in Europe and the Pacific Rim, modified its pricing and promotion over the past two decades, and developed a product offering of over 1,400 data bases.

Maurice Cox, president of CompuServe, is looking toward the future to determine ways of maintaining the growth record of CompuServe. "We must constantly be ready to reinvent ourselves; to capture continuously the entrepreneurial spirit on which the company was built but which must be applied to today's markets and technologies." Cox recognizes that the past success of CompuServe has been built upon focused dominance of the important variables of the marketing mix. Cox wants to evaluate the external environment and internal capabilities and technology to be sure the company is able to continue its success as well as to overcome any barriers or threats that might develop among potential competitors.

Henry W. Block, chairman of the board and chief executive officer of H & R Block, Inc., reflected with great pleasure about CompuServe's record of growth and profitability. He added, "we look forward to continued success as CompuServe moves ahead in the exciting world of technology in the 90s."

Focal Topics

1. How can CompuServe maintain the growth in revenues and profits expected by H & R Block, Inc., during the rest of the 1990s?

2. How would you segment the market and what segments would you recommend for promoting the CompuServe Information Service?

3. What pricing strategy should be implemented by CompuServe? Discuss the merits and weaknesses of your recommendations.

4. Are the changes in advertising appropriate? What promotional strategy would you recommend for reaching target market segments?

5. What other types of consumer research should CompuServe take at this time?

■ ■ ■ ■ ■

Checkfree

■ ■ ■ ■ ■

In 1981 Checkfree was founded by Pete Kight, a visionary entrepreneur who remains president and CEO to this day. Specializing in electronic payment services, Checkfree has two major lines of business. One allows corporations to automatically collect bill payments from consenting customers by debiting the customer's bank account. By 1992, this product had been offered by gas and electric companies, charitable organizations that receive monthly donations, health clubs, cable companies, on-line services, and other monthly billing organizations. The other line allows consumers to pay all bills at home using either a personal computer (PC) or a touch-tone telephone. By 1992, this product was offered direct from Checkfree, in PC and software stores, as part of other computer programs such as "Quicken" by Intuit and the program on managing your money by MECA. It is also offered as a telephone bill payment service marketed with banks such as BankOne and others.

By 1992, Checkfree had annual processing of over $3 billion in payments for more than 1,200 businesses nationwide and over 2 million customers in the United States.

The consumer bill paying service product is called CheckFree. The product is distinguished from the company name by use of the capital F. This bill payment service provides customers with an automated checking account register and a variety of record-keeping functions for tracking the household budget on a PC. CheckFree is a software product that records all pertinent information and sends the information via modem to the Checkfree processing center in Westerville. Checkfree transfers payment funds electronically, if the vendor is on-line, by use of a network linked with the Federal Reserve. If the vendor is not on-line, Checkfree issues a paper check drawn on the customer's bank account. Checkfree has access to the Federal reserve's Automatic Clearing House (ACH). The ACH enables the company to transfer customer payments to companies that are also on-line with the Federal Reserve.

The CheckFree product offers convenience to the consumer by saving time and money, resources which are becoming scarce for many consumers.

It also reduces errors and keeps updated records for budgeting and tax purposes.

Market Situation

Checkfree has identified its target market to be all PC owners with PCs at home. It has also targeted the home office PC market and the Macintosh users. The total number of PC owners in the United States is estimated to be in the range of 20 million or more and is believed to be growing each year. In general, company officials believe that PC owners purchase computers for a variety of reasons, such as work, school, personal record keeping, or just for fun.

CheckFree has grown rapidly. Within 6 months of its introduction in 1989, CheckFree had about 5,000 customers and was adding sixty to seventy more customers each day. Checkfree believes that its current customer base mirrors the "average" PC owner—men between the ages of 35 and 50 who consider themselves PC hobbyists or use their PC for work brought home from the office. It may be possible to identify the market less broadly. Perhaps the market for CheckFree can be further segmented by profession, income, education, and lifestyle.

Product Situation

The initial market release of the CheckFree product occurred in November 1988. The product consists of two components, a tangible software packet at $29.95 and a continuing service fee priced at $9.95 per month. The service charge covers twenty payments per month. There is also a surcharge of $3.50 for each additional set of ten transactions. Checkfree surveyed potential customers and determined that a flat rate was preferred over a variable rate. The company also found that there is some price elasticity and that customers were not interested when the price was significantly above $9.00 per month. In light of these findings, Checkfree established the fixed-step function pricing for a limited number of transactions. Additional services such as research on a subscriber's account or handling disputes with merchants are available for a modest consultation fee.

Checkfree does not expect to make a return from the sale of the software package priced at $29.95. The profitability is expected to be generated from the monthly service fees charged to customers for continued use.

Initially, CheckFree was an MS-DOS based product for use on IBM compatible PCs, but the product was expanded to be available to Apple Macintosh computers as well. In addition, CheckFree customers are required to use Hayes compatible modems to download their payment transactions to Checkfree. The company does offer Hayes modems to customers for $99.00; however, Checkfree does not intend to be in the business of hardware distribution.

One goal of the company is to increase the amount of electronically transferred funds and decrease the amount of written checks. Checkfree will become more profitable by doing this, as the process of issuing checks is labor intensive and costly. These efforts are given strong support by the Federal Reserve through the Fed's promotion of ACH. While promoting its customer product, Checkfree is also trying to convince more companies to become on-line with ACH. This will enable Checkfree to combine the benefits of on-line availability for consumers and companies with automatic bill payment and automatic bill collection.

Competitive Situation

Checkfree's major competition is really the manual use of checks and acceptance of paper checks. Product substitutions come from the banking industry. Many products have been introduced during the last 10 years by financial institutions. Among several promoted were HomeBanking and Pay-By-Phone. These services failed for several reasons:

- The customer had to have an active account with the bank offering the service to be eligible to use the service.

- The customer had to buy or rent specific hardware.

- Pay-By-Phone was not cost effective for the issuing bank, although consumers were receptive to the product.

- When Pay-By-Phone was implemented all transactions were performed manually because the ACH function was not as prevalent as it is today. Pay-By-Phone also could only be implemented on a touch-tone phone.

CheckFree overcomes all of the above through the following:

- CheckFree has the ability to pay customer bills regardless of the customer's financial institution.

- CheckFree may be used on any IBM compatible PC with a Hayes compatible modem as well as other computers.

- Checkfree is on-line with the Federal Reserve and can electronically transmit funds that earlier versions of Pay-By-Phone could not.

Some of the problems that the CheckFree product needs to overcome are the negative associations with the idea of home banking and customer concerns about the security of having their bank accounts directly debited.

Distribution Situation

Recently, CheckFree has advertised through personal computer and on-line related periodicals (see Exhibit 31.1). Interested consumers can receive information on the product by calling a toll-free telephone number indicated in the advertisement. The calls are taken by a telemarketing staff, which does no outgoing calling but answers questions, takes the

■ **EXHIBIT 31.1**   Periodical Advertisement for CheckFree

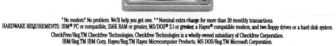

address of the caller, sends out brochures, and takes an order when a caller wants to subscribe. Telemarketing may also mail a demonstration diskette with the CheckFree brochure. This staff consists of four people who have gone through a specified question-and-answer training period.

The telemarketing strategy is to limit the telephone conversations to 3 minutes. Research performed by Checkfree indicates that a conversation longer than 3 minutes will result in a 15- to 30-minute conversation but will not result in an order being taken. Checkfree estimates that 300 calls are received each day. Only three telemarketing representatives may be on the line with potential customers at any one time. Checkfree uses a queue of one and one-half minutes. During this time customers hear a recording telling them to please stay on the line and their call will be handled by the next available representative. Checkfree now also does some outbound telemarketing to dealers and software distributors. Out of the 200 calls, Checkfree estimates on the average that 150 new customers are added daily.

At this point the only information being captured by the telemarketing group is name, address, telephone number, computer type, and how the person found out about CheckFree. The staff earns a straight wage and is not paid commission.

In addition to being sold directly, the software packages are distributed through many of the 7,000 Radio Shack retail stores. Currently, there are some point-of-sale displays and promotions being utilized. The software is offered from the shelf while the demonstration diskette is displayed in some stores. However, the intent eventually is to have the demonstration software running on a computer in the sales area of Radio Shack. A product fact sheet is available at all stores as well.

Checkfree has achieved fairly widespread distribution in software specialty chains, computer superstores, and mass merchandisers such as Sears and Wal-Mart. Other retail outlets include consumer electronic stores such as Circuit City and various office supply stores.

Macroenvironment Situation

A recession or economic downturn could slow down the purchase of new PCs and modems, consequently putting a ceiling on the potential of the target markets. Yet, since the economies of scale are improving, some doubt may be cast on such forecasts. Further research is needed to determine if current PC users would be adversely affected by such economic conditions. In such a case, Checkfree may need to raise prices to combat rising inflation, which usually precedes a recession. In addition, any import fees or changes in the foreign exchange market could increase the prices of hardware and software.

As consumers continue to become PC literate they will continue their search for extended uses of their home PCs. Technological advances such as ACH and Electronic Funds Transfer will increase the chances of success for CheckFree. The strong support of the Federal Reserve for the elimination of paper processing will also enhance the probability of success for Checkfree. As the Federal Reserve pressures the banking industry to move toward increased EFT, support may also come from the banks.

Marketing Strategy

In addition to utilizing retail stores, Checkfree is using a variety of promotional vehicles to promote the CheckFree product. Public relations efforts have given strong support to heightening the awareness of CheckFree. PR activities include newsprint articles in various technical, business, and PC consumer magazines. Several of these publications are listed below.

- *PC Resources*
- *Insight*
- *The Robb Report*
- *Retail Banking Strategist*
- *The Daily Reporter*
- *American Bankers*
- *PC Magazine*
- *Forbes*

- *Ohio Business*
- *Success*
- *Business Week*
- *The Treasury Manager*
- *Business First*
- *New York Times*
- *PC Computing*
- *The Wall Street Journal*

Checkfree has also advertised the CheckFree product on 1,700 electronic bulletin boards across the nation. These bulletin boards reach a variety of PC users ranging from user groups to various computer forums. It is estimated that bulletin boards have reached 500,000 users. Checkfree is also featured on CompuServe, Prodigy, and America Onlines.

To increase public awareness Checkfree company spokespersons attend various speaking engagements throughout the year to promote the new electronic payment service, including trade shows. In addition, Checkfree management meets with editors of computer-oriented magazines, such as *PC Magazine, MAC World,* and *MAC USER.* The company also advertises in these technical magazines.

Part of the message Checkfree is trying to convey is that home bill payment can be done successfully, securely, and without the hassle of switching banks. Extended use of the user's PC is emphasized as well.

A major portion of the sales of CheckFree is through third-party sales or as OEM installations. The most significant is "Quicken," a product of Intuit. Advertising in flight magazines and other media describes "Quicken" and its many money management features, which include CheckFree.

Opportunity and Issues Analysis

Management has given considerable thought to how new products are diffused through the market. In this analysis, several issues have been identified as potential opportunities or potential problems.

Opportunities

- Checkfree has the opportunity to leap ahead of current product substitutes and potential competitors. The key to Checkfree's success will be to offer a sound, secure, easy-to-use product, and to back up the product offering with unbeatable service. In general, people are very protective of their money, credit ratings, and other tangible and non-tangible attributes of money. Most people will feel that they are entrusting Checkfree with their money and the responsibility of paying their bills on time. Therefore, a quality product is only half of what Checkfree must offer; quality service is the other half.

- Consumers' interest in extended current PC use is expected to increase.

- Consumers in the United States overall are increasingly willing to trade money for discretionary time. Events such as more complicated tax returns and desire for increased control over financial assets are also favorable for the success of CheckFree.

Threats

- The relative advantage of EFT for the Federal Reserve and for the banking industry is extremely attractive: decreased float, decreased paper processing, and increased profits. Checkfree should be confident that its potential competitors are not sitting idle while Checkfree continues to perfect its product introductions. The banking industry has quick access to the market; Checkfree should be focused on a winning strategy.

Strengths

- Highly energetic, young, management staff with strong technical backgrounds, combining expertise from innovative and electronic on-line firms such as GE Information Services, CompuServe, Comtrac, and Bank One.

- Financial support in the form of venture capital from four large insurance companies.

- Close proximity to large banking innovators such as Bank One and Huntington Bankshares.

- Access to the Federal Reserve ACH and strong Federal Reserve support.

Weaknesses

- An 800 toll-free number is offered to place orders or receive product literature; however, once the product is purchased the customer is required to call a 614 toll number to receive customer service.

- The only dedicated resources to the marketing campaign are the CEO and the vice president of marketing (excluding telemarketing). This may prove to be difficult to the product roll-out and to reaching the market segments that would utilize CheckFree.

Bill Paying Service

Checkfree's original EFT product is used by companies that have customers paying monthly bills. Some industries, such as health clubs, have a fairly high penetration rate. Other applications which might seem likely candidates have been penetrated but not at as high a rate as Checkfree would like. Examples are electric and gas utilities, where it would seem almost every customer would want the service. By paying a bill with a check initially and submitting a permission form, a customer can receive the bill as he or she would normally but instead of writing a check, an EFT transaction occurs a few days after the bill is issued (providing an opportunity to notify the utility company if there is a problem). Thus, the customer is saving not only the cost of postage and the check but also the time and risk of forgetting to pay or being out of town when the bill is due.

Strategic Alliances

Checkfree has been approached by a number of companies concerning strategic alliances. Some include telephone companies and credit card services. In addition, various chip manufacturers, hardware and software manufacturers, and others might be able to enhance their product with CheckFree.

Checkfree is looking forward to a computerized world and not necessarily an MS-DOS world. For example, the digitalized stylus with a small notebook computer makes possible many enhancements to CheckFree. In the future, consumers may use a notebook computer with a digitalized pen to do many transactions at home, including operations very similar to writing in a checkbook.

As an example of the strategic alliances possible for Checkfree, the company signed an agreement in 1992 with TV Answer of Reston, Virginia, to provide electronic bill payment services via interactive television. With the help of Hewlett-Packard Co., TV Answer plans the most ambitious test of two-way TV to date, attempting to launch a national network using radio signals and satellite technology by 1993. A key service will be the ability to pay utility or retail store bills while watching television. Viewers also could order a pizza electronically or vote on what play the quarterback will call during professional football games.

The centerpiece of TV Answer's technology is a black box, made by Hewlett-Packard, to be installed on top of each subscriber's TV set. The company has committed to placing 1.5 million of the units in some of the largest TV markets during the first year of service. TV Answer is negotiating with programmers of the major networks and cable companies, but it will not be necessary to have the programmers' cooperation to make the system a success. Hewlett-Packard believes it can sell the box for less than $700 to consumers.

Focal Topics

1. From what is known about the diffusion of innovations and this market, who should be the primary market targets for the CheckFree products? For the TV Answer product?

2. What marketing research should be conducted for CheckFree?

3. What promotional program should be used for CheckFree?

4. What new products or strategic alliances do you believe should be developed by Checkfree?

■ ■ ■ ■ ■

Checkpoint

■ ■ ■ ■ ■

Checkpoint was originally incorporated in Pennsylvania in 1969 as a wholly owned subsidiary of Logistics Industries Corporation, but today is based in Thorofare, New Jersey. It is engaged in the development, production, and marketing of Electronic Signatures® systems. Electronic Signatures systems include uniquely identifiable targets which can be assigned to an object or person, and the electronic equipment that recognizes them. The recognized information can then be used immediately or stored for later review, analysis, record keeping, or other functions.

Electronic Signatures systems are provided to the company's customers as Electronic Article Merchandising[SM], EAM[SM] systems, or Electronic Access Control (EAC) systems. EAM systems alert users to the unauthorized removal of protected items such as retail merchandise and library books, but they are used for more than loss prevention. Checkpoint's customers use these systems to bring products back into open areas to which consumers have access, therefore increasing consumer buying. EAM systems make it possible for retailers and libraries to improve customer or patron service, without additional labor, through open merchandising. Open merchandising increases productivity and sales for retailers, while at the same time reducing losses caused by theft. EAC systems restrict access to buildings or areas, such as data processing centers and research and development laboratories, by unauthorized personnel. In addition, EAC systems can provide an automatic record of personnel who have entered specific areas and their time of entry and exit.

Checkpoint's EAM and EAC technologies have produced current products, and the development and convergence of these two technologies are expected to lead to future Electronic Signatures products. The company intends to protect its leadership position in the Electronic Signatures marketplace by pursuing future applications such as self-checkout from retail stores, automatic signal recognition of specified items, and anticounterfeiting devices.

Checkpoint has recently entered into the front-end monitoring (FEM) business. The primary emphasis of FEM is the control of internal theft at the retailer's point-of-sale. The FEM systems record and store on video-tape every transaction at each checkout, as well as the individual transaction data. Customers can generate reports and match questionable transactions to events recorded on the videotape.

Electronic Article Merchandising

EAM systems act as a deterrent to, and prevent the increasing problem of, theft in such establishments as retail stores and libraries. Over the past two decades, retail establishments have recognized that the most effective theft-prevention method is to monitor articles. Other means of theft prevention (special mirrors, security guards, closed-circuit television systems, and surveillance cameras) monitor people, not the articles to be protected, and this limitation among others is addressed by EAM systems.

The retail industry today faces an overcrowded marketplace and rapidly rising costs of occupancy, labor, and operations. In addition, this industry has been plagued with retail sameness and slowed consumer spending. These trends have caused aggressive price discounting, resulting in declining retail profits. These issues when coupled with the growing incidences of theft, create a dilemma of cost control and margin improvement for most retailers. EAM provides solutions.

EAM systems are generally comprised of three components: *detectable and deactivatable* security circuits (embedded in tags or labels), referred to as "targets," which are attached to or placed in the articles to be protected; *electronic detection equipment*, referred to as "sensors," which recognizes the targets when they enter a detection area, usually located in the exit path; and *deactivation equipment* that disarms the target when patrons follow proper checkout procedures.

The most versatile EAM systems use radio frequency (RF) technology. The detection equipment consists of a transmitter and receiver, which together establish an RF field. An active target can interrupt this field and trigger an alarm. With RF technology, deactivation can occur without physically locating or touching the target to be disarmed.

Currently, EAM systems are sold to two principal markets: retail establishments and libraries. Checkpoint has three significant competitors in these markets—Sensormatic Electronics Corporation (Sensormatic) and Knogo Corporation (Knogo), both principally in the retail market, and Minnesota Mining and Manufacturing Company (3M), principally in the library market.

Electronic Access Control

EAC systems restrict access to areas requiring protection from intrusion by unauthorized personnel by granting access only to selected individuals at specified times. Recent developments in Electronic Signatures processing and other technologies have enhanced the sophistication of EAC systems at a low cost.

EAC systems use an "electronic key," such as a push-button key pad or a plastic card with a magnetic strip or magnetic code that is read by an "electronic lock." The most advanced EAC systems utilize plastic cards containing an encoded digital integrated circuit as electronic keys. These can be coded with a personal identification number (PIN). Once the cardholder presents the card containing a PIN, a computer that is also part of the EAC system determines security clearance and access levels. This data, along with time of entrance and exit, can be recorded for later analysis.

Various commercial and industrial markets have applications for EAC. Systems are sold to manufacturers, banks, hospitals, prisons, airports, and governmental installations, which need to protect personnel or assets. The company's major EAC competitors are Cardkey Systems, Inc. (Cardkey), Casi-Rusco, Inc. (Rusco), and Schlage Electronics Inc. (Schlage)

Products

EAM Systems   Checkpoint's principal products are the components of its EAM system, which it markets to both retail establishments and libraries. The EAM system for the retail market is designed to provide protection for a wide variety of consumer items in all types of retail environments, including apparel stores, shoe stores, drugstores, mass merchandise establishments, record and video retailers, and supermarkets. The EAM system for the library market is designed to prevent the unauthorized removal of books and other library media.

EAM system components include four styles of sensors (each including transmitter, receiver, and alarm), and the customer's choice of patented disposable paper targets, reusable flexible targets, and reusable hard plastic targets. The EAM system's transmitter emits an RF signal, and the receiver measures the change in that signal caused by the active targets, causing the system to alarm. For 1991, 1990, and 1989, the percentage of Checkpoint's net revenues from sensors was 31 percent, 36 percent, and 40 percent, respectively, and from targets was 45 percent, 41 percent, and 36 percent, respectively.

In 1989, Checkpoint introduced Counterpoint®, a noncontact deactivation unit which eliminated the need to search for and remove or manually detune disposable targets. Since 1989, the company has expanded its deactivation products with electronic modules that can be installed into numerous point-of-sale (POS) bar code scanners including those manufactured by Spectra-Physics Retail Systems, Symbol Technologies, Inc., Metrologic, Inc., National Cash Register, Inc., and Nippon Denso, Inc. These modules allow the reading of bar code information, while deactivating targets in a single step. These deactivation units allow POS personnel to focus on the customer and minimize errors at checkout. The percentage of net revenues from deactivation units for 1991, 1990, and 1989 was 7 percent, 9 percent, and 9 percent, respectively.

Checkpoint's EAM products are designed and built to comply with applicable FCC regulations governing radio frequencies, signal strengths, and other factors. Its present EAM products requiring FCC certification comply with applicable regulations. In addition, the company's present EAM products meet other regulatory specifications for the countries in which they are sold.

Sensors   Checkpoint's sensor product lines are principally found in retail establishments and libraries. In retail establishments, EAM system sensors are usually positioned at the exit points in the areas in which protected articles are displayed.

In libraries, sensors are positioned at the exit paths, while gates or turnstiles control traffic. Targets are placed inside books and other materials to be protected. A target passing through the sensor triggers an alarm, which locks the gate or turnstile. The target can easily be deactivated or passed around the sensor by library personnel.

Introduced in 1988, the Alpha® sensor product line represented an important step in the evolution of Electronic Signatures processing. It was Checkpoint's first microprocessor-based sensor capable of recognizing unique radio frequency signals. Now incorporated in the QS2000® this microprocessor-based technology brings the company closer to a complete approach to merchandising, by integrating the retailers' three major control problems—pricing, information, and shoplifting.

Introduced in 1990, the QS2000 is the latest evolution in Checkpoint's proven Quicksilver™ sensor product line. With the addition of microprocessor-based radio frequency signal processing, the QS2000 has been engineered to provide excellent target detection with enhanced target discrimination capabilities. The QS2000 analyzes RF signals in its detection zone and can discriminate between unique target signals and environmental interference. This development greatly reduces false and "phantom" alarms while increasing target detection.

In addition to the QS2000 and Alpha sensors, Checkpoint also offers chrome finished Quicksilver sensors and solid-oak Signature® sensors, featuring an earlier generation of components. All of its sensors can be used with the various targets available. Aisle width protection is a function of the target being used. Presently, the maximum aisle width offered by Checkpoint's systems is 6 feet.

Targets   Customers can choose from a wide variety of targets, depending on their merchandise mix. All targets contain an electronic circuit that, unless deactivated, triggers an alarm when passed through the sensors.

Disposable security targets are affixed to merchandise by pressure sensitive adhesive or other means. They range in size from 2.7″ by 3.2″ to 1.525″, enabling retailers to protect smaller, frequently pilfered items.

Disposable targets must be deactivated at the point-of-sale, either manually or electronically, or passed around the sensors. Many disposable targets can be imprinted with standard price-marking equipment. When used with electronic deactivation equipment, they represent the Checklink® concept, developed to combine pricing, merchandising, data collection, and protection in a single step. Targets can be applied at the vendor level, in the distribution center, or in-store. Under Checkpoint's Impulse^{SM} program, described later in this case, tags are embedded in products or packaging at the point-of-manufacture or packaging level.

In 1992, Checkpoint was licensed to sell and provide targets for the Model 4021 label applicator (Pathfinder®) printer manufactured by Monarch Marketing Systems. This product is a sophisticated electronic portable bar code label printer and applicator ideal for use in high volume, mass merchandise, drugstore, and supermarket applications. In addition, Pathfinder has a self-contained keyboard that allows for easy entry of various types of label data, including bar code, price, and size. The Pathfinder has built-in scanning capability that can scan existing package bar codes, then print identical Checkpoint labels for application without obscuring important product information.

Checkpoint has an ongoing business cooperation agreement with Soabar Products Group of Avery International, a supplier of labels and imprinting systems, under which the companies jointly market Cheklink worldwide. In addition, Checkpoint in 1990 signed an agreement with A&H Manufacturing, the dominant U.S. supplier of costume jewelry cards, which granted A&H the right to embed a Checkpoint circuit in cards during manufacturing.

Reusable security targets fall into two categories. *Flexible targets* are plastic-laminated tags, used in a variety of markets, that are removed at the point-of-sale. *Hard targets* consist of a flat plastic case. They are used primarily in the apparel market and present a visible psychological deterrent to theft. Both flexible and hard targets use a nickel-plated steel pin that is pushed through the protected item into a magnetic fastener. These targets can also be attached with a lanyard using the magnetic fastener. An easy-to-use detacher unit removes reusable targets from protected articles without damage.

In 1992, the company introduced Checkpoint ColorTag®, which provides a cost-effective second line of defense against shoplifters. Unauthorized removal of these targets will cause sealed vials of dye to break open, rendering the garment unusable. ColorTag serves as a practical alternative to chaining down valuable merchandise. Ideal for use in department stores, mass merchandisers, and sporting goods stores, ColorTag can be removed quickly and easily at checkout with any standard detacher.

Deactivation Units   Five convenient deactivation configurations—horizontal counter-mounted slot scanners, a vertical mounted scanner, handheld scanners, a weight-scale scanner, and a deactivation pad—are available for a variety of POS environments. These units transmit an audible tone that alerts the user that a target has been detected. The tone stops when the target has been deactivated.

With the exception of the Counterpoint deactivation pad, all of the above scanners read bar code information while deactivating hidden Cheklink targets in a single step. Ideal for high-volume environments, these scanners mount easily at POS and can deactivate multiple targets on a single item.

The Counterpoint deactivation pad is placed at the checkout counter, and targets are deactivated automatically by simply passing protected items across the low profile pad, which audibly signals that targets have been deactivated. There is no need to see the targets in order to deactivate them. Three sizes of pads are available, all of which have a very low profile on the countertop.

EAC The EAC Threshold® product line consists of six systems, ranging from small, relatively simple systems, to large, sophisticated systems that provide a maximum degree of control, monitoring, and reporting.

The Threshold product line features a Distributed Network Architecture™, which means no single point of failure can affect the entire system. These systems are capable of controlling up to 144 doors for access control of up to 50,000 cardholders. The incorporation of alarm monitoring and point control (turning lights on or off) are also integral features of all six Threshold systems.

All EAC systems can also monitor other occurrences, such as a change in the status of environmental systems, motors, safety devices, or any controller with a digital output. While monitoring these controllers, any output can, by a preprogrammed decision, cause an alarm to sound or another event to occur.

Checkpoint has designed a proprietary proximity card and readers system that has advantages, including read distance and read speed, over other card technologies for most applications. The proximity card is comprised of a custom-integrated circuit implanted in a plastic card that is powered by RF energy transmitted from a reader unit (Mirage®) located at the entrance to a controlled door. Access is gained after Mirage verifies a code transmitted by the card. The proximity card cannot be copied or duplicated due to the use of a programmed integrated circuit. In addition, Mirage can be protected from environmental damage or vandalism by installing it inside a wall or behind a glass window. Mirage is used throughout the Threshold product line. Checkpoint's EAC proximity card and reader system has been certified by the FCC to comply with applicable regulations.

FEM Checkpoint recently licensed the exclusive worldwide rights to a front-end monitoring system that is marketed under the name Viewpoint™. Viewpoint will record and store on videotape every transaction at each checkout, as well as the individual transaction data. Viewpoint connects directly to the point-of-sale network using a PC compatible computer and fixed closed-circuit television (CCTV) cameras usually mounted inside domes affixed to a retailer's ceiling. Because all transaction data are stored in the computer's relational data base, users can generate reports and match questionable transactions to events recorded on the tape. The system also features a remote dial-in capability that allows the users to monitor multiple store locations from one site, significantly lowering personnel cost. Viewpoint can be linked to EAM systems in order to record incidents that have caused the EAM system to register an alarm.

Principal Markets and Distribution

Checkpoint sells its EAM systems principally throughout the United States and Europe, and, to a lesser extent, in other areas; it also rents its products in the United States. During 1991, EAM revenues from outside the United States (principally Europe and Scandinavia) represented approximately 29 percent of Checkpoint's net revenues. A significant portion of these international sales were to its primary distributor, Automated Security (Holdings) PLC, whose principal offices are based in the United Kingdom.

Checkpoint markets its products in the United States through its own sales personnel, independent representatives, and independent dealers. Independent dealers accounted for less than 1 percent of the company's net revenues in the United States.

Checkpoint currently employs fifty-seven salespeople who sell its products to the domestic retail market and who are compensated by salary plus commission. Checkpoint's independent representatives sell its products to the domestic library market on a commission basis only. By 1992, there were thirty-three such independent representatives. Three members of Checkpoint's sales management staff are assigned to manage and assist these independent representatives. Of total EAM domestic revenues during 1991, 84 percent was generated by Checkpoint's own sales personnel.

Independent distributors account for 100 percent of Checkpoint's revenues from foreign countries. Foreign distributors sell the company's products to both the retail and library markets. Checkpoint's distribution agreements generally appoint an independent distributor for a specified term as an exclusive distributor for a specified territory. The agreements require the distributor to purchase a specified dollar amount of its products over the term of the agreement. The company sells its products to independent distributors at prices significantly below those charged to end-users because the distributors make volume purchases and assume marketing, customer training, maintenance, and financing responsibilities.

Marketing Strategy

Checkpoint's marketing strategy is to sell to retail market segments that have a well-defined need for EAM, such as mass merchandise, supermarket, apparel, drug, and video markets. Retailers in these market segments have increasingly expressed an interest in expanding their use of open merchandising in order to realize maximum sales and profits.

Checkpoint's strategy is to provide a solution that integrates EAM smoothly, efficiently, invisibly, and inexpensively into the retailer's normal operating procedures. In this regard, Checkpoint has brought to market several new products and has entered into various strategic marketing agreements over the last five years that provide integrated, single-system solutions and encourage EAM system adoption for various retail environments, described earlier in this case. Through these agreements, Checkpoint has emphasized its continued commitment to bring advanced EAM technology into the normal retail environment via easy-to-use, specific solutions that eliminate EAM-related labor. Furthermore, the multiple functionality of product solutions represents an important step toward integrating merchandise security into the total retail management information system, an important consideration and an expressed need of many retailers.

Checkpoint management believes it is the low-cost producer of disposable security circuits by a significant margin and is using this leverage to develop flexible selling and financing techniques that accommodate its customers' needs. In management's opinion, this flexibility combined with the array of new and future product offerings will result in increased market share.

Checkpoint and a group of major national retailers and manufacturers have formed a focus group, referred to as EAM Horizons, to better integrate EAM into the product or product packaging. With this strategy, any EAM-related operational burden on store managers and employees to tag products will be eliminated since the Checkpoint circuit will be embedded in the product or packaging at the point of manufacture or distribution. Checkpoint refers to the source tagging program as "Impulse"^{SM}, because this program supports self-service and impulse buying by consumers. This use of EAM is compatible with the more than 60,000 Checkpoint systems already in service, allowing retailers to use the Checkpoint equipment to improve further their financial results.

In the latter part of 1990, Checkpoint introduced its EAM Impact® Model, a copyrighted financial simulation tool that enables retailers to project the potential benefits of EAM in their operations. Impact is a registered trademark of Management Horizons, a division of Price Waterhouse. Impact is being made available to retailers, retail consultants, and manufacturers free of charge. Retailers enter their own data for such variables as market coverage, penetration level, average shopping frequency, closure rate, and coverage transaction size to determine gross sales. Then, by projecting reduced shrinkage and increases in closure rate and average transaction size resulting from EAM, the model determines the payback period for an EAM investment and the retailers' increase in sales and earnings per store.

Checkpoint has an extensive investment in the protection of its intellectual property. Substantially all of its revenues are derived from products and technology that are patented or licensed, and it is aggressive in protecting rights of these patents and licenses. For its target production, Checkpoint buys from various sources worldwide and completes the manufacturing process in its state-of-the-art production facilities in Puerto Rico. Some components of targets as well as electronic components for proximity cards and readers are manufactured or assembled at Checkpoint's facilities in the Dominican Republic.

Competition

Management of Checkpoint believes that Sensormatic and Knogo constitute its principal competitors in the supply of EAM systems for retailer establishments and that 3M constitutes its principal competitor in the supply of such systems for libraries. These competitors in the EAM industry are larger, well-established businesses and have greater financial resources. In the apparel market, where hard reusable targets are emphasized, Sensormatic and Knogo have enjoyed better penetration than Checkpoint; it is for this traditional EAM market that the competition designed and developed its products.

Checkpoint's product line offers more diversity than its competitors in protecting different kinds of merchandise with soft disposable targets and hard and flexible reusable targets, all of which operate with the same RF system. As a result, Checkpoint management believes it appeals to a much wider segment of the market than does its competitors and competes in marketing its products primarily on the basis of their versatility, reliability, accuracy, and integration into operations. This combination provides many system solutions that allow for protection of various kinds of merchandise from theft. Checkpoint products also compete with other means of merchandise theft prevention, such as surveillance cameras, closed-circuit television systems, security guards, and special mirrors.

Checkpoint believes its RF technology offers many advantages over competitive products. The company distributes a promotional brochure explaining these advantages as well as many of the applications that are possible with its technology. A portion of this brochure is reproduced in Exhibit 32.1. The changing nature of its sales are also reproduced in Exhibit 32.2.

Focal Topics

1. What is the "business" of Checkpoint?
2. What retailers should be the primary targets for Checkpoint?

■ EXHIBIT 32.1 Checkpoint Services for Retailers

EAM IMPACT MODEL
Our FREE Impact Model can help you project
increased sales and profits with Checkpoint Electronic
Article Merchandising. (See page 10 for details.)

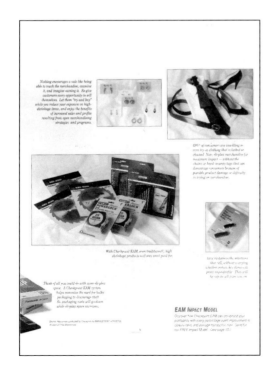

(continued)

How Checkpoint EAM Gives You The Security That Makes Open Merchandising Practical

EAM — the practical result of electronic security.

EAM is the logical extension of Checkpoint's proven electronic security technology. So, if you already own one of the more than 50,000 Checkpoint systems now in operation, you have the building blocks for Electronic Article Merchandising in your store — right now.

And because Checkpoint EAM is in the forefront of open merchandising technology, you will also be able to upgrade your system to employ even more advanced Checkpoint technology to come — without easily obsolescence.

Electronic Article Merchandising Systems from Checkpoint: Simple as 1, 2, 3.

Checkpoint security systems use radio-frequency technology to protect your merchandise.

These systems consist of:

1. Tiny electronic circuits or "signatures" that can be incorporated in merchandise tags, labels, or in the packaging or merchandise itself.

2. Automatic, "non-contact" deactivation devices used to disable the electronic signatures at the point of sale. Deactivators can be provided in standalone countertop pads, or integrated with other POS scanning equipment for "one pass" speed and convenience.

3. Sensors, placed at the exit of a store or department, sound an alarm when someone tries to remove protected merchandise that has not been paid for and deactivated.

Why sales and profits go up...

The typical reaction for curbing shrinkage losses is to lock up the merchandise. Unfortunately, locking up merchandise lowers customer satisfaction levels and curbs sales and profits.

But with Checkpoint EAM, the only locks you will need will be those on the doors of your store. The "invisible" security provided by EAM lets your customers shop in a more interactive atmosphere where sales can flourish.

You will profit from a more inviting environment with less obvious security and fewer barriers to sales. You will also be able to generate more transactions and a higher average transaction size, due to greater consumer interaction and more opportunities for impulse buying.

The convenience of EAM also frees your staff for more profitable activities. So they can offer customer assistance, instead of controlling counter access. Or devote attention to truly interested prospects and sell them, instead of suspecting every shopper.

...and costs go down.

The loss reductions possible through EAM make it practical to stock high-margin, high-turnover products that otherwise might not deliver their desired margins because of high-shrinkage. In fact, the high success rate of EAM can reduce losses for all goods, storewide.

In addition to increasing sales and reducing losses, a Checkpoint EAM system can also relieve your staff of unnecessary security and display-case housekeeping functions. So you may be able to reduce manpower requirements and associated personnel costs while actually improving customer service and satisfaction.

Additional reductions in labor costs may be gained by integrating pricing, inventory bar codes, and security in a single tagging process. And integrated POS functions for scanning and security can speed customer service, while increasing throughput at checkout to reduce manpower costs further.

EAM IMPACT MODEL
Project actual sales and profit gains from EAM in terms of your own operations. Our detailed Impact Model makes it possible. (See page 10.)

(continued)

How A Checkpoint EAM System Can Help You Turn Loss Prevention Into New-Found Sales and Profits

EAM lets you focus on what you do best — merchandising and selling. Unlike the "unlock-show-lock" method of selling high-risk items, it lets consumers sample, compare, and select on their own terms, at their own pace.

And with new Checkpoint Impulse™ technology, you can have restore open merchandising. Impulse is the breakthrough that makes it possible to realize the full potential of Electronic Article Merchandising. It is being developed based on input from leading manufacturers and merchandisers.

With Impulse merchandising, goods will come off manufacturers' assembly lines with tiny Checkpoint signatures already embedded in the packaging or merchandise. As Impulse becomes more prevalent, you will be able to realize the full potential of EAM open merchandising.

The secret is in the signature.

Each Checkpoint electronic signature incorporates miniaturized circuitry that will trigger an alarm as it passes a Checkpoint sensor, if it has not been deactivated through normal checkout procedures. This circuitry is virtually invisible to the consumer — disguised in one of their formats of your choice.

Disposable or Reusable Targets: Available in a variety of styles to match your needs — from economical pre-printed labels to custom-printed designs

Cheklink™ Targets: Available as disposable pressure-sensitive labels or hang tags, these targets integrate pricing, product information, data collection and invisible protection in one label. Imprintable on standard equipment.

Impulse™ Targets: The ultimate in protection, convenience, and flexibility. RF circuits (signatures) are embedded in packaging or in the merchandise itself.

The convenience is at your point of sale.

Checkpoint protection requires no extra effort at checkout. There is no need to locate the target or make direct contact with it. Tagged items may be passed over a Counterpoint® pad to be deactivated automatically. Or deactivation electronics may be incorporated in hand-held scanners, omni-directional scanners, and counter-mounted scanners. In these systems, one pass is all that is required to register the sale and deactivate the security circuit — a labor-saving advantage.

The confidence is in our proven technology.

Checkpoint sensors sound an alarm whenever merchandise with a "live" signature is carried through them. Their proven RF technology assures the most reliable and accurate detection, to bring losses under control and make open merchandising a practical reality.

The support is in our service.

Service begins with our Checkcare™ programs that provide start-up, installation, employee training, and ongoing market support. These programs also include guidance in civil recovery and loss prevention policies and procedures.

Plus, we offer the protection of Checkcare™, our on-site full-coverage customer assurance program. In short, we do what it takes to maximize the open merchandising benefits of a Checkpoint system — and only when you buy it, but as you use it.

EAM IMPACT MODEL
Predict your EAM payback period, including loss and recover your profits. Send for your FREE Impact Model. (See page 10.)

(continued)

HOW TO CALCULATE THE BENEFITS OF OPEN MERCHANDISING IN YOUR RETAIL OPERATIONS

Get your free EAM Impact Model.

There is only one way to predict the profitability of EAM in your retail environment. And that is by modeling the financial conditions of your actual retail operations. That is why we would like to give you a *Free EAM Impact Model* diskette based on the Management Horizons retail IMPACT model.

Your EAM Impact Model will enable you to enter your own data for such variables as *market coverage, penetration level, average shopping frequency, closure rate, and average transaction size* in order to calculate your gross sales. Then, by projecting *reduced shrinkage and increases in closure rate and average transaction size*, it can help you determine the payback period for your EAM system investment and your increases in sales and earnings per store.

You will be able to calculate the realistic benefits of EAM based on increased closure rates and average transaction sizes for the first year, second year, and subsequent years

We believe that when you do your own calculations, using your data, and see the potential results in your environment, you will fully appreciate the benefits of Electronic Article Merchandising

To learn more about open merchandising with Checkpoint EAM, call or write to request your own copy of our EAM Impact Model today. Contact us at:

Checkpoint Systems, Inc.
550 Grove Road
Thorofare, NJ 08086
(800) 257-5540 • (609) 848-1800

A GLOSSARY OF EAM TERMS

Activation — The process of enabling "dormant" electronic signatures to perform in a Checkpoint RF system. In EAM applications where these circuits are embedded in the product or product packaging, this activation would be done at a distribution point before the merchandise is put on display at store level.

Average Shopping Frequency — How often a typical customer visits your store, typically expressed as visits per week or visits per month.

Average Transaction Size — A measure of merchandising success defined as the total dollar amount spent by a customer on a single visit to a store. Average transaction size is computed by dividing the total sales volume by the number of purchases.

Bulk Activation — The ability to make the "dormant" Impulse circuits functional for a volume of products before stocking them on store shelves. This process is accomplished by a Checkpoint activation unit.

Cheklink — The integration of Checkpoint RF technology within the context of other retail labeling and POS procedures. For example, electronic signatures are incorporated within tags or labels that also combine pricing, merchandising, and data collection features. Deactivation capabilities are incorporated in the same hand-held or counter-mounted units used to scan bar code data, for one-step efficiency at checkout.

Closure Rate — The percentage of shoppers who make a purchase during a visit to a store.

Cost of Disposal — An economic and environmental concern related to the increasing expense of waste removal. Smaller, simplified packaging can help control these costs.

EAM Horizons Conferences — A Checkpoint program of retail industry meetings attended by retailers and manufacturers for the purposes of discussing and resolving issues related to the implementation of EAM with Impulse targets.

EAM Impact Model — A spreadsheet developed by Checkpoint (based on the Management Horizons IMPACT model) that enables retailers to project the benefits of electronic article merchandising in their operations. It utilizes user-defined values for factors of economic performance such as penetration level, market coverage, average shopping frequency, closure rate, and average transaction size to calculate store traffic, transactions and gross sales. Gross sales, profitability rate and the shrinkage reduction rate are then applied to determine the sales and profit improvement opportunities.

EAS — Electronic Article Surveillance, a method of monitoring and protecting merchandise by means of an electronically activated alarm system.

Electronic Article Merchandising (EAM) — The Checkpoint Systems strategy of open merchandising made practical through the protection afforded by RF electronic signatures.

Electronic Signatures — RF circuits with a radio wave fingerprint that responds to the transmitted signal of a Checkpoint sensor. In an EAM application, such signatures passing through a sensor system will trigger an alarm.

Greening — The trend toward ecological sensitivity. This affects retailers with regards to packaging size and the amount of materials used in packaging.

IMPACT Model — A simulation of financial performance in retail operations, developed by Management Horizons to help retailers manage profitability related to market coverage, penetration level, average shopping frequency, store traffic, closure rate, transactions, average transaction size, and gross sales.

Impulse — The Checkpoint program of embedding electronic signatures within the product packaging or the product itself, at the point of manufacture.

(continued)

■ **EXHIBIT 32.1** *continued*

A GLOSSARY OF EAM TERMS

Integrated Security — A time-saving, labor-saving method of incorporating security protection within other standard retail operations. For example, electronic security can be implemented during routine packaging or labeling processes and deactivated as a part of routine POS operations.

Integration — The process of assembling a series of elements or processes into a whole system. EAM is the integration of packaging, display, security, and POS efficiencies into a single system designed to improve the profitability of retail operations.

Market Coverage — The customer population in a target market with access to retail store locations and retail promotions.

Non-Contact Deactivation — A convenient means of disabling an electronic security device without the need for locating the target or making direct physical contact with it.

Open Merchandising — Providing shoppers with free access to merchandise, so they can examine it, try it, and serve themselves. The benefits of open merchandising include increased sales opportunities, reduced personnel requirements, and fewer barriers to sales.

Partnering (Partnership) — The exchange of information between a retailer and a manufacturer for the purposes of implementing new product or merchandising ideas.

Penetration Level — The rate of success in capitalizing on market coverage, expressed as that percentage of target market customers who actually visit your store.

POS Deactivation — The process of neutralizing electronic signatures at the point of sale. This can be accomplished as a separate procedure or as one integrated into other point-of-sale operations.

Profit Engineering — The art of defining and managing retail operations for maximum return on investment.

Retail Profitability — The relative return on investment in a retail operation that takes into account factors of marketing, merchandising, and operating efficiencies.

Radio Frequency (RF) Technology — The technology used in Checkpoint electronic signatures for electronic article merchandising. The sensors consist of a transmitter and a receiver that together establish an RF field. When an "active" target interrupts that field, it triggers an alarm.

Self-Service Merchandising — A method of open merchandising that can reduce labor requirements.

Sensor System — Monitoring device used to detect articles protected with security targets. A Checkpoint RF sensor system triggers an alarm when its radio-frequency field is disrupted by active electronic signatures.

Source Tagging — The labeling or tagging of products at the point of manufacture. In a Checkpoint EAM system, this can include embedding Impulse targets into products or product packaging.

Strategic Alliance — A business agreement between two individual companies in an industry or market for their mutual benefit.

Target — An RF circuit used to protect articles with an electronic security system. Checkpoint targets are available as disposable tags, labels, and Impulse™ circuits that feature non-contact deactivation, or as reusable tags.

---

3. What products are the most important for Checkpoint? Where should it concentrate its marketing and production resources?

4. What steps should Checkpoint take to maximize acceptance to consumers of the Checkpoint EAM products?

■ ■ ■ ■ ■

■ EXHIBIT 32.2   Changing Sales Patterns of Checkpoint

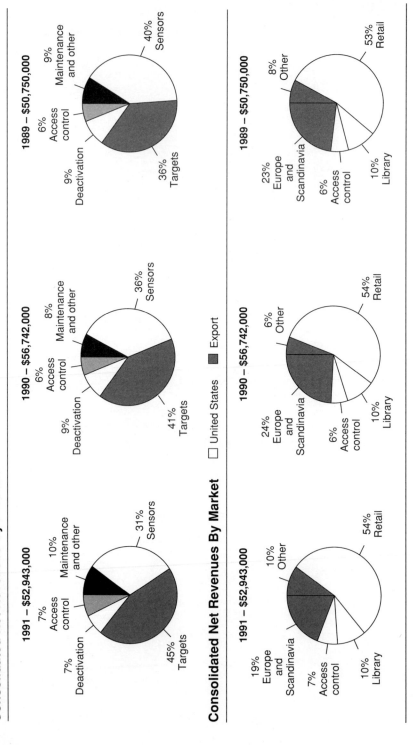

Consolidated Net Revenues By Product

1991 – $52,943,000

- 31% Sensors
- 45% Targets
- 7% Deactivation
- 7% Access control
- 10% Maintenance and other

1990 – $56,742,000

- 36% Sensors
- 41% Targets
- 9% Deactivation
- 6% Access control
- 8% Maintenance and other

1989 – $50,750,000

- 40% Sensors
- 36% Targets
- 9% Deactivation
- 6% Access control
- 9% Maintenance and other

Consolidated Net Revenues By Market   ☐ United States   ■ Export

1991 – $52,943,000

- 54% Retail
- 10% Library
- 7% Access control
- 19% Europe and Scandinavia
- 10% Other

1990 – $56,742,000

- 54% Retail
- 10% Library
- 6% Access control
- 24% Europe and Scandinavia
- 6% Other

1989 – $50,750,000

- 53% Retail
- 10% Library
- 6% Access control
- 23% Europe and Scandinavia
- 8% Other

The J. M. Smucker Company [1]

■ ■ ■ ■ ■

Nearly 100 years ago in a farming community 60 miles south of Cleveland, Ohio, Jerome M. Smucker opened a cider mill for area farmers; later he began making and selling apple butter. His recipe was simple—apples, sugar, and spices. But there were a few special ingredients he threw into the family business—quality, purity and adherence to simple values.

The recipe proved to be a success. This small-time operation grew to be one of the nation's largest producers of jams, jellies, and preserves. By 1992 the company had grown to include brand names such as Smucker's, Mary Ellen, Elsenham, IXL, Dickinson's, and R.W. Knudsen Family. While consumers are still the primary market for Smucker's products, the company also serves commercial food markets.

The J. M. Smucker Co. has about 38 percent market share of the jam and jelly market, according to industry and company officials. By comparison, its largest competitors, Welch's and Kraft, have 12 percent and 4 percent market share, respectively. Despite tough competition, Smucker's continues to increase its market share each year.

In some of its other product offerings—such as ice cream toppings, fruit syrups, and natural fruit juices—Smucker's is also the market leader, although company officials declined to reveal specific market share figures. In addition, the company is the market leader in natural peanut butter.

Market share is not the only success Smucker's has gained over the years. From 1983 to 1992, sales increased from $200.4 million to $483 million, and net income ripened from $12.3 million to $34 million. Analysts predict earnings per share will continue to increase from 13 percent to 15 percent a year. "With some stocks, you can eat well. With others, you can sleep well. With Smucker's you can do both," said Jeffrey Stein,

[1]This case is excerpted from: Sarah Mills Bacha, "Success Spreads at Smucker's," *The Columbus Dispatch*, October 2, 1989, H1; Martha Cooper, Daniel Innis, and Peter Dickson, "The J.M. Smucker Company," *Strategic Planning for Logistics*, 1992, 141–153.

an analyst at McDonald and Company in Cleveland. "This company knows its business."

Smucker's mixes traditional, down-home values of the past with todays business savvy. But sweet success year after year has not spoiled this family-run company. At the Orrville plant, Smucker's runs two shifts 5 or 6 days a week, but not on Sunday. Plant workers, clad in "whites" and hairnets, smile and wave at Paul, Tim, and Richard Smucker, the third and fourth generations to lead the company, as they stroll through the facility. They stop to chat with many of them. Because all three of them started working in the plant as teenagers, they know a lot of the workers well. Just as there have been four generations of Smucker's leading the company, there are other families that have worked for the manufacturer for years.

"They are tucked away in Orrville and out of the mainstream of new greed that seems to be overtaking much of the corporate community," said Elliot Schlang, executive vice president of Kemper Securities Group in Cleveland.

Over the years, the more things have changed on Strawberry Lane due to acquisitions, new products, and financial growth, the more things have stayed the same. The company's top management has been quite stable. Most officers have been with the company for at least 15 years, allowing co-workers to know each other well and work closely together. Top management fosters an attitude of teamwork and communication among functions through cross-functional task forces and committees.

A Tradition of Quality

The process that Jerome Smucker first used to make apple butter is almost the same as the one used today; the modern factory sits on the same site where he first made cider before the turn of the century. In addition, the company's "Basic Beliefs" are still in place. When, Paul, Tim, and Richard Smucker talk about any kind of success that has occurred at the company, they refer to the company's five main principles—*quality, people, ethics, growth and independence*—established four generations ago by the company's founder.

"If you really want to understand the company, that's what it's all about . . . We try to live them on an everyday basis," Tim Smucker said. "They are what make the company what it is today."

While it might sound too good to be true, "this company is genuine," said Martin McDevitt, an analyst with Cleary Gull Relland McDevitt & Collopy Inc. "There is nothing artificial about Smucker's. From its people to its products, they are the highest quality that you'll find anywhere."

"It's a real showcase for how a family-run business in America can work in today's world," McDonald & Co's Stein said.

Key to Smucker's success is its long-standing dedication to quality. The underpinnings of Smucker quality is SQM—Smucker Quality Management program, which is based upon the following philosophies:

- quality is everyone's responsibility
- a commitment to continuous improvement
- open communication
- prevention versus detection
- quality and skills training
- supplier quality

Or more simply stated by Tim Smucker, "If you put quality first, sales, growth, and earnings will follow." The philosophy has paid off.

One blunder in the company's history was its entry into the pickle business in the 1970s. "The pickle was a mistake, and they got out of it fast," McDevitt said. However, he added, "They haven't made what I'd call any strategic mistakes."

Strategic Business Areas

Prior to 1989, Smucker's was structured, both strategically and organizationally, around markets. In 1989, those markets were combined into Strategic Business Areas (SBA). The largest is *Consumer*, which includes the grocery, government, general merchandise, health and natural foods, and gifts and incentives markets. *Foodservice* and *Industrial* are next. Foodservice includes the sales of products to restaurants and to the transportation, healthcare and education industries. In the industrial market, Smucker's supplies other food manufacturers with fruit fillings to be used as ingredients in their own products. According to a spokesman from the National Association of Fruits, Flavors and Syrups, there has been increased growth in the industrial market for fruit fillings found in products like yogurt and cereal. "It's a natural outgrowth of the health-conscious trend," the spokesman said.

The fourth SBA is *Specialty Foods*, which sells gourmet products to specialty and gourmet outlets. *International*, the final SBA, includes Canada, United Kingdom, Australia, and export business.

Marketing

Smuckers is very marketing oriented and is organized so that other business functions support the overall corporate direction. Marketing and sales are organized around the five strategic business areas mentioned earlier: consumer, foodservice, industrial, specialty foods, and international. Operations, logistics, technical services, accounting, and administration serve all five business areas.

The J. M. Smucker Company now ranks as America's number one producer of jams, jellies, preserves, ice cream toppings and fruit syrups. While growth has brought significant change in the company's organization and operations, the strong Smucker brand continues to stand for quality with each new generation of consumers. That continuity over time and across numerous communication channels has been achieved by careful management of the company's consumer marketing efforts: from advertising to consumer promotion to public relations and packaging.

Once limited to the small size, adult variety segment, the company undertook a growth strategy from the mid-1970s and to the mid-1980s that expanded the consumer base from a relatively narrow segment of older, upper income households to also include a higher volume group of families with children consuming larger sizes of jelly.

Smucker's became the category leader in terms of market share by the early 1980s. From a number two position in the mid-1970s, it has more than doubled its market share. Its share is now just under 40 percent and is more than three times that of its nearest branded competitor. Ongoing monitoring of consumer attitudes and perceptions helped guide the strategy year to year. Importantly, consumer feedback continues to point the way as Smucker's extends its market leadership by responding to emerging consumer needs.

New product introductions accelerated from the late 1980s to the present. Low Sugar, Simply Fruit, Light, and Extra Fruit have all been successfully introduced under the Smucker brand. Each has been positioned to respond to consumers' desire for products not only with good taste, but increasingly, with additional health benefits. Smucker's Simply Fruit, a spread sweetened with fruit juice, is targeted for the all fruit niche, which is the fastest growing portion of the jam, jellies and preserves category. "It's been a big success for us," Tim Smucker said.

The company's number one product remains strawberry preserves. But for the jam, jellies and preserves industry, grape jelly is the biggest seller nationwide while strawberry preserves rank second.

Smucker's continues to have a positive brand reputation with the consumer, and leadership on key consumer measures continues. A continuity of national advertising has helped to sustain this important competitive advantage. The company has had a dominant share of voice in the category for more than 15 years. Concentrating in network and cable TV, the company continues to use its well known slogan, "With a name like Smucker's, it has to be good." Created in the early 1960s, it is one of the best known and longest running slogans in use today.

As it grew from a small, regional preserver to a national leader in the U.S. market, the company pursued an "evolutionary" approach in all marketing efforts. By monitoring changing perceptions/needs in the marketplace and avoiding radical shifts, the Smucker brand continues to stand for quality with the consumer. In a slow growth, easy to enter, highly competitive category, it is the trusted reputation of the brand that remains the key to sustained, profitable growth.

Like many U.S. industries, the jams, jellies and preserves business, with annual sales of about $650 million, has not been immune to foreign imports. In response, Smucker's set out to increase its global presence with three strategic acquisitions. In 1988 it purchased the "Good Morning" marmalade line and "Shirriff" ice cream topping and marmalade lines from Kellogg Salada Canada, Inc. Additionally, Smucker's purchased Elsenham Quality Foods Ltd., Elsenham, England, and Henry Jones Foods, Kyabrum, Australia.

With Canadian trade barriers being relaxed, Smucker's sees an opportunity. "We think it's important to have a North American presence, not just U.S.," said William P. Boyle Jr., senior vice president of marketing and president of the international division. "The same thing is happening in Europe. After 1992, there will be virtually no trade barriers. And that becomes a big, attractive market for us."

Boyle said Smucker's intends to sell Elsenham spread products in the United States and abroad. To date, less than 10 percent of the company's sales are international. The new acquisitions "open new opportunities for them that they didn't have before," McDevitt said. "There are certain food-service markets in the United States that they haven't been able to penetrate like upscale restaurants and hotels."

Other acquisitions include the purchase of R-Line Foods, Inc. in Ripon, Wisconsin, a manufacturer of fruit spreads and specialty condiments packaged in small containers and Knudsen & Sons Inc., a leading producer of pure fruit juices. Other growth for the company will come from expanded distribution and new products, Tim Smucker said.

Operations

Smucker's, with 1,900 employees, has twelve production locations domestically and internationally. The three major manufacturing plants are located in Orrville, Ohio; Memphis, Tennessee; and Salinas, California. Juice is produced in Chico, California; peanut butter in New Bethlehem, Pennsylvania; and specialty food products in Ripon, Wisconsin. International operations are in Elsenham, England and Kyabram, Victoria, Australia. Fruit processing plants are in Oxnard and Watsonville, California; Woodburn, Oregon and Grandview, Washington.

At the fruit processing facilities enough fruit is acquired during the fresh fruit season to assure a full year of production. The fruit is then processed, quick frozen and shipped to one of the manufacturing plants to be made into finished product throughout the year. This gives rise to the importance of logistics.

Logistics

The logistics function at Smucker's was created in the late 1970s at the request of management. This organization replaced the prior organization where logistical elements were a part of marketing and operations plans as opposed to an integral part of the product supply chain. This missing link was how to integrate the system from the fields to the stores. The new logistics function was the answer. The procurement and distribution functions, including inventory control and production planning responsibilities, were placed under *logistics*.

Purchasing was centralized under logistics. Certain commodities had always been purchased centrally but it was determined that significant savings could be generated by systematizing purchasing and by aggregating purchases of fruit, packaging, and other material across plants. Central purchasing has led to better control of costs and increased margins.

Logistics is moving into strategic partnering with suppliers and distributor customers. There is visitation to the partner's facilities and vice versa for a better understanding of each other's business. This has led to higher quality products and service, greater efficiencies, and thus, lower costs.

Future Leadership

Although Smucker's went public in 1959, Smucker family members still own the controlling portion of the company's approximately 29 million common shares. There have been acquisition inquiries in the past, but not anymore, Tim Smucker said. The company wants to remain independent and "people know what our intentions are," he said.

To preserve independence and encourage long-term ownership by shareholders, Smucker's has adopted a number of charter amendments. One of these states that if a shareholder owned stock before 1986, he or she gets ten votes per share. A shareholder who bought stock after that, though, has one vote per share until it is held for 4 years. "This reinforces the importance of long-term investment in the company," said Tim Smucker. In 1991, Smucker's also created and issued a second class of nonvoting common shares to increase its flexibility in acquisitions and the ability of insiders to sell shares, if necessary, without diluting their voting strength. As a result of these various provisions, insiders are estimated to control 50 percent or more of the voting power.

Tim and his brother, Richard, are chairman and president of the company, respectively. Their father, Paul, who is chief executive officer and chairman of the executive committee, started working at the company in 1929. Will there be a fifth generation running the company someday? "There are eight children in the next generation," said Tim Smucker. "Four of them have followed in their parents and grandparents footsteps by working in the plant during their summer vacations." Some are pursuing career paths outside the company. "If any of the children want to work for the company, we'd love to have them," Tim Smucker said. But, he added, it's their choice.

Focal Topics

1. How should Smucker's segment the market in the 1990s?
2. Develop an advertising campaign for Smucker's.

3. Smucker's has entered various markets in recent years, often by acquisitions of existing firms. Into what types of products do you recommend Smucker's expand both by manufacturing new products and by acquiring existing companies? Be specific in identifying companies to be acquired.

4. Smucker's has placed emphasis on its logistics function in recent years. Is this justified? How does a superior logistics system affect the company's bottom line and its customer satisfaction level?

■ ■ ■ ■ ■

Harry Rosen

■ ■ ■ ■ ■

It would be difficult to find anyone in Canada who does not know the name and face of Mr. Harry Rosen. He has come to represent quality fashion clothing for men all over Canada and in parts of the United States. Harry Rosen, the man, is approachable, unpretentious, and very popular among his customers. Harry Rosen, the store, is upbeat, exciting, and offers a unique shopping experience to its customers. The man and the store have created high standards in the fashion industry, which competitors have tried to emulate over the last three decades.

A Commitment to Quality

Harry Rosen entered the world of retail with one men's clothing store in 1954. Although he worked diligently on managing the store and making it profitable, he continued to custom tailor suits for many of his customers. His training was in tailoring, a skill he still uses today.

By 1992 Harry Rosen had grown his chain to twenty-four stores located from Quebec City, Quebec, to Vancouver, British Columbia, to Buffalo, New York. The store locations can be broken down as follows:

Location	Number of Stores	Location	Number of Stores
Quebec City	1	Winnipeg	1
Montreal	2	Edmonton	2
Ottawa	2	Calgary	2
Toronto	10	Vancouver	2
London (Ontario)	1	Buffalo, NY	1

The average Harry Rosen is 9,000 square feet in size and is located in an all enclosed shopping center in either a suburb or a downtown shopping complex. Two stores, one in Vancouver and one in Toronto, are a bit larger at 16,000 square feet. The flagship store, by far the largest, is on Bloor Street in Toronto. It is 32,000 square feet and is housed on three levels. Average sales per square foot are over $600.

Harry Rosen strives to be a unique alternative to ordinary shopping in each market it serves, and it succeeds. It operates primarily in markets with a population of 500,000 or more. It plans to grow further in the Montreal market by opening a 16,000 to 30,000 square foot store in downtown Montreal and one in the suburban areas. Much of the company's targeted growth will occur outside Canada in the next decade.

Harry Rosen's philosophy of service, formulated many years ago, is followed today. It begins with members of the sales staff, who understand the meaning of quality. While they make no apology for the rather high price tags, they can and do explain to their customers why the garments are worth their cost.

Harry Rosen's sales associates are trained to sell clothing, accessories, and sportswear by recognizing and meeting the needs of their individual customers. The staff needs to know the details on the vast selection available in the stores. They are trained to understand which look is proper and when, how to accessorize it, how to care for it, and how to fit it. The staff must be willing to listen and observe so that they can understand each customer's requirements of style, size, and price. Finally they must be willing to give advice.

Harry Rosen sales associates execute the special services the company offers its valued customers. For example, an associate can arrange for free alterations on Harry Rosen clothes if a client has lost or gained some weight. Free repairs are offered on buttons and seams. Harry Rosen sales associates will also visit clients at home, evaluate their wardrobes, and suggest what items need to be added to keep their wardrobes up to date. Sales associates also understand the value of their clients' time and will deliver items to offices or homes free of charge. They will also shop for clients if so desired.

Sales associates are also trained to gather as much information on their customers as possible. Some of the information they obtain and record in their computers can be seen in Exhibit 34.1. This information is used to send notes to clients or conduct follow-up phone calls regarding their satisfaction with the products and their shopping experiences. Sales associates are also able to contact customers about new arrivals and special promotions. Most importantly they are able to contact customers who may not have visited a store in recent months to bring them back into the stores.

The training program at Harry Rosen is fairly extensive. It focuses around selling excellence and product knowledge. Associates are also trained in "clothesmanship," including how a good suit is made, how it should be altered to Harry Rosen standards, and how to aid in customer merchandise selection. The Harry Rosen training program also includes a

■ EXHIBIT 34.1   Harry Rosen Sales Transaction Information

HARRY ROSEN CLIENTELE SYSTEM

TITLE	MR
FIRST NAME	John
LAST NAME	Doe
STREET	SHORNCLIFFE AVE
CITY	TORONTO
PROV/STATE	ONTARIO

COUNTRY	CANADA	LANGUAGE	E	ASSOCIATE	444444
POSTAL/ZIP	M4Y1T1	SEND MAIL	Y	STORE	0098

PRIMARY ASSOCIATE   11150 PAWLAK, STEVE AT STORE 98 CENTRAL DISTRIB

LAST STORE SHOPPED   0008 SCOTIA PLAZA

  ASSOCIATE   0011150 PAWLAK, STEVE

  TRANSACTION DATE   MAY 22, 1992   AMOUNT SPENT $85.00

CLIENT SINCE   JAN 16, 1988

PURCHASES

  THIS SEASON $1,416.40   LAST SEASON $1,693.50   LIFE TIME $4,117.90

HARRY ROSEN CLIENTELE SYSTEM
PURCHASE DETAILS

DEPARTMENT	CATEGORY	COLOUR	SIZE	RETAIL	QTY	ASSOC	STR	PURCHASE DATE
P 21 LS VT D	28 J.P. TIL	WHITE	16/2-4	$85.00	1	11150	8	MAY 22 92
P 74 UNDERWE	98 INVALID	ASSORT		$122.50	7	11150	8	APR 29 92
P 63 HOSIERY	53 BRAND LA	ASSORT		$72.50	5	11150	8	APR 29 92
P 63 HOSIERY	51 PRIVATE	BLACK		$13.95	1	11150	8	APR 29 92
P 63 HOSIERY	27 SEDGEWIC	BLACK		$12.95	1	11150	8	APR 29 92
P 63 HOSIERY	20 J.P. TIL	MID GR		$19.50	1	11150	8	APR 29 92
P 21 LS VT D	20 J.P. TIL	WHITE	16/2-4	$170.00	2	11150	8	APR 29 92
P 35 SPORT S	28 J.P. TIL	ASSORT L		$125.00	1	11150	8	APR 29 92
R 5 SUITS	2 ARMANI	TAUPE		$1,475.00-	1	11150	8	APR 20 92
P 5 SUITS	5 HUGO BOS	NAVY	44R	$795.00	1	11150	8	APR 18 92
P 5 SUITS	2 ARMANI	TAUPE	44R	$1,475.00	1	11150	8	APR 18 92
P 27 TIES	5 HUGO BOS	ASSORT		$87.50	1	11150	8	OCT 24 91
P 27 TIES	8 AVANZATA	MID-BL		$65.00	1	11150	8	OCT 24 91
P 27 TIES	1 ZEGNA	ASSORT		$115.00	1	11150	8	OCT 24 91
P 27 TIES	5 HUGO BOS	ASSORT		$95.00	1	11150	8	OCT 16 91
P 66 BELTS/S	51 PRIVATE	ROSE		$60.00	1	11150	8	OCT 16 91
P 66 BELTS/S	0 AVANZATA	BLACK	40	$87.50	1	11150	8	OCT 16 91
P 74 UNDERWE	98 INVALID	ASSORT		$105.00	5	11150	8	OCT 16 91
P 74 UNDERWE	99 INVALID	ASSORT		$26.00	1	11150	8	OCT 16 91

(*continued*)

■ **EXHIBIT 34.1   Harry Rosen Sales Transaction Information** *continued*

P 34	SPORT S	5 HUGO BOS	DARK B	16 1/2	$210.00	1	11150	8	OCT	16	91
P 11	DRESS P	59 GALLERIA	CHARCO	40	$275.00	1	11150	8	OCT	16	91
P 11	DRESS P	8 AVANZATA	DARK G	40	$235.00	1	11150	8	OCT	16	91
P 37	CASUAL	20 J.P. TIL	KHAKI	40	$135.00	1	11150	8	OCT	16	91
P 37	CASUAL	30 H.R.2	BLACK	38	$125.00	1	11150	8	OCT	16	91
P 27	TIES	8 AVANZATA	DARK B		$72.50	1	11150	8	OCT	16	91
P 26	FORMAL	27 SEDGEWIC	WHITE	16-33	$75.00	1	18686	35	JUL	04	91
P 27	TIES	5 HUGO BOS	ASSORT		$87.50	1	20825	9	JUN	14	91
P 27	TIES	5 HUGO BOS	ASSORT		$87.50	1	20825	9	JUN	14	91
P 24	FANCY D	28 J.P. TIL	OLIVE	16-33	$85.00	1	20825	9	JUN	14	91
P 69	FORMAL	98 INVALID	ASSORT		$25.00	1	20825	9	JUN	14	91
P 24	FANCY D	28 J.P. TIL	LT. GR	16-34	$98.50	1	20825	9	JUN	14	91
P 27	TIES	8 AVANZATA	NAVY		$55.00	1	11150	9	OCT	30	90
P 63	HOSIERY	98 INVALID	ASSORT		$90.00	6	11150	9	OCT	30	90
P 11	DRESS P	28 J.P. TIL	CHARCO	42	$195.00	1	11150	9	OCT	30	90
P 27	TIES	8 AVANZATA	LT. GR		$45.00	1	11150	9	OCT	30	90
P 34	SPORT S	53 BRAND LA	BLACK	M	$125.00	1	11150	9	JUL	03	90
P 27	TIES	5 HUGO BOS	ASSORT		$87.50	1	20825	9	JUN	14	91
P 24	FANCY D	28 J.P. TIL	OLIVE	16-33	$85.00	1	20825	9	JUN	14	91
P 69	FORMAL	98 INVALID	ASSORT		$25.00	1	20825	9	JUN	14	91
P 24	FANCY D	28 J.P. TIL	LT. GR	16-34	$98.50	1	20825	9	JUN	14	91
P 27	TIES	8 AVANZATA	NAVY		$55.00	1	11150	9	OCT	30	90
P 63	HOSIERY	90 INVALID	ASSORT		$98.00	6	11150	9	OCT	30	90
P 11	DRESS P	28 J.P. TIL	CHARCO	42	$195.00	1	11150	9	OCT	30	90
P 27	TIES	8 AVANZATA	LT. GR		$45.00	1	11150	9	OCT	30	90
P 34	SPORT S	53 BRAND LA	BLACK	M	$125.00	1	11150	9	JUL	03	90

Courtesy: Mr. Harry Rosen

variety of programs regarding how consumers buy, product knowledge, expense control, merchandise presentation, customer relations, and entrepreneurship.

Harry Rosen — The Man and His Ads

One of the company's critical success factors has been Harry Rosen's involvement in the business. He tries to spend at least four days per year in each store, which helps him keep abreast of changes in consumer needs. It also helps him reach his customers and his staff members and develop relationships with them. He can sometimes be found tailoring clients' suits in various locations if his busy schedule allows.

Harry Rosen has a strong international identity. He actively participates in public relations activities by doing charitable work throughout Canada. He also takes an active role in advertising. He has appeared in numerous

Harry Rosen ads over the last decade, making his face synonymous with the store. He has created a relationship with his customers through his ads.

Recently, the ads have taken on an even more personal flare with the "Ask Harry" campaign. In this campaign, Harry answers his customers' fashion related concerns. Customers write letters to Harry and ask about specific products and fashion trends. He answers them in letter form published in newspaper ads. Every Monday a full page ad featuring an "Ask Harry" ad appears in three Canadian national papers. Although the company has been using the same ad agency for 31 years, it continues to produce new and intriguing ads for Harry Rosen stores.

The "Ask Harry" ads revolve around various issues important to Harry Rosen customers. Exhibits 34.2 through 34.4 show some of these ads. They revolve around issues such as wardrobe essentials for the 1990s and what each brand of suit carried in the stores has to offer. Most often, Harry answers questions about fashion—what is appropriate to wear to the office and which types of suits "travel" best.

Harry Rosen advertising and promotion activities are not limited to the "Ask Harry" ads. The company runs 1,000-line ads approximately fifteen times each season in local markets. This allows the company to tailor messages to specific markets, regions, and stores. Twelve additional ads promoting higher priced products for Scotia Plaza, Bloor Street, and Pacific Centre stores appear in the financial sections of the same national newspapers. Direct mail pieces are sent to current and potential clients twice a year.

Quality Products

There are some men who would agree with the idea that Harry Rosen practically invented the way Canadian men dress for business. "Nice suit. Is it a Rosen?" has become part of the vernacular. Keeping abreast of the times, if not a few steps ahead of them, Harry's suit racks have come to reflect a broadening in tastes and a widening in lifestyle choices.

Rosen philosophy dictates that there is no room for anything less than fine quality garments in Harry Rosen stores. In the fashion industry, quality begins with the cloth, and that cloth must be both the best and affordable, whether it be wool, cotton, or silk. Quality suits wear longer, retain their shape better, and feel and look better on the body. The workmanship must also be superior. The people who make Harry Rosen clothing and sportswear make them to the company's strict guidelines. Seams must be soft yet secure. Linings must be sewn in with all the care that the exterior receives. Buttons and zippers must be the best available. Although many different styles of clothing are sold in the stores, the styling must be classic. No fads will be found in Harry Rosen stores.

Harry feels that all the quality in the world would be worthless if it was not available in the styles, colors, price ranges, and sizes customers need. The goal at Harry Rosen is to provide a selection that will satisfy almost

WHAT IS THE BASIC SUIT WARDROBE FOR THE 90'S?

ASK HARRY

If you started to build a basic suit wardrobe from scratch today, what suit would you start with? How many suits do you need? How much should you pay?

I first answered these questions in an ad back in 1968 and as I look back at what I said then, it isn't much different than what I am about to say now.

Stylewise of course there is much more choice offered today.

Depending on your personal taste, your lifestyle and the image that you want to project, you can choose from the traditional North American looks, the British-inspired classics, the European traditional, and the works of the Italian masters. And amongst those looks there are many individual designer interpretations.

'So come on Harry, answer the question.'

THE SIX SUIT WARDROBE

Start with a dark blue suit, a solid or faint stripe. By keeping any patterns you choose on the subtle side, there is hardly a place – with the possible exception of a coronation or some lesser bash calling for black tie – where it isn't right. Make it single or double-breasted based solely on your preference.

Next a dark grey number. A solid would be the surest bet, but there is no rule that says you can't try a stripe, a herringbone or a sharkskin in either single or double-breasted – but, let me reiterate, in tones of darker grey.

Suits numero three and four. Oxford grey and a mid-dark blue. Here's an opportunity to step into a stripe or classic pic'n pic.

Now we begin to move out a bit. As the fifth suit in the basic wardrobe, I recommend what I couldn't have suggested back in '68 – a suit in olive or an olive/brown in cool tones (a blue dress shirt goes splendidly with either, by the by).

But essentially this is a six-suit wardrobe, and for the final suit you get a choice. 6(a) The Prince of Wales or glen plaid suit in black and white is classic business attire that shouldn't be overlooked. Or, 6(b) a fine houndstooth in black and white.

You might consider your last purchase to be no suit at all. It is the navy blazer, single or double-breasted as

you prefer, worn with oxford grey trousers. In all but the most elegant of professions it is perfectly acceptable office wear on a more relaxed day and of course, wonderful in the evenings.

As a unifying thread running throughout your wardrobe choices, let me stress the importance of fine pure wool fabrics, which look better, feel better and guard their shape longer.

Anything less falls short of the very idea of building a wardrobe of lasting quality.

THE PROPER MIX

And there you have my recommendation: six suits plus maybe a blazer should do the trick. Remember, darker shades are more elegant, more professional, look richer and come with a welcome sense of security; keep the colours and any patterns different from one suit to the next; with the proper mix of shirts and ties you can create the illusion that your six suits are really twelve; that you can change the mood or feel of a suit depending upon which shirt and tie you wear with it. (See our able-bodied staff for a free demonstration.)

So what's the tab for all this? Well I certainly don't expect you to buy everything I've mentioned here in one fell swoop. Indeed, you most likely already own part of the basic wardrobe. But as a guideline I can advise you that suits in a Rosen store begin at $495 and run to $995. (The average would be $595 to $795.) Our shirts go from $55 to $125, ties from $40 to $100.

Before I leave you to peruse your closet, I should clarify that while what I have described is the 'basic six suit wardrobe for the '90s,' it does not necessarily mean that six suits alone will get you to the millenium.

But then again, there are Harry Rosen suits on the streets of Canada today that were bought when we last spoke about the basic wardrobe back in 1968.

Got a question for Harry? Drop him a line. We'll be running lots more 'Ask Harry' ads throughout the season. Please limit your questions to those concerning men's clothing. He's right out of answers to the meaning of life. Write: 'Ask Harry for Help' Scotia Plaza, 11 Adelaide St. W., Suite 200, Toronto M5H 1N1

HARRY ROSEN

PURE VIRGIN WOOL

TORONTO: 11 Adelaide St. W., 82 Bloor St. W., Eaton Centre, Fairview, Oakville Place, Markville Centre, Scarborough Town, Sherway, Yorkdale, Square One. HAMILTON: Eaton Centre. LONDON: Galleria London. MONTREAL: Fairview Shopping Centre, Rockland Centre, Carrefour Laval. QUEBEC: Place Ste-Foy. OTTAWA: Rideau Centre, Bayshore Centre. WINNIPEG: Polo Park. EDMONTON: Edmonton Centre, West Edmonton Mall. CALGARY: South Centre, Toronto-Dominion Square. VANCOUVER: Oakridge Centre, Pacific Centre. BUFFALO: Walden Galleria.

Courtesy: Mr. Harry Rosen

IS THE ALLURE OF A VALENTINO SUIT TOO MUCH FOR A DAY AT THE OFFICE?

ASK HARRY

While it is pure coincidence that they share the same moniker, the work of both Valentinos – the dramatis and the designatoris personae – also share many of the same adjectives when it comes to describing their work. Refined. Sophisticated. Urbane. Classic. One might go so far as to describe a Valentino suit as imbuing a man with a rather romantic air.

Should you wear such a suit to work? My answer is yes, by all means. Flowery descriptors aside, a Valentino suit remains a business suit with a handsome touch of European elan.

The high quality pure wool fabric and tailoring and design are there in spades. Valentino's personal insistence on an end product that is smart and elegant and businesslike is true to demand. In every garment there is balance, perfect symmetry.

Slipping into one will convince you that a Valentino suit achieves a sophisticated look and comfort normally found only in suits that cost more.

So is a Valentino a suit you can buy knowing that you're getting full value for the money and not paying for some 'Fancy Dan's' villa on the Mediterranean? You bet it is.

Is it a suit you can wear to the office? Absolutely. But if a Valentino suit makes you feel like a bit of a Valentino, remember: Only in the movies.

HARRY ROSEN

Write: 'Ask Harry for Help' Harry Rosen Scotia Plaza, 11 Adelaide St. W., Suite 200, Toronto, Ontario M5H 1N1.

PURE VIRGIN WOOL

TORONTO: 11 Adelaide St. W., 82 Bloor St. W., Eaton Centre, Fairview, Oakville Place, Markville Centre, Scarborough Town, Sherway, Yorkdale, Square One. HAMILTON: Eaton Centre. LONDON: Galleria London. MONTREAL: Fairview Shopping Centre, Rockland Centre, Carrefour Laval. QUEBEC: Place Ste-Foy. OTTAWA: Rideau Centre, Bayshore Centre. WINNIPEG: Polo Park. EDMONTON: Edmonton Centre, West Edmonton Mall. CALGARY: South Centre, Toronto-Dominion Square. VANCOUVER: Oakridge Centre, Pacific Centre. BUFFALO: Walden Galleria.

Courtesy: Mr. Harry Rosen

everyone who enters the store. The result reads like a who's who of fine suits. The following is a sample of Harry Rosen's offerings, including some of the finest suits available in the world.

Valentino   Valentino is nothing short of a fabulous suit for the money. Valentino produces high quality clothing that is European-traditional. Its whole character is one of balance, from the astute choice of the finest wool cloth to the colorations and the trademark notch of the lapels. Suits are available starting from (Canadian) $895.

Avanzata   This line, made exclusively for Harry Rosen in Italy, is truly Italian in style. The Avanzata body shape is roomier, the shoulders are wider, and the trousers have a fuller drape. Pure wool cloth ensures that the fuller cut flows elegantly across and down the body. These suits begin at (Canadian) $650.

J.P. Tilford   The J.P. Tilford by Samuelsohn represents the "Stylish Classic" suit. It is respected for its craftsmanship, sophistication, and sensibilities to the requirements of business life. J.P. Tilford is thought by many to be the finest suit of clothes made in Canada today. These suits start at (Canadian) $795.

Harry II   This is Harry Rosen's own rendition of European style. It is positioned to satisfy those who want current fashion on a tighter budget. Harry II is a great looking, contemporary suit with a hint of youthful fabric directions and shape, without an exaggerated silhouette. Suits begin at (Canadian) $495.

Boss   Few words can capture the allure of Hugo Boss. Its distinctly masculine style has captured the attention and loyalty of many men and fashion critics. It can be said that Boss gives today's relaxed tailoring its perfect definition. Suits start at (Canadian) $750.

Sedgewick   Frequently described as the "updated North American classic" and a "remarkable value," the Sedgewick collection is very much a mainstream business look. The line always remains current and stylish through the tasteful addition of styling touches and fresh pure wool fabrics.

All of these suits can be found in all of the Harry Rosen locations, but the larger stores have additional products available. The 16,000 square foot stores offer Ermenegildo Zegna clothing and accessories and complete Armani collections. The Bloor Street location in Toronto features a Cerutti boutique and a Brioni boutique, the company's most expensive tailored clothing line with suits starting at (Canadian) $2,300.

However, the Harry Rosen selection is not limited to suits. In fact sales can be broken down as follows: 43 percent clothing (suits, sport coats, tuxedos, blazers, slacks, dress shirts), 33 percent sportswear, and 24 percent accessories (ties, dress shirts, suspenders, socks, shoes). This ratio is unique for a specialty store because most sell clothing and accessories but little sportswear. Harry Rosen sportswear generates much traffic in the stores and results in many extra clothing sales.

Harry Rosen created a concept many years ago that remains unique to this day. The man and his stores are dedicated to quality in the products they offer and the service they deliver. The company is poised for continued success in the men's fashion industry, both in Canada and in the United States. Mr. Harry Rosen has dressed some of North America's finest dressed men and has created a legend that continues to live in the form of Harry Rosen, Inc. The future looks long and bright for this Canadian company. Just Ask Harry.

Focal Topics

1. How are the roles of men and women in buying men's fashions different? Are the buying behaviors of men and women different, and how do they vary?

2. Customer service is very important at Harry Rosen stores. What additional services would you recommend management consider offering to its customers?

3. Advertising has also played a key role in the success of Harry Rosen, Inc. What types of advertising appeals should be used to target female and male shoppers? How important has the identity of Harry in the ads been in relating to the public and why? If Harry Rosen expands heavily into the United States, how should the ads change?

4. Exhibit 34.1 shows the sales information that is recorded at the time of each transaction. If you were to update this computer program for Harry Rosen, what additional information would you collect? How would you suggest management and sales associates use the information to increase sales and service in the stores?

■ ■ ■ ■ ■

Pick 'n Pay

■ ■ ■ ■ ■

A First World country in the middle of a Third World continent is the way some people have described South Africa. And a first rate company in the middle of South Africa might be the way some people would describe Pick 'n Pay, operators of supermarkets, cash-and-carry wholesalers, and the world's largest hypermarket. Apartheid laws were abolished in 1991 with an affirmation of these changes by national referendum in 1992. Although world opinion was a catalyst for change, much of the continual pressure for a new South Africa came from business leaders. Among the most visible of these was Raymond Ackerman, CEO of Pick 'n Pay.

Pick 'n Pay evolved from a chain of upscale grocery stores to one of the largest food organizations in the southern hemisphere, but not without controversy. Corporate officials travelled extensively through North America, Europe, Australia, and Asia, studying ideas of the best retailers in the world, bringing them back to Africa, hoping to build something better than what could be found in any of those countries.

To some degree they must have succeeded because the Pick 'n Pay Hypermarkets today are the largest in the world. In the Johannesburg suburb of Boxburg, turnover (sales) during the Christmas season hits as high as 2–3 million Rand or approximately $1 million a day, rung up on state-of-the-art NCR cash registers. The stores are models of efficiency and consumer appeal, selling groceries, meats, bakery goods, and a wide line of hard goods, appliances, and clothing. See Exhibit 35.1 for examples of the store.

Counterculture

Senior Pick 'n Pay staff are very conscious of the philosophy that they feel makes their organization different from any other retail chain. They

(Note: This company operates in South Africa, other southern African countries near South Africa, and Australia.)

talk a lot at Pick 'n Pay about their "culture," the deeply ingrained principles by which the company is run. The thoughts of chairman Raymond Ackerman have become in-house jargon—a series of graphic idioms used to describe everything from merchandising philosophy to human relationships.

One executive sees it as a sign that the retail trade has come of age, become a sophisticated industry. Certainly, you can't avoid the feeling, when you enter the doors of the company's head offices, that somehow you have stumbled into some rather exclusive private club. Not only do all managers from the chairman and board members downward wear company ties, a person cannot get out of any office without hearing at least one element of the company litany.

And the litany is not just words. Beneath the relaxed camaraderie and behind the quotable quotes lie a highly developed strategy, a toughness and determination to be top of the heap, and a considerable amount of acumen, all used in pursuit of their goals.

"At our fortnightly directors' meetings," says nonfood merchandising director Alan Gardiner, "we devote a certain amount of time to milking opportunities. We ask the question 'what could make us better?' And I think that maybe it is the strength of the company.

"People at all levels are dedicated to attention to detail and looking at the basics. We don't float off in clouds of euphoria. We are shopkeepers and that's the way we try to operate—from Ackerman downwards."

Supporting the edifice is what Ackerman calls the "four legs of the table"—administration, merchandising, sales promotion, and people.

Pick 'n Pay is a company full of contrasts—a vast empire controlled and administered by a remarkably small head-office staff; a professionally managed, corporate conglomerate that retains the ethos of a family business; and a simple concept fronting a multitude of complex procedures and decisions. It is seen by many on the outside as fast-moving, innovative, and maverick, and by some on the inside as conservative and slow to react. The company has a reputation for egotism and complacency, but staff members consider themselves humble.

"Humble? What makes Pick 'n Pay different?" asks Joint Managing Director Hugh Herman. "An unbroken history of profit and growth for 19 years. We are now the biggest in the country—our results are a helluva lot better than anyone else's. Off a small base we grew fast, and from a large base we are still growing."

Two of the major criticisms of the company have been that it was perceived as a one-man show and that it had no assets. Now, says Herman, "everybody acknowledges that Ackerman doesn't run it single-handed. The management has grown up and it is as good as any management in the country."

The company has assets. A strong property portfolio and assets in the stores—nothing is leased. The net asset value of the share is much higher than it was before, maintains Herman.

He believes its success is the result of a steady and consistent policy and realistic goals "because the company is controlled by the people who work there, it's run from within. One doesn't have to go running to outside boards to get permission." And, he observes, "we're not afraid to copy—you don't have to reinvent the wheel."

Much of Pick 'n Pay's "culture" relates to its stated attitude to its employees. Promotion comes from within as often as possible. As far as senior management goes, the often reiterated "people" theme seems a reality. The one thing that all executives seem to agree on is that their chief executive really means it when he says people are important to him.

At a purely personal level, the stories are legendary of Ackerman phoning from an airport to inquire about the progress of a seriously ill child; of providing money to send an employee injured while in the army abroad for an operation; of checking that flowers have been sent to the bedside of a sick secretary; and of writing letters of appreciation to the staff after each visit to a store.

"We say we are a people's company which isn't really trite," says company secretary Mike Marsden. "I came to this company because of the way Ackerman treated my twin brother, who was working here. I said 'I want to work for a man like that.'

"He says he's never turned anyone away from his door and that's a fact. I can't say it doesn't assist his ends, but his intentions are sincere and honorable."

The spin-off is a group of executives and senior management whose length of service ranges from 9 years to the full 19 years of the company's existence. Another part of the Pick 'n Pay "culture" is long-service badges—gold for more than 10 years, silver for over 5. There are a lot of those around the head office—behind the tea trays and executive desks.

At senior level, the company makes it worthwhile for people to stay. Salaries, perks, and benefits are generous and appreciated by the recipients. What they give in return is a great chunk of their lives. Many of them spend most of their week travelling between the eighteen separate divisions that constitute the decentralized whole.

Even when they do have a brief respite at home, there is no five-day week. "You'll never see this office on a Saturday less busy than on a Friday," says Alan Gardiner. "If people aren't here, they're in a store somewhere else. All executives work six days a week. If you're in the supermarket business, that's a 6-day week job wherever you are."

"Pick 'n Pay people never think of themselves as being workaholics," he maintains, "but without exception, they all put in a really good week's work." It's all part of the "culture." It is also quite a put-off for potential recruits who are unaccustomed to the degree of motivation that has gone into creating that "culture."

"A lot of us got an opportunity when we came to this company which we could never have hoped to get anywhere else," says Gardiner. "You're not eternally grateful, Ackerman gets his pound of flesh, but every day is a new challenge."

Ultimately, all the challenges come down to one overriding obsession—to stay at the top.

The basic strategy has never changed—low prices, high turnovers, narrow margins—the aim simply becomes more difficult to achieve with pressure both from the opposition and from the worsening economic climate.

Running fast enough to stay ahead is becoming a matter of refining systems, increasing efficiency and productivity, and being constantly innovative. The company is increasingly turning to computerization for the answers.

"We try to keep prices low across the board," says Marsden. "We try to keep away from gimmicks. We don't pick on one section of the market only to try and win favour.

"I think we built this company on being extremely credible in the eyes of the consumer. We don't profess to be the cheapest with all lines, but if we don't get a cheaper price we are pretty tough negotiators."

There is no nice guy image when it comes to battling for a better deal. Pick 'n Pay is aware of its ascendancy in the food market, controlling at least 40 percent of the off-take of most products. "When you start negotiating, that's a pretty strong argument which helps you get better deals, which ensures that you can be competitive," says Marsden.

Like his colleagues, he is impatient with the complaint that Pick 'n Pay delays all its payments until the last possible moment. "I believe that when they say we delay payment of our accounts, that is the biggest lot of . . . it's an incorrect statement.

"Our administration is exceptionally good as far as payment is concerned," he argues. "We pay according to what the suppliers are prepared to negotiate." The better the discount, the faster the payment.

"As for paying cash, that's impractical. Cash balances must remain healthy. Warehouses must stick to budgets and we pay strictly on due dates."

He does concede that the company has been "blessed with tremendous cash flow," monitored on a daily basis and invested accordingly.

"We are aware of our cash position. We do cash flows for a year ahead and see that our cash balances are maintained. Closely aligned, we believe in liquidity, as this is a basic part of the manner in which chain store retailers make a profit." So the expensive program of refurbishing that started recently has all been financed from internal resources.

Nevertheless, many suppliers complain about the payment procedures of Pick 'n Pay, reporting that the company does not pay until the last possible time. Suppliers also report that they are asked to provide free merchandise for Pick 'n Pay's numerous promotions and charitable giveaways.

Another element of the Pick 'n Pay "culture" is loyalty to people with whom the company has worked successfully—architects, shopfitters, advertising agencies, suppliers, and banks (the company deals with five major banks and never has more than R25m in any one of them). "We horse trade in the sense that we won't change for a few shekels, but we are tough negotiators. We make them aware of what's going on in the marketplace and in most instances they match the prices." One reason NCR computers are found throughout Pick 'n Pay stores, many people believe, is because NCR helped Ackerman get started and helped make him somewhat of a hero among American retailers at a time when most of America was expressing negative attitudes toward South Africa.

There are those who feel that elements of that precious "culture," which has served the company well, might have to yield to the pressures of the times, that the company only makes changes because of duress. Marsden sees it differently.

"We are questioning and aiming for perfection all the time. We move slowly because there are deep discussions before any decision. We try to be market leaders, but at the same time we ensure that we do it properly."

Politics and the Chicken Price

Raymond Ackerman is not a man who ever believed business in a politics-ridden society could be divorced from the political forces around it. He battled Prime Minister John Vorster for years on the subject of job reservation. Within his company, Ackerman insisted, promotion would be on merit, not on race.

At his insistence, he says, Clovelly Country Club, founded by his father, went multiracial. Ackerman, along with Premier's Tony Bloom, headed the initiative that had ninety-two major businessmen appear in print under the rallying cry "There is a better way," with a call for the abolition of statutory race discrimination, negotiation with acknowledged black leaders about power sharing, full citizenship for all people, and the restoration and entrenchment of the rule of the law.

The move, he maintains, galvanized business, made commerce and industry move, and created "clear, crisp, strong forces against apartheid."

There was also a message for black leaders, to "show them that business was not part of apartheid," and to potential disinvestors, "to show that there was a better way—to lobby and pressurize government about issues like influx control or citizenship."

"If they would pour money into the Urban Foundation or Operation Hunger, or into creating employment, it would be far more moral. We don't need any more hunger.

"I do believe we businessmen can change overseas perspectives, to make them realize that maybe a blanket boycott is as racialistic as a park bench saying 'nonwhites.'"

During the sanctions era, Ackerman travelled the world with an over-sized scrapbook in his baggage. Proclaiming in large red letters "There is a better way," it was his defense against advocates of disinvestment.

In it is a range of press cuttings reflecting Ackerman's views of social responsibility and the role of the business community in general and Pick 'n Pay in particular.

"Externally," he has written, "let's close ranks and show the world that we need money, that we need support and we are worth supporting because of the way we are running our own businesses. Because that's what this country needs." Before South Africa abolished apartheid laws in 1991, Ackerman said, "Internally, let's fight like hell to get apartheid away. Because that, I believe, is the only way that we are going to save our country."

One of the founders of the Urban Foundation, Ackerman also lays claim to a role in the achievement of 99-year leasehold in the country's black townships.

"I have," he says, "a consistent record of fighting the government for change in this country."

Now, he says, he is doing his best to get closer to black colleagues through regular meetings with black business leaders in an attempt to "bridge the gap and hear what the people are really saying."

What are they saying? "There is a lot of anger, but there's a common universality that they don't want killing and violence. Underneath the anger and the criticism—and I've never been so pilloried in my life—what's coming through is they want a power-sharing situation, a peaceful South Africa."

Ackerman is prepared to concede that the statements on abolition of influx control, on detentions without trial, on group areas, came very late.

"Yes, I didn't stand up enough against apartheid," he admits, "but what I have done in my whole business life is stand up for nondiscrimination. There's no halo, no lily-white hands, but I really have tried."

Enlightened self-interest? Certainly, that is a feature of the exercise. Although Ackerman is not above a little self-congratulation, he lays less claim to a halo than those around him who believe he has one.

However, his feelings about the need to right some long-standing wrongs, he insists, are at least as much to do with a commitment to his country and its people as they are to do with profits and high profiles.

"I want to stay in this country and build a business. I want my children to stay. If that's enlightened self-interest, who cares?"

He sees an unbreakable link between the battle for effective political change and the fight for a better deal for the consumer.

"Consumer sovereignty [one of many Ackerman-coined concepts that have become part of the company's lingua franca] is useless without a peaceful South Africa, so the business initiative is the real drive," he insists.

"The consumers in this country want peace and not just groceries at low prices. When I went around the stores last year, people were asking what I was doing about keeping young people in South Africa, giving them hope, not just what my chicken prices were. I realized we had to start taking a lead."

That doesn't mean the profit motive has been buried under an avalanche of altruism.

"I've never pretended I'm not here to make a profit and I don't care about the cynics who say I do what I do just for publicity.

"I believe in it—consumers are squeezed between business and government and the only people who can help are retailers who can fight for them.

"People love to query everybody's motives, it's just an excuse for doing
nothing themselves. I'm old enough now not to worry about that sort of
nonsense," he asserts, defensively aware of those who raise a quizzical
eyebrow at his well-burnished public image.

"Maybe I'm giving myself a few bouquets, but I can't help it. We've
been leaders in consumerism and in cartel-busting." Now he sees an added
role for himself and his colleagues in exerting a force for political change.

"I believe that business has got to run its own business properly, make
a profit, but also play a role nationally because we are the ones providing
the finance for the free-enterprise society, and if we don't stand up, who
the hell will?

"We're not dabbling in politics, politics is our business. 'The business
of business is business' doesn't apply in South Africa. If we don't look
broadly into social and political matters, we won't have a business."

Designs of the Times

A new store is opening in Queenstown and Hugh Herman isn't there. He is
in Johannesburg with his chairman and comanaging director trying (un-
successfully as it turns out) to ward off a strike.

It is the first store opening he has missed since he joined Pick 'n Pay
10 years ago, after many years of association with the company as its at-
torney. Normally the whole board attends each opening—"To the people
who open the store it's very important."

New stores are Herman's business. In his time with the company, he
has been responsible for negotiating all its property leases, and for financing and administering them.

He takes it personally if you don't like one of his pet stores; it's a little
like criticizing a member of the family.

Pick 'n Pay defines three grades of stores: supermarkets, which have
an area of between 4,800 m^2 and 5,000 m^2 and where the emphasis is on
food; superstores—which are at least 8,000 m^2 and incorporate a range of
nonfood products; and hypermarkets, ranging in size from 20,000 m^2 to
23,000 m^2 and are described by Herman as one-floor, self-service department stores.

"We think we've got a good formula," he says. Certainly it is one that
has served the company well. And it's sticking to it, though the new generation of stores—those being built now and old ones that are being refurbished—are modified versions of the formula, changed to keep up with
prevailing consumer needs.

For a company built on food retailing, Pick 'n Pay took its greatest step
into the unknown with the opening of the first hypermarket in 1975. Within
its supermarkets, though, the emphasis is still on food. The difference is

only on what kind of food. Increasingly, fresh produce, vegetables, fish, confectionary, and delicacies are in demand.

While diversification is not really on the cards to any great degree (though the company has acquired a 50 percent interest in the furnishing business Tom Boardman Ltd and sees scope for a chain of twenty or thirty stores), new areas of involvement are not precluded. But they must fit in with the merchandising philosophy of keeping prices down.

"We have stuck to our principles, but we are flexible," says Herman. "We probably want to stick to fields we know and we do have plenty to keep our hands full at the moment."

The major factor behind any decision to go into a new field is to achieve "the greatest possible volume per store and rapid turnover. That's what keeps prices lower and creates the gross profit."

Despite the recession, the drop in spending power, and the black consumer boycotts in several areas, the company records record turnovers each year of several billion rand. "It's a question of being innovative and efficient," remarks Herman, a trifle complacently.

It also requires a considerable amount of capital investment to keep ahead. "But it's worth that because you get the return and you marry customers to you."

What's next in the struggle to keep ahead? There is still enormous scope for growth, says Herman.

"We have ninety stores. Our leading competitors have 180-odd. And, of the major three retailers, we have the least exposure to the black market." That is beginning to change—there are stores now in Mitchell's Plain and Bisho and another is opening in Mmabatho and other areas.

On the drawing boards is a smaller module suitable for downtown and small rural areas—a radical departure from the company's tradition of large suburban stores with more attention to the availability of parking than the proximity of public transport.

There was talk once of the company starting its own dairy "because we couldn't make the existing ones innovative." Under some pressure, the existing ones became innovative and the idea was dropped. But there is no intention of going into manufacturing. "We want to work with manufacturers, not be in opposition. We believe both we and they have an input to make."

One area of rapid change is in the design of supermarkets. Recognizing that supermarkets, "of necessity aren't very attractive buildings," there is a move to brighten them up with colorful hanging plastic decor and high-quality air-conditioning.

"Supermarket shopping is a chore but we've tried within that framework to make it pleasant. We believe it's important to create a relaxed and pleasant atmosphere. We've tried to have plenty of parking and good landscaping," says Herman.

As operations director, Keith Blumgart says: "A supermarket is a poor man's country club. It's something of a social outing to come shopping. A lot of people look at it as a drudgery but for some people it's a pleasant thing to have a decent shop with nice bright colors."

In the new breed of shopping centers the emphasis is on natural light, which brightens the atmosphere . . . and escalates the cost of air-conditioning. Water features and attractively set food courts are included in the design for future developments.

It all fits in with the constantly reiterated twin goals—to make a profit and a contribution to the community. "You get your money back but it also does something for the environment."

One of the most innovative and sophisticated of the new stores is a specialty food "emporium" on the site of Durban's Old Station—described by Hugh Herman as a "supermarket version of Harrolds Food Hall."

Though fewer new stores are opening in these recessionary times, the refurbishing of old ones has become a priority. It's a capital-intensive business that has done nothing for profits but there is always an eye on the long-term gain.

Refurbishment, remarks food merchandise director Peter Dove, "gives you a great opportunity to reposition the store in relation to the consumer. The only problem is that the consumer is changing all the time."

So, the image of the stores must be updated. But the sites are good; the stores are working. "In our whole portfolio there isn't one I would have closed. Every single store is firing," says Herman proudly. But one site has been abandoned—the Sir Lowry Road store, the first supermarket in Cape Town. It is no longer considered a "Pick 'n Pay image store."

In turn with growing demand worldwide, new stores and newly refurbished stores will, says Blumgart, have more facilities for the handicapped and those who find it difficult to shop.

Plans are in the works for setting aside parking areas for the disabled, for providing motorized trolleys that can be booked in advance, for wider aisles, and more space at the checkout counters, and for more accessible toilet facilities in shopping centers.

At other levels, attention is being paid to the development of better trolleys, to equipment that will help staff work more easily, and to improved staff facilities.

Among Blumgart's many portfolios is working with planners, architects, and consultants to ensure that all the stores have "the overall chain feel." The self-service concept, he points out, hasn't changed. "All that's changed is a more modernized approach to everything."

Things to Come

Retailing, says Peter Dove, director of food merchandise, is a form of show business—constantly entertaining, constantly changing, unpredictable, and offering few comfortable formulas.

"With the change in the consumer accelerating, you can't predict anything, but we learn and we learn quite well. We always do it right the second time."

It is very important to get it right because, as in show business, if the retailer doesn't give the consumer what she or he wants, the retailer will be playing to empty houses.

Two of the men in charge of seeing that the stores are offering attractions that will keep the crowds coming in are Dove and Alan Gardiner, director of nonfood merchandise.

The first principle of success, as Dove sees it, is to reflect consumer demand—"and the quicker you can do it, the better. What we've got to do a lot more in retailing is learn more about the consumer and learn to communicate." Already, he is convinced that Pick 'n Pay has its corporate ear closer to the ground than the opposition.

That closeness to the community, he believes, "can be as big a deterrent to our opposition as having the best prices."

A lot has to do with communication, which Dove is heavily involved with. He is the man who oversees the company's advertising; he has a tendency to rage over copywriters who believe that the shopper in the aisles will know what "19h00" means when the company is trying to convey to a mass readership that shopping hours have been extended.

"We are redefining our communication goals, which are all part of getting to the consumer."

Dove believes shopping can be a pleasure and that pleasure is what the customer of the future will demand.

In his particular field, the major change in consumer demand is in the area of fresh food. Customers are becoming increasingly wary of packaged foods and are turning far more to fresh produce. From manufacturers they are demanding more nutrition, more information, and better labelling.

Dove is quite excited about the advent of the consumer who knows what "she" wants (consumers at Pick 'n Pay are always termed "she"), and makes an effort to get it.

The retailer who can offer her what she wants fastest and most effectively will be the winner in the cutthroat battle for profits.

Dove is somewhat puzzled over the stigma that is increasingly attached to the word *manufactured*.

"There is a growing disenchantment with many brands in the marketplace, either because they promise something people don't want any more, or because they promise something they don't deliver."

He's not sure the resistance is fair, but it is the trend. "We have recognized it and are reacting."

So new and newly refurbished stores are designed to give far more space to fresh produce and to bakeries, fish counters, and delicatessens— all bearing only the brand of the store from which they are bought. A special area of the store has been designated as "The Food Court" and carries a selection of products delivered fresh to the store each day and designed to be taken home by the consumer with little or no additional preparation. See Exhibit 35.2 for examples of these products.

■ **EXHIBIT 35.2   The Food Court**
Fresh Prepared Foods at Pick 'n Pay

"The lovely thing about fresh produce is it gives you a better margin, good volumes, and a great image, so it's perfect."

Doesn't it also require more staff? Will the new emphasis affect the self-service ethos on which the supermarket culture was built? Dove thinks not. He has visions of effective prepackaging of much of the fresh produce on offer, turning the traditional "service areas" into a mixture of service and self-service.

Price is still the overriding factor for South African shoppers, Dove believes, whereas abroad, "aspects such as convenience, cleanliness, safety, and food that's good for you and actually tastes good are the criteria."

Ultimately, he foresees that kind of demand coming here too. Although price is becoming increasingly important, "at a later stage the retailer who is communicating on price only won't be communicating effectively enough," Dove contends.

Gardiner must also look not only at price but at variety, quality, and novelty. His many duties include supervising a shopping list for the group of about 500 nonfood items from the United States, England, Italy, Hong Kong, Tunisia, Indonesia, and Japan.

His empire encompasses light bulbs and television sets, underwear and power tools, toys, textiles, kitchenware, sports goods, and petrol.

He, too, must keep his ear attuned to customer needs and changing trends. Novelty is always attractive—at good prices, with the middleman cut out by sending department heads to do their own shopping, they are even more attractive.

In the current tough economic climate, innovative sales promotion becomes ever more important. "You scour the markets of the world to look for new things, whether it's a Rubic cube or a pastel-colored BMX.

"Everytime we try something particularly different, everytime we show some merchandise in which we are the leaders it has an enormous effect, so the more we can do it the better we can do," says Gardiner.

He calls it milking opportunities and he finds these in the most extraordinary places—a readiness to be innovative is just about the most important element in his job.

Gardiner cites one example—the request he had once for a miniature cement mixer that could be used at home by an enthusiastic do-it-yourselfer. He diffidently put the idea to a Taiwanese manufacturer, who created a model for what turned out to be a fair-sized South African market and now exports thousands to the United States.

A major element under Gardiner's care is textiles—clothing and household linen.

That area first came into Pick 'n Pay's ambit with the establishment of the first hypermarket in 1975, and, admits Hugh Herman, "we weren't that good in the beginning. Clothing is not beans."

However, he no longer feels morose when he sees the racks of apparel, and the fact that brand names may not be used has ceased to be a problem. In many cases, the hypermarket label is stitched into the identical garment to that selling elsewhere under a more up-scale name at a more up-scale price.

High fashion under a hypermarket label is not the aim. Trendy colors in basic clothing that is stylish, appealing, and of high quality (and low price) is. "Trendy linen has become a new feature in Gardiner's ever-changing world with the development of a line of coordinate and decor matchmakers.

"That's why it's so interesting for me—one day in textiles, one day in hardware, one day pumping petrol. Having started as a supermarket person—packing shelves, counting cabbages—I was suddenly thrown into power drills and televisions; it's been fantastically interesting."

It has also been fantastically frustrating—Gardiner has been in the front line of the company's battle against cartels. The most extreme example was the petrol story, but—particularly in view of the state of the furniture industry—high-ticket items of furniture follow close behind.

There is pressure on manufacturers from the Furniture Traders' Association, which results in turn in pressure on Pick 'n Pay. "If the manufacturers are closed out by the furniture stores, they lose most of their business," Gardiner points out.

"That's an area we constantly battle—we seem to make progress and then we slip back. As much as the manufacturers are beleaguered so are our suppliers, so they strive for stabilization, which is awful because the consumer suffers."

With some bitterness, he tells the story of a major international supplier extensively supported by Pick 'n Pay in South Africa, who refused to supply the Australian hypermarket. "You try to create relationships and the relationship is as long and as good as it suits the other party," Gardiner observes.

"It's protectionism, those things go on all the time."

That is the story for now, but the secret of successful retailing is being sensitive today to the scenario of tomorrow.

Consumer demands aside, Dove sees the greatest challenges facing retailers in the future as productivity and distribution—making better use both of manpower and of available hours.

"Pick 'n Pay, and probably in general our competitors, have put a lot of emphasis on visual standards at point of sales areas," he says. "We have our hands around fairly good-looking stores and fairly motivated management, but what we don't have control over is distribution and productivity. We are going to have to assess it in depth in the next few years."

Given the increasing congestion of city roads, distribution—getting the merchandise from suppliers to warehouses and from warehouses to store shelves as efficiently as possible—is a major problem.

One solution is to use a lot more of the available hours in the week than the 35 percent being used now. Nighttime should be distribution time, Dove feels. However, to make it so will take a great deal of reeducation and a change in patterns of using the available manpower.

Successful distribution also depends on a better relationship between manufacturers and retailers, "knowing each other's business more and trusting each other more, tightening up the chain of distribution."

Again, it's all part of the race for customer domination. "The exploitable areas of difference are shrinking, that's why distribution and productivity are important."

Better distribution, Dove feels, will go some way to curing what he describes as "a creeping illness in grocery retailing"—being out of stock. The

■ **EXHIBIT 35.3**   Print Advertisement for Pick 'n Pay

Don't let the 20th Century kill the 21st

If you think pollution problems are only for fanatics, think again

In the time it takes you to read this advertisement, several tons of polluting waste will have been discharged into our skies, several more into our oceans, lakes and rivers. The result is a polluted planet that is rapidly becoming uninhabitable.

The problem is worldwide.

Ufa, a Russian industrial city the size of Durban, has been officially declared "unfit for human habitation". The four hundred million cars in daily use pour Carbon Monoxide into the atmosphere right round the clock. Innumerable pieces of debris from spacecraft are in orbit right around the planet.

Uncountable volumes of burnt tobacco fumes are exhaled into the air every day. In 1988 the Polish Government evacuated five villages because the air had become too dangerous to inhale. The Transvaal cities of Vanderbijlpark, Witbank and Middelburg have the most serious pollution problems in the whole of Africa, with Pretoria and Johannesburg as runners-up.

The five warmest years of the past century have all occurred during the Eighties — proof that the "Greenhouse Effect" is already extant and dangerous.

Our planet is choking to death on our own man-made wastes, and when it dies we have no other place to go.

Three interlinked problems: Ozone depletion, Greenhouse Effect and Acid rain

Fifteen kilometres above our heads lies the ozone layer, filtering out the harsher rays of the otherwise friendly Sun.

But Chloro Fluoro Carbons (CFCs) found in old fashioned aerosols, air conditioning and refrigeration systems, and the production of plastics are ozone hostile. They have already torn a hole in the ozone layer six times the size of South Africa. Through this hole pour harsh ultra violet rays to create the "Greenhouse Effect". And the acid rain created by millions of tons of industrial wastes

being thrown into our skies every day is already affecting the growth of crops and natural vegetation, as well as rendering the "Greenhouse Effect" much, much worse.

Ultimately it will prevent the growing of temperate climate crops like wheat while it melts the polar ice caps, thus raising the average sea level. These three interlinked problems, left unchecked, will inevitably destroy our planet. Sooner rather than later.

The last decade: our last chance

Ecological experts are not certain just how serious the damage already is; they are agreed on one key point: if we don't make a concerted, local and global effort to heal our sick planet, the sickness will be irreversible by the end of the 20th Century. The 20th Century will, in effect, have killed the 21st. And all the others to follow.

Working together for a healthier planet

We can heal our planet, our home. If we act now. We should be planting trees, not trash: trees are stationary oxygen factories.

We should be aware of waste and pollution; the production of ozone-hostile products cannot stop at once but we should assist in phasing them out of our lives and our environment.

We must both learn and teach: learn the dangers of NOT reversing the pollution of our planet, and teach those around us. We still have time, we still have hope.

If we protect and heal Mother Nature, she'll keep on protecting us.

If we don't, well it's very dark out there and... it's forever.

Let's learn Let's work

If you have any ideas or suggestions for fighting pollution, from publicity to practical inventions or if you would like a free copy of this advertisement in poster form, write to: **"A Healthier Planet"** P.O. Box 784570 Sandton 2146, Transvaal

14 MAJOR ENVIRONMENTAL ISSUES BEING TAKEN UP BY PICK 'n PAY

Pick 'n Pay, through a lack of awareness, used to be as guilty as anybody of contributing towards pollution of the environment. Not anymore. Now that we know better, Pick 'n Pay is so concerned about global pollution that we have committed ourselves to fighting it. Whatever it costs.

PICK 'n PAY IS RESOLVED TO IMPLEMENT THE FOLLOWING PRINCIPLES:

1. CFCs are out. Our No Name Brands are committed to phasing out CFC material. From August 1989 refrigeration equipment and material containing CFCs will be phased out, and all new stores will be ozone friendly. This will include air conditioners, refrigerators and fire-fighting systems.

2. Paper's in. We'll encourage use of environment-friendly paper products containing nil or minimal chlorine bleached pulp. Plus PDCB-free toilet blocks and the use of recycled paper and paper packaging.

3. If it can be recycled... we'll encourage bottle banks for returnable glass and plastic bottles. We'll encourage the return and disposal of halogenated hydrocarbon solvents, the development of standardised crates for returnable bottles and the collection of waste by free enterprise.

4. Health and safety: major priorities. We're encouraging the development of organic food and drink products with people-friendly additives and preservatives ONLY. Packaging must be child and tamper proof; pesticide levels must be controlled and there must be a universally accepted symbol for environment-friendly products.

5. Phosphates out: washing detergents should be phosphate free.

6. Mercury's out: batteries should be mercury free.

7. Petrol should be unleaded, as well as cheaper.

8. Our service areas must become environment-friendly: plastic containers to be replaced.

9. Waste-inhibiting energy monitors in all stores: in-store computers are programmed to switch off lights and other energy consumers when they're being under-utilised. Natural light will be used wherever possible.

10. New store design will incorporate the latest in environment-friendly technology and architecture.

11. Plant trees, not trash. We're encouraging widespread treeplanting, including the co-sponsoring of the planting of 8 000 trees on Table Mountain.

12. Involving the young: we've recently involved schools in an Environment Competition with substantial prizes in four grades. We also sponsored the clean-up of the Braamfontein Spruit.

13. Creating awareness: in our advertising, in our stores, everywhere we can. We have an ongoing policy of environmental action programmes. Watch the press for details.

14. Assisting the Action Teams: we cheerfully assist any environmental action group with the provision of venues for meetings, facilities for distributing pamphlets in our stores, and any other help we can provide.

Pick ₙ Pay

HYPERMARKETS, SUPERMARKETS & SUPERSTORES

Working together for a healthier planet

inability of the retailer or the manufacturer to predict correctly also plays a part here, though, and increased computerization could well help to counteract the trend.

"There's so much to learn. Pick 'n Pay must be confident and show the other guys they'll always be behind us, but we must show people we do have a lot to learn and we want to learn it.

"We are accused of being egotists, but if there was an egotistical approach that would lead to complacency, and that's one of the biggest dangers we've got to guard against. Management and opposition have to know where we stand and we stand to remain the best—it may sound macho, but it isn't complacent," says Dove.

Focal Topics

1. What elements of the Pick 'n Pay corporate culture have led to the company's success?

2. Is Pick 'n Pay justified in playing a political and social role in South Africa? What should be the role of businesses in changing the laws of a country?

3. What should be Pick 'n Pay's marketing program for the future? Which segments of the South African market should be primary targets? Should Pick 'n Pay expand to other countries? If so, which ones?

4. How should Pick 'n Pay manage relationships with suppliers? What policies should be implemented to increase efficiency in the physical movement of merchandise?

■ ■ ■ ■ ■

This case was originally based on "Pick' n Pay. A Corporate Report. Supplement to Financial Mail," July 11, 1986.

Libbey-Owens-Ford, Co.

■ ■ ■ ■ ■

Automobile sales in the United States account for a large percentage of many raw material and component markets. Some estimates indicate that one out of every eight jobs in the United States may be affected to some extent by auto sales. In the early part of the 1990s, many of the supplier firms to the auto industry were adversely affected by declining sales in the auto industry. One firm that sells a high proportion of its output to the auto industry is Libbey-Owens-Ford, Co. While some firms have failed, this firm has achieved considerable success, not because the overall industry is healthy but because it has taken a strategic approach to logistics planning and customer service.

Background

Libbey-Owens-Ford, Co. (L-O-F) is a large manufacturer and distributor of glass products, primarily for *industrial original equipment and/or consumer replacement applications*. L-O-F is an 80-percent-owned subsidiary of Pilkington, plc., a major glass company in the United Kingdom. Acquired by Pilkington in 1986, a 20-percent interest in L-O-F was conveyed to Nippon Sheet Glass, a Japanese glass company, in 1990. Pilkington has allowed L-O-F to operate relatively autonomously since the purchase, but has introduced some minor changes to L-O-F and its planning process. These changes will be discussed in a later section.

   L-O-F is one of the major glass companies in the world. The company is divided into three divisions, organized by product type: (1) original equipment, (2) flat glass, and (3) after market. The original equipment division is the largest of the three, selling primarily to the U.S. auto industry. General Motors, Toyota, and Nissan are the major customers. Flat glass products appear in any number of applications, particularly in the construction of new buildings and other structures requiring large amounts of glass. The after-market group, or Automotive Glass Replacement (AGR), focuses on selling products to replace broken or damaged glass in automobiles, trucks, and vans. There are two types of auto glass sold: windshield glass and tempered glass used for side and rear windows. The AGR market is quite competitive with a relatively complex channel of distribution. In addition, low levels of brand loyalty are present in the channel. This situation *has elevated customer service performance to a critical role* in achieving the marketing objectives of firms in the market.

The company is organized around product lines, as described above, and is largely *decentralized*. Each of the three divisions has its own planning function and its own logistics function. The focus of the case study reported here is the AGR group, which is located at the L-O-F headquarters. *All functions and top management are also located at headquarters, though most manufacturing is located elsewhere.*

Corporate Strategic Planning

Historical Perspective

Prior to 1990, there was a centralized planning function located at corporate headquarters that was responsible for the planning for all three divisions. In 1990, planning responsibility was dispersed to the divisions so that the planning and operational units were the same. This reduced the probability of the plan sitting on the shelf because it was not constructed by those who had to execute it.

The Planning Process

The parent corporation, Pilkington, requires L-O-F to develop and submit a corporate strategic plan every year. Pilkington requests a *3-year planning horizon* for the strategic plan and a *5-year horizon* for capital expenditures. When the strategic plan is updated, a standard, documented procedure is followed by L-O-F. The planning process lasts about 6 months. An initial plan is completed in about 4 months. After a review of top management, any necessary changes are made and the final plan is completed. The plan considers the primary issues facing L-O-F, how the firm wishes to position itself and the actions that are required to allow the firm to meet its goals. In addition, managers are surveyed for their input regarding the current issues that are related to the strategic plan. All three divisions meet on certain established dates to develop and refine the strategic plan. It is an iterative process with each group putting its own plan together and then blending it with the plans of the other divisions to fashion the final, completed document.

Outside sources are used in developing the plan, including data base and economic information. In addition, the company has recently become more active in surveying customers and considering its performance relative to other firms in the industry. At present there is little or no link between L-O-F's strategic plan and that of its primary customers, though the company is trying to reduce customer inventory levels to make itself more valuable to the customer.

Essentially, Pilkington only asks for financial data information to the strategic plan and furnishes L-O-F with the target completion dates for submitting the plan. L-O-F is trying to develop measures that relate to nonfinancial issues for use within the company. There have already been some attempts to identify the quality of profit. For example, why was the profit made, and, if it fell short of the target, was it the best possible performance under the circumstances?

Logistics Planning

Focusing on the AGR portion of L-O-F indicates that *logistics planning is becoming ever more important to the company*. The pattern and timetable of the AGR/logistics plan follow that of the overall corporate plan. AGR has a mission statement that is used as a guide in the planning process. The general process asks several questions: Where are we? Where do we want to go? Is this a sensible place to go? How do we get there? Did we do it? The plan considers the major issues that face the firm or division and how the division should react to these issues. The question "Did we do it?" refers to *measurement against the plan*. At present, these measures are largely financial in nature, but measures of other issues such as utilization and errors in billing suggest the company is moving toward a blend of financial and nonfinancial measures of performance. Some top AGR executives consider it difficult to measure performance that is not number-based.

The critical issues facing the division are determined through a "team planning" process. Anonymous questionnaires are sent to a selected management level. Both short-term and long-term issues are identified based on the questionnaire responses. These are narrowed to about six major issues. The management group that suggested the issues is then involved in preparing the action plans to address the issues. An alternative approach is to have brainstorming meetings to identify the issues, select the major issues, and work on action plans. This procedure is repeated with different management levels within the division.

Logistics considerations have never been a major part of the plan until recently. Traditionally, manufacturing, marketing, finance, and logistics were viewed in that order with respect to their importance to the firm and the planning process. There have been a number of changes that have caused logistics to be viewed as a more important element in the planning process.

Recent Changes in Logistics

Deregulation has played a large role in drawing more attention to the logistics function at L-O-F. The glass industry became much more competitive during the 1980s, which has also drawn attention to the role logistics can play in positioning the firm strategically. Logistics has been identified as a part of strategic planning within the last 3 years, and it has been recognized that logistics can play an active role in obtaining the market share that the firm desires. *There is a general feeling within the firm that capitalizing on logistics opportunities will be one of the company's main differentiation tools in the 1990s.*

The manager of planning and development and the director of manufacturing and distribution have been two of the champions for involvement of logistics in the strategic plan and the strategic planning process. Both feel that the role of logistics in the company and its importance to the firm's positioning should be identified in the strategic plan. Several executives point to *company involvement in the Council of Logistics Management (CLM)* as a driver to a more active logistics participation in the planning process. As involvement with CLM has increased over the past couple of years, there has been a discovery of a number of things that could be done logistically within the firm and the division to improve the competitive position of the company. Inventory controls, customer service, and network configuration are just a few of the issues that have been recently addressed by AGR due, at least in part, to CLM. However, the decision to integrate logistics into planning came from the corporate planning department in the late 1980s. The change was initiated three years ago and is viewed as a continuous process from now on—never reaching completion. The elevation of logistics has resulted in some significant improvements for AGR in terms of order cycle time, inventory levels, sales volume, and profits.

Not all has been easy. Some of the more significant problems encountered as logistics was integrated center around consensus on the plans of various functions. *It takes a good deal of time to reach consensus among the groups involved in planning.* The problem has not yet been overcome. Future changes that are desired by the AGR group and logistics specifically include more participation from those who will be implementing the plan.

Key Issues

Libbey-Owens-Ford, Co.

CEO as Change Agent

Impact of Logistics

Participation in CLM

Improvement due to Elevation

Consensus Building

Customer Service in Competitive Market

Management Involvement in Defining Critical Issues

Champion of Logistics

Planning Is an Ongoing Process

Key Issues

CEO as Change Agent   The chief executive officer is the real driver in bringing change to the planning process. The corporate planning function has been dispersed to the operating divisions to put planning where the execution occurs.

Impact of Logistics   Identifying the impact of logistics on corporate strategy and performance within the plan itself enhances the perceived value of logistics activities to the remaining functions in the firms.

Participation in CLM   Participation in CLM and CLM-sponsored activities is helpful in terms of indicating which issues should be addressed by logistics in both a strategic and an operational sense.

Improvement Due to Elevation   The elevation of logistics has resulted in considerable improvements to order cycle time, inventory levels, sales volume, and profits for the division.

Consensus Building   Remaining problems include obtaining consensus across functions on a particular plan or course of action. Other problems include: (1) top management has to want integration for integration to occur; (2) some employees see the process as a waste of time.

Customer Service in a Competitive Market   Increased customer service performance is critical in a highly competitive market with little brand loyalty. Complex distribution channels require specialized customer care.

Management Involvement in Defining Critical Issues   Several levels of management are surveyed to identify issues relevant for the particular management level. Six critical issues are selected for more immediate attention. The same group that identified and categorized the issues then develops action plans to address the critical issues.

Champions of Logistics   Top management has to want integration for integration to occur. Two managers in one of the divisions have particularly supported the inclusion of logistics into the strategic plan because of its potential role in positioning the firm in the marketplace.

Planning Is an Ongoing Process   The planning process is viewed as continually evolving and a continuous activity. The plan is not put on the shelf until the next planning period.

Focal Topics

1. What trends in the automobile industry can be forecast for the next 5 to 10 years?

2. What actions should L-O-F take to increase sales to the auto industry? To other industries?

3. What elements of the logistics program at L-O-F are most important to the success of the company?

4. What are the strengths and weaknesses of the company's strategic planning process? What changes do you recommend?

■ ■ ■ ■ ■

The Longaberger Company (B)

■ ■ ■ ■ ■

Since joining the direct-selling industry in the 1970s, the Longaberger Company, producers of famous Longaberger Baskets® and Longaberger Pottery®, has grown dramatically to be counted with firms such as Avon and Tupperware as among the most successful.

The Longaberger Company's founder and chief executive officer, Dave Longaberger, seized the opportunity to enter the basket market in 1972 with hardwood, handwoven baskets like the ones his father and grandfather crafted during the first half of this century. Dave's baskets sold well in stores, but they didn't reach the larger market he wanted until, in 1978, he hit upon the idea of having Consultants hold basket shows in people's homes.

In the comfortable surroundings of a Hostess's home, a Longaberger Consultant could show the basket and its many uses, as well as tell the story of how the Longaberger family made their baskets years ago. The marketing system worked, and by 1980 the company had 91 Consultants and 30 employees involved in the artisan's craft of weaving baskets. The company pulled in approximately $800,000 that year. The firm experienced fires, massive debts, attempts at union organization, litigation, and other problems throughout the 1980s but continued to grow in sales. See Case 27: Longaberger Company (A) for more details.

By 1992, the business was growing exponentially with over 11,500 sales associates representing every state in the union. Over 3,500 employees are involved in producing and distributing the country's premier baskets. At the rate of 16,000 Longaberger Baskets® produced a day along with Longaberger Pottery® and related accessories, the company expected to generate sales in 1992 of approximately $200 million. In recent years, the company's sales have been growing at the rate of 40 to 50 percent a year, even in an economy of recession and general malaise.

The Longaberger Company is family-owned with a commitment to the values and ideals of corporate citizenship. Recently, Dave Longaberger was honored with *Inc.* magazine's "Socially Responsible Entrepreneur of the

Year Award." The company also received a "Take Pride in America Award" from the U.S. Department of the Interior.

The company has been innovative in many of its employee programs. It operates an on-site health clinic, providing free medical services to its employees. The company donated over $1 million to the local high school to build a new addition for science education. It has given large grants to the College of Optometry of a nearby university for research designed to improve vision services to Longaberger's employees. When a historic theater was in danger of being demolished in a nearby town, Longaberger bought the building in order to maintain the historic building and to use it as a cultural and educational location for its employees. The company has been involved in many other community and charitable programs, many of which have served to beautify and revitalize economically the village of Dresden and the surrounding area.

The Longaberger handcrafted hardwood maple baskets and fine pottery are produced by skilled artisans who carry out age-old traditions of craftsmanship. Some of the firm's most popular basket and pottery products are shown in Exhibit 37.1. Handmade to be handed down, each one is initialed and dated by the weaver who created it. As sought-after collectibles, Longaberger Baskets® are not only functional, but have traditionally increased in value.

Sales Organization

They have been called the best sales force in the world; they often refer to their love for the products they sell as an addiction; and the growing cultural phenomenon of which they are a part is sometimes described as a cult.

"Basket cult. That's right; you said it," said Marie Martin, who accumulated 150 Longaberger baskets during her first six years as a sales associate in Chickasha, Oklahoma. Marie is one of the over 11,500 Longaberger Associates nationwide who sell Longaberger Baskets, Pottery, and accessories through in-home shows.

Longaberger's Associates have played a major part in the company's climb from a new and struggling direct-selling company in the 1980s to one of the real movers and shakers in the industry in the 1990s.

"The people who make up our sales family are our biggest asset," said Dave Longaberger. They are tireless, caring, honest, and ethical; and they are crazy about their jobs and Longaberger products." Tami Longaberger Kaido, President of Marketing and Sales and one of Dave's two daughters, agreed. "I have seen several companies and sales field organizations and I can honestly say our Associates are the best in the world," she said.

The Associates are usually first attracted to the company because of its high-quality products and its emphasis on traditional family values. "I live Longaberger," said Gail Young, an Associate since 1986 from Colonial Heights, Virginia. "There is hardly a time I don't think about them."

▪ EXHIBIT 37.1   Products of the Longaberger Company

(continued)

The quality of the products attracts many American women and a few men to become associates, with some owning 800 or more baskets. But the opportunities for personal development and financial growth keep them selling and progressing up the career ladder, not to mention the possibility of a six-figure income when they reach the top.

■ **EXHIBIT 37.1** *continued*

Longaberger Pottery and Dinnerware set a beautiful table for dinner at home with family and friends. It's always a special occasion: a time to talk about the day's activities and share stories of days gone by.

Featured left to right on previous page:
Longaberger Dinnerware
  Salad Bowl
  Dinner Plate
  Bread Plate
  Cup and Saucer
Heartland Muffin Basket
Heartland Small Chore Basket
Heartland Bakery Basket
Background top to bottom:
Small Gathering Basket
Small Juice Pitcher
Medium Berry Basket
Medium Vegetable Basket
Grandma Bonnie's Apple Pie Plate
Small, Medium and Large Mixing Bowls
Large Milk Pitcher

There's nothing quite as sweet as the fragrance from a summertime garden, always providing an abundance of freshly cut flowers in Longaberger Baskets for around the home.

Featured above from left:
Medium Key Basket
Spring Basket with Liner
Small Key Basket
Medium Chore Basket
Tall Key Basket
Background:
Laundry Basket

Featured below from left:
Cup and Saucer
Small Juice Pitcher
Grandma Bonnie's Apple Pie Plate
Dinner Plate
Medium Mixing Bowl
Large Mixing Bowl
Large Milk Pitcher

POTTERY

(continued)

"Direct sales is ideal for the 1990s career woman," said Tami, a working mother herself. "You can work as hard as you want and receive proportionate returns. The decisions and choices are yours." And that is why increasing numbers of entrepreneurs—at a rate of 100 to 125 a week— are taking advantage of the Longaberger opportunity. It offers flexibility,

■ **EXHIBIT 37.1**   *continued*

(continued)

self-esteem, and financial gain without giving up one's family. "You can have it all," Tami said.

The company supplies products to individual contractors who sell Longaberger products throughout the United States. The greatest number of these persons are Consultants who are responsible for personal sales. As

■ **EXHIBIT 37.1**   *continued*

We designed a special line of baskets dedicated to the hard workers of long ago in the heart of America—The Longaberger Heartland Collection® These people took pride in their work and did whatever it took to get the job done. And they did it right... down to every last detail.

This sense of pride and commitment is what we've based The Heartland Collection on, as we still weave each basket one-by-one, with a pair of skilled hands and attention to detail. For a special touch, we've carefully interwoven a shoestring weave to reflect our commitment to continuing the tradition of handcrafted quality in American products.

So share in The Longaberger Heartland Collection and share in the tradition of American pride.

Featured clockwise from the top:
Heartland Medium Key Basket
Heartland Medium Chore Basket
Heartland Medium Market Basket
Heartland Large Peg Basket
Heartland Mini Chore Basket
Heartland Tall Key Basket
Heartland Small Purse
Heartland Small Spoon Basket
Heartland Small Chore Basket

Featured to the right,
clockwise from the top:
Large Market Basket
Medium Market Basket
Medium Market Basket
Small Market Basket

Years ago, the folks in Dresden would meet at the farmers' market to barter their goods. They'd gather around as they exchanged eggs for corn, tomatoes for turnips, or beans for berries... sometimes with a tidbit of gossip here and there. Strolling home, their baskets would be filled with fresh fruits and vegetables.

B A S K E T S

people progress in their careers, they can become Branch Advisors and Regional Advisors and receive profits not only from their personal sales but also a percentage based on the sales of the branch and Branch Advisors they have recruited. The highest level of career development is the Sales Director, who receives profits on personal sales and also on the sales of the Consultants and Regional Advisors that he or she has recruited and continues to supervise. The sales structure and percentages received by each person are shown in Exhibit 37.2.

As of 1992, the typical earnings for a Branch Advisor was approximately $20,000. Regional Advisors typically earn in the range of $50,000,

■ EXHIBIT 37.2   Longaberger Management Sales Structure

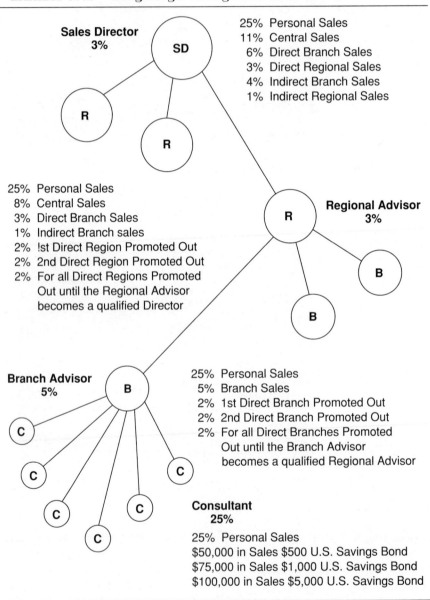

Sales Director
3%

SD

25% Personal Sales
11% Central Sales
6% Direct Branch Sales
3% Direct Regional Sales
4% Indirect Branch Sales
1% Indirect Regional Sales

R

R

25% Personal Sales
8% Central Sales
3% Direct Branch Sales
1% Indirect Branch sales
2% !st Direct Region Promoted Out
2% 2nd Direct Region Promoted Out
2% For all Direct Regions Promoted
    Out until the Regional Advisor
    becomes a qualified Director

R

Regional Advisor
3%

B

B

Branch Advisor
5%

B

25% Personal Sales
5% Branch Sales
2% 1st Direct Branch Promoted Out
2% 2nd Direct Branch Promoted Out
2% For all Direct Branches Promoted
    Out until the Branch Advisor
    becomes a qualified Regional Advisor

C

C

C

C

C

Consultant
25%

25% Personal Sales
$50,000 in Sales $500 U.S. Savings Bond
$75,000 in Sales $1,000 U.S. Savings Bond
$100,000 in Sales $5,000 U.S. Savings Bond

and Sales Directors typically earn approximately $225,000. Each person pays their own expenses from this income.

The company has set up its management system to give unified direction to the entire Longaberger sales field. The objectives, which include uniformity throughout the Longaberger sales field, are designed to allow and encourage growth and the development of a strong sales-oriented management team, as well as the maintenance of communication between the company and the sales field.

The basic sales level is reached by Consultants who receive a discount of 25 percent of all personal sales. Additional benefits include the opportunity to purchase a sample of new products introduced throughout the year at 40 percent of the regular retail price. They also have the opportunity to purchase from two to five baskets for personal or promotional use based on monthly sales at 40 percent of the retail price on a personal order form. This form is valid for 60 days. They also have the opportunity to purchase supplemental baskets (ten items at 40 percent off the regular retail price) on a supplemental order form upon qualifying with $1,000 in sales. This form is valid for 60 days. They also have the opportunity to participate in all company-sponsored incentive programs, including U.S. Savings Bonds, given based on yearly personal sales.

The role of a Branch Advisor is to set a good example through high personal sales each week as well as to recruit and train new consultants while conducting shows of Longaberger products to consumers. After recruiting Consultants, the Branch Advisor is expected to have one-on-one contact with them to inspire, motivate, and give continuous training. Branch Advisors also hold periodic meetings for communication and recognition of Consultants. They also report weekly projections to their immediate Advisor, give assistance as needed to Consultants, attend training and motivation meetings, and hold monthly meetings in their branch.

Qualifications to become a Branch Advisor include service as a qualified Consultant for a minimum of six months as well as the recruitment of a minimum of six active direct Consultants, each qualified with $1,000 of sales. After applying and being appointed as a Branch Advisor, he or she must maintain minimum total sales volume of $6,000 for at least two consecutive months prior to promotion to Branch Advisor. During qualifying months, six of the direct qualified recruits must hold active status. If for any reason a branch has less than six active Consultants, the Advisor has six months to rebuild to obtain six active Consultants. In addition to a 25 percent discount on all personal sales, Branch Advisors receive 5 percent of total branch sales as well as additional benefits such as sample orders, personal orders, and the opportunity to participate in company-sponsored incentive programs. To encourage promoting from within, branch managers are awarded with 2 percent of sales of persons promoted, until the Branch Advisor becomes a qualified Regional Advisor.

The sales plan of the Longaberger Company is different than some other direct-sales firms that make appointments to supervisory positions for life. At the Longaberger Company, appointments require active participation in the management of recruits. Also, when recruits are promoted beyond the Consultant level, bypassing the recruiter, the Advisor no longer receives a percentage of the sales of those persons. Thus, the Longaberger structure provides considerably more involvement and management of recruits than do some other direct-selling structures.

The role of the Regional Advisor is to establish new branches to continue growth and to continue holding enough personal shows to be in tune with what is happening and to receive the income from such sales. The key purpose of holding shows, however, is to recruit and train new consultants. Regional Advisors also maintain good communications through newsletters and phone calls; they also hold periodic meetings to provide sales training and recruiting techniques as well as motivation and recognition. The meetings stress "how to" techniques and use company tools to increase sales and recruiting.

Regional Advisors collect projections on a weekly basis and report them to the Sales Director. The projections are analyzed to improve weaknesses. Regional Advisors are also expected to be supportive of all company programs, to complete change of address and other records, and to attend management meetings and training seminars sponsored by the Director and/or the company.

Qualifications to become a Regional Advisor include success as a Branch Advisor and the ability to establish and maintain a minimum of three active, direct-qualified branches. They are expected to maintain minimum total sales volume of $20,000 for at least two consecutive months prior to promotion to Regional Advisor. After applying, candidates are interviewed by the vice president of Sales for Longaberger and may then be appointed. Regional Advisors are expected to continue recruiting new Consultants to increase sales volume. The appointment continues as long as the Advisor continues to meet objectives although she/he has nine months to rebuild branches if the region falls below the objectives.

The role of the Sales Director is established in consultation with the President and Vice President of Sales at Longaberger. The Sales Director supervises all Longaberger Associates operating with their Directorship, which includes the development of training, management, and motivational programs. They are expected to produce sales that increase annually as well as oversee the preparation of other sales and people-power goals.

A key responsibility of the Sales Director is to continue the entrepreneurial spirit by accepting and implementing the counsel and direction of the company as well as assisting in the development and implementation of company ideas and programs. The Sales Director also identifies and develops candidates for promotion and works with them to qualify, spending a sufficient amount of time in the field at the regions and branches to train, develop, and motivate the Sales Field to higher performance. These people also have responsibilities to gather data and submit reports to the company, keep the company informed on matters relating to sales, programs, and directives, and to direct and coordinate meetings within their directorship in conjunction with the company meeting schedule.

To become a Sales Director, a candidate must be an Advisor for a minimum of three years with a successful proven sales and recruiting program. They must establish and maintain three active, direct-qualified regions and demonstrate strong leadership and sales qualities. In addition to applying and being interviewed by a Vice President of Sales at Longaberger, Sales Directors must maintain a minimum total sales volume of $56,000 for at least two consecutive months prior to promotion. If a Director falls below three Direct Regions, the Director will have a reasonable time to rebuild with standards determined in consultation with the Vice President of Sales.

Central Consultants are those working directly under a Regional Advisor or Sales Director without a Branch Advisor. A Central Branch is any branch working directly under a Director without a Regional Advisor. Direct sales are those made by personally recruited Consultants.

Longaberger Consultants are pleased with the organization for which they work, and Longaberger is committed to keeping it that way. The company realizes that without proper incentive, its Consultants might become unhappy and, thus, experience a decrease in sales. To prevent this, Longaberger conducts periodic surveys of its Consultants and their incentive progam. The results of such a survey conducted in 1988 during a sales meeting are shown in Exhibit 37.3.

The Show

In 1978, Charleen Cuckovich and her family were out for a Sunday drive when they stopped in a small Amish shop in Ohio. While visiting the small shop, she saw a basket that she particularly liked. The shop's owner told her it was made by a man named Longaberger who lived in Dresden. Later she visited the factory to find out more about the beautiful baskets and when she did she saw Dave Longaberger and his daughters, Tami and Rachel. When she saw the weavers making the baskets, she asked one of the weavers if she could have the basket she just finished. When the weaver handed her the basket, Charleen asked her to sign it. A tradition was born that survives today.

Charlene filled her van with baskets and headed home, where she immediately asked her friends to come over and see the baskets she found. When her friends saw them, they wanted some of their own and began to ask her where she got them. Charlene did some investigation of another successful firm called Tupperware, which held parties in homes, allowing those at the party to buy the products. She called Dave Longaberger with the idea.

"As soon as I heard about having a basket party in someone's home, I knew this was it," Dave said. "The idea hit me like an explosion." Longaberger had been struggling to find a better way to sell than through

▪ EXHIBIT 37.3   Longaberger Survey Results

SA = strongly agree   A = agree   N = neither agree, disagree   D = disagree
SD = strongly disagree   NR = no response

	SA	A	N	D	SD	NR	Total
1. In general, current incentive programs motivate me to increase sales either by the fact they help set goals for recruiting or sales.	18.2%	54.6%	18.2%	9.1%			100%
2. The incentive programs for recruiting really do help to motivate me to increase my number of recruits.	9.1%	54.6%	18.2%	18.2%			100%
3. The current incentive programs help me set goals for myself and for my consultants (branches/regions) for sales and/or recruiting.	18.2%	54.6%		27.3%			100%
4. Incentives help me and/or my consultants (regions/branches) to plan during the year in efforts to qualify for any monthly or annual sales or recruiting award.	9.1%	36.4%	18.2%	36.4%			100%
5. I personally think our current incentives are appropriate for Longaberger Baskets for:							
A) Sales:	9.1%	45.5%	36.4%			9%	100%
B) Recruiting:	9.1	54.6	27.3			9	100
6. Evaluate how well the following terms reflect your personal opinion about Longaberger Baskets CORPORATE Incentive Programs.							
a. Free Baskets	63.7%	36.4%					100%
b. Collectibles	45.5	45.5	9.0				100
c. More Money	18.2	45.5	18.2	18.2			100
d. Setting Goals	27.3	36.4	27.3			9	100
e. Sales Promotions	36.4	45.5	9.1			9	100
f. Recruiting Promotions	27.3	54.6	9.1			9	100
g. Getting Consultants	18.2	36.4	18.2	18.2		9	100
h. High Sales Quotas	18.2	36.4	9.1	27.3		9	100
i. Personal Recognition	36.4	36.4	9.1	9.1		9	100
j. Professional Satisfaction	36.4	36.4	9.1			18.1	100
k. Winning pleasurable prizes	36.4	45.5	9.1			9	100

(continued)

▪ EXHIBIT 37.3   *continued*

							Total
l. Excitement of winning	36.4	45.5	9.1			9	100
m. Anticipation of trying to win more incentives	27.3	18.2	45.5			9	100
n. Incentive Travel Prizes	36.4	45.5		18.2		9	100
o. Free incentive gifts	27.3	36.4	9.1	9.1		18.1	100
p. Too many incentives		18.2	18.2	45.5	9.1	9	100
q. Disappointing overall		9.1	36.4	45.5	9.1		100
r. Challenging	9.1	72.8	18.2				100
s. More bothersome than useful		9.1	18.2	36.4	36.4		100
t. They are really of no use to me		9.1	18.2	18.2	54.6		100

7. In general, I personally endorse and promote most of our Longaberger Corporate incentive programs. — 54.6% 36.4% 9.1% 100%

8. In general, I personally work with my people (consultants/branches/regions) to help set regular sales and/or recruiting goals to achieve incentive awards that are offered by Longaberger either monthly or annually. — 27.3% 54.6% 18.2% 100%

9. What percent of the eligible consultants (or branches, regions, or directors) should win in a successful Longaberger Baskets incentive program?

   a. 5% = 0%
   b. 10%   18.2%
   c. 20%   45.5%
   d. 25%   9.1%
   e. 30%   0%
   f. No Opinion   18.2%
   g. No Response   9%

10. Rank by points per answers.

HOW: Lowest number of points for a reason represents highest degree of statement agreement.

Highest number of points – least degree of agreement level.

Number of people responding (×) per preference (=) my total.

		Total
▪ Reason A:	Too difficult to compete or qualify for incentive.	37
▪ Reason K:	I don't have any real complaints or problems with current incentive programs the way they are now.	37
▪ Reason E:	Wrong kinds of prizes: I have no desire for them.	41
▪ Reason C:	Prizes aren't valuable enough to me.	42

(continued)

▪ EXHIBIT 37.3   *continued*

▪	Reason I:	I'd really rather just get free baskets, rather than any other kinds of prizes for incentives.	48
▪	Reason H:	Incentives don't help in my sales efforts.	49
▪	Reason J:	I'm usually just not interested in competing in incentive programs.	49
▪	Reason F:	Too much of the same kinds of incentive programs.	58
▪	Reason D:	Too many incentive programs.	63
▪	Reason B:	Don't understand the rules.	65
▪	Reason G:	My supervisor doesn't encourage me to participate.	65

11. Overall, how would you rate the current corporate Longaberger Baskets incentive programs for 1987 and the ones we've had so far for 1988?

    a. Excellent 18.2%

    b. Good   63.7%

    c. Average 18.2%

    d. Poor

       TOTAL   100%

Comments on Incentives Survey

1. None

2. Some do
Some consultants do not want to recruit. How do we make them want to?
Recruiting baskets
If they want the incentive offered.

3. Can plan month to month. We don't know programs in advance.
If we have lead time.

4. This depends entirely upon the quality of the incentive and the consultants' interest in this. They work for something only if they really want it.

5. April incentive
Basket, plate, prints. Baskets only

6. a. Not the only reward for recruit. Preferred for a sales reward. Two % sponsor or a choice.
   b. None
   c. More sales automatically more money. I don't think they look at it as more money.
   d. None
   e. None
   f. None
   g. None
   h. None
   i. None
   j. None
   k. None
   l. None
   m. None

(continued)

■ **EXHIBIT 37.3**   *continued*

---

n. Prizes or awards which motivate me to reach beyond my normal ability or something to increase my achievement drive.
o. None
p. Too many things to remember.
q. None
r. To some
s. In many cases
t. Many of the incentives that have been previously offered fail in this category.

7. They do not feel the quality of some of the awards are worth working towards. They work for themselves, but work harder for specific incentives, if the incentive was of value to them.

8. None.

9. This depends entirely upon the incentive. Excellent incentives should be offered for high achievers. Recognition type of incentives should be offered for minimum achievement. The value should reflect the performance.

10. a. When weighed against the prize.Consultants and advisors think this.
    b. Too many rules and more bother than worth. Deadlines.
       Some do.
    c. Some feel that way.
    d. Never.
       Like to see qualifying period. Some consultants qualifying for 3 or 4 incentives at a time.
    e. None
    f. None

---

retail stores and this appealed to him. It was a way to sell the handmade, quality baskets that Dave wanted to make, rather than the inexpensive, foreign-made baskets that were common in retail stores. Thus an idea was born that was to become the cornerstone for selling Longaberger products.

Today, Consultants primarily sell through basket parties in association with a Hostess. These parties are called a "show." Show time is excitement time. But it all just doesn't happen magically. The Hostess is a "partner" with the Consultant. She receives a "wish list" as part of the Hostess Benefit Program. The Consultant and the Hostess work together and share the same goals: guests having fun, sales, bookings, and possibly the sponsoring of additional consultants.

The Hostess is coached carefully to achieve success. "Coaching" means preparing, sharing, and caring. The reason the hostess books a show is probably to acquire more products at a discounted price. But she will also have a chance to socialize with friends, entertain in her home, and shop conveniently. The Hostess depends on the Consultant to organize her show and be the expert in helping people have a fun, enjoyable, and informative good time.

Another important aspect of the sales structure is the "Basket Bee" held each summer. This meeting is a combination of product introductions, training, motivation, convention, and the general good fun that used to be associated with a quilting bee. Nearly 5,000 of the firm's Consultants and other people gather each summer in a city near Dresden for this annual event.

Training Programs

The company provides a wide variety of materials and meetings for the training of its Consultants and other Associates, under the supervision of one of Dave's daughters, Rachel Longaberger Schmidt. The heart of the training program is a video-based workbook that takes new recruits step by step through a program that is designed to lead to their success. Because the program involves videotapes and a "Skills for Success" workbook, it can be used for recruits across wide geographic areas and can be used in groups or one on one. It is part of what the company calls the Longaberger University and is designed to help people start their own business with minimum expense and the maximum potential for profitability.

The program consists of six units that have the objective of helping people become entrepreneurs and operate their own business. Sales advisors who have acted as sponsors of the recruits stand ready to assist in answering questions and in motivating and supervising the training process. The Skills for Success program includes the following topics of study:

Unit 1: The Longaberger Heritage

Unit 2: Starting a Longaberger Business

Unit 3: Your Business Lifeline: Hostesses and Bookings

Unit 4: Merchandising Longaberger Products

Unit 5: On with the Show

Unit 6: The Longaberger Career

The six units require 6 to 10 hours to complete and are expected to be completed on the basis of one unit per day. The workbook includes multiple-choice questions on the material so that students can test their retention. The book also recommends IRS and other materials needed for operating a business as an independent contractor. The book features many of the management principles that Dave Longaberger has developed over his career in retailing, manufacturing, and direct sales.

As an example of the materials covered in the training course, Unit 5 teaches principles for organizing a successful show. To carry out these principles, Consultants are taught to use the following tips in each show:

1. Put people at ease.

2. Use humor.

3. Sell yourself.

4. Make the Hostess a star to her guests.

5. Have confidence in yourself.

6. Have confidence in your products.

7. Speak to your group's specific interests and needs.

8. Make frequent eye contact with every guest.

9. Suggest add-on sales.

10. Smile, smile, smile!

Consultants are taught that securing bookings is one of the most important aspects of their Longaberger business. They attempt to schedule at least six bookings per month. By booking shows the first two weeks of the month, the bookings from those shows will usually fill the remainder of the month. Consultants are trained to have a plan of action to handle referrals for future bookings and to prepare materials needed to ensure that everyone enjoys attending the shows. One of Dave's management principles is marketing, merchandising, and selling: If you market yourself, merchandise yourself, you'll have no trouble selling yourself.

The training program includes a wide variety of training and motivational meetings in which sales advisors develop their own materials as well as use those supplied by Longaberger to increase sales each year.

New Products

Longaberger recently introduced another product line, Longaberger Pottery® (see Exhibit 37.1). Handmade quality is a high priority for all Longaberger products. The company's Woven Traditions® Pottery, including a line of dinnerware, is made in two family-owned potteries in East Liverpool, Ohio. The craftsmanship of Longaberger Pottery® recalls traditional pottery-making methods used for centuries.

Longaberger Pottery is made from a specially formulated high-quality clay body. Its durable construction is much the same as the china made for the food-service industry. Elegant in design, with a special embossed band resembling the weaves in Longaberger Baskets®, Longaberger Pottery is safe in the microwave, oven, and freezer. It is distinctive enough to display in a china cabinet and practical enough to use daily on the family dinner table.

Although the pottery products have been well received by Consultants and persons attending the shows, the company has observed that a difference exists between the pottery and basket product lines. Guests attending shows who buy baskets normally pay in the range of $25 to $50 for one or two baskets. Since the pottery is priced at approximately $60 per setting, the total for a four- or eight-piece collection can total several hundred dollars. The company is currently studying the best way to market a product with substantially higher total price than Longaberger Baskets.

Dave Longaberger has always been a visionary. He started in the restaurant business, added a grocery business, and eventually moved to a basket business that few other people believed could be so successful. What else might be in the future?

One possibility is a Longaberger Basket Village. All buildings would take on the appearance of Longaberger baskets and contain shops, restaurants, museums, and theaters. The Village would recapture the history and excitement of various regions of the United States, incorporating the culture, foods, and tradition of American society.

Longaberger family restaurants are also a possibility, since the firm already operates four highly successful restaurants in Dresden, Ohio. The Longaberger Restaurant is a fine dining establishment featuring a buffet or salad bar for lunch and dinner. The walls are lined with hundreds of Longaberger Baskets, nearly every style the company has ever sold, along with the company's pottery selections.

Jayhawks Bar and Grill celebrates Dresden's former high school sports teams, the Jefferson Jayhawks. This upscale but relaxed pub features steaks, sandwiches, and weekly lunch and dinner specials.

Popeye's Soda Shop features a 1950's decor and a menu including sandwiches, dinner entrees, and a full selection of ice cream, sundaes, and shakes. A Breakfast Shop is also operated featuring first quality, farm-fresh breakfast and lunch items.

The Village of Dresden has become one of the major tourist attractions in Ohio. The Longaberger factory is open to the public and especially designed to allow visitors to learn about the handcrafted process by which Longaberger Baskets are produced. The factory attracts many buses, cars, and vans of visitors each day. Nearby, in the Village of Dresden, the Longaberger Museum traces the Longaberger family tradition of basket making for a century. In Dresden's heyday, the museum building housed a bakery where school children watched bakers knead dough and remove fresh loaves from the oven.

Lining Main Street are a variety of shops, featuring distinctive architectural styles and tasteful merchandise, many owned by the Longaberger family. Selections include gifts, decorating accessories, fine women's clothing and jewelry, children's clothing and toys, and quilts. Each store includes items exclusive to Longaberger retail ventures.

Across from the Popeye's Restaurant is the "World's Largest Basket." This focal point, 48 feet long, 11 feet wide, and 23 feet high, has become a traditional picture-taking spot in the village. Ten hardwood maple trees and 2,000 hours of work were required to make this unique attraction. A visit to Dresden means a day of relaxed, enjoyable dining, shopping, and a historic exploration of a village and a craft rich in heritage and beauty.

Focal Topics

1. What are the merits and problems of the Longaberger sales structure? Why has it been so successful? What steps should the company take to maintain or improve its rate of growth in the future?

2. What should Consultants do to maximize the success of the basket shows?

3. What are your recommendations for increasing the sales of Longaberger Pottery?

4. How can Longaberger maintain its growth in sales and profitability in the future? Which, if any, additional products or businesses do you believe the firm should concentrate on?

5. Based on the research presented in Exhibit 37.3 what criteria should be used in recruiting new consultants?

■ ■ ■ ■ ■

Wal-Mart in Mexico

■ ■ ■ ■ ■

It's Saturday afternoon, and the price club is packed. Hundreds of shoppers inch down the aisles, filling improbably huge shopping carts with economy-size cereal boxes and plastic bags of frozen mixed vegetables large enough to feed a small country's army.

Because it's just opened and new in their town, the customers are fascinated—they seem to have arrived in nirvana and not a warehouse market. The formula is working like a charm. As in so many other neighborhoods, the shoppers here are delighted with the opportunity to buy bulk items and economy sizes—paying about 20 percent less than they would at the average supermarket.

What's unusual is that this particular price club—half-owned by Wal-Mart—is not in Dearborn, Short Hills, or Highland Park. It's smack in the middle of Mexico City.

Sam's Wholesale Clubs in Mexico City? That's right. There are two of them so far, only they're called Club Aurrera. Considered by many market analysts to be one of the most visionary retailers in the United States, Wal-Mart entered a joint venture with CIFRA, SA, a Mexican counterpart, last summer to open wholesale clubs in one of the most populous cities on earth. The flagship opened last December, the second unit in February, and—at least in their first phase—they are the talk of the town, retail division, in Mexico City.

But Wal-Mart's venture south of the Rio Grande is not some eccentric exception in international business. In fact, when George Bush and Mexican President Carlos Salinas de Gortari were only in the whispering stages of talks about establishing a North American Free Trade Agreement, the retail giant was already plunging into the land of mariachis, tortillas, and hot chili peppers, along with many other foreign—particularly U.S.—companies.

Following is a list of some of the recent North-South deals, in their respective industries.

Retail   Just as Wal-Mart announced partnership with CIFRA, the San Diego–based Price Company signed an agreement with Comercial Mexicana, the number two Mexican retailer, to open price clubs and import Mexican goods into the United States.

Insurance   Last February, Aetna Life and Casualty signed a contract with VAMSA, a Mexican insurance holding company, to acquire a significant minority equity interest in VAMSA subsidiaries—including Seguros Monterrey, which, with a 30 percent share, is the largest individual life insurance company in Mexico.

Food and Beverage   In October 1991, PepsiCo Inc. acquired an 80 percent interest in Empresas Gamesa, the parent company of Mexico's largest cookie maker, for $320 million. A few months later, Cadbury Schweppes bought the soda water business of the Mexican company FEMSA, SA, for $325 million.

Financial   American Express recently set up a joint venture with Banamex (Banco Nacional de Mexico), Mexico's largest bank, to issue Gold credit cards.

Engineering and Construction   Last August, the Bechtel Group joined with two Mexican companies to provide engineering and construction services to the petrochemical, chemical, and petroleum industries.

Oil   In April 1991, Triton USA of Houston became the first foreign company to be granted an oil-drilling contract off Mexican shores since 1938.

Franchises   Among the companies that have either recently entered or expanded their presence in Mexico are McDonald's, Kentucky Fried Chicken, Colombo Yogurt, I Can't Believe It's Yogurt, Martinizing, Baskin-Robbins, Blockbuster Video, Wendy's, Domino's Pizza, and Pizza Hut.

What makes Mexico such a hot ticket all of a sudden? For U.S. businesspeople, a North American Free Trade Agreement could mean about 85 million potential new customers due south. And for those who want to establish businesses, Mexico also offers inexpensive labor (the minimum wage is about $4 a day), one of the most stable political systems in Latin America, and, in the past two or three years, one of the fastest growing economies in the world.

At press time, the future of the free trade agreement, in negotiation for over a year, was up in the air. However, many authorities on business in Mexico point out that, whether or not a free trade agreement goes into effect anytime soon, the wheels have already been set in motion for foreign investors to come in and start making money.

As Christopher Whalen, Washington-based editor of the newsletter *The Mexico Report*, recently said: "The . . . way to do business in Mexico is . . . to go down and cut your own deal."

Indeed, free trade agreement or not, Mexican President Carlos Salinas de Gortari has made the stimuli of foreign investment and free trade the cornerstone of his administration. Since he took office in 1989, he has changed both infrastructure and legislation to make foreign investment more attractive. Among his policies:

Speed in Applications   "The most important change that Salinas has made," says John S. Wood, commercial attaché to the U.S. embassy in Mexico City, "is that any foreigner who applies to invest here gets a 'yes' or a 'no' in 45 days. If there's no answer after 45 days, it's an automatic 'yes.'"

Percentage of Ownership   Throughout the twentieth century, there have been various laws pertaining to how much of a business a foreigner could own in Mexico. In general, the cap was 49 percent, making the investment less interesting. Although there have always been exceptions to this rule, they are becoming more and more commonplace. Indeed, many businesses can now be 100 percent foreign owned, and some industries that have been completely hands-off—such as oil exploration and insurance—are now inviting foreign participation if only to a limited extent.

Intellectual Property Rights   In the summer of 1991, Salinas brought Mexico's laws pertaining to copyrights, trademarks, and transfer of technology up to what Vincent Lencioni of the American Chamber of Commerce in Mexico calls "a first-world standard." Now, adds attaché Wood, should you be infringed, "you have a good legal leg to stand on."

Wal-Mart is an excellent test case of a recent U.S.-Mexico joint venture. In 1990, before the free trade agreement had become a headline issue, Wal-Mart representatives were already talking with Mexican retail giant CIFRA.

If it is a truism that the largest obstacle for a U.S. company in a foreign country is lack of familiarity with the market, a joint venture with an established local force largely eliminates a foreign business's biggest problem.

Wal-Mart could hardly have chosen a more savvy partner than the high-growth industry leader, CIFRA. With a strong presence in supermarkets, hypermarkets, department stores, and restaurants, CIFRA has a great reputation for sound money management. Its sales topped $2.75 billion in 1991, a 12 percent increase over 1990.

The two companies are splitting the costs (and, they hope, profits) on a 50-50 basis, and the two initial Club Aurrera stores—named after CIFRA's phenomenally successful hypermarket chain—have already created hundreds of jobs in Mexico City, according to a CIFRA source. Retail analysts on both sides of the border are enthusiastic. The consensus is that the stores will do quite well in Mexico City—although perhaps not on the same enormous scale as Sam's Wholesale Clubs in the United States.

"I think it should work extremely well," says Kurt Barnard, publisher of *Barnards' Retail Marketing Report*. "The purpose of wholesale clubs—

■ **EXHIBIT 38.1   Club Aurrera**

to sell merchandise at rock-bottom prices—should be no less attractive in Mexico, or Katmandu for that matter, than it is in the U.S." Retail consultant Walter Loeb adds that success should be ensured given Wal-Mart's "consistency in quality and excellence in technology."

Although also generally encouraging, Mexican market analysts point to three challenges for the wholesale clubs:

The Low Purchasing Power of the Mexican Consumer   Although hopes are high that foreign investment will create not only new sources of work but higher competition, productivity, and economic activity, the fact remains that the majority of Mexican consumers buy small-size products in mom-and-pop stores, even though they are proportionally higher priced. They don't have the ready cash to buy anything larger—let alone the economy sizes and bulk offered in wholesale clubs.

On the other hand, there are more than 18 million people in Mexico City. And it is in the capital that CIFRA has had its greatest success—with a largely upper-middle-class and well-to-do public. Furthermore, Club Aurrera has made great efforts to attract group membership from small- and medium-size businesses, with the hope of reaching a public that might not be able to shop there individually. By opening in Mexico City, Club Aurrera has the chance to reach the largest share of the Mexican market that can afford it.

Innovation of Concept   Mexican shoppers like novelty. When new products or concepts are introduced, from McDonald's hamburgers to instant lottery tickets, the initial success is frequently huge. However, after the novelty wears off, Mexican shoppers often return to stores that are conveniently located or offer sale merchandise. To ensure mid- and long-term success, predict Mexican analysts, Club Aurrera will need to deliver consistently on its promises of low prices and an extensive, attractive assortment of merchandise.

Fragility of Partnership   Both Wal-Mart and CIFRA have been enormously successful by being themselves and have little or no experience in joint ventures. They each have a strong management team, used to getting its own way. Should there be disagreements along the way, the partnership could show signs of strain.

However, although it may be a marriage of convenience, CIFRA and Wal-Mart need each other. The announcement of the free trade agreement and the changes in foreign investment strategy in the Salinas administration have already created a livelier, more stable, and upbeat economy south of the border. Wal-Mart, which doesn't want to miss out on this opportunity, needs CIFRA's knowledge of its market, and CIFRA needs Wal-Mart's American products and technological know-how.

If the first two Club Aurreras are a success, it can be assumed that, considering the enormous growth of Sam's Wholesale Clubs in the United States (181 units in about 10 years), Wal-Mart will not be satisfied with the presence of only two stores in Mexico. Indeed, plans are underway to open a third in the prosperous northern industrial city of Monterrey this autumn. Wal-Mart and CIFRA are also in the planning stages of a program to import Mexican products to the United States.

The advantages of Wal-Mart's early arrival, before either the free trade agreement is implemented or the competition gets to Mexico, are that it will get prime locations, learn about the market before the rest of the pack, and be identified with the wholesale-club concept by customers.

Yet, if Wal-Mart is blazing the trail in the retail business, its example is merely emblematic of a current trend of many U.S. businesses south of the border. Although he was commenting on the Wal-Mart deal, retail analyst Walter Loeb's remarks serve for any number of foreign companies in Mexico: "Their venture is a minimal-risk experiment in becoming a multinational company. If you don't want to try Europe or Japan, you go to Mexico. It's close and you can fine-tune."

Focal Topics

1. What are the economic opportunities or problems for Mexico likely to be in the next decade?
2. Is the decision to enter Mexico likely to be profitable for Wal-Mart?

3. What adaptations, if any, should Wal-Mart make when entering Mexico?

4. What steps should Wal-Mart management take to increase the probability of success in entering Mexico or other markets outside the United States?

■ ■ ■ ■ ■

Reprinted from Delta Air Lines' *Sky Magazine*, July 1992, pp. 81–89, with permission from Mr. David Lida, author.

Paul Ecke Poinsettia Ranch

■ ■ ■ ■ ■

"Mr. Poinsettia" is a name to which Paul Ecke, Jr., readily answers. The Ecke Poinsettia Ranch in Santa Barbara, California, dominates the industry. Mr. Ecke ships millions of mother plants around the world for greenhouses to take cuttings.

Statistics from the U.S. Department of Agriculture indicate that over 33 million poinsettia plants are sold annually, worth $123 million at wholesale. California leads the production by a huge margin followed by Texas and Ohio.

Sales of poinsettias were not always so great. Until the 1970s, poinsettias were sold as fresh flowers. Even the potted plants had a shelf life of only a few days. The red leaves at the top of the plant, called bracts, also tended to fall off as poinsettias were shipped. With help from university researchers, Ecke developed varieties that would stand up to shipping. Research and development has produced varieties today that last for weeks or, under ideal conditions, even months.

As technical problems were generally overcome by the 1970s, the issue facing Paul Ecke Poinsettias was how to increase the sales of this minor, seasonal floral product to a major sales category. Although dominant as a grower of poinsettia stock, the firm was still dependent upon hundreds of floral wholesalers and thousands of florists and other retail outlets to reach consumers.

Publicity

Paul Ecke, Jr., believed that poinsettia usage was limited by a lack of consumer information and promotion. He felt that new shorter sizes, longer lasting quality, and a fresh range of striking colors made poinsettias exceptional potted plants offering diverse opportunities for interior decor and commercial display. He believed that the majority of the public was unaware of these significant changes in poinsettias and that if consumer awareness could be increased, then sales would follow suit. He contacted other poinsettia growers around the country to share promotional ideas and seek cooperative grower efforts. He also pursued promotional programs for the family business at Paul Ecke Ranch through an energetic public relations program.

Paul Ecke might have considered national advertising on television but the costs appeared prohibitive. Instead, Yvonne Owen, public relations director for Paul Ecke Poinsettias, initiated a low-cost, high-exposure public relations (P.R.) program. She said, "Since we're close to Hollywood, and we'd already placed our product in consumer magazines, floral trade journals, and national newspapers, it seemed like a natural progression to go to television. We were trying to get exposure that would benefit the whole industry.

"With television, it's possible to get dramatic results by featuring just a few plants. All we wanted to initially do was get a few poinsettias on the sets, so we approached the TV shows on a 'no-name-mentioned' basis. We were, and still are, promoting the industry, not the individual firm."

The sets of shows such as "The Tonight Show" display the beauty of poinsettias during the holiday season. The "Dinah Shore Christmas Special," the "Bob Hope Christmas Special," and many other national television shows display poinsettias as a major focus, courtesy of Paul Ecke Poinsettias.

The latest public relations push for Paul Ecke Poinsettias has been on television news programs. Yvonne says, "Our goal was to establish a prototype at our own local TV news show so that we could tell other growers how we went about it and encourage them to do the same thing in their local areas." Paul Ecke prepared a plan that could be used by wholesalers or local florists throughout the nation.

The first step is to develop a strategy by local florists. This includes watching the local news or morning talk shows. Usually there is a lack of plants, a good sign for florists. The next step is to find out who is in charge at the station and approach them with an offer. The person in charge is told that the plants are a gift for the season, a mutual exchange, a floral holiday courtesy, and not a promotional venture. Careful, professional arrangements are planned for delivery date, amount of plant material, follow-up care, and plant replacement.

The first time a station agrees to a poinsettia display, the plans are kept simple. Unless the florist is asked to do so, lavish decorations that might overwhelm both the people and the set are avoided. Two or three of the most beautiful plants with saucers and a simple basket or bow are offered.

The plan has been successful in reaching many local stations. In Baltimore, for example, the Allied Florists of Greater Baltimore have donated plants to local television stations for many years. Morning talk shows appear more useful than news shows because the news shows sometimes tend to view the contribution as a promotional venture, whereas the talk

■ **EXHIBIT 39.1   "Superstar Poinsettias" Brochure Photo**
One big plant broadcasts in a department store window.

Reprinted from *Flowers* magazine, August 1982.

shows do not. Occasionally, a local florist will also talk on the show about home plant care.

The national morning news shows have all incorporated poinsettias, lots of poinsettias, into their holiday sets. Famous cohosts such as Joan Lunden, Bryant Gumbel, and Katie Couric find themselves sitting among beautiful poinsettia displays for the entire month of December. Paul Ecke has been able to use this new medium to educate consumers further about poinsettias and how to enjoy them beyond the holiday season. "CBS This Morning" cohosts Harry Smith and Paula Zahn interviewed Paul Ecke in December of 1991 to explain to consumers how to take care of their plants so that they would continue blooming, sometimes even until the next season. At first glance one might think that because consumers view poinsettias as disposable plants the number of plants sold would remain constant or even increase from one year to the next. But some consumers hesitate to purchase poinsettias because they think that they will only last until January. If consumers understand that the plants can be kept beautiful for many months, they might be more likely to purchase them for holiday gifts that will keep giving throughout the new year.

The publicity program includes radio stations. Local florists are brought to the on-air personalities with a message of where they are from and a simple holiday greeting. Often, the next response is a little free air time.

In addition to the value of having broadcast stations as outlets for positive statements, the media contacts have paid off in the ability to counter quickly negative publicity. Although poinsettias are not poisonous, there have been reports that they are, and the positive relationships with stations have resulted in numerous on-air interviews about poisonous plants in which the nature of poinsettias can be clarified.

■ **EXHIBIT 39.2 Poinsettias for Weddings**
Two authors of this book, Kristina and Roger Blackwell, were married in December 1991 amidst dozens of red and white poinsettias.

Product Development

The demand for poinsettias has also been stimulated by the development of new sizes and varieties of the plants. One of the new products is "tubs" or larger forms of display plants. The display poinsettias are sold in 8- to 12-inch containers with plants 2½ to 3½ feet tall, usually with twenty to thirty blooms.

The large display poinsettias are not what the average consumer plans to take home for indoor decorating. But the blaze of red and green produced by a few big poinsettias in a florist's window may be the attraction that brings customers into the shop for a smaller version or for other distinctive products such as poinsettia wreaths, bright hanging baskets, or poinsettia trees.

The ideal market for this "big gun" is probably commercial accounts, especially those seeking large, lavish seasonal displays. Ecke believes that products such as these increase total business in the industry because the products stand out and are very useful and exciting in retail merchandising.

Some florists have had tremendous success selling the big plants for use in a large building or shopping area. It gives these sites showy, sophisticated decorations. Every mall or larger shopping complex has a promotion department. This creates a twofold opportunity, since there are individual merchants themselves as well as the promotional director in charge of major expenditures.

Another new product developed by Paul Ecke is the poinsettia table tree. It differs dramatically from the traditional poinsettia because of the novel tree form. Each poinsettia table tree grows on a single stem, reaching an average height of 30 to 36 inches and has about twenty-five to thirty blooms. According to Ecke, the table tree took about 5 years to develop. Currently it is available only in red, but Ecke hopes to perfect white and pink colors as well.

Traditional holiday decoration is given added dimension by this new poinsettia table tree, which provides an eloquent height to a standard Christmas tree when placed in the home. Ecke suggests that it can be displayed in banks and business lobbies where the public can become aware of this new form of the traditional Christmas flower.

Another new product is miniature poinsettias. Ecke originally developed the idea of putting clusters of miniature poinsettia plants (complete with small soil balls) into handy "Arrangement Paks," and distributed the product to growers and florists throughout the country. These miniature poinsettias are now available in a corsage-type flower, as an expression of the season's cheer and excitement for the wearer. The corsage and boutonnieres are grown from a hardy family and can easily hold up 2 or 3 days.

To promote miniature poinsettias for personal decorating, Ecke goes straight to consumer magazines such as *Cosmopolitan*, *Harper's Bazaar*, and *Gentlemen's Quarterly*. Television hosts and hostesses of Christmas specials are also given poinsettias as body flowers.

■ **EXHIBIT 39.3   Poinsettia Trees for Decorating at Home**

Miniature poinsettias are also sold in clear plastic containers no larger than a paper clip holder. In this form, Ecke calls them "Personal Poinsettias" and they are available in red, white, pink, and marble colors, usually selling for under $5. "It seem to us that there was a market for a carefree-type plant of very, very small size to be used in restaurants, on secretaries' desks, hospital bedside stands—just any place where some color would look good, but there isn't much room to put a big plant," explains Paul Ecke, Jr. "The idea is to put a seasonal symbol any place; with its self-watering property, it can be moved around and there isn't any worry about saucers, water, and spilling." The Personal Poinsettia is watered by a wick similar to that used in a kerosene lantern. The poinsettia is planted in a small amount of soil in the top portion of the container. A string—or wick—positioned alongside the plant's root ball extends into the base of the container, which is filled with water. The plant feeds itself by absorbing water through the string. The only care the Personal Poinsettia requires is additional water when the level gets down to ½ inch from the bottom of the container. There is never a water stress on the plant because of this constant supply of water. Even in low light, the plant will last a month.

Ecke provides recommendations to florists to increase sales of Personal Poinsettias. These suggestions include:

1. Suggest that your customers use the plants at dinner parties. They can place a Personal Poinsettia and a name card in front of each plate for a

▪ EXHIBIT 39.4   Personal Poinsettias

"I'd like a Christmas arrangement that's not too big or too expensive, but would make a nice looking gift and I only have five dollars. Can you help me?"

If requests like that leave your head spinning, don't despair. The Paul Ecke Poinsettia Ranch, Encinitas, Calif., may have the perfect solution. It's called the Personal Poinsettia and, if its test market results are any indication, it's going to be bigger than life this Christmas in Arizona and California. The rest of the nation can expect its debut in 1987.

Packaged in a clear plastic container that's no larger than a paper clip holder, this tiny Christmas plant fulfills all of the above requests. It's attractive—available in red, white, pink and marble colors—and it sells for under $3. Furthermore, it has a self-contained watering system, which means virtually no maintenance is required.

"It seemed to us that there was a market for a carefree-type plant of very, very small size to be used in restaurants, on secretaries' desks, hospital bedside stands—just *any* place where some color would look good, but there isn't much room to put a big plant," explained Paul Ecke Jr., president of the firm. "That's the whole idea. Put this Christmas symbol in a place—any place—and with its self-watering property, it can be moved around and there isn't any worry about saucers, water and spilling.

"That's why we thought the name Personal Poinsettia might be just about right," he added. "It's something that you can just pick up and move around with you as your own personal plant. In an office situation, for example, if you move from one desk to another, you can take the plant with you."

The Personal Poinsettia is watered by a wick similar to that used in a kerosene lantern. The poinsettia is planted in a small amount of soil in the top portion of the container. A string—or wick—positioned alongside the plant's root ball extends into the base of the container, which is filled with water. The plant feeds itself by absorbing water through the string. The only care the Personal Poinsettia requires is additional water when the level gets down to ½ inch from the bottom of the container.

"There's never a water stress on the plant, because it has this constant supply of water," Ecke explained. "Even in low light it'll last a month—meaning it'll hold its foliage and its bracts."

Development of the Personal Poinsettia began five years ago and last year it was test marketed in the Los Angeles area. Like the other Ecke novelty items—poinsettia hanging baskets, trees and arrangement packs—the Personal Poinsettia was an instant success. Ecke believes the plant's wick-watering system and longevity captured consumers' interest.

"People put them in as many different places as you can imagine within an office situation," Ecke said. "And, we had people come back and tell us they put them all over their homes, including their bathrooms."

That fact alone is proof that florists can let their imaginations run wild when selling the Personal Poinsettia this Christmas. The marketing possibilities are limitless.

For instance:
• Suggest that your customers use the plants at dinner parties. They can place a Personal Poinsettia and a name card in front of each plate for a festive table setting. At the end of the evening, guests can take the plants home with them.
• Group several of the poinsettias on a table with candles for an attractive holiday centerpiece.
• Promote them to banks for use in teller windows.
• Offer them to commercial accounts and suggest businesses hand them out with bonus checks or give them to employes as Christmas gifts.
• Tell customers that not only can they enjoy the Personal Poinsettia throughout the holidays, but, at the end of the season, they can snip the flower and wear it as a boutonniere, corsage or hair flower to a New Year's Eve party.

For further information, contact the Paul Ecke Poinsettia Ranch
P.O. Box 488, Encinitas, Calif. 92024, (619) 753-1134

festive table setting. At the end of the evening, guests can take the plants home with them.

2. Group several of the poinsettias on a table with candles for an attractive holiday centerpiece.

3. Promote them to banks for use in teller windows.

4. Offer them to commercial accounts and suggest businesses hand them out with bonus checks or give them to employees as Christmas gifts.

5. Tell customers that not only can they enjoy the Personal Poinsettia throughout the holidays, but, at the end of the season, they can snip the flower and wear it as a boutonniere, corsage, or hair flower to a New Year's Eve party.

Seasonal Demand

Although the peak demand for poinsettias is at Christmas, there is great interest in stimulating demand during other seasons of the year. The firm is seeking ways the plant might be sold for other holidays or to extend the time the plants are sold during the Christmas season.

The Paul Ecke organization has been characterized by innovation and market stimulation. Both product innovation and promotional innovation have been the policy, and the firm intends to continue this progress in the future.

Focal Topics

1. Evaluate the firm's approach to publicity. What changes or additional approaches do you suggest?

2. Should the firm make major expenditures for advertising? If so, what should be the creative and media plan?

3. What new products or new applications should be developed by the Ecke firm?

4. What can be done to stimulate demand other than during the Christmas holiday?

■ ■ ■ ■ ■

P A 6 R T

COMPREHENSIVE CASES

■ ■ ■ ■ ■

■

Miele & Co.

■ ■ ■ ■ ■

In the last year of the nineteenth century the world continued to strive in its quest to develop research and technology for the enrichment of the quality of life. The Wright brothers attempted flying; Madam Curie discovered pitchblende, a mineral containing uranium; and Marconi transmitted across the English channel without the use of telegraph wires. It was also in this year that Carl Miele and Reinhard Zinkann established Miele & Co. in Herzebrock, Germany.

Carl Miele had gained much work experience while working for his father in Herzebrock. His interests shifted from the building materials trade to the development of a superior quality milk separator. He viewed this as a growth market due to the increasing number of separators in the marketplace. Therefore, he concentrated his efforts on the machine design that would give him recognition in this competitive market. During his first meeting with Reinhard Zinkann in 1898, Miele discussed the milk separating business. Soon thereafter they formed Miele & Co., each taking on special responsibilities: Miele, assembly and manufacturing, and Zinkann, distribution.

Production started 4 weeks later in an old corn mill. The young firm employed ten workers and housed only one drilling machine and four lathes. Miele spent many hours working in the factory alongside his employees to oversee production and assure the manufacturing of a high-quality product. Zinkann, on the other hand, spent many hours in the office fulfilling his administrative responsibilities. The first product, the hand driven milk separator "Meteor," was an immediate success. Although competition was fierce in this industry, sales continued to soar due to the sales efforts of Zinkann. By the end of the first year of operation, production and sales had increased from forty to seventy-five units per month.

With the success of the milk separators, Miele and Zinkann searched for a product similar in production processes to add to their product line. The existence of a wood preparation department made the production of wooden washing machines a logical choice. The first Miele washing machine was produced in 1903, making Miele producers of household appliances. It was unknown to the founders at this time what long-term ramifications this action would have on the company.

Business flourished and it became necessary to expand production capacity in order to meet the demand for the separators and the washing machines. Miele soon moved its headquarters to Guetersloh, Germany. This growing city would provide the company with sufficient labor resources and transport facilities because it lay on the main traffic route between Berlin and the Ruhr.

The expanded production capacity translated into the desire for new sales outlets. It was at this time that one of the basic concepts that still guides Miele today was born: form the closest possible contact with one's customers through individual sales offices and customized personal selling and ensure the highest quality product by manufacturing all of the components in-house. Both founders agreed that continued success was dependent upon the quality of the product offered to the customer. They understood the importance of customer satisfaction and its role in repeat purchases. Miele adopted the motto "Always Better," which signified its commitment to innovation and quality enhancement. Although it is no longer inscribed on Miele products as in earlier times, each and every product does contain within it this motto's underlying theme.

The next decade was profitable for Miele, and by 1924 the product line had expanded to include separators, butter machines and churns, small dairy machines, washing and wringing machines and mangles, box and rack wagons, and bicycles. On its twenty-fifth anniversary it was named Germany's largest specialist factory with fourteen sales offices and turnover of 8 million Deutsch Marks. In 1926 the first Miele vacuum cleaner was produced. Unique to the marketplace because of its numerous accessories, this product proved to be very profitable even in its first years of production.

World War I and II were difficult times for all industry in Germany, Miele being no exception. However, the company survived the slowed production and decline in sales and was soon once again growing rapidly. The resurgence of industry in Europe following the reconstruction of the postwar years meant an increase in competition for Miele. It was at this time that the importance of advertising was discovered. Miele chose to project the technical advantages of its products in its advertisements and posters. In order to assist its sales offices and dealers in the push of its products to the customer, Miele devised a way to demonstrate the use of its products to a large group of potential buyers simultaneously. It acquired a 23 meter long bus which was transformed into a mobile exhibition. It created quite a sensation during its attendance at trade fairs all over Europe and soon became internationally recognized, as did the Miele name.

In an effort to increase sales and magnify its current growth rate, Miele concentrated on export sales. Miele appliances were produced under licensing agreements in South America and the Near East. The company was able to adapt its products to the various needs of the markets in which it desired to sell its products. For example, the washing machines sold to missionary stations in Brazil ran on a petrol motor because no power supply was available. This commitment to meeting customer needs gave Miele the competitive advantages needed to capture these relatively untapped markets.

It was in Europe, however, that Miele found it most difficult to gain a foothold. Competitors had adopted the sales networking systems established years ago by Miele. It was decided by Carl Miele, Jr., and Kurt Christian Zinkann, the sons of the founders, that it would be product innovation and superior quality which would differentiate Miele products from those of its competitors. Miele took a strong stand in the industry with its production of Europe's first domestic electric washer in 1929 and with the introduction of Europe's first electronic dryer in 1966. It was the continued high level of innovation and improved product design throughout these years which allowed Miele to achieve dominance in the marketplace. Some of Miele's products are shown in Exhibits 40.1 and 40.2.

Secrets to Growth

Growth in profits has always been a priority at Miele. While its competitors have worried about market share, Miele has refused to become overly excited about anything but its bottom line. It has concentrated primarily on the long run, not changing strategy because of short-term economic conditions such as recessions or its competitors' misfortunes in the marketplace. Instead Miele has concentrated on profits, which have ultimately improved dramatically its standing in the market.

Miele felt that growth could be attained with another extension of its product line. The "Studio-M" customized kitchen provided the company with a way to sell its full line of products packaged in a made-to-order kitchen to its customers. The customer is able to choose from thirty-two various kitchen designs and themes, selecting which appliances, if any, are to be included in the package. The customer is able to choose from a wide variety of dishwashers, ovens, microwaves, ranges and accompanying hoods, refrigerators, washers, and dryers. (See Exhibit 40.3.)

With years of innovation and product line extension, Miele & Co. has become the symbol of quality in the appliance industry throughout Europe, South America, Africa, the Pacific Rim, and the Near East. Today, Miele employs over 15,000 workers in its six factories and over thirty sales offices in Germany and abroad. Advice centers and service depots have been established to provide dealers with advice, publicity, sales, and customer service issues. Although Miele products are priced higher than the majority of its competitors' products, Miele has continued to command increased growth and profitability. Consumers expect to pay more for Miele products, but they also expect to keep them in good working condition for at least 20 years. It is the commitment to quality and detail established by

■ EXHIBIT 40.1   Miele Vacuum Cleaner Products

(*continued*)

■ **EXHIBIT 40.1**   *continued*

Míele   Optional Extras

Turbobrush

The Miele Turbobrush is recommended for routine cleaning of all types of carpeting. The efficient Miele Turbobrush:

- **Compact and maneuverable**
  Sleek, modern design allows Turbobrush to reach under dressers, couches and chairs.

- **Simple operation**
  Eliminates messy wires, extra hoses and expensive repairs, anyone can service. Simply attach to end of wand.

- **Light weight:**
  Only approx. 1½ lbs.

- **Double edge cleaning**
  Suction is channeled to both sides for easy cleaning next to walls.

- **Pile-adjustment**
  custom-sets for low-nap to heavy-shag carpeting.

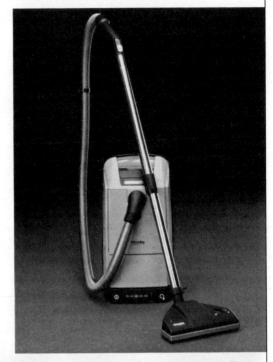

Carl Miele and Reinhard Zinkann over 80 years ago that has given Miele the reputation as the "Mercedes of appliances."

Miele has seemed immune even to tough economic times which spelled trouble for many of its competitors. Miele attributes this to its commitment to high quality, which management believes people are willing to pay for even when cash flow is low, and the service it offers its clients. While

■ **EXHIBIT 40.2   An Array of Miele Products**

Überwachung auf dem Prüfband

Alle Prüfungen bestanden!

Ein fertiger Miele-Geschirr-spüler im Haushalt

Miele strives for technological perfection, some times machines do need servicing. Miele engineers have designed the latest washers and dryers so that the whole front panel of the machine can be opened like a door to make it easy to reach vital parts. Maintenance is much easier and so is the problem diagnosis process because the parts do not have to be reached from the back of the machine.

■ EXHIBIT 40.3   A Model Miele Kitchen

(continued)

■ **EXHIBIT 40.3**   *continued*

In addition to its commitment to service, Miele also places great importance on its human resources. Management believes the quality of its work force is above the industry average, and it develops programs to maintain this level of quality. Miele spends much time and money on continued education of its employees. The company offers all employees from managers to line workers further training programs either in their areas of specialty or in other areas for self-improvement. Even though these programs are voluntary, roughly 33 percent of the total work force attends some sessions each year. Miele publishes a voluminous brochure each year that lists programs offered inside the company and by outside groups. Employees are able to attend as many workshops and training sessions as they wish on company time or on their own.

U.S. Expansion

The current management team at Miele, consisting of Rudolf Miele and Dr. Peter Zinkann, grandsons of the founders, saw the next logical step for Miele as tapping the U.S. market. In 1984 the first U.S. sales office was established in New Jersey with a staff of thirty-three. A subsequent office in San Mateo, California, would later follow with distribution to the Midwest and to the East and West Coasts. The general manager and the executive vice president and CEO oversee the U.S.-based operations. The staff is divided into three categories: sales and marketing, administration, and technical. Four managers within the sales and marketing group are responsible for the East Coast, West Coast, Midwest, and commercial markets, respectively. The administrative group is responsible for inventory control, warehousing, and customer service. The last group helps act as a liaison between the customer and the dealer.

The first product to be introduced in the United States was the vacuum cleaner. Miele found that these products were easier to set up in the dealerships, and they also allowed for the simultaneous establishment of service centers. Miele soon introduced a full range of consumer major appliances including washing machines, dryers, stoves and fans/hoods, dishwashers, ovens, and microwaves. In recent years each product category has accounted for 45 percent of U.S. sales. The remaining 10 percent of total sales were attributed to commercial products. This category consists of commercial laundry equipment and laboratory washing equipment used for the sterilization of test tubes and various laboratory items.

Each product category was pushed through a different channel to the consumer. The vacuum cleaners were sold primarily to small vacuum cleaner dealers. The Miele sales force had to convince the dealer that carrying the higher priced Miele line would prove profitable. The consumer appliance line was distributed first to wholesalers and then to dealerships. Finally, the commercial washing equipment was sold to wholesalers only while the commercial laboratory washers were sold to wholesalers and directly to customers.

Before Miele even sold its first product in the United States, it realized that American consumers would ask: Who is Miele, and why should I buy its products? Name recognition was a problem that Miele no longer had to face in the European market. A recent study revealed the three most recognized brand names in Europe: Mercedes Benz ranked first, BMW was second, and Miele was third. All three names were associated with the highest quality available in their respective product categories. This reputation had been established over the course of 80 years, but unfamiliarity of the Miele name in the U.S. marketplace would prove to be a challenge the company would have to quickly overcome.

When entering new markets, Miele had always positioned its products as the highest priced, top-of-the-line models. It continued this practice in the United States. The top-of-the-line Kitchen Aide washer is priced around $900, while the Miele equivalent is priced between $1,500 and $2,000. The advertising Miele has undertaken reflects the quality and prestige associated with the Miele name. Publications such as *Town and Country* magazine and *Architectural Digest* carry these advertisements frequently to increase awareness and name recognition.

Growth in the United States was slow. However, Miele expected this because it placed much importance on detail and quality. Before selling/shipping Miele products to its dealers, the Miele staff trained the service people and the sales people in each location. The company's theories on customer

■ **EXHIBIT 40.4   A Display of Miele Appliances in a Hypermarket in Brussels**

satisfaction and personal selling were presented to the dealers to ensure the highest quality of service and technological understanding of the products.

The Next Decade

The 1990s will prove to be challenging and exciting for Miele. German re-unification could translate into a new source of profits if Miele can capitalize on this market effectively. While it has a good understanding of the consumer market and its many needs, it faces the challenge of selling to a group of consumers with limited resources.

New European markets are not limited just to the new Germany. They include Poland, Czechoslovakia, Hungary, and Romania. Miele is counting on its reputation in Western Europe and its strong presence in the western market to help boost its acceptance and sales in Eastern Europe.

Regardless of expansion strategy, Mr. Miele states his company's formula simply: Do your own thing, and do it well. Perhaps Miele has managed to do it better than well by doing it better than the competition.

Focal Topics

1. What cultural differences should Miele expect in selling to the American market compared to marketing in Europe? Will the top quality approach of Miele be as successful in the United States as in other parts of the world?

2. What market segments should be Miele's primary targets in the United States?

3. What distribution system should be used by Miele?

4. Develop a promotional program that should be used by Miele, including both media plan and creative strategy. How can Miele develop successfully the same image for quality in the United States as it has in Europe?

5. How can Miele enter successfully the Eastern European market?

■ ■ ■ ■ ■

Center Parcs

■ ■ ■ ■ ■

The year 1968 was a significant time in Europe, especially in Holland. It was the date identified by Allan Fuff in his book *Holland and the Ecological Landscapes* as the beginning of a new environmental movement. Holland in the late 1960s and 1970s became a mecca for environmental planners and landscape architects worldwide. The new landscapes, based on a philosophy of man's relationship to nature, established new images and new techniques, and set standards for landscape design and management that are now the accepted norm in a far more environmentally aware continent.

Land development and management needed a completely new outlook based on ecological principles. Recognizing this, it is no coincidence that the Center Parcs concept was soon developed in Holland. It responded to and helped shape the philosophy that man needs contact with nature for his well-being. Center Parcs was a unique concept in that it offered vacations close to nature in a forest setting, in a manner that embodied the very essence of these new principles. Often viewed as a concept before its time, Center Parcs was, in fact, a generator of ideas, setting new standards of environmental awareness and care in its approach and in its day-to-day operations.

Now, the management of Center Parcs faces a new challenge: the potential of entering the U.S. market. The magic of Disney has been transferred from the U.S. culture to Japan and Europe. The management of Center Parcs is studying how to bring the most successful vacation/resort concept in Europe to the United States.

The Center Parcs Concept

The Center Parcs concept began by responding to the problems experienced by people planning a vacation in Northern Europe's unpredictable climate. It recognized the changing patterns of vacations as leisure time among Europeans increased. The market grew for short break holidays to complement the traditional summer vacation.

The concept started in Holland in 1967 with a "villa in the forest" and has expanded into a unique holiday destination. The Center Parcs formula begins with the combination of high-quality accommodations and an extensive range of indoor and outdoor sports and leisure facilities. Then it adds a mix of restaurants, bars, and retail outlets, all set in a natural environment where woodland and water are considered essential elements. The aim is to create an escape from the hustle and bustle of everyday life and to be at one with nature, with its relaxing and restorative qualities.

Central to the Center Parcs concept is an extensive landscape setting of forest, glades, and water areas. It offers visitors the chance to enjoy contact with nature in a forest environment that absorbs people, buildings, and cars with minimal impact on the landscape.

The grounds include a large lake, forest, hotel with adjacent conference center, registration house, and central atrium. A layout of the grounds is shown in Exhibit 41.1. The atrium contains a tropical forest with stream and live birds, fish, and turtles. It also contains numerous restaurants of many different styles, various retail shops, a supermarket, a disco and open entertainment areas. This open area is used for nightly family entertainment. Guests can also use the indoor tennis courts, badminton courts, and bowling alleys in the atrium. But the atrium's main attraction is the "Subtropical Swimming Paradise," shown in Exhibit 41.2.

■ **EXHIBIT 41.1   Center Parcs's Graphics Layout**

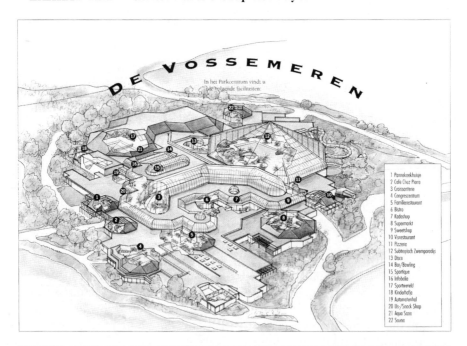

Courtesy of Center Parcs

■ **EXHIBIT 41.2   Center Parcs's Tropical Paradise**

Courtesy of Center Parcs

Guests enter the pool area and may use any of the amenities such as the wave pool, current pool, hot tubs, and water slides.

Guests stay in individual bungalows or in a small number of hotel rooms spread throughout the park area connected by roads and paths. Shuttle buses travel a frequent schedule throughout the park. Guests can rent bikes, which also allow people to travel throughout the grounds freely. Walking, however, is the preferred transportation mode for most guests.

Each bungalow has a kitchen, living room, dining area, fireplace, television, bathroom, shower room (separate from the room with the toilet, which is common in Europe), bedroom(s), and patio. There are no phones in the individual bungalows, but patrons can use public phones in the registration house.

The bungalows tend to have an open structural feel with modern decor. Depending on the size of the party, bungalows have between two and four bedrooms. The bedrooms feature single beds that can be pushed together to accommodate couples rather than queen or king size beds. This makes it easier to accommodate a larger number of people in the bungalow who wish to sleep separately. The kitchens are equipped with a stove, sink, and cooking and eating utensils. The shower room has a sink with a vanity and mirror and a large whirlpool bathtub with a shower head. The living area contains nice, not luxurious, furniture and opens out onto the patio overlooking the park or the lake. The patio comes equipped with lawn furniture and a grill for summer cookouts. A complete list of items furnished by Center Parcs is shown in Exhibit 41.3.

Guest Services and Facilities

Center Parcs tries to have something to appeal to everyone. Regardless of age or degree of physical fitness, guests easily find things to keep them occupied and happy for weeks. A complete list of Center Parcs facilities are shown in Exhibit 41.4. Different parks offer different combinations of facilities to their guests.

The European Center Parcs do not offer maid service during guests' visits; however, a cleaning service is provided before new guests occupy the bungalows. Guests are asked to complete some simple tasks to help in the cleaning process before they leave, including turning the refrigerator to the lowest setting, turning off the central heating, taking the trash out and placing it in the large containers, and stripping the beds and folding the blankets and sheets.

Restaurants

Center Parcs offers its visitors a variety of restaurants and snack shops from which to choose. The atrium contains a higher priced, fancy restaurant where a couple can enjoy a romantic dinner; a few family-style restaurants, one full service and one buffet style; an Italian restaurant; a

I N V E N T O R Y - L I S T

Living room

Item	VM61	VM62	VM63
Armchair	2	2	2
Ashtray	2	1	1
Coffee table	2	1	1
Colour TV	1	1	1
Poker	1	1	1
Radio	1	1	1
Sofa	1	1	1
Vase	1	1	1

Bedrooms

Item	VM61	VM62	VM63
Beds	8	6	4
Bedside tables	6	5	4
Bible	1	1	1
Blankets	16	12	8
Coat hangers	20	16	12
Dressing table stool	1	1	1
Mattresses	8	6	4
Mattress cover	8	6	4
Pillows and pillow cases	10	8	6
Undersheets	8	6	4

Kitchen

Item	VM61	VM62	VM63
Bin	1	1	1
Gas cooker	1	1	1
Ice cube tray	1	1	1
Refrigerator	1	1	1

Dining area

Item	VM61	VM62	VM63
Dining chairs	10	8	6
Dining table	1	1	1

Patio

Item	VM61	VM62	VM63
Patio chairs	8	6	4
Patio table	1	1	1

Cutlery (Kitchen)

Item	VM61	VM62	VM63
Bottle opener	1	1	1
Bread knife	1	1	1
Carving fork	1	1	1
Cheese slicer	1	1	1
Corkscrew	1	1	1
Cucumber slicer	1	1	1
Dessert spoons	12	10	8
Forks	12	10	8
Knives	12	10	8
Potato serving spoon	1	1	1
Sauce ladle	1	1	1
Scissors	1	1	1
Soup ladle	1	1	1
Spatula	1	1	1
Spoons	12	10	8
Teaspoons	12	10	8
Vegetable spoon	1	1	1

Crockery (Kitchen)

Item	VM61	VM62	VM63
Breakfast plates	12	10	8
Cups and saucers	12	10	8
Dinner plates	12	10	8
Plates/soup bowls	12	10	8

Glassware (Kitchen)

Item	VM61	VM62	VM63
Aperitif glasses	12	10	8
Dessert glasses	12	10	8
Duralex dishes	3	3	3
Lemon squeezer	1	1	1
Sherry glasses	8	6	4
Teapot	1	1	1
Tumblers	8	6	6
Wine glasses	8	6	4

Pans (Kitchen)

Item	VM61	VM62	VM63
Casserole - 24 cm	1	1	1
Casserole - 28 cm	1	–	1
Frying pan - 28 cm	1	–	1
Milk pan - 14 cm	1	1	1
Milk pan	1	1	1
Saucepan 24 cm	1	1	1
Saucepan 22 cm	1	1	1
Saucepan 20 cm	1	1	1
Saucepan 18 cm	1	1	1

Children's furniture (in storage area)

Item	VM61	VM62	VM63
Child's bed and mattress	1	1	1
High chair	1	1	1
Playpen	1	1	1

Miscellaneous (Kitchen)

Item	VM61	VM62	VM63
Bread basket	1	1	1
Bread bin	1	1	1
Bread board	1	1	1
Coffee pot	1	1	1
Coffee maker	1	1	1
Colander	1	1	1
Draining board	1	1	1
Egg cups	12	10	8
Kettle	1	1	1
Milk jug	1	1	1
Potato peeler	1	1	1
Potato masher	1	1	1
Simmer plate	1	1	1
Storage tins	3	3	3
Sugar bowl	1	1	1
Table mats	3	3	3
Tin opener	1	1	1
Tray	1	1	1
Washing-up bowl	1	1	1
Washing-up brush	1	1	1
Whisk	1	1	1
Wooden spoon with hole	1	1	1
Wooden spoon	1	1	1

Miscellaneous (Bathroom)

Item	VM61	VM62	VM63
Bucket with lid	1	1	1
Drying rack	1	1	1
Potty	1	1	1
Toilet set	2	2	1
Waste bin	1	1	1

Miscellaneous (Storage room/Bathroom)

Item	VM61	VM62	VM63
Broom	1	1	1
Carpet sweeper	1	1	1
Cleaning pack	1	1	1
Dustpan and brush	1	1	1
Feather duster + pole	1	1	1
Shopping trolley	1	1	1
Sponge	1	1	1
Vacuum cleaner	1	1	1
Window wiper	1	1	1

- **EXHIBIT 41.4   Facilities at a Glance**

FACILITIES AT A GLANCE

FACILITIES	EH	HB	HH	KV	LB	MD	VB	EP	VM	BF
SUBTROPICAL SWIMMING PARADISE										
Jacuzzi	●	●	●	●	●	●	●	●	●	●
Outdoor pool	●	●	●	●	●	●	●	●	●	●
Wave pool	●	●	●	●	●	●	●	●	●	●
Hot-Whirlpool	●	●	●	●	●	●	●	●	●	●
Jungle River					●					
Babies and toddlers pool		●								
Cold plunge pool	●	●	●	●	●	●	●	●	●	
Herbal bath						●				
Rapid tanner	●	●	●	●	●	●	●	●	●	
Solarium	●	●	●	●	●	●	●	●	●	●
Children's pool	●	●	●	●	●	○	●	●	●	
Rippling rapids	●	●			●	●		●	●	
Water slide	●	●		●	●	●		●	●	
Water slide, indoor-outdoor		●		●	●	●		●	●	
Water slope								●	●	
Waterfall	●	●	●		●	●		●	●	
Competition pool			●							
Cascade	●	●	●					●	●	
Wild water cave	●		●	●						
Sun lounge	●	●					●	●		
Salt water pool	●						●			
Swimmers' snack bar	●	●	●	●	●	●	●	●		
Swimmers' bar	●	●	●	●	●	●	●	●	●	
Swimmers' bar in the water						●				
SAUNA AND FITNESS										
Hot whirlpool	●	●	●	●				●	●	
Floatarium	●									●
Facial tanner	●		●				●	●		
Karwendel	●							●	●	
Roman sauna	●									
Sauna	●	●	●	●	●	●	●	●	●	
Sauna bar	●							●		
Sauna garden	●			●		●	●	●		
Sauna garden with jacuzzi	●	●	●				●			
Sauna log cabin			●							
Rapid tanner	●	●		●		●		●	●	
Thalasso	●							●	●	
Turkish bath	●	●	●	●	●	●	●	●	●	
Solarium	●	●		●		●	●	●	●	●
SPORTS										
Badminton	●	●		●		●		●	●	
Basketball				●	●	●	●			
Catamaran	●									
BMX track	●	●	●	●		●		●	●	
Fitness room	●	●	●	●		●		●	●	
Golf									●	
Archery	●	●		●	●	●		●	●	
Marina	○									
Canoeing	○	○	○	○				●	○	
Riding school	30km	●		5km	250m	5km	10km	5km	25km	
Horse riding		●								
Horse stables		●			250m		7km			●
Roller skating							●			
Snooker	●	●	●	●	●			●	●	
Sports café	●	●		●	●	●		●		
Sports hall	●	●		●	●	●		●	●	
Sports field	●	●			●	●		●		
Squash	●	●		●		●		●	●	
Windsurf storage	○	○		○		○		○		
Windsurf hire/Windsurf school	○	○		●		○		○		
Tennis (indoor)	●	●		●		●		●		
Tennis (outdoor)	●	●	●	●	●	●		●	●	
Tennis practice wall						●				
Tennis school										
Jogging track	●			●		●	●	●	●	
Fitness training						●				
Football field	●				●		●	●	●	
Volleyball	●	●		●	●	●		●		
Waterskiing	○									
Watersports	●	●	●	●		●			●	●
Sailing dinghy hire	○		○							
Sailing school	○									

FACILITIES	EH	HB	HH	KV	LB	MD	VB	EP	VM	BF
RESTAURANTS										
Bar/Bowling	●	●	●	●	●	●	●	●	●	●
Bar										
Bistro	●		●	●	●	●	●	●	●	●
Reception rooms	●		●	●	●	●		●	●	●
Café Chez Pierre	●	●	●	●	●		●	●	●	●
Conference centre		●	●	●	●	●		●	●	●
Croissanterie	●		●						●	●
Gelateria		●	●							
Lagoon Bar			●							
Music bar/Disco	●	●		●	●		●	●	●	●
Pancake house	●	●		●	●	●	●	●	●	●
Pizzeria	●	●		●	●	●	●	●	●	●
Plaza/Family Restaurant	●	●		●	●	●	●	●	●	●
Rising Sun restaurant	●			●						
Sports café	●	●		●		●		●		
Grill (Steak Restaurant)	●	●								
Fish restaurant									●	●
Snacks and ices	●	●	●	●	●	●	●	●	●	●
Swimmers' bar	●	●		●	●	●		●	●	
Swimmers' snack bar	●	●	●	●	●	●	●	●	●	●
SHOPS AND SERVICES										
Car wash	●							1km		
Chemist	●									
Bank/Change	★		●	●		●	●	●	●	●
Petrol	●	10km	2km	2km	3km	4km		1km	4km	7km
Bakery	●		●	●	●	●		●	★	●
Boutique								●	●	●
Bijouterie	●		●	●		●		●	●	●
Hairdresser								●	●	●
Post Office	●									
Safe deposit boxes	●	●	●	●	●	●	●	●	●	●
Butcher	●	●	●	●	●	●	●	●	●	●
Off-Licence	●	●	●	●	●	●	●	●	●	●
Sportique	●	●	●	●	●	●	●	●	●	●
Supermarket	●	●	●	●	●	●	●	●	●	●
Sweet shop	●	●	●	●	●	●	●	●	●	●
Launderette	●	●	●	●	●	●	●	●	●	●
Gift shop	●	●	●	●	●	●	●	●	●	●
RELAXATION										
Arcade games	●	●	●	●	●	●	●	●	●	●
Baby-sitting service	●	●	●	●	●	●	●	●	●	●
Billiards	●	●	●	●	●	●	●	●	●	●
Bingo	●	●		●	●		●	●	●	●
Woods	●	●	●		●	●	●	●	●	●
Tenpin bowling	●	●		●	●		●	●	●	●
Darts	●	●		●	●		●	●	●	●
Bicycle hire	●	●	●	●	●	●	●	●	●	●
Deer sanctuary	●	●		●	●	●	●			
Petanque	●	●		●	●	●	●	●		
Children's zoo				●				★		
Kindergarten (3-12 years)	●	●		●	●		●	●		●
Mini-golf	●	●		●		●		●	●	●
Bar/Disco	●	●		●		●		●	●	●
Rowing boat hire			○		●					
Playground	●	●		●	●	●	●	●	●	●
Playing field	●	●		●	●	●		●	●	●
Game and toy hire	●							●	●	●
Table tennis	●	★		●	●	●		●	●	●
Video network	●	●		●	●	●		●	●	●
Fishing	●	●	●		200m	●	3km	2km	●	●
Pedaloes	●	○	○	○		○	○	○	○	○
Beach (lakeside)	●	●		●		●		●	●	
OTHER FACILITIES										
Garage								●		
Canine toilet	●	●	●	●	●	●	●	●	●	●
Hotel									●	●
Information desk	●	●		●	●	●	●	●	●	●
Chapel		●		●	●	●	●	●		
Church			●	●	●	●	●	●		
Parc Plaza	●		●	●	●	●	●		●	●
Conference facilities	●		●	●	●	●	●	●	●	●
Reception facilities	●	●	●	●	●	●	●	●	●	●

EH - DE EEMHOF (NL), HB - HET HEIJDERBOS (NL), HH - DE HUTTENHEUGTE (NL), KV - DE KEMPERVENNEN (NL), LB - DE LOMMERBERGEN (NL), MD - HET MEERDAL (NL), VB - HET VENNENBOS (NL), EP - ERPERHEIDE (B), VM - DE VOSSEMEREN (B), BF - LES BOIS FRANCS (F), ● = AVAILABLE ○ = IN THE SEASON ★ = UNDER CONSTRUCTION

14

seafood restaurant; a Belgian waffle house; and a fast food restaurant with dining facilities. Most of these restaurants are casual to conform to the vacation mode of its guests. One restaurant is designated as an international theme restaurant, where dining gives guests an experience in a different country each night.

Center Parcs provides its guests with yet another food alternative. All guests are invited to shop in the park's grocery store. Guests are able to buy items to prepare in their bungalows for meals or snacks. It gives guests the option to dine in privacy, buy exactly what they want, prepare it as they like, and save on the dining costs of their vacation. The grocery store has its own bakery where many guests buy their breakfast rolls fresh from the oven.

Center Parcs must decide how to best service its U.S. location. it has two primary strategies from which to choose. It can contract with its European suppliers to service and supply its U.S. location, or it can contract with U.S. equivalents.

In the past Center Parcs has been very successful at establishing its own restaurants and retail shops on its park grounds. It manages its own restaurant and retail shops and operates them as profit centers for the parks. This includes hiring and training all employees. With this strategy, Center Parcs controls all of the activities of the profit centers and also keeps all of the profits.

Center Parcs might reduce risk related to entering the U.S. market, however, by forming strategic alliances with established and reputable suppliers of services and products. By contracting with restaurant and grocery chains and food service companies, compliance with local regulations and customs will be simplified. Strategic alliances might be formed with a variety of companies including family restaurants, fast food restaurants, snack shops, a grocery chain, and retail outlets.

Sport Facilities

Center Parcs offers its guest a wide variety of sports activities. The swimming pool equipped with water slides and wave pools is the most popular among guests of all ages. The current streams take daring swimmers on a ride through part of the indoor facility and then outside through part of the park. Swimmers are finally "deposited" back inside the tropical atrium. The indoor atrium also houses four tennis courts and numerous badminton courts, complete with changing rooms and shower facilities.

Nature provides the largest playground for Center Parcs guests. Walking, jogging, and biking on the many trails are the most popular activity. People of all ages can be found during most times of the day and early evenings enjoying the atmosphere of the park. In the summer, it is possible to rent rowboats and venture out onto the man-made lakes within the park grounds.

Center Parcs has reserved a park area for its younger guests. In addition to the traditional playgrounds found in most parks, Center Parcs has added a dirt bike trail for exclusive use by children. They can rent the dirt bikes and protective gear and ride up and down hills, and with parental permission, learn to jump small hills. Although some of these facilities might pose potential harm to some of the abusers of the equipment or facilities, Center Parcs does not staff these areas with personnel. Parents are responsible for their children and are expected to watch them. This is accepted and preferred among European families.

A similar policy exists in the water areas. Very few staff persons are present in the pool area because guests and parents are expected to be responsible for their own safety rather than rely on lifeguards, starters, or others to "police" activities as is often done in the United States.

Green Roots

In contrast to other companies which have only recently realized that green issues are here to stay, Center Parcs's consistently fine environmental record stands alone. Its twelve established villages in the Netherlands, Belgium, France, and Britain provide proof of the standards it sets in environmental care, design innovation, and quality control. Pollution control, recycling of materials, and use of natural resources are important concepts in the design and management of the parks.

Center Parcs has revolutionized the European leisure market. With its introduction of short breaks in forest settings, it attracts discerning guests seeking quality, choice, and close contact with nature. Of paramount importance to Center Parcs is the quality of the forest environment provided—its visual beauty and wildlife diversity. Indeed, nature is the catalyst, the key element that makes the Center Parcs philosophy unique.

One goal of Center Parcs is to bring people and nature together. It manages forest environments that provide not only for a relaxing vacation experience, but which also protect and enrich the countryside. Through its role in creating new habitats, Center Parcs is widely recognized as a beneficial force for nature conservation. It prides itself on its obsession with environmental quality, landscape protection, and nature conservation.

Center Parcs wants to ensure that it maintains its leading position in the area of environmental awareness. The Board of Directors of Center Parcs International has appointed an in-house team, with representatives of each country and from each operational discipline, to coordinate research into new methods of design and construction, the use of environmentally sustainable materials, the continued improvement of habitat management, and the setting of energy conservation standards and quality of water supplies. The team is supported by a professional staff consisting of architects, landscape architects, interior designers, and energy, heating, and water specialists.

The environmental development team has direct responsibility for enhancing the design concept as suggested by research and incorporating new innovations into the village design, including major facilities such as the Subtropical Swimming Paradise, the Parc Plaza, and the sports complex. Funding environmental research that leads to product improvement and continued reinvestment in existing Center Parc villages has been and continues to be a priority for Center Parcs. This ensures that Center Parcs will stay ahead of the increasing demand for higher standards of quality of both the facilities and the environment in which they are set.

Entering the United States

Center Parcs has been very successful in its European locations in the last 25 years. With parks in the Netherlands, Belgium, France, and England, Center Parcs is planning to expand into other European countries and the United States.

Center Parcs is planning on entering the United States in 1993 with its first location in the upper regions of New York state. It has a number of options in adapting to its new environment, and there are many specific areas to consider modifying, such as the bungalows, the common park area, and the retail area. Center Parcs could choose to change its concept to be more American so that the attractions and facilities will be more familiar to American patrons. Or Center Parcs might choose to remain "European" to gain a unique position in the market.

There are many issues Center Parcs is considering before entering the U.S. market. It is through the development and implementation of a long-term strategy for the U.S. market that Center Parcs will achieve long-term success. Its strategic plan will address the competitive environment, differences between the U.S. and European markets, and positioning strategies.

Center Parcs's U.S. Competitors

In identifying potential competitors, Center Parcs is examining *similar* vacation destinations because there are no competitors at this time that offer the same mix of facilities and services that Center Parcs does. Broadly defined, Center Parcs will compete with many organizations for U.S. consumers' vacation dollars and time. A partial list of such competitive forms of vacations might include:

- Federal and state parks
- Amusement parks
- Weekends at hotels
- Aquatic parks such as Sea World
- Water parks such as Wet 'n Wild
- State fairs
- Camps for children

While all of these facilities and activities compete for consumers' time and money, many other such competitors exist. Some indirect competitors for these consumer resources include families choosing to stay home to spend time with family. Consumers may also choose to spend their dollars on products to enhance their leisure time, such as sports equipment, boats, or recreational vehicles.

Center parcs recognizes that there exist some parks that might enter this specific market and become direct competitors by expanding their current facilities. Potential entrants might include Disney, state parks, and various water park facilities. By adding lodging and other family sport facilities they would compete more directly with the Center Parcs concept.

Differences between the United States and Europe

Center Parcs is currently identifying and understanding the similarities and differences between the European and U.S. markets in order to identify necessary modifications of the Center Parcs concept.

Family and Children   The U.S. family unit and the importance it places on children differs from its European counterpart. Americans go on vacation to escape from everyday life, including the problems and demands of their children; therefore, they often leave the children at home rather than take them along or enroll them in "Camp Hyatt" or programs offered by other hotels designed to relieve parents of the needs to be with their children most of the time.

The number of families that are including their children in their vacation plans may be increasing, as may be the importance of family among many consumers. Yet, many parents do not know what to do with their children if they do take them on family vacations.

Working Women   There are more and more women entering the work force everyday and, consequently, the trend toward domesticity has declined rapidly. While there is a similar trend in Europe today, it is not as profound as in the United States. Vacation is a time when the woman of the house wants to be pampered, so she can relax and enjoy her family. Some of the women visiting Center Parcs, however, will not be working women, and their needs and desires may differ from those of the working women.

Elderly   Members of this group tend to be less active than their European counterparts. On average they have relatively high disposable incomes and have the time to vacation. Because they tend to be more sedentary than other markets, they represent the market that might spend a whole week at the parks. While this market tends to be in good health and claims to be more interested in health than in the past, it is not as physically active as the European 65+ age group. While older Europeans are accustomed to walking or riding bikes to the store or for exercise, Americans are not.

Positioning

Center Parcs is considering two different positioning strategies for its U.S. parks: *price positioning and attitudinal positioning.* Price positioning is effective in creating a position of a product or service in the minds of various consumers based on price. In many ways, Center Parcs combines the "return to nature" appeal of camping or visiting parks with the creature comforts and facilities of good hotels. Prices are typically substantially less than resort hotels but more than would be paid for camping in federal or state parks. A major decision facing Center Parcs is how to position the park with respect to price.

Attitudinal positioning emphasizes activities and amenities of Center Parcs to create an image of the park in the mind of consumers, regardless of demographic profile. Regardless of positioning strategy, Center Parcs has focused on what consumers really buy when they visit the park—an *escape from urban reality*, which includes nature, convenience, and fun. Management faces decisions about how to position the park with respect to luxury, the environment, and values relating to family, nature, and perhaps even philosophical (conservational, spiritual) values.

Center Parcs hopes to appeal to many groups of U.S. consumers. They can traditionally be identified in terms of demographics, lifestyles, and psychographics. A study recently completed by Erdos & Morgen identified four distinct groups of frequent leisure travelers, those who have taken five or more leisure trips in the past 3 years and have an income over $35,000 per year. These groups are as follows.

Adventure Enthusiasts With an average age of 43 and an average household income of $65,400, this group makes up 17 percent of the frequent leisure travelers. They averaged 19 trips in the last 3 years and prefer shorter, less expensive trips, often visiting country bed-and-breakfast inns.

Country Club Set This group makes up 14 percent of frequent travelers and is the most affluent of all leisure travelers with an average income of $77,200 per year. They are only a few months older than the "Adventure Enthusiasts" but take longer and more expensive trips, often fly First Class, and stay at first-rate hotels. They are most likely to stay at beach resorts, where many of them golf.

City Sophisticates With an average age of 54, this segment accounts for 15 percent of the total frequent leisure traveler market. Because many are retired, they have the time to enjoy longer trips than the younger groups and the money (an average of $65,300 per household) to enjoy overseas travel.

Family Fun This is the largest segment, 36 percent, of the total leisure traveler market. This group has the lowest household income of the identified groups ($56,900), is somewhat older than the enthusiasts (47), and spends less than half as much as the others on travel. They take fewer and shorter trips, often travel by car, stay in economy motels, and visit friends and family.

Center Parcs is able to segment its market in many ways, not restricted just to the groups listed. While these groups seem important to Center Parcs, it also targets more conventional markets based on age, interest, and other demographical and psychographical information. In Europe, some Center Parcs include excellent meeting facilities and attract small conventions and strategic planning "retreat" types of meetings by business firms and associations. Since some parks include a chapel and prices of accommodations are modest when bungalows are shared by several people, parks attract a number of religious organizations for group meetings and retreats.

Marketing Considerations

Center Parcs is committed to a strong consumer orientation. It frequently conducts consumer research on how to improve its parks, its facilities, and its services. A typical questionnaire used for surveying current customers is shown in Exhibit 41.5

Center Parcs believes it has the ability to build a strong business in the American market with the proper marketing. It is considering the best locations for the first parks in the United States and is committed to purchasing the first locations in Pennsylvania, New Jersey, or New York, probably within easy driving distance of New York City and Philadelphia.

Management is examining various marketing efforts to make the parks successful. Decisions must be made concerning advertising, pricing, and other sales and marketing elements in a total marketing program. These efforts might include cross bookings between European and U.S. Center Parcs locations. The company must also decide if it should use the same name and logo as used in Europe or whether adaptation is needed for the U.S. market.

Some of the most important decisions concern design of the parks to be most effective in the U.S. markets. What modifications, if any, will be needed in the bungalows? What price and attitudinal positioning strategies should be used to serve American lifestyles? What types of merchandising facilities and strategies should be employed? What strategies should be used with respect to food operations? These are just a few of the issues faced by Center Parcs's management in its attempts to translate a highly successful concept in Europe to the American market.

Focal Topics

1. Should Center Parcs adopt an American theme when it enters or should it remain "European"? How might Center Parcs adapt to the U.S. market? Which specific areas should be changed?

2. Who are the primary target markets for Center Parcs? On which basis would you segment the market?

■ EXHIBIT 41.5   Center Parcs Customer Survey

Bungalow-Park / *Nom du Parc* / Bungalowpark:

Bungalow-Nummer / *Numéro du bungalow* / Bungalownumber:

Ankunftsdatum / *Date d'arrivée* / Date of arrival:

1. Wie oft waren Sie früher bereits in einem unserer Bungalowparke? / *Combien de séjours avez-vous déjà faits dans un de nos Parcs?* / How often have you already been to one of our bungalowparks?

0x	1x	2x	3x	4x	5x	6x	7x	8x	9x	10x ou plus or more
										oder mehr

2. Wenn ja, in welchem Jahr und in welchem Monat? / *Si oui, quelle est l'année de votre dernier séjour et le mois?* / If so, in what year was your last visit and in what month?

Monat / *Mois* / Month _____ Jahr / *Année* / Year 19____

---

*Bitte zutreffendes ankreuzen.
*Cocher les bonnes cases.
*Please mark what is applicable

	sehr gut / excellent / excellent	gut / bien / good	mässig / moyen / moderate	schlecht / mauvais / bad
Rezeption / *Réception* / Reception — 1				
Bungalow-Ausstattung / *Confort du bungalow* / Bungalow comfort — 2				
Familien-Restaurant / *Restaurant des familles* / Family-Restaurant — 3				
Bistro / *Bistro - Restaurant à la carte* / Bistro — 4				
Café Chez Pierre / *Café Chez Pierre* / Café Chez Pierre — 5				
Sportique / *Magasin de Sport* / Sportique — 6				
Eis - Snackladen / *Snack -Glacier* / Icecream - Snackshop — 7				
Pfannkuchenhäuschen / *Crêperie* / Pancake restaurant — 8				
Bowling / *Bar - Bowling* / Ten pin-Bowling — 9				
Schwimm-Paradies / *Paradis Aquatique* / Tropical / Swimming paradise — 10				
Supermarkt / *Supermarché* / Supermarket — 11				
Allgem. Eindruck Personal / *Accueil du personnel* / General impression personnel — 12				
Sauberkeit Park / *Proprieté du parc* / Tidiness of the park — 13				

Bitte hier notieren, was Sie als "mäßig" oder "schlecht" empfunden haben. / *Par quoi avez-vous été deçus.* / Please give details of your moderate or bad experiences.

Was kann man noch verbesseren? Und Wie? / *Avez-vous des suggestions?* / Comments, wishes, suggestions?

Welche (Freizeit)-Angebote möchten Sie zusätzlich haben? / *De quelles installations supplémentaires souhaiteriez-vous profiter?* / Which facilities would you like to be added to our park?

	ja / oui / yes	nein / non / no
3. Kommen Sie noch einmal in diesen Park zurück? / *Reviendrez-vous dans ce Parc?* / Will you come to this park again?		
4. In einen anderen Park? / *Irez-vous dans un autre de nos Parcs?* / Will you come again to one of the other parks?		
5. Beabsichtigen Sie, im nächsten Jahr zurückzukommen? / *Avez-vous l'intention de revenir l'année prochaine?* / Do you intend to come back next year?		

6. Welche (Freizeit)-Angebote haben Sie - oder einer der anderen Bungalowbewohner genutzt? (sofern vorhanden) / *De quelle installations avez-vous profité? (si présent)* / Did you or any of the other bungalowguests make use of? (if available)

	ja / oui / yes	nein / non / no
a. Sporthalle / *Halle des Sports* / Sports Hall		
b. Sauna - Türk. Dampfbad / *Sauna - bain turc* / Sauna - Turk. steambath		
c. Tennis-, Squash / *Tennis - squash* / Tennis-, Squash		
d. Fahrradverleih / *Location de bicyclettes* / Bicycle renting		
e. Bowling / *Bowling* / Bowlingalley		
f. Minigolf / *Mini-golf* / Crazy mini golf		
g. Tretboot / *Pédalo* / Peddalos		
h. Kindergarten / *Jardin d'enfants* / Childrens playsch.		
i. Freizeitprogramm / *Animation (spectacles, tournois...)* / Entertainment programme		

---

3. What type of positioning strategy should Center Parcs adopt? How is the decision process of consumers affected by different strategies?

4. How would you alter for the U.S. market the list of specific activities and facilities Center Parcs offers? Suggest specific services to add to or delete from the Center Parcs offerings in the United States.

5. Is the market for week-long vacations the same in the United States as it is in Europe? Why might the week-long stays be more popular in Europe? What should the strategy of Center Parcs be with respect to weekend and week-long bookings?

■ ■ ■ ■ ■

Bank One of Columbus

■ ■ ■ ■ ■

By 1993, Banc One Corporation had moved into the lofty circle of the top ten banks in America based on assets, the result of one of the most impressive records of growth and profitability of any bank in the nation. Starting from a position in the 1960s as the smallest of three banks in the midwestern city of Columbus, Ohio, the bank had passed all others in the nation for the continuous record of increasing profits and dividends. Imaginative and aggressive policies and programs designed to improve customer service have earned the bank notoriety and have allowed it to excel financially. As executive management ponders the future, it realizes the bank must become even more aggressive and creative in the twenty-first century to continue competing as a national banking leader in an ever increasing deregulated environment.

Background

Bank One, Columbus, NA (formerly known as City National Bank), has served the residents and businesses of central Ohio since 1868. As a result of several consolidations in the early 1920s, the bank became the third largest in its area.

In 1968, City National applied for and received permission to establish First Banc Group of Ohio, a registered bank holding company. The spelling of "Banc" was dictated by a regulation prohibiting nonbanking institutions from including the designation "Bank" in their names. During its first decade, the corporation grew to include sixteen banks throughout the state, with total assets exceeding $2 billion.

In the late 1970s, management decided to standardize the names of all member banks, which had kept their original names after affiliating with First Banc Group. In 1979, First Banc Group changed its name to Banc One Corporation and each member bank became the Bank One in its area.

Banc One Corporation was able to acquire a number of profitable and very well managed affiliate banks because of its unique philosophy of running a corporation. (See Exhibit 42.1.) This philosophy, called the "Uncommon Partnership," allowed member banks to continue operating relatively autonomously in their communities. The corporation consolidated data processing and marketing functions but left the management of "people" issues up to the individual banks. In addition, the banks maintained their own Boards of Directors and continued to make virtually all lending decisions. In essence, the "Uncommon Partnership" allowed member banks to enjoy the economies of scale of a national banking organization while offering them the ability to operate on a relatively independent basis.

Banc One Today

By the end of 1987, Banc One Corporation had become the largest banking organization in Ohio, and by the end of 1992, it became the seventh largest in the nation. Today, with more than $76 billion in assets, Banc One operates 60 banks with over 1,300 offices in Arizona, Colorado, Indiana, Illinois, Kentucky, Michigan, Ohio, Texas, Utah, West Virginia, and Wisconsin.

Since 1970, Banc One has ranked among the ten most profitable banking organizations in the country. Net operating income before taxes for Banc One Corporation increased from about $15.5 million in 1968, to more than $514 million in 1991. During that time, earnings per share increased from $1.61 to $2.91. (Exhibit 42.2 provides a financial summary of Banc One Corporation for 1991.)

Targeting a New Market—The Plan

In 1960, executive management developed a new banking strategy. It decided to focus on researching and developing new products and services for the majority of consumers. At the time, this consumer segment of the market virtually was being ignored by most banks, which were concentrating their efforts on developing larger corporate account relationships with businesses and trust customers. Management believed Banc One's new focus would prompt rapid growth and new profitability among its member banks.

This strategic decision caused a number of major changes for Bank One. First, management had to develop a staff that was knowledgeable in data processing and marketing, as well as in brokerage, insurance, and retailing. Management knew that to maximize return on stockholder equity, it would have to consider entering these other financially related businesses.

Second, management decided to allocate up to 3 percent of yearly net earnings toward research and development of new products and services, becoming one of very few banks in the country to actually earmark money for future ventures. With this financial provision in place, there was easy access to funds for experimenting with new ideas and services.

■ EXHIBIT 42.1   Banc One Corporation and Subsidiaries: Affiliates

Affiliates

Banc One Ohio Corporation			Banc One Indiana Corporation	Banc One Wisconsin Corporation*	
28 Affiliates headquartered in:			12 Affiliates headquartered in:	22 Affiliates headquartered in:	
Ohio	Michigan	Kentucky	Indiana	Wisconsin	Illinois
Akron	East Lansing	Lexington	Bloomington	Antigo	Chicago
Alliance	Fenton		Carmel	Appleton	
Ashland	Sturgis		Crawfordsville	Beaver Dam	
Athens	Ypsilanti*		Elkhart	Campbellsport	
Cambridge			Franklin	Clintonville	
Cleveland			Indianapolis	Elkhorn	
Columbus			Lafayette	Freedom	
Coshocton			Marion	Green Bay	
Dayton			Merrillville	Janesville	
Dover			Plainfield	Larsen	
Fremont			Rensselaer	Madison	
Lima			Richmond	Mequon	
Mansfield				Milwaukee	
Marion				Monroe	
Middletown				Neenah	
Milford				Oshkosh	
Portsmouth				Racine	
Sidney				Seymour	
Steubenville				Stevens Point	
Wapakoneta				Waukesha	
Wooster				West Bend	
Youngstown					
Bank One Trust Company					

*Affiliations Pending

Non Bank Affiliates

BANC ONE BROKERAGE
CORPORATION
BANC ONE CREDIT CORPORATION
BANC ONE FINANCIAL SERVICES,
INC.
BANC ONE LEASING CORPORATION
BANC ONE MORTGAGE
CORPORATION
BANC ONE SERVICES CORPORATION

Stockholder Services

Stock Transfer, Dividend Paying and
Dividend Reinvestment Agent:

BANC ONE INDIANAPOLIS, NA
Security Holder Services
111 Monument Circle
Indianapolis, IN 46277
(317) 639-8110

Stock Listing

New York Stock Exchange: BncOne
Ticker Symbol: ONE

Financial Information

1987 financial statements have
been filed with the Securities and
Exchange Commission. The proxy
statement for the annual meeting
will include complete financial reports and the Annual Report Form
10-K. It will be mailed to all stock-
holders of record in March. Investors
desiring additional financial information should direct inquiries to:

Treasurer
BANC ONE CORPORATION
100 East Broad Street
Columbus, OH 43271-0251

This philosophy worked well, and the corporation soon generated a reputation as one of the most innovative new service developers in the country.

Marketing

Executive management also realized that Bank One would have to recruit and develop a fully functioning marketing department. Prior to 1960, few banks in the country had even considered the importance of marketing in their operations. Only a handful of banks had an advertising manager, and even fewer had staff to perform marketing functions.

At Bank One, a marketing staff was hired and initially charged with two main responsibilities. First, the staff would develop advanced services for all potential market segments. This included services for primary customers, as well as services that could be sold to other financially related businesses. Second, it would develop advanced delivery systems for those services. The staff's only restriction was to concentrate its efforts on programs that immediately could be offered from a regulatory point of view.

Advertising

One of the first steps in the development of a marketing function was to hire an advertising manager who could create a new and distinctive image for the bank. The resulting advertising and promotional campaign soon became recognized as one of the most successful bank promotional efforts in the country. Bank One's advertising strategy was initially "product oriented" but eventually shifted to become more "positioning" in nature. (An example of Bank One advertising is included in Exhibit 42.3.)

Advertising soon became crucial for banks. Deregulation, and the introduction of electronic delivery systems for businesses and consumers, had changed basic customer behavior patterns. Because banks could no longer count on potential customers walking into a lobby and asking about new products or services, the total marketing structure and communications process had to be adjusted.

Banc One launched a major advertising and marketing campaign in March 1992, designed to stimulate consumer and small business loans. The television, radio, outdoor, and newspaper ads revolve around the central theme "whatever it takes" to help people with their borrowing needs. Banc One budgeted over $10 million for advertising and related marketing activities in seven states to increase its market share.

One of the 60-second television commercials features an employee who recognized the special needs of some of her branch's deaf customers. The employee used her sign language skills to assist them. The second commercial tells the story of a loan officer who spent Thanksgiving Day in the office to help military personnel take care of their finances before leaving for Operation Desert Shield. Both spots are based on true stories relayed by Banc One employees and are designed to highlight the dedication and special services of its associates.

■ **EXHIBIT 42.2   Banc One Corporation Financial Statements**

BANC ONE CORPORATION
Columbus, Ohio

Consolidated Key Financial Data Summary
Full Year and Fourth Quarter 1991

The columns below labeled "Consolidated" include Bank One, Texas, NA fully consolidated beginning October 1, 1991 to reflect the purchase of the remaining FDIC-owned shares in October for $367 million. The columns labeled "Texas Equity Basis" reflect the investment in Texas and recognition of BANC ONE's share of the Texas income assuming the equity method of accounting had been used for the periods indicated to facilitate comparison with 1990 amounts. Data in 1991 include four Ohio banks from the date of purchase in September 1991 which had total assets approximating $2 billion.

	Year Ended December 31,			Quarter Ended December 31,		
	Consolidated	Texas Equity Basis		Consolidated	Texas Equity Basis	
Earnings—$(thousands, except per share data)	1991	1991	1990	1991	1991	1990
Total revenue	$4,154,129	$3,898,685	$3,506,909	$1,298,651	$1,043,207	$ 937,850
Net income available to common stockholders	514,406	514,406	420,656	139,373	139,373	107,855
Net income per common share	$ 3.20	$ 3.20	$ 2.76	$ .85	$ .85	$ .68
Key Ratios						
Return on average assets	1.56%	1.72%	1.53%	1.27%	1.74%	1.49%
Return on average common equity	16.58	16.58	16.24	16.60	16.60	14.93
Return on average total equity	16.02	16.02	16.20	15.90	15.90	14.90
Average total equity to assets	9.76	10.72	9.45	8.02	10.94	10.02
Tangible common equity to net assets	6.91	9.58	8.88			
Net interest margin[1]	6.09	6.19	5.33	6.02	6.36	5.47
Net funds function[1]	4.68%	4.73%	4.11%	4.50%	4.61%	3.75%
Common Stock Data						
Average shares outstanding (000)	160,598		152,259	163,822		158,893
Ending shares outstanding (000)	167,818		158,835			
Shares traded (000)	69,241		63,717	17,980		25,016
Price:						
High	$ 52.75		$ 33.13	$ 52.75		$ 29.63
Low	24.88		19.00	42.00		19.00
Close	52.63		27.75			
Book value	21.12		18.11			
Common dividend	$ 1.16		$ 1.04	$ .29		$ .26
Income Statement—$(thousands)						
Taxable equivalent interest income	$3,377,415	$3,116,960	$2,869,940	$1,061,924	$ 801,469	$ 755,004
Interest income	3,309,615	3,049,680	2,801,552	1,043,988	784,053	737,826
Interest expense	1,538,943	1,429,447	1,560,646	449,421	339,925	402,256
Net interest income	1,770,672	1,620,233	1,240,906	594,567	444,128	335,570
Provision for loan and lease losses	424,442	397,728	300,332	154,152	127,438	110,847
Other income:						
Income from fiduciary activities	96,092	94,553	88,130	26,081	24,542	22,627
Service charges on deposit accounts	140,969	122,759	105,195	52,221	34,011	27,621
Loan processing and service income	312,053	317,905	280,673	88,416	94,268	75,666
Securities gains (losses)	187	185	(1,389)	937	935	(1,350)
Income from management of collection pool, net	52,889	52,889	53,342	18,779	18,779	18,004
Equity in earnings of Bank One, Texas, NA	57,012	85,372	47,153		28,360	9,066
Other	185,312	175,342	132,253	68,229	58,259	48,390
Total other income	844,514	849,005	705,357	254,663	259,154	200,024
Other expense:						
Salaries and related costs	660,575	603,368	501,224	218,489	161,282	128,345
Net occupancy expense	79,596	70,053	68,508	21,894	12,351	17,710
Depreciation and amortization	79,844	91,068	64,951	22,634	33,858	18,170
Outside services and processing	183,144	164,212	121,196	81,433	62,501	33,925
Communication and transportation	107,975	102,050	84,758	32,792	26,867	22,994
Other	375,097	349,352	262,033	128,523	102,778	79,364
Total other expense	1,486,231	1,380,103	1,102,670	505,765	399,637	300,508
Income before income taxes	704,513	691,407	543,261	189,313	176,207	124,239
Income taxes	(175,047)	(161,941)	(119,888)	(45,005)	(31,899)	(15,716)
Net income	$ 529,466	$ 529,466	$ 423,373	$ 144,308	$ 144,308	$ 108,523

[1]Fully taxable equivalent basis

(continued)

Direct Marketing

In 1987, Bank One created a major new department called Direct Marketing to contact present and prospective customers by phone and mail. The department quickly grew to more than fifty people whose responsibilities included explaining and selling Bank One services directly to individuals

▪ EXHIBIT 42.2 *continued*

BANC ONE CORPORATION and Subsidiaries

Average Balance Sheet Yields/Rates—$(millions)	Full Year[2] 1991			Full Year 1990		Fourth Quarter[2] 1991		Fourth Quarter 1990	
	Ending Balance	Average Balance	Yield/Rate[1]	Average Balance	Yield/Rate[1]	Average Balance	Yield/Rate[1]	Average Balance	Yield/Rate[1]
Short-term investments	$ 2,324	$ 1,074	5.97%	$ 290	8.42%	$ 2,055	5.52%	$ 445	7.88%
Securities:									
Taxable	6,604	4,363	8.69	3,714	9.12	6,569	8.21	3,490	9.16
Tax exempt	1,385	1,320	11.58	1,253	11.94	1,372	10.96	1,271	11.90
Total securities	7,989	5,683	9.36	4,967	9.83	7,941	8.68	4,761	9.89
Loans and leases:									
Commercial	10,276	8,334	10.18	7,795	10.96	10,382	9.67	7,864	10.84
Real estate:									
Commercial	2,117	1,627	9.98	1,190	10.91	2,033	9.46	1,225	10.75
Construction	989	1,049	9.08	1,041	10.36	1,070	8.58	1,100	10.12
Residential	5,300	3,624	10.68	2,464	11.27	5,285	10.20	2,802	11.73
Installment, net	6,381	4,960	12.43	4,108	12.51	6,283	11.49	4,293	11.78
Credit card	4,356	2,961	18.73	1,886	19.04	3,937	18.14	2,248	19.61
Leases, net	779	758	10.79	717	11.27	767	10.41	743	11.12
Total loans and leases	30,198	23,313	11.78	19,201	12.10	29,757	11.23	20,275	12.10
Loan and lease reserve	(539)	(389)		(273)		(525)		(296)	
Net loans and leases	29,659	22,924	11.98	18,928	12.28	29,232	11.44	19,979	12.28
Collection pool	971	289	5.85			1,147	5.85		
Note receivable from FDIC		214	8.81	383	8.81			416	8.81
Total earning assets	40,943	30,184	11.19%	24,568	11.68%	40,375	10.43%	25,601	11.70%
Other assets	5,350	3,677		3,086		4,550		3,249	
Total assets	$46,293	$33,861		$27,654		$44,925		$28,850	
Deposits:									
Non-interest bearing demand	$ 6,729	$ 3,950		$ 3,131		$ 6,124		$ 3,163	
Interest bearing demand	4,172	2,673	4.19%	2,104	4.71%	3,954	4.01%	2,167	4.64%
Savings	10,038	7,231	5.04	5,721	6.13	9,988	4.59	5,859	6.05
CD's less than $100,000	12,837	9,422	6.90	7,746	8.34	13,090	5.89	8,029	8.25
Total core deposits	33,776	23,276	4.84	18,702	5.86	33,156	4.19	19,218	5.81
CD's $100,000 and over	3,281	2,429	6.16	2,286	8.03	3,321	5.40	2,239	7.74
Total deposits	37,057	25,705	4.97	20,988	6.10	36,477	4.30	21,457	6.02
Borrowed funds:									
Short-term	3,623	3,470	5.90	2,985	7.93	3,167	5.03	3,243	7.61
Long-term	703	622	9.28	442	10.04	718	7.87	591	9.92
Total borrowed funds	4,326	4,092	6.41	3,427	8.21	3,885	5.55	3,834	7.96
Total interest bearing liabilities	34,654	25,847	5.95%	21,284	7.33%	34,238	5.21%	22,128	7.21%
Other liabilities	1,096	758		625		962		670	
Preferred stock	269	203		24		270		23	
Common equity	3,545	3,103		2,590		3,331		2,866	
Total liabilities, common equity and preferred stock	$46,293	$33,861		$27,654		$44,925		$28,850	

[1]Rates in many categories are significantly impacted by the inclusion of Bank One, Texas, NA in the fourth quarter 1991 and the four Ohio banks in the third and fourth quarters of 1991.

Credit Quality—$(millions)	1991		1990	Fourth Quarter 1991		Fourth Quarter 1990
	With Texas	Without Texas	Without Texas	With Texas	Without Texas	Without Texas
Ending reserve for loan and lease losses	$ 538.7	$ 425.5	$ 320.2			
Non-performing assets:						
Nonaccrual	405.4	348.3	362.0			
Renegotiated	4.4	4.4	5.7			
OREO	178.4	147.7	75.1			
Total non-performing assets	$ 588.2	$ 500.4	$ 442.8			
Loans delinquent over 90 days	$ 221.3	$ 190.0	$ 114.0			
Gross charge-offs	447.8	414.7	323.4	$ 169.4	$136.3	$ 105.1
Recoveries	87.5	85.4	73.3	27.3	25.2	22.2
Net charge-offs	$ 360.3	$ 329.3	$ 250.1	$ 142.1	$111.1	$ 82.9
Key ratios:						
Reserve to ending loans	1.78%	1.78%	1.57%			
Non-performing assets to ending loans	1.95	2.09	2.17			
90 days delinquent to ending loans	.73	.79	.56			
Net charge-offs to average loans	1.55%	1.51%	1.30%	1.89%	1.87%	1.62%

and businesses. The program has proven so successful that in many cases the Direct Marketing Department outsells all of the branch offices for many of the bank's services. Bank One expects the direct marketing program to continue to expand, becoming the primary means for its affiliates to generate new business.

■ **EXHIBIT 42.3   Bank One Advertising**

We'd love to be here at the game with you, but as usual we're working late.

Stop by tomorrow and let us know how it turned out.

Whatever it takes.

(continued)

■ **EXHIBIT 42.3**   *continued*

(continued)

Branching and Affiliation

If Bank One was going to focus on serving the consumer market, it had to have convenient banking locations where consumers lived and worked. This prompted the bank to launch an aggressive branching program throughout Columbus area suburbs. In 1960, Bank One, Columbus, had seven branches. By 1992, it had fifty full-service and fifteen mini-branch facilities called AutoBanks.

While Bank One was branching out in Columbus, Banc One Corporation was growing by acquiring a larger number of affiliates throughout the Midwest. By 1993, Banc One Corporation member banks had more than 1,300 banking offices located in 11 states and over 55,000 employees. During this period of active growth, tremendous advances were being made in the computer technology used to support the operational areas of banking.

Quality Commitment

Banc One has a renewed commitment to quality. Its affiliates are required to establish a Quality Council, consisting of the bank's president, direct reports, and key staff, which runs the quality planning and objective-setting process. A senior Chief Quality Officer (CQO) is in charge of the group and ensures that the Council is guided to the issues by customer data. All service improvement efforts are concentrated on the dimensions that are important to customers and on Banc One services identified as less than the best in the industry. A quality grid used by Banc One to identify such services is shown in Exhibit 42.4.

After the quality grid is completed, an improvement team is assigned by the Quality Steering Committee to any item identified in the lower right corner of the grid. In addition to providing resources to fund the improvement teams' activities, the Quality Steering Committee selects people to work on quality projects, reviews quality and improvement progress, and adapts reward systems so that quality and bottom line results are acknowledged.

Banc One believes in measuring to reinforce behavior. Measuring performance as well as behavioral quality dimensions reinforces the importance Banc One places on quality. Each employee is measured on the quality of at least one output of his or her job, and managers are measured on the aggregate of all of the quality measures in their realm of responsibility.

It is not only customers who are involved in the quality process; employees are involved as well. Banc One also sets performance standards and measurements of management's response to employees because employees are thought of as customers of management. Employees are surveyed in the same manner as customers and the same grid is used to access quality and performance. Improvement teams are then assigned to address performance issues identified as problematic.

One of the most difficult management tasks is to evaluate the results of any quality effort. Banc One developed one measure which quantifies all of

■ **EXHIBIT 42.3**   *continued*

We certainly can't stop Czechoslovakian acrobats. Nor would we want to.

But we will protect you from bouncing checks.

Our overdraft protection gives you an automatic line of credit that can cover you if your checking account is ever overdrawn.

And best of all, the cost of getting this service is just about the same as what you would have to pay for one bounced check.

We're terribly sorry for any sort of confusion this may have caused.

BANK≣ONE
Whatever it takes.

(continued)

■ **EXHIBIT 42.3**   *continued*

Bank One's overdraft protection will protect you from misteaks.

Get our overdraft protection and we'll cover any checks you write up to your preapproved credit limit. After all, everybody messes up from time to tine.

BANK≡ONE.
Whatever it takes.

(*continued*)

■ **EXHIBIT 42.3**   *continued*

We're looking for business owners who think the 5 o'clock whistle is just a signal to put on another pot of coffee.

If overtime is a normal part of your work day, let our business banking experts take a load off your shoulders. We can help you out with everything from business checking, to loans, to cash management. Give us a call at 576-2200. We can give you just about anything you need. Except sleep.

Whatever it takes.

(continued)

■ **EXHIBIT 42.3**   *continued*

Trying to run your business and handle its finances too?

If you'd like help, talk to our business banking experts. We can assist you with everything from cash management, to business checking, to loans. We'd be glad to come by and talk to you. Just give us a call when you can fit it into your schedule. We know you've got your hands full.

(continued)

■ **EXHIBIT 42.3** *continued*

Here's something to think about as you drive to work eating your breakfast, dictating into your microcassette recorder, listening to the news, and talking on your mobile phone.

We know a business professional like yourself doesn't have a lot of time, so we'll make this quick. If you let us help you manage your finances, you'll have more time to manage the rest of your life. We'll take care of anything you need. Checking. Loans. Trust and investment services. Just give us a call. We'll be glad to stop by when you've got a couple of seconds.

BANK≡ONE.
Whatever it takes.

© 1991 Banc One Corporation

(continued)

■ **EXHIBIT 42.3**   *continued*

First say to your clients,"I'd like to talk a little about banks." When they finish rolling their eyes, read them this.

Bank One has everything you need to make managing your finances easier. Checking, savings, loans. And people that will work with you on things like trusts and investments. In fact, Bank One will do whatever it takes to give you more time to devote to the rest of your life, so you and your clients don't have to waste time on life's less exciting moments. Like discussing banks.

BANK≡ONE.
Whatever it takes.
An affiliate of Banc One Corporation. Columbus, Ohio. Member FDIC

LENDER © 1991 Banc One Corporation

■ **EXHIBIT 42.4**   **Banc One Quality Grid**

		HOW CUSTOMERS RATE EACH QUALITY	
		Low Importance	High Importance
CUSTOMER	High	Ignore	This is why our customers
RATINGS OF	Performance		are OUR customers
THE BANK'S	Low	Ignore	TARGET what our customers
PERFORMANCE	Performance		want FOR IMPROVEMENT

Productivity Views, Vol. 8, No. 5, 1991

the various quality initiatives that take place throughout the company. That measure is customer retention, which is measured in every affiliate and reported on a quarterly basis to executive management. The customer retention factor, dubbed "ROQ" (return on quality), is considered just as important as return on assets and equity in measuring the results of every affiliate.

A New Era—Marketing Begins Product Development

Up until the mid-1970s, banking was a highly regulated and protected business. Products and services were dictated by federal regulations and were, for the most part, the same from bank to bank. Management soon realized, however, that by the end of the decade, major changes would be underway that would deregulate almost entirely the banking business. It was essential that Bank One map out a strategy to direct the corporation into a wider range of income-producing businesses.

The CIF

In the early 1970s, the marketing department decided the first step in its product development effort was to thoroughly understand the structure of business relationships that customers had with the bank. This was difficult since most banks kept their computer files in account sequence, rather than in customer sequence. Such a system could not cross-reference accounts on a total bank basis, which made it virtually impossible to determine how much business each customer did with the bank.

The marketing research department was charged with the responsibility of developing a Central Information File (CIF), which would cross-reference all customer account information. Not only could the system enable staff to determine customers' total relationships with the bank, it could gather specific socioeconomic information about them which could be used to target prospects for additional banking services. Such data could include:

■ Sex

■ Birthdays of family members

- Children (number, ages)
- Home ownership or rental
- Marital status
- Transaction history (all accounts)
- Credit rating
- Reason accounts closed
- Occupation
- Dun & Bradstreet rating
- Zip code
- Income range
- Census tract
- Interest paid last year
- Opening officer
- Real estate tax paid last year

With the CIF system developed, Banc One Corporation began to plan for the total reprogramming of all computer applications to move into a completely automated CIF. A computer program soon became available to complement the CIF. It had a complete set of management report options with which the bank could cross-classify the segments of its business by any CIF variable. For example, if Bank One, Columbus wanted to know the age distribution of its passbook savings accounts, it could place an inquiry in the computer and receive such a report. If it wanted to determine which customers had large demand deposit accounts but no other relationships, that too could easily be reported.

Comprehensive research and use of the new CIF indicated that about half of all customers had only one account with the bank. Bank One considered it essential to "cross-sell" additional services to present customers. With the CIF in place, Bank One was soon able to design a highly specific direct mail campaign based on census tract, effective direct increase business, and cross-selling existing customers on new banking services. Another feature of the CIF was its capability to treat a customer as a "net account." That is, the balance and profitability of a customer could be assessed, rather than merely the balance and profitability of an account (which typically is only a fractional representation of the customer).

The CIF data, coupled with other primary research information, led to the development of a number of new banking services. Several such services are discussed below.

VISA

One of the most significant new services offered by Bank One was the VISA credit card (formerly BankAmericard). This comprehensive credit card program was originally developed and introduced by Bank of America in

California. In the mid-1960s, Bank One officials met with those of Bank of America and convinced them to franchise the service to other banks across the country. As a result of this effort, Bank One became the first bank in the nation to offer the VISA credit card to customers outside California.

Acceptance of the VISA card in Columbus was excellent, and management quickly realized the importance that plastic card services would play in the future of banking. By the end of the VISA program's second year of operation, more than 100,000 customers used the VISA credit card in 8,000 merchant outlets in Ohio. Following this early success, Bank One refranchised the VISA program throughout the Midwest. Today, Bank One processes over 14 million credit cards for 2,500 members, including banks, savings and loans, credit unions, and retailers.

Bank One later expanded its credit card program to include overdraft checking account protection for customers who had both a credit card and a checking account. This "Line O' Credit" program, which protected customers from "bouncing a check," saved customers time, money, and embarrassment. It quickly became a popular Bank One service.

VISA Checking Account Card

In 1975, Bank One was the first bank to introduce the VISA debit card (formerly called Entree), which looked just like a credit card but worked like a check. With the VISA debit card, customers had the convenience of a credit card while using money from their checking accounts to pay for purchases. When Bank One introduced the debit card, it targeted the so-called "convenience users"—customers who charged purchases not so much because of deferred payment, but because it was a convenient substitute for cash.

Bank One was interested in promoting the debit card for a couple of reasons. First, because debit card transactions are drawn from funds on deposit, Bank One did not have to fund outstanding balances as with credit card transactions; and second, because the card was used in place of writing a check, it reduced the bank's check processing expenses.

From the customer's point of view, the VISA debit card offered limited advantages over the credit card, as long as the credit was free. In fact, for the first two years of the VISA debit card program, few customers signed up for the service. But when Bank One introduced a $20 yearly fee for its credit card, a large number of "convenience users" switched to the free VISA debit program.

Electron Card

In the fall of 1983, Bank One became the first bank in the country to introduce the new VISA electronic card to its customers. The electron card could be used in all participating VISA interchange banking machines, in Bank One's own statewide banking machine network, and in point-of-sale terminals for the authorization of purchases. Bank One called its program "Jubilee!"—a unique name that differentiated itself

■ **EXHIBIT 42.5   Description of Bank One's Self-Service Centers**

from the more conservatively labelled programs of competitors. (Exhibit 42.5 describes the Jubilee! machines and their operations.)

New Customer Statements

As Bank One continued basic research efforts, it discovered customers wanted to receive single statements encompassing all of their banking relationships, rather than separate statements for accounts. This led to the introduction of another important service—the "Total Account Bank Statement." This statement lists the monthly details for all accounts owned by a customer on one monthly statement, including checking and savings accounts, loans, and certificates of deposit. (Exhibit 42.6 describes the Total Account Bank Statement in more detail.)

Cash Management Account

In the mid-1970s, Bank One included some advanced features in its credit card processing system to allow other types of financially related businesses, namely finance companies and brokers, to issue credit cards to their customers. Bank One soon became a major processor of these cash management type accounts by providing the service to the nine largest

■ **EXHIBIT 42.6**   Description of Total Account Bank Statement

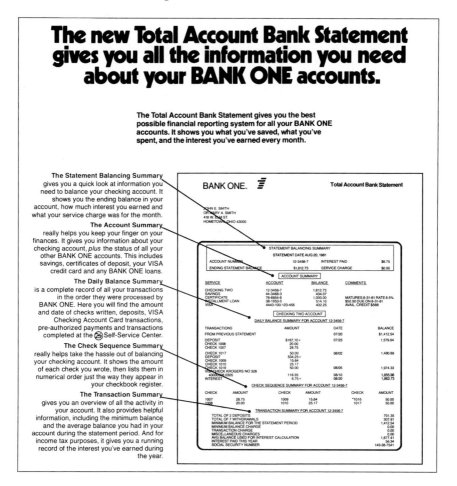

stock brokerage companies in the country. Within a few years, more than a million broker customers used Bank One, Columbus VISA credit cards as part of cash management services.

Cash management accounts (CMAs) permit customers to earn money market interest rates on all of their funds, plus have access to cash and a line of credit through both checks and credit/debit cards. The accounts also typically offer full brokerage transaction capabilities. The minimum opening amount for these accounts ranges from $1,000 to $20,000 and yearly fees can be anywhere from $60 to more than $200. The checking accounts and VISA cards issued to many CMA customers are provided and processed by Bank One. All check and credit card transactions are cleared through Bank One, which then provides individual account information to brokers to be used in monthly customer statements.

Improving Its Delivery of Services

Research conducted by Bank One indicated customers had two basic complaints about service. First, banks were not open during convenient hours. And second, once inside the bank, they had to wait in long lines to complete transactions. It was obvious that Bank One could achieve a significant service differential if these two problems could be solved. Doing so, however, meant radical changes in the bank's delivery of services.

Automated Banking Machines

Bank One first evaluated expanding branch operating hours. It was soon apparent, however, that the return on such an investment would be minimal. Bank One then considered another alternative—automated banking machines.

In 1970, Dallas-based Docutel Corporation introduced an automated cash-dispensing machine that could provide banking services around the clock, every day of the week. After much study, the marketing department concluded that automated banking machines offered a viable alternative to expanded branch operating hours and recommended the machines for Bank One branches. This prompted Bank One's commitment to lead the financial industry in the implementation of automated banking technology.

In the same year, Bank One was the first bank in the nation to introduce automatic cash dispensing machines, called "Cash 'N Carry." A more sophisticated generation of machines was introduced a year later under the name "Bank24." These machines could do much more than just dispense cash 24 hours a day. They could transact deposits, withdrawals, transfer money between checking and savings accounts, and make payments on VISA bills, utility bills, and installment or mortgage loans.

In 1974, Bank One operated the first of two Bank24 branch facilities using both live tellers and the new automated teller machines (ATMs). Eventually some Bank24 machines were relocated outside Bank One branches to give customers access to their accounts when the bank was closed. (Exhibit 42.7 shows alternative architectural schemes for these branches.)

Autobank

An analysis of these Bank24 branches, however, indicated they were larger than necessary. A smaller building could provide essentially the same services at a much lower cost.

In 1978, just four years after it introduced the two Bank24 branches, Bank One developed and introduced the AutoBank. The AutoBank provided the same services as the older, larger Bank24 branches, yet was only 96 square feet in size and cost less than $15,000 to build. Its compact size allowed it to be placed in many convenient locations, such as

■ EXHIBIT 42.7   Examples of Architectural Schemes for Bank24 Branch Facilities

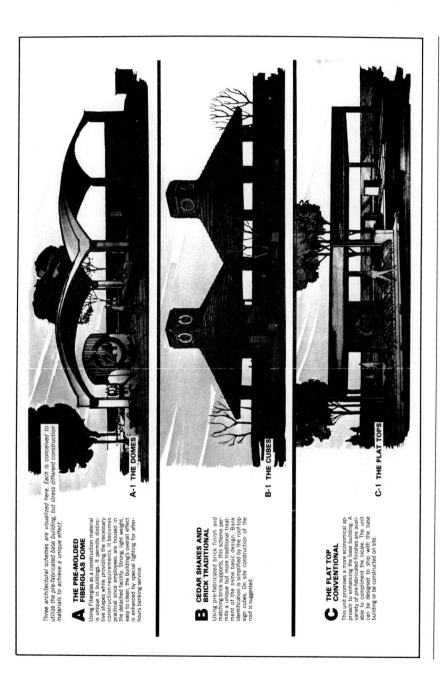

Three architectural schemes are visualized here. Each is conceived to utilize the pre-fabricated base building, but stress different construction materials to achieve a unique effect.

A   THE PRE-MOLDED FIBERGLAS DOME

Using Fiberglas as a construction material is unique in buildings. It permits distinctive shapes while providing the necessary construction requirements. It becomes practical since employees are housed in the detached facility. Strong, light weight, easy to clean, the building's overall effect is enhanced by special lighting for after-hours banking service.

A-1   THE DOMES

B   CEDAR SHAKES AND BRICK TRADITIONAL

Using pre-fabricated brick finish and matching brick supports, this scheme permits a unique but more traditional treatment of the same basic design. Bank identification is simplified by the roof-top sign cubes. On site construction of the roof is suggested.

B-1   THE CUBES

C   THE FLAT TOP CONVENTIONAL

This unit promises a more economical approach to enhancing the base building. A variety of pre-fabricated finishes are available to compliment the locale. The unit can be designed to ship with the base building or be constructed on site.

C-1   THE FLAT TOPS

gas station sites and shopping center parking lots, throughout the city at minimal cost. The new AutoBank locations attracted many new customers to Bank One.

Designing the Branch of the Future

The introduction of the automated teller machine (ATM) in 1970 began to transform the way customers accessed their bank accounts. Activity on the banking machines increased rapidly. By 1987, 40 percent of all customers were using automated teller machines to complete routine transactions. Although Bank One had solved the convenience problem for customers, it now had another problem. Fewer people were entering Bank One lobbbies where customer service representatives had the opportunity to sell additional Bank One services. This also meant there was a great deal of unused space inside many Bank One branch offices.

The Financial Marketplace

This dilemma prompted Bank One to develop a new strategy for its branch office of the future. Taking into consideration the hectic schedules of today's consumers, it decided to bring a full range of financial services, including insurance, real estate, brokerage, and travel all under one roof at the Bank One branch. This "one-stop financial shopping" would hopefully entice consumers back into branch lobbies.

In 1985, Bank One renovated one of its Columbus branches to test this multiple service concept. This new Bank One Financial Center included five services in addition to traditional banking and became so successful that in 1988 Bank One built a new facility and incorporated additional financially related services. This branch, called the Bank One Financial Marketplace, resembled a mini shopping center by featuring virtually every financial service that a customer might want. In addition, Bank One opted to keep its Financial Marketplace open for extended hours, seven days a week. Bank One plans to incorporate successful features of the Financial Marketplace into existing branch offices.

The Computer Revolution—Bank One Excels

Since the inception of computers in the banking industry, Bank One has prided itself on being a leader in computerizing both back-room operations and customer services. Viewing computerization as a means of separating paper work from "people" work, Bank One has worked diligently to stay abreast of new technology. Over the years, the bank has made major additions to its computer center operations. The bank's commitment to state-of-the-art computer technology has allowed Bank One to become a leader in the automation of all banking services, most notably in ATM and point-of-sale technology.

ATMs in the 1980s

Although Bank One led the banking industry in the development of the nation's first automated teller machines in the early 1970s, it was not until the late 1970s and early 1980s that ATM activity heightened. By this time, most major financial institutions had installed ATMs for customer use, and many had banded together to provide regional and national interchange programs, allowing customers access to their accounts even while traveling. Major retailers even began planning to install automatic banking machines.

About the same time, both the VISA and MasterCard national card programs announced plans to install automatic banking machines on a national basis to give cardholders access to their bank accounts from thousands of new locations throughout the country. The two credit card giants recently introduced new technology that would permit member bank cards, such as Bank One's Jubilee!, to be used both in automated teller machines and in point-of-sale terminals located at major retailing outlets.

Such changes have called for Bank One to develop increasingly sophisticated and powerful computer networks and interchanges. By 1993, Bank One had more than 4,000 Jubilee ATMs in 11 states handling the routine banking of more than 8 million customers.

Point-of-Sale

Bank One was also the first bank in the country to test point-of-sale technology. Point-of-sale devices directly transfer money from a customer's account to a merchant's account when a sale is made. Bank One's point-of-sale experiment, which installed sixty terminals in thirty Columbus-area stores, drew more than 250 representatives from banks located around the world to see the experiment.

While more than 10 million transactions were completed on these terminals, Bank One terminated the service. The equipment was too expensive to maintain and install, and grocery stores were unwilling to pay a high enough fee to enable Bank One to recover its investment in the system.

By the mid-1980s, Bank One hoped to provide a similar transaction guarantee service in grocery stores. The stores had begun installing their own inventory control computers and automated check registers. Bank One's strategy was to tap into them. This would allow Bank One to develop the transaction guarantee service, but avoid the large fixed costs of installing hardware.

In the fall of 1987, Bank One began testing such a system in several large Columbus-area grocery stores. This system, which was installed along with inventory control cash registers at several test sites, would determine if Bank One could successfully install a commingled system.

Timing of the test was critical since both VISA and MasterCard had already announced plans to jointly sponsor national point-of-sale systems as early as 1988. To continue its role as a leader in the development of these new systems, Bank One had to be ready to take advantage of the new VISA-MasterCard plan.

Home Banking

On another front, Bank One decided it would have to develop the most sophisticated, yet easy-to-use electronic consumer banking program in the country in order to remain competitive in the coming decade. Bank One's marketing department had been carefully watching the development of the home computer market and the resultant increase in consumer awareness of computer technology.

In early 1980, Bank One introduced an experiment in home banking. This was not simply a pay by phone program, which previously had been introduced by about 250 banks and savings and loans. Bank One's system was more sophisticated, connecting a telephone line to a home TV set to allow the consumer to tap into a variety of information and financial services.

This system, dubbed "Channel 2000" by Bank One, was generically known throughout the industry as Videotex. In a special partnership, Bank One provided financial service delivery capability to about 200 homes in the Columbus area, while another partner provided the information and educational services for the experiment. (An introductory advertisement for the system is shown in Exhibit 42.8.)

Channel 2000 was simple for sample customers to use. After calling the home information service, a "Welcome to Channel 2000" greeting appeared on the screen, followed by a display of the main index for services offered. When "banking" was selected, three types of financial information were available: general financial information, account status information, and two methods of bill payment.

The Channel 2000 experiment allowed test participants to form opinions and change attitudes about in-home banking services. The test also gave Bank One the opportunity to gather a wealth of information for designing future home banking systems. One important finding indicated that nearly 80 percent of Channel 2000's participating customers were willing to pay more than $7.50 per month for the service. Other results helped Bank One define the home banking market—young, well-educated, and affluent consumers commonly categorized as "early adoptors."

Based on Channel 2000 results, Bank One formed VideoFinancial Services, a national corporation that would provide the financial services portion of a complete home delivery information service via a personal computer. VideoFinancial's first joint venture project was with Knight-Ridder newspapers based in Miami, Florida. Together they launched their first complete service, called "Viewtron," in November 1983 in southern Florida, which they expected to be introduced throughout the country over the next several years.

After a year of operation, however, Bank One determined the marketplace was still not ready for the full deployment of home information systems, and discontinued the home banking program. Although the service had avid users, there simply were not enough of them to make the service economically viable, and not enough households had home computers.

BANK ONE

This week BANK ONE and 100 pioneering customers are launching the first major test of delivering banking services directly to the home.

This is an historic week for 100 bank customers who have become participants in BANK ONE's Channel 2000 program…a brand new way of delivering banking services directly to the home by linking the telephone to the standard television set. They're helping BANK ONE develop better services for banking customers all over the country. This project was jointly developed by BANK ONE and OCLC, Inc., the nation's leading provider of computerized library services. Channel 2000 is the first major test of its kind in the United States.

Channel 2000 will let customers pay bills, check on account balances, and get current interest rates and other general financial information. All information will be displayed on the TV screen in the customer's home. In addition to banking use, Channel 2000 will provide access to other valuable community and educational information.

With the cost of transportation and postage getting higher and higher, customers will want more convenient ways to pay bills and complete routine banking transactions. BANK ONE is testing the Channel 2000 now to help make banking more convenient in the future.

BANK ONE

BANK ONE OF COLUMBUS

Member FDIC

Bank One remains optimistic about the future of home delivery of financial information. Broader acceptance is expected as more individuals purchase personal computers for home use.

Excelling in the 1990s

Banc One has followed a growth strategy to which it will continue to adhere in the 1990s: enter markets in which it can be first, second, or third. Being fourth or fifth represents growing for growth's sake, and that is not of interest to the Banc One management team.

Banc One is growing rapidly, but it uses discretion in finalizing deals and avoiding risk. Yet some analysts are concerned about Banc One's profitability during such rapid growth. Some of the recent acquisitions of Banc One Corporation include Valley National Corporation and Team Bancshares at $1.2 billion and $782 million, respectively. But Banc One strives to minimize risk by following the McDonald's rule of consistency; the company tries to create cookie-cutter banks across the United States to capitalize on its knowledge and effective operation of mid-sized local banks. Additional factors included in its success formula are the company's constant focus on steady customers and its management and operational systems. The result is delighted customers.

It is predicted that the 1990s will usher in many new changes for the financial services industry. Banks will follow airlines, trucking, and telephone companies in becoming deregulated by Congress. With deregulation on the horizon, Bank One looks forward to interstate and national branching, and the ability to offer a wide range of new products, such as:

- Insurance services, including brokerage and underwriting
- Stock brokerage services, both discount and full service
- Securities underwriting
- Real estate services, including investment and brokerage
- Data processing and telecommunicating services
- Management consulting services to other banks and customers
- Mutual fund management
- Retail-oriented lease financing

The most important question for Bank One's senior management will be to decide which of these services should be introduced to provide profitable growth through the 1990s.

In order to help in that decision, Banc One decided to test various alternatives by forming strategic alliances with companies already providing some of the nontraditional banking services. Banc One purchased a small merchant banking company in Columbus, Ohio, which became Banc One Capital Corporation. Banc One Capital was big enough to test the merchant banking concept and small enough so that a failure would not cause severe earnings problems. Banc One also started a discount stock brokerage operation, a mutual funds management company, and a major mortgage processing company. Banc One management believes that over time it will be in the best possible position to decide which businesses are likely to succeed and which should be reengineered or eliminated.

Focal Topics

1. What are the primary reasons a consumer chooses a particular bank in preference to a competing bank?

2. Develop a proposal for a continuing consumer research program for Bank One to provide data for the marketing decisions that management must make.

3. What social or economic issues are involved with all the information contained in the Central Information File? How much of this information should be available to customers or others, and how should it be provided?

4. If the electronic delivery systems being developed by Bank One are successful, what future impact will they have on traditional branch offices?

5. How do you visualize the future of automated banking equipment after evaluating the point-of-sale project and the home banking project?

■ ■ ■ ■ ■

Karn Meats, Inc.

■ ■ ■ ■ ■

Karn Meats began as Karn Packing Company in 1971, operating as a small local slaughterhouse selling fresh meats to local markets. The business was started by Jack Karn and his father, William Karn, and was originally a proprietorship before incorporation in 1971. His two sons, Dennis and Dick, entered the business in the 1970s and 1980s, respectively.

In 1983 after the death of their father, the sons reorganized the company as Karn Meats. Annual sales prior to the reorganization were approximately $4 million and have grown under the new leadership to over $50 million. Karn Meats shifted drastically from a local slaughterhouse to a diversified wholesale distributor of a variety of meat products. As part of this change in strategy, the brothers began planning the discontinuation of the slaughter operations. This phase was completed in 1989. The company has grown by expanding geographically from serving local area customers to serving customers throughout the Midwest to become one of the largest independent meat distributors in the area.

Karn Meats employs approximately fifty people; it has managed to increase productivity of its employees from sales of $32 million with fifty-six employees to $52 million with fifty-one employees. Karn has achieved this by investing in capital equipment, including state-of-the-art production facilities, bar-coded inventory control systems, and employee development. But much of its success can be attributed to its high commitment to its employees. It spends much time and money in training its "team." The hands-on management style of the firm's owners keeps management close to employees. The result is high employee commitment to the firm and low employee turnover with nearly one-half of its current employees having been with the company for 10 years or more.

Karn Meats is attempting to change its primary focus from production to one that includes more marketing. This change has contributed to its major physical expansions in recent years. Much of this has centered on grinding meat for use as hamburger by grocery stores and restaurant chains. The firm has also been an innovator by bringing a number of products, such as specialty sausages, smoked turkeys, and cheeses, into its product line, manufactured by other vendors. This has required the addition of substantial amounts of warehouse facilities for frozen and refrigerated products. Karn Meats has entered the food service market while continuing to serve all types of major retail food outlets. Clients in the food service business include individual and chain restaurants and some institutions such as schools and government organizations.

Karn Meats is known throughout the Midwest primarily for its high quality boxed and dressed beef. The company has also successfully introduced a line of high quality hamburger and hamburger patties for institutional and restaurant trades. The company's commitment to innovative technology has paid off. It is the only distributor in the area with a Wolf-king grinding line, a capital equipment item costing nearly $1 million. This machine helps Karn Meats to deliver reliable, high quality ground meats to large users in a manner that few other firms can duplicate.

Karn Meats operates in an industry where a flowchart of channels of distribution can include as many as six players. Products may move from the manufacturer to the wholesaler/distributor to the food broker to the chain warehouse to the chain store and finally on to the consumer. Karn Meats, however, typically receives carcass meat from the manufacturer, grinds it or adds value in other ways, and then sells it to independent grocery stores. While this is a shorter distribution chain, the danger does exist that the manufacturers can acquire the technology to add value themselves and sell to the independent stores directly.

Dick and Dennis Karn have aspirations to expand the company substantially in the future, including the possibility of acquiring firms that would provide product lines or geographic distribution areas that complement the firm's present operations. Both brothers provide a long-term vision for the firm that has changed it dramatically during the past 10 years and provide guiding principles for the future.

The Beef Industry

The beef industry has undergone many changes throughout the last two decades. The 1960s and early 1970s were boom times for beef consumption among Americans, but the 1980s translated into declining sales due to a dramatic shift in diet and health concerns among consumers. Relatively high beef prices were also significant in the first years of decline, but the health trends were more permanent and provided more of a long-term challenge for members of the beef industry.

Consumers have said they want leaner cuts of meat, which the meat industry is supplying. But an adjustment appears to have occurred in this thinking in recent years. Although consumers continue to express strong interest in diet and health issues, they say their decision to serve meat is based primarily on other more traditional concerns. In a survey conducted by the Beef Industry Council in the late 1980s, when asked to rank the attributes that motivate their decision to purchase meat, diet and health factors ranked fourth, behind convenience, taste, and price.

The industry should not, however, be lulled into complacency by the suggestions that diet and health issues are no longer critical. The same study revealed that chicken was a clear favorite with American consumers on most product attributes. While 1988–1989 saw some erosion of chicken's image, it continued to receive a higher overall rating than its meat competitors. Fresh and ground beef now compare well on many attributes; pork, lamb, veal, and processed meats are not yet seen as favorably.

The Beef Industry Council, dedicated to marketing and promoting beef consumption among U.S. consumers, has developed a long-range plan to carry out its mission. It considers various environmental issues that are shaping the market for companies like Karn Meats. Areas the plan addresses include the social/cultural, competitive, technological, legal/political, and economic environments. Appendix 43A represents a complete version of this plan. Appendix 43B contains much data relating to the consumption of red meat and poultry for a thorough understanding of the beef industry.

Many environmental changes have brought about the need to consider expansion into other product categories at Karn Meats. The related lines of lean beef, deli meats, and poultry are likely expansion areas. While lean beef and poultry are being considered by the Karn's management team, the deli line is currently being produced and distributed on a limited basis.

Expansion at Karn Meats
Deli

At the request of some of its boxed, raw meat customers, Karn Meats began to distribute cooked deli meats. As demand for deli meats increased, Karn expanded into a variety of different cooked meats in order to accommodate its customers. The line currently consists of roast beef, several grades of ham, two types of turkey breast, and corned beef. Karn Meats is facing the decision of increasing its deli line from a small scale supplier of independent grocers to a high volume supplier of large grocery chains and other national and regional large scale deli meat users, some of which are currently boxed meat customers.

The deli industry has enjoyed much growth in recent years. The time constrained consumer of the 1990s demands service and convenience, which the deli provides. Grocery stores have increased the presence and prominence of food service areas including bakeries, delis, cheese shops, take-out food, and in-store dining. The deli counter offers customers the convenience taste they crave.

The number of in-store delis grew rapidly in the 1980s and early 1990s. By 1990 approximately 70 percent of all supermarkets had deli counters. As the number of delis increased, so did the number of deli items. Lunch meats and cheeses, the historic deli staple items, quickly were joined by prepared salads, hot entrees, ethnic foods, and vegetarian items. Despite this increase in variety, lunch meat and cheese still represent the majority of deli sales.

Karn Meats has entered an industry that is dominated by several firms that have established a long tradition of excellence and national recognition. The deli meat industry leaders include Hormel, Oscar Mayer, Eckridge, BilMar, and Sara Lee. Over the years, it has become economically advantageous for many of these companies to have their products privately labeled by a meat processor, who specializes in a particular type of luncheon meat. Therefore, many of the national brands are not produced in-house. In fact, it is not unusual for one meat processor to package deli meats for a variety of competitors.

While Karn Meats currently offers some deli items, it is examining other deli items to include in its line of products. According to the American Dairy, Deli & Bakery Association the deli items that have had the largest increases in consumption are chicken breast, turkey breast, and lean/low fat meats. The deli items with decreasing consumption levels were Genoa salami, hard salami, and ribs. The most frequently consumed products from the deli counter are sandwiches, at 2.1 times per week. Closely following are sliced to order lunch meats (1.7 times per week), chicken breast (1.6), fried or roasted chicken (1.3), lean/low fat meats (1.3), ham (1.3), turkey breast (1.2), pizza (1.2), bologna (.9), and shaved meats (.9).

Due to the common origin of many deli meat products and the commodity-like nature of the product, a major differentiation factor is the name of the label. National brands and several regional brands are heavily supported by advertising and promotional campaigns directed toward both the deli shopper and the store's deli meat buyer. The result is a quality image established in the mind of the deli shopper and buyers.

Karn Meats currently is positioned as a lower priced supplier of a select group of deli products. Its options include staying with this low cost positioning or adding value to the products to cultivate a quality image in the deli arena as it has done in the wholesale beef business.

Currently, Karn sells most of its deli line to independent grocers in the Midwest. Many of these retailers are quite small. Karn has received some advice that it should begin to develop a marketing program or other assistance to the independent retailers to help them with their deli operations. Since Karn has no marketing department or personnel assigned to marketing activities other than selling and pricing, such advice would be difficult to implement immediately.

Karn has met little success to date in selling to high volume deli operations such as those in Kroger or other large chains. These chains have centralized buying and marketing programs and some have central commissaries. Other markets that Karn has not yet penetrated include independent delis (not part of a grocery store) and convenience stores (which generally do not have deli operations).

Dick and Dennis Karn are convinced that opportunities exist for the firm by expanding the deli divisions. They face major decisions, however, which include questions about how to increase effectiveness with existing customers as well as the potential of markets other than independent supermarkets. They also face decisions about which products are most likely to be successful and how to source these products. To exploit fully the opportunities in deli operations, Karn Meats also faces organizational and personnel issues; marketing activities are currently developed by Dennis and Dick Karn with the involvement of the sales manager and whatever assistance may be provided by the firm's eight individual salespersons. Decisions about additional personnel must include analysis of how sales or margins might be improved enough to cover the cost of such a person and whether additional personnel costs would better be spent on a marketing person or an additional salesperson.

Lean Beef

Because of the decline in beef consumption among U.S. consumers, lean beef might translate into a real opportunity for Karn Meats. Earlier versions of lean beef products were introduced to the market many years ago, but they did not taste good and subsequently failed. To be successful, lean beef will have to taste as good as regular beef as well as have similar appearance and texture.

In a governmental study, hamburgers, cheeseburgers, and meat loaf were identified as the greatest sources of total fat and saturated fat in the American diet. The desire to eat these items will remain strong in the U.S. market, even if consumption levels are decreasing. Karn Meats feels the need for a low-fat alternative exists among many consumer segments. According to the American Dairy, Deli & Bakery Association, consumers are willing to spend an additional 12.2 percent for low-fat or leaner versions of their favorite food products. Consumers are also willing to spend 12.1 percent and 11.9 percent more for foods lower in cholesterol and calories, respectively.

An initial market research survey conducted in 1991 provided some insight into market potential. The results were encouraging. They indicated that the concept of lean beef appeals to both the higher per capita income and health conscious groups. These groups not only eat away from home frequently, they are more willing and able to purchase "healthy" foods. This may provide Karn with the ability to establish significant market share, a higher selling price, and higher margins. The initial data show that consumers would be willing to buy lean beef to serve at home. However, taste and quality remain of primary importance.

Karn Meats is currently evaluating a marketing research program designed to identify the potential of this market. The research needs to determine to whom the lean beef concept will be attractive and how large the market potential is.

At this point, Karn has thought extensively about the potential for a lean beef product. Working with university sponsored research on lean products and its own experience with beef processing, Karn has produced an experimental product that has excellent taste qualities and can be produced, the Karn brothers believe, without major problems. The major question facing them, however, is how large is the market for lean beef? McDonald's introduced "McLean" products in the early 1990s with very little success, a fact that caused Karn to move cautiously. As part of the caution, Karn is considering research in the form of a questionnaire. Dennis and Dick Karn need to make decisions, however, about who should be included in the survey and other details of marketing research that would help them decide whether or not to enter the lean beef market, a decision that would require a great deal of capital in a company that has expanded rapidly with low margins and thus has very lean capital resources.

Nutrition and Labeling

Karn Meats must address the issue of labeling. If it expands the deli line, should it try to get the Karn Meats name on display in the deli counters or should it be content with supplying the product and having the retailers put their own labels on the products? Karn Meats has a strong reputation in the "meat business" but not in the deli business.

A question facing Karn is the issue of how much importance labels are given in consumer decisions to purchase items from the deli case. Many products are displayed with no label readily observable by consumers. Other products are wrapped in labels identifying well-known suppliers of meat products. Such labels include Eckridge, Hormel, Schaller & Weber, Usinger, and Sara Lee, as well as many regionally known brands such as Longmont. It is believed that customers sometimes look for familiar names because they feel confident of the quality behind the label. Some grocery stores make less use of labels, but may use free-standing price stakes that stand near the meat and identify popular brand names. Sometimes these stakes provide information about the product rather than the manufacturer. It is rare to find deli operations in supermarkets that display any nutritional information, although serving suggestions are occasionally found in the deli case.

Beyond the labels that are actualy on the meat, most deli operators suffer from a shortage of point-of-sale material. The established meat suppliers provide little in the way of cut sheets, flyers, information brochures, and ingredient and nutrition disclosures targeted toward the end user. The burden of disseminating information falls on the deli personnel and manager, who are rarely equipped to handle these tasks.

The number of health-conscious Americans increases every year. Some of these consumers are very concerned about nutrition and may want additional information. They evaluate foods on numerous features, with nutrition being the most important according to a study done by HealthFocus, Inc. in 1990. Exhibit 43.1 shows that health-active consumers ranked nutrition, quality, and taste as the three most important factors in food product choice from a list of eight identified factors.

Health-active consumers, concerned about what they eat and the ingredients in their food products, read labels, according to the HealthFocus study. Health-active consumers expect food companies to provide nutritional information that is easy to read and understand and accurate freshness dating on food packages. Exhibit 43.2 indicates that approximately 70 percent of all health-active consumers are very or extremely concerned about the nutritional information of food packages. It is also apparent that more affluent consumers tend to be more willing to pay premium prices for health benefits and express a greater level of concern for nutrition labeling.

Karn currently provides no counter cards or other labeling materials to the retailers who are its customers. Because of the lack of marketing personnel as well as thin margins, Karn is reluctant to provide materials beyond a label on some of its products. The Karn logo is included on communications to its customers, such as invoices, and on cardboard packages containing products. The nature of the Karn logo is shown in Exhibit 43.3.

■ **EXHIBIT 43.1**   **Importance of Eight Features when Buying Foods (Numbers in graph represent mean scores.)**

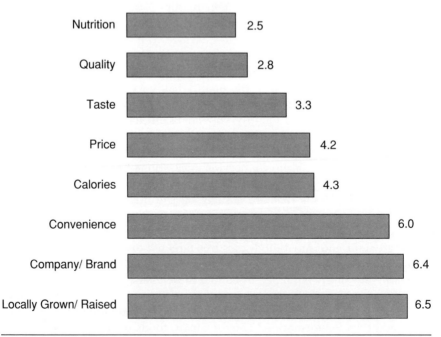

Nutrition	2.5
Quality	2.8
Taste	3.3
Price	4.2
Calories	4.3
Convenience	6.0
Company/ Brand	6.4
Locally Grown/ Raised	6.5

Source: HealthFocus, 1990

- EXHIBIT 43.2 Level of Concern about Nutrition Labeling of Food
  Packages (By different household income groups.)

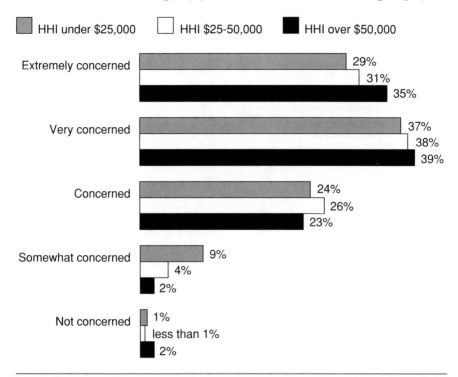

HHI under $25,000   HHI $25-50,000   HHI over $50,000

Extremely concerned — 29% / 31% / 35%

Very concerned — 37% / 38% / 39%

Concerned — 24% / 26% / 23%

Somewhat concerned — 9% / 4% / 2%

Not concerned — 1% / less than 1% / 2%

Source: HealthFocus, 1990

Focal Topics

1. Why has Karn Meats exhibited such rapid growth and success in an in-
    dustry characterized by the failure of many of its competitors? What
    recommendations do you have for the philosophy and organization of
    Karn to maintain growth in the future?

2. Evaluate the decision process that you would expect managers of meat
    departments or deli operations in supermarkets to use in buying from
    vendors such as Karn.

3. Can Karn expand substantially its deli operations? If so, develop a
    marketing program for growing profitably this part of the business.

4. Should Karn develop and market a lean beef product? What research
    should be undertaken to assist in this decision? Prepare a complete
    analysis of the advantages and disadvantages to Karn of adding a lean
    beef product.

5. What other products, markets, or methods offer opportunity for grow-
    ing profits for Karn?

■ ■ ■ ■ ■

■ EXHIBIT 43.3   Karn Logo Used on Labels and Company Materials

Beef Industry Council Long-Range Plan Environmental Analysis

■ ■ ■ ■ ■

Social/Cultural Environment

Short Term Issues

1. Consumers are more health conscious and are changing their eating habits and preferences.
   - Concern about health, weight control, and physical fitness will continue and will stress dietary change, especially in calories and fat.
   - More consumers are exercising regularly and are more likely to have cut down on meat.
   - Although the trend has probably peaked, stressing "light" eating will continue to influence consumer attitudes.
   - Ethnic foods, led by Mexican and Oriental cuisine, will become more popular, especially in the fast food industry.

2. Consumer issues are having an impact on the beef industry.
   - Concern and confusion about fat, additives, preservatives, residues, and antibiotics will make Americans more distrustful of their food supply.
   - Media coverage and animal rights activists make the animal rights issue potentially explosive in the next few years.

Long Term Issues

1. As the "baby boom" generation grows older, it will carry with it size, affluence, active life-styles, and health-oriented values.
   - The largest age segment will be between 25 and 44, and will spend more on consumer goods and be more educated than previous generations. The size and buying power of the over 50 category will also increase.
   - The largest population growth will occur in the 35 to 44 category, followed by the over 65 group.
   - The percentage of the labor force aged 35 to 54 will increase steadily.

- Population growth will continue its rapid rise in the South and West, primarily in Texas, California, and Florida.

2. As their populations grow, minority cultures will strongly influence America's eating habits.
   - Minority segments of the population will grow faster than the overall population.
   - Within five years, the Hispanic population will become the nation's largest minority ethnic group, and will concentrate in specific geographic areas.
   - Hispanics will continue to speak their native language, and Hispanic oriented marketing campaigns can effectively reach them.

3. The revolutionary changes in the American family will influence the manner in which beef products can be effectively merchandised.
   - Fewer households will consist of married couples.
   - The number of women employed outside the home will continue to grow.
   - The average household size will decrease. The number of families with one or no children will increase as will the number of fixed income households over age 65.

4. Changes in consumer attitudes toward health and fitness, changing lifestyles, and animal welfare will be reflected in changing food preferences.
   - Even if the fitness boom dies down, the more basic health concerns about beef will likely continue.
   - Microwave ovens will saturate the market and be used for preparing meals daily.
   - The food-safety issue could prove to be one of the most dominant factors affecting consumer demand for beef, unlikely to fade as just a fad.
   - Concern for animal rights has demonstrated long staying power and will focus primarily on diet, health, antibiotics, and residue issues.
   - Awareness of agriculture as a way of life will continue to fade from the American consumer's consciousness.

Competitive Environment

Short Term Issues

1. Food merchandising at the retail level is undergoing changes that affect the emphasis on fresh meat.
   - Retailers are aggressively merchandising fresh produce; in-store salad, vegetable, fruit, and prepared food bars; delis; and precooked fresh and frozen entrees, taking emphasis off the fresh meat case.
   - Precooked meat products, branded products, chef-prepared meat cuts, smaller package sizes, varieties of cuts, and lean lines of beef products are being merchandised.

- Branded beef products will become much more visible at the retail meat case. This will help promote competition within the meat industry to provide products which better meet consumer demands.
- Meat departments are being merchandised more effectively. Nutrition information programs, video point-of-purchase programs, and a return to a service orientation are being introduced.
- Fresh seafood counters are present in nearly all major retail food markets, although some stores are removing them due to perishability problems. A shortage in fish and seafood in the near future may cause price increases.

2. Beef is experiencing strong competition at the foodservice level.
   - The distinction between foodservice and retail is becoming blurred. Retail markets are beginning to offer more foodservice items.
   - During 1985 to 1986, serving of total beef to commercial foodservice declined 3 percent.
   - Poultry (chicken and turkey) is the primary competition for center-of-the-plate. Beef usage is changing to an ingredient from usage as a center-of-the-plate item.

3. Consumers have more food choices than ever before. Eating style has changed and people are eating a wider variety of foods.
   - Poultry product development has been extremely aggressive and will likely continue in that direction. Many consumers feel poultry outperforms beef in price, value, and healthfulness and is very close in taste.
   - Beef is perceived by some as a heavy, unhealthful nutrient source. Labeling, health claims, and grading issues will heavily impact beef production, processing, and marketing.
   - Fish is being positioned nutritionally as more important than other food products with attention being placed on OMEGA 3 fatty acids.
   - Many food products are using health issues as focal points in their advertising, bringing these issues to the forefront.
   - Residues, food safety, government regulations, and animal welfare may impact beef as the issues become more prominent to consumers.

4. The foodservice industry is undergoing change.
   - Chains continue to dominate the foodservice industry. In 1986, the top 100 restaurant companies accounted for 46 percent of total sales and 26 percent of total units.
   - The restaurant industry has become very competitive, from sources both internal and external.
   - Consumers continue to demand variety, convenience, and lighter, more healthful foods and will put more emphasis on price/value. Take-out and off-premise consumption drove the foodservice market in 1986.

5. It is more difficult to influence consumers to purchase more beef.
  - Consumers are being bombarded with food advertising. The beef industry is competing with other commodities for promotional space.
  - Labeling of meat products as light or natural is unclear to consumers.
  - Consumers will continue to spend heavily on durables as long as lower interest rates continue.

Long Term Issues

1. Competitive pressure from the poultry, fish, and seafood industries will continue to be very strong.
  - Increased efficiency in poultry production, along with consumer acceptance and new poultry product introductions are major forces impacting beef.
  - The poultry industry has increased their market share by taking a strong, continued consumer and marketing orientation.
  - Inspection programs for fish and seafood are being considered, and if implemented, could have a significant impact on their distribution.
2. Improvements have been made in beef-merchandising techniques which will help the beef industry's competitive position.
  - The beef industry has started a strong "blocking" position by introducing new lean beef products and educating consumers about trimming meat to reduce fat and calories.
  - The introduction of new beef products will improve the position of the beef industry. Beef needs to continue monitoring the consumer marketplace in order to respond to consumer demands.
  - Diet, health, and "wellness" issues will continue to be of interest to consumers.
3. Safety and environmental issues will impact beef production.
  - Food safety is important and the beef industry needs to learn how to effectively deal with these issues.
  - There has been competition for water supply in the Western part of the United States. This may be the start of a population migration to areas where the water supply is plentiful.

Technological Environment

Short Term Issues

1. The variety of value-added products now on the market have not been met with comparable or better beef products.
  - Much of the available technology is adaptable to help beef meet the new product challenge.
  - Warmed-over flavor may be a barrier to consumer acceptance of precooked beef. Available technology has not solved the problem.

2. Public pressure in beef production is absolute and resurfaces whenever the issue is publicized.
   ■ Technology is available to produce beef with minimal or no drug use, but it may not be cost effective.
   ■ Residue-free certification is possible.
   ■ In-store spectrometers to detect residues are available but may have limited use due to cost.

3. Microbiological contamination is a serious marketing and regulatory issue for beef.
   ■ Better application of existing technology can help reduce product contamination, but cannot assure absolute safety.
   ■ Food irridation technology exists but faces consumer resistance.

4. The importance of utilizing technology in marketing to the consumer is increasing.
   ■ There is a perpetual need to understand what the consumer perceives as "quality."
   ■ Increased application of existing and potential technology will facilitate response to pressures for nutrient labeling.
   ■ Competing foods are using vacuum and microwave packaging technology which is just beginning to be applied to beef products.
   ■ Detailed information on purchaser demographics is very expensive and limited in availability in spite of usable scanning technology.
   ■ Despite improved production technology, a small but vocal segment of the public is concerned about some current meat industry practices as related to animal welfare.

Long Term Issues

1. Beef production will continue to cost more than poultry production. Genetic engineering, plant automation, and other developing technologies may reduce this differential.

2. Product research may improve the value of the entire beef animal, including by-products presently being underused.

3. The beef industry is not keeping pace with other food marketers in adapting packaging technologies to beef products.

4. The number and variety of beef operations in the U.S. will make dissemination of valuable research and survey information difficult.

5. Research is underway in biotechnological areas such as fat partitioning and growth hormone.

6. Newly developed, synthetic calorie-free fat substitutes may have implications for meat consumption in terms of total fat consumption in daily diet, cholesterol removal from the blood, sale of fats for foodservice or manufacturer food use.

7. Changes in the grading system that will be required to utilize new technologies such as hot fat trimming and hot boning may cause confusion at the consumer level.

Legal/Political Environment

Short Term Issues

1. There is a very real possibility of significant regulatory-related changes affecting the beef industry.
   - Health claims by food producers and their manufacturers have come under closer scrutiny, and it will increase during the next five years.
   - Pressure is increasing to define labeling terminology and standards for products marked under light, lower fat, and natural labels.
   - Balancing the risk of water contaminants, pesticides, fertilizers, and other chemical uses will continue to be an issue.

2. Concern for product safety and consumer health issues is increasing and will receive closer scrutiny.
   - Concerns about bacterial contamination, antibiotic resistant strains, and antibiotic, hormone, and chemical residues continue to gain attention.
   - Improving relations between the beef industry and major diet and health organizations are forecasted for the coming year.
   - Product safety concerns and federal government budget cuts will continue to focus on the U.S. Meat Inspection System.
   - Labor union pressures focusing on food safety, worker safety, and continuous food inspection will continue to escalate.
   - Diet and health organizations are continuing their aggressive policies of developing specific dietary guidelines for the consuming public. In the coming year, the American Heart Association, the National Cancer Institute, and the American Institute for Cancer Research are planning additional reports in this area. Likewise if there is a shift in balance from the USDA to HHS as the leading agency for human nutrition guidelines, there could be an adverse effect on beef's place in the diet.
   - Pressure will continue as fund-raising efforts by diet and health organizations are often based on nutrition premises which are not proven but impact beef negatively.
   - Continued increased passage of state regulations and laws will impact upon interstate commerce and production practices.
   - Petitions filed with the USDA to change the grading system will be acted upon this year.
   - A national cholesterol education program now underway by the National Heart, Lung and Blood Institute is increasing public awareness of the cholesterol issue and dietary change.

- Studies such as the National Academy of Sciences study on nutritional improvements in meat and animal products and the Surgeon General's report telecast in January 1988 impacted the beef industry.
- Animal welfare issues will continue to escalate as biotechnology concerns and current production practices are linked to safety and nutrition claims by consumer activists.

Long Term Issues

1. Regulatory factors will have a major impact on the beef industry.
   - A general trend toward deregulation is likely to continue with a focus on user fees which raise product costs, versus free service which increases public fund costs.
   - Overall import, export, and tariff regulations are likely to loosen between now and 1992, allowing more aggressive pursuit of overseas markets while also increasing competition in the United States from imports.
   - Continuing research on nutrition and health is expected to have significant impact on related policies and health programs.
2. Liability claims against food products will increasingly continue to be brought against product manufacturers.
   - Pressure will increase to label foods with food-safety production practices and international or domestic point-of-origin information in order to trace legal liability.
3. Consumerism issues will produce strong pressures on the beef industry.
   - Continued activities in biotechnology will lead to regulatory hearings and delays in the adoption of new scientific practices.
   - International food marketing policies and regulations will grow in importance to the marketing of beef domestically and internationally.
   - Interaction between urban and rural life-style needs will continue to put greater regulatory pressure on agricultural production.

Economic Environment

Short and Long Term Issues

1. National economic trends will remain generally favorable.
   - The national economy will steadily improve into the early 1990s.
   - Prime interest rates will be more stable with fewer disruptive swings between now and 1992.
   - Unemployment is expected to remain at current levels.
   - Inflation is expected to remain steady, averaging around 4 percent throughout the remainder of the decade.
   - Consumer disposable income is expected to rise steadily into the early 1990s.

- Trade deficits will continue to be high in the short term, but may shrink in the long term.
- Trade restrictions will be slowly reduced by the early 1990s as the world becomes more of an open market. Least cost producers will continue to get most of the business.

2. Economic conditions specifically impacting the livestock industry will experience change.
   - After decreasing through 1988, beef supplies will begin expanding at the end of the decade.
   - The Beef Promotion and Research Act will provide the economic means to greatly enhance beef-industry research and promotion capabilities.
   - The trend toward fewer livestock producers will continue into 1992, being more evident in the stocker and feeder segments than the cow-calf segment.
   - The pace of cropland conversion to pastureland will slow, while the worldwide trend will be the opposite.
   - The nation's agricultural economy will continue to lag behind the national economy; however, it is very uneven, varying by product sector, geographic region, and individual operation.
   - The late 1980s and early 1990s will mark the beginning of a new phase of the technical revolution in agriculture, resulting in sizable productivity gains in some sectors of agriculture.

3. Productivity levels and cost structures within the beef industry will change appreciably.
   - Economies of scale will accelerate consolidation within the meat industry, mirroring current food-industry trends.
   - There will be a major trend toward implementing cost efficient, more productive technologies.
   - The trend toward vertical integration (not necessarily by ownership) in the live stock and meat industry will continue, but the rest of agriculture will return to diversification, especially in the Midwest.
   - Live stock feed costs are expected to remain relatively stable, with increases not expected to exceed the basic inflation rate.
   - Land prices are expected to bottom out and remain stable for the rest of the decade before beginning a gradual upward trend.
   - The beef-price spread between farm and retail is expected to widen over the next five years, but not to exceed the basic rate of inflation.

Data Relating to the Consumption of Red Meat and Poultry

■ ■ ■ ■ ■

Meat Expenditures by Consumer Characteristics, 1989

	BEEF	PORK	OTHER MEATS	POULTRY	FISH	ALL FOODS
BY INCOME						
$ 5,000–$ 9,999	$2.69	$1.85	$1.03	$1.25	$ .68	$41.54
$10,000–$14,999	3.21	1.94	1.78	1.55	1.01	52.82
$15,000–$19,999	3.70	1.89	1.45	1.80	1.44	59.93
$20,000–$29,999	3.87	2.24	1.77	1.83	1.30	70.00
$30,000–$39,999	4.80	2.67	2.04	2.14	1.49	84.14
$40,000–$49,999	4.39	2.27	2.03	2.16	1.63	88.46
$50,000 and over.......	5.34	2.90	2.39	2.88	2.15	113.38
BY NUMBER OF EARNERS						
Single Consumers						
No Earner	1.57	1.00	.80	1.07	.70	33.60
One Earner	1.37	.80	.66	.79	.56	42.15
Two or More Consumers						
No Earner	4.39	2.79	1.73	2.27	1.65	63.22
One Earner	4.50	2.87	1.87	2.20	1.62	73.75
Two Earners	4.53	2.44	2.08	2.18	1.58	85.86
Three or More........	6.58	3.55	2.82	2.90	1.86	109.00
BY SIZE OF CONSUMER UNIT						
One Person	1.44	.87	.71	.89	.61	39.07
Two Persons	3.51	2.19	1.53	1.95	1.44	69.77
Three Persons...........	4.75	2.94	2.06	2.31	1.73	84.86
Four Persons.............	6.05	3.04	2.46	2.73	1.86	96.34
Five or more	6.62	3.78	3.38	2.80	1.81	106.94

(*continued*)

Meat Expenditures by Consumer Characteristics, 1989 *continued*

	BEEF	PORK	OTHER MEATS	POULTRY	FISH	ALL FOODS
BY COMPOSITION OF CONSUMER UNIT						
Husband and Wife, All	5.04	2.82	2.20	2.37	1.73	88.77
Oldest Child Aged:						
Under 6..................	4.36	2.58	1.88	2.06	1.33	84.44
6–17.......................	5.63	3.01	2.61	2.51	1.80	100.01
18 or Over	7.07	3.70	2.84	3.10	2.04	103.59
One Parent With Children						
Aged Under 18.......	3.45	2.28	1.61	1.95	1.13	61.09
Others....................	2.23	1.35	1.02	1.23	.83	47.06
BY REGION						
Northeast...................	3.95	2.17	1.78	2.42	1.67	75.63
Midwest.....................	3.57	2.32	1.73	1.50	.99	67.50
South	3.71	2.30	1.65	1.76	1.26	67.23
West..........................	4.51	2.10	1.76	2.17	1.65	79.08
BY RACE						
White and Other........	3.93	2.13	1.73	1.90	1.33	73.82
Black..........................	3.55	3.09	1.62	2.07	1.58	52.77
BY HOUSING TENURE						
Homeowner	4.37	2.54	1.94	2.11	1.50	80.26
Renter........................	3.03	1.70	1.32	1.57	1.10	55.94
BY TYPE OF AREA						
Urban........................	3.87	2.19	1.70	1.96	1.36	71.88
Rural..........................	3.99	2.49	1.81	1.63	1.31	69.01

Source: U.S. Department of Labor, Bureau of Labor Statistics, 1989 Consumer Expenditure Survey

Average Weekly At-Home Meat Expenditures by Type, 1989

TYPE	DOLLARS PER CONSUMER UNIT
BEEF	$3.89
Ground Beef	1.68
Roasts	.63
Steaks	1.28
Other	.30
PORK	2.24
Bacon	.36
Chops	.56
Ham	.54
Sausage	.30
Other	.48
OTHER MEATS	1.72
Frankfurters	.36
Lunch Meats (Cold Cuts)	1.21
Lamb	.15
POULTRY	1.92
Fresh Whole Chicken	.33
Fresh & Frozen Chicken Parts.	1.14
Other	.45
FISH AND SEAFOOD	1.36
Canned	.35
Fresh and Frozen Shellfish	.32
Fresh and Frozen Finfish	.68

Source: U.S. Department of Labor, Bureau of Labor Statistics, 1989 Consumer Expenditure Survey

Consumer Expenditures for Meat, Poultry and Fish in Grocery Stores, 1989 & 1979

	1989 $ Million	% of Food & Beverages	% of Total	1979 $ Million	% of Food & Beverages	% of Total	% Change 1979– 1989
FRESH MEAT	$26,807	10.9%	8.1%	$21,336	15.4%	11.9%	+26%
Beef....................	20,976	8.6	6.4	16,228	11.7	9.9	+29%
Veal....................	530	.2	.2	637	.5	.4	−17%
Lamb..................	1,175	.5	.4	777	.6	.4	+51%
Pork	4,126	1.7	1.3	3,693	2.7	2.1	+12%
PACKAGED MEATS	13,567	5.5	4.1	12,939	9.4	7.2	+5%
Cured Hams & Picnics.........	2,067	.8	.6	2,238	1.6	1.2	−8%
Packaged Bacon ..	2,102	.9	.6	1,916	1.4	1.1	+10%
Frankfurters........	1,681	.7	.5	1,424	1.0	.8	+18%
Sausages..............	1,217	.5	.4	972	.7	.5	+25%
Other Sausage Products..........	2,944	1.2	.9	2,437	1.8	1.4	+21%
Cold Cuts	3,557	1.5	1.1	3,952	2.9	2.2	−10%
FROZEN MEAT......	202	.1	.1	197	.1	.1	+3%
CANNED MEAT	1,258	.5	.4	1,721	1.2	1.0	−27%
TOTAL ABOVE	41,834	17.1	12.7	36,193	26.2	20.1	+16%
POULTRY...............	11,563	4.7	3.5	5,801	4.2	3.2	+99%
Fresh...................	9,122	3.7	2.8	4,490	3.2	2.5	+103%
Frozen................	2,287	.9	.7	1,235	.9	.7	+85%
Canned	154	.1	*	76	.1	*	+103%
FISH & SEAFOOD	6,384	2.6	1.9	3,394	2.5	1.9	+88%
Fresh..................	3,630	1.5	1.1	1,524	1.1	.8	+138%
Frozen...............	704	.3	.2	465	.3	.3	+51%
Canned	2,050	.8	.6	1,405	1.0	.8	+46%
TOTAL MEAT, POULTRY & SEAFOOD......	59,781	24.4	18.1	45,388	32.8	25.3	+32%
TOTAL GROCERY STORE SALES	329,688	—	100.0	179,717	—	100.0	+83%
Food & Beverages	244,910	100.0	—	138,317	100.0	—	+77%
Non-Foods & General Merchandise	84,778	—	—	41,400	—	—	+105%

Source: Compiled from *Supermarket Business* magazine

Totals may not add due to rounding

Does not include meats sold through service delis or in prepared forms (i.e., frozen dinners, entrees, etc.)

*Less than 0.05

Grocery Stores: Percentage of Meat Sales by Type

	Beef	Pork	Veal	Lamb	Poultry	Fish & Seafood	Processed & Frozen	Other
RETAIL SALES (MIL. $)								
Under $10	41.9%	20.2%	1.6%	1.7%	21.0%	4.0%	6.2%	3.5%
$10–$30	39.3	19.7	1.7	1.8	19.4	4.7	10.5	3.1
$31–$100	39.5	19.5	1.3	1.5	19.2	5.1	8.8	5.1
$101–$250	40.3	16.2	1.9	2.3	21.4	4.4	10.8	2.9
$251–$500	39.7	13.9	1.4	1.6	18.0	4.2	19.5	2.2
$501 +	36.9	15.0	1.4	1.6	19.1	4.3	17.4	4.8
RETAIL AFFILIATION								
Chain	37.3	15.1	1.4	1.7	19.1	4.4	17.1	4.5
Independent	41.1	19.1	1.8	1.9	19.2	4.6	8.7	3.7
HEADQUARTERS REGION								
Northeast	39.6	13.1	2.1	2.9	20.6	5.1	7.9	8.7
Middle Atlantic	40.8	16.8	2.4	1.8	22.5	3.4	10.5	2.1
East North Central	36.4	16.0	1.2	1.2	15.3	6.4	21.7	2.5
West North Central	39.5	16.2	1.2	1.1	15.5	2.7	11.1	12.5
Southeast	38.2	12.2	1.5	2.1	15.8	3.8	20.7	5.9
West South Central	38.6	16.0	1.1	1.3	19.8	3.0	18.4	2.0
Mountain	43.8	12.9	1.1	1.4	14.7	3.5	20.2	2.8
Pacific	35.3	18.5	1.1	1.2	25.2	4.2	11.3	4.2
Average	37.6	15.3	1.4	1.7	19.2	4.3	16.6	4.4

Source: Food Marketing Institute, The Food Marketing Industry Speaks, 1986
May not add due to rounding.

U.S. Average Retail Meat Prices, 1981–90 (Dollars Per Pound)

	1981	1982	1983	1984	1985	1986	1987	1988	1989	1990
BEEF (Choice Grade)	$2.35	$2.38	$2.34	$2.36	$2.29	$2.27	$2.38	$2.50	$2.66	$2.81
Sirloin Steak	2.99	3.06	3.06	3.08	2.96	2.96	3.13	3.29	3.58	3.67
Round Steak	2.86	2.95	2.90	2.91	2.77	2.77	2.89	2.99	3.12	3.32
Round Roast	2.63	2.64	2.55	2.58	2.47	2.44	2.53	2.63	2.76	2.93
Rib Roast	3.03	3.22	3.24	3.35	3.28	3.26	3.54	3.89	4.17	4.49
Chuck Roast	1.82	1.79	1.74	1.68	1.57	1.59	1.68	1.73	1.88	2.09
Ground Chuck	1.80	1.78	1.73	1.72	1.68	1.64	1.71	1.76	1.83	1.97
FRESH PORK	1.52	1.75	1.70	1.62	1.62	1.78	1.88	1.83	1.83	2.13
Pork Chops	2.13	2.39	2.37	2.38	2.34	2.59	2.82	2.77	2.85	3.27
Sliced Bacon	1.67	2.05	1.94	1.86	1.94	2.08	2.14	1.88	1.77	2.13
Smoked Picnic	1.04	1.15	1.05	1.01	1.02	1.06	1.12	1.12	1.10	1.28
Canned Ham	2.46	2.65	2.67	2.56	2.56	2.68	2.80	2.73	2.67	2.77
Fresh Pork Sausage	1.61	1.88	1.87	1.71	1.74	1.91	1.99	1.97	2.00	2.35
Frankfurters	1.77	1.82	1.81	1.80	1.81	1.93	1.99	2.02	2.06	2.29
Bologna	2.11	2.21	2.18	2.13	2.11	2.17	2.19	2.24	2.28	2.51
POULTRY										
Whole Broilers	.74	.72	.73	.81	.76	.84	.78	.85	.93	.90
Frozen Hen Turkeys	.98	.93	.92	.99	1.05	1.07	1.01	.96	.99	.99

Source: U.S. Department of Labor, Bureau of Labor Statistics

Consumer Price Indices, 1982–90 (1982–84 = 100)

	1982	1983	1984	1985	1986	1987	1988	1989	1990
Food at Home	98.1	99.1	102.8	104.3	107.3	111.9	116.6	124.2	132.3
Food Away	95.8	100.0	104.2	108.3	112.5	117.0	121.8	127.4	133.4
All Meats	100.7	99.5	99.9	98.9	102.0	109.6	112.2	116.7	128.5
Beef and Veal	100.6	99.1	100.3	98.2	98.8	106.3	112.1	119.3	128.8
Pork	101.0	100.1	98.8	99.1	107.2	115.9	112.5	113.2	129.8
Other Meats	100.1	99.7	100.1	100.8	103.4	109.9	112.8	116.0	126.8
Poultry	95.8	97.0	107.3	106.2	114.2	112.6	120.7	132.7	132.5
Fish and Seafood	98.2	99.3	102.5	107.5	117.4	112.9	137.4	143.6	146.7

Source: U.S. Department of Labor

- **Consumer Expenditures for Meat, Poultry, and Fish in Grocery Stores, 1979–89**

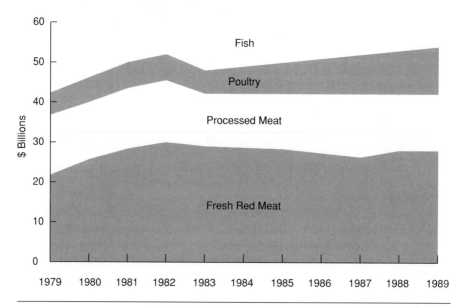